PAKISTAN

PAKISTAN

A Hard Country

WITHDRAWN

ANATOL LIEVEN

PUBLICAFFAIRS
NEW YORK

Published in the United States by PublicAffairs™,
a Member of the Perseus Books Group
Published in Great Britain by Allen Lane,
an imprint of the Penguin Group

PublicAffairs books are available at special discounts
for bulk purchases in the U.S. by corporations, institutions, and
other organizations. For more information, please contact the Special
Markets Department at the Perseus Books Group, 2300 Chestnut Street,
Suite 200, Philadelphia, PA 19103, call (800) 810-4145, ext. 5000,
or e-mail special.markets@perseusbooks.com.

Library of Congress Cataloging-in-Publication Data
LCCN 2011921821
ISBN: 978-1-61039-021-7
E-book ISBN: 978-1-61939-023-1

First Edition

10 9 8 7 6 5 4 3 2 1

In memory of my grandparents,
George Henry Monahan,
Indian Civil Service

Helen Monahan (née Kennedy)

and their son,

Captain Hugh Monahan MC,
5th Royal Gurkha Rifles (Frontier Force)

and in honour of their successors in the civil and military
services of Pakistan, India and Bangladesh

Contents

WITHDRAWN

PART FOUR
The Taleban

List of Illustrations

All plates: Corbis Images

Acknowledgements

This book would not have been possible had it not been for the immense kindness and hospitality of many Pakistanis, who invited me to their homes and talked to me frankly about their lives and their opinions – so many that the great majority will have to go unthanked.

I am especially indebted to Ashraf and Ambrin Hayat and their family in Islamabad. I hope that my prolonged stays with them did not disrupt their lives too much.

Syed Fakr Imam and Syeda Abida Hussain have been most gracious hosts over the years in their various residences, and shared with me their knowledge of politics, history and culture. Najam and Jugnu Sethi have been good friends and kind hosts for an equal time. Naeem Pasha and Kathy Gannon have entertained me more often than I can remember, and Kathy has shared her incomparable knowledge of matters Afghan. Naveed and Saeed Elahi have both given most generously of their time and helped me enormously with advice, information and contacts.

Whether in official service or the media, Maleeha Lodhi has been unfailingly kind, helpful and insightful. Her comments on parts of the manuscript were extremely valuable. I must also thank Shuja Nawaz, Asad Hashim and Hasan-Askari Rizvi for their comments. Of course, responsibility for the contents of this book, and the opinions expressed in it, is entirely my own. Among legions of Pakistani journalists and analysts who have helped me over the years, I must especially mention my old colleague Zahid Hussain, together with Zafar Abbas, Ejaz Haider, Imran Aslam, Behrouz Khan and Mosharraf Zaidi.

In Peshawar, I am most grateful to Rahimullah Yusufzai for all his help, and to Amina Khan and her family, to Brigadier Saad, Brigadier Javed Iqbal, Khalid Aziz, and Fakhruddin Khan. It was also most kind of General Zafrullah Khan and the Frontier Constabulary to invite me to stay in their mess in Peshawar in the summer of 2009. Similarly, I must thank the Vice-Chancellor of Faislabad Agricultural University, Professor Iqraar, for inviting me to speak there and putting me up at the university guest house, Dr Faisal Zaidi and the staff of Broomfield Hall in Multan for inviting me to speak there, Dr Mohammed Amir Rana and the staff of the Pakistan Institute of Peace Studies and Ambassador Tanvir Khan and the Institute of Strategic Studies in Islamabad. I am also most grateful to Professor Ali Khan Shehriyar, Dr Lukas Werth, Dr Shandana Mohmand and their colleagues at the Lahore University of Management Sciences for inviting me to speak, offering very helpful comments on my work and sharing their knowledge of Pakistani society.

General Athar Abbas, Colonel Haidar Malik, Captain Nasireh and other officers of Inter-Services Public Relations helped me greatly by arranging a whole series of meetings with senior military figures. Colonel Ali Awan and Mrs Saira Ahmed of the Pakistani High Commission in London helped not only with meetings but with extremely valuable advice. I am grateful to them and all the officers and men of the Pakistani armed forces who have helped me over the years.

In Sindh, I am deeply grateful to Sardar Mumtaz Ali Bhutto and his family for two very pleasant and interesting stays separated by twenty years, and in particular for inviting me to the boar hunt described in this book; and also to Ellahi Baksh Soomro and other members of the Soomro family for a fascinating stay with them in 1990. The Mayor of Karachi, Mustafa Kemal, gave generously of his valuable time. In Quetta, Nawabzada Aurangzeb Jogezai and Ashfaq Durrani very kindly entertained me in their homes.

I could also not have written this book without the help of assistants and translators in different parts of Pakistan. I am grateful to Zuhra Bahman not only for her help, but also for her family's hospitality. Watching Russian television in Peshawar during the Georgian–Russian war of 2008 was a somewhat surreal experience, but one worth remembering. I am also deeply grateful to Tauseef-ur-Rehman of *The News*, whose insights and contacts in Peshawar helped me enormously. Similarly, to Hasan Kazmi in Karachi, Naeem Daniel of Reuters in Quetta, Ali Gardezi in Multan, and Furrukh Khan and Hirra Waqas in Lahore, who also translated pieces from the Urdu media for me, and to Liz Harris in London.

In Britain, Sir Hilary Synnott, Colonel Christopher Langton, Dr Marie

Lall and Dr Stephen Lyon provided me with help and advice. In the US, Joshua White helped me with his unparalleled insights into Islamist politics in the North West Frontier Province, as did Stephen Tankel with regard to Lashkar-e-Taiba. Lynne Tracey of the US Consulate in Peshawar kindly invited me on a number of occasions. Khatib Alam and Gul Hafeez Khokar of GHK Consulting helped me with advice, introduced me to Faisalabad and impressed me with their achievements in helping to improve administration in that city. This was also true of Riaz Kamlani, Colonel Anwar Awan and the staff of the Citizens' Foundation in the area of education; while the devoted humanitarian service of the staff of the Edhi Foundation has been an inspiration since I first met them more than twenty years ago.

I remain grateful to *The Times* for sending me to Pakistan and Afghanistan in 1988 and allowing me to lay the foundation for this book, and to the Carnegie Endowment for International Peace, the New America Foundation, Bill Benter, the Nuffield Foundation, the Leverhulme Trust and the British Academy for financing different parts of my research in Pakistan from 2001 to 2009.

My thanks are due to my colleagues in the War Studies Department of King's College London for their support, in particular to Professor Mervyn Frost for his kindness in sparing me some administrative duties during the period of researching and writing this book, and to Dr Rudra Chaudhuri, whose insights into Indian policy and generosity in taking over lectures and seminars were a great help in a very busy time.

I am most grateful to Simon Winder, Caroline Elliker and the staff at Penguin for their great helpfulness and patience in what at times (through no fault of theirs) was a difficult editorial process, to Janet Tyrrell for spotting and correcting mistakes and infelicities, and to Clive Priddle and his colleagues at Public Affairs in the US. Natasha Fairweather, Emily Kitchin and Donald Winchester at AP Watt have as always been an indispensable help.

My wife Sasha bore the whole burden of the family during my long absences in Pakistan, and my son Misha absorbed a large amount of (antique) Pakistani weaponry without turning any of it on his father. I hope that before too long they will be able to visit Pakistan with me in more peaceful times.

Acronyms

ANP — Awami National Party, the Pathan nationalist party led the Wali Khan dynasty.

ASI — Assistant Sub-Inspector; a junior police officer.

BJP — Bharatiya Janata Party (India).

COAS — Chief of Army Staff.

DCO — District Coordinating Officer (formerly District Commissioner), the official in charge of the administration of a district.

DIG — Deputy Inspector-General (of police), usually the rank of the officer commanding the police of a district.

FATA — Federally Administered Tribal Areas, the indirectly administered Tribal Agencies along the border with Afghanistan.

FCR — Frontier Crimes Regulations.

FIR — First Information Report.

FSF — Federal Security Force.

IB — Intelligence Bureau, the intelligence wing of the Federal Interior Ministry.

IDP — Internally Displaced Person.

IG — Inspector-General (of police), usually commanding the police of a province.

IJI — Islami Jamhoori Ittehad, an alliance of conservative parties put together in September 1988 to oppose the Pakistan People's Party of Benazir Bhutto.

ISI — Inter-Services Intelligence, the intelligence wing of the armed forces.

JeM — Jaish-e-Mohammed.

JI — Jamaat Islami, Islamist movement founded by Maududi.

JuD	Jamaat-ud-Dawa, the social, educational and charitable wing of Lashkar-e-Taiba (see below)
JUH	Jamiat-e-Ulema-e-Hind.
JUI	Jamiat-e-Ulema-e-Islam, mainstream Islamist movement based in the Pathan areas.
LeJ	Lashkar-e-Jhangvi, anti-Shia Sunni militant group, an offshoot of Sipah-e-Sahaba.
LeT	Lashkar-e-Taiba, militant group focused on jihad against India.
MI	Military Intelligence, the service responsible for counter-intelligence and internal security in the armed forces.
MMA	Muttahida Majlis-e-Amal, alliance of Islamist political parties.
MNA	Member of the National Assembly.
MPA	Member of a Provincial Assembly.
MQM	Muttahida Qaumi Movement or United People's Movement (formerly Mohajir Qaumi Movement), the party of the Urdu-speaking Mohajirs of Sindh.
NWFP	The North West Frontier Province, since 2010 renamed Khyber-Pakhtunkhwa.
PML	Pakistan Muslim League.
PML(N)	Pakistan Muslim League (Nawaz), the party led by the Sharif dynasty.
PML(Q)	Pakistan Muslim League (Qaid-e-Azam), a political alliance mainly made up of defectors from the PML(N) of the Sharifs, and put together in 2002 to support the administration of President Musharraf.
PPP	Pakistan People's Party, led by the Bhutto–Zardari dynasty.
RAW	Research and Analysis Wing (Indian intelligence agency).
SHO	Station House Officer, the commander of a local police station.
SSP	Sipah-e-Sahaba, Pakistan, anti-Shia militant group.
TeI	Tehriq-e-Insaf, party founded and led by Imran Khan Niazi.
TNSM	Tehriq-e-Nifaz-e-Shariat-e-Mohammedi, Islamist militant movement in Swat, since 2008 allied with the Pakistani Taleban.
TTP	Tehriq-e-Taleban Pakistan.

PART ONE

Land, People and History

I

Introduction: Understanding Pakistan

Eppur si muove
(And yet it moves)
(Galileo Galilei)

There have been times during the writing of this book when it seemed that it would have to be titled 'Requiem for a Country'. At the time of writing, the pressures on Pakistan from without and within are unprecedented even in its troubled history. Yet such despair would be premature. Tariq Ali wrote *Can Pakistan Survive? The Death of a State* in 1983, a generation ago. That's quite a long deathbed scene by any standards.[1]

It is possible that the terrible floods of the summer of 2010 have fundamentally changed and weakened the Pakistani system described in this book. This, however, will not be clear for a long while – and in the meantime it is worth remembering the extraordinary resilience that South Asian rural societies have often shown in the face of natural disaster, from which they have repeatedly emerged with structures of local authority and political culture essentially unchanged.

What is certainly true is that if floods and other ecological disasters on this scale become regular events as a result of climate change, then Pakistan will be destroyed as a state and an organised society – but so too will many other countries around the world. Indeed, such a development would reduce present concerns about Pakistan to relative insignificance. In the meantime, however, the floods have obviously damaged Pakistan's national infrastructure, and retarded still further the country's already faltering economic progress.

This book is intended to describe and analyse both Pakistan's internal

problems and the sources of Pakistan's internal resilience. In consequence, it of course deals extensively with the threat from the Pakistani
Taleban and their allies, the roots of their support, and the relationship
of this support to the war in Afghanistan. It also examines the policies
of the Pakistani security establishment towards Afghanistan and India,
since these have had very important effects on domestic developments
in Pakistan. It is not meant, however, to be a study of Pakistan's international position, though the conclusions contain some recommendations
for Western policy.

Trying to understand Pakistan's internal structures and dynamics is
complicated; for if there is one phrase which defines many aspects of
Pakistan and is the central theme of this book, it is 'Janus-faced': in
other words, many of the same features of Pakistan's state and government which are responsible for holding Islamist extremism in check are
at one and the same time responsible for holding back Pakistan's social,
economic and political development.

Pakistan is divided, disorganized, economically backward, corrupt,
violent, unjust, often savagely oppressive towards the poor and women,
and home to extremely dangerous forms of extremism and terrorism –
'and yet it moves', and is in many ways surprisingly tough and resilient
as a state and a society. It is also not quite as unequal as it looks from
outside.

Pakistan contains islands of successful modernity, and of excellent
administration – not that many, but enough to help keep the country trun-
dling along: a few impressive modern industries; some fine motorways; a
university in Lahore, parts of which are the best of their kind in South
Asia; a powerful, well-trained and well-disciplined army; and in every generation, a number of efficient, honest and devoted public servants. The
military and police commanders of the fight against the Taleban in the
Pathan areas whom I met in Peshawar and Rawalpindi in 2008–9 struck
me as highly able and patriotic men by any standards in the world.

The National Finance Commission Award of 2010, which rebalanced state revenues in favour of the poorer provinces, was a reasonable
if belated agreement. It demonstrated that Pakistani democracy, the
Pakistani political process and Pakistani federalism retain a measure of
vitality, flexibility and the ability to compromise. None of these things
is characteristic of truly failed or failing states like Somalia, Afghanistan
or the Congo.

That doesn't mean that Pakistan always smells nice (though some-times it does); and indeed, some of the toughest creepers holding the rotten tree of the Pakistani system together are at one and the same time parasites on that tree, and sometimes smell bad even by their own stand-ards. Nonetheless, tough they are; and unless the USA, India, or both together invade Pakistan and thereby precipitate its disintegration, the likelihood is that the country will hold together, and that if it eventually collapses, it will be not Islamist extremism but climate change – an espe-cially grim threat in the whole of South Asia – that finishes it off.

Support for extremist and terrorist groups is scattered throughout Pakistani society, but as of 2010 mass support for Islamist rebellion against the Pakistani state is so far present only in the Pathan areas, and in only some of them – in other words, less than 5 per cent of the popu-lation. That is not remotely enough to revolutionize Pakistan as a whole. During their rule over the region, the British faced repeated revolts in the Pathan areas, without seriously fearing that this would lead to rebel-lion elsewhere in their Indian empire.

Any Pakistani national revolution would have to gain not just mass but majority support in Pakistan's two great urban centres, Lahore and Karachi; and as the chapters on Punjab and Sindh will make clear, this is unlikely for the foreseeable future – though not necessarily for ever, especially if ecological crisis floods the cities with masses of starving peasants.

When terrorist groups attack India, or Western forces in Afghanistan, their actions enjoy a degree of instinctive, gut sympathy from a majority of Pakistanis – not because of Islamist extremism, but because of Mus-lim nationalism and bitter hostility to the US role in the Muslim world in general and Pakistan's region in particular. Support for a civil war and revolution in Pakistan itself that would turn Pakistan into a revo-lutionary Islamic state is, however, a very different matter from sympathizing with attacks on the US and India. That would mean Paki-stanis killing Pakistanis on a massive scale, and by and large they don't want to. They may well want to kill some set of immediate rivals, but that's another matter.

It is important not to be misled by the spread of terrorism in Pakistan in 2009–10. In many ways, terrorism by the Pakistani Taleban is a sign not of strength but of weakness. If you want to overthrow and capture a state, you need either a mass movement on city streets that seizes institutions, or a guerrilla movement in the countryside that seizes territory, or a revolt of the junior ranks of the military, or some combination of all three. No movement relying chiefly on terrorism has ever overthrown a state. The Pakistani Taleban looked truly menacing when it took over most of the Federally Administered Tribal Areas (FATA), followed by the districts of Swat and Buner. When it blows up ordinary people in bazaars and mosques, it merely looks foul.

Pakistan is thus probably still far from the situation of Iran in the late 1970s or Russia in 1917. Apart from anything else, the army is a united and disciplined institution, and as long as that remains the case, it will be strong enough to defeat open revolt – as it proved by defeating the Taleban in Swat and south Waziristan in 2009. Unlike in Africa and elsewhere, military coups in Pakistan have always been carried out by the army as a whole, on the orders of its chief of staff and commanding generals – never by junior officers. As my chapter on the military will describe, there are very deep reasons for this in terms of material advantage as well as military culture.

The only thing that can destroy this discipline and unity is if enough Pakistani soldiers are faced with moral and emotional pressures powerful enough to crack their discipline, and that would mean very powerful pressures indeed. In fact, they would have to be put in a position where their duty to defend Pakistan and their conscience and honour as Muslims clashed directly with their obedience to their commanders.

As far as I can see, the only thing that could bring that about as far as the army as a whole is concerned (rather than just some of its Pathan elements) is if the US were to invade part of Pakistan, and the army command failed to give orders to resist this. Already, the perceived subservience of the Pakistani state to Washington's demands has caused severe problems of morale in the armed forces. I have been told by soldiers of all ranks that faced with open incursions on the ground by US troops, parts of the Pakistani army would mutiny in order to fight the invaders. With the army splintered and radicalized, Islamist upheaval and the collapse of the state would indeed be all too likely – but even then, the result would be rebellions leading to civil war, not, as in Iran, to a national revolution that would be successful in taking over the whole country.

I hope through this book to strengthen the argument that however great the provocation, the US *must not* contribute to the destruction of

Pakistan – even though, as this book will make clear, neither the Pakistani army, nor the Pakistani state, nor the great majority of Pakistanis will ever give more than very qualified help to the US campaign against the Afghan Taleban, since Pakistanis of every rank and class see these in a quite different light from Al Qaeda and the Pakistani Taleban.

PAKISTAN, AFGHANISTAN AND THE TALEBAN

Pakistan is quite simply far more important to the region, the West and the world than is Afghanistan: a statement which is a matter not of sentiment but of mathematics. With more than 180 million people, Pakistan has nearly six times the population of Afghanistan (or Iraq), twice the population of Iran, and almost two-thirds the population of the entire Arab world put together. Pakistan has a large diaspora in Britain (and therefore in the EU), some of whom have joined the Islamist extremists and carried out terrorist attacks against Britain.

The help of the Pakistani intelligence services to Britain has been absolutely vital to identifying the links of these potential terrorists to groups in Pakistan, and to preventing more attacks on Britain, the USA and Europe. Pakistan therefore has been only a partial ally in the 'war on terror' – but still a vital and irreplaceable one. For we need to remember that in the end it is only legitimate Muslim governments and security services that can control terrorist plots on their soil. Western pressure may be necessary to push them in the right direction, but we need to be careful that this pressure does not become so overwhelming that it undermines or even destroys those governments, by humiliating them in the eyes of their own people.

Finally, Pakistan possesses nuclear weapons and one of the most powerful armies in Asia. This means that the option of the US attacking Pakistan with ground forces in order to force it to put pressure on the Afghan Taleban simply does not exist – as both the Pentagon and the Pakistani military have long understood. Deeply unsatisfying though this has been for the West, the only means of influencing Pakistan has been through economic incentives and the threat of their withdrawal. Economic sanctions are not really a credible threat, because the economic collapse of Pakistan would play straight into the hands of the Taleban and Al Qaeda.

Pakistan's relationship with India has been central to Pakistan's behaviour since 9/11 – as of course it has been ever since partition and independence in 1947. Fear of India has both encouraged and limited Pakistani help to the US in Afghanistan. This fear is exaggerated, but not irrational, and neither are most of the policies which result from it. On the one hand, fear of a US–Indian alliance against Pakistan seems to have been a genuine factor in Musharraf's decision to help the US after 9/11, and was certainly used by him to convince the military and – initially – many ordinary Pakistanis of the necessity of this help. On the other hand, fear of India has been both a reason and an excuse for Pakistan not to redeploy more troops from the eastern border with India to fight against the Taleban in the west.

Lastly, the Pakistani establishment long cherished the hope that it could use Pakistani help against the Taleban to bargain for US pressure on India to reach a settlement with Pakistan over Kashmir. This hope has faded with the refusal (compounded of unwillingness and inability) of both the Bush and the Obama administrations to play such a role; but this refusal, and America's 'tilt towards India', have added greatly to longstanding Pakistani feelings of betrayal by the US.

Pakistan's help to the West against the Afghan Taleban would, however, have been limited in any case both by strategic calculation and mass sentiment. In terms of mass sentiment, the overwhelming majority of Pakistanis – including the communities from which most Pakistani soldiers are drawn – see the Afghan Taleban as engaged in a legitimate war of resistance against foreign occupation, analogous to the Mujahidin war against Soviet occupation in the 1980s.

In terms of strategy, the Pakistani establishment's approach to Afghanistan has long been driven by a mixture of fear and ambition. The fear is above all of Afghanistan, under the rule of the non-Pashtun nationalities, becoming an Indian client state, leading to India's strategic encirclement of Pakistan. This fear has been increased by a well-founded belief that India is supporting Pakistan's Baloch nationalist rebels via Afghanistan, and by what seems by contrast to be a purely paranoid conviction that India is also supporting the Pakistani Taleban.

The greater part of the Pakistani establishment therefore believes that it needs to maintain close relations with the Afghan Taleban, since they are Pakistan's only potential allies in Afghanistan. In recent years, belief in the need for a relationship with the Taleban has been strengthened by the growing conviction that the West is going to fail in Afghanistan, and will eventually withdraw, leaving anarchy and civil war behind – just as occurred after the Soviet withdrawal and the fall of the Communist regime from 1989–92. In the resulting civil war, it is believed, every regional state will have its own allies – and so must Pakistan.

Incidentally, it is worth pointing out that even entirely secular members of the Pakistani establishment do not see the Afghan Taleban as morally worse than the Taleban's old enemies in the Afghan Northern Alliance leaders, with whom the West has in effect been allied since 2001. Their atrocities and rapes in the 1990s helped cement Pathan support for the Taleban. They massacred Taleban prisoners and looted Western aid after the overthrow of the Taleban in 2001, and their role in the heroin trade has helped destroy any hope of the West curtailing that trade since 9/11.

Equally, it is important to note that in the great majority of cases, both in the elites and in the mass of the population, this sympathy or support for the Afghan Taleban does not imply ideological approval, or any desire that Pakistan should experience a Taleban-style revolution – any more than support for the Mujahidin in the 1980s implied much liking for them.

Hence, too, the great difference in Pakistani attitudes to the Afghan and to the Pakistani Taleban. There was never a chance that the Pakistani establishment and army were going to let the Pakistani Taleban conquer Pakistan. The long delay in fighting them seriously was because they were not generally regarded as a serious threat to Pakistan, but were seen as a local Pathan rebellion which could be contained by a mixture of force and negotiation; because many ordinary Pakistanis (including soldiers) saw them as misguided but nonetheless decent people dedicated to helping the good jihad in Afghanistan; because there was deep opposition to the state engaging in a Pakistani civil war for the sake of what were seen to be American interests – especially among all sections of Pakistan's Pathan population; and, finally, because the Pakistani military and its intelligence services were deeply entwined with jihadi groups which they had sponsored to fight against India in Kashmir, and which were in turn entwined with the Pakistani Taleban.

As soon as the Pakistani Taleban were seen by the establishment to be a really serious threat to the central Pakistani state, in the spring of 2009, the army, with the backing of the PPP-led government and much of the establishment in general, took strong action to drive them back. The army's victories over the Pakistani Taleban in Swat and South Waziristan have settled the question of whether Pakistan will survive the Pakistani Taleban's assault (barring once again an attack by the US or full-scale war with India). They have, however, settled nothing when it comes to the question of the army's willingness to fight hard against the Afghan Taleban for the sake of a Western victory in Afghanistan.

TOUGHER THAN IT LOOKS

Failing a catastrophic overspill of the war in Afghanistan, Pakistan will therefore probably survive as a state. The destruction of united Pakistan and the separation of Bangladesh in 1971 are often cited as possible precedents for the future disintegration of today's Pakistan; but this is quite wrong. No freak of history like united Pakistan, its two ethnically and culturally very different wings separated by 1,000 miles of hostile India, could possibly have lasted for long, quite apart from the immense cultural and linguistic differences between the two halves. The tragedy is not that it failed, but that a situation made for a civilized divorce should instead have ended in horrible bloodshed.

West Pakistan by contrast is far more of a natural unity in every way, with a degree of common history and ethnic intertwining stretching back long before British rule. Pakistan in its present shape has already survived considerably longer without Bangladesh (thirty-eight years) than the original united Pakistan managed (twenty-four years).

It is true that 'Pakistan' as a name is a wholly artificial construct, invented by Rehmat Ali, an Indian Muslim student in Britain in 1933, to describe a future Muslim state in the north-west of the then British empire of India embracing Punjabis, Pathans, Kashmiris, Sindhis and the peoples of Balochistan, different parts of which names make up the word Pakistan. 'Pak' in turn means 'pure' in Urdu, and so Pakistan was to be 'The Land of the Pure'.

In the imagination of the coiners of this name, there was no thought of including Muslim East Bengal in this state, so Bengalis had no part in the name; another sign of how completely improbable and impractical was the attempt in 1947 to create a viable state out of two pieces 1,000 miles apart. Certainly most of the Punjabis and Pathans who dominate

West Pakistan never really thought of the East Bengalis as fellow coun-trymen or even true Muslims, shared much British racial contempt for them, and contrasted their alleged passivity with the supposedly virile qualities of the ethnicities dubbed by the British as 'martial', the Pun-jabis and Pathans.

The official language of Pakistan is native to neither of its old halves. Urdu – related to 'Horde', from the Turkic-Persian word for a military camp – started as the military dialect of the Muslim armies of the Indian subcontinent in the Middle Ages, a mixture of local Hindustani with Per-sian and Turkic words. It was never spoken by Muslims in Bengal – but then it has never been spoken by most of the people of what is now Paki-stan either. It was the language of Muslims in the heartland of the old Mughal empire, centred on the cities of Delhi, Agra, Lucknow, Bhopal and Hyderabad, deep in what is now India. Urdu is the official language of Pakistan, the language of the state education system, of the national newspapers, and of the film industry; but the only people who speak it at home are the Mohajirs, people who migrated from India after partition in 1947, and who make up only 7 per cent of Pakistan's population.

However, what is now Pakistan is not nearly such an artificial con-struct as the old Pakistan of 1947–71. It has a geographical unity which in some respects is thousands of years old, being basically the valley of the River Indus plus neighbouring mountains, deserts and swamps. To a much greater extent than most post-colonial states, Pakistan therefore has a core geographical unity and logic.[2] Moreover, most of Pakistan's different ethnicities have lived alongside each other for millennia, have been Muslim for hundreds of years, and have often been ruled by the same Muslim dynasties.

Regional identity may be growing in political importance, with the 2008 elections showing a lower vote for the PPP in Punjab, and a lower vote for the Punjab-based Muslim League in other provinces. All the same, with Pakistanis, there is usually a wheel within a wheel, an identity within an identity, which in turn overlaps with another identity. The only exceptions, the people with a single identity, are some of the Islamists, and some of the soldiers – but by no means all of either. Or as Ali Has-san, a young Lahori executive with a Norwegian company, said to me:

> If I were to jump on a box and preach revolution, with the best programme
> in the world, you know what would happen? First, people from all the

other provinces would say that we can't follow him, he's a Punjabi. Then most of the Punjabis would say, we can't follow him, he's a Jat. Then the Jats would say, we can't follow him, he's from such-and-such a *biradiri*. Even in my own village, half the people would say something like, I can't follow him, his grandfather beat my uncle in a fight over land. If you preach Islamic revolution, most Pakistanis won't follow you because they practise different kinds of Islam and worship different saints. So you see we Pakistanis can't unite behind a revolution because we can't unite behind *anything*.[3]

Or, in the saying common in Pakistan as across the Greater Middle East: 'I against my brother, I and my brother against our cousins, and our family against our *biradiri* and our *biradiri* against other *biradiri*.' Occasionally they end, 'and Pakistan against the world' – but not often.

Not surprisingly then, until recently at least, every attempt to unite large numbers of Pakistanis behind a religious, an ethnic or a political cause ended in the groups concerned being transformed by the ever-present tendency to political kinship and its incestuous sister, the hunt for state patronage. This wooed them away from radicalism to participation in the Pakistani political system, which revolves around patronage – something that is true under both military and civilian governments in Pakistan.

WEAK STATE, STRONG SOCIETIES

Indeed, a central theme of this book is that the difference between civilian and military regimes in Pakistan is far less than both Western and Pakistani analysts have suggested. A fundamental political fact about Pakistan is that the state, whoever claims to lead it, is weak, and society in its various forms is immensely strong. Anyone or any group with the slightest power in society uses it among other things to plunder the state for patronage and favours, and to turn to their advantage the workings of the law and the bureaucracy. Hence the astonishing fact that barely 1 per cent of the population pays income tax, and the wealthiest landowners in the country pay no direct taxes at all. As a state auditor in Peshawar said to me with a demoralized giggle, 'If anyone took taxes seriously, I'd have the most difficult job in the world, but as it is I have the easiest.'

The weakness of the state goes far beyond a dependence on patronage for the survival of governments. To an extent most Westerners would find hard to grasp, the lack of state services means that much of the time, the state as such – as an agent with its own independent will – does not necessarily affect many people's lives very much, either in terms of benefits or oppressions. The presence of policemen, judges and officials may make it look as if the state is present, but much of the time these people are actually working – and sometimes killing – on their own account, or at the behest of whoever has the most power, influence and money at a certain point, in a certain place.

The nineteenth-century British colonial official Sir Thomas Metcalf described the traditional villages of northern India as 'little republics', administering their own justice, deciding their own affairs, and paying only what tribute to the 'state' could be extracted from them by force. This independence has been very greatly reduced over the years, but compared to any Western society a good deal of it still exists in many areas, if not specifically in the village, then in local society generally. Society is strong above all in the form of the kinship networks which are by far the most important foci of most people's loyalty.

For those readers who are *really* interested and have a few brain cells to lose, a brief description of the horribly complex subject of kinship terms and groups in Pakistan is appended to the end of this introduction. Suffice it to say here that the language of kinship – even among people who are not in fact related – permeates most of Pakistan as it does most of South Asia, whether it is a matter of affection, responsibility, asking for favours or asking for protection. The most wonderful expression of this, which perfectly sums up India's mixture of kinship, democracy and hierarchy, is the term with which you may wish to address a relatively menial person in northern India who happens to be in a position to help or harm you (like a bus-conductor): *Bhai-sahib*, or 'Brother-Lord'.

Kinship is central to the weakness of the Pakistani state, but also to its stability, above all because of its relationship with class. Because the Pakistani political elites, especially in the countryside, rely for their strength not just on wealth but on their leadership of clans or kinship networks, kinship plays a vital part in maintaining the dominance of the 'feudal' elites and many of the urban bosses.

By helping to enforce on the elites a certain degree of responsibility for their followers, and circulating patronage downwards, kinship also plays a role in softening – to a limited extent – class domination. Kinship is therefore partially responsible for Pakistan's surprisingly low rating of social inequality according to the Gini Co-efficient, which I will discuss further in Chapter 6.[4] In both these ways, kinship is a critical anti-revolutionary force, whether the revolution is of a socialist or Islamist variety.

The importance of kinship is rooted in a sense (which runs along a spectrum from very strong to very weak depending on circumstance and degree of kinship) of collective solidarity for interest and defence. This interest involves not just the pursuit of concrete advantage, but is also inextricably bound up with powerful feelings of collective honour or prestige (*izzat*) and shame; and, indeed, a kinship group which is seen as 'dishonoured' will find its interests decline in every other way. A sense of collective honour among kin is thus reflected most dramatically in preventing or punishing any illicit sexual behaviour by the kinship group's women, but also in working to advance the political and economic power and public status of the group.

This is a cultural system so strong that it can persuade a father to kill a much-loved daughter, not even for having an affair or becoming pregnant, but for marrying outside her kinship group without permission. You don't get stronger than that. As Alison Shaw and others have noted, the immense strength and flexibility of the kinship system in Pakistan (and most of India too) are shown, among other things, by the way in which it has survived more than half a century of transplantation to the very different climes of Britain. Shaw writes:

> Families in Oxford are therefore best seen as outposts of families in Pakistan whose members have been dispersed by labour migration ... [In Britain] a distinctive pattern of living near close kin has emerged, echoing that of earlier migrations within the Indian subcontinent.[5]

Defence of the honour and the interests of the kinship group usually outweighs loyalty to a party, to the state, or to any code of professional ethics, not only for ordinary Pakistanis, but for most politicians and officials. It is important to understand therefore that much Pakistani corruption is the result not of a lack of values (as it is usually seen in the West) but of the positive and ancient value of loyalty to family and clan.

Since the kinship group is the most important force in society, the power of kinship is inevitably reflected in the political system. Just as in much of the rest of South Asia, a majority of Pakistan's political parties are dynastic. The PPP is the party of the Bhutto family; the PML(N) is that of the Sharif family; and the Awami National Party (ANP) in the Frontier is the party of the Wali Khan family.

The local political groupings which are the building blocks of these parties are themselves based on local dynasties. Hence the phenomenon of a woman such as Benazir Bhutto rising to the top of the political system in an extremely conservative male-dominated society. This was power by inheritance, and says not much more about ordinary women's rights in modern Pakistani society than the inheritance of the throne by Queens Mary and Elizabeth from their father said about ordinary women's rights in sixteenth-century English society.

The only institution which has succeeded to some extent in resisting this in the name of state loyalty and professional meritocracy is the army – and you could say that it has managed this in part only through turning itself into a kind of giant clan, serving its members' collective interests at the expense of the state and society, and underpinned to some extent by ancient local kinship groups among the north-western Punjabis and Pathans.

If the importance of kinship links has survived transplantation to the cities of Britain, it is not surprising that it has survived migration to the cities of Pakistan, especially because in both cases (the British through marriage with people from home villages in Pakistan) the urban populations are continually being swelled and replenished by new migration from the countryside. The continued importance of kinship is a key reason why Pakistan's tremendous rate of urbanization in recent years has not yet led to radical changes in political culture, except – for reasons I will explain – in Karachi.

Largely because of the strength of kinship loyalty, Pakistani society is probably strong enough to prevent any attempt to change it radically through Islamist revolution, which is all to the good; but this is only the other face of something which is not so good, which is society's ability to frustrate even the best-designed and best-intentioned attempts at reform and positive development. Key factors in this regard are the gentry in the countryside and the intertwined clans of business, political and criminal bosses in the towns, all of them maintaining continuity over the years through intermarriage, often within the extended family, almost always (except among the highest elites) within the wider kinship group.

Marriage with members of the same kinship group, and when possible of the same extended family, is explicitly intended to maintain the strength, solidarity and reliability of these groups against dilution by outsiders. Shaw writes of the Pakistanis of Oxford that in the year 2000, almost fifty years after they first started arriving in Britain, there had been barely any increase in the proportion of marriages with non-kin, and that over the previous fifteen years 59 per cent – 59 per cent! – of marriages had been with first cousins; and the proportion in strongly Pakistani cities such as Bradford is even higher:

> Greater wealth was perceived not solely in terms of individual social mobility, although it provides opportunities for this, but in terms of raising the status of a group of kin in relation to their wider *biradiri* and neighbours in Pakistan ... Status derives not only from wealth, mainly in terms of property and business, but also from respectability (primarily expressed by an ashraf ['noble'] lifestyle). One element of being considered a man worthy of respect derives from having a reputation as being someone who honours his obligations to kin. Cousin marriage is one of the most important expressions of this obligation. The majority of east Oxford families have not achieved social mobility and status though massive accumulation of property and business. For them, the marriages of their children to the children of siblings in Pakistan is an important symbol of honour and respectability, a public statement that even families separated by continents recognize their mutual obligations.[6]

It is above all thanks to locally dominant kinship groups that over the years, beneath the froth and spray of Pakistani politics, the underlying currents of Pakistani political life have until recently been so remarkably stable. Civilian governments have come and gone with bewildering rapidity, whether overthrown by military coups or stranded by the constantly shifting allegiances of their political supporters. Yet the same people have gone on running these parties, and leading the same people or kinds of people at local level. The same has been true under military governments. None of these changes of government or regime has produced any real change to the deeper structures of Pakistani politics, because these are rooted in groups and allegiances which so far have changed with glacial slowness.

'FEUDALS'

In the countryside, and to a great extent in the towns as well, the most powerful elements are not individuals – though they are led by individuals – or even families in the Western sense. From this point of view, as from many others, the description of the rural landowners as 'feudals' is false, in so far as it suggests any close comparison with their medieval European equivalents. If this were so, the Pakistani 'feudals' would long since have been swept away by pressure from below and reform from above.

Each individual 'feudal' is quite a small landowner by traditional European standards (500 acres is a big estate in Pakistan), and most of his (or sometimes her) wealth may well now come from urban property. In Punjab at least, the really big landowners lost most of their land in the land reforms of Ayub in the late 1950s and Bhutto in the early 1970s.

In fact, I thought of arguing that there is in fact no such thing as a feudal in Pakistan; but then I remembered wild-boar hunting with the noble landowners of Sindh – a remarkably 'feudal' experience, described in Chapter 8. So what I'll say instead is that while there certainly are 'feudals' in Pakistan in the loose Pakistani sense of that term, there are no feudals in the European historical sense.

A great many leading 'feudal' families, especially in northern Punjab, are not old landowning families at all, but emerged quite recently, often on the basis of urban property or successful corruption when in state service. However, they adopt the same manners and behave politically in the same ways as the old families. Above all, they appeal for support in their own kinship groups, and do so on the basis of the same old politics of patronage and protection.

Indeed, the most powerful remaining 'feudals' in Pakistan owe their power not to the extent of their personal landholdings but to the fact that they are the chiefs of large tribes; and the importance of leadership roles in kinship groups extends down to the lesser gentry as well. It is the way in which individual landowners are embedded in landowning clans (like the Gujjars of Attock, the subject of a classic study by Stephen Lyon) which gives them their tremendous strength and resilience, and allows them to go on controlling the politics of the countryside, and dominating those of the country as a whole.[7]

If the political power of the kinship group in Pakistan depended only on the distribution of patronage, then this power might well have declined over time, given that patronage will always be limited; but it is also rooted in the oldest of social compulsions: collective defence. As one landowner-politician in Sindh told me, in words which were echoed by many other people and provide the title for this book,

> This is a hard country. You need family or tribal links to protect you, so that there are people who will stick with you and sacrifice for you whatever happens. That way you will not be abandoned even when out of government. The tribal people gives even ordinary tribesmen some strength and protection against attack, whether by dacoits, the police, the courts – your tribesmen will get you out of jail, lie for you to the court, avenge you if necessary.

Since British days, outside the Baloch and Pathan areas this has rarely been a matter of the whole clan taking up arms against a rival clan. Rather, in a violent society in which none of the institutions of the state can be relied on to act in accordance with their formal rules, close relations with kinsfolk are essential for help against rivals, against the predatory and violent police, in the courts, in politics, and in the extraction of political patronage – all areas of activity which overlap and depend on each other.

A combination of the weakness of the state and the power of kinship is one critical reason why urbanization has had a much smaller impact on political patterns and structures than one might otherwise have expected. Rather than a new urban population emerging, what we have mainly seen so far is huge numbers of peasants going to live in the cities while remaining culturally peasants. They remain deeply attached to their kinship groups, and they still need their kinship groups to help them for many of the same reasons they needed them in the countryside. Underlying all this is the fact that so much of the urban population remains semi-employed or informally employed, rather than moving into modern sectors of the economy – because these usually do not exist.

And of course while the power of kinship is necessary to defend against the predatory state, it is also one of the key factors in making the state predatory, as kinship groups use the state to achieve their goals of power, wealth and triumph over other kinship groups. As one informed description of the state legal system has it:

> Below the level of the High Courts all is corruption. Neither the facts nor the law in the case have real bearing on the outcome. It all depends on who you know, who has influence and where you put your money.[8]

So the ancient Pakistani kinship groups and the modern Pakistani state dance along together down the years, trapped in a marriage that ought to be antagonistic, but has in fact become essential to the nature of each party.

The problem about all this is that while in one way the power of kinship, underpinning the rule of the elites, has so far maintained the basic stability and even the existence of Pakistan, in other ways the plundering of state resources for patronage which this politics breeds has been extremely bad for the development of the country.

It is striking that the most economically and socially dynamic sections of the Pakistani population are those which have to a greater or lesser extent been shaken loose from their traditional cultural patterns and kinship allegiances by mass migration. This is most obviously true of the Mohajirs of Karachi, who emigrated from India after 1947; but even more important are the Punjabis who fled from east Punjab in the dreadful summer of 1947, and now form the backbone of the Punjabi economy. A much smaller, but in some ways even more striking, group are the Hazaras of Balochistan who fled from Afghanistan in the late nineteenth century, and whose educated middle-class society forms a remarkable contrast to the stagnation that surrounds them.

HOW PAKISTAN WORKS

The original title for this book was 'How Pakistan Works', and one of its core goals is to show that, contrary to much instinctive belief in the West, it has actually worked according to its own imperfect but functional patterns. One of the minor curses of writing on world affairs over the past few years has been the proliferating use of the term 'failed state'. Coined originally for genuinely failed and failing states in sub-Saharan Africa, this term has since been thrown around with wild abandon to describe a great range of states around the world, pretty much in accordance with the writer's prejudices or the need of his or her publication for a sensational headline.

In this respect, it is instructive to place Pakistan in the context of the rest of South Asia. *All* of the states of this region have faced insurgencies over the past generation, which in two cases (Afghanistan and Nepal) have actually overthrown the existing state. Sri Lanka and Burma have both faced rebellions which have lasted longer, covered proportionally far more territory, and caused proportionally far more casualties than has been the case with the Taleban revolt in Pakistan.

India, the great power of the region, is a stable democracy compared to its neighbours; yet India too has faced repeated rebellions in different parts of its territory, some of them lasting for generations. One of these, the Naxalite Maoist insurgency, affects a third of India's districts, and effectively controls huge areas of the Indian countryside – a far greater proportion of India than the proportion of Pakistan ever controlled by the Pakistani Taleban. The Indian Prime Minister, Manmohan Singh, in September 2009 described this insurgency as the biggest threat facing India, and said that to date India had been losing the struggle. A recent book by an Indian journalist describes the greater part of the countryside in several Indian states as effectively 'ungoverned'.[9]

This is not to argue that India is in any danger of breaking up or collapsing. Rather, one should recognize that states in South Asia have not traditionally exercised direct control over much or even most of their territory, and have always faced continual armed resistance somewhere or other. As in medieval Europe, for most of South Asian history government was mostly indirect, and implemented not by state officials but through local barons or tribal chieftains – who often revolted against the king, emperor or sultan if they felt that he was not treating them with sufficient respect and generosity. The world of the Pakistani landowners of today would in some ways have been immediately recognizable to their fifteenth-century English equivalents.

The British introduced a modern state system which all the present countries of the region have inherited. Yet British rule too was to a great extent indirect. Two-fifths of the territory of British India was in fact ruled by autonomous princes who owed allegiance to the king-emperor (or queen-empress) but governed their own states under British tutelage. Even in the areas which came directly under the British Raj, British rule could not have long maintained itself without the constant help of the local landed aristocrats and chieftains, who in consequence often had pretty much of a free hand when it came to their treatment of their own tenants and labourers. As in parts of Pakistan and India today, these local princelings also sheltered and sponsored bandit groups (dacoits) to help in their constant feuds with their neighbours.

When compared to Canada or France, Pakistan inevitably fails. When compared to India, Bangladesh, Afghanistan, Nepal and Sri Lanka, things therefore do not look so terrible. In fact, a good many key features of Pakistan are common to the subcontinent as a whole, from parties led by hereditary dynasties through the savagery of the police and the corruption of officialdom to the everyday violence and latent anarchy of parts of the countryside.

Pakistan is in fact a great deal more like India – or India like Pakistan – than either country would wish to admit. If Pakistan were an Indian state, then in terms of development, order and per capita income it would find itself somewhere in the middle, considerably below Karnataka but considerably above Bihar. Or to put it another way, if India was only the 'cow-belt' of Hindi-speaking north India, it probably wouldn't be a democracy or a growing economic power either, but some form of impoverished Hindu-nationalist dictatorship, riven by local conflicts.

In order to understand how Pakistan works, it is necessary to draw heavily on the field of anthropology; for one of the things that has thoroughly befuddled not just much Western reporting and analysis of Pakistan, but the accounts of Pakistanis themselves, is that very few of the words we commonly use in describing the Pakistani state and political system mean quite what we think they mean, and often they mean something quite different.

This is true whether one speaks of democracy, the law, the judicial system, the police, elections, political parties or even human rights. In fact, one reason why the army is by far the strongest institution in Pakistan is that it is the only one in which its real internal content, behaviour, rules and culture match more or less its official, outward form. Or, to put it another way, it is the only Pakistani institution which actually works as it is officially meant to – which means that it repeatedly does something that it is not meant to, which is seize power from its weaker and more confused sister institutions.

Parts of Pakistan have been the subject of one of the most distinguished bodies of anthropological literature in the entire discipline; yet with the partial exception of works on the Pathans, almost none of this has made its way into the Western discussion of political and security issues in Pakistan today, let alone the Western media. Critically important works like those of Muhammad Azam Chaudhary and Stephen Lyon on Punjab are known only to fellow anthropologists.[10]

Incidentally, this is why in this book I have chosen to describe as Pathans the ethnicity known to themselves (according to dialect) as Pashtuns or Pakhtuns. It was under the name of Pathans (the Hindustani name for them, adopted by the British) that this people is described and analysed in the great historical and anthropological works of Olaf Caroe, Fredrik Barth, Akbar S. Ahmed and others; and it was also by this name that this people was known for more than a century to their British military adversaries. The name Pathan recalls this great scholarly tradition as well as the glorious military history of resistance to British conquest, both of which are crucial to understanding developments among the Pathans of the present age.

When it comes to other parts of Pakistani society, the lack of detailed sociological research means that analysts are groping in the dark, and drawing conclusions largely based on anecdotal evidence or their own prejudices. It is striking – and depressing – that more than eight years after 9/11, by far the best US expert on the vitally important subject of Islamist politics in the North West Frontier Province (NWFP)[11] is a young graduate student, Joshua White – one key reason being that he has actually *lived* in the NWFP.[12] This lack of basic knowledge applies for example to the critical area of urbanization and its effects – or lack of them – on religious, cultural and political patterns.

According to standard theories concerning urbanization in the Muslim world, the colossal movement of Pakistanis to the cities over the past generations should have led to fundamental cultural changes, reducing the power of the old political clans and traditional forms of Islam, and strengthening modern and radical forms of Islam and modern mass parties. But is this really happening? My own impressions would tend to suggest that things are much more complicated, for reasons that will be discussed in this book. But they are only impressions. Systematic studies of these questions have not been carried out for almost a generation.

As a result of this lack of basic information, too often in Western analysis, when local forms differ from the supposed Western 'norm' they are not examined, but are treated as temporary aberrations, diseases to be cured or tumours to be cut out of the otherwise healthy patient's system. In fact, these 'diseases' *are* the system, and can only be 'cured' by a revolutionary change in the system.

The only forces in Pakistan that are offering such a change are the radical Islamists, and their cure would almost certainly finish the patient off altogether. Failing this, if Pakistan is to follow Western models of progress, it will have to do so slowly, incrementally and above all organically, in accordance with its own nature and not Western precepts.

THE NEGOTIATED STATE

In the course of Pakistan's sixty-year history, there have been several different attempts radically to change Pakistan, by one civilian and three military regimes. Generals Ayub Khan and Pervez Musharraf, military rulers in 1958–69 and 1999–2008 respectively, both took as their model Mustafa Kemal 'Atatürk', the great secular modernizing nationalist and founder of the Turkish republic. General Zia-ul-Haq, military ruler from 1977 to 1988, took a very different course, trying to unite and develop Pakistan through enforced adherence to a stricter and more puritanical form of Islam mixed with Pakistani nationalism. Zulfikar Ali Bhutto, founder of the Pakistani People's Party and civilian ruler of Pakistan in the 1970s, for his part tried to rally the Pakistani masses behind him with a programme of anti-elitist economic populism, also mixed with Pakistani nationalism.

And they all failed. Every single one of them found their regimes ingested by the elites they had hoped to displace, and engaged in the same patronage politics as the regimes that they had overthrown. None was able to found a new mass party staffed by professional politicians and ideologically committed activists rather than local 'feudals' and urban bosses and their followers. Indeed, with the exception of Bhutto none tried seriously to do so, and after a short while Bhutto's PPP too had ceased to be the radical party of its early years and had become dependent on the same old local clans and local patronage.

The military governments which took power promising to sweep away the political elites and their corruption also found themselves governing through them, partly because no military regime has been strong enough to govern for long without parliament – and parliament is drawn from the same old political elites, and reflects the society which the military regimes wish in principle to change. Western demands that such regimes simultaneously reform the country and restore 'democracy' are therefore in some ways an exercise in comprehensively missing the point.

To have changed all this, and created a radical national movement for change like that of Ataturk, would have required two things: firstly a strong Pakistani nationalism akin to modern Turkish nationalism – something that ethnically divided Pakistan does not have and cannot create; and, secondly, a capacity for ruthlessness to equal that of Ataturk and his followers in suppressing ethnic, tribal and religious opposition. For the pleasant Western story of Turkey's ascent to its fragile democracy of today ignores both the length of time this took and the hecatomb of corpses on which the modern Turkish state was originally built.

With the exception of the dreadful atrocities perpetrated in East Bengal in 1971 – committed against people whom the Punjabi and Pathan soldiery regarded as alien, inferior and Hindu-influenced – the Pakistani state has not been able to commit abuses on a really massive scale against its own people, either because, in the case of Punjab and the NWFP, its soldiers were not willing to kill their own people, or, in Sindh and even Balochistan, because it always in the end had to make compromises with the local elites.

One of the most striking things about Pakistan's military dictatorships is in fact how mild they have been by the historical standards of such dictatorships, when it comes to suppressing dissent and criticism among the elites. Only one prime minister (Zulfikar Ali Bhutto) and a tiny handful of politicians have ever been executed in Pakistan – far fewer than have been killed in feuds with each other. Few senior politicians have been tortured.

Of course, the poor are a different matter, but, as noted, they get beaten up by the police whoever is in power. Perhaps the single most important social distinction in Pakistan is that between what Graham Greene called the 'torturable classes' and the 'untorturable' ones.[13] This view has support from a surprising source. As General Musharraf writes in his memoirs, 'Whatever the law, civil or military, the poor are always the victims of oppression.'[14]

Nor indeed has the Pakistani state ever faced rebellion in West Pakistan on a scale that would have provoked massacre in response – though that could be changed by the Taleban insurgency in the Pathan areas which began in 2004 and gathered strength in 2008 and 2009. India has faced much more serious rebellions, and has engaged in much larger-scale repression in response.

But in India, as in Pakistan, the state is not responsible for most human rights abuses. This is something that human rights groups in particular find hard to grasp, since they stem from a modern Western experience in which oppression came chiefly from over-mighty states. In Pakistan, however, as in India, the vast majority of human rights abuses come not from state strength, but from state weakness. Even when they are committed by state policemen, they are not on the orders of the government, but are the result of individual policemen or groups of police preying on the population as their ancestors did for centuries. Take the police chief in the interior of Sindh, who told me, 'I try to stop my boys raping women and torturing people to death. Beyond that, you have to be realistic. Anyway, we need to raise more money from the people just to do our job half-way properly.'

No one can seriously imagine that when police rape a woman or torture a suspected criminal in their custody, that this is the will of Prime Minister Manmohan Singh of India or President Zardari of Pakistan. They can be accused of not doing enough to stop such abuses – but their ability to do so is very limited. So Pakistan – and indeed South Asia and much of Latin America – demonstrates the frequent irrelevance of democracy even in an area where we instinctively think that it makes all the difference, namely human rights. The overwhelming majority of human rights abuses in Pakistan stem from a mixture of freelance brutality and exploitation by policemen, working either for themselves or for local elites; actions by local landlords and bosses; and punishments by local communities of real or perceived infringements of their moral code.

The murder of women in 'honour killings', the giving of young girls in marriage as compensation in the settlement of clan feuds, the dreadful cases of gang rape as a punishment which have taken place in recent years in southern Punjab, Sindh and Balochistan are the work of families, or local clans and their collective leaderships, not of the state. Atrocities by local dominant clans and the police are also entirely characteristic of much of neighbouring democratic India. As regards the police, this is starkly revealed in a report by Human Rights Watch of August 2009.[15]

Not for nothing was an old Hindustani popular term for banditry *'padshahi kam'*, the imperial trade. This indicated not only that ordinary people could usually see no difference between bandits and soldiers, but that they often changed places. Unpaid soldiers became bandits; successful bandits became soldiers of conquering armies, and their leaders became kings.

According to standard Western models, and to the Pakistani constitution that derives from them, authority stems from the sovereign people through elections, and then spreads downwards from the government through hierarchical structures, which transmit orders from above, from superior to inferior officials, in accordance with laws made by parliament or at least by some formal authority.

In Pakistan, only the armed forces work even in the second half of this way. For the rest of the state, the law, the judiciary and the police, authority is a matter of constant negotiation, with violence or the threat of it very often one of the cards that can be played on either side. The negotiated nature of the Pakistani state was summed up for me in a grim anecdote from a retired general who in the 1990s was responsible for commanding anti-dacoit operations in Sindh.

A subordinate had run a dacoit gang to earth on the estate of a parliamentarian from the then ruling party, and wanted to send troops in to get them – which would have led to furious protests from the governments in Islamabad and Karachi, and most probably the immediate release of the men arrested. His commander overruled him, and instead invited himself to lunch with the landowner concerned. At the end of a convivial meal, he passed his host a note and said that he'd be personally obliged for his help. The next day, four of the dacoits were handed over to the army with a message from the landowner-politician saying that the general could shoot two of them, but could he please charge the other two before the courts.

'Any two?' I asked, somewhat faintly.

No, he said which two we could shoot. Probably they had offended him in some way, or they were not from his tribe. As to the other two, he knew perfectly well that his influence meant that the courts would never convict them, and they would be released after a few months. The courts are useless when it comes to criminals in this country if the criminals have any connections – they are bribed, or scared, or both. That is why if you really want to deal with a miscreant, the only way is to kill him out of hand. This is a hard country, and this is the way things are here, sadly.

This negotiated nature of the state also applies to the workings of democracy. For democracy is representative not only of the people, but of all those classes, groups and institutions through which the popular will is refracted until it eventually finds some kind of distorted reflection in elected institutions. In other words, democracy usually reflects not so much 'the people' or 'the electorate' as the distribution of social, economic, cultural and political power within a given society. The nature of Pakistani society, and the weakness of real democratic development, are shown among other things by the lack of real, modern, mass political parties, with their own cadres of party workers.

A while spent pondering on these themes should bring out why so much Western analysis of Pakistan misses the mark, because it expects institutions with names like 'the law' and 'the police' to work as they are meant to work in the West, according to rules rather than negotiation. Similarly, Western language about 'corruption' in Pakistan suggests that it can and should be cut out of the political system; but in so far as the political system runs on patronage and kinship, and corruption is intertwined with patronage and kinship, to cut it out would mean gutting Pakistan's society like a fish.

This of course is precisely what the Islamist revolutionaries would like to do. The modern Islamist political groups are trying to replace the clan and patronage politics of the 'feudal' landowners and urban bosses with their own version of modern mass politics, so far with only very limited success. With the partial exception of the Jamaat Islami, the Islamist political parties have themselves been swallowed up by the patronage system. As for the Pakistani Taleban (the Tehriq-e-Taleban Pakistan, or TTP), they are so far a primitive collection of guerrilla and terrorist groups, which would be completely at sea if they found themselves responsible for Peshawar, let alone Lahore or Karachi.

Of course, they do draw a great deal of their strength from the glaring inequities and oppressions of the Pakistani system, and above all the justice system. It is true, as I have said, that ordinary Pakistanis are themselves part of endless conspiracies to pervert the course of justice – but it is also true that they feel they have no choice, given the nature of the justice system. The state's law is felt by many ordinary people not just to be rigged in favour of the rich, and hopelessly slow, corrupt and inefficient, but also to be alien – alien to local tradition, alien to Islam, the creation of alien Christian rulers, and conducted by the elites for their own benefit.

So, as this book will describe, when ordinary people speak of their reverence for the Shariah, and their respect for the Taleban when they introduce the Shariah, this should not necessarily be taken as active support for the Taleban's complete programme. Rather it is a mixture of a reverence for the Shariah as part of the word of God, dictated to the last Prophet, with a vague yearning for a justice system that might be cruder than that of the state, but would also be quicker, less biased in favour of the elites, and conducted before the eyes of the people, in their own language. Mixed in with this is a great deal of somewhat veiled anti-elitist feeling, which in the eyes of parts of the Pathan tribal populations helps fuel mass acceptance of Taleban attacks on the local *maliks* and khans, or tribal bosses and local landowners.

But then, the Pathans have always been the most culturally egalitarian people of Pakistan. Among the masses elsewhere, the progress of the Islamists has so far generally been very limited when it comes to gaining active mass support. One key reason for their failure to date is the deeply conservative nature of much of Pakistani society; for – quite contrary to most Western perceptions – Islamist mobilization often thrives not on backwardness, but on partially achieved modernity. Thus, to judge by all the economic evidence about poverty and landownership, radical Islamist groups preaching land reform ought to be flourishing in the Pakistani countryside.

In fact, the only areas where they have had any significant success (outside the Pathan territories) are where a sectarian (Sunni versus Shia) or tribal element comes into play. This is partly because of clan solidarity, but also for the simple reason that the only people who could lead such a radical Islamist movement in the countryside are the local mullahs, and they are in effect chosen by the local 'feudal' landowners – who do not exactly favour radicalism of any kind, least of all involving land reform.

In the cities, things are freer, but even there most attempts at political mobilization from below are stifled by the grip of the political bosses and the kinship groups they lead, as well as by the politically apathetic condition of society, and by divisions along religious lines. In other words, while there is certainly a great deal of economic, social discontent in the Pakistani population, being discontented is not at all the same thing as being able to do something about it. As of 2009, the perennial discontent of the urban masses in most of Pakistan continues to express itself not in terms of political mobilization behind new mass movements, but sporadic and pointless riots and destruction of property – including most notably the buses in which the rioters themselves have to travel every day.

According to the standard Western version, by which the Western way is the only way to modernity, the key ideological struggle in Pakistan is between Westernized modernity (including democracy, the rule of law, and so on) and Islamic conservatism. A more accurate way of looking at it would be to see much of Pakistan as a highly conservative, archaic, even sometimes quite inert and somnolent mass of different societies, with two modernizing impulses fighting to wake it up.

The Western modernizers have on their side the prestige and success of the Western model in the world in general, and the legacy of British rule, including a vague belief in democracy – but are crippled both by the conservative nature of Pakistani society and by growing popular hatred for the US and its Western allies.

The Islamist modernizers can draw on a much more ancient and deeply rooted tradition, that of Islam – but are crippled by the conservative nature of Pakistani society, by Pakistan's extreme fissiparousness, by the failure of their programme elsewhere in the Muslim world, and by the fact that the vast majority of the Pakistani elites reject their model, for cultural as well as class reasons. Both Westernizers and Islamists see the battle between them as apocalyptic, and ending with the triumph of good or evil. Yet there is a fair chance that Pakistan will in effect shrug both of them off, roll over, and go back to sleep.

A GAMBLE ON THE INDUS

Pakistan cannot however afford to do so, because time is not on Pakistan's side. In the long run, the most important thing about the people

29

of Pakistan is not who they are or what kind of religion they follow, but that whoever they are, there are too many of them for the land in which they find themselves – and more of them all the time. In 2010, the population was estimated at between 180 and 200 million, making Pakistan the sixth largest country on earth in terms of population. It had risen from 131 million at the census of 1998, 34 million at the census of 1951 (four years after independence) and only 19 million at the British census of 1911 – and is today ten times what it was 100 years ago. Officially, population growth now stands at 2.2 per cent a year–which would seem to be a serious underestimate.

Pakistan's inability to bring this rate down more quickly reflects state weakness, social conservatism, lack of education (above all among women) and the ability of the religious parties to play on popular prejudices. Since Ayub Khan in the late 1950s, no Pakistani government has dared to promote family planning seriously, and the reduction that has occurred has happened because of socio-economic change and urbanization, not through state action.

The huge youth bulge making its way through the Pakistani population means that this population will continue to grow steeply for a long time to come (in 2008, 42 per cent of the population was estimated as under the age of fourteen). If present trends continue, then by the middle of the twenty-first century, according to World Bank projections, Pakistan may have as many as 335 million people.[16]

This is far too many people for Pakistan's available water resources to support, unless the efficiency of water use can be radically improved. If the old Indian economy used to be described as 'a gamble on the monsoon', then the entire Pakistani state can be described as 'a gamble on the Indus' – and climate change means that over the next century this may be a gamble against increasingly long odds. The capricious power of water in this area is demonstrated by the remains of numerous cities – starting with those of the Indus Valley civilization 4,000 years ago – that have been either abandoned because rivers have changed their course, or been washed away by floods, as so many towns and villages were by the great floods of 2010.

At an average of 240 mm of rainfall per year, Pakistan is one of the most naturally arid of the world's heavily populated states. Without the Indus river system and the canals flowing from it, most, even of Punjab, would be semi-desert and scrub-forest (called 'jungle' in Pakistan) – as it was before the British began their great irrigation projects.

This is apparent if you fly over the country. Once the five great rivers of Punjab and the Kabul river flowing from Afghanistan have paid their tribute to the Indus, the vast majority of cultivated land in the southern end of Punjab and the whole of Sindh is only what can be irrigated from the Indus. Beyond these lands, all is brown, yellow and grey, dotted with the occasional oasis provided by natural springs or more often tube-wells. Only 24 per cent of Pakistan's land area is cultivated – the great majority through man-made irrigation systems. The rest is pastoral land, or uninhabited: desert, semi-desert, and mountain.

Chronic over-use, however, means that many of the natural springs have dried up, and the water table is dropping so rapidly in many areas that the tube-wells will also eventually follow them into extinction. That will leave the Indus once again; and in the furore surrounding the debunking of the exaggerated claim that the glaciers feeding the Indus will disappear by 2035, it has been forgotten that they are nonetheless melting; and if they disappear a century or two later, the effects on Pakistan will be equally dire, if no serious action is taken in the meantime radically to improve Pakistan's conservation and efficient use of water.

If the floods of 2010 are a harbinger of a long-term pattern of increased monsoon rains, this on the other hand would potentially be of great benefit to Pakistan – but only potentially, because to harness them for agriculture requires both a vastly improved storage and distribution infrastructure, and radical measures to stop deforestation in the mountains and to replant deforested areas. Otherwise, increased rainfall will risk more catastrophes like that of 2010, with the water rushing off the deforested hillsides in the north to swamp first the valleys and then the plains. It should be added, though, that an absolutely essential part of existing infrastructure did work during the floods: the great barrages along the Indus and its tributaries. If these had broken, several of Pakistan's greatest cities would have been inundated, and the death toll would have been vastly higher than the 1,900 who lost their lives.

This dependence on the Indus is the greatest source of long-term danger to Pakistan. Over the next century, the possible long-term combination of climate change, acute water shortages, poor water infrastructure and steep population growth has the potential to wreck Pakistan as an organized state and society. Long-term international aid projects in Pakistan should be devoted above all to reducing this mortal threat, by promoting reforestation, repairing irrigation systems and even more importantly improving the efficiency of water use. Human beings can survive for centuries without democracy, and even without much security. They cannot live for more than three days without water.

The extent of the water crisis that is already occurring will be described in the chapters on Sindh and Balochistan. As two of the authors of the World Bank's very worrying 2004 report on Pakistan's water situation write:

> The facts are stark. Pakistan is already one of the most water-stressed countries in the world, a situation that is going to degrade into outright water scarcity due to high population growth. There is no feasible intervention which would enable Pakistan to mobilize appreciably more water than it now uses ...
>
> There are no additional water resources to be exploited and agricultural water use must decline to enable adequate flows into the degrading Indus River Delta. Pakistan's dependence on a single river system makes its water economy highly risky ...
>
> Groundwater is now being overexploited in many areas, and its quality is declining ... There is little evidence that government (or donors, including the World Bank) have re-engineered their capacity and funding to deal with this great challenge. And here delay is fatal, because the longer it takes to develop such actions, the greater will become the depth [beneath the earth] of the water table.[17]

According to a 2009 study by the Woodrow Wilson Center drawing on a range of different works, by 2025 population growth is likely to mean that Pakistan's annual water demand rises to 338 billion cubic metres (bcm) – while, unless radical action is taken, Pakistan's water availability will be around the same as at present, at 236 bcm. The resulting shortfall of 100 bcm would be two-thirds of the entire present flow of the Indus.[18]

And this frightening situation would have come about even before the potential effects of climate change begin to kick in. These effects could be to turn stress into catastrophe by the end of the twenty-first century. Well before Pakistan reaches this point, however, it is likely that conflict over access to the shrinking Indus will have raised tensions between Pakistan's provinces to levels which will be incompatible with the country's survival.

If anyone thinks that the condition of Pakistan will be of little consequence to the rest of the world in the long run, they should remember that a hundred years from now, if it survives that long, Pakistan will still possess nuclear weapons, one of the biggest armies in the world, one of the biggest populations in the world and one of the biggest diasporas in the world, especially in Britain. Islamist radicalism, which has already existed for hundreds of years, will also still be present, even if it has been considerably reduced by the West's withdrawal from Afghanistan.

All of this will still mean that of all the countries in the world that are acutely threatened by climate change, Pakistan will be one of the most important. Moreover, what happens to Pakistan will have a crucial effect on the rest of South Asia, where around one-fifth of the world's entire population live and will live. Those Indians who would be tempted to rejoice in Pakistan's fall should therefore consider that it would almost certainly drag India down with it.

The World Bank has valuable programmes in place, on which much more could be built. For example, at present, Pakistan harvests a good deal less of its rainfall than neighbouring areas of India, and only a fraction of China's harvest per cubic metre of rainfall. Intensive effort is needed to improve this performance – something which does not require expensive high-tech solutions, but rather a mixture of spadework and better, more innovative management.

Concentrating development aid on the improvement of Pakistan's water infrastructure has the added advantage that such improvement is highly labour-intensive, and provides a range of jobs, from masses of ordinary workers with spades to highly trained engineers. This means that benefits from international aid will flow immediately to many ordinary people and be immediately apparent to them. By contrast, most US aid in recent decades, though often very useful to the economy as a whole, has not been visible to ordinary people and therefore has had no political effects in terms of attitudes to the US.

THE PAKISTANI ECONOMY

There would be no point in talking about any of this if Pakistan were in fact the hopeless economic and administrative basket-case that it is so often made out to be. This is not the situation, however. Pakistan has never followed the 'Asian tigers' in radically successful modern development, and shows no signs of doing so, but for most of the time since 1947 its rates of growth have been substantially higher than India's. Pakistan would be a far more developed and prosperous state today but for the economic disaster of Zulfikar Ali Bhutto's nationalization programmes of the 1970s, which led to a steep drop in growth.

After another period of economic stagnation in the 1990s (worsened by US sanctions imposed as a punishment for Pakistan's nuclear programme), under the Musharraf administration from 1999 to 2008 economic growth returned to a rate of between 6.6 and 9 per cent a year, before dropping again as a result of the global economic recession.

Certainly, most people in Pakistan are poor; but all the same, as a result of this economic growth, together with the effects of Islamic charity and the circulation of state patronage to the kinfolk and followers of successful politicians, Pakistan lacks the huge concentrations of absolute poverty to be found in India's cities and countryside. In fact, the absolutely poor and defenceless people in Pakistan are often the same as in India – the descendants of the old 'untouchable' castes, who – seeing nothing for them in India – remained in Pakistan at partition but have never escaped their traditional poverty and marginalization. There are however far fewer of them in Pakistan.

From this point of view as so many others, Pakistan has a rather medieval look. The state is very bad at providing modern services such as clean water, medicine, public transport and education, because it is too weak either to force much of the population to pay taxes or to control corruption on the part of its own officials. In part as a result of the lack of education, ordinary people are also very bad at organizing themselves to demand or create such services. Certain groups are outside the system altogether, and have no access to protection, patronage or charity. On the other hand, the system does ensure that the great majority of the population does at least have enough to eat.

And where the state decides that a particular development project is of great national importance, it can in fact partially isolate it from the corruption of the rest of the system and ensure that it is built successfully. This was true of the vast extension of dams and irrigation in the 1950s, and in recent years the construction of the port of Gwadar and the fine motorways linking the great cities of northern Pakistan.

Pakistan's GDP as of 2009 stood at $167 billion, making it the 48th largest economy in the world (27th if adjusted for purchasing power). Despite the image of Pakistan as an overwhelmingly rural society, and the dominance of political, social and cultural patterns drawn from the countryside, agriculture as of 2009 accounted for only about 20 per cent of GDP. The 'service sector' accounted for 53 per cent (most of it in informal, very small-scale businesses and transport), with industry at 26 per cent. However, around 60 per cent of the population continued to live in the countryside, helping to explain the continued power of the rural elites. Most of Pakistani industry is made up of textiles and food processing. In 2007–8 Pakistani exports stood at $18 billion, the majority of them textiles.

Pakistan also contains certain islands of high technology – above all the nuclear industry, which (whatever you may think about its strategic implications) is a very remarkable achievement for a country with Pakistan's economic profile, and shows what the Pakistani state can achieve if it really sets its mind to it, and can mobilize enough educated, honest and committed people.

It is miserably clear, however, that – as with the other South Asian countries – the greater part of the Pakistani economy has not made the breakthrough to modern development and seems nowhere near doing so. As of 2009, GDP per head stood at a mere $1,250 (before adjustment for purchasing parity). Between 1960 and 2005, per capita income as a proportion of that of the USA actually fell from 3.37 to 1.71 per cent. Some 23 per cent of the population live below the poverty line. Underlying this lack of development is a literacy rate which in 2010 stood at only 55.9 per cent, above all because of the complete absence of education for women in much of the countryside.

LIVING IN PAKISTAN

If the West and China want to help improve this picture, they need to develop an approach to Pakistan which recognizes the supreme importance of the country but is based on a real understanding of it, and not on fantasy, whether of the paranoid or optimistic variety. This book is an attempt to strengthen such understanding. It is based on travels to Pakistan dating back to my time there as a journalist for *The Times* (London) in the late 1980s, and on five research trips in 2007–9 lasting a total of six months, during which I visited all Pakistan's provinces and major cities.

It should be said that, with the exception of my stays in some of the Pathan areas, at no point during my visits did I feel under any direct physical threat, except from the execrable local driving – and if you were going to be too affected by that you'd have to avoid visiting about half the world. Moreover, the Pathan areas are only a small proportion of Pakistan as a whole. It is worth stressing this, because one reason why Pakistan is so little known and so badly misinterpreted in the West is that so many analysts and commentators are too afraid to go there, or, if they go, to travel outside Islamabad. This reluctance to visit Pakistan is true even in Britain, which is organically linked to Pakistan by the large Pakistani diaspora; and it is largely unjustified – not to use a stronger word for this behaviour.

Of course, an unescorted visit to the tribal areas, or a prolonged stay in Peshawar in unprotected accommodation, might very well prove fatal; but it is entirely possible to live for months on end in a dozen other different Pakistani cities, and most of the Pakistani countryside, without in my view running any very serious risk. Researchers, analysts and officials dealing with aid to Pakistan need to do this if they are to do their jobs properly.[19]

My own recent researches in Pakistan have been not nearly as long as I would have wished, owing to teaching commitments and a short deadline for this book; but they did give me the chance to talk to hundreds of ordinary Pakistanis from every walk of life, most of whom had never been asked for their opinion before by any Pakistani or Western observer or organization. The views of these voiceless masses form the heart of this book, and I have tried to reflect them as faithfully as I can and draw from them an understanding of Pakistani reality.

This has not always been easy. I remember a conversation with an elderly leader of the Awami National Party in Peshawar in 2008. In his garden were a pair of strikingly graceful long-legged grey birds with crests. I asked him what they were. 'Flamingos,' he replied.

'Um, I don't *think* so, sir . . .'

'No, you are right of course, they are not flamingos. They migrate to Russia in summer, sensible birds, and then come back here again to lay their eggs. We hoped one of them was female and would lay eggs, but it turns out they are both males. So they fight all the time or stand at opposite ends of the garden sulking.'

'Like Pashtun politicians, sir, perhaps?'

With a deep laugh: 'Oh yes, yes indeed, unfortunately! But what are they called now in English? We call them *koonj*.' Turning to his staff, he asked, 'What are *koonj* in English?' And with absolute, unquestionable conviction, one of them replied:

'Swans!'[20]

So if in the course of this book I have sometimes mistaken flamingos for swans, or indeed pristine Pakistani political swans for ugly ducklings, I can only plead in self-defence Pakistani society's ability to generate within an astonishingly short space of time several mutually incompatible versions of a given event or fact, often linked to conspiracy theories which pass through the baroque to the rococo.

Conflicted Pakistani relations with reality notwithstanding, I am deeply attached to Pakistan, which has provided me with some of the best moments of my life; and Pakistan's people have treated me with immense kindness and hospitality. Pakistan is one of the most fascinating countries of my acquaintance, a place that cries out for the combined talents of a novelist, an anthropologist and a painter. But after twenty years of intermittently covering Pakistan, this is a clear-sighted affection. I have good friends among the Pakistani elite, but I also take much of what they say with several pinches of salt – even, or especially, when their statements seem to correspond to Western liberal ideology, and please Western journalists and officials.

The problem goes deeper than this, however. Western-style democracy has become so associated over the past generation with human rights, wealth, progress and stability, that to accept that a country cannot at present generate stable and successful forms of it is an admission so grating that both Westerners and educated Pakistanis naturally shy away from it; Westerners because it seems insulting and patronizing, Pakistanis because it seems humiliating. Both, therefore, rather than examining the reality of Pakistan's social, economic and cultural power structures, have a tendency to reach for simple explanations concerning the wicked behaviour of malignant forces, whether the generals, the 'feudals', the mullahs or the Americans.

Seen from a long historical perspective, things look rather different. Modern democracy is a quite recent Western innovation. In the past, European societies were in many ways close to that of Pakistan today – and indeed, modern Europe has generated far more dreadful atrocities than anything Islam or South Asia has yet achieved. In the future – who can say? The virtues of courage, honour and hospitality, in which Pakistanis excel, do after all have their permanent worth.

It may also be worthwhile in this context to recall the words which the science fiction novelist John Wyndham put into the mouth of a professor asked to give advice on future careers in a world threatened by radical climate change. He had two recommendations: 'Find a hilltop, and fortify it'; and 'Enlist in a regiment with a famous name. There'll be a use for you.'[21] Pakistan has plenty of famous regiments, and local chieftains have been fortifying hilltops for thousands of years. They may yet cope better with the future than the successful elites of today's world.

A NOTE ON KINSHIP TERMS

That kinship is of critical importance in Pakistan is something on which all the academic experts agree – which is nice, because they tend to agree on nothing else about the subject. For me, the definitive word was said 100 years ago by the great British civil servant and ethnographer Sir Denzil Ibbetson. After an official career lasting decades in the Punjab, he wrote:

> An old agnostic is said to have summed up his philosophy in the following words: 'The only thing I know is that I know nothing, and I am not quite sure that I know that.' His words express very exactly my own feelings regarding caste in the Panjab. My experience is that it is almost impossible to make any statement whatever regarding any one of the castes we have to deal with, absolutely true though it may be for one part of the province, which shall not presently be contradicted with equal truth as regards the same people in some other district.[22]

Thus the English term 'tribe' can be translated into several different local words, which overlap with other English meanings. *Qaum* can mean tribe, people, ethnicity or even nation. *Zat* is related to the Indian word *jati*, for a 'sub-caste' in Hinduism. 'Tribe' can also mean several very different things in different parts of Pakistan. Among the Baloch tribes (not just in Balochistan but in Sindh and southern Punjab as well), a tribe means something like the old clans of Scotland, a tightly knit group under an autocratic chieftain.

Among the Pathans, however, while tribal membership is a tremendously important marker of identity and status, the tribes are divided into endless rivalrous sub-tribes, for which new leading men emerge in every generation. Meanwhile in Punjab, the Rajputs, Jats, Gujjars and others were presumably tightly knit nomadic tribes in the distant past, but long ago spread out and intermingled territorially across the whole of what is now northern India and Pakistan (the Gujjars have given their name to a state in India as well as a city in Pakistan, among many other places).

Originally assimilated to the Hindu caste system as *kshatriyas* (the warrior caste) thanks to their conquests, many Jats, Gujjars and Rajputs later converted to Islam or Sikhism. Within Pakistan, they have no collective overall political identity at all, but have a certain community of sentiment, including a strong sense of superiority to everyone else, and a strong preference for marrying each other. An appeal to fellow Rajput or Jat feeling may gain some limited help when all else fails. More important in terms of loyalty and mobilization is the local sub-clan, as in Chauhan Rajput, Alpial Rajput and so on. The Sayyids and Qureishis are groups peculiar to Islam, being (ostensibly) descendants of the Prophet and his clan, and therefore of Arabic origin. Yet their role and status in South Asian Muslim society has certain limited affinities to that of the Brahmins in South Asian Hindu society.

Meanwhile, other kinship groups are descended straight from the lower castes of the Hindu system. These include the *kammi* artisan and service groups of the towns and villages; and below them, the old untouchables and tribals, who are so far down the system that no one even bothers much if they are Muslim, Hindu or – what most really are – pre-Hindu animist. As in India, these last are the most vulnerable groups in Pakistani society, liable to be preyed on economically and sexually by local dominant lineages and by the police.

As to effective political roles within kinship groups and in wider politics, this spreads outwards from the *khandan* – denoting both the immediate family and the extended family (often a joint family, in which several brothers and their families live together under one roof) – to that hellish concept, invented for the confusion of mankind: *biradiri* (related to the Indo-European root for 'brother'), which is supposed to denote the descendants of one common male ancestor. To judge by my interviews, however, *biradiri* can be used to mean almost any kind of wider hereditary kinship link depending on context. In this book, I have therefore used 'kinship group' or 'kinship network' rather than *biradiri* when speaking of such wider groups.

2

The Struggle for Muslim South Asia

*Then We made you their successors in the land, to see how you
conduct yourselves*
(The Koran, Surah Yunus 10, verse 14)

*When we lowered the boat of our existence
Into the river run with pain
How powerful our arms were,
How crimson the blood in our veins!
We were sure that after just a few strokes of the oars
Our boat would enter its haven.
That's not how it happened.
Every current was treacherous with unseen maelstroms;
We foundered because the boatmen were unskilled;
Nor had the oars been properly tested.*

*Whatever investigations you conduct;
Whatever charges you bring,
The river is still there; the same boat too.
Now you tell us what can be done.
You tell us how to manage a safe landing.*

(Faiz Ahmed Faiz)[1]

This chapter is not intended to provide a history of the territory of what
is now Pakistan – something that would take several books (a chron-
ology of the main events of Pakistan's history is, however, included as

an appendix to this book). Rather, this chapter will try to draw from the history of the region, and of Islam in South Asia, those events and elements which are of greatest relevance to the situation in which Pakistan finds itself today: notably, the intermittent but recurrent history of Islamist mobilization against Western forces in the region; recurrent attempts by different administrations radically to change Pakistan; and an equally recurrent pattern of governmental failure which is common to both civilian and military regimes, and results from a combination of state weakness and entrenched kinship loyalties, religious allegiances and local power structures.

'ISLAM IN DANGER'

As with the Muslim world more widely, the single most important thing to understand about patterns both of Muslim history and of Muslim consciousness in South Asia is the tremendous rise of Muslim power up to the seventeenth century, and its steep decline thereafter. Before 1947, the glorious history of Muslim rule and cultural achievement in South Asia helped make it impossible for Muslims to accept a subordinate position in what they saw as a future Hindu-dominated India. By the same token, for a long time after independence and to a degree even today, Pakistanis have felt that they not only must compete with India, but must compete *on an equal footing*; and that to accept anything less would be a humiliating betrayal.

This history also contributes to the fact that, in the words of Iqbal Akhund,

> The Pakistani Muslim thinks of himself as heir to the Muslim empire, descended from a race of conquerors and rulers. There is therefore a streak of militarism in Pakistan's ethos, even at the popular level.[2]

By 1682, when Ottoman Muslim troops were battering the walls of Vienna, the Mughal empire ruled (albeit often very loosely) almost the whole of South Asia. The Mughals built on previous Muslim sultanates of Delhi that had ruled most of north India since the thirteenth century. Even after the Mughal empire began to fall to pieces in the first half of the eighteenth century, great Muslim successor dynasties in Awadh,

Bengal, Bhopal, Hyderabad and Mysore continued to rule over most of what is now India.

While Muslim soldiers conquered, Muslim missionaries converted – but much more slowly. Outside what is now Pakistan, only in Bengal was a majority of the population over a large area converted to Islam. A central tragedy of modern Muslim history in South Asia has been that, as a result, the greatest centres of Muslim civilization in South Asia were established in the midst of Hindu populations, far from the areas of Muslim majority population. The decline of Muslim power, and the partition of 1947, left almost all the greatest Muslim cities, monuments and institutions of South Asia as islands in an Indian sea, towards which Pakistanis look as if from a distant shore towards a lost Atlantis.[3]

The old Muslim dynasties of South Asia were as a rule not severely oppressive towards their Hindu subjects. They could not afford to be, given Hindu numerical predominance and the continued existence of innumerable local Hindu princes. At the popular level, Hindu and Muslim religious practice often merged, just as in Europe Christianity took on many traditions from local pagan religions. At the highest level, the Mughal Emperor Akbar (1542–1605) founded the Din-i-Ilahi (Divine Faith), a syncretic cult containing elements of Islam, Hinduism and Christianity.

Nonetheless, in the Muslim kingdoms there was no doubt which religion was foremost in the state, as the great mosques which dominate the old Muslim capitals testify, and were meant to testify. The Din-i-Ilahi cult failed completely to root itself, while – like all attempts to dilute or syncretize Islam – provoking a severe backlash from orthodox Muslim clerics, which undermined Akbar's authority. The last great Mughal emperor, Aurangzeb (1618–1707), responded to the increasing problems of his empire with a programme of strict religious orthodoxy.

As elsewhere in the Muslim world, the decline of Muslim power from the early eighteenth century on produced a complex set of religious and cultural responses – the great majority of which, however, had the same ultimate goal, namely to strengthen the power of Muslims in the face of their enemies, and to strengthen Muslim unity in the face of the Muslims' own divisions.[4] From the later eighteenth century, Muslim fears were focused above all on the rise of the British (in 1803 the Mughal emperor became a British pensionary).

Since those days, religious forms of Muslim resistance to Western power have been a constant in South Asian history, ebbing and flowing but never disappearing. From the mid-nineteenth century on, they have been joined by a very different response, that of Westernization. It is important to note, however, that the great majority of Westernizers have justified their programmes in public by arguing that they were necessary in order to strengthen their communities, their countries or the Muslim world in general against their non-Muslim enemies. In other words, these figures were no more necessarily pro-Western in geopolitical terms than were the Westernizers of Japan. This is something that the West would do well to remember, given our congenital illusion that anyone who shares aspects of our culture must necessarily agree with our foreign policy.

The Muslim religious response to Western power has always been a highly complex mixture of conservative and radical elements. Many of these have been reformist – but reformist in the sense of the Protestant Reformation in Europe, not of modern Western 'reform'. They have also shared the 'fundamentalism' of parts of the Protestant tradition, in the sense of a return to the 'fundamentals' of the original religious scriptures. All have stressed the need for Muslims to wage the 'greater jihad' of spiritual struggle and personal and social purification as well as the 'lesser jihad' of war against Islam's enemies.

Underpinning intellectual and political responses by Muslim elites has been a diffuse but widespread sense among the Muslim masses of 'Islam in danger'. This has contributed to episodes both of mass mobilization and of savage local violence against non-Muslims (or other Muslims portrayed as non-Muslims). These combined in the developments leading to the creation of Pakistan in 1947.

This sense of an endangered Islam has long been fuelled not only by local or even regional events but by developments in the wider Muslim world (for example, in the later nineteenth and early twentieth centuries, the fall of the Ottoman empire in the face of attack from Christian powers). The role of the Ummah in the minds of most South Asians therefore might be seen as vaguely analogous to that of 'Christendom' in the European Middle Ages: not something that could ever trump local powers and allegiances and lead to a universal *state*, but nonetheless a potent idea with important cultural, intellectual, emotional, political and international consequences – not least in the form of the Crusades.

With the disappearance of France and Britain as ruling powers in the Muslim world, the focus of Muslim fears concerning Western threats to the wider Muslim world naturally shifted to the new state of Israel (in occupation of Islam's third holiest shrine, as Pakistanis are continually reminded by both their mosques and their media) and Israel's sponsor, the United States.

In Pakistan, however, hostility to the US was for a long time damped down by the fact that Pakistan was facing far more pressing dangers, against which the US provided at least a measure of security: India and the Soviet Union. Thus, in the 1980s, President Zia's Islamization programme contained no hint of anti-Americanism, for the obvious reason that the US was both an essential ally in fighting against the Soviet occupation of Afghanistan, and an essential financial sponsor of Pakistan and Zia's administration. Zulfikar Ali Bhutto made considerable play with anti-American sentiment and with the idea of Pakistan as a leader of the Muslim world (including his rhetoric of a Pakistani 'Islamic bomb'), but his own anti-Americanism owed more to the fashionable left-wing thought of the time. The collapse of left-wing nationalism in the Muslim world in the last quarter of the twentieth century has left the Islamists as the last political homeland of anti-American (and anti-colonial) sentiment.

After 1989, a series of developments shattered the previous obstacles to anti-Americanism in Pakistan. First, the Soviet withdrawal from Afghanistan and the subsequent collapse of the Soviet Union itself removed Pakistan's value to the US as an ally. Instead, free rein was given to groups in Washington that feared Pakistan's nuclear programme to press for sanctions on the country. The prominent role of the Israel lobby and pro-Israeli politicians such as Congressman Stephen Solarz in these moves helped increase existing anti-Israeli feeling in Pakistan, and focus attention on the US–Israel alliance. The anger this caused in Pakistan was exacerbated by the way in which the US abandoned all responsibility for the consequences of a war in Afghanistan which it had done so much to fuel, leaving Pakistan facing a civil war on its borders and a continuing refugee problem.

Of even greater importance has been Washington's increasing 'tilt to India', replacing the mutual hostility that characterized most of the period from 1947 to 1991. Seen from Pakistan, this was reflected first in Washington's willingness to punish Pakistan as well as India for the nuclear race in South Asia, despite the fact that in both 1974 and 1998 it was actually India which first exploded nuclear devices. Moreover, because of its far smaller economy and greater dependence on exports to the West, the US sanctions of the 1990s hit Pakistan much worse than India, and were in fact largely responsible for the economic stagnation of that decade.

Since 9/11, the US has sought a quasi-alliance with India, amid much talk in the US of building up India as a force against both China and Islamist extremism. The US has abandoned any pretence at parity in its approach to the Indian and Pakistani nuclear programmes, and has sought active nuclear partnership (albeit with qualifications concerning security) with India. The US has put immense pressure on Pakistan concerning sponsorship of militant and terrorist groups in India and Indian-controlled Kashmir, but has repeatedly backed away from any attempt to put pressure on India to reach a settlement of the Kashmir conflict – notably when, in early 2009, pressure from India and the Indian lobby in the US led to India being swiftly dropped from the responsibilities of the Obama administration's regional special envoy, Richard Holbrooke.

Also of great importance in creating anti-American feeling in Pakistan has been the belief that Washington has supported authoritarian governments in Pakistan against their own people. In the past, this belief was stimulated by US aid to Generals Ayub, Zia and Musharraf. Today, it is focused on US help to President Zardari – which just goes to show that US administrations have no preference for military government or indeed any kind of government in Pakistan as long as that government *does what the US wants*.

Pakistanis also tend greatly to exaggerate the degree of hands-on control that the US can exert over Pakistani governments. In fact, the relationship with the US has always been one of mutual exploitation heavily flavoured with mutual suspicion. Ayub went to war with India and cultivated relations with China against US wishes; Zia diverted US aid to Pakistan's particular allies among the Afghan Mujahidin; successive Pakistani administrations developed a nuclear deterrent in the face of strong pressure from Washington; and since 9/11 Pakistani governments have only very partially acceded to US wishes in the 'war on terror'. However, in Pakistan facts are rarely allowed to get in the way of a good conspiracy theory, and the widespread belief among Pakistanis is that the US runs their country as a neo-colonial client state.

As a conclusive blow to pro-US sentiment in Pakistan came the US invasions of Afghanistan and Iraq. In the immediate wake of 9/11, to judge by my researches in Pakistan in 2001–2, the US move into Afghanistan was accepted with surprisingly little protest by most Pakistanis, and there was some willingness to accept Al Qaeda's responsibility. The invasion of Iraq, however, and the mendacious arguments used by the Bush administration to justify the invasion, appeared to confirm every Muslim fear about the American threat to the Muslim world.

The disastrous impact of this invasion in Pakistan is reflected in the fact that it retrospectively destroyed the justification for the Afghan war as well, as far as most Pakistanis are concerned. This shift is reflected in the fact that, to judge by my own interviews and those of other Western colleagues, an absolutely overwhelming majority not just of the Pakistani masses but of the Pakistani elites believe that 9/11 was not in fact carried out by Al Qaeda but was a plot by the Bush administration, Israel, or both, intended to provide a pretext for the US invasion of Afghanistan as part of the US strategy of dominating the Muslim world.

Whenever a Westerner (or, more rarely, a sensible Pakistani) attempts to argue with this poisonous rubbish, we are immediately countered by the 'argument' that 'Bush lied over Iraq, so why are you saying he couldn't have lied about 9/11?'[5] The US invasion of Iraq, coming on top of US support for Israel and growing ties to India, greatly strengthened the vague and inchoate but pervasive feeling among Pakistanis that 'Islam is in danger' at the hands of the US.

The effects of all this on the desire of Pakistanis to make sacrifices in order to help the US in the 'war on terror' should hardly need emphasis. Instead, from the widespread hostility to the Afghan Taleban in 2001–2, by 2007–9 the perception of them on the part of the vast majority of ordinary Pakistanis with whom I spoke at that time had become close to their view of the Afghan Mujahidin during my time in Pakistan in the late 1980s: not nice people, or ones they would wish to see ruling Pakistan – but nonetheless brave men waging a legitimate war of resistance, or defensive jihad, against an alien and infidel occupation of their country.

Naturally, therefore, there has been intense opposition within Pakistan to the Pakistani military helping the US by attacking the Afghan Taleban in Pakistan's border areas. For a long time, this opposition extended to the Pakistani militants in the region, who were seen as simply attempting to help their Afghan brethren carry on their legitimate struggle. This opposition diminished somewhat as the extent of the militant threat to Pakistan became apparent in 2008–10, and the Pakistani media became much more hostile to the Pakistani Taleban. It remains, however, a very powerful strain of public opinion, and opposition to the military campaign against the Pakistani Taleban, and hostility to the US alliance in general, have done terrible damage to the administrations of both President Musharraf and his successor President Zardari.

RELIGIOUS AND SECULAR RESPONSES

The specific religious forms that resistance to the West has taken have of course changed considerably over time, while nonetheless preserving an organic continuity. In the eighteenth and much of the nineteenth centuries, a prominent part was played by Sufi orders and local religious leaders belonging to those orders – just as in the resistance of the Muslim Caucasians to Russian conquest under Imam Shamil, and that of the Algerians to French conquest under Abdul Qadir. Today, the Wahabi-influenced Taleban and their like are attacking the shrines of the very saints who formerly fought against the British, French and Russians – but nonetheless they are their heirs as far as anti-Western action is concerned.

Shah Waliullah (1703–62), the most significant intellectual Muslim figure of the era, was an Islamist reformist who preached the use of independent reasoning (*ijtihad*), but directed towards a return to a purer form of Islam based on the Koran, and towards the strengthening of Muslim states and mobilization for armed jihad to restore Muslim power in South Asia; a jihad which he and his followers – like their successors today – saw as 'defensive'. Jihad against the British was declared and implemented by the great Muslim ruler of Mysore in southern India, Tipu Sultan.

Shah Waliullah's teaching inspired both the Deobandi tradition which in recent years has inspired political Islamism in Pakistan, and more immediately Syed Ahmed Barelvi (1786–1831), who tried to lead a jihad against growing Sikh rule in the Punjab. Interestingly, he and his 600 followers became the first of a number of figures – of whom Osama bin Laden and Al Qaeda are the latest – to move from elsewhere to the Pathan tribal areas, both because the absence of government provided what we would now call a 'safe haven', and because the legendary fighting qualities of the Pathan tribes seemed to make them prime recruits for jihad.

Like many of his successors, however, Syed Ahmed Barelvi discovered that the tribes also have their own traditions and their own agendas. He was abandoned by most of his local Pathan allies after he tried to replace the traditions of the Pathan ethnic code of *pashtunwali* with strict adherence to the Koran, and, together with his closest disciples, was killed in battle by the Sikhs at Balakot. He is remembered by jihadi Islamists in the region as the greatest progenitor of their tradition, though the precise circumstances of his end tend to be glossed over. Following Shah Waliullah's defeat and death, his grandson Muhammad Ishaq quit India in disgust for Arabia.

Because of their radical fundamentalism and Arabian links, Syed Ahmed, his followers and descendants were given a name by the British which also has profound echoes in the present day: that of 'Wahabi', after the ferociously puritanical fundamentalist movement founded by Muhammad Abdul Wahab in Arabia in the late eighteenth century, and adopted by the House of Saud as their religion. As with the attribution of 'Wahabism' to the Taleban today, this was only partly accurate. Shah Waliullah had studied in Arabia, in part under teachers who taught Wahab; but his teaching and that of his descendants differed from Wahabism in significant respects.

However, the Wahabis' capture and savage purging of Mecca and Medina (including the destruction of 'heretical' shrines and even that of the Prophet himself) had made them a name that was useful for both supporters and opponents of jihad: supporters because of their reputation for courage and religious rigour, enemies because of their reputation for barbarism and their ferocious attacks on Muslims from other traditions. As in South Asia and the former Soviet Union today, the term 'Wahabi' therefore came to be thrown about with abandon to describe a variety of supporters of jihad and advocates of fundamentalist reform of Islam. All the same, those fighting against the Taleban and Al Qaeda today would do well to remember that, though new movements in themselves, they have roots going back hundreds of years in Arabia and South Asia, and 180 years among the Pathan tribes.

The critical moment in the Muslim response to British rule came with the great revolt of 1857, known to the British as 'the Indian Mutiny'. This revolt itself stemmed in part from the British abolition the previous year of Awadh, the last major semi-independent Muslim state in north India. In Lucknow, mutinous soldiers proclaimed the restoration of the

Awadh monarchy, and, in Delhi, they made the last Mughal emperor their figurehead. Across much of north India, radical Muslim clerics preached jihad against the British.

In consequence, although a great many Hindus took part in the revolt, the British identified Muslims as the principal force behind it, and British repression fell especially heavily on Muslims and Muslim institutions. The two greatest Muslim cities of north India, Delhi and Lucknow, were ferociously sacked and largely destroyed by the British army and its Punjabi auxiliaries, with many of their leading citizens killed. The last vestiges of the Mughal empire were wound up, and many Muslims dismissed from the British service.

In the decades following the revolt, the Muslim elites, as the former ruling class of much of India, suffered especially from changes introduced by the new British administration which replaced the East India Company. English replaced Persian as the language of administration, and English-language universities increasingly replaced traditional Muslim centres of education.

Intentionally or unintentionally, British rule also came to favour the Hindu upper castes above the old Muslim elites. Hindus moved with greater ease into the British educational institutions, and hence came to dominate the lower ranks of the civil service. The growth of Calcutta, Bombay, Madras and Karachi as commercial entrepôts favoured the Hindu trading castes. Most disastrously of all, the gradual introduction of representative institutions from the 1880s on revealed just how heavily Muslims were outnumbered by Hindus across most of India.

Muslim responses to these challenges continue to shape the Pakistani state, and Pakistani public debate of today. Some of the responses centred on secular education and mobilization, some on different forms of religious renewal. Different movements – or the same movements at different times – emphasized competition with Hindus, or co-operation with them against British rule. As for the idea of a separate Muslim state in South Asia, this emerged only at the very end of British rule, and in a very ambiguous form. However, whatever approach they adopted, the vast majority of Muslims who became politically engaged did so in separate organizations from the Hindus. In the early days of the Indian Congress, some of its more radical Hindu leaders opposed Muslim membership.

In the very broadest terms, the main tendencies of Muslim response to British colonialism can be divided into three: that stemming from or related to Shah Waliullah and his preaching of religious renewal and resistance; that epitomized by Sir Syed Ahmed Khan (1817–98); and that of the mass of the Muslim population, including the local rural elites.

These latter basically got on with their lives and with extracting whatever benefits they could from British rule (notably, in northern Punjab, in the form of military service and settlement in the new canal colonies), while at the same time being subject to occasional waves of unrest when fears as to the safety of their Muslim identity were aroused. Local factors also sometimes produced armed revolts by specific Muslim groups – chiefly in the Pathan areas, but also in the 1920s on the part of the Moplahs of the Carnatic in southern India, and in the 1940s on the part of the Hurs, religious followers of the Pir Pagaro, a hereditary saint in Sindh.

Sir Syed Ahmed Khan was a Mughal aristocrat who sided with the British in 1857, though he also bitterly criticized their policies. Although himself a deeply religious man, Sir Syed advocated the need for Indian Muslims to collaborate with the British, and to learn the ways of Western modernity in order to develop as a people and compete successfully with the ascendant Hindus. Sir Syed founded what he intended to be 'the Muslim Cambridge', the Mohammedan Anglo-Oriental College, at Aligarh – another of those key Muslim institutions now left behind in India.

In 1888, Sir Syed laid down the basic principle on which Pakistan was created – though without at that stage dreaming of territorial separation. He stated that 'India is inhabited by two different nations', which would inevitably struggle for power if the British left:

> Is it possible that under these circumstances two nations – the Mohammadan and the Hindu – could sit on the same throne and remain equal in power? Most certainly not. It is necessary that one of them should conquer the other and thrust it down. To hope that both could remain equal is to desire the impossible and the inconceivable.[6]

The founder of Pakistan, Mohammed Ali Jinnah, and his closest associates, therefore stood in the direct tradition of Sir Syed; a tradition which saw the Muslims of the subcontinent as a kind of nationality defined by language (Urdu) and religiously influenced culture, rather than by religion as such. The priority given to fear of the Hindus naturally inclined this tradition to oppose the Hindu-led Indian independence movement, and to ally with the British against it.

In Pakistan, this tradition of nationalist modernization has been followed by two of Pakistan's military leaders, Ayub Khan and Pervez Musharraf, and by Zulfikar Ali Bhutto. Ayub could also be seen to have replaced Britain with America as the Muslims' inevitable (if unfortunate) ally in their struggle with 'Hindu' India.

In a vaguer sense, Sir Syed's programme of broadly Western modernization remains the ideology of the Pakistani civil service and of the educated wealthy classes – though their commitment actually to do much about this is another matter. Some members of this tradition decided in 1947 to throw in their lot with India rather than Pakistan, and are now to be found scattered through the worlds of Indian politics, administration, the universities and especially the arts.

Under British rule, the Islamist tradition of Shah Waliullah naturally opposed collaboration with the British and stood for anti-colonial resistance – though, given the realities of British power, this was inevitably mostly by peaceful means. This led to the paradoxical result that some of the most fervent proponents of jihad – like Maulana Abul Kalam Azad (1888–1958) – were also advocates of close co-operation with Hindu Indian nationalists against British rule (Azad ended as an Indian National Congress leader and independent India's first Minister of Education). This tradition therefore opposed the partition of India and the creation of a separate Pakistani state, in part because they were attached to the idea of a universal Muslim Ummah and opposed any move to divide it further along national lines.

It is entirely logical therefore that Pakistan's largest Islamist party, the Jamaat Islami, should have opposed the creation of Pakistan in the name of loyalty to the Ummah; and today should be especially committed to Muslim causes in the wider world, including the 'jihads' in Palestine, Chechnya and Kashmir – also in the name of defending the universal Ummah, rather than narrow Pakistani national interests. President Musharraf, by contrast, explicitly condemned this approach in his speeches after 9/11, emphasizing the need for Pakistanis to put Pakistan first.

THE GENESIS OF PAKISTAN

The last generation of British rule saw two Muslim mass political movements in South Asia, the Muslim League and the Khilafat movement. The Muslim League, founded in 1906 and heavily influenced by Sir Syed's tradition, began as an elite movement to defend Muslim interests, extract concessions from the British, and either oppose or co-operate with the Indian National Congress as tactical advantage dictated. It only became a true mass movement in the last years of British rule.

Though founded in Dhaka, in what is now Bangladesh, by far the strongest support of the Muslim League was in the heartland of Muslim Urdu-speaking culture, in the United Provinces between Delhi and Allahabad (now the Indian state of Uttar Pradesh). A key moment in its foundation came in 1900 when the British agreed that Hindi (Hindustani in the 'Hindu' Devanagari script) should be placed on an equal footing with Urdu (Hindustani in the 'Muslim' Arabic script) as an official language, with the clear implication that given Hindu numerical preponderance, Urdu would eventually be edged out of government altogether.

The other great Muslim movement under British rule was much more in the tradition of Shah Waliullah, being both explicitly religious and much more radical. This was the Khilafat (Caliphate) movement, from 1919 to 1924, one of whose leaders was Maulana A. K. Azad, mentioned above. This took place in alliance with the Indian National Congress, now led by Mohandas Karamchand Gandhi, and was the chief Muslim aspect of the unrest which gripped India after the end of the First World War. However, as its name suggests, the formal catalyst of the movement was a purely Muslim one, and reflected allegiance to no South Asian cause, but to the universal Ummah.

South Asian Muslims rallied behind the movement in protest against the impending abolition of the Caliphate, or titular leadership of the Muslim world, which the Ottoman sultans had claimed. The Caliphate issue became the rallying cry for protest against the British and French subjugation of the entire Middle East and destruction of the last Muslim great power, as well as of course against British colonial rule in India, and a range of local Muslim grievances. The Jamaat and other Islamist groups in Pakistan today see their hostility to the US today as directly descended from this Islamist anti-colonial tradition. As Mahatma Gandhi himself wrote in 1922:

> The great majority of Hindus and Muslims have joined the [anti-British] struggle believing it to be religious. The masses have come in because they want to save the khilafat and the cow. Deprive the Mussulman of the hope of helping the khilafat, and he will shun the Congress. Tell the Hindu he cannot save the cow if he joins the Congress and he will, to a man, leave it.[7]

The Khilafat movement was led by two clerics, the brothers Maulana Mohamad Ali Jauhar and Maulana Shaukat Ali, and generated a wave of religious enthusiasm among South Asian Muslims. For that reason it was disliked by Mohammed Ali Jinnah, who stood in Sir Syed Ahmed's tradition of tactical co-operation with the British, and to whom religious fanaticism was deeply antipathetic. So great was this religious enthusiasm that in 1920 some 20,000 Indian Muslims attempted to emigrate to Afghanistan, as the last independent Muslim state left standing in the region. They were eventually expelled by the Afghan authorities after having been robbed of many of their possessions – not the first or the last time that the hopes of South Asian Islamists concerning the Afghans have been disappointed.

The rhetoric of the Khilafat movement was heavily influenced by that of jihad, and the movement's violent edge led to increasing tension with Gandhi and the Congress. The movement finally collapsed in the face of British repression, and the Caliphate was eventually abolished not by the colonial powers but by Kemal Ataturk and the new Turkish secular republic.

The mass religious enthusiasm which powered the Khilafat movement eventually flowed into the very different strategy of the Muslim League, led in the 1920s by Sir Muhammad Iqbal (1877–1938) and from 1936 by Jinnah. A radically simplified account of League strategy in these years would be that it involved selective co-operation with the Congress to put pressure on the British to grant more extensive powers of legislation and self-government to India and the Indian provinces, and selective co-operation with the British to limit Congress's power and ensure Muslims a guaranteed share of the new legislatures and governments.

The idea of creating a separate state for Muslims in South Asia came only very late. It was first raised by Iqbal in 1930 – and he still envisaged that this state would be part of a wider Indian Confederation. Shortly afterwards, the name 'Pakistan' was coined for this proposed state. The so-called 'Two Nation Theory' had in a way been implicit in Muslim League ideology from the beginning. This theory holds that Indian Hindus and Muslims have the characteristics of two different ethno-cultural nations. As the example of Lebanon, Northern Ireland and other countries where what are in effect different nations live in one country under a set of arrangements for coexistence, this does not however necessarily dictate territorial separation.

The decisive moment for the demand for Pakistan as a slogan came with the Government of India Act of 1935 and the elections of 1937 which followed. Prior to the elections, Congress had made informal promises to the League that the two parties would form coalition governments in provinces with substantial Muslim minorities. As it turned out, however, Congress's victories were so overwhelming that – most unwisely – the Congress leadership decided that it did not need to share government with the League, and reneged on its promise.

This Congress 'treachery' convinced Jinnah and the other leaders of the League that Muslim parties would be excluded from power in a Congress-ruled independent India, and Muslims reduced to a wholly subordinated community. In the background to all these moves and counter-moves were recurrent 'communal riots', in which local issues and religious prejudice led Hindus and Muslims to attack each other, often resulting in heavy casualties.

The eventual result was the Lahore Resolution of 1940, in which, at Jinnah's call, the Muslim League set out the demand for an independent Muslim state. However, Jinah still spoke not of full separation but rather of 'dividing India into *autonomous* national states' (my italics); and as the distinguished South Asian historian Ayesha Jalal has convincingly demonstrated, this demand was not quite what it seemed.[8] As late as 1939, Jinnah was stating that although Hindus and Muslims were separate nations, 'they both must share the governance of their common homeland'.

Jinnah in the end was bitterly disappointed with the 'moth-eaten' Pakistan that he eventually received. Not merely did this exclude almost all the great historic Muslim centres of India, but it left out those areas of north India where support for the Muslim League and the demand for

Pakistan had been strongest; and yet for demographic and geographical reasons, there was no way that an independent Pakistan could ever have included these areas. Furthermore, all the evidence suggests that Jinnah and the League leadership were completely unprepared for the realities of complete separation from India. This was to have tragic consequences when Pakistan was created.

Rather, it seems, Jinnah was using the slogan of Pakistan for two purposes: to consolidate his own control over the League, and as a threat to force Congress to concede what he – and most Muslims – really wanted. This was a united India in which Muslims would be guaranteed a share of power, which in turn would guarantee their rights. On the one hand, this would be a highly decentralized India in which the provinces (including the Muslim-majority provinces) would hold most of the power – a goal shared by the Muslim and indeed Hindu elites of Punjab and Sindh. On the other hand, Muslims would be constitutionally guaranteed a 50 per cent share of positions in the central government, and a large enough share of the central legislature to block any attempts to change the constitution or introduce policies hostile to Muslim interests.

In 2010, such goals may not seem particularly outrageous. In the cases of Northern Ireland, Bosnia, Lebanon and parts of Africa we have become accustomed in recent decades to constitutional arrangements guaranteeing 'power-sharing' between different ethno-religious groups, and heavily qualifying strict majoritarian democracy. However, these demands proved unacceptable to the Congress. They threatened Congress's power, Hindu jobs and the plans of Congress leader Jawaharlal Nehru for state-led economic development, something which depended on a strong centralized state. There was also a well-based fear that a loose Indian confederation would soon collapse into appalling civil war. In the end, therefore, Congress preferred – however unwillingly – a smaller but strong and united Congress-dominated India to a larger but weak, decentralized and endangered Indian confederation.

In 1947, with British rule disintegrating and Hindu–Muslim violence increasing, the British agreed with Congress and the League on independence and partition. Pakistan was to consist of two halves separated by almost 1,000 miles of Indian territory: in the east, the Muslim-majority areas of the province of Bengal; in the west, the Muslim-majority areas of the province of Punjab, together with Sindh, the North West Frontier Province and adjoining tribal and princely territories.

To some extent, the movement for Pakistan may have escaped from Jinnah's hands. As his famous speech to the Pakistani constituent assembly had it, in Pakistan,

> Hindus would cease to be Hindus and Muslims would cease to be Muslims, not in the religious sense, because that is the personal faith of every individual, but in the political sense as citizens of the state.

This passage makes clear that Jinnah expected Pakistan to be a Muslim-majority but essentially secular country in which Muslims would be the 'people of state', but large Hindu and Sikh minorities would exist and would have a share of power. Pakistan would also therefore still be part of a wider South Asian unity, in cultural, social and economic terms, with the possibility of some form of confederation between equal partners emerging later.[9]

However, since Muslim numerical weakness meant that Jinnah and the League could not block Congress's plans by democratic and constitutional means, they were critically dependent on Muslim street power; and this street power was largely mobilized using the rhetoric of Islam (with strong jihadi overtones harking back to the Khilafat movement) and of communal fear. This then collided head-on with Hindu and especially Sikh street power mobilized in the name of their respective fears and visions.

Jinnah spoke of a secular Pakistan, but on the streets the cry was the Muslim profession of faith:

Pakistan ka naaraah kya?
La illaha illallah
(What is the slogan of Pakistan?
There is no God but God)

This is still the slogan of the Islamist parties in Pakistan concerning the country's identity. The wave of mass religious enthusiasm that powered the Muslim League in the last years before partition led Peter Hardy to describe it as 'a chiliastic movement rather than a pragmatic political party'.[10] The Pakistan movement therefore was one in which a secular-minded leadership in the tradition of Sir Syed Ahmed Khan coexisted uneasily with mass support motivated above all by the cry of 'Islam in danger', and by vague dreams of creating a model Islamic society.

A combination of this religious fervour with Jinnah's original plan to balance against the Hindus in an Indian confederation was responsible for the most disastrous aspect of the new Pakistan, namely the uniting of West Pakistan (the present Pakistan) with Muslim East Bengal. This union made absolutely no geographical, historical, economic or strategic sense, and was bound to collapse sooner or later. Apart from anything else, East Pakistan was indefensible in the face of serious Indian attack, as the war of 1971 proved.

The union of West and East Pakistan was dictated in the first instance by the need to keep all Muslims together so as to form the largest possible block against the Hindus within an Indian confederation. Thereafter, the quite different idea of independent Pakistan as the homeland of all the Muslims of South Asia, and the source of their safety and progress, meant that enormous political and emotional capital was invested in trying to maintain Pakistan as one state – when two friendly allied states would have made so much more sense.

Throughout the 1950s and 1960s the need to balance, conciliate or suppress the Bengalis of East Pakistan exerted a malign influence on Pakistan's development. The first protests in the East were in defence of the Bengali language, and in opposition to the extension of Urdu as the state language. From there, opposition turned into demands for greater autonomy, and finally into a programme of de facto separation.

The fact that East Pakistan, though much smaller geographically and economically, held a small majority of Pakistan's population helped make democracy impossible, as it would have implied a Bengali domination which most of the West Pakistanis simply would not accept. This contributed to the breakdown of Pakistani democracy in the 1950s, and the military coup by General Ayub Khan in 1958. Ayub then tried to prevent Bengali domination by abolishing the provinces of West Pakistan and lumping them together in 'one unit', alongside the other 'unit' of East Pakistan. This in turn greatly increased local discontent in West Pakistan.

Ayub's successor, General Yahya Khan (who took power in 1969), reduced tension in West Pakistan by abolishing 'one unit' and restoring the provinces, but failed altogether to conciliate East Pakistan. The West Pakistani establishment – including Zulfikar Ali Bhutto, founder of the

Pakistani People's Party (PPP) – were prepared to accept neither a loose confederation with East Pakistan, nor the democratic domination of the Bengali majority in a united Pakistan.

During the years of protest against Ayub's rule, Sheikh Mujib-ur-Rehman had emerged as leader of the Awami League, representing Muslim Bengali nationalism. Mujib's 'Six Point' programme was a return to the original platform of the Muslim League in British India, demanding maximum autonomy for East Pakistan and reducing Pakistan to a loose confederation. Bengali radicalism had been increased by repeated clashes in East Pakistan between demonstrators and troops, and a catastrophic cyclone in November 1970 in which up to 1 million people died and the government was accused of negligence.

In the December 1970 national elections, the Awami League won 160 out of 162 seats in East Pakistan, and an absolute majority in the national parliament. The PPP won 81 seats out of 138 in West Pakistan. Mujib therefore demanded the right to form the national government, with confederation the inevitable result. This was acceptable neither to Yahya Khan and the army, nor to the Punjabi elites, nor to Bhutto, who demanded an equal share in government on the basis of his party's majority in West Pakistan, and who forged an alliance with hardline military elements in Yahya's administration to resist Bengali demands.

A series of moves and counter-moves took place in the following months, accompanied by increasingly violent mass protests and clashes with the military in East Pakistan. Then at midnight at the end of 25 March 1971, the military launched a savage campaign of repression in East Pakistan (Operation Searchlight). Thousands of students, professionals, Awami League leaders and activists and East Pakistani police were killed, amid dreadful scenes of carnage and rape.

This revolting campaign was the most terrible blot on the entire record of the Pakistani army, and was made possible by old and deep-seated racial contempt by the Punjabi and Pathan soldiery for the Bengalis, whom they also regarded as not true Muslims but crypto-Hindus. It is worth noting that, despite recurrent episodes of military repression, nothing remotely as bad as this has ever happened in West Pakistan, where this racial and racist tension between army and people does not exist to anything like the same degree. Indeed, unwillingness to fire on their own people has been one factor in undermining the will of the soldiers to confront the Taleban.

Memory of the March 1971 massacres in East Pakistan has been largely suppressed in the Pakistan of today, since for obvious reasons neither the military nor the political parties (including the PPP, which after the death of Bhutto was headed for a while by General Tikka Khan, who as commander in East Pakistan launched the campaign of killing there) nor the newspapers, which justified or ignored the killings, have any desire to recall them.

The campaign led to the mutiny of East Pakistani troops (the Bengal Regiment) and a mass uprising in the countryside. Millions of refugees fled from East Pakistan to India with dreadful tales of the Pakistani army's behaviour. Eight months later, with international opinion now ranged against Pakistan, Prime Minister Indira Gandhi of India ordered the Indian army to invade East Pakistan, and in two weeks 96,000 hopelessly outnumbered Pakistani troops there were forced to surrender. An attempt to save the situation by invading India from West Pakistan was beaten off with ease. East Pakistan became the independent state of Bangladesh, and was recognized by the international community.

Because of the vision of Pakistan as both a united Muslim homeland and an ideal Muslim state, the loss of Bangladesh has been seen by most West Pakistanis as a catastrophe which called into question the 'two nation theory' of Muslims as a South Asian nation equal to 'Hindu' India, and therefore the very meaning of their country.

In actual fact, it was only the terrible circumstances of the end of united Pakistan that were a catastrophe. Separation itself was inevitable sooner or later, and left West Pakistan a geographically coherent state whose peoples were also much more closely linked by ethnicity and culture. Pakistan has indeed demonstrated this by surviving, despite so many predictions to the contrary, and by the fact that despite a variety of local uprisings, until the rise of the Taleban it has never faced a challenge remotely on the scale of East Bengali nationalism.

THE NEW PAKISTANI STATE

In West Pakistan, however, despite the cynicism instilled by the later decades of Pakistani history, the initial idealism of the Pakistan movement, and its real achievements, should not be underestimated. Without them, Pakistan might not have survived at all. In Pakistan's first years, despite political turmoil, many Pakistanis displayed a level of energy and public service that they have never since recovered. These qualities were largely responsible for their country's success in overcoming the quite appalling problems generated by partition, the disruption of trade and the transport network, millions of refugees and growing tension with India. As Ian Talbot writes:

> [M]any of the refugees regarded their journey to Pakistan as a true *hijrat*, an opportunity for a renewal of their faith ... Those who have grown cynical over the passage of time in Pakistan will be surprised by the widespread manifestations of social solidarity and improvisation, reminiscent of Britain during the Blitz in the Second World War, which marked the early days of the state's existence.[11]

The late Akhtar Hamid Khan (a former British Indian civil servant and founder of the famous Orangi urban regeneration project, who moved to Pakistan after partition), told me in 1989 that 'ridiculous though that may sound now', he and many younger educated Muslims had genuinely believed that Pakistan could be turned into a sort of ideal Muslim socialist state, drawing on Islamic traditions of justice and egalitarianism as well as on Western socialist thought. In the lines of the Punjabi poet and Muslim Leaguer Chiragh Din Joneka:

> The Quaid-e-Azam will get Pakistan soon,
> Everyone will have freedom and peace.
> No one will suffer injustice.
> All will enjoy their rights.[12]

In fact, however, as with later attempts at radical reform, the first years of West Pakistan also turned into the story of the digestion of the Pakistan movement by local political society and culture, based on 'feudalism', kinship and conservative religion – an experience that was to be repeated under the administrations of Ayub Khan, Zia-ul-Haq and Musharraf. All, in their different ways, tried to bring about radical changes in Pakistan. All were defeated by the weakness of the Pakistani state and the tremendous undertow of local kinship networks, power structures and religious traditions.

Any hope in the immediate aftermath of independence that reformist elements in the Muslim League might prevail against these traditions was destroyed by the premature deaths of Jinnah (barely a year after independence) and his prime minister, Liaquat Ali Khan.[13] Without them, the Muslim League quickly disintegrated. This marks a critically important difference with India, which helps explain why these two offspring of the British Indian empire have had such different political histories.

In India, the charismatic leader of the independence movement, Jawaharlal Nehru, survived in power until 1964, and founded a dynasty which dominates Indian politics to this day. Thanks largely to Nehru, the Congress Party also survived as a powerful force. Indeed, although a 'democracy', until the 1960s India was in some respects (like Japan for more than five decades after the Second World War) a de facto one-party state. In Pakistan, no such party existed.

Even had Jinnah lived, however, it is questionable whether the Muslim League could have continued to succeed politically as the Congress did. The League had its origins, its heart, and by far the greatest part of its support in the north of what was now India. Until shortly before independence, Punjab and Sindh were ruled by local parties dominated by great landowners, in alliance with their Hindu and Sikh equivalents (in Punjab) and with Hindu businessmen (in Sindh). The North West Frontier Province was ruled by a local Pathan nationalist party in alliance with Congress, and Balochistan by its own local chieftains, several of whom opposed joining Pakistan.

The leaders of the new Pakistani state and army were acutely aware of the thinness of loyalty to the new state across most of its territory; and this too helped create the mentality of a national security state, distrustful of its own people, heavily reliant on its intelligence services, and dependent ultimately on the army to hold the country together.

The Muslim League was only able to supplant the local Sindhi, Punjabi and Pathan parties towards the very end of British rule, when the imminent prospect of an independent Hindu-dominated India stirred up profound fears in the Muslim masses of the region. And even then, the League was only able to prevail because it was joined by large sections of the local landowning elites – the first of the compromises between reformist parties and traditional local elites which has been one of the dominant themes of Pakistani history. In consequence, the hopes of more radical elements of the League for land reform were soon buried.

All the same, at the start the top ranks both of the Muslim League and of the bureaucracy were dominated by men from what was now India. This included Jinnah and Liaquat, and a large proportion of the senior ranks of the civil service. This added an additional degree of distance from local society to what were in any case not an indigenous state structure and legal system, but ones bequeathed by the British empire.

One might almost say that the composition and the achievements of the Pakistani state in its first twenty years were mostly non-Pakistani: a state structure created by the British and largely staffed by officials who had moved from the old Muslim territories in India, outside the new Pakistan; a British-created and British-trained army; and an industrial class mainly made up of Gujaratis, also from India. In the decades since, this state has been brought into conformity with the societies over which it rules.

In language too, the new state created a double distance between itself and the population. The new national language, inevitably, was supposed to be Urdu, the language of the Mughal court and army, and of the Muslim elites and population in north India. It was not, however, the language of any of the indigenous peoples of West Pakistan, let alone the Bengalis of East Pakistan.

The strategy of forcing these populations to go to school in Urdu spurred local nationalist resentments in Sindh and the NWFP; all the more so as Urdu was not in fact the language of the top elites. These had come, under British rule, to speak English, and in Pakistan English – of a kind – has remained the language of the senior ranks of government, of high society and of higher education. The baleful effects of this on the legal system will be examined in the next chapter; while the idea that an Urdu education confers social prestige does not long survive any conversation with young upper-class Pakistanis, whose snobbish contempt for Urdu-medium pupils is sometimes quite sickening. So Urdu found itself squeezed from both above and below.

ATTEMPTS AT CHANGE FROM ABOVE

Since the disintegration of the Muslim League in the early 1950s, Pakistan has seen four attempts at radical transformation, three of them in the secular tradition of Sir Syed Ahmed Khan, and one in the Islamist tradition stretching back to Shah Waliullah. Three of these attempts have been by military administrations, and one by a civilian administration.

However, in a sign that Pakistani history cannot be divided neatly into periods of 'democracy' and 'dictatorship', the civilian administration of Zulfikar Ali Bhutto was in many ways more dictatorial than the military administrations of Generals Ayub Khan and Pervez Musharraf, just as for most of his time in power Musharraf's rule was if anything milder than the 'democratic' government of Nawaz Sharif that he overthrew in 1999.

Both main 'democratic' parties when in power have used illegal and dictatorial methods against their opponents – sometimes in order to suppress ethnic and sectarian violence, and sometimes to try to maintain their own power in the face of multiple challenges from political rivals, ethnic separatists and the military. In the gloomy words of a Pakistani businessman:

> One of the main problems for Pakistan is that our democrats have tried to be dictators and our dictators have tried to be democrats. So the democratic governments have not developed democracy and the dictatorships have not developed the country. That would in fact have required them to be much more dictatorial.

But whether civilian or military, and more or less authoritarian, as pointed out in the introduction all Pakistani governments have failed radically to reform Pakistan – in consequence of which, Pakistan, which was ahead of South Korea in development in the early 1960s, is dreadfully far behind it today. However, it is also worth pointing out that they did not fail completely: Generals Ayub Khan, Zia-ul-Haq and Musharraf presided over periods of fairly successful economic growth, and Zulfikar Ali Bhutto's rule, though economically disastrous, freed many Pakistanis from their previous position of complete subservience to the rural elites, and gave them a degree of pride and independence which they have never since wholly lost. In consequence of these achievements, if Pakistan is not South Korea, it is also not the Congo – which is saying something, after all.

Two Pakistani military governments tried to change and develop Pakistan in the general spirit of the Westernizing traditions of Sir Syed Ahmed Khan. I therefore have grouped the administrations of General Ayub Khan (1958–69) and General Pervez Musharraf (1999–2008) in one section. Ayub Khan came from a background that to some extent exemplifies the ethnic complexity of Pakistan: born in the NWFP, from a Pathan tribe but a Hindko-speaking Hazara family of small landowners.

In a way, however, this was irrelevant. Coming from a military family (his father had been a Rissaldar-Major in the British Indian army), and having spent almost his whole adult life in the British Indian and then the Pakistani military, like Musharraf and a great many Pakistani officers his personal identity was completely bound up with his professional one as a soldier.

While Ayub's family had been in the British military service, Musharraf's had served the British as administrators. Like Musharraf's father, Ayub had studied briefly at Aligarh University, which Sir Syed founded. Both men derived from this tradition a strong dislike of Islamist politics, and from their military backgrounds a loathing of politicians in general; yet both found that, in order to maintain their power, they had to rely on parliamentary coalitions made up of some of the most opportunist politicians in the country. In contrast to other military and civilian rulers of Pakistan, both men were personally kindly and tolerant, yet both headed increasingly repressive regimes.

In striking contrast to most successful civilian politicians in Pakistan and throughout South Asia, neither they nor Zia-ul-Haq founded political dynasties or tried to do so. This was in fact impossible, above all because, although they ran what were in certain respects personal dictatorships, they were none of them personal leaders of what has been called the 'sultanistic' kind, and did not personally control the institution that brought them to power.

Rather, they came to power as the CEOs of that great meritocratic corporation, the Pakistan army; and the board of directors of that corporation – in other words the senior generals – retained the ultimate say over their administration's fate. This marks the degree of the army's 'modernity' compared to the political parties. Both Ayub and Musharraf left office when the other generals decided it was time for them to go. As to Zia, no one knows who was responsible for his assassination.

Both Ayub and Musharraf were committed secular reformers. Ayub in particular was bitterly hostile to the Islamists, and removed the 'Islamic' label from the official name of the Republic of Pakistan. He promoted women's education and rights, and was the only ruler in Pakistan's history to have made a really serious attempt to promote birth control, correctly identifying runaway population growth as one of the biggest threats to the country's long-term progress. Like his reformist successors, however, Ayub was forced to retreat from much of his reformist programme in the face of the Islamists' ability to mobilize much of the population in protest at interference with their values and traditions, and the traditional landed elite's ability to block any moves that threatened their local dominance.

Like Musharraf and Zulfikar Ali Bhutto, Ayub Khan expressed great admiration for the reformist secular policies of Kemal Atatürk, founder of the Turkish republic; but all three of them failed to implement anything like Atatürk's programme, for all the reasons that have made Pakistan since independence so different from Turkey since the fall of the Ottoman empire.

Apart from anything else, Atatürk and his movement rode to power on the back of military victory against the Greek, Armenian and French troops which had invaded Asia Minor at the end of the First World War. Ayub's attempt at military victory over India in 1965 ended in failure, and the wave of nationalist fervour that he had aroused then blamed him for the inevitable compromise peace, and contributed greatly to his downfall. In the process, Ayub discovered the severe limits to America's alliance with Pakistan, to which he had committed his administration. Musharraf's experience in this regard was even harsher.

Both Ayub and Musharraf followed strongly free-market economic policies, though, compared to Musharraf's, Ayub's administration did far more to build up the industry and infrastructure of the country. In one respect, Ayub went further than Musharraf, and further than any other government except that of Zulfikar Ali Bhutto in the 1970s. Ayub's administration introduced a land reform in 1959 which, if it fell far short of India's and was largely frustrated by the big landlords, nonetheless contributed to the break-up of the biggest 'feudal' estates, and their transformation in northern Punjab (though barely elsewhere) into smaller-scale commercial holdings.

Ayub's land reform in turn helped spur the successful 'Green Revolution' in the area. However, this commercialization of agriculture, and the spread of mechanized farming, also led to new unemployment and dispossession among agricultural workers and marginal tenants. These moved to the cities and swelled mass unrest against Ayub.

In 1962, Ayub created the Convention Muslim League as a political party to prop up his rule in the face of political pressure that he could not crush through repression (because of his own character, the weakness of the Pakistani state, and the fact that the opposition adoped as its presidential candidate the iconic figure of the Qaid-e-Azam's sister, Fatima Jinnah). Ayub's 'party' was an alliance of independent local notables and bosses, and in no sense either a mass movement or a modern political party staffed by full-time professional officials and volunteers.

The Convention Muslim League was therefore part of the familiar pattern whereby would-be reformist administrations have to depend on traditional – and strongly anti-reformist – power-holders to maintain their rule. This has always inevitably involved turning a blind eye to their corruption, and rewarding them with patronage which has under-mined good government and the state budget. This was just the same with the Pakistan Muslim League (Qaid-e-Azam), or PML(Q), the 'King's Party' that Musharraf put together to support his rule and con-test the elections of 2002. This party was made up chiefly of defectors from Nawaz Sharif's Muslim League (N), and was a typical grouping of opportunist landowners and local bosses. Musharraf was therefore also forced to follow the old pattern.

Thus in his first years in power Musharraf pursued anti-corruption and revenue-raising strategies which won praise from Transparency International and international financial institutions. In advance of the parliamentary elections of 2002, however, a whole string of cases for corruption, non-repayment of loans and tax evasion were dropped against politicians whose support Musharraf needed.

In consequence, tax collection, which had edged up to 11.4 per cent of GDP in 2001, fell again to its historic rate of around 10.5 per cent – low even by the standards of the developing world. Given Musharraf's need for the courts to legitimize him and elected politicians to support him, it seems questionable whether he should really be called a military dictator at all. He was certainly a very weak one by international and historical standards.

Musharraf followed Ayub in attempting to increase the power of local municipal bodies elected on a non-party basis. In both cases, this strategy had both an opportunistic and an honourable side. The oppor-tunistic element was the desire to weaken the opposition political parties by reducing the powers of the national and provincial parliaments, and reducing their access to local patronage.

However, these moves also addressed a very real problem, which exists in India as well as Pakistan. This is that in both countries local elected bodies have traditionally had very weak powers. Real local authority has remained where it was established in British colonial days, in the hands of unelected civil servants whose powers are vastly more sweeping than those of their Western equivalents (including not just powers that in the West belong to elected municipalities, but some of those of the judiciary as well). Even under 'democracy', as far as most of their citizens are concerned, the Pakistani and Indian states therefore function more like 'elected authoritarianisms'. The weakness of local government is especially damaging in the cities, where it hinders the development of new kinds of reformist urban politics.

On the other hand, whereas in British days these civil servants were at least independent of politics and in a position to guarantee minimally honest administration, today they are not just responsible to the national and provincial governments, but are subject to endless pressure from elected politicians at the national and provincial levels. This gives tremendous powers of patronage and harassment to these politicians and their parties, but is extremely bad for honest and effective administration. One consequence is the constant transfers of officials on political grounds, meaning that very few have the chance ever to get to know their districts or areas of responsibility properly.

Ayub's 'Basic Democracy' scheme, and Musharraf's 'Devolution' were both meant to address these problems by giving real power to local elected bodies. In Musharraf's case, he also tried to strengthen the position of women by reserving a third of elected municipal seats for them. However, in both Ayub's case and Musharraf's, after they fell from power their civilian successors simply swept away these reforms, with no attempt to distinguish the good from the bad sides, in order to restore their own power and patronage.

In Musharraf's case, however, his devolution was also widely criticized because he had weakened the police, contributing to several embarrassing collapses of local police forces in the face of Taleban attack. Musharraf had done this by removing the police from the authority of the District Commissioner (the old British 'Burra Sahib', now renamed in rather politically correct Blairite fashion the 'District Coordinating Officer'), and placing them under the elected councils.

This was meant to address a terrible problem in Pakistan (and still more in India): the extreme unaccountability of the local police, which has contributed to so many ghastly atrocities against ordinary people. The problem was that the local councils proved wholly incapable of taking responsibility for the police. In consequence the latter, with no one to force them to take action, developed a strong tendency when faced with any crisis simply to do nothing – not only because of natural somnolence, but out of fear that they would have to take the responsibility if something went wrong. In other fields of administration, too, the newly elected politicians proved too weak and inexperienced to exercise their powers properly – though they might have learned to do so given more time.

There is something therefore both strange and tragic about Musharraf's devolution and its abolition: strange that a 'military dictator' should actually have weakened the state's powers of repression; tragic that elected 'democratic' governments should have undermined democratic progress by weakening local democracy; but above all tragic that a reform with some truly positive democratic and modern aspects should have foundered on the traditional hard realities of South Asian society. Local government reform was therefore part of Musharraf's declared spirit of 'Enlightened Moderation', which, though never systematically developed or implemented, nonetheless stood in the direct tradition of Sir Syed Ahmed Khan. Some of Zia's Islamization measures were rolled back, and, as noted, a strong attempt was made to improve the political role of women.

Until 9/11 Musharraf continued to support Islamist militants fighting in Kashmir against India, but at the same time confirmed his secular credentials by taking tough action against Sunni extremist groups which in previous years had conducted a savage campaign of sectarian terrorism against Pakistan's Shia minority. In 2008–9 these groups allied with the Pakistani Taleban, and extended their terrorism from the Shia and Ismailis to Sunni Muslims from the Barelvi and Sufi traditions, as well as attacking state targets.

Musharraf's administration differed from Ayub's in two ways – one good, one bad. The good one was that – once again, very surprisingly for a military dictatorship – Musharraf introduced a radical liberalization of the media, something that he was to pay for heavily when the media turned against him in 2007. This reflected the fact that, as a great many senior Pakistanis who dealt with him personally have told me, until things began to fall apart towards the end of his rule, Musharraf was a far more open personality than either Ms Bhutto or Mr Sharif, and was genuinely committed to a form of liberal progress.

The bad difference from Ayub lay in the field of economic policy, and was perhaps a matter of Western influence as much as bad judgement on the part of Musharraf and his economic team. In Ayub's day, Western development thinking was focused on the need to build a country's industrial base; and Ayub responded with a very successful programme of industrial growth. By Musharraf's time, however, the Washington Consensus and the capitalist triumphalism that followed the fall of Communism had shifted Western attitudes to a blind faith in market liberalization and an increase in mass consumption. So while Musharraf's economic boom did lead to real growth in the economy and a real rise in state revenues, it was also much more shallow than growth under Ayub and left a much smaller legacy.

Musharraf's finance minister and (from 2004) prime minister, Shaukat Aziz, nonetheless conducted for several years what seemed to be a strikingly successful economic policy. GDP growth, which when Musharraf took over had stood at 3.9 per cent (only a percentage point or so over the rate of population growth), from 2003 to 2008 stood between 6.6 per cent and 9 per cent. Shaukat Aziz's strategy, however, failed to deal with the underlying problems of the Pakistani economy.[14] In 2008, the advent of the world economic crisis led to a sharp drop in the economy, while acute electricity shortages revealed not only incompetence by the new PPP government but also the failure of the Musharraf administration to develop the country's energy infrastructure.

Given Musharraf's personal honesty (in marked contrast to most of his predecessors) and progressive credentials, it is in fact depressing to note how little his administration achieved in nine years in terms of changing Pakistan; though perhaps just helping to keep the country afloat in such times should be considered an achievement in itself.

ZULFIKAR ALI BHUTTO

Bhutto's government from 1971 to 1977 marked the only time a Pakistani civilian administration has sought to bring about radical changes in the country. His most enduring legacy was the creation of the Pakistan People's Party (PPP), one of the dynastic parties (with populist trappings) that continue to dominate South Asian politics. By contrast, Bhutto's attempts at radical reform largely met the same fate as those of

his military counterparts – though with far more tragic personal consequences for Bhutto.

Bhutto's combination of intense 'feudal' and familial pride with an
often vindictive hatred of the Pakistani upper classes has been attributed by many to the fact that his mother, Sir Shah Nawaz's second wife,
was a convert from a Hindu family, inevitably – though probably
wrongly – alleged by his enemies to have been a dancing girl. The miser-
ies resulting from this for a sensitive child in an intensely snobbish and
anti-Hindu milieu can easily be imagined. Later, the scurrilous and mendacious viciousness with which the anti-Bhutto press used his mother's
origins against him must surely have increased his own savagery towards
his critics and opponents.

Bhutto was, however, also a child of his era, one in which left-wing
nationalism was at its height in the 'Third World'. When Bhutto founded
the Pakistan People's Party (PPP) in 1966, Nasser was in power in Egypt,
Sukarno in Indonesia, Nkrumah in Ghana, and Mao was the darling of
the left-wing intelligentsia in much of the world. In neighbouring India,
Mrs Gandhi was preparing to break the hold of the old Congress bosses
on her father's party by a populist campaign much of which was very
close to that of Bhutto. Bhutto's slogan of '*roti, kapra aur makan*' ('bread,
clothes and housing') was echoed by Mrs Gandhi's of '*gharibi hatao*'
('abolish poverty'). So Bhutto seemed to himself and others to be riding
the wave of the future – though even before he took power Nkrumah
had fallen and Nasser had been crushingly defeated by Israel.

The basic dynamics of Bhutto's strategy were simple enough, and
familiar enough from many such regimes elsewhere in the developing
world. The intention was to bring about a socio-economic revolution
from above in Pakistan, and to create rapid economic growth through
the nationalization of industry and state-directed development. In the
process, the support of the Pakistani masses for Bhutto and his party
would be consolidated, and the PPP would become the permanent party
of power, with Bhutto as the lifetime charismatic national leader who
would then pass on this power to his descendants. Unlike the military
rulers, Bhutto was therefore a would-be 'sultanistic' dictator, personal
and dynastic rather than institutional.[15] For Bhutto to achieve his goals,
the grip of the existing elites on politics, the economy and the bureaucracy would have to be broken, when necessary by ruthless means.

It was highly unlikely that this programme could ever have worked in terms of developing the country – as so many other international examples demonstrate. However, as these examples also demonstrate, Bhutto's approach might have worked much better when it came to consolidating his own power and that of his party; he could have ruled for a generation, instead of fewer than six years.

The two differences between Pakistan and more successful examples of authoritarian nationalist populism are that for such regimes to succeed in gaining a real, semi-permanent grip on power they have to create powerful, organized parties staffed by new men and not the old elites; and, even more importantly, *they have to control their armies*. Very often indeed, like Peron, the populist leaders come from the ranks of the army themselves. Bhutto did not come from the military and, as will be seen, the military itself does not allow personal dictators from its ranks to establish dynastic rule. Nor was Pakistani society capable of generating a true mass political party, independent of kinship loyalties and local power elites.

On the side of social and economic change, however, Bhutto acted rapidly and radically. In 1972, all major industries and banks were nationalized. This created a hostility to the PPP on the part of the capitalist classes which has continued long after the PPP abandoned every shred of real left-wing economics, and which largely explains business support for the PPP's opponents in the new Muslim League.

Much more importantly, nationalization was economically disastrous. The move led to a flood of capital flight from Pakistan and a drastic fall in private investment for which the Pakistani state did not have the resources to compensate. Private investment in manufacturing dropped from an average of Rs992 million in 1960–65 to Rs682 million in 1971–6, while public investment rose only from Rs57 million to Rs115 million. By 1974–7, average economic growth per year had plunged to 2.7 per cent, less than the annual growth of population. This compared to average annual growth of 6.8 per cent in 1959–69, under Ayub Khan. Overall, Bhutto's populist economic strategy was therefore a disaster from which it took Pakistan an entire generation to recover.

This was partly because state control of the large-scale commercial economy proved such a lucrative source of political patronage that for a long time it was continued in several areas by succeeding administrations. Direction of the state companies was handed over as patronage to PPP supporters from inside and outside the bureaucracy, a task at which they proved both incompetent and corrupt. Nationalization contained a provision for partial workers' control in the form of workers' committees which were supposed to work together with management. In practice these proved largely a dead letter. Over the succeeding decades, both trade union power and worker commitment to the PPP eroded, until by 2009 they were hardly visible in most sectors.

Despite the genuine radicalism of Bhutto's measures in these areas, they did not go far enough for the left-wing radicals within the PPP. The socialist finance minister Mubashir Hasan had wanted the nationalization of urban land, and the collectivization of agriculture – something that would have led to counter-revolution and bloody civil war across the country. When Bhutto reformed his cabinet in October 1974, Dr Hasan and other left-wingers were excluded, and replaced by an influx of 'feudal' landowners who had rallied to the PPP in the hope of patronage, especially in the nationalized industries.

In the field of land reform, Bhutto was a good deal less radical than in the area of industry – but still more radical than any other Pakistani administration but Ayub's. By a law of 1972, ceilings for landownership were reduced to 150 acres of irrigated land and to 300 acres of unirrigated land, from 500 and 1,000 acres, respectively, under Ayub's land reform; still big farms by Pakistani standards, but nothing resembling the huge estates of Pakistan in the past, or indeed of Britain and America today.

This reform did indeed push agriculture in northern Punjab further in the direction of medium-sized commercial farming; and in Punjab and the NWFP, many of the great 'feudal' political families of today derive their wealth not from agricultural land, but from urban rentals; for many noble families either had patches of land around the edges of the old cities, with villas, orchards and pleasure gardens, or were wise enough to invest agricultural profits in urban land; and ten acres covered with houses and shops is easily worth a hundred times the same acreage in the countryside.

In much of Pakistan, however, Bhutto's land reform was to a great extent subverted. Above all, great landowners would on paper distribute parts of their land to junior relatives and retainers, rewarding them with a share of the proceeds while in practice continuing to control them. Especially in Sindh and southern Punjab, the kinship system yet again worked as a critical element of what has wrongly been called 'feudal' power. Finally, and inevitably, Bhutto's reform turned a blind eye to many of the holdings of Bhutto's own landowning supporters, and own family. My travels with Bhutto's cousin (and governor and later chief minister of Sindh under Bhutto), Sardar Mumtaz Ali Bhutto, will be described in Chapter 8. He is a magnificent figure, a splendid representative of his class and caste – and about as much of a radical agrarian reformer as the Earl of Northumberland *c.*1300 CE.

Land reform faltered still more towards the end of Bhutto's administration, as his power crumbled, his party split, and he became more and more dependent on sections of the old landowning elites to keep him in power – a pattern which, as already argued, echoed the experience of Ayub and prefigured that of Zia-ul-Haq and Musharraf. Growing reliance on the landowning elites reflected Bhutto's failure to consolidate his power through the creation of a disciplined, organized mass party and an effective seizure of the mechanisms of state coercion. Instead, repression under Bhutto took the form of sporadic terror against individual opponents and their families – something that only succeeded in infuriating the state establishment and the other political parties, without breaking their power.

Bhutto was well aware of the need to create a disciplined cadre party. Ironically enough, he had given precisely this advice to Ayub Khan when he was serving in his government (and Bhutto's plans for the PPP in some ways echoed Ayub's hopes for Basic Democracy). But to create such a party across Pakistan it would have been necessary to pay and to motivate its local cadres in such a way as to make them a power in their own right, and independent of local social and economic power structures. That has never been possible in Pakistan, because the state is too poor and weak, and local bosses, kinship groups and religious affiliations are immensely strong. Moreover, no party in Pakistan has been able to generate the ideological fervour required to turn its cadres into purely obedient and disciplined servants.

The only exceptions are the Jamaat Islami and the Mohajir Qaumi Movement – and for reasons that will be explored in Chapters 6 and 8, they have only been able to do this on a local basis. Bhutto's failure to create a disciplined party also meant that local PPP leaders used the breakdown of state authority to set up their own private armed groups and local fiefdoms, and to engage in violent turf battles with each other as well as with the PPP's opponents.

Lacking an effective mass party with real control over society, Bhutto was forced back on instruments of state control. He managed to a great extent to bend the bureaucracy and judiciary to his will, though in the process causing personal hatred which contributed to his death. The police were another matter. As successive Pakistani leaders have found – including in the struggle against the Taleban – the Pakistani police, though often savage enough on an individual basis, are an extremely unreliable force when it comes to mass repression. One reason for this is sheer laziness, exacerbated by bad pay. 'Would you risk your life and run around in this heat for the pay we get?' was the response of many policemen to whom I suggested a more active approach to fighting crime, and, as in the rest of South Asia, it often seemed to me that 'Brutality Tempered by Torpor' wouldn't be a bad motto for the force as a whole.

More importantly, from a force under the British which was to some extent independent of society and under state control, the Pakistani police at ground level had already become a force colonized by society; that is to say, whose officers and men as often as not were working in alliance with local kinship groups, landowners and urban bosses, classes which they naturally therefore were very unwilling to attack.

Bhutto therefore set up his own paramilitary group, the Federal Security Force (FSF), staffed by PPP loyalists drawn from the most thuggish elements of the police and military; and by doing so, he can be said to have signed his own death warrant. It is not clear whether Bhutto gave specific orders to this force concerning the savage victimization of opponents and their families, but at the very least he played the role of Henry II concerning the murder of Thomas à Becket ('Who will rid me of this troublesome priest?').

On the other hand, just as the PPP was not the Soviet or Chinese Communist Party, so the FSF was not the NKVD. It was not remotely strong enough to terrorize Pakistani society as a whole into submission. It was, however, strong and vicious enough to raise hatred of Bhutto in sections of the elite to a degree not seen of any Pakistani ruler before or since. Hence in part the difference between Bhutto's fate and that of Ayub, Musharraf and Nawaz Sharif when they were overthrown. Ayub was allowed to live on in peaceful retirement in Pakistan; Sharif was eventually permitted to go into exile with his family fortune intact, and later returned to politics.

Zia would have allowed Bhutto to take the same path into exile; but when the deposed leader made it clear that he was determined to return to power, and when mass rallies made it clear that he had a real chance of being re-elected, both Zia himself and all the leading figures who had helped bring Bhutto down knew very well what would happen to them, and more importantly their families, if he did in fact return to office. Bhutto's execution removed that threat, and by its very uniqueness stands as a reminder to Pakistani leaders of Machiavelli's lesson that in many societies men will far more easily forget an injury to their interests and even their persons than an assault on their honour.

ZIA-UL-HAQ

It was easy for Bhutto's executioner and successor Zia-ul-Haq to portray his administration as the antithesis of Bhutto's, since he himself was Bhutto's personal antithesis. Zia was Pakistan's first ruler from the middle class, born into the family of a junior British civil servant from east Punjab. Zia himself entered the officer corps of the British Indian army in the Second World War. In 1947 his family became refugees from India, something that strongly marked his world view. In sharp contrast not only to Bhutto but to Pakistan's other military rulers to date, he was a deeply pious Muslim.

Unlike both Bhutto and his military predecessor Ayub and successor Musharraf, Zia attempted to change Pakistan along Islamist lines. This reflected not only Zia's own profound personal religious convictions, but also a nationalist belief (which has been shared by some more secular figures within the military and civilian establishment) that religion is the only force which can strengthen Pakistani nationalism and national identity, keep Pakistan from disintegrating, and motivate its people to give honest and dedicated service to the nation and society.

In most of his goals, however, Zia failed as completely as Bhutto and Musharraf, despite the harshly authoritarian character of much of his rule. He thereby demonstrated once more the underlying and perennial weakness of the Pakistani state, even at its most dictatorial. Pakistani political and social culture was not transformed along official Islamic lines; in fact, Zia's Islamizing measures proved generally superficial (though intermittently very ugly, especially as far as women were concerned) and were eventually largely reversed by Musharraf.

Soon after Zia's death in 1988, a woman lawyer in Lahore, Shireen Masoud, told me that, though she had loathed Zia's regime, most of the Western coverage, reflecting in turn Pakistani liberal opinion, had greatly overestimated its impact on Pakistani society.

> Zia changed a lot less than people think. After all, as far as ordinary people are concerned, this was already a very conservative society, and he didn't make it more so. Feminists complain about the Hadood Ordinances, and rightly, but most people have always imposed such rules in their own families and villages. As to the elites, they have gone on living just as they always did, drinking whisky and going around unveiled. This isn't Iran – Zia was a very religious man himself and also not from the elites so he probably would have liked to crack down on this kind of thing, but in the end he had to keep enough of the elites happy. The one area where he really did change things and force religion down our throats night and day was on state TV and radio – but that's because it was the only place that he really could control.[16]

No new dedicated and religiously minded elite emerged. Instead, Zia, like his predecessors and successors, found himself making deals with the same old elites. Pakistani nationalism was not strengthened, and the state did not grow stronger.

Like the military's Inter-Services Intelligence (ISI), which was responsible for distributing arms, money and training to the Mujahidin, the Islamist parties in Pakistan also profited enormously from the money directed to helping the Afghan jihad, a good deal of which was directed via them. In other ways, however, they were dissatisfied with Zia's rule. They had hated Bhutto, and Zia's Islamization programme ought to have made them his natural allies; but both the administration and the Islamists were too weak, and too different in their agendas, to be able to create a strong foundation for a new kind of Pakistani state.

General Zia declared Pakistan to be an Islamic state. He reversed Ayub's measures limiting the role of Islam in the state, and greatly extended the formal Islamizing measures which Bhutto had adopted in a (vain) attempt to appeal to the Islamist parties. However, Zia conceived his Islamization programme as top-down, and almost entirely in terms of strengthening state power through an increase in the disciplinary aspects of Shariah law. Meanwhile, throughout the state services and society in general, honesty, morality and duty were to be strengthened through the preaching of religion. Islamic ideas of the promotion of social justice and social welfare, and of encouraging people to organize themselves to seek these goals – key to the success of Islamist politics elsewhere in the Muslim world – were almost entirely absent; inevitably so given the essentially authoritarian cast of Zia's mind and strategy.

Zia's approach therefore left the Islamist parties deeply unsatisfied. The Jamaat Islami in particular has also always had a certain real though complex belief in democracy, and became increasingly disillusioned with Zia's dictatorship. On the other hand, for Zia to have formed an alliance with the Islamist parties successfully to transform Pakistani society would also have required them to have been far stronger and more deeply rooted across that society. This in turn would have required much larger, more developed and more confident middle classes in Pakistan.

As subsequent chapters will explore, the great variety of different kinds of Islam in Pakistan makes the creation of a real national Islamist movement extremely difficult. As they will also describe, Zia's official Islamization wholly failed to overcome these differences, and in fact made them much worse. There were bitter disagreements even among Sunni clerics belonging to different theological schools as to which version of Islamic law should be adopted, and Shias rose in protest against what they saw as an attempt to turn Pakistan into a Sunni state. Coupled with fears created by the Shia Islamic revolution in Iran, this left another malignant legacy of Zia's rule: enduring violence between Sunni and Shia militant groups.

So rather than the creation of a new state, Zia was left with the same strategy that all the rulers of Pakistan have sooner or later adopted: a combination of reliance on the state bureaucracy, army and police with handing out state patronage to the rural and urban elites in order to win their support. The economy recovered to a great extent from the disasters of Bhutto's rule, but the boom of the 1980s under Zia proved as shallow as that under Musharraf – based above all on US aid and remittances from the Pakistani workers who flooded to the Gulf states in response to the oil boom. This was in contrast to Ayub, whose administration did build up Pakistan's real economy, though at a high social cost.

Zia did, however, leave certain legacies. Within Pakistan, he created a new and enduring party, to which was given the glorious name of the old Muslim League (though apart from Pakistani nationalism there was no continuity). Initially just another patronage-based alliance of landowners and urban bosses created by the military for its own purposes, this party subsequently developed a real identity of its own, and has been central to Pakistani politics ever since. Like Bhutto, who developed his power base as a member of Ayub Khan's administration before breaking with his mentor, so the man charged by Zia with leading the new Muslim League, Nawaz Sharif, later broke with the military that had created him.

Created to counter the Bhuttos' PPP, the growth of the Muslim League has led since 1988 to the emergence of what is in effect a two-party political system at the national level (though only very rarely can either party win an absolute majority of seats) – a system which survived Musharraf's attempt to eliminate both parties between 1999 and 2007.

But while this two-party balance – like those of India and Bangladesh – has demonstrated its resilience, neither party has demonstrated its ability to provide good government to the country, let alone radical reform. The 'democratic' period of the 1990s was a miserable episode from the point of view of governance, apart from the privatization and economic stabilization measures introduced by the second Muslim League administration from 1997 to 1999. Both PPP and Muslim League governments used illegal methods against political opponents, and savage (though perhaps unavoidable) ones to contain ethnic and sectarian violence.

The PPP's economic and social populism remained at a level of pure rhetoric, with the government of 1988–90 distinguishing itself as the only Pakistani government not to pass a single piece of new legislation. The Muslim League's Islamist policies also remained largely symbolic, contained no element of the social justice and progress which is the hallmark of such policies at their best (for example in Turkey), and often seemed designed mainly to boost the personal authority of Prime Minister Nawaz Sharif.

Both PPP and Muslim League governments were corrupt, owing chiefly to the perennial need to reward kinsfolk and supporters. For example, the PPP Speaker of the National Assembly from 1993 to 1997 (and prime minister after 2008), Syed Yusuf Raza Gilani, created or freed no fewer than 500 jobs in various parliamentary services to give to his supporters. The PPP leadership under Benazir Bhutto (and her husband Asif Ali Zardari) went beyond patronage and limited corruption into outright kleptocracy.

Despite their high claims both main parties have been the prisoners of Pakistan's political society and Pakistan's political culture. As later chapters will analyse, the first has made them dependent on patronage systems necessary to reward local power-holders. The second has meant that, whatever their 'democratic' pretensions, both parties in fact function as dynastic autocracies, with no internal elections and all key decisions and appointments made by the head of the dynasty and his or her closest relatives and advisers. At the time of writing, there is no sign that either of these parties is capable of transcending these deeply ingrained patterns of Pakistani life.

PART TWO

Structures

3

Justice

*From the unwritten comes the law which is sanctioned by use,
because long-lasting customs, which are approved of by agreement of those who are used to them, resemble laws.*

(Code of Justinian)[1]

A visit to the Mohmand Tribal Agency in September 2008 (described
further in Chapter 11) summed up for me the attitudes of most ordinary
Pakistanis to the official judicial system, and how the Pakistani Taleban
have been able to exploit this to their advantage. As Tazmir Khan, a
farmer, told me, to the approval of the other local men sitting with him,

Taleban justice is better than that of the Pakistani state. If you have any
problem, you can go to the Taleban and they will solve it without you
having to pay anything – not like the courts and police, who will take your
money and do nothing.[2]

Strikingly, his views were supported by the steward and the mullah
of the local *malik* landowning family whom I was visiting, and in whose
dusty, sun-drenched yard we were sitting – men who were, if by no
means members of the elite, then not part of the truly downtrodden
masses either. The steward, Shehzad, spoke approvingly of a recent case
of Taleban justice:

Last week, a woman and her husband from Shapqadar were killed. She
was a prostitute and he was selling her. So the Taleban warned her twice,
then arrested them, killed the husband, cut off her nose, gouged out her
eyes and drove a car over her.

The mullah, Zewar, retorted that,

> I agree that she should have been killed, because she had committed crimes, and after all hundreds of people are being killed in this fighting every day. But not the way they did it, by cutting her nose and eyes. That is against the Koran and the Shariah.

However, he added that he too supported the Taleban because they bring quick and fair justice, even if it is often rough:

> The Taleban's work in our area has been good. If you have a problem you can go to them and they will decide your case justly in three days. If you go to the police station, they will take all your money and decide the case in twenty years. In Pakistan, only the rich get justice. So people are coming here from Charsadda and even further to get justice from the Taleban.[3]

From this, it can be gathered that the harshness of Taleban justice, so often denounced in the West and by Pakistani liberals, does not necessarily repel local people, whose local traditions of justice are themselves often very harsh indeed, especially as far as women are concerned. As the mullah pointed out, the punishment of the prostitute and her husband was closer to the *pashtunwali* (the traditional ethnic code of the Pathans) than to the Shariah. Even clearer was the entire local population's absolute loathing for the state judicial system; and this was an attitude which I found among ordinary people across Pakistan.

However, it would be wrong to see the Pakistani population simply as innocent victims of a vicious judicial system run from above for the benefit of the elites. Rather, justice in Pakistan is an extension of politics by other means, and everyone with the slightest power to do so tries to corrupt and twist the judicial system to their advantage in every way possible.

Thus cases brought before the state judicial system are key weapons in the hands of individuals and groups fighting for national and local power; and in both the state and the traditional systems of justice, outcomes are determined largely by political considerations. That means kinship, wealth, influence and armed force, but also sometimes and to some extent the ability to win over public opinion in general. The means to do this have changed over time, with the modern media now playing an important role in some cases.

In the various traditional systems of justice, the powerful always had colossal advantages, albeit occasionally qualified by considerations of religious morality expressed through the influence of the Shariah. In the Pakistani state judicial system derived from the British, to this built-in bias against the poor and weak is added the appalling slowness and complexity of the system, and the ruinous costs extracted by a largely predatory judiciary and police.

All of this is well known to every Pakistani, and fear and even hatred of the state judicial system is general among the mass of the population – even among those who are exploiting the system assiduously to attack their enemies. As an Urdu couplet (with parallels in many languages round the world) has it,

> The day a lawyer was born Satan said with joy,
> 'Allah has made me today the father of a boy.'[4]

Yet at the same time, whether stemming from the teachings of Islam or from innate and universal human cravings, there exists among Pakistanis a deeply felt desire for a better form of justice. This has led to admiration in the educated classes for courageous human rights lawyers such as Asma Jehangir, and to the (alas, exaggerated) hopes attached to the Lawyers' Movement which began in 2007 against President Musharraf and has continued in a lower key against President Zardari.

For many ordinary Pakistanis, however, this hunger for justice focuses on the Islamic code of Shariah; and as subsequent chapters will describe, at least up to the spring of 2009, the Taleban's claim to spread Islamic justice was central to the growth of their popularity in the Pathan areas, and to the unwillingness of most Pakistanis elsewhere to support military action against them.

In the words of Imran Aslam, president of Geo TV:

> Ask ordinary people here about democracy, and they can't really explain it; but ask them about justice, and they understand it well, because unlike democracy issues of justice are part of their daily lives. Also, a sense of justice comes from Islam – a third of the names of God have something to do with justice, fairness, harmony or balance. Issues of electoral democracy have no necessary relation to this, because in Pakistan electoral democracy has little to do with the will of ordinary voters.[5]

It would be quite wrong, however, to see the Pakistani masses faced with the state justice system as simply the passive, sheep-like victims of predatory lawyers, judges, policemen and political elites. This is true, but it is also true that the vast majority of Pakistanis (and Indians) with even the most limited power to do so have contributed to the wreckage of the state judicial system by their constant efforts to twist it to their own individual or group purposes. One reason for this is the continual struggles for power which permeate Pakistani society – struggles in which politics and property are often inextricably mixed. In turn, these struggles generate and are generated by the lack of mutual trust that permeates Pakistani society, between but also within kinship groups.

An additional and disastrous factor is also present. However much, in England in the past, men may have bribed or intimidated judge, jury and witnesses, while at the same time swearing hypocritically into their beer that the law was an ass, they still had a feeling that, however corrupted, the law was *English* law, with its roots in England and stretching back to the very beginnings of English history.

No Pakistani can feel that his state law is Pakistani law in this sense, for the obvious reason that it isn't. It is British law, as transmitted by British rule to the empire of India, adapted to the purposes of ruling India, and somewhat modified by Pakistani governments and parliaments since independence. All over the former colonial world, modern legal systems have been undermined by the fact that they were imposed from outside, have never been fully accepted by the mass of the population, and often clash with that population's traditional codes.

This is also true to some extent in much of neighbouring India. In Pakistan and other parts of the Muslim world, however, the state judicial system faces a dual challenge to its legitimacy: from traditional, informal and unwritten local practices (and the moral orders and loyalties they reflect) called in Urdu *rivaz*, and from another great formal, written legal code, that of the Shariah.

The state code and the Shariah are both by nature 'great traditions' in the legal sense, strongly and essentially opposed to the 'little traditions' of the old local and kinship-based codes. They are in competition with each other to replace those codes, though both have at different times and in different ways sought accommodations with them. Indeed, the Taleban in the Pathan areas owes much of its success to its successful blending of Shariah and *pashtunwali*.

Both the state legal code and the Shariah are reformist and progressive codes in the context of Pakistani customary justice, especially as far as women are concerned. As will be seen in subsequent chapters, the

86

most ghastly atrocities against women in Pakistan have been committed as a result of judgments under customary laws, not the Shariah. In the face of the – let us be frank, often barbarous – tribal traditions of the Baloch and the Pathans, the Islamic code stands where it stood when it was first created by the Prophet Mohammed to civilize the pagan tribes of early seventh-century Arabia. This is something which British imperial administrators in the region fully recognized and sought to exploit.

The competition of judicial codes is intimately related to the weakness of the state in Pakistan, and Pakistan's difficulties in developing as a modern society and economy. For the idea of the modern state is largely bound up with the idea of the population being subject to one legal code, to which the state itself and its servants are (in theory at least) also subject. This code is laid down by one legislative authority, and administered by one hierarchy of judicial authorities. Any officially sanctioned deviations from this code are fairly minor matters of religious jurisdiction. Unsanctioned deviations are ipso facto not just illegal but illegitimate. The population of Pakistan by contrast has a choice between the law of the state, the law of religion (the Shariah), and local folk, tribal or community law.

People move between these three codes depending on circumstance and advantage, often pursuing their goals through several of them simultaneously – as well as through violence or more often the threat of it. The authorities which are supposed to implement the state law in conjunction with the Shariah, very often end up following community law or even turning a blind eye to violence. Often this is because they have been corrupted or intimidated, but often, too, it is because the police concerned share the cultural attitudes of the populations from which they are recruited. So the nature of Pakistan as a 'negotiated state', in which authority is a matter of negotiation, compromise, pressure and violence, not formal rules, is exemplified by the area of law and justice.

THE CUSTOM OF THE COUNTRY

State law and the Shariah are both formal, written codes. Customary laws (which can also be described as community, familial or 'folk' laws) are informal and unwritten, but immensely strong, because they reflect the cultures of the people. These laws, as implemented by bodies of local elders and notables or the leading males of families, reflect the basic attitudes of the population across the South Asian countryside, and to a remarkable extent in many of the cities as well.

These laws are weaker in northern Punjab than elsewhere, but still present even there, as Muhammad Azam Chaudhary's study of justice in a village in Faisalabad District makes clear. For a very large part of the rural population, these codes, and not the state law or the Shariah, govern rules of inheritance, the regulation of marriage and sexual relations, and the punishment of a range of 'crimes' or the resolution of a range of local disputes. Local people, and Western commentators, are generally convinced that these laws correspond to Islam or are even part of the Shariah – which is not at all the case.

The most famous, the most extensive, and the best studied example is the *pashtunwali*, the ethnic code of the Pathans, but every traditional Pakistani, Indian, Bangladeshi and Nepali community has its own version. The only large population in Pakistan which has completely shed allegiance to traditional codes are the Mohajirs of Karachi, precisely because they were migrants who moved during and after 1947 from very different areas of India.

These informal systems of justice take many different shapes, but in all cases both the shapes and the outcomes are closely influenced by local kinship and power relations. In the Western systems of justice derived from or influenced by Roman law, and in all the legal codes around the world which in modern times have been based on Western codes, all crimes should be punished, and the purpose of the law and the criminal justice system is – in principle – to abolish crime altogether. These are also the basic principles of the Pakistani state legal system, because this system is based on that of Britain.

The traditional codes of Pakistan are based on quite different aims: the defence of collective honour and prestige; the restoration of peace, and the maintenance of basic order. In this much of Pakistan resembles many other heavily armed kinship-based societies. Since these kinship groups always really saw themselves at bottom as independent sovereign groups, it is logical that the laws that grew up out of these societies should in key respects resemble traditional international law more than modern national law: that is to say they are based on diplomacy as much as rules; they usually aim at compromise not punishment; and the possibility of pressure and violence continue to lurk in the background.

This is in part because ideas of honour (*izzat* or *ghairat*) and dishonour are fundamental to the culture of most parts of Pakistan. A man, or a family, who fails to avenge certain types of insult or injury by violence will be dishonoured in the eyes of their community and themselves, and nothing can be worse than that. Dishonour means lack of prestige, and lack of prestige means that the family's prospects will be diminished in every way.

A British colonial judge, Sir Cecil Walsh, described 'that great and fateful word *izzat*' as follows, in terms which also imply its direct link to violence:

> Every Indian, from the highest to the lowest, has his izzat, or name to keep. After his son, it is his most cherished possession, and if it is injured, he is an unhappy man. And in such a sensitive race there is nothing easier to injure than the izzat. The injury may be purely imaginary, but it is no less keenly felt ... He will neither forget it nor forgive the man who did it.[6]

In the evocative local phrase, a worthy and respected man 'does good *izzat*' – *accha izzat karna* – or in the Pathan territories, 'does *pashto*'; that is to say 'follows the path of honour'. This is not just a matter of individual actions and decisions, but a whole way of living one's life; just as a woman is expected to 'do *ghairat*' in her dress, mode of behaviour and above all, of course, sexual conduct.

Walsh speaks of *izzat* as an individual matter, but it is equally important to families, extended families and clans. Indeed, most crimes committed in defence of *izzat* (and for that matter, most crimes in general) are collective crimes, as other family members join in to help or avenge their injured kinsman in battle, to threaten witnesses, to bribe policemen and judges, or at the very least to perjure themselves in court giving evidence on behalf of relatives. This is not seen as immoral, or even in a deeper sense illegal. On the contrary, it takes place in accordance with an overriding moral imperative and ancient moral 'law', that of loyalty to kin.

As Walsh himself recognized:

> In England, a very large proportion of crime is committed single-handed, and the average number of offenders per crime must be under two. The

average number per crime in the United Provinces must be nearer ten than two ...[7]

Violence is not frequent, or Pakistan would be in chaos; but it is fair to say that the possibility of it is often present somewhere in the background. Muhammad Azam Chaudhary writes that:

> The decision to go to the police/courts involves a risk of blemishing the *izzat*. You often hear 'if you are a man, brave and strong, come forward and fight directly. Why do you go to uncle police', and that the real *badla* [revenge] could only be inflicted directly or by close relatives and not by the police or courts. But, on the other hand, if going to the police is only for the purpose of harassing the opponent and impoverishing him, it could become a source of adding to one's *izzat*, especially by winning a court case against one's rival. This competition of winning the cases in the courts between rivals leads to ... 'addiction to litigation'.[8]

During a visit to Sindh in 1990, a member of a great local landowning and political family in Shikarpur told me:

> If neighbouring landowners see that you are weakening, there are always a lot of people to take your place, and they will hit your interests in various ways, like bringing lawsuits to seize your land or your water. If you can't protect yourself, your followers and tenants will ask how you can protect them. A semblance of strength must be maintained, or you're finished. The trick is to show your armed strength without getting involved in endless blood-feuds ... Such rivalries between families and clans are also conducted in the law courts, but the ultimate decision always lies with physical force ...
>
> In the countryside here in Sindh, a man from a strong tribe can go about unarmed, when no one else can. This will only change if a proper judicial system is established here in Sindh ... Western education changes attitudes to some extent, but people still feel a strong attachment to their tribe. It does make some of the sardars more relaxed though, less likely to demand retaliation at the drop of a hat. Junaid [his younger brother], when he presides over jirgas, tries to take a moderate line, and to seek compromise with other tribes instead of blood. Other sardars and tribal notables do the same. That is why, although the jirgas here are not officially recognized, the government and police use them all the time to settle disputes, and

prevent them getting out of hand. On the whole the feudals are more favourable to bring tribal feuds to an end, because they are not carried away by emotion, and see that in the end no one wins. Also, a Kalashnikov can kill more people in a week than were previously killed in a year, so things can more easily get out of hand. All the same, no sardar, however rich, can afford to be seen as a coward by his people . . .

Agha Tariq, PPP Development Minister, shot a man from a Mughal family in broad daylight 500 metres from here. He had a love marriage with a girl from Tariq's family without permission – the girl has disappeared, so they must have killed her too. To kill Tariq or someone from his family in return, the Mughals would have to have tribal backing to protect them and give evidence for them. But they are basically a middle-class service family. The brother is in customs in Karachi. They are wealthy and well-connected in Karachi and even Islamabad, but they don't have the local influence and prestige necessary to get away with killing, even in revenge. So they filed a case in court, but Tariq and all his followers got sworn alibis – some were supposedly in hospital, some even got the police to swear that they were in gaol at the time for traffic offences. They'll never be convicted. And they won't be unpopular with the people here because of it either – people respect men who defend their family's honour. Even in jail such people are respected more by the other criminals, as people who have done the right thing, maintained their honour.

And the speaker, by the way, was no rural thug, but a senior official of a European-based bank.

Customary laws differ considerably among the different regions and ethnicities of Pakistan. Within the same village too, judgments according to customary law can take place at different levels and in different fora, according to the case in question. Everywhere, however, the basic unit is the same, just as it is in Pakistani rural and to a lesser extent urban societies: the 'patriarchal' extended family: 'patriarchal', though as innumerable Pakistani and Indian daughters-in-law are bitterly aware, behind the patriarchal façade, the grey eminence, the greatest tyrant and the most ruthless enforcer of custom in these families is quite often the senior female.

According to the traditional ideal, *all* cases involving only members of one extended family should be settled within that family, and by a patriarch relying on the consensus of the family. A situation in which different members of the same extended family appeal to outside judicial authority – whether state or communal – in disputes among themselves is generally felt to be a disgrace for the family as a whole. Disputes between extended families should also ideally be settled by negotiations between their wise and experienced patriarchs.

When it comes to issues of sexual behaviour and family 'honour', a majority of cases are in fact settled at this level – all too often by the death of the woman concerned at the hands of her own family. According to all the customary codes, when this happens wider justice has no role to play at all; and alas, across most of Pakistan the state authorities receive little or no help from local communities in pursuing these cases, most of which go unreported (the same is true across very large parts of India).

If however a case involves people from different extended families (or relations within one extended family break down irretrievably), then outside help will be invoked by one or both parties to the dispute – either to prevent violence or to restore peace after violence has occurred. This help usually involves a mixture of mediation by some respected local figure or figures with judgment by a group of 'elders'. In Punjab, as in north India, such a group is usually known as a *'panchayat'* (from a Hindustani word originally meaning 'council of five'). In the Pathan areas, Sindh and Balochistan, the name commonly used is the Pathan word for such a council of local elders and notables, 'jirga'.

Among the relatively well-defined and structured Pathan and Baloch tribes, such councils have a fairly regular appearance, and among the Baloch and other tribes influenced by their culture, the jirgas are presided over by the sardar (hereditary chieftain) of the tribe concerned or a close relative. In Punjab they are much looser and less informal. If a case involves members of the same local *biradiri*, then the *panchayat* concerned will represent that clan involved; if members of different clans, then representatives of the whole village (or at least its dominant landholding elements) will be present. More rarely, representatives of different villages will meet to discuss disputes between them.

Membership is informal and ad hoc, and emerges from a local consensus as to who is worthy of taking part. In the Pathan and Baloch areas especially, a respected local religious figure may play a mediating role. The local village mullah, however, does not have any right to do so ex officio – a sign of the low respect in which these figures have traditionally been held. Judgments also generally emerge informally from local consensus.

This is especially true when the alleged perpetrator of a given 'crime' is some universally despised figure, or one who has committed an action which directly threatens the wellbeing of the whole community – for example, a miller who mixes sawdust into his flour. Such people may be punished by fines, by collective ostracism, or by some form of public ritual humiliation, like being paraded around backwards on a donkey with a blackened face (a South Asian version of the collectively imposed 'rough music' in traditional English villages which gave rise to the expression 'face the music').

Very often the jirga or *panchayat* really only ratifies a communal decision which has in effect already been made. This is equally true of the greatest of all jirgas, the traditional *loyah jirga*, or grand national assembly, of Afghanistan. In disputes involving two families or clans, this decision in turn will be based not on any strict definition of formal justice, but rather on a whole set of shifting elements in which considerations of equity, of relative power and above all of communal peace will all play a part. Judgments will inevitably involve relative winners and losers; but because communal peace and family prestige are both of the essence, considerable care will usually be taken to 'save face' on all sides, and to arrange compromises. Here, compensation rather than punishment is of the essence.

As Imran Aslam of Geo TV continued:

> Pakistan works at one level which is informal. You could call it the informal moral economy, which keeps hitting back against the elites. Attitudes to the law are part of this ... One thing that ordinary people here fault the state's Anglo-Saxon legal system for is that there is no compensation. Yes, they say, the law has hanged my brother's killer, but now who is to support my dead brother's family – who by the way have ruined themselves bribing the legal system to get the killer punished? Both the traditional justice systems and the Shariah are all about mediation and compensation, which is an important part of their appeal for ordinary people.[9]

Some of the British themselves recognized these objections to their system; and from the time when they first introduced the modern Western legal system and modern Western administrative, and later representative, institutions to their Indian empire, some of them also sought to give a recognized and honourable place to traditional forms. One of the greatest and most thoughtful of British officials, Sir Mountstuart Elphinstone, sought to safeguard and recognize customary law, because of the need for government 'to escape the evil of having a [British] code unsuitable to the circumstances of the people, and beyond the reach of their understanding'.[10]

Since independence, a number of attempts have been made in both India and Pakistan to bring the jirga or *panchayat* into the regular state judicial and representative system. In India, '*Panchayati Raj*', or basic democratic self-government, was for a long time the official Gandhian programme of the Congress Party. Attempts under Ayub Khan and Musharraf to create basic democratic institutions in Pakistan – paradoxically as an underpinning of military rule – both failed in the face of the opposition of the political elites.

When it comes to the judicial system, this issue in Pakistan must be divided into the informal and the formal level. At the informal level, policemen in much of Pakistan (but especially the tribal lands) frequently resort to customary judicial practices for the simple reason that – as so many of them stressed to me – given the reality of Pakistani society and police weakness, it would be impossible to operate half-way effectively without them. In particular, it is quite impossible to prevent, contain or end tribal feuds without recourse to tribal jirgas.

As the chief of police in Larkana District in Sindh told me in 2009 (echoing precisely what the police chief in the neighbouring district of Shikarpur had told me twenty years earlier):

> We try to work between the [state] legal system and the tribal system. When the tribes fight each other, I try to first pressurize them by raids, arresting known violent characters or in extreme cases even the sardars themselves, and holding them for a while. Then having taught them a lesson about not going too far, I get both sides around a table to negotiate. You can contain tribal violence by prompt police action, but to solve a conflict, you always end up with a jirga; because you can only end feuds if the two sides agree between themselves to end them . . . We are not like the army; we can't just shoot people until they obey us. In the end we live among the people and have to work with local people. If we don't, the whole system collapses.

Statements like this exemplify the nature of Pakistan as a 'negotiated state', and also the way in which the Pakistani police (and, indeed, much of the civil service) are still basically a colonial-era police force, or even a medieval one: dedicated chiefly not to the pursuit of crime as such, but to the maintenance of basic peace and order. In fact, the Pakistani police still operate on the basis of the British Indian Police Act of 1861, only slightly modified. This act was introduced in the immediate wake of the Indian revolt of 1857, and its structures and regulations were drawn up on the basis of those governing the paramilitary police force in Ireland, also charged with holding down a restive population.

The element of negotiation in police work applies not only to major tribal feuds, but also to quite minor cases. Thus in the Tehkal police district of Peshawar in August 2008, an investigating officer described to me a recent case in which two neighbouring families had fought each other. He said that they probably had longstanding issues with each other, but that the fight itself was the product of pure exasperation, heated to boiling point by a local electricity breakdown in the Peshawar summer.

After an endless wait, an electricity repair crew was bribed by both families to turn up, but naturally had to go to one of them first. An argument erupted which turned to blows, and then pistol shots, leaving two dead on one side. 'Who started it?' I asked. 'God knows,' the policeman replied. 'They both say the other did. Does it matter? They weren't criminals, just ordinary people who got a rush of blood to the head. That's very common in this country.'

The men of the winning side fled to relatives in the Khyber Agency of FATA, from which it is (especially now) virtually impossible to recover criminals. The investigating officer said that the police tried ('a bit') to arrest the men by asking the Khyber Tribal Agency for help and putting pressure on relatives who remained in Peshawar to get them to return and turn themselves in,

> but in the end we encouraged the family of the dead men to ask for a jirga to arrange a settlement and compensation, and both sides swore to accept its decision. They were paid Rs10 million, I think, and in return they swore on the Koran not to seek revenge. Then they came to us and we dropped the case ... Rs5 to 20 million is the range of compensation for a murder, but sometimes the compensation can be in vehicles or property. *Swara* [the infamous Pathan and Baloch custom of handing over young girls in compensation] is greatly diminished these days because of education, at least in the towns.

While the police at ground level are resorting to informal justice to get things done, some senior officers are thinking seriously about how the entire system can be changed so as to bring it more into line with popular expectations of justice, and improve its effectiveness at the same time. Malik Naveed Khan, the thoughtful and able inspector-general (i.e. commander-in-chief) of the police in the NWFP, took time off from fighting the Taleban in July 2009 to give me a fascinating lecture on the subject of 'restorative justice'. This is a growing trend in approaches to criminal justice in a number of countries (including New Zealand), with certain parallels to traditional South Asian approaches.

Naveed Khan has set up public committees attached to police stations in parts of the NWFP, composed of respected local people co-ordinated by the local police chief to arrange reconciliation and compensation in a range of cases up to and including murder. Unlike in the informal jirgas, these committees are not able to make decisions (reprisal killing, the giving of women, and so on) which contradict Pakistani state law. In his words,

> If we can regulate the jirga system and make it official, then we can prevent such illegal decisions while keeping the best aspects of the old system. After all, no one but the lawyers really wants to bring cases to court if they can avoid this. It is an immense burden to everyone concerned, including the police who here in the NWFP are in a life and death struggle with the Taleban. What is more, no one sensible wants to send people to jail – often not even the victims of crime, if they can be compensated by the perpetrator. Prison only turns accidental criminals into professional ones, and anyway, all too often in Pakistan for whatever reasons they are let out again after serving only a small part of their sentence.[11]

There is, however, a range of obstacles to the full integration of informal justice structures into the formal justice system. The first is obviously the economic interest of judges, lawyers and policemen, all of whom would stand to see their incomes from bribes and fees greatly diminished. This is related to the point that the informal justice system cannot work properly if disappointed parties are always in a position to appeal from local consensus to the police and the state courts – which, unlike the local community, can bring overwhelming force to bear in particular cases, at least if they are bribed enough.

A second obstacle is that because they are ad hoc and informal, jirgas and *panchayats* usually have to be based on small village or tribal communities in which people know each other, know who has sufficient local respect to serve on a jirga, and also understand well both the personal characters of the parties concerned and the reality of power relations between them. This is less and less possible in Pakistan, where the population, and the urban share of it, are both growing enormously.

This problem was brought home to me when in 2009 I visited Mingora, capital of Swat, after more than twenty years. The people of Swat still remember the autocratic but fair judgments of their former ruler the Wali, under a system in which the ruler presided personally over all serious cases, and knew personally every significant figure in his land. But when the Wali ruled Swat the whole territory had fewer than 500,000 people. Now Mingora alone (which I remember as a small country town) has almost that number – more than London or Paris in the eighteenth century. In a population this size, it is impossible to follow the old ways based on personal knowledge and local consensus.

The existence of a parallel, legally unrecognized set of judicial institutions relying on local codes obviously calls into question the whole project of creating a unified modern state, which is why since early modern times royal authorities in Europe and elsewhere tried to stamp out these institutions and practices and replace them with a uniform code and uniform institutions staffed by centrally appointed judicial officials. This has been a challenge for India as well as Pakistan. In the words of the Indian legal anthropologist M. P. Jain:

> There is one other very important reason as to why custom should now be abrogated. Most of the customs are tribal or communal and sectarian, and so long as custom survives these class dictinctions are also bound to survive. It would lead to a better integration of the people, if the sense of separation of each community arising out of its distinctive customs were removed.[12]

Finally, in one key respect the question of the judicial role of jirgas and *panchayats* raises in acute form the clash of cultures between the Pakistani masses and the Westernized educated elites which dominate the state and the senior ranks of the judiciary – which in turn raises a fundamental question about Pakistani democracy. This question relates to the treatment of women.

Especially among the Pathans and Baloch (including the Baloch tribes of Sindh and southern Punjab), tribal jirgas are regularly responsible for ordering punishments of women which are absolutely odious not only to modern Pakistani state law and Westernized sensibilities, but to the Shariah and strict Muslim sensibilities as well; but which, unfortunately, enjoy the support of the vast majority of the members of the communities concerned – or at least the males.

These jirga decisions include: the execution of women for 'immorality', and even for perfectly legal and religious marriages with men from other tribes; the giving or exchange of minor girls in compensation as part of the settlement of feuds; and, more rarely, orders of gang-rape as a punishment. This last, however, is almost always limited to actions by one locally dominant kinship group to teach another one its place – as in the particularly monstrous case of the rape in 2002 of Mukhtar Mai, a woman of the Gujjar *biradiri* in the Muzaffargarh district of southern Punjab, on the orders of a jirga of the Mastoi, a local Baloch tribe. This is a tactic often used by superior castes in India as well to crush and humiliate the lower castes.

This issue raises yet again the question of whether Pakistan is really (as most observers believe) insufficiently democratic, or whether on the contrary it is in fact too democratic for its own good – in so far as the views of a largely illiterate, obscurantist and often violent population are in a position to prevail over those of the educated elites, and the state is too weak to enforce its own official law.

For it should be remembered that in eighteenth- and nineteenth-century Europe, key advances in judicial progress, and administration in general, which laid the foundations for modern European civilization, were carried out by small enlightened aristocratic and bourgeois elites. These often had to use authoritarian methods to crush the resistance of the mass of the population. They certainly never believed for a moment that the masses should be consulted about elite actions.

This issue also raises the question of the difference between a truly 'feudal' elite and one based on the leadership of kinship groups. A truly feudal elite – and one which did not have to stand in elections – might eventually summon up the will to be true to its own modern education and ensure that measures protecting women (of which there are plenty in law) are actually enforced. An elite dependent on the consensus of kinship groups to be elected to parliament cannot do so – especially because even in the most autocratic Pakistani culture, that of the Baloch tribes, there is in the end almost always some rival would-be chieftain waiting within the chieftain's family to challenge him if his support in the tribe dwindles.

The reality of all this was brought home to me by the Sardar of one tribe in Balochistan – a Pathan tribe, but which, unlike the Pathans of the NWFP and FATA, had been heavily influenced by autocratic Baloch traditions. If his very candid and all-too-human account of his approach seems less than heroic, I invite you, dear Reader, to ask yourself whether you or I would really do so much better.

This Sardar is a 'Nawabzada', the descendant of a tribal chieftain who fought against the British, but later compromised with them and was given the title of 'Nawab' – another sign of the old Frontier tradition whereby yesterday's enemy is today's ally, and vice versa. His tribe straddles the Afghan frontier, but in Afghanistan his influence, though present, is greatly reduced. The Sardar's grandfather sat in the Pakistani Constituent Assembly of 1947.

The walls of the Sardar's mansion in Quetta are festooned with the heads of mountain goats and photographs of ancestors bristling with guns, swords and facial hair. The resemblance in terms of both hair and general expression was rather marked. The Sardar's own facial hair is more limited – a moustache and a pair of small sideburns, which together with his long curling hair gave evidence of student years in London in the late 1960s. He spoke of his time in London with deep regret as 'the happiest time of my life', but with a disarming smile, admitted that 'in the end, I just could not bear to live my whole life in a place where, when I walk down the street, people do not bow and say, 'Salaam aleikum, Sardar Sahib'.

The Sardar described his judicial role as follows:

In my tribe, the poorest man if he gets into trouble will be helped by his fellow tribesmen, led by me and my cousins. Even if he drives a rickshaw or sells boot polish he can look anyone in the eyes because he has a chief and a powerful tribe behind him . . .

Every month, hundreds of people come to me or my cousins to have their problems solved. If it is a simple case, we make decisions ourselves. If more difficult, we call a jirga, and from the jirga people are chosen as a committee to look into the case. We choose people depending on the nature of the case. If it is a transport problem, we choose people with transport experience. If business, then businessmen. If the parties to the case want it to be judged according to the Shariah, we include a mullah. We make the judgment, and we enforce it.

For example, a few months ago one boy from the tribe killed another boy. We are arranging compensation. They are both from our tribe, so that was quite easy. A more difficult case recently was when one of our women was raped by two young men from another tribe. We caught the men, and our tribal jirga met, and called witnesses according to the Shariah and modern law. We consulted with the elders of the other tribe. They offered money compensation but we can only take this in cases of murder or wounding. To take it in cases of the rape of our women would disgrace us. Then they said, you can kill the older boy, but please spare the younger one. So we decided to kill the older boy, and slit the nose and ears of the younger one . . . The older one was twenty-something, the younger is sixteen . . .

'Rough justice,' I suggested.

Yes, but if we had gone to the government law it would have taken years, and in that time they would have been free to roam the streets raping more girls and laughing at us. Relations between the tribes would have got worse and worse, and maybe in the end many people would have been killed. This is our tribal system which has existed for ages. If it had been bad, it would have been abandoned by the people. It is a hard decision, but we need to make sure that no one will think of killing or raping our people again . . .

This system helps keep the peace and stops feuds getting out of hand. For example, we have just settled a feud with another tribe in south Punjab, over land. Six years ago, there was a clash. Two people were killed on each side, and four of our men are in jail in Multan for this. Our jirga has negotiated a settlement with the other tribe, and they agreed to drop the charges. So this week we are going to Multan to bring our men from jail. We will give a feast for the jirga of the other tribe at which we will formally forgive each other, and in two weeks, they will give a feast for us.

'Is this according to Pakistani law?' I asked.

There is no law! If there were a real law in this country, why would all these people come to me for help? I don't go looking for this work. I have important business in Karachi that I have to leave behind to do this. People come to my cousins and me because they respect us, not just because of our titles but because they know our character and know that we are fair. I depend on my people's respect only. After all, I have no official position, and no support from the police or the courts . . .

I asked him about the punishment of women in 'honour' cases, and how far – since he had previously spoken bitterly about the backwardness and lack of education of his fellow-countrymen – he was able to bring his own more enlightened views to bear.

Sometimes there is no need to set up a committee of the jirga. If it is a very simple case and I know what the tribe thinks, I can just say, 'This is the decision!' But issues involving women are never simple, and I always have to think about what the opinion of the tribe will be. The tribal set-up is very hard, not just towards women but towards men as well. Remember, no one in this country has real rights . . .

Because I have travelled and am educated, taking these decisions over women is not easy for me. I have to think and think about how to handle them. There are certain things I will not permit. For example, the first decision I made on becoming Sardar was that I will not allow the giving of girls in compensation. That is still very common in our system but I will not allow it. I will order money given instead, if necessary much more money.

Also I will not punish a girl for wanting to marry or not to marry some-one, as long as it is a proper marriage. If a couple run away together to get married without their parents' permission, I will put pressure on the parents to agree to the marriage, not to kill them. I may fine the boy's family though so as to save the face of the girl's family.

With such female problems I am very cautious. To be honest I try to avoid them whenever I can. If I can solve them without bloodshed, then I do so. Otherwise I send the case to my cousins to decide.

'And do they share your more enlightened principles?' I asked.

Well, that is up to them. But I do try, you know, when possible, and this has sometimes involved me in arguments with my own tribe. I can say in the end to the jirga and the parties in a case: 'I don't agree to your verdict. This is my decision and if you don't like it, you can go to state law.' But

I can't do this often or no one would obey me any more. I only do it sometimes in women's cases, because after all I am a father with daughters. If
it's a business issue and I disagree with the jirga, I won't take a stand – after
all, businessmen can always get their money back somehow . . .

I cannot say whether this Sardar did in fact try hard in 'women's cases';
but at least he seemed aware that he ought to. As will be seen in Chapter
8, the other Sardars I met in Balochistan simply defended tribal custom
tout court; they also claimed to be modern and educated men, and – of
course – 'good democrats'.

THE POLICE

The problems affecting the police and the official judicial system in
Pakistan are so many and so great that it is hard adequately to describe
them, but one single word that explains many of the others is yet again
'kinship'. In the words of a police officer in central Punjab:

Families and clans here stick together, so if you really want to arrest one
person here and prosecute him successfully, you may need to arrest ten, or
threaten to arrest them – the original suspect plus three for perjury, three
for bribing the police and judges, and three for intimidating witnesses. And
if the family has any influence, the only result will be to get yourself transferred to another district. So I'm afraid that it is often much easier just not
to arrest anyone.

Take the FIR [First Information Report] system. If two individuals or
families clash, and someone is killed, the dead man's family will lodge an
FIR with one police station saying that he was wantonly murdered, and
the other family will lodge an FIR with another police station saying that
they were attacked and acted in self-defence – and they may be telling the
truth. The police and the courts have to judge between them on the basis
of evidence, every bit of which is probably false in one direction or another.
So either the case goes on for ever, or it is resolved in favour of which side
has more power and influence.

If it's an especially bad case and you are sure of what happened, you
may be able to bargain with the family or with local politicians to give
you the man you want. But then of course you will have to give them

something in return, or let one of their members off in some other case. This is typical give and take – what we call here *lena dena*.

The problem for the police and the courts begins with lying. Astonishingly – at least, it astonished me – it is not permitted in Pakistani courts to swear on the Koran (that is, the Book itself, not in the words of the Koran) when giving evidence. I asked Sayyid Mansur Ahmed, vice-president of the Karachi Bar Association, why ever not. 'It's very simple,' he replied with a cheerful smile. 'Most people would swear and then lie anyway. That would bring religion into disrepute – and you are not supposed to do that in Pakistan.'

British officials working in the field recognized this problem and attributed it to their own system, drawing a contrast yet again with traditional local jirgas and *panchayats* where, since everyone knows everyone else and the basic facts of the case, outrageous lying is pointless. In the words of General Sir William Sleeman, commander of the campaign to suppress *thuggee*:

> I believe that as little falsehood is spoken by the people of India, in their village communities, as in any part of the world with an equal area and population. It is in our courts of justice where falsehoods prevail most, and the longer they have been anywhere established, the greater the degree of falsehood that prevails in them.[13]

Denzil Ibbetson, the great colonial administrator and ethnographer of the Punjab, writes of the ordinary Baloch being naturally frank and honest in his statements, 'except where corrupted by our courts'.

Once again, the people doing the lying and manipulating would in most cases not feel that they were acting immorally; rather, that they were obeying the higher moral law of loyalty to kin. And, once again, there is no essential difference in this regard between the big 'feudal' politician and the small tenant farmer. They all, each according to their station and resources, do their utmost to help relatives and allies by deceiving, corrupting or pressuring the police and the courts. Pressure can be directly physical (especially in the case of the Islamist extremist groups) but more often it comes through political influence.

This goes up to the very top. Thus in 2009 I was sitting in the office of the inspector-general of police in one of Pakistan's provinces, when a call came through from the province's chief minister – who was roaring so loudly that I could hear him through the receiver from several feet away. He was complaining that a superintendent of police had arrested a dacoit (bandit) leader at the rural mansion of one of his party's provincial deputies.

The unfortunate inspector had to promise an inquiry, the dacoit's immediate release and the immediate transfer of the offending police officer to another province. And this chief minister, by the way, has a personal reputation for efficiency, hard work and relative honesty. A senior officer in Punjab told me that around half of the 648 station house officers (chiefs of local police stations) in the province are chosen by local politicians through influence on the Punjab government, to serve their local interests.

Furthermore, the state judicial system is not merely politically reactive, but is also regularly used as an active weapon. A great many artificial cases are brought deliberately by politicians to attack rivals, and by governments against their opponents. The manipulation of such cases and their outcomes is also a key tactic of the ISI (Inter-Services Intelligence) in managing elections by forcing particular candidates to withdraw or to change sides.

A situation of nearly universal mendacity and political pressure concerning their work would place an intolerable burden on even the best-equipped, best-trained, best-paid and best-motivated police force in the world – and the Pakistani police (like the Indian) are very, very far from being any of these things.

The miserable conditions in which ordinary policemen work was brought home to me by a visit to a station house in the suburbs of Peshawar in August 2008 (responsible for an area where there had been eighteen murders so far in 2008). I spoke with the sub-inspector in charge of the investigation unit in the room where he and the other officers sleep and eat during the day and night that they spend at a time on duty. It was a slum, with bare concrete walls, stained with damp from the leaking roof. My visit was during a power cut – the ordinary police of course have no generators – and in the monsoon the whole station was a hot fug of rot and sweat. The officers' clothes hung on pegs, and there was a mirror for shaving. That, with their charpoys (string beds) and a couple of chairs, was all the furniture.

The sub-inspector is a big, very tough-looking middle-aged man with enormous fists – not a good person to be interrogated by. I asked him what the police in the NWFP need most. He gave a harsh laugh.

Where to begin? First, we need better pay and incentives. Look at the motorway police. Everyone says how honest and hard-working they are – well, that's easy, they are paid twice what we get. We need better accommodation – look at this place. We need better vehicles, better radios, better arms, bullet-proof vests. Tell me, could any police force in the world work well given what we have to rely on? Would you risk your life fighting the Taleban for the pay we get?

He told me that at that time there was one fingerprinting machine for the whole of the NWFP; and, as his seniors candidly admitted, it was almost completely useless, both because of the inadequacy of the archiving system and because the ordinary police have no training in taking fingerprints. This is also true for the greater part of Punjab and the whole of interior Sindh. And indeed, all this is irrelevant, since the police have no training in how not to ruin all evidence by trampling over a crime scene. This is generally the case even of the Interior Ministry's special service, the Intelligence Bureau. It helps explain the shambolic nature of the investigation into Benazir Bhutto's assassination, which has generated so many conspiracy theories.

To lack of equipment and lack of training can be added lack of numbers. Visitors to Pakistan who see large numbers of police guarding official buildings or accompanying politicians may think this is a heavily policed society. In the main cities, large numbers of police can indeed be called upon if required; but in the Punjab countryside, there is one police station for approximately every fifty villages (incidentally, the figures in much of rural India are even worse). Most policemen with whom I spoke had no real idea how many people there were in their areas – or even, very often, how many serious crimes had been committed there over the past year.

The result of all this, as well as of lack of incentives – and a certain doziness, exacerbated by the heat – is that most of the time the police are purely reactive. You *never* see a speeding police car in Pakistan (whereas you do occasionally see speeding ambulances and fire engines) unless, once again, it is accompanying a senior politician. The police wait in their stations for cases to be lodged with them, and, in the case of murder, for bodies to be brought to them – which naturally makes any forensic examination of the crime scene out of the question, even if the police had the training or equipment to carry it out. Since the population is mostly illiterate, the police can often write down whatever they like on the FIR, and get the witnesses to sign it. Unless the police see some money in it for them, this often means that cases are simply never registered at all.

A standard part of the police investigation technique is the torture of suspects, relatives of the suspects, and witnesses. Most police officers are completely candid about this in private. A senior officer in Punjab told me:

> I am trying to introduce fingerprinting, forensic examination and so on, but there is a cultural problem. The response of the ordinary SHOs [Station House Officers] is, 'Oh, this is just another hobby-horse of our over-educated senior officers. I prefer the reliable method: put the suspect on the mat and give him a good kicking. Then he'll tell us everything.'

The investigating officer I spoke with in Peshawar described a recent carjacking case in which the suspect had absconded to the Mohmand Agency with the vehicle.

> So we arrested his father, and put pressure on him to get the car back. If he had been a young man, naturally we would have beaten him till he told us where it was, but, since he was old, we didn't torture him. We just threatened him in other ways, with cases against other people in his family – everyone in this society is guilty of something. We told him that we would talk to the Political Agent in Mohmand and get his family home there demolished if he didn't help us. So in the end he sent someone to bring the car back.

Together with the general police tendency to take bribes in return for every service, it is hardly surprising therefore that people avoid the police as much as possible, and try to resolve crimes in informal ways. As to the idea that it makes any difference in this regard whether Pakistan is ruled by a civilian or military government, the Peshawar investigator answered that question categorically. I visited his station house the day after Musharraf's resignation as president. I asked him if his use of torture would change now that Pakistan was a 'democracy' again. If I had turned into a purple elephant his look could not have been more blank with amazement. I had asked not just a meaningless question, but one with no connection whatsoever to any reality he knew.

None of this however is necessarily timeless or set in stone. Some dedicated and intelligent senior officers are working hard to improve things, and the national motorway police, mentioned by the sub-inspector, are an example of what the Pakistani police can be when the circumstances and conditions are right. Their high pay makes them resistant to bribes, and because they are commanded from Islamabad they are immune to local political pressure. Perhaps equally importantly, they work in a context – that of Pakistan's splendid modern motorways, with their gleaming service stations and roadside cafés – which gives them legitimate pride in their country and their service.

In consequence, they are amazingly honest and efficient. My driver was given a ticket for speeding on the way from Islamabad to Lahore – with no suggestion that he could be let off in return for a bribe – and I heard numerous members of the elite complain with astonishment that the same thing had happened to them. Then again, Pakistan's motorways often seem in a way to float over the country without being connected to it, so it is natural that their police should be the same.

THE COURTS

Suspects in Pakistan who survive investigation by the police find themselves before the courts – and may the Lord have mercy on their souls. 'May God save even my worst enemy from disease and a court case,' as a Punjabi saying has it. At least as bad as the problem of corruption is that of delay. Indeed, if there is a classical legal phrase that ought to be nailed above every Pakistani (and Indian) courtroom, and perhaps to the foreheads of South Asian judges and lawyers, it is 'Justice Delayed is Justice Denied.' When I visited the city courts in Quetta, Balochistan, a majority of the people with whom I spoke outside had cases which had been pending for more than five years, and had spent more than Rs200,000 on legal fees and bribes – a colossal sum for a poor man in Pakistan.

These problems do not apply only to court cases. One old man had had to come every day for six days, despite paying several bribes, simply in order to get a property transfer registered. This means that a great many people, especially in the countryside, prefer to arrange all such transfers and inheritance arrangements informally – which means that there can then be no recourse to official law if things go wrong.

The inordinate length of time taken by South Asian legal cases is in part related to corruption, but also to a host of other factors in which local influence and intimidation, lack of staff, a grossly overloaded system, cynical manoeuvres by lawyers, and sheer laxness, laziness and incompetence on the part of both the judiciary and the police all play a part.

Moreover, of course, delay breeds overloading and overloading breeds more delay, in a sort of horrible legal combination of *circulus vitiosus* and *perpetuum mobile* (to use two Latin phrases that might usefully replace those legal ones so beloved of South Asian lawyers). As of May 2009, there were more than 100,000 cases pending before the Karachi city courts alone, with 110 judges to try them (in a city of some 17 million people) – which makes for an easy enough calculation. Some of the courts are supposed on paper to attend to more than 100 cases a day. Every day, around 1,200 prisoners should be delivered to the courts in Karachi, but there are only vehicles and holding cells for 500.

To deal with the issue of Pakistani delays in the way that the English legal system (belatedly and in part) improved the almost equally dreadful state of the law in early nineteenth-century England would require the isolation of particular causes. That is hard to do, because there are so many causes, and the legitimate (or at least unavoidable) and the illegitimate are so mixed up together. A central problem is the scandalous number of adjournments, of which it is not at all uncommon to encounter several dozen in one single case.

An adjournment may be given for any number of reasons, including it seems for no reason at all except that one or other lawyer asks for it. And these reasons may be legitimate (for example, there really is an acute shortage of vehicles to bring prisoners from jail to court) or may be the product of corruption, influence, intimidation, personal friendship or just the easygoing attitude to members of their own class that characterizes most of South Asian officialdom. As a retired judge told me:

> It doesn't do for a judge to be too hard with the lawyers. We all know each other and there is a sort of family feeling in the legal profession. And a judge who makes himself really unpopular with the lawyers will find his promotion blocked by rumours and whispers, or may even be accused of corruption, rightly or wrongly. So many judges take a live-and-let-live

attitude when they really ought to be pulling a lot of lawyers up very hard indeed, especially when it comes to non-attendance and requests for adjournments for specious reasons . . . Though it is also true that the system is so terribly overloaded that it simply couldn't work properly even if everyone did their duty.

Central to the near-paralysis of the judicial system are the embittered relations between the judiciary and the police. Of course, this exists to some extent in all societies, but in Pakistan it has reached a level which, as will be seen, can become literally violent. It should be obvious from this chapter why the judiciary have good reason to distrust cases brought by the police. Equally, the police can point to numerous instances where they have finally prosecuted well-known murderers and gang leaders, who have then been acquitted by the courts on specious grounds, or whose cases have dragged on for years with no result.

As a result, as many policemen told me: 'If you really want to deal with a powerful miscreant in this country, you have to kill him.' This has contributed to the taste of the Pakistani and Indian police – urged on by provincial governments with a particular commitment to tackle crime – for 'encounter killings' (extra-judicial executions by the police under the pretence of armed clashes). The inability of the courts to get convictions has been particularly disastrous when it comes to tackling Islamist extremists, who, even when proceeded against by the state, are often released for lack of evidence.

The case of the gang-rape of Mukhtar Mai, mentioned above, shows the police, the courts and the political system at their interactive worst. The crime occurred in 2002. In 2010 she is still waiting for justice; and this was both an extremely simple case (legally speaking) and an extremely high-profile one in which the Pakistani and international media and human rights organizations took a close interest, and which the PPP government which took power in 2008 promised to expedite.

One key aspect both of the incompetence of the judiciary and the alienation of the mass of the population from the judicial system is that, owing once again to the British Raj, the system is conducted mainly in English sprinkled with Latin. The alienation of the population comes from the fact that the overwhelming majority of the population do not understand English. The incompetence comes from the fact that neither do many of the system's staff – at least, not well enough to do their jobs half-way properly.

In January 2009 in the Bar Association in Multan, southern Punjab, I listened with wry amusement as the president of the Association, Mehmood Ashraf Khan, dictated legal notes to his clerk to write down. The clerk (or *munshi*) was an old, old man with a grey beard and a wool hat, and it may in part have been lack of teeth as well as lack of English that made him stumble over his words.

> 'The following prisoners are required to be implemented as respondents,' said the lawyer.
> The clerk repeated slowly, writing as he spoke, 'The following prisons are retired to be . . .'
> 'Required!' snapped the lawyer.
> 'Are required to be imprem, indem . . .'
> 'Implemented!'

Of course, it would have helped greatly if the lawyer had done his writing himself, but that would presumably have offended against one of the most basic and universal rules of South Asia – that the elites do not perform manual labour. In fact, many of the lawyers whom I meet speak – and therefore presumably write – very poor English. As a result of this and the inadequacy of most Pakistani legal training, a great many simply cannot master even moderately complex briefs, or prepare their cases in ways that will allow them to be understood easily and decided expeditiously. This is of course a godsend for defence lawyers.

Evidence in the courts can be given in Urdu or provincial languages, but then has to be translated into English to be recorded. In a courtroom in Karachi in May 2009 I watched while a woman gave evidence – in a case of child kidnapping – in Urdu and the judge translated it into poorish English to a clerk writing beside him in longhand (the case then had to be adjourned because the public prosecutor did not turn up). Everything had to be repeated to make sure that it was accurate, and the judge and the defence lawyer repeatedly corrected each other's English. The lawyers can speak to the judge in either English or Urdu, but the lawyers make their arguments in English and the judge delivers his judgment in English – so that unless someone translates for the accused, they will most of the time not know what is happening to them.

I asked a weary but thoughtful woman judge, Amina Nasir Ansari, why the whole system couldn't be moved to Urdu:

In the first place, because law is based on precedent, and all our records going back to British days are in English. If we abandoned English, there would be no solid basis for our judgments. We would have to start everything over again and God knows where that would take us. And secondly, because of the language issue in this country. In Punjab, most courts do in fact operate in Urdu, though everything still has to be translated into English for the records, and all communications are in English. But here in Karachi, if we moved to Urdu our Sindhi brothers would complain, and vice versa.[14]

The basic reason why this court was operating in English was carved into its ornate neo-classical façade: the letters GRI, which no one in the court could decipher for me but which stand for *Georgius Rex Imperator*: George V, King of England and Emperor of India.

According to old photographs, when the court was first built it stood alone, looking out onto a broad avenue. Today, it faces a traffic-choked road, and its façade towers over a bazaar. Indeed, the bazaar appears to have invaded the forecourt itself, with touts, hawkers, police, prisoners and their families, booksellers and lawyers all surging around in a slow-moving maelstrom. Workers of the Saylani Welfare Trust were distributing food from a small field-kitchen to prisoners and their families – an action enjoined by the Koran, and a small example of the private charity which does so much to soften the hard edges of life in Pakistan.

In this busy throng, by far the most exotic sight was the lawyers, who were all dressed in their uniforms of black jackets, white shirts and dark ties, on a day when the temperature in Karachi touched 45° centigrade – like penguins in hell. The women lawyers were also dressed in black jackets, but with white *dupattas* (scarves). Sitting in the bar-room, I asked the youngish vice-president of the Bar Association, Sayyid Mansur Ahmed, why the lawyers kept their jackets and ties on all the time when they weren't in court. He looked at me in astonishment. 'It is our uniform, our identity, our symbol,' he replied. I pointed out that my sister (a barrister in London) does not wear her wig outside the courtroom, and certainly wouldn't in this heat.

Yes, but there is a big difference between Karachi and London. There are so many people here who want to be lawyers. We have to show that we are special. I feel that our jackets show that we are advocates, because only advocates are allowed to wear them. Our seniors teach us that it doesn't matter how hot it is, the common people will see the jacket and know that you are an advocate, and respect you.

Outside, the wall was plastered with campaign posters for elections to various positions on the board of the Bar Association. 'Please Vote and Support Muhd. Adil Khan Advocate – For Prestige of Lawyers', one of them read.

Elitism is one of the curses of Pakistan's official judicial system, but also the source of whatever progressive elements it contains. The police are divided into three cadres, with hardly any movement between them: the ordinary constables and NCOs; the junior officers; and the senior 'gazetted' officers (around one in 800 of the total) who are recruited by examination, and rank alongside the senior civil service. This of course is derived directly from the British system, where the British senior officers were divided from their Indian officers, and those in turn from the rank and file. Today's senior officers (assistant superintendent and above) have often studied criminology in the West.

As for the legal system, this is essentially the English Common Law, as introduced by the British. For obvious imperial reasons, however, the British empire left out the ancient democratic element of the English system, namely the jury. Pakistan and India have continued this autocratic tradition, partly because of the ingrained contempt of the elites for the illiterate masses, and partly because of better-based fears that juries would split bitterly – and then violently – along lines of kinship, sect or ethnicity.

Informal *panchayats* and jirgas are therefore the only democratic legal institutions in Pakistan. But there is a problem, which raises key issues of democracy and progress in Pakistan. Leaving aside their domination by local elites, these informal courts are at best only representative of half the population – the male half. Women are virtually never represented. On the other hand, in the official legal system, women have a small but slowly growing place: some 500 lawyers in Karachi are women, out of 9,000 in all, and there is a sprinkling of women judges.

Under the lash of progressive lawyers including women such as Asma Jehangir (Chairwoman of the Human Rights Commission of Pakistan), the official system has repeatedly issued judgments and injunctions protecting women's rights, even if political pressure and its own failings mean that it usually cannot actually deliver justice in individual cases brought before it. Left to itself, the informal judicial system would, by the democratic will of its (male) representatives, sweep away modern women's rights altogether.

Hence the repeated judgments of the higher courts declaring jirgas and their judgments illegal, even as the police rely on them constantly to reconcile disputes and keep order. This is the dilemma on the horns of which Pakistani liberals are impaled, but which they themselves do not dare to recognize: that their progressive programme, though couched in democratic terms, is opposed in key respects by the overwhelming democratic majority of (male) Pakistanis.

THE LAWYERS' MOVEMENT

For a time in 2007–8, it seemed as if a bridge might be created between the Pakistani judicial elites and the masses, that mass support might be generated for a liberal programme in Pakistan, and that the judiciary itself might find the will radically to reform its own judicial system. This vision was embodied in the Lawyers' Movement, which played a key role in bringing down the administration of President Pervez Musharraf, and may well contribute to doing the same to President Asif Ali Zardari.

The Lawyers' Movement originated in attempts by the Chief Justice, Iftikhar Chaudhry, in early 2007, to place limits on President Musharraf's power – including the alleged 'disappearance' of Pakistanis to US custody. Musharraf's consequent dismissal of the Chief Justice led to a protest movement of lawyers against his rule, which was supported on the streets by hundreds of thousands of people. After Musharraf's resignation, the movement continued in a lower key against Zardari.

Echoing much of the Western media, the *New York Times* described the Lawyers' Movement as 'the most consequential outpouring of liberal, democratic energy in the Islamic world in recent years'.[15] Pakistani liberals, too, initially saw it as marking a breakthrough in Pakistani history, the mobilization of a section of the educated middle classes as a political force in their own right, and with mass support.

It may be that in the long run the Lawyers' Movement will indeed be seen to have marked the start of a new and better era in Pakistan's history. As of 2010, however, it seems that many of the media analyses of the movement have missed a number of important aspects of what has happened. The first is that historically the law in Pakistan has resembled the hen in the old Pathan proverb: 'a bird belonging to the man who seizes it'.

This was very apparent during Pakistan's period of 'democratic' rule in the 1990s. In 1993, fearful of the new power and independence of the Supreme Court, and its apparent leaning to Sharif in 1993, the PPP government sought to pack the Supreme Court and Punjab High Court with its own nominees. The result was a stand-off in which the government refused to implement the Supreme Court's orders and lawyers boycotted the sittings of PPP-appointed judges, paralysing much of the judicial system.

This episode was followed by an even worse assault on the judiciary by the next Nawaz Sharif administration of 1997–9. When the Supreme Court attempted to challenge a law passed by his government giving the police a virtual amnesty for extra-judicial executions, Nawaz Sharif launched a ferocious campaign against them, including the invasion of the Court by Muslim League thugs. By the end of 1997 the head of the Supreme Court had been forced from office along with President Farook Leghari, who had tried to defend the Court's independence.

These episodes make it rather odd that both Pakistani and Western commentators should have described Musharraf's clash with the Supreme Court in 2007, and the Lawyers' Movement that followed, as 'unprecedented', the support of the PPP and Muslim League for the dismissed Supreme Court to have been part of a genuine movement for democracy, and Musharraf's moves against the Court as the result of 'military dictatorship' rather than the familiar workings of Pakistan's power politics.

Every military and civilian regime has sought to win over the higher courts and, failing that, to intimidate them into acquiescence in unconstitutional and illegal actions. The movement to defend the independence of the Supreme Court in 2007–9 may represent a radically new departure, as its supporters hope. The problem is, however, that by 2009 the Court and the Lawyers' Movement had to some extent become political allies of Nawaz Sharif and his PML(N) opposition.

In consequence of this and of the Supreme Court's moves to abolish the National Reconciliation Ordinance and resume charges of corruption against PPP ministers, the judiciary came under strong attack from liberal journalists and commentators who had previously raised the cry of judicial independence against Musharraf. Liberal circles close to the ruling PPP were full of talk of conspiracies between the judges and the military, and of how the judiciary (and the mainstream media) would have to be 'tamed' again.

As already described, Nawaz Sharif when in power in 1997–9 also removed the then Chief Justice by unconstitutional and even violent means. It may be that subsequent events have changed his attitude – or it may not. And it may be that if Mr Sharif returns to power the Supreme Court will prosecute further illegal acts by his administration even though they have been political allies – or it may not. The Lawyers' Movement gives good hope of this, but no certainty.

The idea of the Lawyers' Movement as a 'progressive' force also needs qualification. It is true that prominent liberal lawyers such as Munir Malik and Latif Afridi in Karachi were part of the leadership of the movement. However, much of the local leadership, and the rank and file, were made up of deeply conservative provincial lawyers who detested Musharraf above all for his support for the US and moves for reconciliation with India. As Mr Mehmood Ashraf Khan told me:

> I also sympathize with the Taleban movement. They brought peace and justice to Afghanistan in response to the will of the people ... In Pakistan, too, the Taleban have introduced the Shariah and have punished the persons involved in kidnapping, drug dealing, and so on. They have always been loyal to Pakistan, and terrorist attacks here are not their work ... Or, if they have carried out such acts, it is only in response to killings by the government like at the Lal Masjid [Red Mosque]. If your family and friends are killed and the legal system cannot help, then you have the right to fight back. At the Lal Masjid thousands of innocent women were killed. I believe that this was really done by Jews and Christians to create civil war in Pakistan ... They say that the Taleban are burning girls' schools, but very little of this is being done by the Taleban. Most is being done by other forces to discredit the Taleban. India has dozens of consulates in Afghanistan, not to help the Karzai administration, but to help the Taleban to destroy Pakistan ...[15]

So if the Pakistani courts have repeatedly released extremist leaders and terrorist suspects, this is not just because they have been intimidated by the extremists or the government. Considerable sympathy on the part of judges and lawyers is also often present, as for the assassin of Governor Salman Taseer in January 2011.

I also have to say that both conservative lawyers like Mehmood Ashraf Khan and liberals like Munir Malik in their conversations with me displayed on many issues a contempt for logic, rationality and basic rules of evidence – no worse than the rest of the population, but these people are senior lawyers. Mr Malik too shared to the full the belief that the US, India, Israel and other countries were – for reasons that he could barely explain himself – supporting the Pakistani Taleban, and were responsible for their terrorist outrages.

Just as important as any of this – indeed, fundamental to Pakistan's hopes of progress – is whether the Lawyers' Movement represents a solid mass movement for reform, or just another desperate search for a magic key that would miraculously solve Pakistan's problems without anyone having actually to work steadily to achieve change. In the *New York Times* article mentioned above, James Traub described the lawyers he met at a demonstration as 'apparently deranged' by enthusiasm for their cause, and some of the slogans I saw raised would certainly support that view. 'Restoration of Chief Justice Means Salvation of Pakistan' read one placard above the Bar Association in Multan. 'Independent Judiciary Will Solve Every Problem' read another.

On the whole the evidence as of 2010 concerning the future of the Lawyers' Movement is pretty discouraging. To put it at its simplest, masses of ordinary Pakistanis supported the Lawyers' Movement not because of its programme, but because it seemed the only force able and willing to challenge the increasingly hated rule of President Musharraf; just as they supported it later out of hatred for President Zardari. This certainly did not reflect popular admiration for lawyers as a class, or the official law as an institution.

Moreover, the masses could not in fact have supported the Lawyers' Movement's liberal programme anyway, because the movement did not have one. The lawyers' only collective programme has been the independence, power and prestige of the judiciary – which is an excellent thing in principle, except that the judicial system is one of the most flawed institutions in Pakistan, and consequently loathed by the masses.

Unfortunately, although individuals such as Mr Ashraf Khan have brought forward some very valuable proposals for judicial reform, the

Lawyers' Movement as a whole has not generated any serious movement among lawyers for reform of their own judicial system – something that is absolutely essential if mass support for the movement is to be maintained in the long term, but would be very uncomfortable for many lawyers. Indeed, most of the members of the movement with whom I spoke did not seem to understand what I was driving at when I asked about this, let alone think that it was in any way important.

In his *suo moto* (by his own motion, i.e., not in response to a case brought before the Court) judgments in 2007–9, Chief Justice Chaudhry undoubtedly righted a number of individual wrongs, and garnered a great deal of popularity by hauling police chiefs and bureaucrats before the Court and humiliating them publicly. He also appears to have a genuine commitment to the supremacy of the law, at least as defined by himself. His personal style in this it must be said was entirely autocratic, as was that of other senior leaders of the Lawyers' Movement whom I met – on both the conservative and liberal sides.

The question is once again whether this was part of an attempt at systemic change, or whether Chaudhry was simply playing the role that you can see politicians and their assistants playing in every political office in Pakistan – responding to appeals for help against the police in return for promises of political support. Moreover, by 2009 the use of *suo motos* by Chaudhry and other senior judges was beginning to extend far beyond their judicial competence, with, for example, judgments being issued ordering the government to reduce prices of essential goods. If continued, this will inevitably bring the courts into conflict with any government – and it is not clear where public sympathy will lie in future.

At a lower level, individual lawyers and groups of lawyers express their views in more direct ways. During the Lawyers' Movement, lawyers beat up opponents and fought with police. After the restoration of the Chief Justice, some took their victory as a licence to continue this violence in individual cases. During my stay in Lahore in August 2009, a group of lawyers beat up a police officer who had testified against their client in front of the court. When this was shown on television, the next day they beat up the camera team responsible. From various parts of the country came reports of judges using Contempt of Court judgments to muzzle the press and intimidate opponents, to help friends and relatives. As a Lahori friend remarked cynically,

Well, what do you expect? The army wears uniforms and beats up people, and so do the police, so of course the lawyers wear their black jackets and beat up people. It is what you do if you have power in this country.

THE SHARIAH

Faced with all this, it is hardly surprising that ordinary people dream of a completely different and better system of justice, or that for many these hopes should focus on the Shariah. All over Pakistan there was majority support among the ordinary people with whom I spoke for agreements with the Taleban to establish the Shariah in certain areas (like the Nizam-e-Adl agreement of February 2009 for Swat), and in the Pathan areas that support was overwhelming – though that only made many people's disillusionment greater when they saw that the Taleban were not interested only in bringing Islamic justice, but also sought power for themselves.

People on both sides of the Afghan–Pakistan frontier remember how in the 1990s the Afghan Taleban, on the ideological basis of the Shariah, restored order out of the chaos created by the victory of the Afghan Mujahidin in 1992. The Islamic Courts' Movement in Somalia has much of the same appeal.

In fact, the Afghan Taleban fulfilled the vision set out for me by a *qazi* (Islamic judge) in the Afghan province of Paktika in 1989. Looking at the complete absence of regular government in the areas 'liberated' by the Mujahidin, I asked him whether he was not afraid of anarchy when the Communist regime in Kabul fell and the Mujahidin took over completely. 'No,' he replied, 'because we Pashtuns have our own code, the *pashtun-wali*, which resolves conflicts and maintains order. It doesn't stop all feuds, but it prevents them going too far. And if that fails, then we have the Shariah, Islamic law, which everyone respects and which it is my job to implement.'

But what is this 'Shariah' that ordinary people say they want, and that the Taleban claim to be implementing? Here, a great deal of careful unpicking is necessary. At one level, believing Muslims are simply required to declare their support for the Shariah, because its ultimate basis is to be found in the Koran, which is the word of God delivered through His Prophet. On the other hand, people also use 'Shariah' as a sort of code for a better, simpler, more equal, more honest and more accessible form of official justice, without really knowing in detail what they mean by this, or what the various forms of Shariah really contain. For example, when faced with the idea of amputation of the hand as a standard punishment for theft, most people (outside the harsher Pathan areas) reject this outright, some nevertheless pointing out approvingly the Shariah's detailed provisions for compensation and reconciliation.

Formally speaking, the introduction of Shariah law in Pakistan is quite unnecessary, because a series of laws beginning with Zulfikar Ali Bhutto in the 1970s have declared that all Pakistani laws must be in conformity with the Shariah. In practice, however, this is irrelevant. Legally, it has only added to the confusion and contradiction that marks Pakistan's legal scene. Much more importantly, however, it misses the point that the campaign for the Shariah is not so much about the *content* of the law as about popular *access* to the law, the *speed* of the law, and who gets to *enforce* the law.

In trying to make the Shariah the system of justice throughout Pakistan, and to make local mullahs the judges, the Taleban are going far beyond anything that existed before. Before the British came, the Shariah was of course the official code of Muslim states in South Asia, but in practice its implementation was restricted to the cities and seats of government. Beyond, everything was governed by local customary law, albeit formally in the name of Islam.

But then again, it is not really the Shariah that the Pakistani Taleban and their allies are trying to implement in the areas they control, but a mixture of the Shariah and the *pashtunwali* – and this also marks a change between the old Taleban in Afghanistan before 9/11 and the 'Neo-Taleban' that has emerged in response to the Western presence. Between this mixture of the *pashtunwali* and the extremely harsh Wahabi version of the Shariah favoured by the Taleban, more progressive aspects of the Shariah are absent from the Taleban programme. In the Shariah itself, however, they remain marked when compared to the tribal codes of Pakistan. The Shariah was in consequence admired and even promoted by British officials. As the British gazetteer for Balochistan in 1906 has it:

> The position of widows has been further strengthened by the following
> important decision given by Sir Hugh Barnes, agent to the Governor

General, in November 1892 in the case of Lukman Kakar versus the Crown:

> As regards a widow's power of choosing a husband, Muhammadan law must not be over-ridden by local inhuman and ignorant custom and, in all disputes regarding widow remarriage brought before the courts in British Balochistan or the Agency territories, the Courts of law should follow the provisions of Muhammadan law, in so far as that law gives to widows full liberty and discretion to marry whom they please; and no case of this kind should be submitted to a jirga for settlement without a clear direction that on this point of a widow's freedom of choice, no curtailment whatsoever will be permitted of the liberty and discretion which Muhammadan law allows her.[17]

Under the British, the Muslim Shariah Act of 1937 abrogated (officially, that is) customary laws with reference to Muslims and applied to all Muslims instead the provisions of the Shariah as regards all issues of personal law, marriage and inheritance. In justifying this, the British government of India cited the formality and certainty of the Shariah compared to the informality and endless variations of customary codes. However, according to M. P. Jain:

> A much more sound reason to abrogate custom was that under it the position of women in matters of inheritance was inferior to that under Muslim law . . . The abrogation of customary law was a result of the agitation carried on by such bodies as the Jamiat-ul-Ulema-i-Hind [a forerunner of the contemporary JUI], an organization of Muslim religious men. Support was lent by many Muslim women's organizations which condemned the customary law as adversely affecting their rights.[18]

Educated women in the Pathan areas of Pakistan are still well aware of this difference. Thus in May 2007 I provoked a fascinating discussion among students of Peshawar University concerning the Taleban's promotion of a strict version of the Shariah, whether this conflicted with the traditions of the *pashtunwali* and, if so, which should take precedence. At first, the great majority tried to argue that there was no conflict between the two traditions, and their professor cut in with 'Well, the main point is that all my customs, whether they are good or bad, are different from those of Punjab' – at which there was another tremendous burst of applause.

When, however, I pressed them to state a preference between the Shariah and the *pashtunwali*, twelve chose the *pashtunwali* and fourteen the Shariah, with the rest not voting. The striking thing was that most of the men chose the *pashtunwali* and *all* the girls chose the Shariah. They did not state their reasons, but they seem obvious enough. Restrictive though they appear to Westerners, the provisions of the Shariah proscribe the most savage provisions of the *pashtunwali* as far as women are concerned – like the odious practice of giving girls as part of the settlement of feuds between families – just as the Koran was intended to reform the savage tribal traditions of seventh-century Arabia.

The Shariah also guarantees a share of inheritance to girls, while the *pashtunwali* gives it only to boys; and furthermore it guarantees rights to wives in the case of divorce. This progressive aspect of the Shariah was also something that the Information Secretary of the MMA (Muttahida Majlis-e-Amal) Islamist alliance (then forming the government of the NWFP) stressed to me in an interview later that afternoon, emphasizing that his party stood for Islamic progress against tribal barbarism.

For all that, there is no chance of the Shariah as preached by the Taleban sweeping Pakistan, for the same reasons that the Taleban themselves cannot sweep Pakistan. The first is that while the ruling elites may be willing to make any number of local compromises with the Shariah, they will fight hard and successfully to prevent Islamist revolution.

That leaves open the possibility that moderate Islamist forces in Pakistan might develop a new form of the Shariah like that of the modern state in Iran, more adapted to the contemporary world. But this will be extremely difficult in Pakistan, because the different Islamist groups in Pakistan cannot agree on which form of the Shariah is in fact valid. While Iran has a unitary and centralized form of Shia Islam, Pakistan – quite apart from its Sunni–Shia divide – has a multifarious collection of different forms of Sunni Islam. This critical obstacle to Islamist revolution will be explored further in the next chapter.

NOT QUITE AS BAD AS IT LOOKS

Re-reading this chapter, I feel that it needs a certain correction. Naturally a description of a country's criminal justice system will focus on crime, but it would be a mistake to draw from the above the idea that

Pakistani society is in a state of permanent chaotic violence. A number of things need to be kept in mind. The first is that the jirga and *pan-chayat* mechanisms described in this chapter are explicitly dedicated to regulating and containing violence, and usually do so successfully. Local saints and their descendants also play a part in this regard.

As Stephen Lyon has pointed out, one also needs to watch out for local hyperbole. If you believed all the stories you hear concerning violence in the countryside, 'there would hardly be a man left alive or a women left un-raped'.[19] Political violence aside, most of Pakistan is not in fact very violent or crime-ridden by the standards of many US cities, let alone those of Mexico or Brazil. In fact, given levels of poverty, the level of ordinary crime (as opposed to crime stemming from politics, religion or 'honour') is in many ways remarkably low.

One reason is that this society is mostly dominated by landowning and business politicians who, while they have to be prepared to order killings if really necessary, have generally inherited their positions, not murdered their way to them in savage gangland wars. They generally have to obey some sort of local moral consensus, which approves courage in defence of your *izzat*, but which certainly does not approve unrestrained murder and theft. Another factor is the relative (though of course only relative) lack of extreme class divisions, mentioned in the Introduction.

It is quite true that in much of Pakistan, tribes and chieftains operate as autonomous armed forces – but that was true of medieval Europe, and it did not prevent the great achievements of that period in terms of both culture and commerce. To paraphrase the words of various 'feudal' acquaintances and tribal chieftains, for by far the greater part of the time, the point of armed force is not war but deterrence – to show that you are strong so as *not* to have to fight. In a paradoxical way, therefore, to use violence may be a sign of weakness, and also of lack of self-control. This virtue is not prized as much as physical courage, but it is still highly prized, since the consequences of lack of self-control can be both per-sonally fatal and bad for your kinship group's prestige.

Finally, the rather miserable picture of the police and courts painted in this chapter is equally true of by far the greater part of India; indeed, because of caste divisions, parts of India are considerably worse as far as police atrocities are concerned. The same is true of the dominance of cus-tomary law. In fact, throughout most of this chapter (except, obviously, those parts dealing with the Shariah), I could, without any substantial inaccuracy, have substituted the words 'Indian' or 'South Asian' for 'Pakistani'.

This is awful for much of the Indian population, and has contributed directly to the growing Maoist insurgency among low-caste and tribal peasants in much of the Indian countryside; but it has not so far prevented the great recent economic achievements of the Indian state. The difference with Pakistan is that in India there is no coherent and unified cultural alternative to the modern state and its legal structures, which also operates as a standing moral reproach to those structures. In Pakistan, in the view of many believers, there is the way of Islam, reflected in the Shariah. This code for every aspect of life and society is the subject of the next chapter.

4

Religion

Don't compare your nation with the nations of the West
Distinctive is the nation of the Prophet of Islam
Their solidarity depends on territorial nationality
Your solidarity rests on the strength of your religion
When faith slips away, where is the solidarity of the community?
And when the community is no more, neither is the nation.

(Sir Muhammad Iqbal)[1]

Verily God will not change [the condition of] a people, until
they change what is in themselves.

(The Koran, Shura 13, verse 11)

Since 9/11, international discussions of Islam in Pakistan have focused mainly on the threat from religious extremism and terrorism. In these discussions, a dangerous intellectual mess is often created by the mixing up of words such as 'extremism' and 'militancy' with the very different concepts of 'fundamentalism' and 'conservatism'.

Long before 9/11, however, much of the discussion of Pakistani Islam, inside and outside Pakistan, concerned whether Pakistan, having been founded as a refuge for the Muslims of South Asia, should or should not be an Islamic state; or, on the other hand, why Islam had allegedly failed to keep West and East Pakistan together, and was continuing to fail to help develop Pakistan as a united and successful society.

On the first point, I have already argued that, while terrorism is obviously present and frightening, Islamist extremism in Pakistan presents little danger of overthrowing the state unless US pressure has already split and crippled that state. The religious barriers to the spread of extremism will be outlined in the present chapter.

The second question is whether or not the state should have an official Islamic character, which will go deeper than the formally Islamic nature it has possessed since the constitution of 1973 (under the government of the 'liberal' Z. A. Bhutto) declared Islam the state religion. This is an important issue – but not nearly as central as many analysts have assumed. It makes no difference to the beliefs and behaviour of the vast majority of the population, which are deeply conservative and steeped in different Muslim traditions.

It is worth noting from this point of view that the PPP, generally regarded as a 'secular' party, is in fact in some areas of Pakistan partly religious in its appeal, in that many of its local politicians come from the families of hereditary saints, and owe much of their local power and prestige to this ancestry. Of course, though, this is a very different kind of religious appeal from that of the Islamist parties.

The point, therefore, is that the Islam of the Pakistani masses contains very *different* traditions. The Islamic character of the state would only be a real issue for most of the population if that state were to imitate Saudi Arabia or Iran and try to impose one monolithic version of Islam. However, the Pakistani state is too weak to achieve this even if it wanted to – as Zia-ul-Haq's failure demonstrated.

A related issue is that of whether a strong formal state commitment to Islam is necessary to hold Pakistan together, as Islamists (and some non-Islamists) claim, or whether, on the other hand, as secular analysts would argue, this has already been tried and failed. Here, many of the analysts and reporters have been looking at the wrong things in the wrong places. Popular (as opposed to official) forms of Islam do in fact play a key role in holding Pakistan together, but often in ways which are very different from those that the forces of Islamist reform (whether moderate or extremist) would wish; just as in India Hinduism plays a far greater role in Indian unity than liberals wish to recognize, but a very different role from the one that Hindu nationalists would wish to create.

As in Europe in the past, even some Pakistani statesmen whose own religious practice has been very lax have wished to promote religion in public life as a way of trying to improve appallingly low levels of public ethics in the state services and among politicians – especially as the

Western codes of public service left behind by the British have gradually eroded. This in turn is part of the crucial question for Pakistan of whether it is possible to create loyalties and ethics which transcend those of loyalty to kin. Clearly, Islam in Pakistan has so far failed in this regard, though things would be even worse without its influence.

Closely connected with this unsuccessful role of religion, however, is another, much more effective role of Islam which is hardly noticed outside the country, but should be: that of softening the misery of Pakistan's poor through charity. Levels of trust in Pakistani state institutions are extremely low, and for good reason. Partly in consequence, Pakistan has one of the lowest levels of tax collection outside Africa. On the other hand, charitable donation, at almost 5 per cent of GDP, is one of the highest rates in the world.

Just how much of this is motivated by religious beliefs cannot be quantified, but, given the religious faith of most Pakistanis, it must be a great deal, in accordance with the commandment in the Koran that:

> Righteousness is not that ye turn your faces towards the east or the west, but righteousness is, one who believes in God, and the last day, and the angels, and the Book, and the prophets, and who gives wealth for His love to kindred, and orphans, and the poor, and the son of the road, beggars, and those in captivity; and who is steadfast in prayer, and gives alms.[2]

Thus the Citizens' Foundation, the most widespread and effective educational charity in Pakistan (with more than 600 schools and 85,000 pupils), is a non-religious organization, but a majority of its founding members from the business community are practising Muslims – though they come from all the different branches of Islam represented in Pakistan and do not use any religious element in their public appeals.

Charities with a religious character also tend to be more favoured and more trusted by the population. It is also true of Pakistan's most famous private charitable institution by far, the Edhi Foundation, which is non-religious; however, Abdus Sattar Edhi is himself a deeply religious man, known by the public at large as *Maulana* (a Muslim distinguished by his piety and learning) even though he is not a Muslim scholar and in fact greatly dislikes being called this.

There is no sight in Pakistan more moving than to visit some dusty, impoverished small town in an arid wasteland, apparently abandoned by God and all sensible men and certainly abandoned by the Pakistani state and its own elected representatives – and to see the flag of the Edhi Foundation flying over a concrete shack with a telephone, and the only ambulance in town standing in front. Here, if anywhere in Pakistan, lies the truth of human religion and human morality.

FEUDING THEOLOGIANS

As to modern Islamist politics in Pakistan, the most important question to be asked is not why they are so strong, but why they are so weak. Think about it. Across much of the Middle East and the Muslim world more widely, Islamist political parties and reformist movements are making progress. Such a party rules in Turkey, and others would probably come to power in Egypt, Syria, Algeria and Morocco if those countries held democratic elections. Iran of course experienced an Islamist revolution, albeit of a specifically Shia kind, as did the Shia of Lebanon.

Pakistan has always had a political system which is far more open than those of most other Muslim states; it has levels of poverty which would seem to cry out for a mass reformist movement in the name of Islam; and it has inherited from India before 1947 one of the leading intellectual traditions of Islamist modernism and reformism. Yet with brief exceptions, the Islamist parties have always performed miserably in the polls, and are no nearer today than they ever were to creating a mass political movement that would successfully pursue a truly Islamist system in Pakistan, whether by peaceful or revolutionary means.

The truth is that, while most forms of Islamist radicalism have ancient roots, they are also modern, and a response to modernity. Most forms of Pakistani Islam for their part are traditional and conservative – far too conservative to support a revolution, and far too diverse to submit themselves to a monolithic version of Islam. This in turn derives in part from the fact that Pakistan remains in many ways a very rural society, where even the rapidly growing cities are still heavily rural in culture, owing to the constant flow of migrants from the countryside.

Islamist radicalism, whether of old or new varieties, has always been a basically urban phenomenon, and derived from old and new patterns of urban society and culture. In Pakistan, the rural masses can occasionally be stirred up to furious panic by the cry of 'Islam in danger', as they were in 1947, but only two radical forces have established a long-running presence in parts of the countryside. The first are the Sunni sectarian extremists of the central and southern Punjab, who have succeeded in appealing to Sunni tenant farmers and the lower middle classes against the local Shia elites. Where, however, the landed elites are Sunni, they help prevent the spread of the Islamist parties through their control of the appointment of mullahs to local mosques, which they use to bar anyone with a hint of social radicalism.

The other case of Islamist success in rural areas is the Pakistani Taleban in parts of the tribal areas and the NWFP – a success which is due above all to specifically Pathan factors and traditions, and the impact of developments in Afghanistan. As of 2010, the Taleban and the Sunni sectarians have forged an alliance which is carrying out terrorist attacks across much of Pakistan; but to overthrow the Pakistani state would be quite a different matter, and something of which they are, in my judgement, incapable unless the US indirectly gives them a helping hand.

Theologically speaking, all the Sunni Islamist groups, from the relatively moderate and democratic Jamaat Islami to the Taleban and other extremists, are drawn from one of two traditions: the Deobandi, named after a famous madrasah founded in Deoband (now in Uttar Pradesh, India) in 1866; and the Ahl-e-Hadith ('People of the *hadiths*', or traditions attributed to the Prophet), a branch of the international Salafi (fundamentalist-reformist; *salaf* meaning forerunner or spiritual ancestor in Arabic) tradition, heavily influenced by Wahabism, and with particularly close links to Arabia dating back to the original foundations of this tendency in the sixteenth century CE.

The Ahl-e-Hadith are more extreme than the Deobandis, and less concerned with questions of modern social justice and development. Both traditions, however, can be broadly described as fundamentalist, in that they advocate a return to the pure teaching of the Koran and the Prophet; reformist, in that they advocate radical reforms to both contemporary Muslim society and much of contemporary Islam; and puritan (in the old Anglo-American sense), in their concern for strict public morality and their dislike of both ostentatious wealth and the worship of saints and shrines.

There is a difference between the two in this regard, however. The Ahl-e-Hadith loathe the Sufi and saintly traditions in general. The Deobandis – whose tradition is largely descended from the thought of Shah Waliullah, himself a member of the Naqshbandi Sufi order – praise the saints themselves (and used to claim miraculous powers for their own greatest Deobandi teachers), but condemn the ways in which the saints are worshipped, and the belief that they can intercede with God.

The Deobandi tradition gave birth to the Tablighi Jamaat, by far the greatest preaching organization in the Muslim world (indeed, in the whole world), which each year draws millions of people to its great rallies at its headquarters in Raiwind near Lahore. The Tabligh was founded in India in the 1920s as a revivalist movement dedicated to strengthening scriptural Islamic practice among Muslims and resisting the efforts of Hindu preachers to draw them back into the Hindu fold. In recent decades the Tabligh leadership has strongly emphasized its apolitical character and has firmly distanced itself from extremism and terrorism; but its networks and gatherings have been used by radicals as a cover for meetings and planning.

However, until recently a majority of Sunni Pakistanis, in so far as they were aware of belonging to any particular tradition within Islam, belonged neither to the tradition of the Deobandis nor of the Ahl-e-Hadith but to that of the Barelvis (who call themselves the Ahl-e-Sunnat, or people of the teaching of Mohammed and his companions), named after a madrasah founded in 1880 in the town of Bareilly – also now in Uttar Pradesh, India. Barelvi religious attitudes, which are linked to those of leading Sufi orders, are far closer to popular Islam as it has usually been followed in South Asia. This popular Islam includes in particular a belief in the intercession of saints with God, the validity of miracles by the saints, worship at the shrines of saints (though not strictly speaking worship *of* the saints), and local traditions attached to the saints.

The Barelvis therefore might be called Catholics to the Deobandis and Ahl-e-Hadith's puritans – with the crucial distinction that far from being grouped in one hierarchical organization, the Barelvis are a very loose and fissiparous grouping which cannot really be described as a 'movement' at all. Their rivals, though historically fewer in number, have generally had the edge when it comes to organization.

Despite repeated attempts, the Barelvis have never created a large and enduring political party of their own, though they have played a leading part in all the wider Muslim mass movements in India and Pakistan. Barelvi parties formed part of the MMA Islamist alliance which governed the NWFP and Balochistan from 2002 to 2008, and supported that alliance's calls for the introduction of Shariah law and a variety of Islamic regulations. However, both of Pakistan's main Islamist parties today, the Jamaat-Islami (JI) nationally and the Jamiat-e-Ulema-e-Islam (JUI) in the Pathan areas, are drawn from the Deobandi tradition.

The greater radicalism, and anti-Westernism, of the Deobandi theological tradition can be traced in part to its urban, social and institutional origins, which differ from those of the Sufi and Barelvi traditions. British rule made little difference to the practice of Islam in the South Asian countryside. Except in the case of the most outrageous abuses, the British never meddled with the shrines, and as long as local *pirs* did not rise in revolt the British tried to co-opt them.

It was quite otherwise in the cities. As the last chapter, on justice, described, the role of formal Islamic justice in the countryside was always very limited. In the old Muslim states, however, the *qazis* (Islamic judges) and *ulema* (Islamic scholars; singular *alim*) ran the justice and higher education systems in the cities, and played a crucial role in the administration of the Mughal empire and other kingdoms. The destruction of those kingdoms, and the introduction by the British of British systems of law (with the exception of personal law) and higher education dealt a shattering blow to the power, prestige and income of the *ulema* and *qazis*. Inevitably, many were radicalized in response.

The decline of the urban clerics from their status under the Mughal empire was highlighted for me by the contrast between the Badshahi (Imperial) mosque in Lahore, and its state-appointed imam or chief cleric. The mosque is Pakistan's greatest and most splendid architectural monument, and from its completion in 1673 to 1986 was the biggest mosque in the world. Its imam, however, lives in a cramped and shabby lower-middle-class house in its shadow. He sat on his bed while I interviewed him – a burly figure with a booming voice who dwarfed his small bedroom.

His circumstances of course could reflect religious austerity; but other things suggested a man who essentially was a very minor government functionary: the deference he paid to my companion, a local PML(N) politician; the continual repetition – evidently from a very well-worn official record for the consumption of Western visitors – of his commitment to peace, religious harmony, birth control and so on; and his bringing out of a tattered photo album showing his attendance on behalf of the Pakistani state at various international inter-religious conferences. Despite his international diplomatic role, he spoke almost no English, thereby marking his de facto exclusion from all Pakistan's elites. I'm afraid that I was strongly reminded of meetings with officially sanctioned – and officially controlled – religious figures in the former Soviet Union.

I visited the imam during Moharram 2009. Twenty years earlier, I had also been in Lahore's inner city during Moharram, to visit young activists of the Jamaat Islami. They all came from the educated lower middle classes. They were a pleasant lot, well-mannered, hospitable and keeping whatever fanaticism they possessed well veiled before a guest. What I took above all from my visit to their homes was the intensity of their families' struggle to save themselves from sinking into the semi-criminal lumpenproletariat, and the way in which religion – and the Jamaat allegiance and discipline in particular – helped in that struggle. These boys spoke with deep feeling of the lure of street crime, heroin smuggling and heroin addiction. Not far away the Hira Mandi – the red-light district – beckoned as an attraction for men and a fate for women.

Something that one also takes away from visits to the lower and lower middle classes in Pakistan's cities is the singularly repulsive nature of the semi-Western, semi-modern new culture these cities are liable to breed, especially concerning the treatment of women – a mixture of Western licentiousness with local brutality, crudity and chauvinism. This culture threatens women with the worst of all worlds, in which they are exposed to exacerbated male lust without the protections afforded by traditional culture, and in which their children are exposed to a range of new dangers and temptations. This is why the support of women forms such an important background to many of the Islamist groups, and why all the intelligent Islamist leaders with whom I have spoken (that is, not the Taleban) have stressed an Islamic women's education programme as a core part of their programme.

In these depressing social and cultural circumstances, adherence to a radical Islamist network like the Jamaat provides a sense of cultural security, a new community and some degree of social support – modest, but still better than anything the state can provide. Poverty is recast as religious simplicity and austerity. Perhaps even more important, faith provides a measure of pride: a reason to keep a stiff back amid continual humiliations and temptations.

Faith also has its physical expression and impact through architecture, as the beauty and grandeur of the Badshahi mosque reminded me.

In the blaring, stinking, violent world of the modern 'third world' Muslim inner city, the mosque provides an oasis of calm and reflection. The harmonious serenity of its traditional architecture contrasts with the ugly, vulgar clash of Western and Pakistani kitsch which is the style of so many of the elites, let alone the masses. Like the Catholic churches of Central America described by Graham Greene in *The Lawless Roads*, the mosque may be the only beautiful work of human creation that most people ever see, and the haven not only of beauty but of an ordered and coherent culture, and a guide to living.

THE LIMITS TO RADICALISM

On the other hand, the Islamist parties have never been able to break out from their relatively narrow cultural and ethnic bases to appeal successfully to the mass of the Pakistani population. For this a number of factors are responsible. Firstly, their religious culture is in fact alien to that of a majority of Pakistanis. This is changing as a result of social development and urbanization – but the lack of modern economic development, and therefore of truly modern urbanization in Pakistan (as opposed to migration from the countryside which brings rural culture with it), means that this change is not happening nearly as fast as might have been expected. The lack of modern development also means that unlike the Islamist Justice party in Turkey, the religious parties in Pakistan do not have support from modern educated business and technical classes, and have not been able to develop new thinking and new solutions to Pakistan's myriad social and economic problems.

Secondly, the Islamist parties – or at least the Jamaat, since the JUI has become in effect just another patronage machine – challenge the deeply embedded structures of power, property, patronage and kinship which dominate Pakistani politics and government. This is clearest in their hostility to the hereditary descendants of saints who dominate large swathes of the Pakistani countryside and play an important part in all Pakistani regimes.

Having failed to consolidate real mass support in the population, the Islamist parties have found themselves outflanked from both directions. On the extremist side, their more radical supporters have been drawn away by violent jihadi groups like the Taleban in the Pathan areas, and

Jaish-e-Mohammed, Lashkar-e-Taiba, Sipah-e-Sahaba and others in Punjab. Meanwhile, at the moderate end of their spectrum, pragmatic Islamists who wish to share in state patronage have been drawn to support first the military regime of President Zia-ul-Haq and then the Pakistani Muslim League (PML) of the Sharif brothers, both of which promised Islamization of Pakistan without any of the social and economic change for which the Jamaat stand.

The Taleban meanwhile have been led into violent attacks on the shrines of saints and on the *pir* families who are descended from the saints. They and their allies have attacked Barelvi religious leaders who have condemned them and opposed their takeover of particular mosques. For example, on 12 June 2009 they assassinated a leading Barelvi cleric of Lahore, Mufti Sarfraz Naeemi, who had spoken out against them, and in 2005 had issued an edict against suicide bombings. On 1 July 2010 suicide bombers carried out a massive attack on the famous and beloved shrine of the saint Data Ganj Baksh in Lahore (see below), killing dozens of worshippers and galvanizing Barelvi religious figures into an unusual display of united protest.

Taleban attacks on shrines are motivated partly by religious hostility. The Wahabis have been bitterly opposed to shrines since their very beginnings in the eighteenth century, and first leapt to international notoriety when they captured Mecca and Medina and destroyed the shrines and tombs there, not sparing even that of the Prophet himself. Particular hatred between Wahabis and Shia dates back to the Wahabis' sack of the great Shia shrines of Karbala, Iraq, in 1802. In Saudi Arabia today, shrines continue to be banned and Sufi orders persecuted.

Taleban hostility to the shrines also stems from the role played by these families in the local elites, which means that the Taleban have to attack and destroy them in order to seize local power. However, as of 2010, the evidence suggests that far from gaining wider support, these attacks have in fact alienated large numbers of people who were initially attracted by the Pakistani Taleban's support for the jihad in Afghanistan, advocacy of the Shariah and actions against local criminals. As I was told by people I interviewed on the street in Peshawar in the summer of 2009, among Pathans this was especially true of the Taleban bomb attack on 5 March 2009 which damaged the Peshawar shrine of the Pathan saint Pir Rahman Baba (Abdur Rahman Mohmand, 1653–1711 CE), who like a number of Sufi saints is revered not only for his spiritual power but as a poet of the local vernacular language and has been called the 'Pashto nightingale'. Data Ganj Baksh too is beloved by Punjabis and indeed by Muslims all over South Asia.

The attacks on these shrines was therefore a mistaken strategy, which some other Taleban were clever enough to avoid. Thus at the shrine of Pir Haji Sahib Taurangyi in the Mohmand Tribal Agency (some of whose descendants will be described in a later chapter), the local Taleban were careful not to attack the shrine but to co-opt it, stressing that the saint had been a leader of jihad against the British Raj just as the Taleban were fighting the British and Americans invaders and oppressors in Afghanistan, and their 'slaves' in the Pakistani government.

SAINTLY POLITICIANS

In attacking the saints, the Islamist extremists – though they refuse to recognize this themselves – are striking at the very roots of Islam in South Asia. One might say that the beginnings of South Asian Islam were the Book and the Saint. In principle the Saint was the bearer of the Book, but in practice it often did not work out quite like that. The Book is of course the Koran, and to a lesser extent the *hadiths*, or traditional statements and judgments of the Prophet and stories concerning him, recorded (or invented) and more or less codified by early generations of Muslim scholars.

The Koran is the absolute, unquestionable foundation of Islam, and since Islam's earliest years every movement seeking to reform Islam from within has been 'scripturalist', or 'fundamentalist' in the sense of emphasizing a return to the pure spirit of the Koran, just as Christian fundamentalists (for whom the term was coined in the nineteenth century, by the way), have sought to do in the case of the Bible.

The saints were the Muslim preacher-missionaries, mostly from the tradition loosely called 'Sufi' (a very complex and often misleading term). In South Asia, the saints are known by the Arab term *shaikh*, and they and their descendants by the Persian one *pir* (old man). As much as the great Muslim conquering dynasties, the saints actually spread Islam to many of the ordinary people of South Asia, just as, thousands of miles away, their equivalents were doing in Morocco and elsewhere.

In the process, they, their shrines and their cults took on many local Hindu features, which made them beloved of the local population, but intensely suspect to fundamentalists. The latter have also long accused the cult of the saints of involving *shirk*, or the worship of figures other than the one God – perhaps the worst sin in the entire Islamic theological canon. Nonetheless, most of the population, especially in the countryside, came to see the saints as embodying the only Islam they knew. Moreover, the saints were usually from families claiming to be descendants of the Prophet (Sayyids), and in some cases had themselves come directly from the Arab world. This gave them immense prestige as bearers of Islam from its source, which continues to this day.

The local and decidedly non-Koranic aspects of the saints' cults were due not only to the influence of the surrounding Hindu world. They have also reflected what seems to be a feature of almost every human society at one time or another, namely a desire for accessible sacred intermediaries between the human individual and his or her supreme, unknowable God. The Arabic phrase usually translated into English as 'saint' literally means 'friend of God'. In the words of an early twentieth-century British officer:

> The general idea of our riverain folk [the traditional settled rural Muslim population of Punjab, which had to live near the rivers to draw water for irrigation] seems to be that the Deity is a busy person, and that his hall of audience is of limited capacity. Only a certain proportion of mankind can hope to attain to the presence of God; but when certain individuals have got there, they may have opportunities of representing the wishes and desires of other members of the human race. Thus, all human beings require an intervener between them and God.[3]

The legends of the early saints contain many stories of their battles with Hindu priests and kings, in which their superior powers prevail, the priests are routed and the kings defeated in battle or converted. Most of what is now Pakistan was converted to Islam only very slowly, however, and long after it was conquered by Muslim dynasties.

In the words of the great scholar of South Asian Islam, Francis Robinson:

> The holy men were . . . the pioneers and frontiersmen of the Muslim world, men who from the thirteenth century played the crucial role in drawing

new peoples, pagans, Hindus, Buddhists, Shamanists, into an Islamic cultural milieu. According to tradition, nine saints introduced Islam to Java; wandering holy men, we are told, first brought Islam to West Africa. What the holy men did, it appears, was to find points of contact and social roles within the host community. They shared their knowledge of religious experience with men of other spiritual traditions. They helped propitiate the supernatural forces which hemmed in and always seemed to threaten the lives of common folk. They interpreted dreams, brought rain, healed the sick and made the barren fertile. They mediated between rulers and ruled, natives and newcomers, weak and strong.[4]

Stories of miracles grew up, first around the saints and then around their tombs and, as in the Christian world of the Middle Ages, the tombs became shrines (*khanqahs*) and places of pilgrimage, where people hoped to benefit from access to the saint's *baraka* (*barkat*), or spiritual power. The death anniversaries or *urs* of the saints (from the Persian word for marriage, commemorating their 'marriage' with God at death) became great 'fairs'. As with Hindu temples and Sikh *gurdwaras*, the *langars* (free kitchens) attached to the shrines play an important part in feeding the local poor, as well as pilgrims.

Muslim Pakistan, like Hindu India, is bound together by pilgrimages and allegiances to shrines and saints which stretch across provincial and linguistic boundaries. These bonds can be traced visually by the sayings and symbols of particular saints which often form part of the wonderfully extravagant decoration of the lorries which cross the country from one end to another, creating a 'sacred geography' that spans the whole of Pakistan.[5] Sufism and the shrines play a very important part in the popular poetry of local languages, above all in Sindh – where the saint Abdul Latif of Bhit is regarded as Sindh's national poet – but also in Punjabi and Pashto.

The culture of the shrines thus permeates Pakistan. Zulfikar Ali Bhutto sometimes presented himself to his followers as a divinely inspired guide and teacher, as does Altaf Hussain of the MQM (called by his followers 'Pir Sahib'). The mausoleum of Zalfikar Ali Bhutto and his daughter Benazir near Larkana is consciously modelled on the shrine of a saint. At PPP rallies, I have seen party supporters shaking their heads violently from side to side in the manner of ecstatic devotees at saintly festivals. Saints have also been pressed into military service. During the 1965 war with India, stories circulated of saints catching Indian bombs in their hands.

As in the Christian world, the shrines grew wealthy on the strength of donations from pilgrims and, above all, land grants from monarchs, noblemen and tribes. However, in the Muslim world there is a crucial difference from that of Christianity (at least since the Catholic Church in the eleventh century began to insist successfully that priests and bishops could not marry): namely, that unlike Christian saints, most Muslim saints married and had children, and that in the world of Muslim saints spiritual power is hereditary. This power 'is distributed among all the progeny of the saint and harnessed by the few who fulfil religious obligations and meditate on the tomb of the saint in order to perform miracles'.[6]

Not just the shrines themselves, but the *pir* families of the *sajjada nashins* (literally, 'he who sits on the prayer carpet') who were their guardians therefore became major landowners, exercising both religious and spiritual power in their neighbourhoods; sometimes performing miracles, often mediating local disputes and interceding with rulers, and occasionally going to war. They attracted whole local tribes as adherents and defenders, and intermarried with other Sayyid families to form powerful networks of kinship and patronage. Once again, in Pakistan it is not wealth alone, but wealth plus either kinship or spiritual prestige, or both, that gives political power.

The shrines and their guardians have therefore always vastly outclassed in prestige the menial and often despised village mullah, just as the shrines and monasteries of medieval Europe cast the humble village priest deep into the shade. The power of the *pirs* in Sindh and southern Punjab, and their role in combating the Taleban in the Pathan regions, will be discussed in later chapters.

These *pir* families remain of immense political importance in much of Pakistan, and especially in the PPP; as witness the fact that, as of 2010, the Prime Minister, Syed Yusuf Raza Gilani; deputy prime minister, Makhdoom Amin Fahim; foreign minister, Syed Mahmood Qureshi; and minister for religion, Syed Ahmed Qazmi are all from *pir* lineages, as are leading party supporters like Syeda Abida Husain. However, members of *pir* lineages are also to be found in prominent positions in other mainstream parties, like Makhdoom Faisal Saleh Hayat of the PML(Q) and Makhdoom Javed Hashmi, Makhdoom Ahmed Mehmood and, greatest of all, the Pir Pagaro of Sindh, all of whom at the time of writing are supporting the PML(N).

Thus, back in 1988, a PPP politician from the family of the *pir* of Hadda in Sindh, Syed Parvez Jillani, recounted to me the legends of Hadda, including one which told how the fish of the River Indus would come to worship his cousin the *pir* (a legend presumably taken originally from the worship of a Hindu river-god). He described the absolute, unquestioning devotion of the *murids* of Hadda to the *pir* and his family. Then, as a good PPP politician, he added:

> The difference between us and the other *pirs* is that we are in favour of bringing education to our *murids*, and that we have always played a democratic role – we were always for the PPP. That is why the defeat of the Pir Pagaro does not worry us. Our people would never betray us, because we have always worked with the masses and spoken for the rights of the poor. And we have always spoken out on Sindhi issues.[7]

The point is of course that, as this interview clearly indicates, in practice the *pirs* and their families cannot genuinely advance either local education or local democracy, as this would strike directly at the cultural and social bases of their own power. This brings out again the tragic tension in Pakistan between the needs of modern progress and the needs of social and political stability. The traditions and structures which prevent Islamist revolution and civil war also help keep much of the population in a state of backwardness and deference to the elites.

As these particular PPP *pir* families also demonstrate, they play a very valuable role in bridging the Sunni–Shia divide and hindering the rise of sectarian extremism. These *pir* families are publicly Sunni, but are generally known to be in private largely Shia (like the Bhuttos and Zardaris). Many saints, their traditions and their descendants in Pakistan are therefore not bound by the Sunni–Shia divide, but can be Sunni, Shia, or something undefined in between. This makes them very different from the Islamic scholars and judges of the towns, whose entire tradition is concentrated on precise learning and the drawing of precise distinctions on the basis of written sources.

It would be a mistake, however, to see the cults of the saints as purely rural or as purely derived from the past, and therefore – an assumption which is often derived consciously or unconsciously from the other two – doomed gradually to be eclipsed either by Western-style secularism, or by the modernist Islamism of the new urban radicals. Some of the greatest and most ancient Pakistani shrines, in Lahore and Multan, were created by their founding saints in great cities and have large followings among local businessmen (a point discussed further in the chapter on the Punjab). Others were originally in the countryside, but have been incorporated into Pakistan's mushrooming cities.

Nor are the shrines of Pakistan only about the worship of long-dead saints and their descendants. New local preachers are emerging all the time. Sometimes they emerge from the followers of existing shrines, like Pir Mir Ali Shah, who in the 1930s and 1940s greatly increased the fame of the ancient shrine of Golra Sharif near what is now Islamabad. In several cases in recent decades preachers have succeeded in establishing new and famous places of pilgrimage. A notable example is the shrine of Pir Hazrat Shah at Ghamkol Sharif in the NWFP. Hazrat Shah established himself there in 1951, and gained a reputation for holiness, preaching and miracles which attracted many followers, especially in the Pakistani armed forces.

The network of this shrine extends to large parts of the Pakistani diaspora in Britain. As Pnina Werbner has documented, the growth of this shrine's following in Britain formed part of a movement which saw the influence of the scripturalist 'Deobandi' school pushed back among British Muslims in the 1970s and 1980s.[8] The madrasah at Golra Sharif also sends preachers to Britain.

However, there are lots of new *pirs* unknown beyond their immediate neighbourhoods. Any Muslim can claim to be a saint, on the basis of a vision, or the appearance of another saint in a dream. To make good the claim, however, requires above all personal charisma, natural authority, psychological insight and good judgement in giving advice and solving local disputes. An ability to perform miracles or – depending on your point of view – a lot of luck are definite assets. Most such newly emerged figures never do become more than small local holy men. A few attract much more considerable followings. Often, this will be a process stretching over generations, with an impressive disciple succeeding the original *pir* and attracting yet more support.

Thus Pir Hasan Baba, a new saint in Lahore, who died in the 1950s, was the chosen successor of a previous *shaikh*, and Pir Hasan's prestige in turn was consolidated by his successor, Hafiz Mohammed Iqbal, who died in 2001. Together, they attracted a considerable following in the

Lahori middle classes and intelligentsia. Hasan Baba was by origin an Englishman drawn like many others to Sufi mysticism. Their followers are building a shrine for them on the site of the small, ordinary house where Hasan Baba (a small government clerk) lived and preached from the 1930s to the 1950s, and where they are both buried.

Reflecting the class and culture of its devotees, the shrine (which I visited in August 2009) is a beautiful building constructed from traditional materials, and designed by a leading Lahore architect – and follower of these saints – Kamil Khan. 'Nothing like this has been built in Pakistan or India since the fall of the Mughal empire,' the engineer, Rizwan Qadir Khwaja, told me. Reflecting the trans-communal nature of the shrines, the overall design is modelled on that of the famous Shia shrine of Ali in Najaf, Iraq, although Pir Hasan Baba was, technically at least, Sunni. As Mr Khwaja told me,

> In Pakistan, you often find that a wife is Shia, the husband Sunni. And in the past this was never a problem, but now extremists want to divide us. Sufism and Sufi shrines play a very important role against this, by bridging Sunni and Shia. When someone asks me if I am Sunni or Shia I reply that like my saints I really do not care. It is irrelevant. I think only of the will of God.[9]

Followers of Pir Hasan and Hafiz Iqbal also went out of their way to stress these saints' respect for other religions, that Hafiz Iqbal had called Pope John Paul II 'a true saint', and so on. 'A problem in Islam is that the Koran is too explicit and rigorous, unlike other scriptures, so there is less room for flexibility,' as one of the devotees told me – a statement calculated to cause apoplexy in many more-rigorous Muslims.

This shrine and its followers gave a strong sense of a living and growing tradition, and – like Qawali music – of a very strong cultural and emotional force. Mr Khwaja said, 'We are not trying to invent something new, but to breathe new life into old traditions,' and they seemed to have done just that. As to the miracles attributed to these saints, as a modern rationalist I could not help smiling at them – but as a Catholic (however faded) I have to recognize their central place in all religious traditions.

Like these saints, South Asian saints in general belong to one or other Sufi order, and their whole tradition has been called a Sufi one. This can be rather misleading for Western audiences whose ideas of Sufism are derived chiefly from Omar Khayyam (via Edward FitzGerald) and Idries Shah. The idea of Sufism as a vaguely deist, New-Age-style philosophy with lots of poetry, alcohol and soft drugs is also immensely appealing to members of Pakistan's Westernized elites, whom it permits to follow a Westernized and hedonistic lifestyle without feeling that they have broken completely with their religion and its traditions.

This image of Sufism as representing a sort of latitudinarian and pacific moderation has led to a US strategy of supporting Islamist Sufis in the Muslim world against radicals – whereas in reality a more helpful strategy in the 'war on terror' might be to use the FBI to support American Methodists against American Pentecostals. The unpopularity of the US is such among ordinary Pakistanis – including Barelvis and followers of the saints with whom I have spoken – that US moves in this direction are a great asset to radical enemies of Sufism. As to the supposed 'moderation' of the Barelvis, the assassin of Governor Salman Taseer, who committed his crime in defence of Pakistan's blasphemy law, is a Barelvi and was defended by most Barelvi clerics. The Barelvis are in fact deeply conservative reactionaries and are therefore opposed to modern Islamist revolution *and* to liberalism.

Sufis have often been at the forefront of movements insisting on stricter religious observance and obedience to the Koran, as in those fighting against European colonialism. The famous Qawali form of ecstatic devotional music (brought to Western audiences by great artists like Nusrat Fateh Ali Khan) stemmed from Sufism and is performed at many shrines – but has been banned by the Naqshbandi Sufi order.

In the sixteenth century, some Sufi leaders denounced the Mughal emperor Akbar's attempt to create a new syncretic cult. In the late seventeenth and early eighteenth centuries, others supported the harsh Islamizing policies of the Emperor Aurangzeb. In the eighteenth century, the great Islamist reformer Shah Waliullah (mentioned in Chapter 1) was a member of the Naqshbandi Sufi order and, in the late nineteenth century, followers of his tradition founded the Deoband theological school, whose adherents today form the backbone of Islamist radical politics in Pakistan.

While these are often harshly critical of the shrines and their followers, their madrasahs are believed often to have private links to particular Naqshbandi shrines, showing the persistence of the shrine's power and influence. As Carl Ernst has remarked, many of the leaders of modern

Islamist radicalism came originally from backgrounds heavily influenced by Sufism.[10]

Shah Waliullah's tradition of defending Islam against the West has – in their own perception – been continued by the adherents of Pir Hazrat Shah in Britain, who in 1989 helped lead the movement of protest against the publication of Salman Rushdie's *Satanic Verses*. The classical teachings of all the recognized orders of Sufism have always taught that a knowledge of and obedience to the Shariah are essential if one is to become a *shaikh* or his *murid*.

In Pakistan, the cults of the saints, and the Sufi orders and Barelvi theology which underpin them, are an immense obstacle to the spread of Taleban and sectarian extremism, and of Islamist politics in general. This is not because the shrines or the Barelvis have powerful political parties of their own, like the Jamaat Islami (JI) and Jamiat-e-Ulema-e-Islam (JUI) of the Deobandi tradition. Every attempt at creating such parties over the decades has foundered on the deep rivalries and jealousies between (and indeed within) the great *pir* families, and also on the fact that, unlike the modern Islamist radicals, the shrines and the Barelvis have no uniting political ideology at all beyond loyalty to their own traditions.

Rather, when it comes to combating radicalism the importance of the shrines lies in two things: first, in the way that the different cults and traditions – especially in so far as they overlap with those of the Shia – make impossible the kind of monolithic Sunni Islam of which the Jamaat in one way and the Taleban in another dream. Second, and equally important, is the way in which the *pir* families are entwined with and help support and legitimize dominant landowning clans across much of the Pakistani countryside, and parts of the traditional business elites in the towns.

The *pirs* are therefore an important part of the dense networks of elite power and patronage which have been an immense and so far insuperable obstacle to revolution in Pakistan. Politically speaking, *pirs* behave in the same way as the great majority of other politicians. They use their network of influence to gain patronage and protection for their followers. Quite contrary to the conventional Western image of Sufism, therefore, one of the most important roles of the Sufi shrines in Pakistan has always been in the eminently practical area of politics.

Pirs with real personal religious prestige are at an advantage in being able to command support beyond their own lineages, and also some-times to command a more unconditional loyalty. Often a key step in the rise of a newly emerged urban *pir* is when he gains a local politician as a follower – just as in the past, a saint's reputation would be made by the public respect of a local prince, or even – in the greatest cases – the sultan himself. Thereafter, the politician and the saint rise (and to a lesser extent fall) together, each contributing to the alliance from their respective spheres. *Murids* have been known to commit murders on the orders of their *pir*, either for his own sake or that of one of his political allies.

There are therefore two sides to the *pirs* and shrines: their political, property-owning and sometimes criminal role co-exists with the benefi-cial spiritual and social functions described by Lukas Werth, a leading scholar of Sufism:

> Many of the new *pirs* are not frauds. Ordinary people take great comfort from them. They give them an outlook on life, and an inspiration. They create an emotional counterweight against the constant troubles of life here, the calamities that everyone has to face, the sorrow and the sheer mess of life. They provide a place of spiritual rest for the people. They also educate children – which is more than the state does most of the time – calm down local fights, reconcile husbands and wives, parents and children, or brothers who have fallen out.[11]

A Sindhi intellectual friend drew attention to another side of the cults of the shrines:

> The negative side of mysticism and saint worship is that it makes people passive, respectful of their superiors and believing that everything comes from God or the saint and should be accepted. This is especially damaging in Sindh, because we are a traditional, agrarian and backward society and mysticism helps keep us that way. We need an industrial revolution to take us out of this feudal domination of which the *pirs* are part. But people in Sindh love their *pirs*, and our whole culture is bound up with them. Even I am deeply influenced by this, though I loathe the political and social role of the *pirs*.

The *pirs* and the shrines are therefore also an obstacle to modern reform, democracy and development in Pakistan. It is true that *pirs* provide at least psychological help for poor people facing disease, when no help whatsoever is forthcoming from the state or the regular medical services.

Some shrines are especially popular with women, who often come to pray to be given children, or to be cured of various ailments.

This is especially true of psychiatric problems. These are thought by the mass of the population to be due to possession by devils, and people suffering from them are brought to the shrines to be exorcized. It may indeed be that for disturbed women in particular, the licence given to them at the shrines to defy all normal rules of behaviour by dancing ecstatically and screaming either prayers or demon-induced obscenities does indeed provide an essential therapeutic release from their horribly confined and circumscribed (physically as well as emotionally) lives. On the other hand, it is unfortunately also true that many *pirs* actively discourage people from seeking regular medical help, telling them to come to them instead. Occasionally ghastly stories surface of small-time rural *pirs* ordering their devotees to perform black magic and even human sacrifice.

SHRINES AND SUPERSTITION

The 'superstition' of the shrines and Sufi orders is one reason why radical secular reformers in the Muslim world have been deeply hostile to them; another, as far as modern nationalists are concerned, is that they advance the idea of a loyalty to their leaders which transcends that of the nation-state. Thus in Turkey, Kemal Ataturk launched a ferocious persecution of the shrines and the Sufis, and imposed restrictions which have been lifted only in recent years.

This was an ambiguity of which the British rulers of India were fully aware. On the one hand – like many Muslim rulers earlier – they regarded the shrines and the landowning *pir* families as forces for stability and potential sources of support for imperial rule. In Punjab, they took care to incorporate the *pir* families into what they defined (along British lines) as the 'landowning gentry', and to reward them with consultation, honours and sometimes new land grants.

The British saw the *pirs* as barriers to the anti-British revolutionary movements of the Wahabis and some of the reformist Muslim preachers. Successive Pakistani governments have also relied on the *pirs* for local support and influence. General Zia-ul-Haq, with his personal sympathy for modern Islamist culture, was believed to be hostile to the shrines, but took little action against them, beyond following previous (unsuccessful) policies of trying to regulate and partially control their finances through the Waqf Board (statutory body which administers religious endowments).

On the other hand, in their Protestant souls the British shared the Islamist reformers' views concerning the culture of the shrines, and despised the superstition, obscurantism, corruption and intoxication which they saw flourishing at the shrines and among their adherents; and, indeed, the parallels they drew between popular Muslim worship of the saints and the failings of 'Popery' in the West were often quite explicit.

In Major O'Brien's view, 'All [Punjabi Muslims] alike are sunk in the most degrading superstition, and are in the most abject submission to their spiritual pastors or pirs.'[12] The political needs of imperial rule aside, British officialdom much preferred the scripturalism, legalism and relative modernity of the urban Islamist reformists, and – as the last chapter described – sometimes favoured the Shariah against the local customary law, on progressive grounds.

Certainly some of the great shrines in Pakistan could be described (like Russia's) as 'an offence against the Protestant state of mind'. This is especially true of those with large followings of *qalandars* or *malangs* (the South Asian equivalent of the dervishes of the Arab world and Turkey), wandering holy beggars with certain affinities to the Hindu *saddhus*. Much of the contempt felt by the British and the Islamists for the shrines stems from the character of the *malangs,* and especially the *musth malangs – musth* indicating a mixture of intoxication and madness.

Like many educated Sufis, Mr Khwaja of the following of Pir Hasan Baba expressed strong disapproval not only of the scripturalist enemies of Sufism, but also of many of the Pakistani *pirs* and their followers:

> Unfortunately, at the lowest level, some of the new saints and many of the *malangs* are fakes and are just in it for business. There are so many of them out there bringing a bad image on us. *Malangs* sell drugs, run prostitution rackets and things like that. And the political hereditary *pirs* are also a problem. They discredit the Sufi tradition with their corruption and politicking. A true Sufi saint cannot be fat, healthy and rich. He has to be poor and simple, and living in poor conditions. But humanity has always worshipped false gods, and Pakistan is no different. Surely if you look at the hereditary *pirs*, you can see clearly all the false gods that they worship.

Some of the *malangs* I have met, especially at smaller rural shrines, do indeed tend to support British and Islamist prejudices: filthy, stoned to the gills, and surrounded by retinues of giggling half-naked little boys as degraded-looking as themselves. One *malang*, however, justified their use of drugs to Katherine Ewing in words some of which could have come from recent reports by medical experts to the British and American governments:

> Alcohol works on the outside – it makes a man violent and blinds his senses. Charas [hashish] works in the inside. It makes him peaceful and opens his spirit to God. So a *malang* should avoid alcohol as he should avoid women. Alcohol will cut him off from God but charas brings him close to God. That is why we *malangs* use it.[13]

This is part of the *malangs'* proclaimed belief that their exclusive concentration on God and their particular saint requires them to 'place [themselves] outside the world' and the world's normal social rules. The *malangs* and *qalandars* therefore are known as the '*be-shar*' ('without law') Sufis, as opposed to the *pirs*, who marry and have children, and follow (in theory) the rules of the Shariah.

At some of the large urban shrines attempts have been made to prevent the public smoking of hashish by devotees. This is especially true of the clean, orderly shrines round Islamabad and Rawalpindi, with their strong following among officials, others such as Ghamkol Sharif with strong military connections, and all shrines that I know of belonging to the Naqshbandi order of Sufis. At other great shrines, however (especially during their annual *urs*, and at the sessions of prayer, chanting and dancing that take place every Thursday evening), to refuse to inhale hashish you would have to give up breathing altogether.

This is certainly true of the two great shrines in Sindh – Bhitshah and Sehwan Sharif. On visiting Sehwan, I couldn't help grinning when I thought of the contrast between the prevailing physical atmosphere and the would-be spiritual atmosphere (one of unutterable official pomposity) which breathed from the booklet about the shrine and its saint, full of pious phrases from ministers, that I had been given by the local government.

Sehwan Sharif is situated on the right bank of the Indus in central Sindh and, like Hadda, is associated with some legends derived from Hindu river worship. A village of low-caste Hindus still exists nearby. Sehwan's founding saint was Shaikh Syed Usman Marwandi (1177–1274), a Persian known as Lal Shahbaz (the Red Falcon) Qalandar, having – according to legend – once turned himself into a falcon to rescue his friend and fellow-saint, Baba Farid of Pakpattan, from execution. Most of the leading saints of Sindh, including Shah Abdul Latif, were from the tradition Lal Shahbaz Qalandar founded. Politicians take good care to honour the saint, and the golden gates of his shrine were donated by Zulfikar Ali Bhutto.

The first thing that strikes you on approaching Sehwan Sharif (or in my case looking down on it from the guest house where the local government had kindly housed me, situated castle-like on a nearby hill) is the fairground atmosphere. The shrines of the saint and his leading disciples, and many of the streets between them, are lit by thousands and thousands of coloured fairy-lights. The carnival continues in the streets themselves, which are a sort of bazaar-apotheosis – that is to say, a normal South Asian bazaar, but with *more* of everything: more music, more light, more crowds, more smells (attractive and otherwise), more religious charms and souvenirs, more beggars and more thieves. Twice in the course of my visit I felt a hand steal into one of my pockets, where I had taken good care not to put my wallet or documents.

So in some ways Sehwan is Pakistan- (or India-) plus. Another aspect of this and other shrines however is very different indeed from the normal life of Pakistan, but helps explain the shrines' popularity and social role: the behaviour of women. In Sehwan, groups of ordinary women pilgrims stride around with extraordinary (for Pakistan) freedom and self-confidence, unaccompanied by their menfolk though often with small children in tow. They even smile at you – without, I hasten to add, being prostitutes, though female and male prostitution is said to flourish around some of the shrines.

The tomb of the saint is surrounded by family groups of women and children praying and chatting. In the courtyard, where the drumming and dancing in honour of the saint takes place, one section is roped off (but not screened) for women. On the evening when I visited the shrine, most of the women were sitting quite decorously with their *dupattas* (scarves) pulled over their hair, chanting softly and moving their heads gently to and fro in time to the music. In the middle of them, however, three women were swaying and shaking their heads feverishly like maenads, with unbound hair flying around their faces – most probably some of the psychologically troubled people (women especially) for whom the shrines provide a real if questionable therapy.

The rest of the courtyard is packed with dancing, swaying men. At intervals, servants of the shrine force their way through the crowd spraying scented water to cool people down, but the heat is indescribable and the dancers drenched in sweat. In the middle of the courtyard stand huge skin drums, and relays of volunteers come forward to beat them. Rather charmingly, my official guide, a very staid-looking middle-aged government clerk with glasses (and the inevitable pen stuck to the outside of his breast pocket as a symbol of his status), seized the drumsticks at one point and beat out a tremendous tattoo.

Most of the men in the courtyard were ordinary folk, but the front ranks of the dancers are made up of *malangs* (or dervishes, as they are often called in Sindh), with long, wild hair and beards – thousand-year-old hippies – stretching their arms above their heads and pointing their fingers at heaven, very like at a pop concert. The smell of hashish was everywhere.

The Shia element was very apparent, both in the Shia family groups around the tomb, in the drumming, which was very reminiscent of that I had heard at the great Shia festival of Ashura in Lahore four months earlier, and in the chants of 'Ya Ali'. Some of the *malangs* were clearly as crazy as the women dancers. One was draped in chains from head to foot. Another was dressed in women's clothes, with a headdress made from animal skins and feathers, like a pagan shaman.

Quite what Lal Shahbaz himself would have made of all this we do not know – though above the gates stands a picture of the saint himself dancing, holding a sitar. What we do know is what the spectrum of 'fundamentalist' Muslim groups think of this kind of thing – and the answer of course is more or less what seventeenth-century puritans thought about Catholicism, minus the Pope and the bishops. As should be clear, the scenes at some of the shrines in Pakistan contain just about all the elements necessary to make a puritan feel nervous.

PURITANS, FUNDAMENTALISTS, REFORMISTS: THE JAMAAT ISLAMI

There could not be a greater contrast with Sehwan Sharif than the head-quarters of the Jamaat Islami party – the only truly national Islamist party in Pakistan – at Mansura in Lahore. Like a number of institutions in Pakistan – the military especially – the appearance of Jamaat offices seems deliberately created to be as different as possible from the general mixture of dirt, disorder, colour, poverty and ostentation that is the public face of Pakistan.

The only hint of fun I have ever seen with the Jamaat has been its younger members playing cricket – and indeed there are aspects of the Jamaat of which Dr Arnold of Rugby would thoroughly have approved; they are clean-living, muscular Muslims. With the Jamaat, everything is disciplined, neat, orderly, plain, clean, modest and buttoned-up: a puritan style, with faint echoes of the barracks and strong ones of the boarding school. Its members also dress and behave in this way – a style which reflects both their ideology and their generally lower-middle-class urban origins and culture.

Jamaat activists certainly dress and behave very differently from the far rougher, largely rural Pathan members of the other main Islamist party from the Deobandi tradition, the Jamiat-e-Ulema-e-Islam (Council of Islamic Clerics, or JUI). The JUI's parent party in undivided India, the Jamiat-e-Ulema-e-Hind, was founded in 1919 as part of the Khilafat movement against British rule.

The JUI split off in the 1940s to support partition and the creation of Pakistan. In Pakistan, however, the JUI has become an almost exclusively ethnically Pathan party, and so I have dealt with it in a later chapter, on the Pathans of Pakistan. In addition, the JUI no longer has a significant intellectual aspect, and has to a considerable extent become just another Pakistani patronage machine on behalf of its followers – as one of its leaders candidly admitted to me.

The Jamaat Islami is a very different kind of party, much more impressive and in its way more frightening – so impressive indeed that its lack of political success is all the more striking. The Jamaat has excellent Islamist intellectual credentials, having been founded in Lahore in 1941 by Syed Abu Ala Maududi (1903–79), one of the leading thinkers of the international Islamist canon. Indeed, in some ways the Jamaat is too intellectual for its own good.

Maududi and the Jamaat were strongly influenced by the Deobandi tradition of hostility to British rule, and attachment to the idea of the universal Muslim Ummah. They also deeply distrusted the secularism of Jinnah and other Muslim League leaders. On these grounds, they initially opposed the creation of Pakistan, preferring to struggle for a more perfect Muslim society within India.

After partition became inevitable, Maududi and his chief followers moved to Pakistan. For a long time, the party kept a strongly Mohajir character (Maududi himself was born in Hyderabad, India). The cultural influence of relative Mohajir openness and progressivism (a key example of the role of migrants in promoting whatever social and economic dynamism exists in Pakistan), as much as Jamaat ideology, may have accounted for the more enlightened and modern aspects of the Jamaat, especially concerning women.

Maududi took his intellectual inspiration from Hasan al-Banna and the Muslim Brotherhood (Ikhwan-ul-Muslimeen) of Egypt and the Middle East, but carried their ideas considerably further. His plan for the Jamaat was very much that of al-Banna for the Ikhwan: 'A salafiyya message, a Sunni way, a Sufi truth, a political organization, an athletic group, a scientific and cultural link, an economic enterprise and a social idea.'[14]

As these words indicate, the Islamist vision of this tradition is an all-embracing one, based on the belief that Islam is 'a system for the whole of human life'. Maududi took this further, developing a reformist agenda with certain socialist elements, strongly condemning modern capitalism and arguing that the Muslim tradition of *zakat* corresponds to modern Western ideas of social insurance. The Jamaat's statement on its website (in rather poor English, for the Jamaat) emphasizes above all issues of social injustice, suffering and corruption:

> Have a look at our dear homeland injustice and mischief has become order of the day. God created man equal but a handful people have grabbed more land they needed and amassed, money in excess of their needs for, they want to live a luxurious life. And, such people have enslaved other fellow human beings by keeping them poor and ignorant, we have weakened our fellow compatriots by denying them their due rights. And thus have deprived their lives even of trifle joys, Corruption together with adulteration is prevalent. Bribery is must even for a legal thing. Police always acts beyond any norms of decency and emptying the purses is the only way to get justice from a court of law. Standard of the education is all time low and morality and ethics too, are no better. Obscenity is all permeating. The armed forces instead of conquering the enemy have conquered its own nation many a time by declaring Martial Law in the country.

Bureaucrats who are supposed to be public servants have become public bosses.[15]

Gulfaraz, a Jamaat student activist studying political science at Peshawar university and with the neat, Islamic-modern Jamaat look (trimmed beard and spotless *kurta*) emphasized hostility to 'feudalism' and the 'feudal' domination of the other parties, as one of his key reasons for joining the Jamaat:

> This is the root of all our problems that this small group of feudals and their businessmen allies control everything. It is because India got rid of them through land reform that India can be a democracy today. In all the other parties, the people who say they want change are in fact from within the feudal system, so obviously these parties can't change anything. That is why we need student unions, trades unions, NGOs that can give rise to new, democratic parties ... In Jamaat, this feudal and dynastic system doesn't exist. Our leaders are elected all the way down to the student groups, and they never pass the leadership to their children.
>
> My reasons for joining the Jamaat were first religion, and then social justice and democracy. I only did it after a lot of thought. My family are ANP, and I am the only one of my brothers and sisters to join the Jamaat. It happened gradually. I went to college and met Jamaat members and was impressed by them and how they worked. Once you are affiliated, you learn political awareness and organization skills as well as religious awareness. Then as student members you go to other colleges to organize public debates and spread the Jamaat message.[16]

On the other hand, while the Jamaat has always strongly denounced 'feudalism', in practice its support for land reform has wavered to and fro and has never been more than lukewarm at best.

The Jamaat has enjoyed its greatest success among the educated classes, and has made gaining influence in the universities and the media a key part of its strategy – a sort of Islamist version of the reform-Marxist 'long march through the institutions'. However, this also reflects the party's failure to appeal to the masses in general, or to transcend the 5 per cent or so of the electorate which has been its average for the past sixty years.

Although its leaders often come from old *ulema* lineages, the Jamaat remains a party of the aspiring urban lower middle classes, and especially of their educated elements. Apart from the hostility of Pakistan's dominant classes, and lack of a clan and patronage base, the party also suffers from the fact that its entire puritan and intellectual style is rather alien not just to the mass of the rural population but to the urban proletariat as well, with their vulgar, colourful popular culture, love of Indian movies, extensive use of hashish and alcohol, and surprisingly frank attitude to sex (except of course as far as their own womenfolk are concerned).

The fact that the old urban middle classes are constantly being swamped by new migrants from the countryside casts a certain doubt on whether – as some analysts have predicted – Pakistan's rapid urbanization necessarily means an increase in adherence to the Deobandi tradition as opposed to the Barelvi, and with it an increase in support for the Jamaat and other Islamist groups. For this to happen, a sufficient number of former migrants and their descendants would have to be not just urban, but upwardly mobile – anecdotal evidence suggests that the influence of Tablighi Jamaat preachers, for example, is strongly correlated with a rise in the social scale from the proletariat to the lower middle class. The problem is that the lack of sociological research and detailed surveys means that this is indeed only anecdotal evidence.

The Jamaat's disdain for the mass of the population was very evident when I visited their headquarters in the great Punjabi industrial city of Faisalabad to see if they were benefiting from the workers' anger at power cuts and unemployment. The Jamaat's district leader, Rai Mohammed Akram Khan, seemed surprised that I thought appealing to the workers was important, and spoke contemptuously of their lack of education and 'real Islam', including their love of illicit liquor:

> We don't want to rally the masses behind us, because they don't help us. They can launch strikes and demonstrations but they are disorganized, illiterate and can't follow our ideology or stick with our strategy. We want our party workers to be carefully screened for their education and good Muslim characters, because if we simply become like the PPP and recruit everyone, then the Jamaat is finished ... We don't care if we can't take over the government soon as long as we keep our characters clean. Only that will help us one day to lead the people, when they realize that there is no other way of replacing the existing system.[17]

The Jamaat believes that the Koran and Shariah, properly interpreted and adapted, hold the answer to every social, economic and political question. It differs however from other Islamist movements in its acceptance of the principle of *ijtihad*, which allows the reinterpretation of lessons of the Koran and *hadiths* (within certain limits) in accordance with human reason and in answer to contemporary problems. The Jamaat shares its belief in *ijtihad* with the Shia tradition; and indeed, Jamaat leaders have often spoken to me of their admiration for the Iranian revolution and the system it has created, which they say resembles Maududi's idea of a 'theo-democracy'. One of the more positive aspects of the Jamaat's record has been its strong opposition to anti-Shia militancy in Pakistan.

In contrast to Khomeini's movement in Iran, however (but recognizing Pakistani realities), Maududi's and the Jamaat's approach to Islamist revolution in Pakistan has been gradualist, not revolutionary. They have stood in most elections, and condemned the administration of President Zia (which in other respects they supported) for its lack of democracy. This is despite the fact that Maududi imbued the Jamaat with certain aspects of modern European totalitarianism. He was also quite open about the fact that his idea of the Jamaat's revolutionary role owed much to the Russian Communist idea of the Bolshevik party as a revolutionary 'vanguard', leading apathetic masses to revolution. The Jamaat, and more especially its semi-detached student wing, Islami Jamiat Talaba, have frequently engaged in violent clashes with rivals.

The Jamaat's relationship with democracy is complex. It pursues quasi-totalitarian ends by largely democratic means, and internally is the only party in Pakistan to hold elections to its senior offices – all the other parties being run by autocratic individuals or dynasties. The Jamaat and the Mohajir-based MQM are the only parties to possess really effective party organizations, and the only ones with successful women's wings. Indeed, I have heard it said that Munawar Hasan's wife (leader of the Jamaat women's organization) is 'the real leader of the party'.

In this, the Jamaat is also close to the Iranian revolution. Its leaders like to emphasize that they believe strongly in women's education, employment and full rights and opportunities, 'but in harmony with their own particular rights and duties'. At least in speaking with me, Jamaat leaders strongly condemned aspects of the Afghan Taleban's treatment of women and the Pakistani Taleban's destruction of girls' schools. I got the feeling that this also reflected the disdain of educated people from an ancient urban – and urbane – Islamic tradition for the savage and illiterate Pathan hillmen.

However, while intermittently condemning Taleban terrorism against Pakistani Muslims (though also frequently in private blaming it on the security forces), the Jamaat have consistently opposed any military action against the Taleban. Statements by the party's *amir* (leader, or, strictly translated, 'commander') on the Jamaat website in December 2009 summed up the party stance very well: 'Munawar and Liaqat Baloch strongly condemned the suicide bomb attack on the Peshawar press club and termed it an attack on press freedom'; but at the same time, 'Operation in Waziristan to have horrible consequences, and the nation will have no escape', and 'All Islamic and Pakistan-loving forces must unite against America.'[18]

Without taking up arms themselves, the Jamaat have also shown considerable sympathy for militancy. A large proportion of Al Qaeda members arrested by the Pakistani authorities have been picked up while staying with Jamaat members, though the party leadership strongly denies that this reflects party policy. The Hizbul Mujahidin, a Kashmiri militant group which has carried out terrorism against India, is in effect a branch of the Jamaat. In the course of the 1990s, however, its role in Kashmir was eclipsed by the more radical and militarily effective Lashkar-e-Taiba, and it has never carried out attacks in Pakistan.

The greater radicalism of the Jamaat was displayed during the Red Mosque crisis of 2007. The JUI condemned the actions of the Red Mosque militants and called for them to reach a peaceful compromise with the authorities. The Jamaat by contrast gave them strong backing – while continuing to insist that it stood for peaceful revolution in Pakistan. Moreover, a considerable proportion of the leadership of the Swat wing of the Pakistani Taleban (the former Tehriq-e-Nifaz-e-Shariat-e-Mohammedi, of whom more in later chapters) started with the Jamaat, although admittedly they left it because of its insufficient radicalism.

The ambiguities of the Jamaat's position, and the divisions among its members, were amply demonstrated when I visited Mansura in January 2009. First I spoke with the head of the party's youth wing, Syed Shahid Gilani. The lights went out during our talk, and he turned on a torch so that I could continue to take notes, making the spectacles of his three co-workers flicker like fireflies in the dark – a pretty reflection of Jamaat intellectualism. While bitterly critical of US strategy and the US 'occupation' of Afghanistan, Gilani was also harsh in his condemnation of the Taleban:

> We don't accept the Taleban as a model. The Afghan Taleban offended the whole world; and in any case they didn't believe in a political system, only in their own rule. Can you imagine the Taleban in power here in Pakistan? Impossible! The Pakistani Taleban mean anarchy – anyone with a couple of hundred men with weapons can take over cities ... So we should fight them, because we have to give protection to the people who are falling victim to their terrorism, and also because we can't have a state within the state. We can't accept that Pakistan is split into different zones under different parties. It would mean the end of the country. The writ of the state must run everywhere.[19]

Perhaps not coincidentally for these views, Gilani is a Punjabi from the great military centre of Rawalpindi. The then secretary-general of the Jamaat (elected its leader a few months later), Syed Munawar Hasan, gave a very different impression when I went on to talk with him. This was a notable meeting in that it was the only time in all my years of meeting with them that I have seen one of the Jamaat leaders – normally so calm and polite – lose his temper, because I had forced him into a corner over the Jamaat's policy towards terrorism and violent revolution (though let it be said he apologized afterwards and offered me some more biscuits). I asked him repeatedly if the Jamaat denounced terrorism against fellow Muslims and violent revolution. He replied (in response to repeated questions):

> It is because of America that these terrorist attacks are happening. America is the biggest terrorist in the world ... I do not fear the TTP [Pakistani Taleban]. I only fear the US ... Before 9/11 there was no terrorism in Pakistan. Once America has left Afghanistan our society will sort itself out ... We are not for the TTP but against America ... .[20]

MILITANTS

The Jamaat's ambivalence towards the violent militants probably reflects not only the party's own divided soul, but also the fact that the party leadership is worried about being outflanked by those militants, and losing its own younger and more radical supporters to them. The leader of the single most spectacular Islamist action outside the Pathan areas – the creation of an armed militant base at the Red Mosque (Lal Masjid) in the capital, Islamabad – Abdul Rashid Ghazi, had indeed at one stage been associated with the Jamaat Islami, before leaving in protest at what he called their cowardice and political compromises. His whole personal style, however, remained very close to that of the Jamaat – and very different from that of the Pathan Taleban up in the hills. This gave me a very uneasy sense of the ease with which Jamaati activists might shift into violence.

Together with Peter Bergen of CNN, I interviewed Ghazi in April 2007, some two months before his death when the Pakistan army stormed the mosque complex. Ghazi was a slight man of forty-three years, with round spectacles, a spotless white *shelwar kameez*, and – for public consumption at least – a quiet, reserved and amicable manner. In his youth – a bit like St Augustine – he had initially defied his father's wish that he study to become a cleric, and took an MSc in International Relations at the Qaid-e-Azam University. He later had a junior job with UNESCO. He seems to have been radicalized by his father's murder, but even more by the US invasions of Afghanistan and Iraq after 9/11.

Although Ghazi was a veteran of the Mujahidin jihad against the Soviets, he was not, on the face of it, the kind of man to go down fighting in a desperate last stand, until you remember that many dedicated Communists in the old days looked just the same. In fact, in the view of a Pakistani journalist who interviewed him not long before the military assault, he himself by the end would have chosen to surrender; but this would have meant that international militants in the building would have been handed over to the USA (eighteen of them were among the dead, according to official figures); and for him this was too much of a humiliation. His brother tried to escape dressed as a woman and was captured, only to be released two years later on the orders of the Supreme Court. Ghazi himself was killed in battle.

Peter and I were taken to the office across the broad courtyard of the complex, crowded with male and female volunteers whom we were not allowed to interview. There were few obtrusive signs of defence, but during the attack on the mosque it was discovered that the militants had burrowed a set of tunnels and concrete bunkers beneath it. The army showed an array of weapons that it had captured there, including heavy machine-guns, rocket-propelled grenade-launchers, sniper rifles and belts for suicide bombs.

The office where we met Ghazi was small and dingy, with grubby cream-coloured walls, a row of computer screens on a long table, and broken, uncomfortable chairs on which we perched awkwardly. It all felt very far from the luxurious mansion where I had lunched that day with a leading pro-government politician – and the contrast was perfectly deliberate. All the Islamist leaders I have met, militant or otherwise, have lived with a kind of ostentatious modesty.

Ghazi's background helps explain how the movement at the Red Mosque got off the ground so easily, and why the government was so slow to try to stop it. His father, Maulana Mohammed Abdullah, the founder of the mosque, had been at the heart of the Pakistani establishment, and the mosque itself was the first to be built in Islamabad when the site was chosen for the new capital in the 1960s. 'In those days, around here was just jungle. This mosque is older than Islamabad,' he told us. In 1998, his father had been shot in the courtyard that we had just crossed, something that Ghazi blamed on the ISI (even as Pakistani liberals were accusing the ISI of backing Ghazi).

The overall line that Ghazi put across to Peter and me was very close to what I had heard from Jamaat leaders over the previous days, and indeed since. His words, in certain respects, also reflect those of the leaders of the notorious anti-Indian militant group Lashkar-e-Taiba (see below). Concerning America's role, Ghazi's statements would indeed be agreed with by the overwhelming majority of all classes of Pakistani society. This indicates the greatest opportunity for the more intelligent, non-sectarian Islamist militants. This is not that they will be able to win a majority of the population over to their theological and ideological revolutionary agenda, which is shared by only a small minority of Pakistanis. Rather, they may be able to exploit US and Indian actions to mobilize much larger numbers of Pakistanis behind their Islamic and Pakistani nationalist agendas, which have some degree of sympathy from the great majority of their fellow countrymen.

Unlike the JUI, the Jamaat refused to condemn the Red Mosque movement, and the attack on the mosque was one factor in driving the party into more radical opposition to Musharraf. Ghazi's views also illustrate the very great differences between different strands of Islamism in Pakistan – except on one point: hostility to the US, India and Israel. Thus, like the Jamaat, Ghazi laid great emphasis on his family's commitment to women's education, though partly on pragmatic grounds. He said that he had argued with the Taleban in Afghanistan about this:

> My father established the first female madrasah in this country. Now, more than 6,000 of the 10,000 students here are women. It is the same education for men and women, but girls have a reduced course of four to six years, while men study for eight. There is a good reason for this. If you educate a man, you have educated only one person; but if you educate a woman you have educated a whole family. In this, we differ from the Taleban in Afghanistan . . .
>
> The Taleban were not the right people to rule. They did not have the expertise. All the same, there were many good things to their credit. Under the Taleban, you could travel in safety from one end of Afghanistan to another. The Taleban started as a reaction against the crimes that were being committed in Afghanistan, and then turned into a movement. We too perhaps. We are a reaction to a criminal system in this country. We do not want to rule. But if we are not recognized, then maybe we too will turn into a movement.[21]

Ghazi denounced the MMA Islamist alliance (while making an exception for the Jamaat): 'They are opposing us, just like the MQM and other political allies of Musharraf. The MMA are just products of this Pakistani system. They do not stand for real change.' A few days later, a JUI minister in the MMA government of the Frontier, Asif Iqbal Daudzai, told me in Peshawar that:

> We support the basic demands of the Lal Masjid [Red Mosque] group: anti-corruption, the return of democracy, a ban on pornography, and laws based on the teachings of Islam. But we question their credibility as a democratic force and the way they are going about things is wrong. Passing new laws is the business of the parliament and government. Islam doesn't allow anyone to impose their views by force, and the Constitution of Pakistan already defends both the basic rights of every person and the supremacy of Islam. The point is not to have a revolution, but to implement the existing constitution correctly.[22]

On the question of support for violence, Ghazi himself appeared to waver to and fro – just like the Jamaat, in fact. And as with the Jamaat and the JUI, whether this was from real doubts and internal conflicts of his own, calculated ambiguity, a deliberate desire to deceive, or a mixture of all three was not entirely clear.

> Our view is that suicide operations in Afghanistan and Iraq are *halal* [legitimate] because they help stop the aggressor from continuing his aggression. After all, US soldiers have travelled thousands of miles to kill innocent people. But such operations should not themselves kill civilians ... And terrorist attacks should not take place in Pakistan. You have to understand, though, that the people who are doing this are doing it from frustration and revenge. It is like a younger brother whose brother has been killed and who runs amok, forgetting about the law.

He gave what seemed a carefully tailored message to the American people:

> Americans should think and think again about their government's policy. If you talk to us and try to understand us, you can win our hearts. But if you come to attack us you will never win our hearts and will also never conquer us, because we are very determined people. How much have you spent on this so-called war on terror? Trillions of dollars. If you had spent this on helping develop Pakistan and Afghanistan, we would have loved you and never attacked you. But this is the stupidity of Bush, I believe, not of all Americans.

Among the various armed militant groups operating in Pakistan by 2007 Ghazi's was therefore towards the more moderate end of the spectrum. It is notable that like the Jamaat he rejected sectarian anti-Shiism, since this has formed the bridge linking the Taleban among the Pathans with the Sipah-e-Sahaba and Lashkar-e-Jhangvi in central and southern Punjab (this alliance will be described further in Chapter 7 on Punjab).

In 2009, these groups contributed greatly to the spread of terrorism from the Pathan areas to Punjab. This included attacks on high-profile military targets which could hardly have been planned without at least low-level sympathizers within the military itself. Militant anti-Shiism has also encouraged parts of the Jaish-e-Mohammed (JeM) to turn against the Pakistani state and ally with the Taleban – though it seems that in 2009 the Jaish split and much of it remains loyal to the Pakistani state. This split is said to have been due to the influence of the Pakistani intelligence services, which after 1988 trained and equipped the Jaish and other groups to conduct armed attacks and terrorism in Indian Kashmir, and which retain close links with them.

Western officials have often attributed the recruitment of militants in Pakistan to the enormous increase in the number of madrasahs (religious schools) during and after the Afghan war. This, however, seems to be in part a mistake. A majority of known Pakistani terrorists have in fact attended government schools and quite often have a degree of higher education – reflecting yet again the basis for Islamism in the urban lower middle classes rather than the impoverished masses. It is true that, as the chapter on the Taleban will explore further, a large number of Taleban fighters have a madrasah education – but that largely reflects the fact that in the tribal areas government schools are very rare. The communities concerned would have supported the Taleban anyway, madrasahs or no madrasahs.

A very large number of ordinary Taleban fighters have had no education at all, and their recruitment owes less to specific Taleban education than to the general atmosphere prevailing in their villages. Concentration on the role of madrasahs by Western policy-makers is not wholly mistaken, but it nonetheless reflects a very widespread mistake in Western analysis: namely, the tendency to look at Islamist groups and their strategies as instruments which can be isolated and eliminated, rather than phenomena deeply rooted in the societies from which they spring.

5

The Military

For men may come, and men may go, but I go on for ever.
(Alfred Lord Tennyson, *The Brook*)

Different sections of Pakistani society have different images or mirrors of paradise, which they try to create to the best of their ability on this earth, and that serve as havens from the squalor and disorder – physical and moral – by which they are surrounded. For believers, this image is of course the mosque, or, for the devotees of saints among them, the shrines.

As throughout the arid parts of the earth, almost everyone sees paradise as a garden, and those with the money to do so try to recreate on a small scale the great gardens of the old Muslim rulers. For the upper classes, paradise is an international hotel, with its polished cleanliness and luxury, its hard-working, attentive staff, its fashion shows and business presentations, in which they can pretend for a while that they are back in London or Dubai.

For the military, the image of paradise is the cantonment, with its clean, swept, neatly signposted streets dotted with gleaming antique artillery pieces, and shaded by trees with the lower trunks uniformly painted white. Putting trees in uniform might seem like carrying military discipline too far, and the effect is in fact slightly comical – like rows of enormous knobbly-kneed boys in white shorts. However, the shade is certainly welcome, as are the signposts and the impeccably neat military policemen directing the traffic in an orderly fashion.

The buildings of the cantonments are equally impressive inside. In the poorer parts of Pakistan, the contrast with civilian institutions – including those of government – is that between the developed and the barely developed worlds. In Peshawar, the recently refurbished headquarters of the XI Corps gleams with marble and polished wood, and has a fountain playing in its entrance hall, while government ministers work from decaying office blocks with peeling walls and broken stairs. In the military headquarters, every staff officer has a computer. In the government offices, most ministers do not (and in many cases would not know how to use them if they did).

The cantonments are not just about providing pleasant and orderly surroundings for generals. They also contain a range of services for the ordinary soldiers and their families of a quality totally unknown as far as ordinary people in the rest of Pakistan are concerned. The US armed forces, which also devote great attention to looking after the families and dependants of their servicemen, have been called 'the last vestige of the Great Society' in the US (a reference to President Lyndon Johnson's social welfare programme in the 1960s). The Pakistani armed forces could well be called the only element of a great society that has ever existed in Pakistan.

AN ARMY WITH A STATE

The cantonments were originally built by the British as absolutely conscious and deliberate statements of difference and distance from the society that surrounded them, their straight lines symbolizing order and rationality; and quite apart from the British-Indian architecture that still dominates many of the cantonments, this sense of difference and distance is still very present. In the words of a senior officer of Inter-Services Intelligence (ISI) with whom I talked in 2009:

> Under the British, the military was kept in cantonments very separate from society. That was a good model, because in Pakistan there is a permanent threat of politicization and corruption of the military. We fear this very deeply and try to keep ourselves separate. Within purely military institutions, things are honest and closely controlled. This is a matter of honour for officers and people keep tabs on each other. Corruption comes wherever there is interaction with civilian bodies.
>
> We have a great fear of the politicians interfering in military promotions and appointments. This could split the army and if you split the army you destroy the country. Look at what happened under Nawaz Sharif's last

government. Karamat [General Jehangir Karamat, then chief of army staff] accepted a lot from Nawaz, but in the end the army couldn't take any more. Whenever a civilian government starts trying to interfere in this sector, we have to act in self-defence.

This of course is quite against democratic rules; but before condemning the military for this, it is worth acknowledging the very real dangers presented by political splits in the military – and asking oneself the question whether, given their records, one would really want the likes of Nawaz Sharif and Asif Ali Zardari to be responsible for military appointments.

Commitment to the army, and to the unity and discipline of the army, is drilled into every officer and soldier from the first hour of their joining the military. Together with the material rewards of loyal service, it constitutes a very powerful obstacle to any thought of a coup from below, which would by definition split the army and would indeed probably destroy it and the country altogether. Every military coup in Pakistan has therefore been carried out by the chief of army staff of the time, backed by a consensus of the corps commanders and the rest of the high command. Islamist conspiracies by junior officers against their superiors (of which there have been two over the past generation) have been penetrated and smashed by Military Intelligence.

Military morale has come under unprecedented strain from the war in Afghanistan and the very widespread feeling among ordinary Pakistanis that the military have become servants of the Americans. So far, however, discipline has held, and in my view will continue to do so unless the US does something that ordinary soldiers would see as a direct affront to their honour.

The Pakistani military, more even than most militaries, sees itself as a breed apart, and devotes great effort to inculcating in new recruits the feeling that they belong to a military family different from (and vastly superior to) Pakistani civilian society. The mainly middle-class composition of the officer corps increases contempt for the 'feudal' political class. The army sees itself as both morally superior to this class, and far more modern, progressive and better-educated.

In the words of Lt-General (retired) Tanvir Naqvi:

The run-of-the-mill officer feels very proud of the fact that the army is a very efficient organization and is therefore a role model for the rest of the country in terms of order, discipline, getting things done and above all patriotism. He is very proud of Pakistan and very proud of the army.[1]

This belief is also widely present in Pakistani society as a whole, and has become dominant at regular intervals. As Nawabzada Aurangzeb Jogezai, a Pathan tribal chieftain and politician in Balochistan, told me in accents of deep gloom concerning his own political class:

> In Pakistan, only one institution works – the army. Nothing else does. Look at the difference between Quetta City and Quetta Cantonment. When people here enter the cantonment, their whole attitude changes. You straighten your tie, do up your shirt, leave your gun at home, become very polite. When you cross the military checkpoint again, you go back to being the same old bandit. Because in the city order is kept by the police, who are weak, corrupt and shambolic and dominated by the politicians, but the cantonment is run by the army, and in the end, this country is always saved by the army. The politicians themselves call for this when they have made enough of a mess of things or want to get their rivals out of power. Look at the PPP. Now they say that they are for democracy and against military rule, but in 1999 Benazir distributed sweets [a traditional sign of rejoicing and congratulation] when the army overthrew Nawaz Sharif.[2]

These feelings in the mass of the population are always diminished by periods of direct military rule, when the military has to take responsibility for the corruption and incompetence of the state system as a whole. However, admiration for the military always comes back again, as their relative efficiency in their own area is contrasted with the failings of civilian politicians. This was the case for example during the floods of 2010 – only two years after the last military ruler left office – when the military's rescue and relief efforts were compared with the incompetence, corruption and above all indifference of the national and provincial governments and the civilian bureaucracy. As this chapter will bring out though, this relative military efficiency is only possible because the military has far more resources than civilian institutions.

It is unfortunately true that whatever the feelings of the population later, every military coup in Pakistan when it happened was popular with most Pakistanis, including the Pakistani media, and was subsequently legitimized by the Pakistani judiciary. As Hasan-Askari Rizvi writes of the coup of 1999: 'The imposition of martial law was not contested by any civilian group and the military had no problem assuming and consolidating power.'[3] In his book on the Pakistani military, Shuja Nawaz describes how, when his brother General Asif Nawaz was chief of army staff during Nawaz Sharif's first government in the 1990s, some of Mr Sharif's own ministers would come to see his brother to complain about the prime minister and ask the military to throw him out and replace him with someone else.[4]

It is possible that developments since 2001 have changed this pattern. This is due to the new importance of the independent judiciary and media; the way that the military's role both in government and in the unpopular war with the Pakistani Taleban has tarnished their image with many Pakistanis; and because Pakistan's history of military coups has taught both the PPP and the PML(N) the dangers of intriguing with the military against their political opponents. It seems highly likely that in 2009–10 Nawaz Sharif would have made a determined push to use mass protest to bring down the PPP national government, had he not been sure that this would inevitably bring the military back into the centre of politics, and therefore later risk repeating the experience of 1999 when the military ousted him from power too. General Kayani and the high command also deeply distrust the Sharifs.[5]

However, this change is not proven yet, and depends critically on how Pakistani civilian governments perform in future. On that score, by the summer of 2009, only a year after Musharraf's resignation, many Pakistanis of my acquaintance, especially of course politicians who had failed to find a place in the Zardari administration or the PML(N) government of Punjab, and in the business classes, were once again calling for the military to step in to oust the civilian administration of President Zardari. They did not necessarily want the military to take over themselves, but to purge the most corrupt politicians and create a government of national unity or a caretaker government of technocrats.

Civilian governments themselves have often asked the military to step into aspects of government, because of its greater efficiency and honesty. For example, in 1999 Prime Minister Nawaz Sharif, faced with a disastrous water and power situation, put the military in charge of these sectors in order to bring some order and enforce the payment of fees. Both the Sharif and Musharraf administrations also used the military in the field of education, to search for 'ghost schools' (ones which are officially listed as operating, but in fact do not exist because the money for them has been stolen by officials, local politicians or both). In July 2009, the military – in the person of Lt-General Nadeem Ahmed, commander of the First Corps at Mangla, and his staff – were put in charge of co-ordinating relief and reconstruction in Swat and elsewhere.

Apart from its inherent qualities and a strong measure of popular support, the military's power comes from the fact that it has far greater financial resources than any other state institution – indeed, than almost all the rest put together. Voltaire remarked of Frederick the Great's Prussia that 'Where some states have an army, the Prussian army has a state.' In view of the sheer size and wealth of the Pakistan military and associated institutions compared to the rest of the state, much the same could be said of Pakistan – especially if the nuclear sector is included.

By world standards, the scale of the Pakistani army is very great. As of 2010, it had 480,000 men (with another 304,000 serving in paramilitary units), almost as large as the American, and far bigger than the British army. These are not the demoralized conscripts of Iraq in 2003 or the rag-tag Taleban militias of Afghanistan in 2001, but highly motivated volunteers. Fears of the effects on international terrorism if Pakistan were to collapse have focused on the fate of the country's nuclear deterrent; but a more immediate – and absolutely inevitable – result would be the flow of large numbers of highly trained ex-soldiers, including explosives experts and engineers, to extremist groups.

The Pakistani army is the world's largest after China, Russia – and India, which is of course the rub. In the Middle East, South-East Asia, Africa or South America, Pakistan would be a regional great power. India, however, eclipses it on every front. The Indian army as of 2008 had 1.1 million men, twice Pakistan's numbers; but the Indian military budget, at the equivalent of $23.5 billion, was almost seven times Pakistan's $3.56 billion, just as India's GDP, at more than 1 trillion dollars, was eight times Pakistan's $126 billion.[6]

Pakistan's military spending in that year made up some 17.5 per cent of the government's budget. This was a radical reduction from the 1980s, when the military proportion of Pakistan's budget was around 60 per cent. With India spending on the military 14.1 per cent of a vastly greater 2008 budget, Pakistan's expenditure was not remotely enough to compete with India. Meanwhile, this military spending has gravely undermined the ability of both India and Pakistan to provide essential services to their citizens.

THE MILITARY FAMILY

The Pakistani military likes to think of itself as a big family – and in some ways it is more like a Pakistani big family than it likes to think. Its success as an institution and power over the state comes from its immunity to kinship interests and the corruption they bring with them; but it has only been able to achieve this immunity by turning itself into a sort of giant kinship group, extracting patronage from the state and distributing it to its members.

Much Pakistani corruption is obviously about personal gain. Equally important, however, is corruption as patronage – the recycling of state money by politicians to win, retain and reward supporters, and (which comes to the same thing) to help members of the politicians' kinship groups. Outright individual corruption in the Pakistani military is, as one would expect, centred on weapons procurement and those branches of the military dealing with civilian businesses. The most notorious case (or, at least, the most notorious that was exposed) in the past twenty years involved the chief of the naval staff from 1994 to 1997, Admiral Mansur-ul-Haq, who was convicted of taking massive kickbacks from a submarine contract and was eventually sentenced to seven years in jail, which he managed to have radically reduced by paying back most of the money. Such cases, however, seem to be relatively rare – and, by the standards of Pakistan in general, remarkably rare.

A journalist in the Sindhi town of Larkana explained this lack of outright corruption in the military as follows:

> One friend of mine, a colonel in the army, is about to retire. He has been allocated a plot of land in Islamabad, which he can either build a house on or sell for a big profit, and there is also a job in the Fauji Foundation. So he doesn't need to steal. Another friend, an SSP [Senior Superintendent of Police], will also retire soon, and he will have nothing but his miserable pension to live on, so he has to secure his retirement through corruption.

A military friend told me of some retired military men, like Colonel Shafiq-ur-Rehman, who have become well-known Pakistani humorist writers, 'but they write humour, not satire, because they are happy, live comfortably and play a lot of golf'.

In the Pakistani military, as in some Western defence establishments, one can almost speak of 'illegal' and 'legal' corruption. The first is theft pure and simple, as in the case of Mansur-ul-Haq. The second is benefits to servicemen – and, much more importantly, to retired servicemen – not accessible to the rest of the population. In this, it is worth noting, Pakistan is not so different from the US, where senior officers and officials on retirement step into senior jobs with private corporations dealing with the military, and use their military knowledge and connections for personal gain.

Concerning the military patronage system, public criticism in Pakistan has focused on three areas: the appointment of retired officers to senior jobs in the administration and state-owned corporations (true, but also true in the US, albeit to a lesser extent); the ability of officers to buy land through instalment plans on easy terms in Defence Housing Associations (or to be allocated a free plot after thirty-two years' service); and military-controlled businesses. Some of this criticism is fair, but some reflects ignorance both of military needs and of Pakistani realities.[7]

Thus the Pakistani military, like all militaries, suffers from the problem of a sharply tapering promotion pyramid as officers and soldiers get older, and the need to retire large numbers of officers in their forties or fifties into an economy which cannot provide nearly enough middle-class jobs to support them. Access to plots of land is in itself a reasonable way of ensuring a decent retirement, and is part of a South Asian tradition going back to British and indeed Mughal days. Also reflecting this old tradition is the military's grant of land to wounded soldiers and the families of soldiers killed in action.

The state also reserves certain junior categories of state service for ex-soldiers, including 50 per cent of places for official drivers.[8] Officers of the rank of captain or its equivalent are also allowed to transfer to the senior ranks of the civil service and police if they pass the relevant examinations. Apart from this regular system, however, over the years a great many retired or serving senior officers have been appointed to positions in the diplomatic service, the bureaucracy, state-owned industrial and power companies and the administration of universities. In February 2008, General Kayani ordered that all serving (but not of course retired) officers resign from positions in the civilian sector.

General Naqvi justified the system of land purchase to me in words that have been used by other officers to justify the patronage system as a whole:

The officer in general sees himself as leading a frugal life compared to the civilian officials, let alone the politicians and businessmen. An officer's career may seem privileged, but it involves a nomadic life, living for long years in freezing or boiling garrisons in the middle of nowhere, not being able to look after your children after a certain age because they have to be sent off to school and live with your parents. Wages have gone down radically compared to the private sector over the past thirty years, though you are still quite handsomely rewarded at retirement. That is why it is so important to have the possibility to buy land for a house over a long period and on easy terms . . .[9]

The problem is that the military's power within the state (or importance to the state) has meant that over the years the state has given these Defence Housing Associations (DHAs) free land in what used once to be outer suburbs of cities but are now among the most expensive pieces of real estate in Pakistan. In the case of the Lahore DHA, according to the BBC, the real value of a plot increased in the six years from 2000 to 2006 from $65,000 to more than $1.5 million.[10]

Inevitably, officers are buying their plots at subsidized rates and then selling them at market ones; and generals, who can acquire up to four plots depending on their rank (or even more at the very top – Musharraf had seven), are making fortunes – perfectly legally. Like US generals taking jobs with arms companies, this might be said to come under the heading of behaviour which isn't illegal but damned well ought to be; and is indeed attracting some criticism within the military itself. In the words of Major-General (retired) Mahmud Ali Durrani,

They should have given every officer just one plot and then there would have been no criticism, but people got greedy. When I was a captain, I was the only officer I knew who had a car of his own (a present from my father) – and I couldn't afford to buy a new tyre! Everyone used to bicycle to work. But then society and the middle classes became more affluent, and the officers felt that they had to catch up. The army couldn't afford higher pay, so they looked for other ways.[11]

With the exception of the state-owned armaments companies, Pakistan's military businesses were created to look after retired and disabled soldiers. The foundations were laid by the British Military Reconstruction Fund for retired and wounded Indian soldiers during the Second

World War. In 1953, the Pakistani military decided to invest their share of the remaining funds in commercial ventures, with the profits still being used for the same purpose.

In 1967 the resulting complex of industries and charitable institutions was renamed the Fauji Foundation. By 2009, the Fauji Group (the commercial wing) had assets worth Rs125 billion ($1.48 billion), and the Fauji Foundation (running the welfare institutions), Rs44 billion. A popular misconception notwithstanding, the Group's commercial activities are not exempt from taxation, and in 2005–6 they paid Rs32.4 million in taxes. Its spending on welfare, however, is tax-exempt as a charity.

The Fauji Board is headed by the chief secretary of the defence ministry (a civil servant), and made up of serving senior officers. The chief executive is a retired general. The Fauji Group started in textiles, and now owns or has shares in fertilizer, cement, cereal and electricity plants, security services and experimental farms. Fauji cornflakes confront many Pakistanis every day for breakfast. As of 2009 the group employed 4,551 ex-servicemen and 7,972 civilians. It obviously is a lucrative – though limited – source of patronage for ex-officers and NCOs.

When servicemen retire, only they themselves (and not their families) are guaranteed military health care. The Fauji Foundation, with a budget of around Rs4 billion a year, therefore provides health care, education and vocational training for the children and dependants of ex-servicemen, and for the parents, widows and families of soldiers killed or disabled in action.

Men actually serving are helped by the welfare trusts of the army, navy and air force, with help for their families' education and support for amenities like sports clubs. The Army Welfare Trust has total assets of some Rs50 billion ($590 million), and owns among other things 16,000 acres of farmland, rice and sugar mills, cement plants, and an insurance company. Unlike the Fauji Foundation, the welfare trusts benefit from lower rates of tax and other state subsidies.

As of 2009, the Fauji Foundation runs 13 hospitals, 69 medical centres and mobile dispensaries, 93 schools, 2 colleges (one for boys and one for girls), and 77 technical and vocational training centres. Since its creation, it has provided Rs3.2 million stipends to the children of soldiers. It also runs a private university, with a proportion of funded places for the children of ex-servicemen. Having spent some time visiting military hospitals and talking with soldiers who have been disabled in the fight with the Taleban, I must confess that all this seems to me both necessary and admirable. In addition, the Fauji industries have a reputation for being well run and looking after their workforce.

The chief objections raised against them are threefold. Firstly, that the military should not be involved in commercial business on principle. This seems to me just another case of insisting that Pakistan rather selectively follow Western models. Since the 1990s, the Chinese military has divested itself of its formerly huge *direct* commercial holdings, but it has done so by spinning these off into independent companies run by retired officers – similar to those of the Fauji Foundation. The Chinese economic model is emerging as a serious rival to that of the West in Asia, so there is no particular reason why the Pakistani military should be judged according to Western patterns in this matter.

The parallel with China is also interesting from another point of view. As the Chinese, South Korean, Taiwanese (and even to some extent Japanese) examples show, high levels of corruption and of state links to private companies are entirely compatible with the highest rates of economic growth. What appears essential, though, is that the corruption be informally regulated, limited, and above all predictable; and that both the corruption and the relationship with companies exist in an atmosphere which demands that patronage produce economic *results*, and not merely the endless circulation of money and sinecures. If Pakistan could move towards this kind of corruption, it would have taken an immense step towards economic, political and indeed moral progress.

This argument also partially answers one of the most serious objections to the industries owned by the military: that the Fauji and Army Welfare Fund industries' link to the state gives them unfair commercial advantages. It is true that the Welfare Fund has benefited from subsidies, but at least they appear to have been ploughed back into its industries and not simply stolen, as has been the case with so many state loans to private business.

Moreover, if the military businesses were deriving really massive competitive advantages from the state, it should be above all rival businessmen who complain, and in my experience this is not the case. On the contrary, 'it is better that the military is involved in industry – it helps them understand industry's concerns', as an industrialist friend told me. Only half-jokingly, he suggested that rather than the Fauji

Group being run by a retired general, it should be a requirement for generals being considered for chief of the army staff that they should have *previously* run the Group – 'that way, our next military ruler would be an experienced businessman'.

It would also be quite unfair to see the role of ex-soldiers in society as chiefly the result of state patronage. As in some Western societies – but to a far greater extent – retired soldiers are also prized by private businesses and NGOs for the qualities of discipline, honesty, hard work and indeed higher education that they have acquired during their military service – qualities which alas are not so common in wider Pakistani society.

Thus one of the most moving and convincing tributes to the military that I have seen was paid by the Citizens' Foundation educational charity, mentioned in the last chapter. The Foundation, which is funded by a mixture of business and individual contributions, largely employs ex-officers as its administrative and directing staff. This is both because of their reputation for efficiency and honesty, and because the soldiers, having spent so much of their lives in garrisons, are prepared to go and work in the countryside and small towns, in a way that most educated Pakistani civilians are not.

There has, however, been one very dark spot on the military's involvement in the economy. This was the use in 2002–3 of the paramilitary Rangers to brutally suppress protests by tenants on agricultural land owned by the military at Okara in Punjab after the terms of their tenancy were arbitrarily changed. This behaviour was no worse than that of the 'feudal' politicians whom officers profess to despise – but also no better. The Okara case indicates the improbability of the military ever returning to the land reform agenda of Field Marshal Ayub Khan and of launching a serious assault on the 'feudal' elites – of which the army itself has to some extent become a part. It was apparently, however, a unique case, which has not been repeated on military-owned land elsewhere.

The imperative to look after retirees and soldiers' families is especially strong in the Pakistani military because of the central role of morale in Pakistani military thinking. Recognizing from the first that the Pakistani armed forces were going to be heavily outnumbered by the Indians, and that Pakistan could only afford limited amounts of high technology, a decision was made to rely above all on the morale and fighting spirit of the soldiers. This emphasis also reflected self-perceptions of Muslim

Punjabis and Pathans as natural fighters, and the legacy of British belief in loyalty to the regiment.

As part of the effort to maintain strong morale, the Pakistani armed forces offer both high pay and excellent services – services that are good by world standards, not just the miserable ones of Pakistan in general. They offer these services not just to the soldiers and their immediate families, but to retired soldiers and the parents of soldiers. The effect has been to make military service very attractive indeed for many ordinary Pakistanis, and to ensure a high quality of recruits.

The family aspect of the Pakistan military was illustrated for me by a visit to the Combined Military Hospital in Peshawar in July 2009, an old red-brick British building with Pakistani additions. Until the fighting with the militants began, its biggest task was delivering babies – 1,321 of them in 2008, 'because Pakistani soldiers are very vigorous, you see', as Colonel Bushra, the female head of the family wing (and indeed a grandmotherly kind of officer), told me with a twinkle.[12]

When I visited the hospital, of its 600 beds, 47 were occupied by the parents of soldiers, some 60 by children, and around 40 by non-military civilians. The hospital and its seventy doctors provide important additional services to the horribly underfunded and overloaded civilian medical services of Peshawar, with specialist paediatric and intensive care units, incubators for premature babies (four when I visited), and so on.

It was not just the equipment, but also the cleanliness and general atmosphere of the hospital that were striking after some of the truly ghastly state medical institutions I had visited in Pakistan. And the effort needed to maintain both cleanliness and diligence in the middle of the South Asian monsoon will not need emphasizing to anyone who has lived through monsoons in the plains.

As the hospital commander, Brigadier Khalid Mehmood, in an interview on the same day, told me, 'All this is so that when the soldier is fighting at the front, he knows that his family are being looked after at home. This is crucial for maintaining the morale of the soldiers, on which in the end everything else depends. This means not just medical services, but also education, and help with finding jobs when the soldier retires.'

The brigadier also exemplified the other family aspect of the Pakistani military. He is by origin an Awan from Gujjar Khan in the Potwar region of Punjab, still the most important Pakistani military recruiting ground, and his father, grandfather, uncle and father-in-law were all officers. Most of the wounded officers I met were also from families with previous military connections.

To create services and surroundings like this hospital, two things are necessary: a strong sense of collective solidarity and *esprit de corps*, with the dedication and honesty that this creates; and *a great deal of money*. Neither element can exist without the other. The Pakistani military is a striking institution by the standards of the developing world, and an absolutely remarkable one for Pakistan. Pakistani military discipline, efficiency and solidarity have repeatedly enabled the Pakistani military to take over the state, or to dominate it from behind the scenes. They have used this power in turn to extract enormous financial benefits for the armed forces.

However, the military's collective spirit has meant that in general these resources have not simply been recycled into patronage or moved to bank accounts in the West, as would have been true of the civilian politicians. They have mostly been used for the benefit of the armed forces; and these rewards in turn have played an absolutely critical part in maintaining military morale, discipline and unity.

The effects have been similarly Janus-faced. The military has repeatedly overthrown Pakistani 'democracy', and the scale of military spending has severely limited funds available for education, development, medical services and infrastructure. If continued, this imbalance risks eventually crippling the country and sending Pakistan the way of the Soviet Union – another country which got itself into a ruinous military race with a vastly richer power. On the other hand, the rewards of loyal military service have helped to prevent military mutinies and coups by junior officers – something that would plunge Pakistan overnight into African chaos, and usher in civil war and Islamist revolt. As Tan Tai Yong writes of the British Indian army, in terms very relevant to the forces of Pakistan today in their fight with the Pakistani Taleban:

> Clearly, the tasks of securing the reliability of the Indian Army did not merely pertain to military discipline and punishment; the maintenance of its social base – the soldier at his home – was equally, if not more important, as 1857 showed. One could plausibly argue that it was in the soldiers' homes and villages, and not in the regiments, that the loyalty of the army was often won or lost. Similarly, the maintenance of the recruiting ground did not merely entail ensuring a constant supply of recruits. More than

that, it demanded the safeguarding of the interests of the general military population – recruits, serving soldiers, pensioners and their dependants – as a whole.[13]

This is hardly an academic issue. Since 9/11, the Pakistani military has been forced into an alliance with the US which a majority of Pakistani society – including the soldiers' own families – detests. At least until 2007–8, when the Pakistani Taleban emerged as a direct threat to Pakistan itself, much of the military was extremely doubtful about military action against Pakistani militants, seeing this as a campaign against fellow Pakistani Muslims for the good of and on the orders of the US. As a lt-colonel fighting the Pakistani Taleban in Buner told me in July 2009,

> The soldiers, like Pakistanis in general, see no difference between the American and the Russian presences in Afghanistan. They see both as illegal military occupations by aliens, and that the Afghan government are just pathetic puppets. Today, also, they still see the Afghan Taleban as freedom-fighters who are fighting these occupiers just like the Mujahidin against the Russians. And the invasion of Iraq, and all the lies that Bush told, had a very bad effect – soldiers think that the US is trying to conquer or dominate the whole Muslim world. But as far as our own Taleban are concerned, things are changing.
>
> Before, I must tell you frankly, there was a very widespread feeling in the army that everything Pakistan was doing was in the interests of the West and that we were being forced to do it by America. But now, the militants have launched so many attacks on Pakistan and killed so many soldiers that this feeling is changing . . .
>
> But to be very honest with you, we are brought up from our cradle to be ready to fight India and once we join the army this feeling is multiplied. So we are always happy when we are sent to the LOC [the Line of Control dividing Pakistani and Indian Kashmir] or even to freeze on the Siachen. But we are not very happy to be sent here to fight other Pakistanis, though we obey as a matter of duty. No soldier likes to kill his own people. I talked to my wife on the phone yesterday. She said that you must be happy to have killed so many miscreants. I said to her, if our dog goes mad we would have to shoot it, but we would not be happy about having to do this.

Between 2004 and 2007 there were a number of instances of mass desertion and refusal to fight in units deployed to fight militants, though mostly in the Pathan-recruited Frontier Corps rather than the regular army. By early 2010, more than 2,000 Pakistani soldiers and paramilitaries had been killed. In these morally and psychologically testing circumstances, anything that helps maintain Pakistani military discipline cannot be altogether bad – given the immense scale of the stakes concerned, and the appalling consequences if that discipline were to crack.

HISTORY AND COMPOSITION

Given the circumstances of its birth, it is somewhat surprising that the Pakistani military survived at all – and, at the same time, it was precisely because Pakistan's birth was so endangered that the new state came to attach such central importance to its military, and from the first gave the military such a disproportionate share of its resources. As Pakistan's first prime minister, Liaquat Ali Khan, stated in 1948, 'the defence of the state is our foremost consideration. It dominates all other governmental activities'.[14] This is a statement with which almost all subsequent governments (civilian and military) would have agreed. It is still true today – though the defence of the state is now belatedly being seen in terms of defence against religiously inspired revolt as well as against India and ethnic separatism.

From the first, therefore, the leaders of the Pakistani state felt acutely endangered from within and without: from India of course, but also from Afghanistan with its claim to Pakistan's Pathan territories, and equally importantly by internal revolt. This combination of threats led to the creation of what has been called Pakistan's 'national security state'. The same sense of external and internal threats has led to the creation of a powerful national security establishment in India also – but on a far smaller scale compared to the Indian state as a whole, and with a far smaller role for the uniformed military.

Relative size and geography have contributed greatly to the sense of danger, often spilling over into paranoia, which characterizes the Pakistani security establishment. With the exception of the barren and thinly populated bulge of Balochistan in the south-west, Pakistan is basically a long thin country on either side of the River Indus. Its second largest city, Lahore, is virtually on the Indian frontier, and the crucial highway linking Lahore and Karachi is, for long stretches, within 50 miles of Indian territory.

This led in the past to a frequent obsession with strategic depth in the Pakistani military, which has had particularly damaging effects on Pakistani policy towards Afghanistan – seen as a potential source of that increased depth. In February 2010, the then COAS (Chief of Army Staff), General Kayani, publicly defined 'strategic depth' as meaning 'a peaceful and friendly Afghanistan', and offered to help train the Afghan National Army.[15] However, most of the Pakistani military see such a stable and friendly Afghan state as unachievable, and an Indian-influenced and hostile government in Kabul as a real possibility. So a Taleban-controlled territory under Pakistani influence remains the Pakistani high command's reserve position.

Before being too harsh on the Pakistani military over this, one should remember that it is the job of militaries to be paranoid, and that the US security establishment in its time has generated remarkable levels of concern over infinitely smaller potential threats than those faced by Pakistan. The sense of strategic disadvantage and embattlement has been with the Pakistani military from the start. Partition left Pakistan with hardly any of the military industries of British India, with an acute shortage of officers (especially in the more technical services) and with a largely eviscerated military infrastructure.

The institutional and human framework inherited by Pakistan, however, proved resilient and effective. This framework remains that created by the British. As the history of law, democracy, administration and education in Pakistan demonstrates, other British institutions in what is now Pakistan (and to a lesser extent India as well) failed to take, failed to work, or have been transformed in ways that their authors would scarcely have recognized. The British military system, on the other hand, was able to root itself effectively because it fused with ancient local military traditions rather than sweeping them away (as was the case with education and law).

By a curious paradox, the Indian revolt of 1857, the defeat of which dealt a shattering blow to Muslim power and civilization in South Asia, also laid the basis for the future Pakistani army. The mutiny of most of the soldiers from the traditional British recruiting grounds of Bihar and Awadh left the British extremely unwilling to trust soldiers from these regions again.

By contrast, Muslim and Sikh soldiers from the recently conquered Punjab mostly remained 'true to their salt' – in the case of the Muslims, in part because the British had delivered them from the hated rule of the Sikhs. To this was added British racial prejudice, which saw the tall, fair-skinned Punjabis and Pathans as 'martial races', providing military material far superior to the smaller and darker peoples of the rest of India. This was a strange belief, given that by far the most formidable Muslim opponents the British Raj ever faced, the armies of Tipu Sultan, were from South India – but it is a prejudice that is completely shared by the Punjabis themselves, Pakistani and Indian alike.

By the 1920s, Punjab, the NWFP and Nepal (i.e. the Gurkhas) were providing some 84 per cent of the soldiers of the British Indian army. On the eve of the Second World War, almost 30 per cent of all soldiers were made up of Punjabi Muslims alone. These in turn were recruited chiefly from the Potwar (Potohar) area of north-western Punjab adjoining the NWFP, where the chief British military headquarters and depot at Rawalpindi was situated. The Jat, Rajput, Awan, Gakkhar and Gujjar tribes of this region continue to provide a majority (though a diminishing one) of Pakistani soldiers today.

Punjabi domination of the army (not to nearly the same extent of the air force and navy, but these are much smaller services) is a central element in complaints from the other provinces about Punjabi domination of Pakistan as a whole – an issue which will be discussed further in Chapter 7 (on Punjab). This accusation is somewhat overstated, at least as far as the senior ranks are concerned. Of Pakistan's four military rulers, only Zia-ul-Haq was a Punjabi.

The British land-grant system, derived from the Mughals but based on the new giant irrigation schemes of the 'canal colonies', has passed into Pakistani practice. It was intended most of all to provide a loyal and reliable source of recruitment of the Viceroy's Commissioned Officers (VCOs), who constituted the backbone of the British Indian army, and under new names continue to play a key role in that of Pakistan. At a time when the officer corps was monopolized by the British, the native VCOs served as the essential link with the ordinary soldiers (colloquially known as *jawans* – 'boys' or 'lads').

This remained true for a considerable time in the army of Pakistan. The vast increase of officers of middle- and even lower-middle-class origin means that it is less so today, but the bulk of the soldiers still come from traditional rural backgrounds, have often not travelled far beyond their own villages, and find the rhythms, the disciplines and the technicalities of military life very alien. Though of course this is much less so than in the past, the Pakistani army still makes the process of introducing them to military life a more gentle and prolonged one than in other military services, and one in which the Junior Commissioned Officers (JCOs) and NCOs are central. This in turn is part of the belief in morale and the regiment as family which is central to the whole Pakistani military system – and, once again, is of critical importance today, given the issue of how far the military can be isolated from the feelings and passions of the society that surrounds them.

The idea of the regimental family has been tested in recent years by the army's attempts to create a more truly national army by increasing the (previously tiny) numbers of Sindhi, Mohajir and Baloch recruits and reducing the dominance of north-west Punjab and the NWFP. This has involved, among other things, the creation of new military cantonments in Sindh and Balochistan, and a propaganda drive to encourage volunteers. As Lt-Colonel (retired) Anwar Awan told me:

> Twenty years ago a Sindhi in the infantry would have been seen as like a girl flying a fighter aircraft – absolutely impossible. But now we have three girls flying fighter aircraft, and more and more Sindhis are joining the army. So you see in the Pakistani military, nothing is impossible![16]

In fact, the effectiveness and determination of this programme are difficult to judge. The military are extremely cagey about releasing figures for ethnic proportions in the military, while critics from the other provinces claim that the whole business is mere window-dressing. According to Shuja Nawaz, who obtained internal army documents, 65 per cent of the army by 1990 was made up of people from Punjab (some 10 per cent more than Punjab's proportion of Pakistan's population), 14 per cent of people from the NWFP and FATA, 15 per cent of those from Sindh and Balochistan, and 6 per cent from Kashmir (reflecting the large numbers in paramilitary units along the Line of Control).[17]

It should be noted that 'from Sindh' is not the same as 'Sindhi', as ever since the British rewarded retired Punjabi soldiers with land grants in the new canal colonies in Sindh, Punjabi settlers there have contributed a disproportionate number of recruits. A more significant shift may be within Punjab itself, where more soldiers (and an even higher number of officers) are now recruited from southern districts that previously provided very few soldiers. Anecdotal evidence from conversations with military officers suggests that the change in ethnic balance over the past twenty years has been extensive enough to cause a certain amount of worry, both concerning future career prospects for military families from the Potwar region, and concerning regimental unity and morale.

The lt-colonel with whom I spoke in Buner told me that his battalion of the Punjab regiment contained roughly equal numbers of Punjabis and Sindhis (despite the territorial names of Pakistani infantry regiments, they are not based on deliberate recruitment from particular territories), as part of the general principle that no unit should have more than 50 per cent from one province, except Punjab – naturally. The colonel is the sixth generation of his family to serve in the military, and his father was, like himself, an officer of the Punjab Regiment. The family are Awans from Chakwal in the Punjab – another classic military recruiting ground.

Echoing the views of other Punjabi and Pathan officers with whom I spoke, the colonel expressed unease about the effects of increased recruitment of Sindhis, both on the army and his own family:

> To increase the number of Sindhis and Baloch, we had to lower educational and fitness standards, because in those provinces education is less and poverty is worse. Perhaps this does not matter too much – we look after our soldiers' education and health, and in the end 30th Punjabi will fight for 30th Punjabi, not for anyone else – the old British regimental spirit is still very strong with us. But I do feel that some important standards have been compromised, and that is bad and causes resentment.

Colonel Awan (himself another Potwari from Chakwal), who served as chief of the army's training centre at Sukkur in Sindh, told me that:

> It was a great problem at first getting Sindhis to join, but now many are coming in – native Sindhis, not just local Punjabis. And at first it is true that we had to go soft on discipline problems because of local culture. When Sindhis go to the local town twenty miles away, they say 'we are going abroad'. The Sindhi soldiers used to rush back to their villages at every opportunity. But now there is no problem with Sindhi officers, and less and less with the men. And after all, if we have to compromise a bit on standards, still we have to look at the wider canvas and think about the integration of the country. We also have to cast our net wider because the Potwar region itself is changing as a result of economic development,

education, and people going to work in the Gulf . . . The army is no longer the only road to get ahead, even for village kids from Chakwal.

Nonetheless, the tens of thousands of men (and some women) in the Pakistani officer corps make the armed forces Pakistan's largest middle-class employer by far. In recent decades, it has also become perhaps the greatest agency of social advancement in the country, with officers originally recruited from the lower middle classes moving into the educated middle classes as a result of their service with the military.

One sign of this is the way that knowledge of English – that quintessential marker of Pakistani social status – improves as officers move up the ranks. To judge by my experience, the Pakistani military almost has a new variant of an old British army adage (about marriage): lieutenants need not speak very good English; captains may; majors should; colonels must. In the process, the officers also acquire increasing social polish as they rise.

The military therefore provides opportunities which the Pakistani economy cannot, and a position in the officer corps is immensely prized by the sons of shopkeepers and bigger farmers across Punjab and the NWFP. This allows the military to pick the very best recruits, and increases their sense of belonging to an elite. In the last years of British rule and the first years of Pakistan, most officers were recruited from the landed gentry and upper middle classes. These are still represented by figures such as former Chief of Army Staff General Jehangir Karamat, but a much more typical figure is the present COAS (as of 2010), General Ashfaq Kayani, son of an NCO. This social change reflects partly the withdrawal of the upper middle classes to more comfortable professions, but also the immense increase in the numbers of officers required.

Meanwhile, the political parties continue to be dominated by 'feudal' landowners and wealthy urban bosses, many of them not just corrupt but barely educated. This increases the sense of superiority to the politicians in the officer corps – something that I have heard from many officers and which was very marked in General Musharraf's personal contempt for Benazir Bhutto and her husband.

I have also been told by a number of officers and members of military families that 'the officers' mess is the most democratic institution in Pakistan, because its members are superior and junior during the day, but in the evening are comrades. That is something we have inherited from the British.'[18]

This may seem like a very strange statement, until one remembers that, in Pakistan, saying that something is the most spiritually democratic institution isn't saying very much. Pakistani society is permeated by a culture of deference to superiors, starting with elders within the family and kinship group. As Stephen Lyon writes:

> Asymmetrical power relations form the cornerstone of Pakistani society ... Close relations of equality are problematic for Pakistanis and seem to occur only in very limited conditions. In general, when Pakistanis meet, they weigh up the status of the person in front of them and behave accordingly.[19]

Pakistan's dynastically ruled 'democratic' political parties exemplify this deference to inheritance and wealth; while in the army, as an officer told me:

> You rise on merit – well, mostly – not by inheritance, and you salute the military rank and not the sardar or *pir* who has inherited his position from his father, or the businessman's money. These days, many of the generals are the sons of clerks and shopkeepers, or if they are from military families, they are the sons of *havildars* [NCOs]. It doesn't matter. The point is that they are generals.

However, hopes that this might lead military governments to adopt radical social and economic policies (as has occurred with some Middle Eastern and Latin American militaries) have never come to anything. Whatever the social origins of its officers, the military establishment is part of the social elite of the country, and – as has been seen – the armed forces control major industries and huge amounts of urban and rural land. Finally, most of the progressive intelligentsia – whose input would be needed for any radical programme – have always rejected alliance with the military.

The social change in the officer corps over the decades has led to longstanding Western fears that it is becoming 'Islamized', leading to the danger that either the army as a whole might support Islamist revolution, or that there might be a mutiny by Islamist junior officers against the high command. These dangers do exist, but in my view most probably only a direct ground attack on Pakistan by the US could bring them to fruition.

It is obviously true that, as the officer corps becomes lower middle class, so its members become less Westernized and more religious – after all, the vast majority of Pakistan's population are conservative Muslims. However, as the last chapter explained, there are many different kinds of conservative Muslim, and this is also true of the officer corps. In the words of General Naqvi:

> Officers suffer from the same confusion as the rest of our society about what is Islamic and what it is to be Muslim. The way I have read the minds of most officers, they certainly see this as a Muslim country, but as one where people are individually responsible to God, for which they will answer in the life hereafter, and no one should try to impose his views of religion on them. Very few indeed would want to see a Taleban-style revolution here, which would destroy the country and the army and let the Indians walk all over us . . .
>
> Many officers still drink, and many don't. They don't bother each other, unless people misbehave when drunk. So among those who drink, great store is set by being able to handle your drink, and not drinking on duty. There is no toleration at all for that. Liquor used to be allowed in the officers' messes and clubs until Bhutto banned it. Now officers drink together at home, at private parties . . .[20]

General Musharraf exemplified the kind of officer who was well known to like a whisky and soda but was never (to the best of my knowledge) known to get drunk.

On the whole, by far the most important aspect of a Pakistani officer's identity is that he (or occasionally she) is an officer. The Pakistani military is a profoundly shaping influence as far as its members are concerned. This can be seen, among other things, from the social origins and personal cultures of its chiefs of staff and military rulers over the years. It would be hard to find a more different set of men than Generals Ayub, Yahya, Zia, Musharraf, Beg, Karamat and Kayani in terms of their social origins, personal characters and attitudes to religion. Yet all have been first and foremost military men.

This means in turn that their ideology was first and foremost Pakistani nationalist. The military is tied to Pakistan, not the universal Muslim Ummah of the radical Islamists' dreams; tied not only by sentiment and ideology, but also by the reality of what supports the army. If it is true, as so many officers have told me, that 'No army, no Pakistan', it is equally true that 'No Pakistan, no army'.

In the 1980s General Zia did undertake measures to make the army more Islamic, and a good many officers who wanted promotion adopted an Islamic façade in the hope of furthering this. Zia also encouraged Islamic preaching within the army, notably by the Tablighi Jamaat. However, as the careers of Generals Karamat and Musharraf indicate, this did not lead to known secular generals being blocked from promotion; and in the 1990s, and especially under Musharraf, most of Zia's measures were rolled back. In recent years, preaching by the Tabligh has been strongly discouraged, not so much because of political fears (the Tabligh is determinedly apolitical) as because of instinctive opposition to any groups that might encourage factions among officers, and loyalties to anything other than the army itself.

Of course, the army has always gone into battle with the cry of *Allahu Akbar* (God is Great) – just as the old Prussian army carried *Gott mit Uns* (God with Us) on its helmets and standards; but, according to a moderate Islamist officer, Colonel (retired) Abdul Qayyum:

> You shouldn't use bits of Islam to raise military discipline, morale and so on. I'm sorry to say that this is the way it has always been used in the Pakistani army. It is our equivalent of rum – the generals use it to get their men to launch suicidal attacks. But there is no such thing as a powerful jihadi group within the army. Of course, there are many devoutly Muslim officers and *jawans*, but at heart the vast majority of the army are nationalists, and take whatever is useful from Islam to serve what they see as Pakistan's interests. The Pakistani army has been a nationalist army with an Islamic look.[21]

However, if the army is not Islamist, its members can hardly avoid sharing in the bitter hostility to US policy of the overwhelming majority of the Pakistani population. Especially dangerous as far as the feelings of the military are concerned has been the US 'tilt towards India', which associates the US closely with all the hostility, suspicion and fear felt by the soldiers towards India.

To judge by retired and serving officers of my acquaintance, this suspicion of America includes the genuine conviction that either the Bush administration or Israel was responsible for 9/11. Inevitably therefore, despite the billions of dollars in military aid given by the Bush administration to Pakistan (which led to the army being portrayed not just by Islamists but by sections of the liberal media as 'an army for hire'), there was deep opposition throughout the army after 2001 to US pressure to crack down on the Afghan Taleban and their Pakistani sympathizers. 'We are being ordered to launch a Pakistani civil war for the sake of America,' an officer told me in 2002. 'Why on earth should we? Why should we commit suicide for you?'

In 2007–8, this was beginning to cause serious problems of morale. The most dangerous single thing I heard during my visits to Pakistan in those years was that soldiers' families in villages in the NWFP and the Potwar region were finding it increasingly difficult to find high-status brides for their sons serving in the military, because of the growing popular feeling that 'the army are slaves of the Americans', and 'the soldiers are killing fellow-Muslims on America's orders'. Given the tremendous prestige and material advantages of military service in these regions, this was truly worrying.

By late 2009 the sheer number of soldiers killed by the Pakistani Taleban and their allies and, still more importantly, the increasingly murderous and indiscriminate Pakistani Taleban attacks on civilians, seem to have produced a change of mood in the areas of military recruitment. Nonetheless, if the Pakistani Taleban are increasingly unpopular, that does not make the US any more popular; and if the US ever put Pakistani soldiers in a position where they felt that honour and patriotism required them to fight America, many would be very glad to do so.

INTER-SERVICES INTELLIGENCE, KASHMIR AND THE MILITARY–JIHADI NEXUS

The issues of religious orientation and attitudes to the US obviously lead to the question of the military's links to Islamist extremism, both inside and outside Pakistan. These links are obvious, but their origins have sometimes been misunderstood. The Islamists were initially intended to be tools, not allies; and the goal was not Islamist revolution as such, but to further Pakistan's national interests (as perceived and defined by the Pakistani military and security establishment), above all when it came to attacking those of India.

A common definition of tragedy is that of a noble figure betrayed and destroyed by some inner flaw.[22] The Pakistani military is in some ways an admirable institution, but it suffers from one tragic feature which has been with it from the beginning, which has defined its whole character and world view, which has done terrible damage to Pakistan and which could in some circumstances destroy Pakistan and its armed forces altogether.

This is the military's obsession with India in general, and Kashmir in particular. Of course, Kashmir is by no means only a military obsession. It was Zulfikar Ali Bhutto who once said that 'Kashmir must be liberated if Pakistan is to have its full meaning', and Pakistani politicians share responsibility for encouraging ordinary Pakistanis to see jihad in Kashmir as legitimate.[23] Nonetheless, both the military's prestige and the personal experiences of its men have become especially focused on Kashmir.

Speaking of the average Pakistani officer of today, General Naqvi told me:

> He has no doubt in his mind that the adversary is India, and that the whole *raison d'être* of the army is to defend against India. His image of Indians is of an anti-Pakistan, anti-Muslim, treacherous people. So he feels that he must be always ready to fight against India.[24]

Pakistan was born in horrendous bloodshed between Hindus, Sikhs and Muslims; and, within two months of its birth, fighting had broken out with India over the fate of the Muslim-majority state of Kashmir. This fighting has continued on and off ever since. Two out of Pakistan's three wars with India have been fought over Kashmir, as have several smaller campaigns. These include the bitter, 25-year-long struggle for the Siachen Glacier (possibly the most strategically pointless fight in the entire history of human conflict) initiated by India in 1984.

The vast majority of Pakistani soldiers have served in Kashmir at some point or other, and for many this service has influenced their world view. Kashmir therefore plays for Pakistan the role of an *irredenta*, and has joined a long historical list of such obsessions: like France with Alsace-Lorraine after 1871, Italy with Trieste after 1866, and Serbia with Bosnia after 1879. The last case, it may be remembered, led the Serbian military to sponsor terrorists who, by assassinating the Austrian Archduke Franz Ferdinand, sparked the First World War.[25]

Kashmir is not a specifically military obsession. It is very widely shared in Punjab, and to a lesser extent in the NWFP and FATA, from which many volunteers for the Kashmir struggle have been drawn ever since 1947, but far less in Karachi, Sindh and Balochistan. This belief has been kept alive in part by the belief (which is true but – as in so many such cases – irrelevant) that democracy and the past resolutions of the UN are on Pakistan's side; and by anger at Indian atrocities against Indian Muslims, both in Kashmir and more widely.

In both the Pakistani and the Indian militaries, the commitment to fight for Kashmir has been reinforced over the years by the sacrifices made there: some 13,000 dead on both sides in the wars of 1947 and 1965, together with around 1,000 dead in the Kargil battle of 1999, and some 2,400 (mostly from frostbite and accidents) in the twenty-five years of the struggle for the Siachen. That is without counting the thousands of civilian dead in 1947, and the 50,000 (according to Indian official figures) or more than 100,000 (according to Kashmiri groups) civilians, militants and Indian security personnel killed or missing in the Kashmiri insurgency which began in 1988.

Washington's growing alliance with India since 2001, and abandonment of the previous US stance on the need for a plebiscite on Kashmir's fate, has therefore caused intense anger in the Pakistani military. The military's obsession with India and Kashmir is not in origin Islamist, but Pakistani Muslim nationalist. With rare exceptions, this has been true even of those senior officers most closely involved in backing Islamist extremist groups to fight against India, like former ISI chief Lt-General Hamid Gul.

Most have used the Islamists as weapons against India without sharing their ideology. Similarly, the deep hostility of men like Gul or former chief of staff General Aslam Beg to the US comes from anger at perceived US domination and subjugation of the Muslim world, not from radical Islam – a feeling to be found among many entirely secular and liberal figures in institutions such as Al Jazeera, for example.

That does not necessarily make their hostility to India any the less dangerous though. I had a rather hair-raising glimpse of the underlying attitudes of some ISI officers in 2008 when I asked a senior ISI public relations official (and seconded officer) to tell me who he thought were the most interesting analysts and think-tanks in Islamabad. He recommended that I see Syed Zaid Hamid, who runs an analytical centre called 'Brasstacks' (after the huge Indian military exercise of 1987, seen in Pakistan as a prelude to Indian invasion).

Mr Hamid also presents a programme on national security issues on the News One television channel. He fought in Afghanistan in the 1980s with the Afghan Mujahidin, and, though he told me that he had never been an ISI officer, there can be no doubt that he was close to that organization. He described the ISI as 'the intellectual core and centre of gravity of the army. Without the ISI, the army is just an elephant without eyes and ears' (this phrase caused extreme annoyance among some military friends to whom I repeated it).

Mr Hamid described himself to me as 'a Pakistani neo-con', and there really is something neo-conservative about his mixture of considerable intelligence, great fluency in presenting his ideas and geopolitical fanaticism and recklessness. Like some neo-cons of my acquaintance in Washington, his favourite word seemed to be 'ruthless'. Despite his background, he had a geekish air about him, and spoke with nervous intensity.

On the Taleban, he echoed the Pakistani security establishment in general (at least when they are speaking off the record), emphasizing the difference between the Pakistani Taleban, who were in revolt against Pakistan and had to be defeated, and the Afghan Taleban, who had never attacked Pakistan and were an essential strategic asset. However, he stressed repeatedly that he was a Pakistani nationalist, not an Islamist, and said that he himself would have far preferred to see Pakistan allied to the late Panjshiri Tajik leader Ahmed Shah Masoud, 'Afghanistan's only liberal leader'.

On strategy towards India, his views were the following:

> We say that if India tries to break up Pakistan by supporting insurgents like the Baloch nationalists then our response should be to break up India. In any case, we owe them payback for what they did to us in East Pakistan . . . India is not nearly as strong as it looks. The faultlines of the Indian Federation are much deeper than those of Pakistan: Kashmir, the Naxalites, Khalistan, Nagaland, all kinds of conflicts between upper and lower castes, tribals, Hindus and other religions and so on. If we were to support these insurgencies, India would cease to exist.[26]

I hasten to add that, Kashmir aside, there is in fact no evidence that the ISI is supporting any of these insurgencies within India. Nonetheless, this kind of attitude is deeply troubling, especially because India's growing problem with the Naxalite Maoist peasant rebellion means that Mr Hamid's words, while horribly dangerous, are not as stupid (seen from the perspective of an ultra-hardline Pakistani) as they might first appear.

To understand ISI attitudes, and Kashmir strategy in particular, it is necessary to understand that they saw victory over the Soviets in Afghanistan very much as their own victory. It became their central institutional myth. Because of the huge funds flowing from the US and Saudi Arabia to help the Mujahidin, which the ISI administered and used for its own purposes, the Afghan jihad of the 1980s was the key episode in giving the ISI an autonomous financial base and boosting ISI power within the military and the state as a whole.

The ISI became quite convinced that what they had done to the Soviets in Afghanistan they could do to India in Kashmir, using the same instruments – Islamist militants (the fundamental political and geopolitical mistakes involved in this belief should hardly need repeating). The spontaneous mass uprising of Kashmiri Muslims against Indian rule from 1988 on (initially in protest against the rigged state elections of the previous year) seemed to give a great chance of success. However, to a much greater extent than in Afghanistan, these militants were to be recruited not just in the country concerned, but from within Pakistan (and to a lesser extent the wider Muslim world).

The ISI's Kashmir strategy reflected the longstanding Pakistani strategy of promoting Kashmiri accession to Pakistan, and not Kashmiri independence. They therefore used pro-Pakistani Islamist groups to sideline the Jammu and Kashmir Liberation Front, which initially led the Kashmir uprising. This strategy included the murder by the ISI-backed Islamist militant groups of a considerable number of JKLF leaders and activists – even as these were also being targeted and killed by Indian security forces.

The Islamist radical groups, madrasahs and networks which had served to raise Pakistani volunteers for the Afghan jihad had always hated India, and were only too ready to accept Pakistani military help, including funding, weapons supplies, provision of intelligence, and the creation of training camps run by the Pakistani military.

However, just as in Afghanistan first the Mujahidin and then the Taleban escaped from the US and Pakistani scripts and ran amok on their own accounts, so the militants in Kashmir began to alienate much of the native Kashmiri population with their ruthlessness and ideological fanaticism; to splinter and splinter again into ever-smaller groups and fight with each other despite ISI efforts to promote co-operation, and to prey on Kashmiri civilians. Lashkar-e-Taiba's greater discipline in this regard was reportedly one factor in the increasing favour shown to it by the ISI.

Finally – though it is not clear if this was really a departure from the script, as ISI officers claim in private, or was planned by the ISI as the Indian government believes – the militants began to carry out terrorist attacks on Indian targets outside Kashmir (starting with an attack on Indian soldiers at the Red Fort in Delhi in December 2000). This last development in particular ensured that in the wake of 9/11 Pakistan would come under irresistible US pressure to abandon its active support for the Kashmiri jihad and crack down on its militant allies.

In January 2002, Musharraf formally banned Lashkar-e-Taiba and Jaish-e-Mohammed, and ordered an end to militant infiltration into Indian Kashmir from Pakistan. From mid-2003 this ban on infiltration has largely been enforced, leading to a steep reduction in violence in Kashmir. As a result, in November 2003 India and Pakistan agreed a ceasefire along the Line of Control in Kashmir, and initiated a dialogue on a possible settlement over Kashmir, which will be discussed further in the Conclusions.

The Pakistani military remained firmly convinced that India would never agree to terms even minimally acceptable to Pakistan unless at least the threat of future guerrilla and terrorist action remained present. Meanwhile, their continued hostility to India was also fuelled by attacks on Muslims in India, and especially the infamous Gujarat massacres of 2002, which were orchestrated by the BJP state government (and which claimed, it should be pointed out, at least ten times as many victims as the Mumbai terrorist attacks, while receiving perhaps one-tenth of Western media notice).

By 2008, as the Taleban insurgency against Pakistan itself gathered pace and an increasing number of ISI officers and informants fell victim to it, the ISI itself had also begun to see the need for a new approach to some of its militant allies within Pakistan. In the meantime, however, various developments had made it far more difficult for the Pakistani military to take effective action.

The military had helped the militant groups root themselves more deeply in Pakistani society, especially in parts of Punjab, exploiting not just the military's financial assistance but the prestige of taking part in a jihad which most Punjabis saw (and were encouraged by the military to see) as legitimate. The extensive charitable and educational network developed by Lashkar-e-Taiba/Jamaat-ud-Dawa with military encouragement also served as a way of employing fighters withdrawn from the Kashmir battle. By 2009, the Jamaat-ud-Dawa's own resources had made it independent of ISI financial support.

The military is genuinely concerned that if it attacks these groups it will drive more and more of them into joining the Pakistani Taleban – as has already occurred with Sipah-e-Sahaba, Lashkar-e-Jhangvi and some sections of Jaish-e-Mohammed. According to Stephen Tankel, some members of Lashkar-e-Taiba/Jamaat-ud-Dawa did press the organization to revolt against the Pakistani government when Musharraf sided with America after 9/11, but their demands were rejected by the leadership and they left the organization. Since Lashkar-e-Taiba remained focused on Kashmir (and, after 2006, on Afghanistan), and did not attack Pakistan, the ISI did not move against it.[27]

On 14 January 2010, Jamaat-ud-Dawa condemned the killing of Muslims by suicide bombing as un-Islamic and said that such attacks 'played into the hands of the US, Israel and India'. It is important to note that LeT and JuD's hatred and fear of India may act as a deterrent against their joining in revolution in Pakistan – at least, a JuD spokesman whom I interviewed in January 2009 stressed repeatedly his organization's loyalty to Pakistan as the state that 'defends Muslims of South Asia against Indian Hindu conquest and oppression'. He promised therefore that the JuD would do nothing to destroy Pakistan.

Pakistani officials have told me that their greatest fears of mass revolt in Punjab concern what would happen if Lashkar-e-Taiba/Jamaat-ud-Dawa were to swing against the state and use their extensive network to mobilize and organize unrest. This they say is one key reason (along with their anti-Indian agenda, which they do not mention) for not taking the sweeping measures against the organisation that the US is demanding. As the commissioner of one of Punjab's administrative divisions said to me in January 2009:

> We have to worry that if we do what you say and crack down on them that some of them at least will turn to terrorism against Pakistan in alliance with the Taleban. After all, they have the ideology and the training. The

last thing we need now is yet another extremist threat. And, after all, is it really in your interest either to cause revolt in Punjab? This province alone has three times the population of the whole of Afghanistan, and don't forget that the army too is recruited from here.

These officials also do not add that one way of keeping LeT quiet in Pakistan is to allow (or even encourage) its activists to join the Afghan Taleban to fight against Western forces on the other side of the Durand Line.

In Jaish-e-Mohammed, by contrast, militants pressing for a jihad against the 'slave' government of Pakistan prevailed against the counsel of the group's leadership. The suspected involvement of Jaish-e-Mohammed (JeM) activists in the attempt to assassinate Musharraf in December 2003 (apparently with low-level help from within the armed forces) led to a harsh crackdown on parts of the group by Pakistani intelligence. On the other hand, ISI links with the group meant that other parts remained loyal to the Pakistani state – though only, perhaps, because they were allowed to help the Taleban in Afghanistan and to retain at least their potential to attack India.

Moreover, their long association with the militants, first in Afghanistan and then in Kashmir, had led some ISI officers into a close personal identification with the forces that they were supposed to be controlling. This leads to a whole set of interlocking questions: how far the Pakistani high command continues to back certain militant groups; how far the command of the ISI may be following a strategy in this regard independent from that of the military; and how far individual ISI officers may have escaped from the control of their superiors and be supporting and planning terrorist actions on their own. This in turn leads to the even more vital question of how far the Pakistani military is penetrated by Islamist extremist elements, and whether there is any possibility of these carrying out a successful military coup from below, against their own high command.

Since this whole field is obviously kept very secret by the institutions concerned (including Military Intelligence, which monitors the political and ideological allegiances of officers), there are no definitive answers to these questions. What follows is informed guesswork based on numerous discussions with experts and off-the-record talks with Pakistani officers including retired ISI officers. It is also worth remembering that even in Western democracies (notably France and the US) intelligence services have had a tendency to develop both institutional cultures and institutional strategies of their own; and also that the nature of their work can make it extremely difficult to control the activities of individual agents – especially of course after they retire. A number of retired middle-ranking ISI officers are reported to have openly joined LeT and other militant groups.

Concerning the ISI, the consensus of my informants is as follows. There is considerable resentment of the ISI in the rest of the military, owing to their perceived arrogance and suspected corruption. This sentiment was crystallized by a notorious case in 2006 when ISI officers harassed the family of a highly decorated retired brigadier after a clash between his grandchildren and the children of the head of the ISI's political wing. However, when it comes to overall strategy, the ISI follows the line of the high command. It is after all always headed by a senior regular general, not a professional intelligence officer, and a majority of its officers are also seconded regulars. The present chief of army staff, General Ashfaq Kayani, was director-general of the ISI from 2004 to 2007, and ordered a limited crackdown on jihadi groups that the ISI had previously supported. Nonetheless, ever since the Afghan war the ISI has been building up a separate corporate identity and ethos, which has bred a willingness to pursue separate tactics and individual actions without consulting the high command.

Concerning the Afghan Taleban, the military and the ISI are at one, and the evidence is unequivocal: the military and ISI continue to give them shelter (though *not* much actual support, or the Taleban would be far more effective than they are). There is deep unwillingness to take serious action against them on America's behalf, both because it is feared that this would increase Pathan insurgency in Pakistan, and because they are seen as the only assets Pakistan possesses in Afghanistan. The conviction in the Pakistani security establishment is that the West will quit Afghanistan leaving civil war behind, and that India will then throw its weight behind the non-Pathan forces of the former Northern Alliance in order to encircle Pakistan strategically.

In these circumstances, 'It's not that we like the Taleban, but they are all we've got,' as Mr Hamid told me, reflecting the private statements of several officers. As these words suggest, in the great majority of Pakistani officers a willingness to shelter the Afghan Taleban does not indicate any affection for them – while on the Taleban side, the memoirs of the former Taleban official and ambassador to Pakistan, Mullah Abdul Salam Zaeef, are filled with the most virulent hatred for Pakistan in general and the ISI in particular.

Concerning the Pakistani Taleban and their allies, however, like the military as a whole, the ISI is now committed to the struggle against them, and by the end of 2009 had lost more than seventy of its officers in this fight – some ten times the number of CIA officers killed since 9/11, just as Pakistani military casualties fighting the Pakistani Taleban have been more than double those of the US in Afghanistan.

Equally, however, in 2007–8 there were a great many stories of ISI officers intervening to rescue individual Taleban commanders from arrest by the police or the army – too many, and too circumstantial, for these all to have been invented. A senior civilian counter-terrorism officer told me that his agency has repeatedly arrested members of terrorist groups who have turned out to have ISI links. He also said that his counter-terrorism operations have received very little co-operation from the ISI – though that, he said, was often in his view more from institutional rivalry (so familiar from relations between the CIA and FBI in the US) than from a deliberate desire to protect terrorists.

It seems clear, therefore, that whether because individual ISI officers felt a personal commitment to these men, or because the institution as a whole still regarded them as potentially useful, actions were taking place that were against overall military policy – let alone that of the Pakistani government. Moreover, some of these men had at least indirect links to Al Qaeda. This does not mean that the ISI knows where Osama bin Laden (if he is indeed still alive), Aiman al-Zawahiri and other Al Qaeda leaders are hiding. It does, however, suggest that they could probably do a good deal more to find out.

Concerning the threat of terrorism against the West (as opposed to attacks on Western forces in Afghanistan), the Pakistani military and civilian intelligence services have been extremely helpful to Britain in particular, as British intelligence officers testify. Problems in this co-operation appear to be due to lack of co-ordination between Pakistan's different agencies, and the lack of an overall counter-terrorism strategy by the Pakistani state, rather than to any ill-will towards Britain or sympathy for the terrorists.

However, on the question of support for terrorism against India, it is obvious that not just the ISI but the military as a whole is committed to keeping Lashkar-e-Taiba (under its cover as Jamaat-ud-Dawa) at least in existence 'on the shelf'. Reflecting these continuing links, up to 2010 Lashkar-e-Taiba has been careful to oppose militant actions in Pakistan itself, arguing that 'the struggle in Pakistan is not a struggle between Islam and disbelief', that the Pakistani state is not committing Indian-style atrocities against its own people, and that true Islam should be spread in Pakistan by missionary and charitable work (*dawa*) not jihad. Echoing statements by Mullah Omar, the leader of the Afghan Taleban, LeT/JuD leaders have also argued that fighting fellow Muslims in Pakistan is a distraction from the true jihads in Kashmir and Afghanistan. The group has also taken a strong line against sectarian violence within Pakistan.[28]

As part of its programme of missionary and charitable work, and of spreading its influence by these means, the group has built up an impressive network of schools, hospitals and social welfare organizations in northern Pakistan. In 2005, it played an important part in relief work after the Kashmir earthquake, and the efficiency and honesty of its officials won praise from doctors and aid workers despite their lack of sympathy for the group's ideology. Evidence is contradictory on whether the 2010 floods have allowed JuD to build up their prestige in the same way. Some accounts claim that this is so, but others say that the sheer scale of the catastrophe swamped their efforts, and that any boost to their popularity was local and limited. After the Mumbai attacks, the Pakistani state was forced by US and Indian pressure to take over the supervision of Jamaat-ud-Dawa's formal educational and welfare organization – but many of the same people work there as in LeT, and the group is also thought to have an extensive informal network which the state has left alone.

Because of this, and much more importantly of the popularity of its fight against India among the great majority of the population, Lashkar-e-Taiba has struck deep roots in Punjabi society. This is despite the fact that its Ahl-e-Hadith theology is alien to most Punjabis. This theology draws Lashkar-e-Taiba closer to Saudi Arabia and indeed to Al Qaeda, with whose leaders it was once closely linked.

From my talks with Pakistani military and intelligence officers it is clear to me that, having done so much to build up Lashkar-e-Taiba, the Pakistani security forces are now very afraid of the creature they helped create, of its possible sympathizers within their own ranks, and of the dreadful consequences if it were to join with the Taleban and the sectarians in revolt against Pakistan.

Jamaat-ud-Dawa's extensive international network in the Pakistani diaspora also leads Pakistani officers to fear that if they attempt seriously to suppress the group it will launch successful terrorist attacks in the West, with disastrous results for Pakistan's international position. This is something that up to mid-2010 the Pakistani intelligence services have done much to help prevent. While the Pakistani Taleban and their allies have begun to sponsor such attacks (like the abortive one on Times Square in New York in May 2010), groups still allied to the Pakistani state have not.

However, Lashkar-e-Taiba members certainly have contacts with Al Qaeda, and helped Al Qaeda operatives escape from Afghanistan after the defeat of the Taleban, and gave them shelter within Pakistan. As Stephen Tankel writes:

> Ideologically, for all of its strategic restraint following 9/11 Lashkar is, after all, a jihadi organization with a long history of waging pan-Islamic irredentist campaigns. Indian-controlled Kashmir may be the group's primary ideological and strategic target, but it has never been the apotheosis of Lashkar's jihad.[29]

Men trained by LeT and still associated with members of the group have been implicated in terrorist plots in Europe, North America and Australia, though the group's leadership does not seem to have been involved. They have also taken part in actions within Pakistan which their leaders have deplored. The world of Sunni Islamist extremism as a whole functions not as a hierarchical organization, or even as interlocking organizations, but rather as a net with nodes.

All the groups and individuals within this net hate the US, Israel, India and indeed Russia alike, though they have different targets at different times. Despite LeT's strategic decision to concentrate on India, there is no ideological barrier to its members taking part in actions against the West. The jihadi world could even be called a kind of cloud of interplanetary gas in which individuals join some clump for one operation and then part again to form new ad hoc groups for other attacks. This also makes it extremely hard for the ISI to keep tabs on the individuals concerned, even when it wants to.

By far the biggest terrorist attack carried out by LeT itself was that in

Mumbai in November 2008. The great majority of the Pakistani experts and retired officers whom I know do not think that the Pakistani high command, either of the ISI or the army, was involved in ordering Lashkar-e-Taiba's terrorist attack on Mumbai in November 2008. They point out in particular that, while deliberately targeting Westerners greatly boosted LeT's prestige among international militants, it would have been an unprecedented, reckless and pointless strategy for the Pakistani high command, ensuring a furious reaction from the international community.

Equally, there is an overwhelming consensus that this operation could not have been planned without ISI officers having been involved at some stage, and without the ISI knowing that some sort of operation was being planned. Whether the operation then continued as it were on autopilot, was helped only by retired officers, or whether the junior officers concerned deliberately decided to pursue it without telling their superiors, is impossible to say at this stage. The American LeT volunteer David Headley, who was involved in the preparations for the Mumbai attacks, has testified under interrogation that ISI officers were involved in the planning, but could not say whether they were acting independently or under orders from above.

Certainly the ISI and the military as a whole made strenuous attempts – in the face of incontrovertible evidence – to deny that LeT had carried out the attacks. While the Pakistani authorities could do a great deal more to restrict and detain LeT activists and leaders, it is extremely difficult to put them on public trial – for the obvious reason that they would then reveal everything about the ISI's previous backing for their organization.

THE PAKISTANI NUCLEAR DETERRENT

The question of military links to Islamist terrorists raises particular fears in the West because of Pakistan's possession of nuclear weapons. The horrendous consequences if such a weapon did fall into terrorist hands makes this a natural fear, but one which has led to a considerable degree of exaggeration and even hysteria in the Western media as far as Pakistan is concerned.

Given Pakistan's lack of economic development, the Pakistani nuclear deterrent is the most remarkable achievement of the Pakistani state. It may also in certain circumstances lead to that state's downfall. This is obviously because of the risk of a nuclear exchange with India and the destruction of both countries; and perhaps even more importantly because of the fears that Pakistan's nuclear weapons have raised in the US. These fears are in part based on mistaken information and analysis, but they are nonetheless real.

For a long time, the US turned a partially blind eye to Pakistan's nuclear weapons programme. The reasons for this were that every Pakistani administration since the early 1960s – military and civilian alike – was involved in this programme, and several of those administrations were, at different times and for different reasons, key US allies. Moreover, until the 1990s at least, India, and not Pakistan, was generally seen in Washington as the culpable party in driving a South Asian nuclear race – partly because during the Cold War India was seen as a Soviet ally, but also because India did indeed lead the race and carry out the first nuclear tests in 1974 and 1998.

From 1989 and the Soviet withdrawal from Afghanistan, it is untrue to say that the US was indifferent to Pakistan's nuclear programme. After a ten-year interval brought about by Pakistan's help to the US in combating the Soviet occupation, the US administration permitted the re-imposition of the terms of the Pressler Amendment, mandating sanctions against countries which could not certify that they were in compliance with the Nuclear Non-Proliferation Treaty.

These sanctions were imposed on both India and Pakistan, but hurt Pakistan very much more, given its smaller size and more vulnerable economy. Indeed, the imposition of these sanctions is one of the chief Pakistani arguments concerning America's 'betrayal' of Pakistan once the Soviet withdrawal diminished Pakistan's apparent strategic importance to the US.

Fear of India has always been the driving force behind Pakistan's nuclear programme. Rhetoric of an 'Islamic bomb' reflects pride in Pakistan's role (in this if nothing else) as the leading country of the Muslim world, and has also been used when dealing with other Muslim countries over nuclear issues. According to every Pakistani soldier and official with whom I have spoken, though, it reflects neither the core motive nor the strategic intention behind Pakistan's nuclear deterrent. As a senior retired general told me,

Look, we knew from the mid-60s that India was seeking the bomb. Given that, any Pakistani who did not want to get the bomb too would have been either a complete fool or a traitor. We needed the bomb at all costs for exactly the same reason NATO needed the bomb in the Cold War, faced with overwhelming Russian tank forces threatening you in Europe. So how can you criticize us?

Part of the problem in South Asia, first in trying to prevent a nuclear arms race and then in managing it, has always been that, unlike in the Cold War between the US and the Soviet Union, this was never a straight two-way competition. Rather, ever since the Sino-Indian war of 1962, and the first Chinese nuclear test at Lop Nur in 1964, India has been largely motivated by rivalry with China – a rivalry that combines strategic and emotional elements. India's desire to achieve a balance with China makes it impossible to devise an agreed balance between India and Pakistan – unless of course China were to extend a nuclear shield to Pakistan.

As early as 1965, Zulfikar Ali Bhutto told a Western journalist that if India were to acquire a nuclear bomb, 'then we should have to eat grass and get one, or buy one of our own!' As prime minister after 1971, Bhutto was instrumental in getting Pakistan's nuclear programme off the ground – a programme which naturally gathered momentum immensely after India carried out its 'Smiling Buddha' nuclear tests in 1974.

Bhutto also began the co-operation with Libya on nuclear development that continued through the 1980s and '90s until Libya revealed and abandoned its programme as part of its effort for reconciliation with the US after 2001. Secret dealings with Libya, North Korea and Iran were greatly extended under the direction of Dr A. Q. Khan, a metallurgist working in Holland's nuclear industry who returned to Pakistan in 1976 with information stolen from his then employers.

A. Q. Khan has been well described by Shuja Nawaz as 'part brilliant and hard-working scientist, part patriot, and partly self-serving, publicity-seeking egomaniac'.[30] The success of his publicity campaign has indeed been such as to make it very difficult to assess his real importance to the development of Pakistan's bomb. Where he was clearly of critical importance was in acquiring essential technology, expertise and material from abroad, as part of barter with states dubbed 'rogues' by Washington. Since 9/11, these links have naturally attracted immense interest from the US. Before 9/11, Musharraf had already removed A. Q. Khan from his position as chief of the nuclear programme in March 2001. He was later placed under (a very liberally defined) house arrest.

The extent of US pressure on Pakistan over the nuclear proliferation issue has been modified by two facts well known to US intelligence. The first is that A. Q. Khan is not an Islamist, but a secular Pakistani nationalist. His wife is of Dutch–South African origin. There is no evidence at all of any links between him and Al Qaeda or other terrorist organization.

The second fact is that, while A. Q. Khan certainly profited personally from some of his deals, at no stage was he a truly 'rogue' element. Rather, as my military acquaintance quoted above told me, every Pakistani president and chief of the army staff knew in broad outline what A. Q. Khan was doing. They might not necessarily have approved in detail – but then again, they took good care not to find out in detail. 'He had been told, "get us a bomb at all costs", and that is what he did.'

As far as US intelligence is concerned, this means that, on the one hand, they cannot really pursue A. Q. Khan for fear of unravelling their relationship with the entire Pakistani military and political establishment. On the other hand, the fact that this establishment was always ultimately in charge means that US fears concerning potential terrorist access to Khan's network are less than the Western media have sometimes suggested. As a result, the private US line to Pakistan on nuclear links to 'rogue states', in the off-the-record words of a US official, has been 'We know what you did and we will let you off this time. But don't do it again. Since 9/11, everything has changed. If you do it again, we will have no choice but to hit you very hard.'

The most worrying aspect by far of the A. Q. Khan network concerns not the network as such, or the proliferation to Iran and North Korea (which are also not about to commit suicide), but the links to Al Qaeda before 9/11 of two Pakistani nuclear scientists, Sultan Bashiruddin Mahmood and Chaudhry Abdul Majeed. Neither of these men was part of the A. Q. Khan network or concerned with the weapons programme as such, and it would be impossible for people like this to produce a nuclear bomb. If, however, terrorist sympathizers in the nuclear structures could get their hands on radioactive materials, what such figures could do is help terrorists to produce a so-called 'dirty bomb'. This is the greatest fear of US diplomats, as revealed by WikiLeaks.

It is certain that if there ever seemed a serious chance that Pakistan's nuclear weapons were going to fall into the hands of Islamist radicals, the US would launch some kind of strike to capture or disable them. Barring a split in the army and the collapse of the Pakistani state, such a danger is in fact minimal. There is no chance at all of the Pakistani military giving them to terrorists. The Pakistani army exists to defend Pakistan. That is its *raison d'être*. A move which would ensure Pakistan's destruction for no strategic gain would contradict everything the military stands for. Moreover, these weapons are Pakistan's greatest military asset. 'We are not going to cut off our own crown jewels and give them to terrorists,' an officer told me.

Nor is there any chance – once again, unless the state and army had *already* collapsed – of terrorists somehow seizing the weapons, which are the most heavily defended objects in Pakistan, and protected by picked men carefully screened to eliminate extremist sympathizers of any kind. The weapons are not on hair-trigger alert, and a majority may well be disassembled at any given time. According to a report of 2007 by the International Institute for Strategic Studies (IISS) in London:

> A robust command and control system is now in place to protect Pakistan's nuclear assets from diversion, theft and accidental misuse. For the most part, these measures have been transparent and have worked well. Indeed, Pakistan's openness in explaining its command and control structures goes beyond the practices adopted by most other nuclear-capable states ... Responsibility for nuclear weapons is now clearly in the hands of the National Command Authority and its constituent bodies. General Khalid Kidwai and the Strategic Plans Division he commands have gained national and international respect for their professionalism and competency.[31]

Incidents such as the terrorist attack on the military headquarters in Rawalpindi are not a precedent, because this was a suicide attack – whereas if you want to steal a nuclear weapon, you obviously don't just have to get in, you have to get out again, carrying it.

The greatest danger may be not Pakistani realities but US fears. That is to say, the risk that the US might launch a strike on Pakistan's nuclear deterrent prematurely, thereby precipitating precisely the scenario that the US fears – since such an attack would so radicalize the army and destabilize the state as to run a really serious risk of bringing about mutiny and state collapse.

Another danger is that the growth of India's nuclear forces will leave Pakistan in a position where it feels that it has no alternative but to seek new technology on the international black market. Such a move, if discovered – as it certainly would be sooner or later – would bring about the collapse of relations with the US and the imposition of Western sanctions, risking economic collapse, an increase in radicalization, and possibly revolution.

Finally, there is the ultimate nightmare scenario (other of course than a nuclear exchange between India and Pakistan) of a successful attack on a US target using a weapon of mass destruction. If the aftermath of 9/11 is anything to go by, the effects of such an attack would be temporarily at least to deprive the US establishment of its collective wits, and remove any restraint in US strategy.

Even if such an attack turned out to have no Pakistani origins, Pakistan's possession of nuclear weapons would undoubtedly place Pakistan squarely in America's gun-sights. Very likely, this is precisely what the perpetrators of such an attack would be hoping – since a US attack on Pakistan would be the shortest road to victory for Al Qaeda and its allies that could be imagined, other than a US invasion of Saudi Arabia.

The most dangerous moment in my visits to Pakistan since 9/11 came in August/September 2008, when on two occasions US forces entered Pakistan's tribal areas on the ground in order to raid suspected Taleban and Al Qaeda bases. On the second occasion, Pakistani soldiers fired in the air to turn the Americans back. On 19 September 2008 the chief of the army staff, General Kayani, flew to meet the US chief of the joint staffs, Admiral Mike Mullen, on the US aircraft carrier USS *Abraham Lincoln*, and in the words of a senior Pakistani general 'gave him the toughest possible warning' about what would happen if this were repeated.

Pakistani officers from captain to lt-general have told me that the entry of US ground forces into Pakistan in pursuit of the Taleban and Al Qaeda is by far the most dangerous scenario as far as both Pakistani–US relations and the unity of the army are concerned. As one retired general explained, drone attacks on Pakistani territory, though the ordinary officers and soldiers find them humiliating, are not a critical issue because they cannot do anything about them.

US ground forces inside Pakistan are a different matter, because the soldiers can do something about them. They can fight. And if they don't fight, they will feel utterly humiliated, before their wives, mothers, children. It would be a matter of honour, which as you know is a tremendous thing in our society. These men have sworn an oath to defend Pakistani soil. So they would fight. And if the generals told them not to fight, many of them would mutiny, starting with the Frontier Corps.

At this point, not just Islamist radicals but every malcontent in the country would join the mutineers, and the disintegration of Pakistan would come a giant leap closer.

6

Politics

*Men went there [to the British parliament in the eighteenth cen-
tury] to make a figure, and no more dreamt of a seat in the
House in order to benefit humanity than a child dreams of a
birthday cake that others may eat it; which is perfectly normal
and in no way reprehensible.*

(Lewis Namier)[1]

*The fidelity of the martial classes of the people of India to their
immediate chief, whose salt they eat, has always been very
remarkable, and commonly bears little relation to his moral virtues or conduct to his superiors . . . He may change sides as often
as he pleases, but the relations between him and his followers
remain unchanged.*

(Sir William Sleeman)[2]

Patronage and kinship form the basic elements of the Pakistani political
system – if water, chemically speaking, is H_2O then Pakistani politics are
P_2K. Political factions are very important, but they exist chiefly to seek
patronage, and have kinship links as their most important foundation.
Factions which support individual politicians or alliances of politicians
are not usually made up chiefly of the kinsfolk of these leaders, but the
politicians concerned almost always need the foundation of strong kinship networks to play any significant role.

By contrast, ideology, or more often sheer exasperation with the
regime in power, might be compared to the energy propelling waves
through water. These waves can sometimes assume enormous size, and

do great damage; but after they have passed the water remains the same. In Pakistan, waves of public anger (or, much more rarely, public enthusiasm) can topple regimes and bring new ones to power; but they do not change the basic structures of politics.

It is possible that the floods of 2010 have brought about a major transformation of this system, by so damaging local agriculture and infrastructure that the old patronage system is hopelessly short of benefits to distribute, and by driving so many rural people into the cities that traditional patterns of kinship allegiance and social deference cease to operate. If this proves to be the case, then the analysis set out in this chapter – and indeed in this book – will be a historical portrait of Pakistan as it existed in the first six decades of its existence, rather than a guide to the future.

However, it is still too early to draw this conclusion. The patterns and traditions concerned are very old and very deeply rooted in local society. They have adapted to immense upheavals over the past 200 years, and are likely to be able to do so in the face of future upheavals, unless ecological change is so great as eventually to threaten the very basis of human existence in the region.

So one can most probably continue to speak of certain long-lasting and enduring features of the Pakistani political system. Among these is the fact that the alternation in power of civilian and military regimes has also been carried along by a sort of deep political wave pattern common to both. In the case of military regimes, the wave that has buoyed them up has lasted longer, because they have had more autonomy from political society and not been so dependent on parliament; but in the end they too have plunged into the trough between the waves and been overwhelmed.

The pattern has worked like this. Every new Pakistani government comes to power making two sets of promises, one general, one specific. The general promises are to the population, and are of higher living standards, more jobs, better education and health services, and so on. The specific promises are to smaller parties and to individual politicians, who are offered individual favours to themselves, their families or their districts in return for their political support.

The problem is that the poverty and weakness of the state make this process rather like trying to get a very skimpy blanket to cover a very fat man, and a man, moreover, who will never keep still but keeps twisting and turning in bed. In other words, there just isn't enough patronage to go round. This is even a circular process, because a large part of the favours that governments hand out are meaningless but expensive ministerial posts (more than sixty in the civilian governments of the 1990s and after 2008), tax breaks, corrupt contracts, state loans (which are rarely repaid), and amnesties for tax evasion and embezzlement – all of which helps keep the state poor.

As a result, governments simply cannot keep most of their promises, either to the masses or to the political elites. As time goes on, more and more of the political elites find themselves disappointed, and unable in turn to pass on favours to their followers and voters – which means the likelihood of not being re-elected. What is more, even giving a serious favour to a political family is not enough. In parts of the countryside, local politics is structured round competition between particular landowning families, branches of the same family, or family-based factions. That means that the state favour not only has to be large, but has to be visibly larger than that given to the local rivals. No contract or ambassadorship will compensate for seeing your enemies become ministers, with all that means in terms of ability to help local friends and allies.

Meanwhile, at the level of parliament, Pakistan's deep ethnic, regional and religious divisions mean that no party ever succeeds in gaining an absolute majority, even if it is army-backed; and even if it could, it wouldn't mean much, because for most politicians party loyalty means little compared to personal advantage and clan loyalty. So governments find that their parliamentary majorities are built on shifting sand.

Sooner or later, the 'outs' have come together and found that they outnumber the 'ins'; and also find that the state's failure to improve the lot of the population means growing discontent on the streets, or at least a public mood of disillusionment which inclines more and more people to support whoever is in opposition. As Abida Husain, a great Punjabi landowner-politician, said to me candidly: 'You know, a normal Pakistani with a normal human heart can't be really pro-government no matter what the government is, because governments always look indifferent to the hardships of the people.'[3] This permanent mood of simmering mass irritation with government is catalysed by specific events or developments – economic crises, especially gross instances of corruption or autocracy, foreign policy humiliations or all of them together.

As politics has become disorderly and government unmanageable, the army and senior bureaucracy have engineered the downfall of a civilian government and replaced it either with a new civilian government or with their own rule; or, after the military themselves have been in power for a few years, they have managed a transition from their own rule back to civilian rule; and the whole cycle of patronage has begun again. Developments since the 1990s, and both main parties' fear of renewed military rule, may have modified this pattern to some extent, but I very much doubt that they have fundamentally changed it.

It would be quite wrong to see these features of Pakistan as reflecting simply the absence of 'modern' values of democracy and the law. Rather, they also stem from the continued presence of traditions of overriding loyalty to family, clan and religion (often in a local form, which is contrary to the precepts of orthodox Islam as well as the Pakistani legal code) and to the rules of behavior that these loyalties enjoin. Similarly, 'corruption' in Pakistan, as in so much of the world, is not the kind of viral infection instinctively portrayed by much of Western analysis.

In so far as it is entwined with patronage and family allegiance, corruption is an integral part of the system as a whole. In fact, to reform Pakistan radically along the lines of how Western states supposedly work would require most of the population to send itself to gaol. Corruption cannot therefore be 'cured'. Rather, as in South Korea and other societies, it may over time be possible to change it organically into less destructive forms of patronage. To quote a local proverb, 'Dishonesty can be like flour in salt or salt in flour. It's a question of the proportion.'

As far as most of the political parties are concerned, these do not exist in the form taken as the norm in the West. With the exception of the MQM and the religious parties, all of Pakistan's 'democratic' political parties are congeries of landlords, clan chieftains and urban bosses seeking state patronage for themselves and their followers and vowing allegiance to particular national individuals and dynasties. Most of these individuals inherited their positions from their fathers or (more rarely) other relatives. Where new individuals gain political power, they invariably found political dynasties of their own, and seek to pass on their power, influence and followers to their sons (or occasionally daughters).

Thus the Pakistan People's Party is built around the Bhutto dynasty, the Pakistan Muslim League (Nawaz) around the Sharif dynasty, and the Awami National Party around the Wali Khan dynasty. The smaller building blocks of these parties are also local political families. These often break away to form new alliances with other families, or to create a new small party based on one leader and his family, like the PPP (Sherpao), founded by a dissident local PPP politician from the Frontier, or – on a much larger scale – the Pakistan Muslim League (Qaid-e-Azam), created by the Musharraf administration but put together and led by the two Chaudhury brothers from Gujrat.

As will be seen, ideology does play a certain part in political loyalties, but outside the Jamaat Islami it is not dominant. Furthermore, a long-term loyalty to one party, sometimes taken by observers to reflect ideological allegiance, may in fact be reflective of something more like a medieval allegiance: an obstinate personal loyalty to a particular lead-ing family. In many ways, the kind of politician who is personally admired today (for more than simply his or her ability to gain patron-age for supporters) is still very close to the Pathan chief described by Mountstuart Elphinstone more than 170 years ago:

> Proud, high-spirited and obstinate; frugal, but not sordid in expense, steady
> in his attachment to his party, and strict in conforming to the notions of
> honour which prevail among his countrymen . . .[4]

Long-term loyalty to one party can also reflect the fact that the indi-vidual and family concerned have no alternative, because they have burnt their boats as far as all the other potential loyalties are concerned. Thus in my travels round Pakistan, I have quite often been told in private (sometimes by the politicians themselves): 'Of course, So-and-So Khan would like to join the ruling party; but he can't, because the Sharifs [or the Bhuttos] will never forgive him for what he did to them when he was in government'; or, sometimes, because a rival local faction, or set of cousins, is so firmly entrenched in one party that their local rivals have no choice but to stick to the other, come what may.

In the Pakistan of 2010, there are only two areas where this is not the case: the Federally Administered Tribal Areas (FATA), which were never fully part of the state patronage system, and much of which have been removed from state control by the Pakistani Taleban; and to some extent the MQM-controlled areas of Karachi, where the removal of the Mohajirs from their ancestral roots in India, and the disruption of their kinship networks, as well as their old urban culture, has produced a more 'modern' form of ethnic party politics.

THE MILITARY AND POLITICS

The nature of the Pakistani political system has made possible three military seizures of power, and the long periods of military rule that have followed. Even more common have been military attempts to manipulate politics from behind the scenes, to influence and put pressure on journalists, to bring down civilian governments that have fallen out with the military, and to shape the results of elections.

Retired officers, or serving officers speaking off the record, are usually quite unapologetic about the military's role in politics. As Admiral (retired) Arshad Gilani told me in November 1990:

> Democracy has failed – it is not suited to our temperament. It took Western countries hundreds of years to develop and we have only had forty. The military is the only force in the country which has some discipline, which can guarantee stability and economic growth. If there has been army rule for most of Pakistan's history it is not the military's fault. Benazir complains that the military did not give her a chance – well, grow up. This is a serious game. Let's accept that no force that has power wants to give it up. If the PPP wants to keep power, then it has to prove itself to be better at government than the army.[5]

Because real political power is spread among so many local actors, and depends so heavily on patronage, this also places limits on the ability of the military to control things for long – because, as I've said, there just isn't enough patronage to go round. On the other hand, both civilian governments and the ISI have other means of influence, as sketched for me by Murtaza Jatoi, son of the caretaker chief minister of Sindh, in 1990:

> If this were a political government running a political campaign, then PPP candidates would have no water for their land, all the state loans to them would be called in, there would be raids on Asif Zardari's home and those of his relatives to pick up known dacoits taking shelter there, and every vehicle with a PPP flag or sticker would be pulled over to see if its licence is in order or its tyres in proper shape. That's how governments in power run elections here.[6]

The key military institution for the manipulation of politics is of course Inter-Services Intelligence (ISI). In private, the army is unabashed about the need to keep an eye on politics as part of internal security in general. As a retired senior general pointed out to me with considerable justification, since its foundation the Pakistani state has been faced with parties in the NWFP, Sindh and Balochistan which have been committed to breaking up the country, and have also had close links at different times with India, Afghanistan and the Soviet Union. 'No country in our circumstances could do without a strong domestic intelligence service,' he told me. He pointed out that while the ISI has helped Pakistani military regimes against their domestic opponents, the Intelligence Bureau (IB) has been used by different civilian regimes, first in one direction, then in another, 'to the point where they have become almost paralysed as a force to defend Pakistan' (not of course a judgement with which the IB would agree).

In July 2009 one of the ISI's senior officers gave me an account of its political role and its limits, an account which needs to be taken with several pinches of salt, but which is nonetheless interesting:

> I just have to laugh when I hear these conspiracy theories about how the ISI controls everything in Pakistan. If that were true, don't you think that General Zia would still be in power? Or that Nawaz Sharif and his party would have stayed our loyal servants instead of becoming our enemies?
>
> As to political manipulation, I must tell you that every single civilian government has used us and the IB to target their political rivals and to rig elections, so their complaints about this are also a bit of a joke ...
>
> We have never controlled elections either on behalf of civilian governments or the military – Pakistan is much too big and we aren't nearly strong or numerous enough for that, and we also don't have the money. Remember how much money is involved in winning one Pakistani assembly seat, and then multiply it by hundreds. What we have sometimes done is pushed a bit – usually if things were moving in that direction anyway. There are various ways in which we can help get the result we want in some individual constituency. But across the whole country, no.

This is certainly a very considerable understatement of the ISI's ability to influence politics, but it is accurate on some points – firstly, the fact that the civilians themselves have used the intelligence services for unconstitutional ends. As Iqbal Akhund, adviser to Benazir Bhutto, admitted, 'From early in Pakistan's history, rulers lacking support from a strong political party relied instead on the intelligence agencies to consolidate their rule.'[7] A key role in building up the ISI's political wing was played by Z. A. Bhutto. Ten years later, under Zia, this section of the ISI played a key part in putting together the new Muslim League and the IJI political alliance that ran against Z. A. Bhutto's daughter Benazir.

My ISI contact was also truthful when he said that the ISI has to work with the grain of the existing political system, and not against it; and that, during elections, its heavy power is usually brought to bear to produce results in particular parliamentary constituencies, rather than across the board – which means that they can have a big effect in a close-run race, but cannot stop a really big political swing, whether to the PPP in 1988 and 2008, or the Muslim League in 1997. As the leading Muslim League politician Chaudhury Shujaat Hussain told me in 2008: 'The army and the ISI will only go with you as long as enough of the people are with you. They are like a horse that carries you only as long as you have strength in your own legs.'[8]

One important group whom the ISI can influence very heavily, however, is the senior bureaucracy, because a negative security report from the ISI will blast their careers. This means that while, ever since Z. A. Bhutto's time, civil servants have been subjugated by the politicians, there is no possibility of a serious movement to resist military influence or a military takeover emerging in the bureaucracy.

A picture of some ISI political tactics emerged in 2009 with revelations from a former ISI officer, Brigadier Imtiaz, about his organization's role in bringing down the PPP government of Benazir Bhutto in 1990 ('Operation Midnight Jackal'). This involved, among other things, bribing PPP deputies to defect from the party, and a whispering campaign to the effect that she was about to be sacked by the president for corruption, and therefore that her MPs and ministers should switch sides in order to keep their positions.

HOW THE SYSTEM WORKS

Generally portrayed by both Western and Pakistani analysts as wholly negative, the Pakistani political system is in fact two-sided. On the one hand, it is very bad for the overall economic development of the country, for reasons summed up for me in 1988 by former Finance Minister Mehboob-ul-Haq, and equally true twenty years later:

> Growth in Pakistan has never translated into budgetary security because of the way our political system works. We could be collecting twice as much in revenue – even India collects 50 per cent more than we do – and spending the money on infrastructure and education. But agriculture in Pakistan pays virtually no tax because the landed gentry controls politics and therefore has a grip on every government. Businessmen are given state loans and then allowed to default on them in return for favours to politicians and parties. Politicians protect corrupt officials so that they can both share the proceeds.
>
> And every time a new political government comes in they have to distribute huge amounts of state money and jobs as rewards to politicians who have supported them, and in short-term populist measures to try to convince the people that their election promises meant something, which leaves nothing for long-term development. As far as development is concerned, our system has all the worst features of oligarchy and democracy put together.
>
> That is why only technocratic, non-political governments in Pakistan have ever been able to increase revenues. But they cannot stay in power long because they have no political support ... For the same reasons, we have not been able to deregulate the economy as much as I wanted, despite seven years of trying, because the politicians and officials both like the system Bhutto put in place. It suits them both very well, because it gave them lots of lucrative state-appointed jobs in industry and banking to take for themselves or distribute to their relatives and supporters.[9]

It is important to note that the speaker had been finance minister under the 'military dictatorship' of General Zia-ul-Haq (no relation); but, as he candidly admitted, this regime had been almost wholly unable to change these basic features of the Pakistani system. Lack of revenue, and the diversion of what revenue there is to political patronage, are especially disastrous for Pakistan's ability to develop its national infrastructure – something which in the area of water conservation could in future literally threaten the country's very survival.

On the other hand, the Pakistani system creates immense barriers to revolutionary change, including that offered by the Taleban and their allies; and these barriers are formed not just by the raw power and influence of 'feudals' and urban bosses, but also by the fact that, for a whole set of reasons, the system requires them to use at least some of that influence and patronage for the good of poorer sections of the population.

As Stephen Lyon and others have emphasized, patronage in Pakistan should not therefore be seen as the preserve of the elites, and as simply a top-down relationship. A mixture of the importance of kinship loyalty and the need for politicians to win votes, and – on occasions – to mobilize armed supporters, means that quite wide sections of society have the ability to exploit and even distribute patronage to some extent. Quite poor people can thus form part of 'human resource networks' and mobilize some degree of help or protection from their superiors. Even the very poorest in the villages often benefit from the *deg* tradition, whereby local landowners and big men distribute free food to the entire village to celebrate some happy event, to boost their local prestige through public generosity, and by the same token to try to cast local rivals into the shade.

People gain access to patronage by using their position within a kinship network to mobilize support for a politician who then repays them in various ways when in office, or by using kinship links to some policeman or official to obtain favours for relatives or allies. In certain circumstances, this can benefit whole villages through the provision of electricity, roads or water. Of course, everyone complains bitterly about this in public when others do it successfully, while following precisely the same strategies themselves. In the words of Professor Iqraar, vice-chancellor of Faisalabad University:

> The problem with Pakistan's political and government system is not so much feudalism as what I would have to call South Asian political culture in general. Everyone here seeks personal and family power by all means and then misuses it. The feudals just have more of it, that's all.

Rather than being eaten by a pride of lions, or even torn apart by a flock of vultures, the fate of Pakistan's national resources more closely resembles being nibbled away by a horde of mice (and the occasional large rat). The effects on the resources, and on the state's ability to do things, are just the same, but more of the results are ploughed back into the society, rather than making their way straight to bank accounts in the West. This is an important difference between Pakistan and Nigeria, for example.

As this parallel suggests, part of the reason is the nature of the resources concerned. Unless you are right at the top of the system and in a position to milk the state as a whole (like Zardari in the PPP governments of the 1990s), to make really large individual fortunes in the poorer parts of the world today requires the ability to make, extract or steal something which can then be sold in the economic metropolises of the world – in Nigeria's case, oil.

Pakistan exports textiles and agricultural products, together with limited amounts of steel and copper – not the kind of goods or raw materials that can generate this kind of fortune. Even its most successful legitimate businessmen do not have really large fortunes by international standards because the things they make and export do not generate that kind of profit. Nor can even the biggest Pakistani landowners hope to make huge fortunes from their lands. Urban landowners enjoy large rents – but rents which are still limited by the overall poverty of the country; as witness the fact that even Karachi has hardly any skyscrapers worth the name.

In fact, very often to make a fortune in Pakistan means finding some way to milk the state – including of course international aid flowing to the state, which is one of the principal ways in which the Pakistani elites make money from the West. What is more, given the lawless nature of Pakistani society, you usually also need influence over the state (especially the police and the courts) to defend what you have from predatory neighbours or the forces of the state themselves.

This has a whole set of crucially important consequences. First of all, it usually sets a limit on how much you can take. Most politicians are not in power for very long, and partly for the same reason (because their political patrons lose office) most officials are not left for long in the most lucrative positions. Furthermore, an individual minister or official who steals an outrageous amount for himself will attract the envy of colleagues, who will try to replace him so that they can share.

Thus the great majority of senior politicians of my acquaintance have some sort of property in a posh part of London, which in most cases was certainly not paid for out of legitimate earnings. Most have flats in Knightsbridge or Kensington, or houses further out; and so have good reason not to condemn other people with flats in Knightsbridge. However, families like the Bhuttos, who buy whole country estates in Britain on the strength of their profits from government, will attract unfavourable notice, and earn a bad reputation which can have a serious effect on their political fortunes.

Even more importantly, if to make a lot of money generally means gaining influence over the state, to gain influence over the state generally means procuring some kind of political power. Political power requires supporters – individuals and families with power of their own, gunmen to protect you, and ordinary people to vote for you; and followers have to be rewarded. In other words, a very large proportion of the money made from corruption has to be recycled downwards through patronage or straight gifts – because otherwise the ability to extract corruption would itself dry up. The patronage system therefore has a strongly cyclical aspect, which once again strengthens its anti-revolutionary character.

If the political power of the kinship group in Pakistan depended only on the distribution of patronage, then this power might well have declined over time, given that patronage will always be limited; but it is also rooted in the oldest of social compulsions: collective defence. But while the power of kinship is necessary to defend against the predatory state, it is also one of the key factors in making the state predatory, as kinship groups use the state to achieve their goals of power, wealth and triumph over other kinship groups. So the ancient Pakistani kinship groups and the modern Pakistani state dance along together down the years, trapped in a marriage that ought to be antagonistic, but has in fact become natural to each.

This system has a critical effect on Pakistan's remarkably low inequality rating according to the Gini Co-efficient, measuring the ratio of the income of the poorest group in society relative to the richest. In 2002, according to UN statistics, the figure for Pakistan was 30.6, compared to 36.8 for India, 40.8 for the US, and 43.7 for Nigeria. Part of the reason is obvious if you sit down with someone from a Pakistani political family and work out their income and expenditure. By the time you have accounted for payments to servants, gunmen and supporters (in the biggest families, sometimes even permanently hired musicians, to sing their praises), for political transport (including constant travel to weddings and funerals) and political hospitality, and shared the rest among several relatives, even in some very powerful families what is left does not usually amount to a large income by world standards, unless the family has a member who is actually in senior office at the time.

All this can also be illustrated visually by the houses of leading Pakistani political families. Of course, these are very luxurious indeed by the standards of the vast mass of the population. However, when it comes to size, at least, the grandeur of these houses can sometimes be exaggerated – because they contain far more people than initially meets the eye: political workers, servants and family members themselves.

Take an unusually large but otherwise typical example: the rural home of Makhdoom Faisal Saleh Hayat, a leading politician from a Shia *pir* family in Jhang, who started with the PPP before switching to the PML(Q) in order to join the Musharraf administration, and as of 2010 is back in opposition. At first sight, the frontage of this vaguely neoclassical monstrosity is on the approximate scale of Buckingham Palace, a resemblance strengthened by the glaring floodlights by which it is illuminated at night.

A closer look reveals something closer to Sandhurst or West Point. It is in fact a giant political barracks, and the great majority of the rooms are bleak, barely furnished sleeping cells for political workers and visiting supporters, and bleak halls for political consultations. Similarly, as with most of the houses of politicians, the lawn in front is not part of a private garden, but is an arena for political rallies and entertainments.

Then there are the servants. Every big 'feudal' family I have visited has far more of them than it actually needs. It doesn't pay them much – but then again, according to strict free market capitalist rules, it doesn't need to employ most of them at all. One reason is of course to display wealth and power through the number of one's entourage. The other was summed up for me by a lady in Lahore:

> Oh, what I wouldn't give for one hard-working servant with a vacuum-cleaner instead of having to pay and keep an eye on ten who sit around eating and staring into space and getting into all kinds of trouble which we have to get them out of again. But of course it's impossible. They all come from my husband's village, and some of their families have been in our family's service for generations. If we sacked them, the whole village would start saying how mean and treacherous we are.[10]

Her husband was not a politician – but his brother was, which comes to the same thing; and he needed to be elected from his village and district, in the face of rival politicians from his own kinship group appealing to inhabitants of 'his village' for their support.

One can, however, be too cynical about this. This lady's old nurse-maid, to whom the family was devoted, was now looking after her own children. There was thus a commitment to look after the nursemaid's family, which was emotional and indeed familial, and not just political. During my stays with Pakistani elite families, I have seen servants treated with appalling arrogance; but I have also seen those elite families paying for their servants' children to be sent to school, making sure that they go to the doctor when they are ill, that the daughters have at least modest dowries, and so on.

Finally, there are the families themselves. According to the cultural ideal prevalent across most of Pakistan, the ideal family is the joint extended family of patriarch, sons and sons' families resident together in the same house (albeit often with separate cooking-spaces). As so often, this cultural value also has a practical political underpinning in collective familial solidarity and self-defence against rivals and enemies. This is connected to the fact that among rural landowning families a mixture of land reform and the subdivision of land by inheritance means that many estates are the collective property of several brothers and other relatives, but are administered jointly for the sake of economic efficiency and political weight.

Joint families are by no means an aspect only of rural society. Even many very wealthy and powerful urban families, for example the three sons of the late General Akhtar Abdur Rehman (chief of the ISI under Zia-ul-Haq) and their children in Lahore, still live together; and obviously the size of any house has to be divided by the number of people in it.

Thus in conservative joint families, the hidden presence of large numbers of women and children may be revealed by muffled howls of joy, sorrow or imprecation from behind closed doors. In more liberal ones, those doors may open to disgorge a seemingly endless flow of relatives – and it is remarkable how even a very large room may suddenly seem quite small when filled with two or three mothers, a grandmother, some-times a great-grandmother, a couple of nursemaids, a horde of children and an entire assembly line of aunts – all of whom have to be fed and clothed, and, in the case of the children, educated, and jobs found for the boys and dowries for the girls.

In grander and more liberal families, this increasingly also means jobs for the girls – including elected positions. This change was given a tremendous push by Musharraf's requirement that members of the national and provincial assemblies possess college degrees. Musharraf's educational requirement eliminated a good many male politicians, but, since the law was cancelled by the new PPP government in 2008, the effects may not prove long-lasting.

On the other hand, the move of women into politics reflects other factors. Even more than elsewhere, being a politician in Pakistan requires a particular set of qualities of which the women in a given family may have more than the men. Their choice by the family is also an extension of the fact that in Pakistani 'feudal' families the political representative of the family was never necessarily the eldest son, but whichever son seemed fittest to be a politician. Thus, while the younger brother or even wife may stand for election, the elder brother or husband may keep a more secure and equally lucrative job as a civil servant, policeman or whatever.

In 2002, a senior customs officer from a big landowning family from Sarghoda sketched for me what this meant for 'feudal' politics, in the context of his family's general political strategy. There was obviously no question of his giving up his own job to run for election, since customs is not only among the most lucrative areas of state service, but one where it is possible to do a great many political favours:

> There are three branches of my family, and we rotate the seats in our area between us. My uncle has held one seat for the Jamaat, but the Jamaat is now in alliance with the PPP, so my wife is now standing for the PPP. She was chosen because I am a civil servant and can't run and my brother is working abroad. Our sister doesn't have a degree, so it had to be my wife.

The ideal Pakistani political family thus has its members in a range of influential occupations: a civil servant, a policeman, a lawyer, a business-man and, if possible, representatives in several different political parties. As a member of a rival family said admiringly of a great political 'feudal' family in Sindh, 'the Soomros have been everyone else's teachers at keeping one member of the family in power whatever happens. They have someone in each party, but they are also all loyal to each other.' The Saifullahs, a leading business family of Peshawar, probably hold the record for this, placing different brothers, sons and nephews in mutually hostile political parties, while retaining an inexorable commitment to family solidarity and family collective advantage.

It would be a mistake, however, to focus too heavily on the top elites when it comes to understanding how Pakistan's political system works, and how it has proved so remarkably stable. As subsequent chapters on Pakistan's provinces will explore, different parts of Pakistan vary greatly when it comes to the autocratic power of great landowners – and where they possess quasi-autocratic power, as in Balochistan, Sindh and parts of southern Punjab, this is due above all to their role as tribal chiefs or hereditary *pirs*. Even in these regions, the chieftains – if they are wise – will pay a great deal of attention to the opinions, the interests and the *izzat* of the second-tier tribal leadership, and will be careful to show them public respect.

This is partly because, even in Balochistan, when it comes to leadership Pakistani tribalism is closer to ancient Irish tribalism than to Scottish tribalism. The latter, at least in the romanticized version, involved blind loyalty to a hereditary chief, invariably the eldest son. In Irish tribes, the leading men of the tribe elected as chief whichever male member of the royal family they thought most suitable – as in Pakistan, a fecund source of bloody family feuds. In consequence, a majority of Pakistani chieftains know very well that dear old uncle Ahmed over there in the corner, so very nice and respectful, is all too ready to seize the leadership if the chance offers itself.

More important for Pakistan as a whole is the fact that politics in large areas of the Punjab and the NWFP are no longer dominated by great individual landowners. This is partly because of land reform and the subdivision through inheritance of formerly great estates, and partly because of social mobility due to economic change. The key rural politician in these areas is a relatively small landowner (with perhaps 100 acres or so), deeply embedded in a powerful local landowning clan, with influence over the police and administration.

Such landowners are very often local urban politicians too, because they own urban property from which they derive most of their income, even while their prestige and ability to mobilize kinship links continue to come from rural landownership and their leading position in landowning clans. Sometimes, the enormous expansion of the towns means that the lands of local landowning lineages have been swallowed up, greatly increasing their wealth in the process but leaving their approach to politics and kinship unchanged. As Abida Husain told me: 'Very little of our income actually comes from land any more, but land is our essential link to the people and our voters.'[11]

The cultures of leading groups in northern Punjab and the NWFP have also always had a more egalitarian and meritocratic tinge, as with the Pathans and the Jats. In these groups, it is often more accurate to talk of 'big men', risen through personal wealth and character, rather than hereditary chieftains. Thus back in 1988, I asked a Punjabi Jat member of parliament (for the PPP) to explain how exactly it was you became a Chaudhury like him (the name for a respected and influential figure among the Jats), since I had noticed that in many cases it was not by inheritance. 'It's very simple,' he replied. 'You become a Chaudhury among the Jats when you can call yourself a Chaudhury without all the other Jats laughing at you!' Very often, as he and many others told me, the decisive moment in a family's rise was when they became sufficiently locally powerful to get into a political party as a candidate, and on that basis to get a government job – 'after that, they can make their fortunes by corruption'.

In Sindh and southern Punjab, most of the important political families are old, with a minority of newcomers. In northern Punjab, it tends to be the other way round. However, in a great many ways these new families tend to merge into established 'feudal' patterns of power. Just as with the English aristocracy and gentry of the past, this is partly through inter-marriage. Some of the greatest aristocratic families of Punjab turn out on examination to be intermarried with new business dynasties.

As in England, this is partly because of the immense social and cultural prestige attached to owning land – something which has defined the identity and self-image not only of the 'feudal' classes, but of the landowning tribes and clans from which they spring. Above all, however, the new families tend to become 'feudal' because the system requires them to follow the same kind of political strategies, based on strong kinship groups and the factions built around them, and the gathering and maintenance of support through patronage and protection.

On the other hand, urbanization and economic development have given ordinary people in much of northern and central Punjab greater opportunities to exploit the system for their advantage. The power of the really big landowners and tribal chiefs has been much reduced, and has shifted to lower and much more numerous strata of rival landowners and local bosses. This gives people more chance to extract benefits by switching between them. Urbanization has also reduced the role of kinship, though not as greatly as standard models predict.

A combination of the weakness of the state and the power of kinship is one critical reason why urbanization has had a much smaller impact on political patterns and structures than one might otherwise have expected. For in the cities, albeit not as much as in the countryside, you also need protection from the police, the courts and politically linked urban gangs.

Moreover, rather than a new urban population emerging, what we have seen so far is huge numbers of peasants going to live in the cities while remaining culturally peasants. They remain deeply attached to their kinship groups, and they still need their kinship groups to help them for many of the same reasons they needed them in the countryside. Underlying all this is the fact that so much of the urban population remains semi-employed or informally employed, rather than moving into modern sectors of the economy – because these usually do not exist.

How kinship works politically in the cities was well summed up by a young office worker whom I asked in 1988 how he intended to vote in the forthcoming elections. He was from central Karachi, but of Punjabi origin:

> I voted PPP in the last elections because it was the will of my uncle, the head of our family, though actually I think the Muslim League has done a better job in government. In previous elections, sometimes he said to vote PPP, sometimes Muslim League, depending on what they promise him, whether they have fulfilled promises in the past, and which of his friends or relatives is now important in that party. He owns a flour mill. He helps us find jobs, gives us the transport to take us to the polling booths, so it is natural that we give him our vote in return. He is respected because of his wealth and because his mother and aunt are the two eldest ladies in our family. Everyone listens to them on family matters. They arrange marriages and settle quarrels. They are very much respected, so uncle is too. But he decides in political matters. The women can't do that because they don't go out of the house. They can't even remember which candidate is which. If you ask them the next day, they have forgotten which is which. That is why we have symbols for parties. They can't read or write, so we tell them about politics. But I must obey my mother in all personal things. If she had said I can't take up this job, then I can't.

It is also worth noting that, as this passage reflects, while women play no role in the outward political behaviour of the family or clan, they are central and can even be dominant when it comes to its internal politics and the balance of prestige and power between its members. If this appeared in public, it would be a matter of shame and ridicule; but as long as it remains within the extended family, family *izzat* (honour, or prestige) is not threatened.

Anecdotal evidence (which you would be ill advised to ask about in detail) suggests that this can also sometimes be true of sexual relationships. In common with the traditions of the Jat caste from which many Punjabi Muslims were converted, an affair which, if it took place with an outsider, would be punished with death or mutilation, may be tacitly or even explicitly condoned if it is with a close relative by marriage. Or as a Punjabi saying has it, 'the honour of the family remains within the family.'

As the above account brings out, kinship remains of immense importance even among educated people in Pakistan's cities, if only because in the case of fairly recent migrants (i.e. most people), the ties to ancestral villages remain firm. For that matter, as described in the Introduction, these ties stay strong even when the migration was not to a Pakistani city but a British one, and took place fifty years earlier.

Some of the ways in which the political traditions of the countryside continue to pervade the cities, while also having been changed by them, were illustrated for me by a series of interviews with ordinary people and political workers in the chief Potwari city of Rawalpindi in the summer of 2009. In the 1950s, Rawalpindi's population was still less than 200,000. The building of Islamabad nearby, however, together with the enormous growth of the Pakistani army, whose GHQ is in Rawalpindi, meant that it grew even faster than other cities; according to the census of 2006 its population then was just over 3 million. The overwhelming majority of its inhabitants therefore are migrants from the countryside or their children.

One of these recent migrants with whom I talked was Mudassar, a taxi driver from the nearby area of Gujjar Khan, belonging to the Alpial clan or *biradiri* of the Rajputs. He was illiterate, and gave his age as 'about twenty-two, I think', but he had a humorous thinker's mouth under his big moustache. In the last elections, he had worked as a driver for the campaign of PPP politician Raja Pervez Ashraf – a small piece of local kinship patronage. Pervez Ashraf is a leading local Rajput landlord, businessman and politician who became Minister for Water and Power in the new government. Because of its role in local patronage, this is one of the most politically important jobs in government. I asked Mudassar why he had supported Pervez Ashraf. 'Because he paid me,' he replied (very courteously stifling the obvious temptation to add 'you idiot'):

> And also because he is from the same Rajput *biradiri* as my family, and my family and most of my village voted for him. We still support Raja Pervez Ashraf, though we are not happy with Zardari and the PPP government in general ... Because after the elections he has brought new roads to our area and laid the first gas pipelines, which we have never had before though we are so close to Islamabad. And he shows us respect. Every week he comes to our village or a neighbouring village to meet us and hear our complaints, and to give us moral support. If someone is facing a court case or has trouble with the police, he helps us.

I asked him whether Raja Pervez Ashraf being an Alpial Rajput meant that Mudassar's family and village would always vote for him no matter what. 'Of course not,' he replied:

> If Raja Pervez Ashraf does not act justly towards us, and take care of the poor people of Gujjar Khan as he promised, and if he doesn't come to us to show respect and listen to us, then we will vote for someone else ... Yes, we will always vote for a Rajput, but there are other Rajput leaders in Gujjar Khan.[12]

This reminded me of a famous remark by a Pakistani 'feudal' landowner summing up the changes in electoral politics since the 1950s: 'Once, I used to send my manager to tell my tenants to vote the way I wanted. Then, I had to go myself to tell them to vote how I wanted. Now, I have to go myself to ask them to give me their vote.'[13] Or, in the words of Amir Baksh Bhutto, son of Mumtaz Ali Bhutto and cousin of Benazir: 'We're the biggest landowning family in Sindh' (by most accounts it's actually the Jatois, but still). 'If the *waderos* still had absolute power do you think I'd be driving through this bloody desert, begging people to give me their vote? I'd sit at home, wouldn't I, and wait for people to come and present themselves.'[14]

It would not necessarily be correct to see this as a wholly new phenomenon, reflecting growing 'modernity'. To some extent, it may also be a new version of a very old pattern familiar from late-feudal Europe and many other systems, whereby great local families rise or decline according to fortune, the characters of their leaders, their choice of allegiances, and their ability to cement local alliances and retain local loyalties in the face of rival lords seeking to draw their followers away. As the British *Gazetteer* of 1930 for Attock District records of one great lineage which had failed to do this,

> Gradually the great power of the Pindigheb family was frittered away. First the Langrial family was allowed to secede. Then the Khunda, Kamlial and Dandi families broke away . . . During this troubled time the ruling family contained no men of power. The chiefs were lazy, licentious and incompetent and from a love of ease let great opportunities slip past. But they are still the nobility of the *tehsil*.[15]

A POLITICIAN'S LIFE

As these remarks suggest, Pakistani politicians now have to work very hard for their votes. In many ways, they have to work much harder than their Western equivalents, because 'here, everything is politics', as I have often been told. This does not just mean court cases, bank loans, police and civil service appointments, contracts, and so on; but also most of social life – births and funerals are very important events for political deal-making and alliance-maintenance, and, as for the arrangement of marriages, this is of course inherently political. All this is like enough to the existence of lords in the European Middle Ages – with the difference that Pakistani politicians also have to try to master much more complicated matters of administration and business; and usually try unsuccessfully. Those rare ones who have the education to do so may not have the time. The sheer amount of *time* required to perform the necessary functions of a Pakistani politician – including those in office – may be one factor behind the poor quality of Pakistani government.

Part of this is an even more intensive version of the obligation incumbent on many Pakistanis (and especially Pathans) to attend all the births, marriages and funerals even of distant relatives – all of which have a 'political' aspect within the family, and therefore potentially at least in wider politics as well. As numerous friends have complained, this is crushingly exhausting and time-consuming even for people with no political ambitions; but a failure to turn up to the marriages or funerals even of very distant cousins will be taken as an insult which will severely affect future relations.

Then there is the time consumed by the workings of the patronage system. Iqbal Akhund, a bureaucratic observer of the creation of the PPP-led government in 1988, remarked that:

> Ministers were besieged in their homes from morning till night by petitioners, job-hunters, favour-seekers and all and sundry. It was the same inside the National Assembly, where every minister's seat was a little beehive with members and backbenchers hovering around and going back and forth with little chits of paper. How the ministers got any work done is a mystery, but in any case policy took a back seat to attending to the importunities of relatives, friends and constituents.[16]

Twenty years later, in the summer of 2009, a businessman from Multan described to me a recent dinner given by the Multan Chamber of Commerce in honour of the Foreign Minister, Makhdoom Shah Mahmood Qureshi, who is a member of a leading *pir* family from Multan:

> As soon as the speeches were over and people went to the buffet, Shah Mehmood was besieged by people wanting things:
>
> 'Oh, Qureishi Sahib, my nephew has been arrested on a false murder charge, you are such a great man, it will take one phone call from you only.'
>
> 'Oh, Minister Sahib, you remember that business about a loan, still they are making trouble.'
>
> 'Oh, Makhdoom Sahib, you promised to help my brother with promotion in his department, but he has been passed over. The minister, he is your good friend. Please call him, my family will be so grateful.'
>
> And you know, if these are important local people who have helped him in the past, or close relatives, then he will have to help them – or he will have no political future in Multan. And if it is a difficult case with other influential interests involved, or an important position, then he won't be able to depute it to his staff. In order to show respect all round and get the result, he will have to make the call himself. And so here we are in the middle of a really dreadful international crisis for Pakistan, and our Foreign Minister will be spending half his time dealing with things which in a properly run country wouldn't be his business at all, instead of doing his real job for Pakistan.

Being a politician in Pakistan therefore has its particular strains; yet, on the other hand, since every major landowner needs to attract and keep followers, deter rivals and maintain influence over the administration, in many ways every landowner is a politician. To be successful at this requires particular qualities, as described to me by a banker from the great Soomro landowning family in Sindh in 1990:

> You need a strong family or tribe behind you, and you also need to play a role in politics, so as to gain influence over the government, the police and the courts. When you grow up, you decide or it is decided for you whether you will go into politics. There is no fixed rule in the great families which son or cousin should go into politics. Junaid is my youngest brother. It depends on who seems best suited to it. But someone always has to.
>
> Me, I'm not suited to it. I like a regular life as a banker, getting up at eight to go to the office, coming back at six. Junaid can be woken up at 1 a.m. any night by one of our tenants or followers: 'Sir, I have a problem with the police' – and of course every one wants precedence. You have to be always on call, and you have to judge person by person who to help, and how much to help, and how quickly. Some friends will wait and stay your friends, others not. It's a disorganized kind of game, and everything depends on circumstances. You also have to be patient and careful. Many are not suited to it. You need to have the right temperament and like the game to succeed at it and if, like me, you give it up, sometimes you miss it, like a drug.
>
> And the power of single lords or landowning families is now fading. You also need to attach yourself to a party, with some kind of ideology. Then even when you are in opposition you will still have friends in the bureaucracy, and your enemies will remember that you may be in government again, and will be more careful with you.
>
> But going into party politics also makes the game even more dangerous, because when the government changes you can be imprisoned, or even killed. The brothers in my family are a surgeon, a banker, a lawyer and a politician, and we've all gone to jail. You have to be motivated to do this – standing in chains before a military judge, for fifteen straight days. The people of our class are not usually tortured, but a selected few are. More common is murder, which can be blamed on criminals. And then there is mental torture – fake executions, waking you up repeatedly at night. But

there is this to be said for it: it hardens you. And life in this country is difficult whatever you do, so there is no room for weaklings.[17]

So while Pakistani politicians in general get a pretty bad press, and deservedly so, it is sometimes possible to feel sorry for them. They are often not saints, but they often need the patience of saints, as well as the courage of wolves, the memory of elephants and the digestion of crocodiles.[18] This last requirement was brought back to me by my last political journey with a Pakistani politician, in Sindh in the spring of 2009.

My host was one of the Bhuttos – in fact the hereditary chief of the Bhutto tribe, Sardar Mumtaz Ali Bhutto. He is a cousin of the late Benazir, but no love is lost between the two branches of the family. Mumtaz Ali was chief minister of Sindh in the first years of Zulfikar Ali Bhutto's administration but, in a familiar pattern, was forced to resign when it seemed that he might become a rival. Since then, he has headed his own small and moderately Sindhi nationalist political party, and was only briefly Chief Minister again in the caretaker government of 1996–7.

Yet his lands and wealth, his name, his status, his personal prestige and the faint possibility – even at the age of seventy-six – that he might once again hold senior office mean that he is still a force to be taken into account by other local politicians. Also of importance is the fact that he has an able and energetic eldest son, so that it is clear that the dynasty is not going to fade, and that by helping him people are stockpiling potential reciprocal benefits for the future.

Small though his party is, my travels with him had something of the air of a minor triumphal procession, with delegations coming to meet his convoy in towns and villages, throwing rose petals over his landcruiser, chanting his slogans and bowing to kiss his hand, and children running out for the free *tamasha* (show). For a while we were accompanied by an escort of young men on motorbikes and scooters waving the party flag. This took me back to the great motorized cavalcades of past election campaigns in Pakistan that I had covered; and, looking even further back, one could almost glimpse through the clouds of dust turbaned and helmeted riders on horseback, with pennants waving from their lances.

A rather macabre, but absolutely typical aspect of our progress to the Sardar's ancestral estate was that it was repeatedly interrupted by condolences. Three times we called on local landowning and political families whose patriarchs had just died. In Europe, for an uninvited guest like me to intrude on private grief in this way would seem grossly insensitive, but these events are anything but private. They are in fact a central part not just of social life but also of political life, an occasion to demonstrate political loyalty or at least connections, to see and be seen. Not, however, to talk. It took me a long time during my first stay in Pakistan to get used to gatherings of men sitting in dead silence, broken only by the occasional murmurs of the eldest son and the chief guest. The movement of jaws is not for speech, but for food – and such food! As Mumtaz Ali Bhutto told me:

> If you want to keep well fed in the countryside here, just keep going to condole with people; and if you are a politician you have no choice anyway. This is supposed to be a purely private journey not a political one, but you see how it is. If this were an election campaign, we'd have been offered twelve meals a day. The trick is to nibble just a little bit everywhere.

Meanwhile, I studied the decor of the houses we visited, an amazing mixture of exquisite old-style local taste, appalling Western taste and what might best be described as contemporary Bollywood Neo-Moghul stage-set taste. With summer fast approaching, all the curtains were drawn against the heat and glare outside, so that the rooms were lit only by glaring strip-lights. Throughout Pakistan, this gives most homes – even some of the most luxurious ones – the curious impression of third-class cabins in the bowels of a cruise ship.

Some of the decor was not conducive to maintaining gravity. One of my favourite items was an enormous toy tiger sitting on a table in the middle of a drawing-room where we had gathered to condole. Its eyes looked directly into mine – glassily, but not much more so than those of the other guests, who also gave a strong impression of having been stuffed. As the respectful silence wore on and on, I was seized by an almost irresistible desire to offer the creature some kebab and try to strike up a conversation.

Even more impressive was the bedroom of the eldest son and political heir of another mournful house, where the guests of honour were ushered to use his toilet. The room contained only two furnishings: an enormous neo-rococo bed decorated with huge bunches of flowers, fruit and ostrich feathers, all painted in imitation gold leaf; and, hanging over the bed, an equally enormous photograph of the young politician himself.

This too was obviously a room for official entertainment, a local version of Louis XIV; but who on earth, I wondered, could possibly be the local version of Madame de Maintenon?

It would be a grave mistake, however, to laugh at the *waderos* of Sindh. As the chapter on Sindh will demonstrate, they are very much in control of their own society, and look like remaining so for the foreseeable future. The secret of their success is a mixture of wealth and the deference ensured by their status as clan chiefs, local hereditary religious figures, or a mixture of the two. One local landowner we visited seemed barely above the level of the larger peasants in terms of wealth, living in a bleak concrete house with bare concrete walls and floors; yet he turned out to be a *pir*, and a significant political influence in the local Shia community.

THE MEDIA

In the twenty years between my stay in Pakistan in the late 1980s and the writing of this book, by far the most important change on the Pakistani political scene (other than the rebellion of the Pakistani Taleban) has been the proliferation of television and radio stations during Musharraf's period in power. By 2009 there were around eighty Pakistani TV channels, twelve exclusively for news and current affairs. Indeed, several middle-class people said to me that 'news has become our entertainment', though they admitted that this was probably the effect of novelty and would sooner or later wear off. Five channels were devoted to religion.

In the 1980s, Pakistani television was completely state-controlled and was of a quite excruciating dullness (as indeed was state TV in India). Newspapers and magazines were the main sources of news and analysis, but, although they had occasional lively discussions and sometimes exposed scandals, their journalists were hopeless at following up and researching stories.

Musharraf had good cause to curse the media he had allowed to form. In the later years of his rule it was above all due to the support of some of these channels – notably Geo, a branch of the Jang media group – that the Lawyers' Movement gathered public support and even briefly became something like a mass movement. This alliance of journalists and lawyers gave many people the idea that a new middle-class political force that might transform the political system had been forged in Pakistan; or, at the very least, that the media would play a critical role in making and breaking governments, reducing the traditional role of kinship and patronage.

In 2008–9, however, liberal intellectuals and their English-language media outlets (like the *Friday Times* and *Daily Times* of Lahore) turned against much of the rest of the new media, accusing them of sympathy for the Taleban and bias against the PPP administration of President Zardari. There was much muttering among liberals of my acquaintance about establishment conspiracies to manipulate the media, and about the way in which Musharraf had created a 'Frankenstein's Monster'.

The error of the liberals and many Western analysts was to forget that, in the words of Dr Mosharraf Zaidi, 'Pakistan's media is guilty of being a microcosm of the society that it reports on, reports for and reports to. It is a reflection and an extension of Pakistan at large.'[19] Liberals had assumed that a new media, dominated by educated middle-class people, would inevitably therefore reflect liberal and (by implication) pro-PPP and pro-Western positions.

This ignored the fact that a very considerable portion of the educated middle class is conservative and even Islamist by sympathy; as noted in the chapter on religion, the Jamaat Islami has long had a determined and rather successful strategy of targeting universities, partly precisely in order later to get its students into influential professions like the media. As Imran Aslam, head of Geo, told me:

> When in the '90s I started *The News* as Pakistan's first desktop publication, my print media colleagues and I didn't have a clue about the technology involved. We had Apples sitting on the desks and we didn't know what to do with them. We had to hire people to help. And you know what? The only people we could find were from the Jamaat Islami. They'd been trained in the '80s with CIA and ISI help to support the Afghan Mujahidin with propaganda. So the people who the liberals see as Yahoos were explaining to the media elites what hotmail was.[20]

Even more importantly, the middle classes and the journalists among them are just as suffused with hostility to the US and its presence in Afghanistan as the rest of society. Depressingly, this has also meant that I have heard as many cretinous conspiracy theories about America from journalists as from ordinary Pakistanis – indeed more, because the journalists' background gives them more raw material with which to weave their fantasies. In fairness, however, I must say that liberal journalists are just as bad, with the difference that their baroque conspiracy theories are directed at the army.

The media are therefore a microcosm of the Pakistani middle classes, and reflect their views. One sign of this is television's approach to religion. Many liberals are horrified by the number of religious programmes on TV – though as of 2009 this is only five out of around eighty, which is roughly the US proportion. It is equally true that Jamaati supporters with whom I have spoken have been horrified by the content of many of these programmes.

This is partly because of a response to audience wishes and the strong element of popular religion, involving the worship of saints and other 'Hindu superstitions'. It is also because, owing to privately owned television's innate need for controversy and excitement, a considerable amount of debate and disagreement about religion appears on TV – once again, accurately reflecting the conflicting views of Pakistani society, but infuriating the orthodox. I was told about (though haven't been able to trace) one lively exchange on a phone-in programme on religious rules when a Sunni cleric told a woman that it was sinful to paint her nails, and his Shia colleague asked him why, in that case, he himself was dyeing his beard!

It was indeed surprising that middle-class journalists from classes which generally have a traditional reverence for the army (if only because so many of their relatives are officers) should have turned against the Musharraf administration so radically in 2007–8 – especially since they had generally begun by supporting him. This can be partly be explained by a genuine middle-class respect for the law and desire to defend the independence of the judiciary; but it can also be explained by the fact that respect for the army is closely connected with nationalism. As in the judiciary itself, Musharraf's perceived subservience to the US and obedience to 'US orders to kill his own people' had already begun to cripple his prestige with the middle classes before the Lawyers' Movement rose against him. The same perception of being 'America's slave', together with corruption, explains the growing hostility of much of the media to the Zardari administration in 2009–10.

This hostility to the US, rather than extremist feeling as such, explains the rather shocking toleration for the Pakistani Taleban shown by much of Pakistani television up to the spring of 2009. This did not take the form of outright propaganda, but rather of playing interviews with Taleban spokesmen, and military or official interviews, on an equal basis and without commentary; and, in the reporting of terrorist acts, of frequent references to conspiracy theories which might excuse the Taleban from responsibility.

This was not a matter of cynical manipulation – as far as I can see, from a great many interviews with journalists, they believed these theories implicitly themselves. There was therefore a reciprocal effect, with the media sucking up public prejudices and playing them back to the public, strengthening them in the process. In the spring of 2009, however, there was a real change. The military did some tough talking to media owners and journalists, and thereafter most of the media have been much more supportive of the campaign against the Pakistani Taleban – while continuing, like the rest of society, to oppose action against the Afghan Taleban.

As to the media's future role in politics, there are two key issues: mass mobilization, and the righting of wrongs. On the first, television is indeed likely to play an important part in encouraging various kinds of protest and stirring up support for movements against the alleged crimes of unpopular and dictatorial regimes. However, if the past is anything to go by, this may just as well be against civilian as military regimes.

On the exposure of wrongs, the media have indeed played an increased role. When it comes to justice for wrongs, the media's ability is naturally limited to its capacity to embarrass, since punishment is a matter for the government, the police and the courts. Thus, I heard of a case in northern Sindh where three young 'feudals' had raped a nurse in a local clinic. On the insistence of her colleagues, the police arrested the youths concerned. Of course, I was told by a local journalist,

> Their political relatives got them released again very quickly, and they will never go to jail for what they did. But in the meantime the media had filmed them handcuffed in the police station. So at least their families were embarrassed, and maybe that meant they gave them a damned good beating when they got home.

On the other hand, despite extensive media coverage, the criminals in the monstrous case of the rape of Mukhtar Mai and persecution of her family, and the burial of girls alive in Balochistan (described in Chapter 9), have not been brought to justice years after the event, because of the political power of those responsible.

The use of the media to embarrass politicians could also become a weapon of political misinformation and attack between different parties, factions and individuals. This has always been the case on a small scale but the new force of television vastly increases the possibilities. The media as weapon (though, in this case, of legitimate self-defence) was brought home to me by a Christian journalist friend in one of the rougher parts of Pakistan. He had got into a parking dispute with the followers of a notoriously ruthless local chieftain. I asked him whether this wasn't dangerous, especially given the way in which Christians in the area had been persecuted. No, he replied, because the Sardar and his men knew that he was a journalist and a friend of the other leading journalists of the area. 'We journalists stick together and defend each other. So if they did anything to me, stories about all the bad things he and his family have done would be all over television, the papers and radio.'

It is still too early to say whether the new media form a really important new force, or whether they will only be a new element of the old scene, and will essentially be ingested by the traditional system – as has happened to so many forces before them. At the very least, though, the media are encouraging a wider range of people to think and talk about public issues than has been the case in the past – which is presumably a good thing, depending on what they think and say.

THE PAKISTAN PEOPLE'S PARTY (PPP)

As you drive towards the Sindhi town of Larkana from the north, a shining white lump appears on the flat face of the plain and gradually grows to enormous dimensions. It is the mausoleum of the local Bhutto family of landowners and tribal chieftains, who in recent decades have made an impact considerably beyond their ancestral territory. Reflecting this impact, the mausoleum is a squatter but possibly even bigger version of the Taj Mahal in gleaming white marble. It is built over the site of the ancient Bhutto family graveyard, and was started under the first government of Benazir Bhutto after 1988 as a monument to her executed father. Now she rests there herself.

The mausoleum is arranged on two levels. When it is finished, the upper one, under the huge dome, is supposed to be for the general public; the lower one, containing the actual tombs, will be for VIP visitors only. But perhaps one should say *if* it is finished, rather than when; for it has a curious look of having been designed to be a ruin. As of mid-2009, after twenty years of construction repeatedly interrupted by the PPP being ousted from government, both levels were unfinished, with scaffolding everywhere, the floors a patchwork of rough concrete and uneven, badly laid marble slabs, the stairs uneven to the foot, and heaps of unused building materials lying around. The mixture of pomp and shoddiness made a depressing contrast with the beautiful carvings and calligraphy of the older Bhutto tombs.

On the walls of the basement, posters proclaim the allegiance of various PPP politicians and would-be politicians. One, from Pervaiz Menon, head of a PPP chapter in the US, read:

> Once Athens bled and mourned death for Socrates, twice the persecution of beloved Bhuttos, for his death transcends the greatest tragedy in Asian history ... The integration of human sufferings begins within a promise to conquer the unknown, the unleashed giant.

Whatever that was supposed to mean. But as so often in South Asia, solemnity is not really the local style. I spoke harshly to my guide about his lighting a cigarette beside the tombs, but my concern for decorum was quite unnecessary. As at some of the shrines described in the chapter on religion, extended families were picnicking among the tombs, their small children running around squeaking, and sometimes competing in jumping over the smaller graves: in the midst of death we were in life.

Outside the mausoleum is a scene which also exactly recalls the shrines of saints (and the Catholic Mediterranean): a small hamlet of stalls selling quasi-religious memorabilia mixed with cheap toys and jewellery, and with the local equivalent of hymns – speeches by the various Bhuttos – booming over loudspeakers. Also familiar from shrines everywhere is another reputed use of the mausoleum – as a discreet meeting-place for lovers.

None of this is specific to the Bhuttos or Pakistan. South Asia is a region of hereditary political dynasties: the Nehrus-Gandhis in India, the Bandaranaikes in Sri Lanka, and the rival families of Sheikh Hasina and Begum Khaleda Zia in Bangladesh. The violent nature of South Asian politics means that most of these dynasties have their martyrs:

Mrs Gandhi and her son Rajiv in India, the father of Sheikh Hasina and husband of Khaleda Zia, and of course Zulfikar Ali Bhutto and his daughter Benazir.

These dynasties have proved extraordinarily resilient. They have survived the violent deaths of their leading members, repeated failures in government, repeated failures to deliver on promises to the masses and, in many cases, the abandonment of whatever genuine ideology they ever possessed.

This reflects at a higher level the kinship allegiances which permeate most South Asian political societies; and the fact that, in most cases, these societies have not developed classes and groups that can generate parties based on ideology and mass organization rather than on family allegiance. As a PPP politician, Aftab Shaban Mirani, told me in 1990, 'It is impossible to destroy the PPP. Individual politicians can be split from it, but the nucleus will always remain the house of Zulfikar Ali Bhutto.'[21]

Most of Pakistan's parties, large and small, are led by dynasties. None of the others however – not even the Sharifs, described in the next section – approaches the monarchical atmosphere surrounding the Bhuttos. I had a taste of this back in 1988 at a press conference with the new Minister of State for Information, Javed Jabbar. The words 'grace' and 'gracious' tripped from his lips so often that they came to seem like royal titles – which in a way is exactly what they were:

> After eleven years of darkness, a woman leader has come to power who is brave, bright, brilliant, gracious, to overthrow the forces of darkness. I would like to thank the Prime Minister for her most gracious act in appointing me to the ministry . . . Thanks to her, every few days there is a moment which will become historic. I am privileged to have sat in the first cabinet meeting led by a woman Prime Minister, which she presided over with her customary grace . . .[22]

This was not personal sycophancy so much as general party style, which tends to be overripe even by the flavourful standards of South Asia. A book by a PPP supporter, *The Ideals of Bhutto*, reads in part as follows:

> What is Bhuttoism? It is a clarion call to establish a welfare democratic state. It is the power of people. It is an enlightened, modern, moderate and egalitarian society. It is the end of religious extremism, sectarianism, parochialism and terrorism . . .

Jeeay Bhutto [Long Live Bhutto, or Victory to Bhutto] is a banging slogan raising the dead to life. It awakens the slumbered souls. It has a meaning. Long live Bhutto signifies his unending mission. This mission can never die. It is a permanent principle of paramount importance. It reminds us of democracy. It cuts the roots of fascism. It severs the branches of feudalism, militarism and mullahism . . .[23]

Benazir Bhutto herself described the slogan as follows:

Jeeay Bhutto. It's a lovely word. It's warm and wonderful. It lifts the heart. It gives strength under the whip lash . . . It means so much to us, it drives us on. It makes us reach for the stars and the moon.[24]

As described in Chapter 1, the basic elements of the party's style and image were established by Zulfikar Ali Bhutto, with his combination of a populist appeal to the masses in politics with the personal style of a rich Westernized aristocrat. This combination was not originally hypo-critical, for Bhutto had a love–hate relationship with his own 'feudal' class. However, as far as the landowners were concerned, his initial brief radicalism did not last long and was soon replaced by political alliances with great 'feudal' families in Sindh and southern Punjab.

Not merely was it naturally out of the question for members of this class to pursue economically progressive agendas on the part of the PPP, but the nature of their local power also made it impossible for them to support socially progressive agendas (especially in the area of women's rights), even if they had wanted to – since this would have offended the deeply conservative kinship networks on which they depend for support. In fact, the uttermost limit of the progressivism of many PPP land-owner-politicians in this regard is that they keep one younger Westernized wife for public show at their home in Karachi or Lahore – while two or more wives from arranged marriages with first cousins are kept firmly in purdah back on their estates.

A Sindhi PPP leader whom I interviewed in 1990, Dr Ashraf Abbasi (a doctor by profession), was candid about the political realities:

We have no choice but to adopt candidates like U. Khan and A. T. [names disguised for obvious reasons], though of course we know that they are both murderers. Who else can we work with here in the interior of Sindh? Of course we don't want them, when we have good, loyal party workers on hand. But the voters themselves support them and demand that we take them, because they are the heads of powerful clans and because people here respect men who have *danda* [armed force; literally a cudgel]. So we have to think which candidates can pull in votes along these lines. All the same, it is only the PPP of all the parties which can mobilize voters at all along any other lines than *biradiri*, tribes, force and money.[25]

The PPP still contains middle-class professional party workers like Dr Abbasi – for example, the former president of the Sindh party, Taj Haider, and the president of the Punjab party (as of 2010), Rana Aftab Ahmed. Without men like this to hold together some party organization, the party could not have survived its long years out of power.

However, as far as rural Sindh is concerned, nothing has changed in the PPP over the past twenty years – because, as later chapters will recount, little has changed in the economy, society, culture and politics of the Sindhi countryside, which is the PPP's most essential base. For example, as of 2010, the PPP Federal Education Minister, Azar Khan Bijrani, a Sindhi tribal chief and landowner, had been charged in the Supreme Court because a tribal jirga over which he presided had handed three minor girls over in marriage to another tribe as part of the settlement of a dispute; but the case against him had been suspended indefinitely.

The tribal court of another local sardar and PPP politician, Abid Husain Jatoi, had declared that a Jatoi girl and a Soomro man who eloped together should both be killed. The Sindh High Court intervened to protect them, but the resulting scandal did not prevent Jatoi from becoming Provincial Minister of Fisheries and Livestock. None of this differed in any way from the stories I had heard about PPP ministers and other politicians during my visits to the province more than twenty years earlier.[26]

As a journalist in the Bhutto stronghold of Larkana said to me, with commendable restraint: 'It is surprising for the civil society of Pakistan that people like this are inducted into the federal and provincial cabinets.' This is not to say that the PPP is any worse in this regard than the other parties – but it is also no better. Such behaviour is part of the stuff of local society in Sindh (and most other regions of Pakistan as well) and has continued unchanged under both civilian and military governments.

Despite all this, a certain romance between the Bhuttos and many

Pakistanis has continued. As far as the poor are concerned, a journalist friend told me, it is because

> Zulfikar Ali Bhutto is the only Pakistani leader who has ever spoken to the poor as if they mattered, and made them feel that they mattered. No one else has done that. So though in fact he did little for them, and Benazir nothing at all, they still remember him with respect, and even love, and something of this still sticks to the Bhutto name.

But for many ordinary Pakistanis, the identification between Z. A. Bhutto's heroic image and that of the Pakistan People's Party, which he founded, was cemented by his death. His daughter Benazir's beauty and combination of feminine vulnerability with personal autocracy confirmed the Bhutto image. Meanwhile, the Westernized intelligentsia (who are tiny in proportion to the population, but influential in the elite media, and in their effect on perceptions in the West) largely stick with the party because they have nowhere else to go, politically speaking – and often, because they have family or marital links to leading PPP families. Sherry Rehman, the PPP Information Minister in 2008–9, gave me her reasons for supporting the party, which are those of many educated women I have met (excluding the bit about helping the poor, which most no longer bother to claim):

> I am with the PPP because it is the only mainstream federal party that has consistently maintained the secular ideals of Mohammed Ali Jinnah. And the PPP addresses first the needs of the oppressed, poor, vulnerable and minorities including women. The party was led by a woman who gave her life for her ideals, and women in the party are regularly involved in top decision-making. This is a major appeal for women. The PPP is the only party which has not been ambiguous about their rights.[27]

The question facing the party after Benazir's assassination is whether it can survive the leadership of her distinctly less charismatic widower, Asif Ali Zardari (who is also of course not a Bhutto by blood) – at least long enough for their son or daughter to grow up and inherit the family mantle. Zardari had never held any party position, and inherited the co-leadership of the party (jointly with their underage son Bilawal, born in 1988 and so aged twenty in 2008) in the strictest sense of the word inherited – according to the terms of Ms Bhutto's will, the original of which neither the party nor the public was allowed to see!

As of 2010, Zardari was widely viewed by PPP politicians and party workers as a potentially disastrous liability, owing to the circumstances of his inheritance, a lack of legitimacy stemming from the fact that he is not a Bhutto, his reputation for kleptocracy, his personal arrogance and his reliance on a coterie of personal friends and advisers rather than on established leading figures in the party. A crushing additional blow was given by his government's miserable record during the floods of 2010, and especially the fact that at the height of the crisis he visited his family's chateau in France rather than returning home to take charge of the relief effort. The eclipse of the 'party stalwarts' has also undermined the party's reputation for physical courage – a highly valued quality in Pakistan – in the face of persecution. This had done much to maintain the party's image.

The unpopularity of Zardari in the PPP is leading to frantic attempts to build up the image of his son Bilawal (who, interestingly, is often described by PPP supporters as if he were Benazir's son only and not Zardari's too). Repeatedly from PPP politicians and workers in Sindh I heard extremely improbable stories about his courage, intelligence, openness to ordinary people, and even close resemblance to Z. A. Bhutto.

Who knows, all of this might even come to be true in future. Bashar al-Assad, Rajiv Gandhi and even more improbably Sonia Gandhi all inherited political positions very much against their will, and for which they appeared completely unsuited – and yet proved good at them. However, the PPP may not have the time. As one PPP female politician said: 'Our problem is that we need Bilawal to grow up ten years in one year, and that isn't physically possible, unfortunately.' As of 2010, because of his parents' exile and his education in the West, Bilawal Bhutto-Zardari does not even speak enough Urdu to give public speeches in that language, let alone in Sindhi; and the ability to give speeches in the language of ordinary people is perhaps the one thing a populist party cannot do without.

However, until 2010 at least, outright revolt against Zardari within the PPP had been kept in check partly by the flow of US aid, some of which he was able to distribute as patronage, but more importantly by the fact that with Benazir's children not yet in a position to succeed, getting rid of him would leave the party with no dynastic leadership at all – at which point it would risk disintegrating altogether as a result of feuds between rival factions.

Zardari aside, the PPP suffers from certain potentially disastrous long-term weaknesses, but also from some enduring strengths. These latter could mean that even if it suffers a crushing defeat at the next elections due in 2013 it may well eventually bounce back again, as it has done several times in the past.

The first PPP weakness is that its socialist policies, on which Z. A. Bhutto founded the party's appeal, have become a completely empty shell, no longer even seriously veiled by populist rhetoric. The PPP is in fact the most distinctly 'feudal' in its composition of any of the major parties. This does not necessarily matter much as long as none of the other parties is offering anything better in terms of economic change, but it does mean that the party has lost a great deal of ground among what used to be a key constituency, the working classes of Punjab. With kinship politics somewhat less important among them, little realistic access to patronage and major cultural differences with the Jamaat Islami, this section of the population does not generally vote for the PPP's opponents, but rather is less and less likely to vote at all. I found this to be true of the workers I met in the great industrial city of Faisalabad, described in the next chapter.

On the other hand, another major Punjabi urban constituency in terms of numbers, the traditional lower middle classes, does vote heavily – and in general votes heavily anti-PPP. It does so because of the traditional hostility of business to the PPP, but even more importantly because this class is the heartland of Deobandi Islamist culture, which tends to detest the Westernized style of the PPP leadership.

If this class grows continuously, at the expense of the rural classes, as a result of urbanization and social change, then the PPP in Punjab may be doomed to inexorable electoral decline. This has already been the case in Lahore. During my stay in the late 1980s the PPP had a great deal of support there, but in 2008 and 2009 it was hard to find a single would-be PPP voter on the street, even in former PPP strongholds.

This is not at all certain, however. As already stressed, because of links to the countryside and because of the informal nature of much of the economy, the growth of urban populations does not necessarily mean the urbanization of culture, or the extension of traditional lower-middle-class culture to the new lower middle classes. What would terribly damage the PPP among these classes as a whole, and indeed among much of the Pakistani population, is if the perception of the Westernized culture of its top leadership becomes permanently linked to a perception of subservience to the US. This would also mark a complete break from the legacy of Z. A. Bhutto, whose popularity was founded on a mixture of populism and ardent nationalism, with a strong anti-American tinge.

As repeatedly emphasized in this book, while radical Islamism in Pakistan is very limited, hostility to the US is overwhelming, even among PPP politicians who are benefiting from US aid. As a PPP member of the National Assembly from Sindh told me in Hyderabad in April 2009:

> We used to be very liberal, pro-Western people, but American behaviour and attitudes are forcing us to develop our own identity, because we cannot simply be your servants. The Taleban are religious fanatics but so is Bush and many Americans. Worst of all, the Americans are forcing us to make mistakes and we are suffering as a result, and yet still they are blaming us for not doing enough. America faced only one 9/11. Due to our helping America, we in Pakistan are now facing 9/11s continuously with so many dead, and American policies are continuously making things worse, killing people, helping the Taleban and spreading disorder . . . Many people here think the reason can only be that the Americans are creating all this disorder deliberately because they want to establish military bases here against China and Iran.

President Zardari's alliance with the US has proved lucrative in terms of aid, but is widely detested by the population. On the other hand, a government of Nawaz Sharif and the PML(N) would probably have little choice but to follow essentially the same policies, so that over time this perception of the PPP might fade.

The PPP also has certain long-term strengths, though they are not those featured in party propaganda. Despite a decline in Punjab, it still remains more of a national party than its chief rival the Muslim League (N), and far more than any other party but the Jamaat – whose limitations have already been described. While the Muslim League in power can always pick up some Sindhi allies by offering patronage to local 'feudals', Sindhi feeling as such has nowhere to go but the PPP unless it is to move into outright rebellion against Pakistan – which most Sindhi politicians do not wish to contemplate, for reasons that will be brought out in the chapter on Sindh. As the Sindhi PPP politician quoted above told me after reciting a litany of complaints about Zardari:

> But even with all the mistakes and even crimes of Zardari, in the interior of Sindh people love the Bhuttos. And anyway, we have no options. Who else can we Sindhis vote for? ... It is also unfair to compare Zardari to Bibi [Benazir Bhutto]. Nobody can compare to her. All the other leaders are pygmies by comparison.

It remains to be seen if anger in Sindh at the PPP government's failure during the floods of 2010 has been enough to shatter this dynastic loyalty.

Finally, the PPP can appeal to members of religious traditions that have reason to fear Sunni Islamist ascendancy, and which see the Muslim League as increasingly associated with Deobandi and Ahl-e-Hadith culture: followers of the Barelvi tradition, devotees of the shrines and of course the Shia. The Bhuttos and Zardaris are both Shia, and many of the leading figures of the party come from *pir* families with strong Shia leanings.

In the past, this has not marked a clear Sunni–Shia split between the main parties. Kinship, personal and factional rivalries divide all Pakistan's religious traditions. The PML(N) contains many Shia and Barelvis, and the Sharifs have been careful to show great respect and support to the leading shrines. However, the savage attacks by the Pakistani Taleban and their Punjabi sectarian allies on shrines in 2010, and the apparent closeness to the sectarians of some of the Sharifs' leading allies, mean that Shia and Barelvis may begin to desert the PML(N), possibly dealing it a heavy blow in certain areas.

The PPP leadership for its part knows very well that it would be crazy to make an openly Shia appeal in an overwhelmingly Sunni country, in which outright, declared Shia (as opposed to devotees of shrines which bridge the Shia–Sunni gap) may be as few as 10 per cent. The Bhuttos, Zardaris and other families therefore follow Sunni rituals in public – in accordance with the old Shia tradition of *taqiyya*, which permits Shia to disguise their real beliefs if threatened with persecution. Nonetheless, the PPP does seem to have a degree of permanent residual support in some minority religious groups – a point to which I will return in the next chapter, on Punjab.

THE PAKISTAN MUSLIM LEAGUE (NAWAZ) (PML(N))

On the whole, however, and for many years now, Pakistani vote swings have been powered less by enthusiasm for the party in opposition than exasperation with the party in power. In other words, the future of the PPP will depend heavily on how its main rivals, the Muslim League of the Sharifs, perform when they are next in government. If the PML(N)'s past record is anything to go by, the PPP will have plenty of opportunities to exploit public discontent. Indeed, anger at the PPP-led national government in Punjab over failures of the flood relief effort in 2010 was to some extent balanced by anger at the PML(N)'s provincial government for the same reason.

When trying to define the identity of the Muslim League, I quoted Benazir Bhutto on the slogan *Jeeay Bhutto* to a Pakistani friend, and asked him what the PML(N)'s equivalent would be. '*Parathas*,' he replied like a shot, referring to the fried flat-bread much loved in Punjab. 'Just listen and you'll hear how right it sounds for them: "Long live *parathas*." It's a lovely word. They're warm and wonderful. They lift the heart . . .'

This is of course a shockingly frivolous comment, and I sincerely hope that no Pakistani reader is so utterly lost to political seriousness as to laugh at it. This joke was, however, also intended to make a serious point concerning one of the greatest strengths and greatest weaknesses of the PML(N), namely their strongly Punjabi character.

It is the party's base in Punjab and in Punjabi sentiment that allowed it to liberate itself from its original military masters and to survive eight years in the political wilderness after Musharraf's coup in 1999. On the other hand, this means that its vote in other provinces has been very limited, and it has never been able to rule in Sindh except through local alliances of opportunist 'feudals'. In the NWFP, however, Sharif's criticism of the US and distancing from the struggle with the Taleban may pay permanent electoral dividends.

Punjabi culture largely explains the particular charismatic appeal of Nawaz Sharif to many ordinary Punjabis, so absolutely incomprehensible to most Western observers and indeed to Pakistani liberal intellectuals. His rough but jovial personal style goes with this, as does the fact that, while frequently wooden and tongue-tied in English, he apparently speaks very effectively in Punjabi.

Leaders of the party like to stress that it had its beginnings in the mass opposition movement to Z. A. Bhutto in 1976, and especially in the outrage of the conservative Punjabi middle classes at Bhutto's socialism, Westernization and autocracy. The self-image of the core PML(N) is therefore of a 'moderate conservative and Muslim, but also modern middle-class party', as the PML(N) Information Secretary, Ehsan Iqbal, put it to me.[28] The key role in putting the Muslim League together in the mid-1980s, and in choosing Nawaz Sharif to run it, was however played by the military administration of Zia-ul-Haq, and the ISI.

Nawaz Sharif (born 1949) and his younger brother Shahbaz are the sons of an industrialist of Kashmiri-Punjabi origin who moved to Pakistan in 1947 (there will be more on the family in the next chapter), and who moved to Saudi Arabia when his industries were nationalized under Z. A. Bhutto. The family's Punjabi middle-class origins, Pakistani nationalism, hatred of the Bhuttos, links to Saudi Arabia and (in the father's case) personal piety all endeared them to Zia. In 1985 Nawaz Sharif was made Chief Minister of Punjab (a position held as of 2010 by Shahbaz), and in 1991 became Prime Minister of Pakistan for the first time.

The Sharifs' business origins and pro-business policies mean that businessmen favour their party. Indeed, every single one I have met has done so, irrespective of whether they have been secular or conservative in their personal culture. This link to business has given the PML(N) a clear edge over the PPP when it comes to economic policy and efficient government in general. As a leading industrialist in Lahore (one of the most cultivated and cosmopolitan figures I have met in Pakistan) told me:

> The PPP have repeatedly chosen very weak economic teams, because they are feudals and populists, while the Sharifs are businessmen by upbringing and have carefully cultivated the business elites. The PPP have not had one good period in government as far as economic policy is concerned; whereas Nawaz Sharif's team has always been good – it was crafted by that old sage Sartaj Aziz. So businessmen certainly trust the Muslim League more. The genesis of this difference is [Zulfikar Ali] Bhutto's brutal nationalization, which left a legacy of distrust for the PPP among businessmen that has never gone away . . .
>
> But we certainly don't have full confidence in the Muslim League. Unfor-

tunately, Nawaz is not the most stable of characters, as his past record in government shows, and his brother is a good number two, a good administrator, but not a leader or visionary. Shahbaz is willing to stay on his feet for sixteen hours straight kicking ass and giving orders, but ask him about an export-led growth strategy and he won't have a clue. Whereas Nawaz does have a kind of vision for Pakistan, but he is impetuous, careless and can be cruel . . .

On the other hand, another reason why businessmen trust Nawaz is that if you cross him as a businessman, he gets annoyed but he does not retaliate against you or your business – against journalists who criticize him on the other hand he can be very harsh. When I publicly criticized his budget in '99 he was very angry but did not loose the police or the income tax authorities on me – there was no case of an out of order tax inspection or the police flagging down my car and so on; the typical pressure tactics here. And I have never heard that he has done this to any other businessmen.

I asked a former minister in Nawaz Sharif's governments of the 1990s to sum up his character. 'Not at all educated but very shrewd, intelligent, determined and courageous. But unfortunately also autocratic, impulsive, reckless and hot-tempered, which has often been his downfall', was the response.

Shahbaz Sharif for his part has had a good personal reputation for efficiency, hard work and personal honesty as Chief Minister of Punjab (while of course employing just the same patronage incentives as everyone else in his political strategy). He also seems to be good at picking and listening to good advisers. He exemplifies something that I have often heard said about the PML(N), in different forms, that 'their real ideology is managerialism'. As with his brother, this goes with a considerable reputation for autocracy and ruthlessness.

The number of 'encounter killings' of criminals by police in Punjab soared after Shahbaz Sharif became Chief Minister in 2008, though I was told that he also gave strict orders that care be taken that only genuinely violent criminals were to be killed. When I interviewed him in Lahore in January 2009, he was impressively briefed on a great many policy issues compared with the PPP ministers I met, some of whom seemed to be wandering through government in a kind of dream, interspersed with purely ritualistic statements about their policies and ideals.

Party representatives like to stress the middle-class nature of the PML(N) as against the 'feudal' Bhuttos. 'Mian Sharif [Nawaz's father] was often called *Mistri* [blacksmith] either as a term of affection or an insult,' I was told. 'But he didn't mind. He used to say, "I am a small man, but God gave me these big hands so that I can work iron."'

Dr Saeed Elahi, a PML(N) member of the Punjab assembly, told me, echoing the Sindhi PPP leader quoted above:

> The middle classes in Punjab see us as their party culturally and in every way; and the poor, well, they think that we have at least brought about some good development for them, more than anything the PPP have ever done. But while the cities have solid PML(N) support and we can choose good middle-class candidates, the countryside is still dominated by *biradiris*, and by feudals, tribal chieftains and *pirs*, so we have no choice but to choose feudals with their own followings.[29]

In most of rural Punjab the party's leaders are therefore close to those of the PPP in terms of social origin, and the PML(N)'s strategy for gaining and keeping support through patronage does not differ significantly from that of the PPP.

The Muslim League, however, have stressed both their moderate Islamist and their nationalist credentials, seeking thereby to contrast themselves with the 'Westernized' Bhuttos. In 2007–10, the Sharifs also distanced themselves from the alliance with the US and the campaign against the Pakistani Taleban, without categorically opposing them. Thus in July 2010, following a Pakistani Taleban attack on the great shrine of Data Ganj Baksh in Lahore which killed forty-five worshippers, Nawaz Sharif echoed Imran Khan in calling for peace talks between the government and the Pakistani Taleban:

> If Washington says it is prepared to talk to the Taliban who are willing to listen, then a similar initiative should also come from Islamabad. We should not only see what decision they [the Western countries] will make about our fate. We should decide our own fate . . . Peace is the priority and for that, ways can be found.[30]

In March 2010 his brother Shahbaz stated publicly:

> General Musharraf planned a bloodbath of innocent Muslims at the behest of others only to prolong his rule, but we in the PML-N opposed his

policies and rejected dictation from abroad and if the Taliban are also fighting for the same cause then they should not carry out acts of terror in Punjab [where the PML-N is ruling].[31]

These statements are an obvious attempt to get the Pakistani Taleban and their allies to stop attacking Punjab and concentrate on other provinces instead. This may not do much for the Sharifs' standing in those provinces, and as of 2010 also does not seem to be working. The PML(N) government's failure to prevent massive terrorist attacks in Punjab may well undermine its prestige as a 'party of law and order', and while many Punjabis with whom I have spoken continued to support talks with the Pakistani Taleban even after they began to attack Punjab, it is not certain that this will continue if they kill more and more innocent people and target such beloved sites as Data Ganj Baksh.

The PML(N)'s support for talks and distancing from the US form part of a strategy, emphasized to me by the PML(N)'s Information Secretary, Ehsan Iqbal, of seeking to undermine both the Pakistani Taleban and the Jamaat Islami by drawing away their supporters into mainstream politics. PML(N) leaders estimate that in the February 2008 elections, which the Jamaat boycotted, 40 per cent of Jamaat voters nonetheless turned up to vote PML(N).

The party is making no visible headway in winning over the violent radicals, who have long since moved beyond the reach of Pakistani mainstream politics. As regards the Jamaat, however, this strategy does seem to have had considerable success; and to judge by my interviews, the soaring popularity of the PML(N) in opinion polls in 2008–9 owed a good deal to the perception that the Sharifs 'would defend Pakistani interests against America, not sell them like Musharraf and Zardari', as a Lahori shopkeeper told me. This perception was also boosting PML(N) popularity in the NWFP, increasing the party's chances of permanently expanding beyond its Punjabi base.

All this has led to fears among Western observers and Pakistani liberals alike that in government the PML(N) will turn Pakistan away from the alliance with the US, and towards a much more Islamist system at home, akin to that introduced by General Zia. There are nevertheless limits to how far the party can go in either of these directions. More perhaps than any other group in Pakistan, the industrialists who support the Sharifs know the disastrous economic costs of a radical break with the US.

Businessmen also know how dependent Pakistan will be on US aid, and, although they will undoubtedly try for greater distance, in the end their policies towards the Afghan Taleban are likely to be much the same mixture as those of Musharraf and Zardari. The Sharifs' business and 'feudal' support also means that unlike the Jamaat and the Taleban they cannot even flirt with ideas of Islamist social and economic revolution.

When they come to power, the Sharifs will also probably continue a tough line against the Pakistani Taleban, along the same lines as their past toughness with sectarian extremists in Punjab (as described in the next chapter). This is not so much a matter of ideology as of a passionate commitment to being in charge and suppressing revolts against their government. When I asked a senior PML(N) figure about whether the party would show any toleration to the spread of Islamist extremism in Punjab, he barked at me:

> This is *our* province, and we mean to keep it that way. We are responsible for government and development here. Apart from anything else, our whole image is built on order and good administration. Of course we are not going to allow any terrorism and disorder by miscreants here, no matter if they say they are doing this in the name of Islam and against America.

Finally, in terms of their personal culture, while the Sharifs are quite far from the Bhuttos, they are also very far from the buttoned-up, puritanical Jamaat, described in Chapter 4 on religion. Close associates have described them as not personally bigoted, and generally relaxed about religion. They like good food, ostentatious luxury and above all women, for whom both brothers have a considerable appetite which they hardly trouble to disguise. They are, however, strict about not drinking alcohol.

This may well seem a hypocritical mixture, but unlike the open Westernization displayed by some of the PPP leadership, and the strict Islamism displayed by the Jamaat, it may be rather close to the basic attitudes of a majority of male Punjabis – who, as described in the next chapter, are also far from puritanical in their basic attitudes to life, while regarding themselves of course as good Muslims and insisting on strict behaviour by their own women. Imran Aslam of Geo described what he called 'the Sharifs' Pakistan' as

Conservative with a small 'c'. It is a form of religion that gives stability and comfort but is not fanatical, and is at peace with itself – unlike our psychologically and culturally tortured liberals, and equally tortured Islamists.[32]

The Punjabi conservative attitude to the Sharifs may therefore be compared to the conservative attitude of the American South to the youthful George Bush's escapades with drugs, alcohol and women (except that the Sharifs are no longer youthful). The fact that they are nonetheless seen as part of the same conservative culture (unlike the democratic 'liberal elites') somehow absolves them from blame. Even Nawaz Sharif's well-publicized affairs with Indian (Muslim) actresses will not do him much harm among most men in a province where so much of the male population watches Bollywood movies and – unless Punjabis are differently constructed from men anywhere else in the world – dream of sleeping with their female stars.

On the other hand, because of this luxurious lifestyle, the elite composition of most of its top leadership, and the basic realities of kinship and patronage politics, the PML(N) stands no chance either of crafting a social and economically reformist agenda for Pakistan, or of transforming itself into a modern mass party. The Sharifs lack the openly monarchical style of the Bhutto-Zardaris, but both brothers are natural autocrats whose autocratic tendencies helped destroy their government and bring about the military coup of 1999.

As in the PPP, there are no internal elections in the PML(N), and everything comes down in the end to choices and decisions by the Sharifs and their advisers. The PML(N) is therefore yet another dynastic party, with the usual problem that the next generation of Sharifs (Shahbaz's son is the heir apparent to the party leadership) are rather unknown quantities in terms of ability – though they are better placed in this regard than the Bhutto-Zardaris.

THE MUTTAHIDA QAUMI MAHAZ (MQM)

The fossilized nature of the PPP and PML is shown up especially starkly by the contrast with Pakistan's only truly modern mass political party, the MQM, which will be further described in Chapter 8. I have included the MQM in this chapter as a counter-example to the other main parties, and because the MQM itself has aspirations to be a national party.

The MQM's character as a middle-class party stems from its ethnic background in the Mohajir population of Karachi and Hyderabad. It has sought to transcend this identity and capitalize on its modern middle-class character to become a progressive party across the whole of Pakistan. It has appealed to the middle classes in the name of progressive (but not anti-capitalist) anti-'feudal' and anti-Islamist (though not of course anti-Islamic) values, against the PPP, the Muslim League and the Jamaat Islami alike.

To this end, in 1997 the MQM dropped its original name of Mohajir Qaumi Mahaz (Mohajir People's Movement) and renamed itself the Muttahida ('United') Qaumi Mahaz, 'in order to further national development and a nationwide campaign against feudal domination'.

This MQM strategy has, however, failed, partly because the social and cultural conditions which produced the MQM in Karachi do not exist in the rest of the country. The other urban middle classes have not been shaken free of traditional kinship allegiances and rural links, as the Mohajirs were shaken free by their exodus from India; and, indeed, with the very partial exceptions of Lahore and Faisalabad, there is no other modern urban centre to support modern urban politics. Equally, the MQM has not been able or willing to transcend its ethnic nature and loyalty, for which it was founded and which has brought it into ferocious conflict with other Pakistani ethnicities.

The MQM's appeal to the mass of Pakistanis may be restricted still further by its strong stand against the Taleban, which reflects a mixture of genuine hostility to Taleban ideology, ethnic hostility to the – allegedly pro-Taleban – Pathans of Karachi, and a strong play for American and British support. The MQM has identified Karachi as an essential route for US and NATO supplies to Afghanistan and is determined to exploit this strategic opportunity to the best of its ability.

The MQM has been in and out of coalition governments, both in Islamabad and in Sindh. Having initially boycotted elections under President Musharraf (himself a Mohajir) as a protest against his military coup (leading to a brief period of renewed Jamaat Islami rule of the city of Karachi), the party later made a deal with him and took control once again of the municipality. At the time of writing, the MQM is in coalition with the PPP and ANP in Sindh, but given its past record there can be no doubt that it will also be willing to enter into coalition with Nawaz Sharif, or indeed anyone else. This in turn means that with the help of the MQM and a sufficient number of opportunist Sindhi 'feudal' politicians, a new government in Islamabad can usually succeed through patronage in putting together a provincial government in Sindh as well.

The MQM demonstrates one of the 'Indo-Pakistani' political trends mentioned in the Introduction: an ethnic political movement which emerged through violence and still intermittently uses great violence against its enemies, and which has had violent clashes with the state, but which also over time has been co-opted by the state through repeated deals and grants of patronage, and which has abandoned its most radical demands. Thus the MQM now never raises its original demand of a separate province of Karachi, knowing that this would make it impossible for even moderate and opportunist Sindhi politicians to form coalitions with the MQM.

It would be quite wrong to see the MQM as just another bunch of corrupt, opportunist and brutal ethnic politicians. They are a remarkable party by any standards, and a very remarkable party indeed for Pakistan. The loyalty of their activists is especially impressive. One of them, Nasir Jamal, a greying, rather intense thirty-four-year-old who joined the party when he was sixteen, described to me how his family had fled first from India to East Pakistan in 1948, and then to Pakistan from the new Bangladesh, and then from the new Bangladesh to Karachi in 1974. 'We felt that we had lost everything twice over and no longer had any country of our own at all.'

> When the MQM was created, there was a crisis of identity for all those like us who had migrated from India. We felt that we had no identity because we had no land of our own, unlike the Sindhis, Punjabis or Pathans. But the MQM gave us our identity, and if I could describe it in one sentence, the MQM is a passion for us. Identity is self-respect, freedom, honour. I now feel that I am also something, that there are some things that are in my hands, that I am helping my community to solve their problems, if only in a small way.[33]

Iftikhar Malik sums up the MQM's leading features as follows:

> [A] comparatively recent, totally urban, predominantly middle-class party with a specific ethnic consciousness, characterized by wider literacy,

meticulous organization, effective propaganda campaigns and an impressive level of youth organization.[34]

He lists their 'inherent weaknesses' as 'personality-centred politicking, factionalism, intolerance towards other ethnic communities, and coercive tactics against the media' (if the latter can be described as a 'weakness' rather than an ugly but effective manifestation of strength). I can confirm much of this from my own observations. Certainly the fear of the MQM on the part of journalists is very striking. Even at the height of the killings in Karachi during my stay in April 2009, it was very difficult to find any explicit criticism of the party in the mainstream media; and time and again, when I interviewed local journalists or analysts, they said that all their words could be 'on the record' – except the bits criticizing the MQM. They were full of stories about how closely the MQM monitored their movements, including supposedly my own during my visit to the city. Some of these stories sounded to me highly paranoid, but they were certainly widespread and believed.

Dr Malik's essay was written in 1995, and fifteen years on a couple more things need to be added. The first is that despite the factionalism of which he speaks, and which has been very evident in the MQM in the past, the party has retained an impressive public unity compared to any other party in Pakistan. One reason for this may be precisely the extraordinary cult of personality that has been created round the figure of Altaf Hussain – while at the same time his absence in London, following an assassination attempt, allows a reasonable degree of autonomy to the second-rank leadership.

The other thing about the MQM that has become more apparent since the 1980s is their capacity for effective and progressive government. Although Karachi has more than doubled in size over the past twenty years, the city has not lapsed into the shambolic misery that many predicted. It is in fact not merely the best-run city in Pakistan (with the possible exception of Faisalabad) but one of the best-run larger cities of South Asia, without the appalling mass poverty that characterizes most Indian and Bangladeshi cities.

Communications and public services have considerably improved under the MQM's municipal government – once again, something to set against the growing violence and misery of the Pathan areas of northern Pakistan. Finally, businessmen in the city confirm that while the MQM is not without corruption, its leaders' corruption is both on a smaller scale and more orderly than that of the leaders of other parties, and sometimes at least is for the party rather than the individual concerned. 'They take, but they deliver,' as one banker put it to me.

The MQM built on its highly disciplined and ruthless student organization – both derived from and modelled on that of the Jamaat – to extend its organization throughout Mohajir society, with the partial exception of the richest and most cosmopolitan elements, which had dominated Karachi politics in the 1950s and 1960s. Unlike any other party – except yet again the Jamaat – women are critical to the MQM's organization, and have indeed kept the party going when its male leadership was in jail or on the run.

Women are especially important in the MQM's social welfare wing, the Khidmat-e-Khalq Foundation, which helps people with everything from repairs to their homes to the education of their children and dowries for their daughters. The party's organization thus permeates Mohajir society. Social work and social organization, at least as much as violence and intimidation, are central to the power and resilience of the party, and its enduring grip on the support of most of the Mohajir population, which has survived all the vicissitudes of the past twenty years and many years out of office. The MQM's professionalism and modernity are reflected in its website, MQM.org, which lists its branches and achievements, as well as providing party videos and songs to actual or potential supporters. The websites of the PPP (ppp.org.pk) and the Muslim League (pmln.org.pk) do not begin to compare. Once again, the MQM and Jamaat (itself largely of Mohajir origin) are the only parties in Pakistan that do this in any systematic way.

Crucial to the nature and success of the MQM's social and political organizations is that they are staffed and led by people of the same origins as those whom they are helping. I visited their local headquarters in north Karachi's sector 11B, responsible for 12,000 MQM members out of a population of around 1.3 million. A small, scrupulously tidy place, well equipped with computers, printers and photocopiers, its walls were lined with ordered files of information on local issues and letters from the population – and with pictures of Altaf Hussain, of which there were no fewer than twelve in one room alone.

The local mayors (*nazims*) who had been invited to meet me seemed a good cross-section of the Mohajir middle classes: an electrical engineer, a salesman for Philips, a software manager and a couple of shopkeepers. Basharat Hasnia, a middle-aged man with a dark, deeply lined, thoughtful face, said:

> The MQM is a party for lower-middle-class people, in a country where most parties are run by feudals. Their representatives are not really elected but selected according to their land, money and clan. The MQM gives us a voice against these people, as well as helping us solve the problems of our own city and neighbourhoods.[35]

MQM leader Altaf Hussain himself is of humble origin, and was once a lower-middle-class student and part-time taxi driver. Apart from his brilliant qualities as an organizer, Altaf Hussain possesses an immense charisma among his followers. This is reflected in the name they have given him: 'Pir Sahib', intended to recall the blind devotion of *murids* to their saint. Oskar Verkaaik quotes the sincere words of a Karachi worker:

> We are like robots. Pir Sahib holds the remote control in his hands. When he tells us, Stand up, we stand. When he says, Sit down, we sit down. We don't use our brain. If we would, we would be divided.[36]

Some of the mystique which surrounds Altaf Hussain – including his public image of austerity and asexuality – recalls Mahatma Gandhi and other Hindu religious-political figures, though he certainly has not practised non-violence. The MQM sometimes refer to themselves as 'the Altafians'. Since he went into exile in 1992 after an assassination attempt on his life, his image has been maintained from London via videos, DVDs and recordings – and may indeed have been maintained all the better by his physical absence.

His charisma has puzzled many non-Mohajir observers, given his dumpy appearance, undistinguished face and high-pitched though oddly compelling voice; but his mass appeal seems to lie precisely in the fact that his is the charisma of the ordinary. Looking at Benazir Bhutto, ordinary Pakistanis felt that they were looking at a great princess who had descended from a great height to lead them. Looking at Altaf Hussain, lower-middle-class Mohajirs feel that they are looking at an exalted version of themselves.

The key to the nature and success of the MQM lies not just in their middle-class composition – for a considerable part of the support of the

PML(N) is made up of the Punjabi middle classes. Equally important is the fact that migration from India shattered the two fundamental and tightly connected building-blocks of the other Pakistani parties: kinship, and domination by local urban and rural magnates, whose power and prestige are derived not just from wealth but equally importantly from their positions of leadership within particular kinship groups – or from a combination of land and religious status, as in the *pir* families. Members of formerly great Muslim families from India do still play an important part in Pakistani social and cultural life, but their political power was naturally destroyed by migration and their loss of property.

Meanwhile traditional kinship and religious links were violently disrupted by a process which took Muslims from all over India, separated them, and threw them down at random in what in effect were completely new cities of Karachi and Hyderabad. As Chapter 8 on Sindh will explore further, this experience, together with the mostly urban tradition of most Mohajirs before 1947, has allowed this community to break out of the web of elite domination and patronage politics which continues to enmesh every other Pakistani party but the Jamaat.

There are two sad and frightening things about this: that to bring this political possibility about took an immense upheaval, a divided country, the displacement of millions of people, and the deaths of hundreds of thousands; and that the party created as a result, though undeniably 'modern' compared to the other Pakistani parties, has about it more than a touch of the 'modernity' of some notorious lower-middle-class European nationalist parties before 1945 – also famous for their successful social work and strong organizations. Compared to this kind of modernity, there may be something to be said for 'feudalism' after all.

PART THREE

The Provinces

7

Punjab

Lahore – the ancient whore, the handmaiden of dimly remem-
bered Hindu kings, the courtesan of Moghul emperors – bedecked
and bejewelled, savaged by marauding hordes – healed by the
caressing hands of successive lovers. A little shoddy, as Qasim
saw her, like an attractive but ageing concubine, ready to bestow
surprising delights on those who cared to court her – proudly
displaying royal gifts.

(Bapsi Sidhwa)[1]

PAKISTAN'S PROVINCIAL BALANCE

Unlike India, Pakistan has one province – Punjab – which with almost
56 per cent of the population can to a certain extent dominate the country. No Indian province comes anywhere near this in terms of relative
weight – though if all the Hindi-speaking states worked together as a
bloc they would approach Punjab's weight in Pakistan. Punjab also
provides most of the army, and without Punjabi support no military
government of Pakistan would be possible.

Yet at the same time, whatever the other ethnicities may sometimes
allege, Punjab is not nearly strong or united enough to create a real
'Punjabi Raj' over the whole country, an effective, permanent national
regime based on Punjabi identity. Pakistan is in this, as in other ways,
more like India than immediately appears.

India is held together as a democracy (or at least a constitutional system, since Indian administration often does not work in ways that the
West thinks of as 'democratic') in large part precisely because it is so

big and varied. Many years ago, I asked an Indian general if he and his colleagues ever thought of creating a military dictatorship, as in Pakistan. 'We're not that stupid,' he replied.

> Democracy in India is a damned mess, but it gives the system the flexibility it needs to survive. It means that rebels who can't be killed can always be bought off by being elected to government, and given jobs and favours for their relatives. This country is so big and so varied and so naturally chaotic, if you tried to introduce an efficient dictatorship in India it would actually destroy India within a year.

If you emphasize the word 'efficient' and add the word 'Punjabi', then the same is true of Pakistan. No national government can simply crush the warlike, heavily armed Pathans. All have preferred instead to co-opt them through service in the army and bureaucracy, and into government through elections. The Pathan territories of the North West Frontier Province (NWFP) and the Federally Administered Tribal Areas (FATA) have always been administered overwhelmingly by ethnic Pathan officials. Nor can any Punjab-based regime dream of ruling over the megalopolis of Karachi, with all its rival ethnicities, by simple dictatorial means. There too, co-option and compromise are essential. So while Pakistan's Punjabi core makes it different from India, and more susceptible to dictatorship, it is like enough to India to make sure that its dictatorships can't work in an effectively dictatorial manner.

So the balance between the provinces also forms part of what I have called Pakistan's 'negotiated state'. There is a real element of Punjabi dominance, but fear of breaking up the country on which Punjab itself depends means that this dominance always has to be veiled and qualified by compromises with the other provinces. Thus in 2009–10, in a considerable achievement for Pakistani democracy and the PPP government, the centre and the provinces agreed on a new national finance award rebalancing revenue allocation in favour of the poorer and more thinly populated provinces. Punjab, with some 56 per cent of the population and around 65 per cent of the revenue generation, was allocated 51.74 per cent of revenue.[2]

Sometimes, however, these compromises are damaging not only to Punjab's interests but to those of Pakistan as a whole. For example, it is absolutely essential for Pakistan to develop greater, more reliable and more ecologically responsible sources of electricity. It is now more than fifty years since the idea of a great hydroelectric dam at Kalabagh on the Indus was first mooted. The site is eminently suitable as far as hydro-electricity is concerned; yet for that entire half-century the project has been stymied by opposition from the NWFP and Sindh, which fear that they would lose water to Punjabi industry. And that has continued to be the case through no fewer than three periods of military rule, the project decried by provincial nationalists as expressions of Punjabi dominance!

More than ten years after immense coal reserves were discovered beneath the Thar desert in Sindh, as of 2009 plans to develop them were still in limbo because of disagreements between the Sindh and federal governments, and because the federal government was both unwilling and constitutionally unable to impose its will on Sindh, for fear of split-ting the Pakistan People's Party and creating a new surge of Sindhi nationalism. But this was not only a problem of civilian rule. Musharraf in his nine years in government also failed to push through this project. In this way, Pakistan's delicate ethnic balance, and the endless negotia-tions it entails, contribute to the sluggish pace of Pakistan's development.

On the other hand, the maintenance of this balance has helped ensure that with the exception of some of the Baloch, who think that they would do well on the strength of their gas and mineral reserves, very few political or intellectual groups in Pakistan and Pakistan's provinces actu-ally want to break the country up, whether because they are genuinely attached to it (in the army, the bureaucracy and much of the Punjab); because they hope to take it over and use it as a base for a wider pro-gramme (the Islamists); because they are afraid of Indian domination (Punjabis); because they are afraid that Pakistan's break-up would lead to a dreadful civil war with other ethnicities (the Sindhis and Mohajirs, and even the Pathans, since the Hindko-speaking minority in the NWFP is strongly opposed to Pathan nationalism); or simply because the alter-native looks so much worse (the Pathans, when they look across the border into Afghanistan). So one of the biggest factors holding Pakistan together is fear.

However, it isn't the only factor by any manner of means. The differ-ent 'ethnic' groups of Pakistan are often very intermingled, to the point where the standard definitions of ethnicities or nationalities within Pakistan sometimes seem almost as artificial as Pakistan itself. Thus Sindhis, Pathans and Baloch complain frequently of Punjabi domina-tion, especially under military rule; yet the army, or at least the other ranks, have until recently not represented 'Punjab' at all, but rather the Potwar plateau, half a dozen districts in the north-west of Punjab, bordering on the North West Frontier Province – the same area from where the British recruited their soldiers. Some other parts of Punjab have been almost as poorly represented in the military as Sindh.

For that matter, Punjab, Sindh and Balochistan are in their way also 'artificial'. It is a mistake to see them as Czechs, Hungarians or Poles under Habsburg rule, increasingly self-conscious nations with an earlier history of nationhood, which with the collapse of the empire easily formed national states. Linguists dispute how many different dialects of Punjabi there are, but certainly Seraiki, in the southern third of Punjab, could just as well be a language in its own right. The Baloch for their part, while having some kind of ethnic unity with a common tribal code, are divided into two completely different languages, one of them descended from the Dravidian of southern India, presumed to be the language of the Indus Valley civilization 4,000 years ago.

And linguistic divisions are not the most important ones. Particular religious allegiance counts for as much; still more do endless combinations of family, clan and lineage. Like the Sayyids, these often trace their ancestry back to somewhere else, whether in legend or fact. Even where the Rajputs came from originally is not known. As the eighteenth-century Indian Muslim reformist theologian Shah Waliullah stated proudly of his Sayyid ancestry,

> I hail from a foreign country. My forebears came to India as immigrants. I am proud of my Arab origin and my knowledge of Arabic, for both of these bring a person close to the 'Master of the Ancients and Moderns', the 'most excellent of the prophets sent by God', and 'the pride of all creation'. In gratitude for this great favour I ought to conform to the habits and customs of the early Arabs and the Prophet as much as I can, and abstain from the customs of the Turks and the habits of the Indians.[3]

As far as personal pride and identity are concerned, to be a Sayyid usually comprehensively trumps being a Punjabi or a Sindhi.

Many of the great landowning families of Sindh and southern Punjab are the descendants of Baloch tribesmen who conquered the local peasantry centuries ago, still speak Baloch at home, and owe allegiance to saints whose following is as widely spread as the Baloch tribal migrations which shaped these local societies.

As for the Pathans, as will be described in Chapter 10, though they have a very strong ethnic identity, their deep and rivalrous tribal allegiances and their division between Pakistan and Afghanistan mean that they have never been able to turn this into a strong modern nationalism – something in which they resemble certain other tribal ethnicities such as the Somalis.

Finally, Karachi, the country's greatest city, is itself a major source of unity, since it includes not only indigenous Sindhis and Mohajirs from India, but also huge populations of Punjabis and Pathans. In fact, Karachi is the third largest Pathan city after Kabul and Peshawar, and probably the fourth or fifth largest Punjabi city. More Baloch may live in Karachi than live in Balochistan. These different populations in Karachi often loathe each other, but they also depend on the city for their livelihoods, and their more responsible (or self-interested) leaders and the businessmen who fund them do not want to destroy those livelihoods for the sake of nationalist dreams.

In Europe, the USA and Japan during the nineteenth century it was above all the modern state education system that deliberately created a sense of nationhood among the ordinary people of these countries, most of whom had previously had little sense of belonging to any identity beyond their village, region, local religious allegiance and kinship group.[4] In Pakistan, state education barely reaches most of the population; and education in the religious schools or madrasahs obviously influences people more to a sense of being part of the universal Muslim world community or Ummah than to a sense of being Pakistanis – just as the Church schools of medieval Europe were designed to turn boys into Catholics, not into Germans or French.

But then none of the different bits of Pakistan's education system is designed to make children into Sindhis or Punjabis either. So it would probably be wrong to see Pakistan as necessarily following a classical Western course in this matter, or to assume that because Pakistan's national identity is weak, other, inherently stronger identities are waiting in the wings to break the country up.

Rather, therefore, than an early disintegration, the greatest threat would once again seem to be that long-term ecological degradation – especially in the area of water resources – will over time so increase tensions between different regions, and so reduce the ability of the regional elites to contain these tensions, that national government becomes unworkable. By this stage the situation may have become so bad that effective provincial government will also be unworkable.

DIFFERENT PUNJABS

In the case of Punjab, not only the great majority of the Punjabi establishment but a great many ordinary Punjabis identify their provincial identity with that of Pakistan as a whole; and this identification is one of the things which makes writing about Punjabi identity and Punjabi attitudes to Pakistan so difficult. Apart from the fact that there are simply so many more Punjabis than others, and of more varied kinds, the identities of most of Pakistan's other nationalities are to a considerable extent shaped by their differences with the Punjabis (except for the Mohajirs), and their ambiguous relationship with the Pakistani state.

Many Punjabis, by contrast, believe that they *are* the state, and if they define themselves against anybody else, it is against India. An adviser to Chief Minister Shahbaz Sharif with whom I spoke in January 2009 was unabashed in his declaration that 'if anything is ever to get done in Pakistan, Punjab has to take the lead. We determine the direction of Pakistan.' As a senior official (of Mohajir origin) remarked sourly, 'The difficulty about writing on Punjab as a province is that they think and behave as if they are the whole damn country.' This Punjabi commitment to Pakistani nationalism has profoundly shaped Pakistan, and is indeed responsible for Pakistan's survival as a state. And the overthrow of that state can never happen in peripheral areas such as Waziristan, Balochistan or even Karachi. It would have to happen in Punjab.

One sign of Punjabi commitment to Pakistan, to the point in some cases almost of submersion in Pakistan, is that (in sharp contrast both to the other Pakistani provinces and to Indian Punjab), Pakistani Punjab has not been committed to the development of Punjabi as a provincial language. Instead, successive state governments have promoted the national language, Urdu, as the language of education and administration throughout Punjab. Urdu is also far more prevalent in society. Whereas Sindhis and Pathans almost always speak Sindhi and Pashto among themselves, educated Punjabis usually speak Urdu with each other, when they are not speaking English.

Sir Muhammad Iqbal, the great Urdu poet, philosopher and prophet of Indian Muslim nationhood, came from Sialkot in western Punjab. Pakistan's two greatest writers, Faiz Ahmed Faiz and Saadat Hasan Manto, were both Punjabis (albeit in Manto's case from a Kashmiri family) but both wrote mainly in Urdu. Punjab's finest writer of the present day, Daniyal Mueenuddin, writes in English.

So while Punjabi dialects continue to be spoken at home and there is a rich and living folklore in Punjabi, almost all public life is conducted in Urdu or English. The spread of Urdu is also encouraged by Pakistani television, by the Pakistani cinema ('Lollywood', because based in Lahore) and indeed by the passionately beloved Indian cinema from Bollywood, which uses Hindi – and despite assiduous nationalist efforts in both India and Pakistan to change the languages, spoken Hindi and Urdu remain basically the same language.

Much older influences than Pakistani nationalism are also at work here. Although quite distant from the Urdu-speaking heartland of the old Mughal empire, Punjab was still far more culturally affected by it than were Sindh or the Pathan areas. Equally importantly, Punjabi is not in fact the language of large parts of Punjab – or even of most of it, depending on how you define 'Punjabi'.

According to a traditional Punjabi statement, 'Language changes every 15 miles' – just as it did in Europe until the rise of modern mass education and entertainment in the nineteenth century. So 'Punjabi' is itself broken up into numerous dialects. Meanwhile, people in most of the southern third of Punjab, from Multan down to the Sindh border, speak a completely different language, Seraiki, which while related to Punjabi is closer in some respects to Sindhi.

A movement for a separate Seraiki-speaking province has existed for many years, but has never got anywhere much. One reason for this is the entrenched opposition of the Punjab establishment, backed by the fear of national governments in Islamabad of the appalling can of worms which such a move might open (a new Mohajir demand for a separate province of Karachi leading to fresh Mohajir–Sindhi violence, for starters).

Probably even more important is the fact that the Seraiki-speaking area also contains numerous other dialects, or languages (like Haryani) which might be part of Punjabi, Seraiki, Urdu, Sindhi – all or none of them. Until 1955, much of southern Punjab was covered by the former autonomous princely state of Bahawalpur, many of whose inhabitants continue proudly to claim their own special identity, and even that they speak their own language separate from Seraiki. Other identities also cut across the Punjabi–Seraiki divide: these include religious affiliation (whether of the different Sunni sects, Shiism or the following of a particular saint) and wider kinship group (Jat, Rajput, etc.).

Many Seraiki-speakers are in fact by origin from Baloch tribes. How for example is one to define former President Sardar Farooq Khan Leghari in terms of identity? Is he a Punjabi (the province where his clan holds its land); a Seraiki (by language); a Baloch (by ethnic descent and tribal identification); a Punjabi-speaking Pathan (by marriage); a Pakistani (having worked as a Pakistani official, spent most of his life in national politics and ended as president of Pakistan); or, at bottom and perhaps most importantly of all, hereditary chieftain of his branch of the Leghari tribe? So 'Punjab' contains numerous overlapping identities, in a way that helps heavily to qualify 'Punjabi' dominance over Pakistan as a whole.

LAHORE, THE HISTORIC CAPITAL

For a land which cradled one of the very first human urban civilizations, Pakistan is remarkably lacking in historic cities, and even those that do exist often have few historic monuments. What war has spared, the rivers have often destroyed, either by washing away cities or by changing course and leaving them isolated and waterless.

The great exception is Lahore, ancient capital of Punjab. The old city of Lahore contains one of the greatest Mughal mosques, and one of their greatest forts, as well as a host of lesser monuments, including the tombs of both Sultan Qutb-ud-Din Aybakh (died 1210 CE), founder of the Muslim 'Slave Dynasty' which ruled from Delhi, and of the Mughal emperor Jehangir. Lahore also contains some of the greatest monuments of British rule in the former Indian empire.

In fact, Lahore looks and feels much more like the capital of a major state than does Islamabad – and in the view of Pakistan's non-Punjabi ethnicities Lahore also often behaves that way. It is some ten times the size of Islamabad, and Pakistan's largest city by far after Karachi – just as the province of Punjab is home to almost 56 per cent of Pakistan's population (more than 100 million people) and forms its industrial, agricultural and military core. Punjabis on average are considerably richer than the inhabitants of the other provinces (though, as will be seen, with huge regional variations within Punjab). In Sindh, Balochistan and the NWFP, more than half the population is listed as being below the poverty line. In Punjab, the figure is around one-quarter. If Pakistan is to be broken from within by Islamist revolt, then it is in Punjab that this would have to happen, not among the Pathans of the Frontier; for Pakistan is the heart, stomach and backbone of Pakistan. Indeed, in the view of many of its inhabitants, it *is* Pakistan.

As described in Chapter 6, the old Punjab elites (themselves often not so old, having been in many cases the product of British land grants) have been greatly changed in recent decades by the entry of very large numbers of 'new men' into their ranks. However, these new families have frequently intermarried with old families from the same 'castes', and some of those old families also retain considerable wealth and, more importantly, great local power through the leadership of their clans and kinship networks, or the inheritance of shrines and religious prestige.

This can give Punjabi politics a united and clannish air, and covering Punjabi elections in the company of well-born and well-connected Punjabi journalists can be a bit like attending a family party, albeit a pretty quarrelsome one: 'Will Booby or Janoo get the family seat this time, do you think? Will Bunty get a ministry at last? And isn't it soooo *sad* about Puphi Aunty's marriage?'[5]

The participants and household members do not even necessarily have to be human. During my last visit, I listened as a great Punjabi aristocratic and political lady conducted an impassioned phone conversation about Punjab politics. I was increasingly bewildered by the fact that not only did the conversation keep switching between English and Urdu, but an increasing number of horses seemed to be wandering into it along with the name of the Chief Minister and other leading Punjabi politicians. When my hostess got off the phone, I asked her if she was planning to make one of her horses Chief Minister. That would be an *excellent* idea, she laughed, but no, the conversation had been about something much more important – the composition of the Board of the Lahore Race Course.

At its worst (which is admittedly much of the time), Lahore high society is all too close to the 'Diary of a Social Butterfly', the weekly satirical column by Moni Mohsin in the *Friday Times*, which she has put together in a book of the same name.[6] Though brilliantly funny, this column is in a way quite unnecessary, because the picture of this society which appears on the society pages of the *Friday Times* and its sister publications is in fact beyond parody.

For the absolute epitome, the *non plus ultra* of this set (in Karachi as well as Lahore), readers might want to buy a book of portraits of society figures by the society and fashion photographer Tapu Javeri, entitled – in pretentiously lower case - *i voyeur: going places with haute noblesse*, and decorated with captions to portraits like 'on the sperm of the moment'. This is the hard-partying world portrayed in Mohsin Ali's brilliant, grim novel *Moth Smoke*.

However, at its best, there is also in Lahore a mixture of elegance and intelligence which could make it one of the great cities of the world (if they could only fix the roads, the drains, the public transport, the pollution, the housing of most of the population, the electricity supply, the police ...). The Lahore museum, with its magnificent Buddhist and Mughal works of art, is the only museum in Pakistan of international stature, and casts the rather sad Pakistani National Museum in Karachi into the shade.

This was the 'Wonder House' of Kipling's *Kim*, which famously begins with Kim perched on the great cannon, Zam Zama, in the road outside the museum, of which Kipling's father was the curator. Kipling worked for a Lahore newspaper, and some of his finest stories are set in Lahore, as are those of many of Pakistan's greatest writers and poets. Lahore is a city of the imagination, in a way that bureaucratic Islamabad and dour, impoverished Peshawar cannot be, and Karachi has not yet had the time to become (though writers like Kamila Shamsie are working on it). The Lahore University of Management Sciences (LUMS) is in parts at least the best university not only in Pakistan, but in South Asia.

Most unusually for Pakistan, which as a society exemplifies the principle of 'private affluence and public squalor', Lahore, although it contains some fairly awful slums, also has some fine public gardens, though admittedly ones bequeathed by the Mughals in the case of the Shalamar Gardens, and the British in the case of the Lawrence Gardens (now Jinnah Bagh). Strolling through the Jinnah Bagh in September 2008 on my way from breakfast with friends in a stylish and charming café called 'Coffee Tea and Company' to visit a modern art gallery, past uniformed schoolchildren, girls in brightly coloured *shelwar kameezes* like parrots tossing balls to each other, and neatly dressed middle-class couples, I reflected on the idiocy of portraying Pakistan as a 'failed state'. It was hardly a scene reminiscent of Grozny or Mogadishu.

The contrast was all the greater with Peshawar, which I had just left, and where the sense of threat from the Pakistani Taleban was palpable. Indeed, it was sometimes difficult to remember that Peshawar and Lahore were in the same country. I remember my shock – and then amusement at my shock – on seeing what I first took to be a fattish Pathan boy in a Pathan cap and jeans on the back of a motorcycle in Lahore – only to realize that it was in fact a girl; which in Peshawar would be a truly dangerous combination, and in other Pathan areas a potentially fatal one.

Then again, you could say that my reflections on the success and stability of Lahore were only the result of my becoming lahorized (or perhaps lahorified, to rhyme with glorified), because this is very much the way that the Lahore elites feel, and for many years it led them into a very dangerous complacency vis-à-vis the militant threat.

With the exception of some journalists, most of my Lahore elite friends did indeed treat developments in the Pathan areas as if they were happening in a different country a long way off. This was still apparent even in January 2009, despite serious terrorist attacks in Islamabad and Rawalpindi. By July 2009, however, this complacency had been shattered by major attacks in Lahore itself, on the Sri Lankan cricket team and the police academy. Many more have followed. However, as this book has been at pains to point out, terrorism and insurgency are two very different things. Terrorist attacks can do great damage to Pakistan, but to overthrow the state would require an immense spread of the rebellions which broke out in some of the Pathan areas between 2001 and 2009. Above all, to seize power in Pakistan, Islamist militancy would have to seize Lahore.

During my visits to Lahore in 2007–2009, I was deeply worried by the lack of support among the mass of the population for tough action against the Pakistani Taleban – even in July 2009, by which time opinion in the elites had shifted very significantly. On the other hand, I could not find much significant support on the streets for the Taleban's actual programme of Islamist revolution, even among the poor and the lower middle classes, the social heartland of Islamist radicalism in Punjab.

In January 2009, during the holiday which marks the festival of

Moharram, I strolled across the park surrounding the Minar-e-Pakistan, the monument to Pakistan's independence next to the Old City, mingling with the crowds and talking to people of different classes (from rickshaw drivers to members of the middle classes, but excluding the elite) about their views of their government, the economic situation, the Pakistani Taleban, the war in Afghanistan and anything else that they wanted to talk to me about.

This was a time when anti-Western feeling in Pakistan was running even higher than usual, owing to the Israeli attack on Gaza; and, as I have remarked elsewhere in this book, while it is difficult enough to argue with anti-Western Pakistanis when they are in the wrong, it is even more difficult to do so when they are in the right. So as might have been expected, I came in for a great deal of impassioned and radical-sounding rhetoric. Support for a military offensive against the Pakistani Taleban was extremely weak, and sympathy for the Afghan Taleban's fight against the 'US occupation' of Afghanistan was universal.

Habib, an old scooter-driver, declared to murmurs of approval from the other drivers that,

> The military should stop fighting against the Taleban in Swat and Bajaur. We are all Muslims after all. The Taleban are just trying to spread real Islam and bring peace and justice, and I don't know why the army is trying to stop them. All over the world Muslims are under attack from the Jews and Americans, in Palestine, Afghanistan, everywhere. The Taleban are right to fight them.

Every single person I spoke with opposed Pakistani help to America in Afghanistan. Asghar, an educated, English-speaking youth in a baseball cap, declared, to the applause of his friends:

> We have two opinions in our society: the government, which is for America, and the people, who are against America. How can any Muslim support US policies when they are helping Israel kill innocent Muslims? That is why the Taleban are carrying out terrorism in Pakistan, because of this gap between the government and the people. So we all think that the government should negotiate with the Taleban to end this conflict.

That said, a couple of serious qualifications need to be entered. The first is that in the great majority of cases people only started talking about the Taleban and the fight against them when I mentioned these themes (this was one thing which had changed by July, when Lahore had already come in for terrorist attacks). If I only asked what they were most concerned about, the overwhelming majority started talking about inflation and jobs.

The other thing worth pointing out is that at no stage in the course of that morning did I feel the slightest concern for my own safety, except from the cricket balls, which were whizzing in all directions from the dozens of informal and anarchical cricket matches that were going on and that clearly interested most of the young men present far more than my questions. Even when one group of kids started chanting Taleban slogans, there was an air of clowning for the camera about the proceedings, and the chanting was accompanied by an offer of a soft drink 'because you are our guest and it is so dusty here'. By contrast, in a crowd like that in some of the Pathan areas, I would have had real reason to worry that I might have been beheaded and my head used as the ball.

If there is no revolutionary mood among the masses in the heartland of Punjab, revolution also seems highly unlikely in the face of the power of Punjab's entwined landowning, business, military and bureaucratic elites, and the deep traditionalism of most of the population. Nevertheless, Punjab has also long been home to very strong strains of Islamic revivalism. The headquarters of the Tablighi Jamaat, the world's greatest Muslim preaching organization, is in Raiwind, 20 miles to the south-west of Lahore. The Tabligh have always stressed their peaceful and apolitical nature; but 10 miles to the north-west of Lahore is Muridke, the headquarters of the Jamaat-ud-Dawa, mother organization to the Lashkar-e-Taiba, which played a leading role in the jihad against India in Kashmir, and carried out the November 2008 terrorist attacks on Mumbai.

For reasons that have deep roots in history, militant groups – and especially LeT/JuD – do have widespread support in Punjab, at least when they attack the Indians in Kashmir or the West in Afghanistan. Their popularity has been one factor in discouraging the Pakistani state from attacking them in turn, lest they join with the Pakistani Taleban. From 2008 on, some of these groups did just that, and started to launch terrorist attacks in the very heart of Pakistan. These attacks are unlikely to destroy the Pakistani state, but they can do terrible damage, and perhaps force the state either to compromise with the militants, or to adopt ferocious measures of repression in order to crush them.

PUNJABI HISTORY AND THE IMPACT OF MIGRATION

Punjab is *panch aab*, the 'Land of the Five Rivers': the Indus, and its four great tributaries, the Chenab, Ravi, Sutlej and Beas. As its name suggests, the northern parts of the province at least have a degree of geographic and historical unity, reflected in the Punjabi language. The southern parts of Punjab were converted to Islam, beginning more than 1,000 years ago (largely by Sufi preachers). Thereafter the region was usually ruled by Muslim rulers based elsewhere, mostly in Delhi, but sometimes in Afghanistan or even Persia.

The only Punjabi state to rule over the whole of Punjab was that of the Sikhs, a radical movement within Hinduism that (although heavily influenced by both Islamic monotheism and local Muslim Sufi traditions) arose in reaction against Muslim rule in the late sixteenth century. In the course of the eighteenth century, the Sikhs conquered more and more of Punjab from the decaying Mughal empire, and under their greatest ruler, Ranjit Singh (ruled 1801–1839), united the whole of Punjab, including Multan to the south, in one state. However, some 60 per cent of Ranjit Singh's subjects were Muslims.

After Ranjit Singh's death, the British conquered Punjab in two wars in the 1840s. These saw some of the hardest-fought battles the British ever had to undertake in India; yet, by a curious paradox, the Punjab was to become the heartland of British military recruitment in the Indian empire, with results for the state and society that have profoundly shaped the whole of Pakistan to this day, and provide some of the foundations for military power in Pakistan.

As related in Chapter 5 on the military, the British created a powerful synthesis of modern Western military organization with local traditions, and underpinned this with a system of land grants to reward loyal soldiers and recruiters. The British military system was entwined with the vast irrigation projects started in central Punjab by the British; the new 'canal colonies', in what had formerly been wasteland, were intended

1. Mohammed Ali Jinnah, founder of Pakistan

2. Field Marshal Mohammed Ayub Khan, military ruler 1958–69

3. Surrender of the Pakistani forces in East Pakistan, Dhaka, 16 December 1971

4. Zulfikar Ali Bhutto, Prime Minister 1971–77

5. General Muhammad Zia-ul-Haq, military ruler 1977–88

6. Pakistani soldiers on the Siachen Glacier, Kashmir, August 2002

7. Asif Ali Zardari (*left*) and
Bilawal Bhutto-Zardari,
with the portrait of the late
Benazir Bhutto (2007)

8. Benazir Bhutto
(1989)

9. Poster of the Bhutto-Zardari family (2010)

10. Nawaz Sharif (*left*) and Shahbaz Sharif (2008)

11. General Pervez Musharraf
(*right*), military ruler 1999–2008,
with US Vice-President Dick Cheney,
Islamabad, 26 February 2007

12. General Ashfaq Kayani,
Chief of the Army Staff,
November 2007

13. President Asif Ali Zardari with President Mahmoud Ahmedinejad (*centre*)
of Iran and Hamid Karzai of Afghanistan (*left*), Tehran, 24 May 2009

14. MQM women activists with pictures of Altaf Hussain (2007)

15. MQM Rally in Karachi (2007)

16. The aftermath of the suicide attack by the Pakistani Taleban on the Lahore High Court, 10 January 2008

17. A demonstrator with a placard of Osama bin Laden, Karachi, 7 October 2001

18. A demonstration in support of the Afghan Taleban, Karachi, 26 October 2001

19. Jamaat Islami demonstrating in Peshawar against US drone attacks, 16 May 2008

20. Mahsud tribesmen meet for a jirga to discuss US drone attacks, Tank, 20 April 2009

21. Pakistani soldiers in South Waziristan, October 2009

22. A terrorist attack in Peshawar, 5 December 2008

23. Destruction caused by the floods in Azalkhel, NWFP, 9 August 2010

24. A terrorist attack by Lashkar-e-Taiba in Mumbai, India, November 2008: the aftermath of the attack on the railway station

25. Muslim Khan,
Pakistani Taleban
spokesman, Swat,
28 March 2009

26. Pakistani
Taleban supporters
celebrate
promulgation of
the Nizam-e-Adl
agreement, Swat,
16 April 2009

27. A Taleban patrol in Swat, April 2009

28. Pakistani soldiers on guard in Swat, September 2009

29. Hakimullah Mahsud, Amir (leader) of the Pakistani Taleban, Orakzai Tribal Agency, 9 February 2010

30. A victim of a suicide bombing, Kohat, 7 September 2010

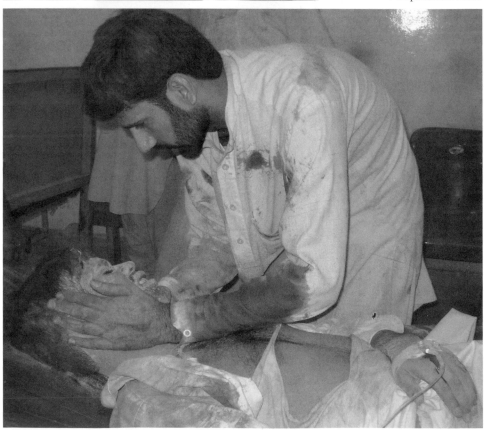

not only greatly to increase food production (which they did) but to provide both men and horses to the British Indian army.

The development of electoral politics from the 1880s led to political mobilization along religious lines. There were periodic explosions of communal violence, such as the riots in Rawalpindi in 1926 over the building of a cinema next to a mosque. However, British patronage, common agrarian interests and fear of communal violence meant that until the very last years of British rule, Punjab politics was dominated by the Unionist Party, which brought together Muslim, Hindu and Sikh landowners and their rural followers.

As independence approached in 1945–7, the Unionists collapsed under the triple blows of Muslim League agitation for Pakistan, Sikh agitation for a Sikh-dominated province or even independent state (something that was to resurface in the Sikh extremist rebellion against India in the 1980s), and the refusal of Jawaharlal Nehru and the Indian National Congress to accept a confederal India with a semi-independent position for Punjab. Exacerbated by the haste of the British withdrawal, and some perverse decisions by the Radcliffe boundary commission, the result was the appalling bloodletting that gripped the province after March 1947, and resulted in a crescendo of violence in the weeks following independence and partition in August.

In the resulting massacres on both sides, between 200,000 and 1 million people lost their lives in Punjab and Bengal (modern scholarship tends to support the lower figure), and more than 7.5 million Punjabis became refugees. The human cost is commemorated in innumerable memoirs and writings, including the greatest piece of fiction yet to come from Pakistan, *Toba Tek Singh* by Saadat Hasan Manto. Lahore, which had been in the middle of the northern belt of Sikh and British Punjab, was left almost on the Indian frontier – something which has contributed to its inhabitants' obsession with the Indian threat. In the 1965 war the Indians came close to capturing the city.

The ethnic impact of the migration from India on Pakistani Punjab was far less than on Sindh, where the migrants came from completely different parts of the British Indian empire – in Punjab, refugees were settled among fellow Punjabis. The scale of the movement however was immense. Out of the more than 7.25 million people who moved from India to Pakistan, 5.28 million moved from east (Indian) to west (Pakistani) Punjab. After 1947, these refugees made up just over 25 per cent of the population of Pakistani Punjab, one of the highest proportions of refugees in an area in recorded history.

This forced migration built on already existing Punjabi traditions of peaceful economic migration to develop new land and new businesses, which already under the British had taken hundreds of thousands of Punjabis to settle in the new canal colonies of Sindh (which were created in the 1930s, two generations after those of Punjab) and to work as shopkeepers and artisans in Balochistan. From the 1950s on, these traditions took hundreds of thousands more to the terraced houses of Leeds, Leicester and Oxford.

The east Punjabi refugees of 1947 brought two things with them to their new homes in west Punjab (mostly homes and lands abandoned by fleeing Hindus and Sikhs). The first was relative economic and social dynamism created by the shock to their old settled ways. Because they moved to another part of the same province, and en masse as whole village communities, the element of disruption was less than in the case of the Mohajirs in Sindh.

Nonetheless, the experience of being uprooted, and the consequent undermining of the old landowning elites, meant that the Punjabi migrants also were to some extent shaken out of their old patterns. Those who were unable to find land in the countryside settled in the cities, entering new trades and professions. This strengthened the element of independence and egalitarianism already present in some of the northern Punjabi castes – especially the Jats, who like to say of themselves, 'The Jats bow the knee only to themselves and God.'

The other thing that the refugees naturally contributed was a particularly intense hatred and fear of India, which remains far stronger in Punjab than in Sindh or the NWFP – just as on the other side of the new border, Hindu refugees from west Punjab came to play an especially important role in anti-Muslim politics. This fear has helped strengthen the refugees' identification with Pakistan, and therefore that of Punjab as a whole. Of the educated Punjabi migrants, a high proportion joined the officer corps. They played a particularly prominent role under General Zia-ul-Haq – himself from Jullundur in east Punjab, like his ISI commander, General Akhtar Rehman. A majority of the leadership of the violently anti-Shia Sipah-e-Sahaba Islamist militant group (now allied in revolt with the Pakistani Taleban) have also been from east Punjab.

The refugees therefore played a vital role in creating what Abida

Husain has called, with some exaggeration, 'Pakistan's Prussian Bible Belt': that is to say, the combination of tendencies towards economic dynamism, social mobility, militarist nationalism and Islamist chauvinism to be found in northern and central Punjab.

These tendencies, and the overall impact of the refugees, have been qualified however by much older traditions in Punjab, a mixture exemplified by the city of Lahore. As noted, the headquarters of Islamist radical groups are close to the city. The main headquarters of the Jamaat Islami party, Mansura, is in one of Lahore's suburbs. Yet Lahore also contains numerous shrines of saints, including one of the greatest not only in Pakistan but in South Asia, Data Ganj Baksh, the object of a Taleban terrorist attack on 1 July 2010.

Data Ganj Baksh (original name Abul Hassan Ali Hajvery) was an eleventh-century Sufi preacher from Ghazni in Afghanistan who played a key part in converting people in northern Punjab to Islam. His shrine became famous for miracles, and for many centuries he has been the most beloved of Lahore's many saints. 'He is our very own link with God,' I was told by Mukhtar, a worshipper at the shrine from Mianwali in western Punjab near the border with the NWFP.

However, the shrine now looks much less like an ancient inner-city shrine than it did when I first visited it in the 1980s. Then, like most old shrines, it was surrounded by houses, and you approached its gate through a narrow crowded lane. The buildings of the mosque dated back to Mughal times and were far too small for all the worshippers from Lahore's immensely expanded population. In the late 1980s and early 1990s, therefore, when Nawaz Sharif was chief minister of Punjab, he rebuilt the shrine at immense cost, including the creation of a strikingly modernist mosque by a Turkish architect, an underground parking lot, and a huge forecourt on the edge of a main road, to create which several streets of houses had to be bought up and demolished.

This says something very interesting about overlapping Punjabi identities and the relationship between religion and politics. Like many traditional Punjabi commercial families, the Sharifs are by origin Kashmiris who moved to Punjab centuries ago. In 1947, they migrated from east Punjab to Lahore, where Nawaz Sharif was born in 1949. Partly from older family tradition, and partly perhaps because of the impact of migration, Nawaz Sharif's father joined the Ahl-e-Hadith, a religious tradition with strong Wahabi leanings. This is an affiliation which later strengthened, and was strengthened by, Sharif ties to Saudi Arabia, where Nawaz Sharif's father went into business after Z. A. Bhutto nationalized his industries in the 1970s, and where Nawaz took refuge after being overthrown by Musharraf. Nawaz Sharif therefore has been widely suspected of sympathies with radical Islamist theology.

However – presumably in order to consolidate their position in their new home, Lahore – Nawaz Sharif's family married him to a girl from a leading Kashmiri family of Lahore's Old City. In a reflection of this Old City culture, Kulsum Sharif is the niece of Bohlu Pehlewan, an Indian wrestling champion before partition. Like most of the old Kashmiri families of Lahore, her family are by tradition Barelvi Sunnis, and followers of Lahore's saints and especially of Data Ganj Baksh. In a sign of the way that allegiance to the saints often cuts across sectarian divides, she named their two sons Hassan and Hussain – the two greatest names of the Shia tradition.

It may be assumed, therefore, that Mrs Sharif and her family had some impact on Nawaz Sharif's decision to spend a fortune (admittedly of state money) rebuilding the shrine of Data Ganj Baksh. A political calculation was also no doubt involved – the desire to increase Muslim League support among the saint's followers in Lahore and elsewhere. In an amusing example of jumping on the bandwagon (or possibly Mr Sharif trying to kill two birds with one stone), followers of *another*, modern Lahori Sufi saint (mentioned in Chapter 4), Hafiz Iqbal, claimed that their saint was actually responsible because he appeared to Mr Sharif in a dream and told him to help his brother Data Ganj Baksh.

Whether this story was initiated by Hafiz Iqbal's followers in order to appeal to the Sharifs, or the Sharifs in order to appeal to Hafiz Iqbal's followers, I cannot say (nor of course would I wish for one moment to discount the idea that saints could in principle appear to Mr Sharif). The point however is that religion and politics are deeply intertwined in Lahore – but in ways that often cut clean across what at first sight are people's formal religious affiliations.

Another famous example of a Punjabi, and especially Lahori, tradition that spans religious divides is that of the Basant festival (from the Sanskrit word for spring), which takes place in February. This Hindu festival is supposed to have been incorporated into popular Muslim practice by medieval Sufi saints. It is celebrated in Lahore and elsewhere in Punjab by the flying of a multitude of brightly coloured kites.

In consequence, Basant is naturally hated by the puritan reformers of the Deobandi and Wahabi traditions. However, official moves in recent years to restrict the celebration of Basant have been mainly due to a different, rather depressing cause, namely, the tradition of coating the strings of kites with ground glass, so as to cut the strings of rival kites. Every year, a number of people (especially children) are killed or injured when cut strings fall back to earth, or when they bring down electricity wires.

PUNJAB'S REGIONS

Geographically and economically, one can divide Punjab into three main regions (though blurring together at the edges and with numerous sub-divisions within them). The first, north-central Punjab, contains Lahore, the old agricultural areas along the rivers, and most of the new canal colonies created by the British. It has Punjab's (and Pakistan's) most productive agriculture, which also benefited more than any other area of Pakistan from the 'Green Revolution'. In the first half of the 1960s, agricultural growth in the main canal colony districts of Faisalabad, Multan and Montgomery (Sahiwal) increased by 8.9 per cent a year, and these three districts alone came to account for almost half of Punjab's entire agricultural production.[7]

Although water shortages today pose a growing and possibly even existential threat to Pakistan, it should be remembered that, as the canal colonies demonstrate, water is also something in connection with which men in the past have achieved great triumphs in this region. This was true not only of the original construction of the canals by the British, but also of their tremendous extension by the new Pakistani state in the 1950s. This included, among other things, the construction of the Tarbela reservoir and dam, the largest earth-filled dam in the world.

Finally, when in the 1960s the canals began to produce a crisis of waterlogging and salination in the canal colony areas, the state took quite effective action to drain the land, improve the efficiency of the canals and limit over-use of water. Salination is still a problem in parts of Punjab and Sindh, but it is a limited one – unlike the over-use of aquifers, which if it continues unchecked will render parts of Pakistan uninhabitable. These past achievements are another sign that Pakistan is not the hopeless case that it is so often made out to be. What it achieved once it can achieve again, given leadership, a recognition of the problem, and a little help from its friends. Whereas in the past Pakistan and especially Punjab were well ahead among developing countries in terms of water storage, in recent decades both have fallen behind badly as a result of under-investment and political wrangling over dam construction.

As of 2004, Pakistan had only 150 cubic metres of water storage capacity per inhabitant, compared to 2,200 cubic metres in China. The contruction of small earthen dams to trap rainwater has improved the situation somewhat in the years since then, but Pakistan is still far behind India in water storage, let alone China and the developed world.[8]

The farmers of the canal colonies have for more than a hundred years demonstrated their versatility and commercial drive. This was shown again by the speed with which they adopted many of the techniques of the Green Revolution. It should in principle, therefore, be possible to get them to adopt more water-efficient ways of growing crops. The problem is that this would almost certainly require them to be pushed towards water efficiency by water-pricing – and this is such a politically explosive subject that no government, civilian or military, has so far been willing to touch it. Nonetheless, it is not beyond the bounds of possibility, at least once people begin to see real agricultural disasters starting to develop elsewhere as a result of water shortages.

Alongside Lahore, the central region contains Punjab's greatest industries, centred on the textile centre of Faisalabad (founded by the British as Lyallpur) and other cities. The importance of the great 'feudal' landowning families in this region has been greatly reduced in recent decades, and its politics are dominated by smaller landowners and new families risen through commercial success or (corrupt) government service. This region is closely linked to Kashmir, from where the families of many urban Punjabis (including the Sharif family) originally migrated. This has helped cement the commitment of many people in this region to the struggle against India in Kashmir. Punjabi speakers from Pakistani Kashmir also dominate the Pakistani diaspora in Britain.

The second region is the Potwar (or Potohar) plateau of north-west Punjab, extending from the Salt range of hills to the Indus River and the Pathan lands, which have exerted a strong cultural influence here. A good many of the Potwari-speaking inhabitants of this region are in fact from originally Pathan tribes, like the ancestors of the cricketer-politician

Imran Khan Niazi, but consider themselves to be Punjabis. This is an area of poor, arid soil which the canal colonies did not reach. As in Balochistan and parts of Sindh and the NWFP, in much of the Potwar region the water table is dropping rapidly because of both excessive and inefficient use by agriculture, and the booming needs of the mushrooming twin cities of Islamabad–Rawalpindi. Water shortages in turn are driving farmers off the land to swell these urban populations still further. This is at present a low-level, undramatic movement, but its importance in worsening living standards should not be underestimated – as anyone who has seen Pakistani rural women carrying containers of water for long distances in the heat of summer can easily appreciate.

The Potwar region has few great landowners but numerous landowning clans, with bigger farmers exercising leadership – a development encouraged by past land reforms, which led landowners to split their lands between different members of their families. This marks a difference from central and southern Punjab, where (as in Britain) landowners tried to keep their estates in the hands of one son, and put other sons into the army, the civil service or business. Politics here is no longer 'feudal', but it is still critically dependent on kinship and leadership within kinship groups.

Owing to the poverty of its soil, the Potwar region has long exported its labour in one way or another. The British recruited most of their Muslim soldiers from the Potwar area, and until recently a large majority of the Pakistani army was also recruited from these few districts. The strong Pathan influence in this region has created concerns that Taleban influence could spread here from the NWFP. This could undermine the willingness to fight of the ordinary *jawan* (young man), or even in the worst case lead to mutiny. A great many people from this region are working in the Gulf, and the remittances that they send home help support the region economically and increase their families' independence from local landowners.

The biggest city of the region is Rawalpindi, which now has more than three million people but was a tiny village until the British developed it as their military headquarters to cover the Afghan frontier (though it is close to the site of another city erased by war, the great Gandharan Buddhist centre of Taxila). The choice of this region by Ayub Khan for his new capital, Islamabad, reflected its better climate but also no doubt a desire to base the capital in an area with solid military ties.

The third great Punjabi region is the south. This area overlaps but is not identical with the Seraiki-speaking belt, and in certain ways includes parts of central Punjab such as Jhang. It is defined more by cultural and economic patterns than by language. With a much smaller share of the canal colonies, the south was less affected by the greater social mobility and economic dynamism they brought in their train, and also received relatively fewer refugees from east Punjab. It also contains fewer egalitarian Jats than the northern and central parts of Punjab, and more Baloch, with their traditional deference to their autocratic chieftains.

In consequence, southern Punjab is far more 'feudal' than the north, in ways that connect it culturally to Sindh. Also linking this region to Sindh is the very strong tradition of worshipping saints and shrines, in many cases the base for great 'feudal' families of hereditary saints, or *pirs*. The shrines bind together many local Sunnis with the Shia, who have a major presence in this region. However, this presence, and especially the high proportion of the local 'feudals' who are Shia, has also helped stir up some bitter sectarian chauvinism against the local Shia.

Given all these divisions within Punjab itself, can one really speak of Punjabi domination of Pakistan, or of a Punjabi identity as such? The answer is less than the other provinces like to claim, but more than the Punjabis themselves like to pretend. To a great extent, of course, there is no establishment conspiracy about Punjab's domination of Pakistan – with some 56 per cent of the population and some 75 per cent of the industry, it naturally outweighs the other provinces, just as England naturally dominates the United Kingdom. This industry is no longer only limited to textiles and food processing. Sialkot is a major international centre of sports goods and somewhat weirdly (but presumably by extension through bladders) of bagpipes. Gujrat produces high-quality shoes and medium-quality electrical goods. No industries of this scale and sophistication exist in any of Pakistan's other provinces, with the obvious exception of the city of Karachi.

When representatives of other provinces denounce Punjab for its 55 per cent quota of official jobs, they conveniently forget that this is actually slightly *less* than Punjab's share of the population, just as, following the seventh National Finance Commission Award of 2010, Punjab's share of state revenues is considerably below its share both of population and of revenue generation. The great majority of Pakistan's national leaders (including three out of four of its military rulers) have not been Punjabis.

A widespread opinion exists among the Punjabi elites that the province is in fact 'leaning over backwards' to accommodate the other provinces, even at the cost of both Punjabi and national development.

This feeling in Punjab contributes to support in the province for the Sharifs and the Muslim League. As one of the Muslim League's leaders told me in November 1988, after the elections in which the PPP had won power in Islamabad and the IJI alliance (led by the Muslim League) in Lahore:

> There has been a tremendous growth in provincial awareness in Punjab. The province is looking for its own leader. This is necessary to balance the other provinces, which in the past have blackmailed Punjab – 'if you do not give us more water we will break up Pakistan' and so on. We are 62 per cent of the population of Pakistan, but have only a 45 per cent share of jobs in the state services. We have taken the role of a generous uncle to the other provinces.[9]

On the other hand, the leader in question was Chaudhury Shujaat Hussain of Gujrat; and, after Musharraf's coup against Nawaz Sharif's government in 1999, Chaudhury Shujaat and his brother, Chaudhury Pervez Elahi, abandoned the Sharifs to join Musharraf's administration and take over the government of Punjab themselves. So, as always in Pakistan, collective identities (whether provincial, ethnic, religious or whatever) are constantly being trumped by personal and family loyalties and ambitions.

If the Punjabi elites functioned as a united whole with a common agenda, then they certainly could dominate Pakistan absolutely for a while; but as the sensible ones realize, in the long run they would also destroy Pakistan, because of the furious resentment this would cause in the other provinces. There is little likelihood of this happening, because, as the previous account of Punjab's divisions should suggest, the Punjabi elites are themselves very divided, and have very different agendas.

There does seem to be a sort of loose community of sentiment favouring Punjab among many senior Punjabi army officers and bureaucrats – though one which is endlessly cut across by personal and political ties and ambitions, and by considerations of *qaum* (community) and religious affiliation. As a senior official in Islamabad told me:

> You have to argue twice as hard to push through any project in one of the other provinces; and if I want to push through a project to help a city in

one of the other provinces, I always have to be careful to balance it with one helping a Punjabi city; but it doesn't work the other way round. Any Sindhi-based national government has to lean over backwards to show that it is not disadvantaging the Punjab in any way.

Concerning official jobs, according to the quota Punjabis have less than their proportion of the population, but they are over-represented in the senior jobs. That is partly because they are better educated on average – and that also means that they dominate the merit-based entry and the quota for women.

He also said that I should be aware that he is a Mohajir, and therefore possibly biased himself.

The closest Pakistan came to a united Punjabi establishment was under Zia-ul-Haq, when a Punjabi military ruler created a Punjab-based national political party under a Punjabi industrialist (Nawaz Sharif). However, the alliance between the military and the PML(N) frayed in the 1990s and collapsed completely when General Musharraf overthrew Nawaz Sharif's government in 1999. Since then, relations have been at best extremely distrustful.

In turn, there are deep differences between northern Punjabi industrialists (who tend to support either the PML(N) or military regimes), and southern Punjabi 'feudals' (who tend towards the PPP). Punjabi industrialists, however, cannot dominate military regimes, as witness their failure to achieve their infrastructure and energy needs under both Zia and Musharraf. Finally, the Muslim religious leaders in Punjab are so fractured along theological, political, personal and regional lines that it does not make sense to speak of them as an establishment at all.

Punjabis from north-central Punjab certainly feel superior to the other nationalities in Pakistan, and this feeling – of which the others are well aware – helps to keep ethnic relations in a permanent state of mild tension. The Punjabis from these regions are quite convinced (and it must be said, with good reason) that they are harder working, better organized and more dynamic than anyone else in Pakistan except the Mohajirs; and while Punjabis respect Mohajirs, since the latter are not farmers they cannot really be fully fitted into the traditional Punjabi view of the world (as a very unkind saying about the Punjabi Jats has it: 'Other peoples have culture. The Jats have agri-culture').

For the Sindhis, Punjabis tend to feel a rather amused and tolerant contempt, as for pleasant and easy-going but lazy younger relatives. For the Baloch there is contempt without the tolerance, as primitive tribesmen sponging off Punjabi charity. For the Pathans, however, Punjabi sentiments are very different, in ways that may have an effect on their attitudes to the Taleban and the war in Afghanistan.

Punjabis believe (once again with good reason) that they are more modern and economically dynamic than the Pathans. Yet in Punjabi Muslim culture there is also an ingrained cultural and historical respect for the Muslim pastoral warriors who repeatedly swept across Punjab from Afghanistan, and from whom many Punjabis – especially in the upper classes – are or claim to be descended; and the Pathans, however savage, are widely seen as Muslim warriors *par excellence*, whose prowess has been celebrated in Pakistani literature and propaganda in all the modern wars from Kashmir to Afghanistan.

This identification with the pastoral tradition gives rise to the public and formal (as opposed to private and familial) eating habits of the Punjabis, including in hotels and restaurants; a tradition whereby the green vegetable is almost a publicly persecuted species: part of a heroic effort by a people of mainly bean-eating sedentary farmers to portray themselves to visitors, each other and most of all themselves as meat-eating nomadic herdsmen.[10]

However, the fact that Pathan armies also repeatedly raped, looted and burned their way across Punjab (contributing to the province's lack of historic cities) makes this Punjabi respect for Pathans a somewhat wary one. As a Punjabi lady acquaintance said to me of the Afghan Mujahidin back in 1988: 'I know they are very brave people, fighting for their country against the great Russian army and so on, but I must say I'm glad they are based in Peshawar, not Lahore.' Or as an old southern Punjabi proverb used to have it: 'The son of a Pathan is sometimes a devil, sometimes a demon.'

INDUSTRIALISTS

Driving in Punjab can be a slightly surreal experience. Magnificent (but usually almost empty) new motorways coexist with the same old potholed two-lane 'highways', where the SUVs of the wealthy jostle perilously with the bullock carts and camels of the poor. The motorways are patrolled by the astonishingly honest and efficient national motorway police. The other roads are patrolled (or rather not) by the same old Punjab police.

The same element of surrealism goes for the contrasting sights along the road. Driving to Faisalabad from Multan in the evening, we passed mile after mile of primeval-looking mud villages, with the occasional electric light illuminating some home or roadside stall. My need to stop and retire behind a tree became increasingly urgent, but my driver would not permit it. 'No stop here sir, here very bad people. Baloch, dacoits.' Just as I was preparing to throw myself from the car and into the arms of any bandits who might happen to be passing, a mirage came into sight, blazing with lights like a solitary fairground in a desert: 'Welcome to Paris CNG Station' it said, and offered not merely gas, but a business centre with fax and e-mail and a lavatory with flush toilets.

Business and administration in Faisalabad are rather the same. Faisalabad is the Punjabi industrial and migrant city *par excellence*, at the heart of the canal colonies; and by many indices is Pakistan's most modern and successful city. With a GDP in 2005 of $27 billion (according to Price Waterhouse Cooper) Faisalabad has the third highest GDP in the country after Karachi and Lahore, and the second in terms of per capita production and income; it vies with Karachi for the reputation of having Pakistan's most efficient municipal administration, without Karachi's feral ethnic politics; and it is the heart of Pakistan's biggest export industry, that of textiles.

However, every time you begin to think that you really are visiting 'the Manchester of the East', you are apt to be brought back with a thump to the realities of kinship-based politics, dysfunctional administration, ineffective law, irrational economic policies, mass illiteracy, obscurantist mass culture, and media and academia addled with lunatic conspiracy theories, and (in the case of the English-medium institutions) often barely understanding the language in which they operate. If Faisalabad is clear evidence of Pakistan not failing as a state, it is certainly not evidence that Pakistan is ever going to succeed as one.

Faisalabad earned its proud title of 'Manchester of the East' when Manchester, England, was still the textile capital of the West; and its self-image has a certain nineteenth-century utilitarianism about it. In talking with me, Faisalabadis used the word 'practical' so often to describe themselves and their city that it was easy to think oneself in the world of industrial England in the age of Dickens; especially, it must be said, given the living conditions of the working class.

Literacy in Faisalabad is still between 40 and 50 per cent according to the city government. This is a grotesque figure for a city and region that hopes to become an industrial giant of Asia, and one that reflects both the historic failings of repeated Pakistani and Punjabi governments and the cultural attitudes of the local population – above all when it comes to education for women.

Faisalabad was founded in 1880 as Lyallpur, and named after the then British Governor of the Punjab. It was renamed Faisalabad in 1977 after the late King Faisal of Saudi Arabia, who had displayed considerable generosity to Pakistan. Like the town of Montgomery (now Sahiwal) to the south, it was created by the British as the commercial and administrative centre of one of their new canal colonies, on what had previously been an almost uninhabited area of arid jungle and semi-desert. Patches of this still remain, where either the canals never reached or salination has destroyed the land's fertility again.

The original town was laid out in the shape of a Union Jack, with streets radiating from a central clock-tower, in a sort of Victorian gothic-saracenic style. In 1902 it still only had 9,000 people, but thereafter the growth of commercial farming and cotton cultivation, South Asia's great tradition of textile production, and the settlement of east Punjabi refugees after 1947 led to explosive growth. Today, the city has almost 3 million people and the district more than 5 million – and, being Faisalabad, these statistics may even be accurate. A large proportion of the population – some say a majority – are east Punjabis who replaced local Hindus and Sikhs who fled in 1947. Faisalabad is therefore, partly at least, another example of the economic dynamism of these migrants, even while it also reflects their cultural conservatism.

Faisalabad's municipal government is home to a strategic policy unit, the only effective city institution of its kind (so far as I know) outside Karachi, the leaders of which seemed models of efficiency and dedication. With the help of GHK, a British-based public policy consultancy, and assistance (now alas ended) from the British Department for International Development (DIFID), the unit has developed a number of new projects to revolutionize the city's administration and provision of services. Its work is based largely on a mixture of satellite imaging of the district backed by an intensive programme of local inspection. As a result, for the first time the government is developing an accurate picture of the city, the spread of population, the provision of services, and so on.

Perhaps most importantly, as Gul Hafeez Khokar of GHK told me, it is now possible at the click of a mouse to see whether a planned road or school has actually been built or not: 'This is a check on corruption, because the city government can now check immediately whether a planned road has been built, or the money stolen. And on the other hand, if it has been built, then it doesn't need to be commissioned all over again – something that happens all the time in Pakistan.'

The digital map will allow more efficient provision of services, and hopefully prevent disasters like that of 2007 in a Faisalabad slum when local community pressure on the politicians led to the city government increasing the flow through water pipes to the area. Because it had no idea how many pipes were actually there, it increased the pressure too much and burst the pipes. The result was an outbreak of gastro-enteritis in which several dozen people died. Until the digital mapping project started, the government could not even properly tax gas stations in the city, because it did not know how many there were. It is possible to see all this when the computers are working; but, when I was there, they were not, because the electricity had failed; and, although the local government has its own generators, the money had run out to provide them with fuel.

According to Mr Khokar, 'Things are improving. Not as fast as we would like, but still they are on track.' One key reason for this is that in 2008 the new PML(N) government in Punjab did not withdraw its support from the project, even though it had been initiated under Musharraf and the PML(Q) government of Punjab. This marks a change from the usual – and disastrous – Pakistani practice, which the PML(N) government has followed in other areas.

Some of Faisalabad's cotton industry is also truly impressive. The Chenab mill at Nishatabad is the biggest of eight mills in the Chenab group, with 4,000 workers (out of 14,000 in the group as a whole) and an output in 2008 worth $130 million. The mill is capable of turning out 12,000 individual garments a day. The group owns the stylish (and extremely expensive) Chen One chain of clothes shops and shopping malls in Pakistan, and supplies Macy's, J. C. Penney, Debenhams, Ikea and Laura Ashley, among other international outlets. I am no expert on textile production, but the mill gave a completely modern impression, with apparently well-fed women working on huge, smoothly running machines in giant air-conditioned workshops. One that I visited was producing frilly women's underwear, and I have never seen so much pink in such a large space at the same time. The headquarters building could have been an unusually stylish office in Singapore or Frankfurt. None of this is the kind of thing one sees in a 'failed state'.

When I visited Faisalabad last in January 2009, however, boasts of the city's success were interspersed with bitter complaints about its present economic state (admittedly, a local journalist also warned me that 'Faisalabad is known as "the city of opposition" because our industrialists are not happy whatever happens'). Local anger and worry focused above all on the electricity shortages which at that time were crippling the city's industrial production and exports.

Just as even very moderately well-off families in Pakistan pay a fortune for private generators to avoid the constant load-shedding, so the bigger mills and factories have had to develop their own power plants and import the fuel for them privately. The problem is that not only is this extremely expensive, but in Pakistan's and even Faisalabad's – semi-modern economy, the big mills rely for supplies of many of their semi-finished goods on small local mills and even piece-workers, who are completely dependent on the state electricity grid. Chenab's managing director (and son of its founder, Mian Mohammed Kashif Ashfaq) told me that this is true even of his group.

Above all, though, the problem when I last visited the city was electricity, and the lack of it seemed likely for a while to provoke mass riots that could even have toppled the national government, a conflict in which the industrialists and their workers might have found themselves on the same side. The head of Faisalabad district council, Rana Zahid Tauseef (himself a textile industrialist), complained bitterly:

> My customers in the US, UK, Australia need guaranteed commitments that I will keep my contract to supply them. Yes, my firm has a good reputation so they may wait one week or even six but finally they will say, 'You are not reliable, you live in a shit country, I can't order from you any more.'

How can we possibly compete with other countries if we can't rely on our own electricity grid?[11]

Quite apart from the issue of electricity supply, the working conditions in the smaller workshops – or rather sweat-shops – bear no resemblance to those at Chenab Mills. The contrast is absolutely jarring – as if, while visiting a factory in Lancashire today, you were to be transported by a wicked witch with a taste for education back to a factory in Lancashire in 1849. And for all the modernity of parts of Faisalabad, the 'old' centre around the clock-tower is a typical Pakistani inner-city slum, in which the roads are not even paved.

Concerning the clock-tower, I experienced a small example of how constant mass migration from the countryside continually undermines the development of a civic identity and urban culture in most of Pakistan's cities. My driver, a recent migrant to Faisalabad from a village (but a village only 10 miles away), could not find the tower in the dead centre of town, even when I showed him a postcard of it.

The industrialists heaped curses on the administration of President Zardari for incompetent purchasing decisions and favouring agriculture over industry; but they also had harsh words for the previous Musharraf administration and especially his Prime Minister (previously Finance Minister, from 1999 to 2004), Shaukat Aziz.

In the words of Azem Khurshid, a mill owner:

In terms of our recent leaders, Musharraf was the best of the worst. He appointed some good people and got us out of debt. But he and Shaukat Aziz were obsessed with empty growth figures and with how many cellphones and fridges people were buying. Beyond Gwadar and the motorway, they did nothing for the infrastructure of the country, including electricity generation, on which industry depends – and we are paying the price for it today. We are suffering from all those years of the Washington Consensus which our leaders followed blindly. Now the West is revising its approaches but it will probably take years to filter through here, and we have already lost years which we should have spent building up our real economy ...

And then Musharraf made his compromise with the feudal politicians, and that of course meant favouring agriculture at the expense of industry, and the PPP government is dominated by feudal landowners. Even the Sharifs, though they are industrialists themselves, have to favour the feudals because they have the seats in the countryside and you can't win a majority without them. So throughout Pakistani history, state resources have gone to buying feudals and their families and followers, and not on turning Pakistan into a modern economy.

The obvious question is why, with their wealth, intelligence and economic dynamism, the industrialists and businessmen themselves have not been able to gain greater influence over state policies. After all, even the PPP is no longer explicitly hostile to private industry (as it was in the days of Z. A. Bhutto) and the other major forces are strongly in favour of industry: the PML(N) because the Sharifs are industrialists themselves, the MQM because industry is part of their vision of a modern, successful Karachi, and the military not only because it too believes strongly in modernizing Pakistan, but also because indirectly (thanks to the Fauji Foundation and Army Welfare Trust) it is itself a major industrial force.

The answer seems to lie partly in a combination of sheer lack of weight within society, and an absence of kinship networks. For all that the textile industry dominates Pakistan's exports and is absolutely crucial to its balance of payments and ability to import essential goods, its share of the economy is relatively small, and its workers form a small part of the population as a whole – and this is especially true of modern industries like Chenab Mills.

For every semi-modern city like Faisalabad, there are dozens of medium-sized towns (which in Pakistan means towns with populations of hundreds of thousands of people), where the entire local economy is based on small shops and stalls, small family-owned workshops, and mostly fairly primitive food-processing. In these towns, kinship remains of central political importance, and the political scene is dominated not by modern businessmen but by interlinked clans of urban and rural notables living mainly off rents. The constant swamping of settled urban populations by new waves of migrants also plays a key role in preventing the growth of truly urban politics.

The business community is also fractured along lines of kinship, and by the rivalries and bitterness caused by past political alignments, and the victimization by governments of businessmen who have backed the other side. This has made many industrialists wary of becoming involved in politics at all. 'Businessmen are afraid to get involved with politics because they are afraid that their businesses will be targeted with tax raids, land claims, court cases, deliberate electricity cuts and so on,' Mr Khurshid told me.

Most importantly, perhaps, unlike most of the 'feudals', the industrialists and businessmen in politics have no mass kinship groups to fall back on – and their workers are hardly likely to behave like a clan and guarantee them a permanent vote bank. Because so many city-dwellers have only recently arrived from the country, even in the cities kinship networks often remain vital to power and influence. Money and property are of course very important, but not all-important. Even in Faisalabad city and district, a majority (though a small one) of members of the national and provincial assemblies are from landed families. These are not huge 'feudals', and they usually draw most of their wealth from urban land, but they are still primarily landed notables rather than urban businessmen or professionals.

All of this might have been set aside if the military and the industrial elites had formed a solid alliance to develop the country, as has been the case in a number of developing economies in the past (Germany and Japan are the most famous, if not the happiest examples). This looked as if it might be happening when Zia-ul-Haq re-created the Muslim League and put Nawaz Sharif in charge of it. But in the ten years after Zia's death, first the army refused to back the Muslim League against the PPP, then the Muslim League tried to gain dominance over the military, and then the military under Musharraf shattered the alliance for good by overthrowing Nawaz Sharif. Musharraf, to stay in power, compromised with the same old 'feudal' elements in Punjab, and all chance of a military–political–industrial alliance for development was lost.

That leaves the Islamists. In Turkey, the moderate Islamist party (in its various incarnations) rose to power with mass support, but also very much on the shoulders of provincial business and industrial elites. If anywhere in Pakistan, Faisalabad would seem to be the place where the beginnings of such a development might be found. But, as mentioned earlier, the Jamaat Islami there seems hopelessly tied to its lower-middle-class constituency – which is barred from seeking working-class support by class and cultural factors, but is also too poor and uneducated (compared to its Turkish, Egyptian or Iranian equivalents) to generate any kind of coherent modern social and economic policies.

In the words of a local administrator: 'It would be very difficult for the Islamists to make much headway in Faisalabad, because they have no answer to practical problems like gas and electricity, and this is a very practical place. We are Punjabi businessmen here, not Pathans – warriors, dreamers, fanatics.' Despite the intense anger of many Faisalabad workers at electricity cuts and growing unemployment, during my stay in the city I found no one who seemed to think that there was any serious chance of the Pakistani Taleban successfully appealing for their support and setting off a mass revolt in Faisalabad.

SECTARIANS AND TERRORISTS

It is quite otherwise in different parts of central and southern Punjab. If Punjab – and Pakistan – were to be broken from within by Islamist extremism, then the process would start here, in the belt between Jhang and Bahawalpur, with the ancient city of Multan at its heart. Here, Islamist militancy may be able to make serious inroads with the help of local sectarian forces which since the 1980s have been attacking the local Shia community. The Pakistani Taleban have formed an alliance with these sectarian groups which in 2009–10 led to increasing terrorism in Punjab. Because of poverty, madrasahs in southern Punjab are more important than in the north, where the state education system has a bigger presence (in rural areas, the literacy rate is less than 25 per cent); and these madrasahs have long been a key recruiting ground for militant groups.

Throughout the 1980s and 1990s, madrasahs sent many fighters first to the Mujahidin in Afghanistan, and then to the jihad in Kashmir; so groups like Lashkar-e-Taiba and Jaish-e-Mohammed, formerly backed by the Pakistani military to fight in Kashmir, have a strong presence in southern Punjab. Hundreds of recruits from this region were killed in Kashmir, and as in the Frontier their graves have become local places of pilgrimage. As elsewhere, association with the Kashmiri and Afghan jihads has been absolutely critical to increasing the prestige of local militants.

However, the main jihadi groups in Punjab are not yet in revolt against the Pakistani state; and, precisely because the most important extremist forces in southern Punjab are sectarian forces, it seems to me extremely unlikely that they will be able to start a rebellion that could conquer the region, as the Taleban were able for a number of years to take over large parts of the FATA and Swat. Their ideological programme is bitterly resisted not only by the Shia but by all the local Sunni who are deeply attached to their local shrines and traditions – like Data Ganj Baksh; and their social radicalism will be equally savagely resisted by most of the local elites. This picture would change only if Lashkar-e-Taiba/Jamaat-ud-Dawa were to ally with the TTP – and failing a really determined crackdown on them by the Pakistani authorities, they seem unlikely to do so. I have been told by officials that precisely because their core agenda is anti-India, this gives LeT's leaders an especially acute sense of the Indian threat, and discourages them from taking actions that would weaken or even destroy Pakistan.

What the extremists in this region can do, however, is carry out bloody terrorist attacks, which they have been doing for many years against the Shia. By mid-2010, this extremist alliance had also repeatedly shown its ability to carry out serious terrorist attacks in Punjab against the state and the general public – though it is important to remember once again the crucial difference between terrorism and successful rebellion.

A certain latent tension has existed between Sunni and Shia in this region for a long time, owing to the tendency of successive regimes, ending with the British, to reward Shia nobles – some, like the Turkic Qizilbash, from far away – with great land grants in areas populated by a mainly Sunni peasantry. However, despite occasional denunciations of the Shia as heretics by Sunni preachers, until the 1980s this tension remained very limited.

As the *Multan Gazetteer* of 1923 stated: 'Generally speaking there is very little bitterness between the Sunni and Shia sects, and in the ordinary intercourse of life there is little to distinguish the two'[12] – something that could certainly not have been said of Shia–Sunni relations in other South Asian Muslim cities like Lahore, Quetta and Lucknow. But as Sunni peasants moved into local towns in the mid-twentieth century, a new Sunni lower middle class emerged which saw its access to jobs and patronage blocked by the Shia elites and their clients. A degree of resentment at Shia dominance is therefore widespread. As a (personally enlightened) head teacher in Multan told me: 'There is a feeling among many people here that the Shia stick together, protect each other and give each other the best jobs – like the Freemasons in England.' Anti-Shia groups also built on the successful campaigns from the 1950s to the 1960s to have the Ahmedi sect declared non-Muslim.

In the early 1980s several factors came together to create a wholly new level of sectarian violence, starting in the Jhang district of central Punjab. The Iranian revolution gave new confidence and prominence to the Shia minority in Pakistan, and raised fears in the establishment that they might become a revolutionary force. Many Shia firmly believe – though without any actual evidence – that Washington encouraged the administration to attack the Shia, out of fear that they could spread Iranian-style revolution.

President Zia-ul-Haq had already become bitterly unpopular with many Shia for the execution of Zulfikar Ali Bhutto (a Shia), and for his promulgation of Islamic laws for Pakistan based purely on the teachings of the Hanafi Sunni sect. This move led to massive Shia protests orchestrated by the radical Shia organization the Tehriq-e-Nifaz-e-Fiqah Jafferia, which forced the government to back down and concede to the Shia their own separate code in certain respects.

These developments in turn stoked the anger of certain Sunni groups, and may have led Pakistani intelligence services to favour the creation of Sunni sectarian forces in response. There is, however, no actual evidence of this, and it is entirely possible that these forces simply bought some of the arms which flooded into Pakistan to arm the Afghan Mujahidin – especially as these were being funded by state and private money from Saudi Arabia, with its strong traditional hostility to Iran and Shiism.

Later, the sectarians also forged links with groups participating in the Kashmir jihad, and probably received guns from them – another case of the Frankenstein syndrome or, rather, of Frankenstein's monster wandering off, making friends with other monsters, and starting whole families of little monsters.

The result was the creation in Jhang in 1985 of the Sipah-e-Sahaba Pakistan (SSP), as a breakaway group of the Jamiat-e-Ulema-e-Islam (JUI). The SSP began a programme of attacks on local Shia targets, in the name of declaring the Shia non-Muslims and making Pakistan an officially Sunni state like Saudi Arabia. Local police told me that, in a few cases, local Sunni businessmen owing debts to Shia creditors or with business disputes with Shia rivals paid the SSP or LeJ (Lashkar-e-Jhangvi) to kill them.

Over the years the SSP's activities spread beyond Jhang to take in southern Punjab and other areas of the country where old Sunni–Shia tensions had been latent, including Quetta, Peshawar and the Kurram Agency of FATA, where tribal conflict between the Sunni Bangash and Shia Tori tribes dates back some 300 years. In recent years, the SSP and their even more radical offshoot the LeJ have also extended their anti-Shia campaign to take in Ahmedis and Christians. Radical Shia fought back through the Tehriq-e-Jafferia and other groups, and in the 25 years to 2010 more than 6,000 people have been killed in sectarian clashes and terrorism, with the dead in a rough proportion of three Shia to two Sunni. Individual leaders and activists on both sides have been killed, mosques have been bombed, and on occasions bazaars frequented by people of the rival community have also been attacked.

It should be noted that, unlike with the jihadi groups fighting in Kashmir and Afghanistan, since General Zia's time at least there has been no evidence of Pakistani governments backing the anti-Shia militants. The PPP is naturally extremely hostile to them, if only because the Bhuttos and Zardaris are Shia, and so are (in private at least) many of the PPP's chief supporters among the landowners of central and southern Punjab. Despite the apparent sympathy of some leading members of the PML(N) for the anti-Shia militants, when Nawaz Sharif was Prime Minister in the late 1990s, his government launched a crackdown against them during which many were killed. The response was an attempt by the LeJ to kill Mr Sharif. The Musharraf administration continued this assault on the Sunni sectarians, and banned the SSP and LeJ in January 2002.

These repeated attacks by the state are a key reason why the SSP and LeJ (unlike the militants fighting in Kashmir such as the Lashkar-e-Taiba) have themselves increasingly attacked the state as well as the Shia and Christians, and as of 2009 have formed an alliance with the Pakistani Taleban. The wave of terrorism they have launched in Punjab also gives one more sympathy for the Pakistani state's deep unwillingness to add to the number of their terrorist enemies by attacking the even more formidable Lashkar-e-Taiba. As a senior official in Faisalabad told me in January 2009:

> I am seriously worried about the spread of militancy from Jhang to the rest of Punjab. It is true that so far LeJ and SSP have been only sectarian, but they

can switch. The same is even true of Lashkar-e-Taiba and Jamaat-ud-Dawa, even though we have backed them all these years. We have to worry that if we do what you say and crack down on them that some of them at least will turn to terrorism against Pakistan in alliance with the Taleban. After all, they have the ideology and the training. The last thing we need now is yet another extremist threat.

The fact that despite crackdowns by successive Pakistani regimes the sectarian extremists have been able to survive is another reflection of the weakness of the Pakistani state, and especially of the police and judiciary. In the words of a police officer in Jhang district in 2002:

> There are hundreds of thousands of SSP and Lashkar-e-Jhangvi sympathizers in this region and we aren't America – we can't arrest them all and send them to Cuba. We have to stay more or less within the law. It's different for the hard-core terrorists who we know have killed people – them, we can sometimes just kill. But there are so many more people who may have given them shelter, or who may be going to become terrorists, but who haven't actually done anything yet. Under the anti-terrorism laws, we can hold people for three months, but after that we have to go to the High Court, and the court will demand evidence that we usually don't have, because witnesses just will not come forward – you can understand why. Only very rarely do the courts allow us to hold people permanently in preventive detention. And of course the judges are also frightened. That is why they let out Azam Tariq, though everyone knows he has ordered God knows how many murders . . .
>
> Everyone says that it is because the police sympathize with the militants, but I can tell you that is definitely not true at the senior level – junior policemen, yes, in some cases. But you know twenty-two policemen have been killed by these bastards in Jhang alone in the past ten years. The superintendent of a jail where SSP prisoners were being held was even kidnapped in front of his own jail and killed. That kind of thing scared the police, and for a time we became quite inactive in this part of Punjab. That was especially true in the early '90s, but in recent years we have become much tougher.

As he freely admitted, the difficulty of getting convictions means that if the police get an order to deal firmly with some sectarian leader, their response often is to kill him. Several leaders of the SSP have indeed been killed, either with or without official complicity. In 1990, one of the group's founders, Maulana Haq Nawaz Jhangvi, was killed by Shia terrorists, as was his successor Maulana Zia-ur-Rehman Farooqi. In October 2003, after attempts to convict him for terrorism had failed, SSP leader Maulana Azam Tariq was shot dead by unidentified gunmen a hundred yards or so from a police checkpoint in Islamabad where he had been stopped for half an hour.

Officially, the killing was blamed on Shia militants, but both the private accounts of my official friends and the circumstances of the killing make it clear that the Pakistani state was involved. This was also almost certainly true of Azam Tariq's successor, Allama Ali Sher Haideri, who was killed in an ambush in Khairpur, Sindh, in August 2009, once again ostensibly by Shia militants. The killing came two weeks after an anti-Christian pogrom orchestrated by the SSP in the Punjabi town of Gojra, which killed eight local Christians and severely embarrassed both the national and provincial governments. Private claims by intelligence officials that this was official retaliation for Gojra therefore seem credible.

When covering the 2002 parliamentary elections in Pakistan, I travelled for a while with a Shia politician in central Punjab. According to both official and unofficial sources (speaking off the record), the SSP had made a plot to ambush and kill her, possibly emboldened by the fact that Azam Tariq had been released from jail shortly before and was standing in the elections.

The local police received categorical orders that sectarian attacks on politicians during the elections were to be prevented. The police response? They took three Lashkar-e-Jhangvi activists (whom they suspected but were not able to prove had been responsible for several previous murders of Shia) into a field at night and shot them 'while resisting arrest', and let SSP and LeJ know that if they launched attacks during the elections there would be many more such 'encounter killings' of their members. I asked an official acquaintance whether a strong warning wouldn't have been enough. 'This was a strong warning, the only warning these people understand,' he replied.

In consequence, for many years the sectarians have also been launching attacks on state targets, which in turn has increased state hostility to them. Terrorism by SSP and LeJ increased enormously after the storming of the Red Mosque in 2007 (in which fighters linked to SSP were killed) radicalized Islamists across Pakistan, while US drone attacks killed Punjabis from the sectarian parties fighting for the Taleban in the FATA and Afghanistan.

In July 2009, a huge explosion destroyed part of a village in Multan district and killed seventeen people when an arms cache in the home of a local madrasah teacher with links to the SSP and the Pakistani Taleban blew up accidentally. In the following months, the growth of terrorism in Punjab seems largely to have been the work of SSP and LeJ militants linked to the Pakistani Taleban, rather than of the Taleban as such. According to credible reports, Pakistani intelligence responded in typical fashion with a mixture of arrests, extra-judicial executions, and attempts to split the militants and draw more 'moderate' Sipah-e-Sahaba members into allegiance to the state. This also appears to be the strategy of the PML(N) government of Punjab. Whether it will have any success is at the time of writing wholly unclear.

MULTAN

A famous Persian couplet about Multan sums up some of the reasons for Sunni militant support there, and the immense obstacles to it: 'In four rare things Multan abounds / Heat, dust, beggars and burial grounds.' The notorious heat and dust of summer have no great impact one way or the other, but while the beggars reflect the area's poverty, the burial grounds are those of local Sufi saints and their followers. Multan was the first part of present-day Punjab to be converted to Islam, starting in the tenth century, and the conversion was largely carried out by these saints.

It is impossible to miss the saints in Multan. Their tombs literally tower over the old city on its hill, and give Multan its fame. Several are faced with the equally famous blue Multani tilework. The shrine of Shah Rukn-e-Alam is a particularly striking combination of grim fortress and soaring fantasy. The lower parts consist of walls and towers of massive unadorned brickwork, which act as the base for a beautiful tiled dome.

Despite horribly destructive sieges by the Sikhs and British, and the whims of the Chenab River, which now flows several miles away, a combination of the strategic hill and pilgrimages to the saints' tombs has meant that Multan has always been rebuilt in the same place. It is indeed the oldest continuously inhabited city in Pakistan, and visitors are shown the spot on the old walls where Alexander the Great was wounded during his attack on the city. This might conceivably be true, though the attraction of the spot for tourists is sadly diminished by the fact that it now faces yet another concrete semi-slum which over the years has swamped what used to be a Mughal garden.

Worship of the saints is the greatest local obstacle to the spread of Sunni radical ideology in southern Punjab, just as the political power of the great landowning families – Gilani, Qureishi, Khakwani and Gardezi – who are the saints' descendants and custodians of their shrines (*pirs*) means that a radical takeover would require a massive social revolution. At the time of writing, both the Pakistani Prime Minister, Syed Yusuf Raza Gilani, and the Foreign Minister, Syed Shah Mahmood Qureshi, are from Multani *pir* families. They are both from the PPP, but began in the PML(N), and other branches of their family are still in that party.

The shrines and the *pir* families illustrate a key obstacle to the propagation of sectarian hatred in Punjab, which is that no one knows how many Shia there actually are, because in a great many cases no one can ascertain – including quite often the people concerned themselves – who is Shia and who is Sunni. The Sufi shrines, their custodians and their followers play an important part in this by constantly preaching against the Sunni–Shia divide and stressing that 'our saint preached that there should be neither Sunni nor Shia, but only worshippers of God' – as I was told at many shrines.

Apart from the stricter followers of the saints, masses of ordinary local people worship at the shrines and are influenced by this feeling. As for the *pir* families themselves, some of the Gardezis are openly Shia, as is their shrine. The Qureishis and Gilanis are generally thought to be Shia, but practise Sunni worship in public. Then there is a variety of traditional local arrangements, either based on status, or intended to dampen sectarian conflict and extend the alliance networks of particular clans. Thus I was told that the local Khosar tribe (like the Legharis, of Baloch origin but now Seraiki-speaking) worship the local saints and take their wives from Shia families, while the men of the tribe remain Sunni. Sayyids (descendants of the Prophet, including all the *pir* families)

by definition only marry other Sayyids, and this rule is far more important than sectarian divides.

I visited the shrine of Shah Yusuf Gardezi in Multan together with a
member of the Syed Gardezi family, a student at the local Broomfield
Hall School where I had given a talk. The shrine is home not only to the
tomb of the original saint but to those of members of his family and
leading followers – including the lion and snake which accompanied
him to Multan, and come in for their own share of respect. Presumably
when paying respects to a lion the question of whether the creature was
a Shia or Sunni lion is not uppermost in the mind of the worshipper.

Though openly Shia, the shrine is therefore also worshipped at by local
Sunni. The stories of miracles I heard about the shrine were told to me
by local Shia and local Sunni. A senior official in Multan told me that
during the Shia festival of Ashura (10th Moharram) in Multan, when
the administration issues licences to carry *taziyas* (imitation mausole-
ums of the martyred Imams made of wood and paper, like small towers)
in procession, '90 per cent of the licences went to people calling themselves Barelvi Sunnis'.

Less encouraging was what my Gardezi guide told me in January
2009 about his school. Broomfield Hall is very much the school of the
local elite (not the very top elite, who would go to the famous schools
of Lahore, but their close relatives). He said that three quarters of the
boys in his class sympathize with the Pakistani Taleban: 'They say that
they are good Muslims oppressed by America and the Pakistani army.'
He said that one seventeen-year-old son of a local businessman

> is trying to grow a big beard to look what he calls proper Muslim. He says
> he is a Wahabi. I don't think he really knows what that means but he
> certainly hates us Shia. He says that he would like to go to America and
> blow himself up together with Americans. He makes me laugh, though it
> isn't really very funny.

Most of this is doubtless adolescent posturing, but as far as anti-
American sentiment among the students goes, there can be no doubt.
When I spoke to the senior classes, they were full of the same crazed
conspiracy theories as the rest of society. In their view, it has been proved
that the Jews were responsible for 9/11; that a Jewish conspiracy exists
to dominate the world; that the US has occupied Afghanistan in order
to invade Pakistan, Iran and Central Asia, and so on, and on.

The vast majority of Broomfield's students of course have far too much to lose ever to join an extremist group; but sentiments among poor people on the street were just as extreme – and they have far less to lose. As in the rest of Punjab, in January 2009 in Multan I found some sympathy for the Pakistani Taleban among most of those people I asked who declared themselves to be Sunni (I made a point of asking my interviewees' sectarian affiliation, though many refused to answer, in some cases giving adherence to a saint as the reason). Concerning the idea of military action against the Taleban (Pakistani or Afghan) a majority of Sunni and even some Shia were opposed. This may have changed since then, but I doubt it has changed completely.

However, the Shia (together with smaller minority Muslim groups like the Bohra, who also fear persecution by Sunni radicals) were the only section of the population with many members willing to support military action. Shia and Bohra were also the only former PPP voters on the streets in Multan, many of whom still said that they would vote for Zardari and the PPP at the next election. As of that date at least, the local Sunni seemed to have deserted the party en masse.

Then again, one should not make too much of this. Several of the Shia and Bohra also said that they were sick of the PPP and Zardari and would vote PML(N) at the next election, and a good many Sunni, if not a majority, denounced the Pakistani Taleban and said it was right to fight against them. All my interviewees, Sunni, Shia and Bohra alike, denounced the US and its presence in Afghanistan, but then that is true even in the most anti-militant circles in Pakistan. Furthermore, this was among the lower-middle-class shopkeepers in the bazaars of Multan city, where one would expect Sunni militant feeling to be stronger, and where people (including the Shia middle classes, for economic reasons) are more likely to vote PML(N). After the 2008 elections, of Multan district's six national assembly seats, three were held by the PPP, two by the PML(N) and one by the PML(Q). Two of the PPP's Members of the National Assembly (MNAs) and the PML(Q) MNA were from *pir* families. The PLM(N) MNAs were a small landowner and a local businessman.

In the countryside of Punjab south of Multan, *pirs* and their shrines are still very widely revered, and kinship groups and their hereditary landowning chieftains remain politically dominant. This, the Seraiki language, and the presence of large numbers of Baloch tribes bind southern

Punjab closely to Sindh, the subject of the next chapter – more closely in many respects than to northern Punjab. Rural Sindh contains very little support for Islamist militancy of either the jihadi or the sectarian variety; but like southern Punjab and Balochistan – and unlike northern and central Punjab – most of Sindh also contains few signs of economic and social change and dynamism.

8

Sindh

We all knew it would start up again – the shootings on a massive scale, the unnatural silence in the evenings, the siege mentality – but for the moment, for today, Karachi was getting back on its feet, as it had always been able to do, and that didn't just mean getting back to work, but getting back to play: friendship, chai, cricket on the street, conversation . . . In the midst of everything that was happening, Karachi had decided to turn round and wink at me. And in that wink was serious intent: yes, the city said, I am a breeding ground for monsters, but don't think that is the full measure of what I am.

(Kamila Shamsie)[1]

On the late afternoon of 29 April 2009 in Karachi I visited the local headquarters of the Jamaat Islami party and spent a couple of hours talking with the head of their social welfare organization; then went on to Zeinab Market in the old downtown area to buy some presents, and spent another hour or so haggling over tablecloths and shawls; then to another shop to buy a new suitcase, and back to my hotel for a shower and a meal, and to call my family.

That done, I turned on the television to see if anything important had happened during the day, and discovered that yes, it had – thirty-four people had been killed in gun battles and targeted shootings over the previous few hours in outlying parts of Karachi; and no one whom I'd met in the centre of town had thought it worth mentioning, or had changed their behaviour in any way as a result.

What was even more striking was that this experience echoed one of almost twenty years before, when I was visiting Karachi as a journalist in August 1989. Then, too, a gun battle erupted in another part of town, of which I and everyone I met were unaware until I was tipped off by a local journalist. On that occasion, if I remember rightly, there were only six dead.

The fighting then was between fighters from the Mohajir majority in Karachi and others from the Sindhi minority in the city (but majority in the province as a whole). In 2009, the fighting was between Mohajirs and Pathans. Otherwise, at first sight, *plus ça change* . . . Nothing about the Rangers (a paramilitary corps under the army, acting as a reserve force of order in the city) trying to separate the two sides had changed, nor the alert, tense, rather contemptuous glances they cast over the local population from behind the light machine-guns mounted on their jeeps. Nor had anything at all changed in the handful of mostly ill-equipped and dirty hospitals to which the wounded were ferried. There have been several more such battles in 2009 and 2010.

All this is a long way of saying that Karachi is a deeply divided city, but also a very big city, with a remarkable capacity to tolerate episodes of great violence. In 1989 the population was already 8 million, bigger than London's. By 2009, it had swelled to a megalopolis of around 18 million – or at least that was the estimate Karachi's mayor gave me and uses as a basis. Other opinions from officials ranged from 15 to 20 million. Obviously, a city which is not sure of the existence of several million people isn't going to miss thirty-four very badly; and indeed, visiting the affected areas in the following days, it was not easy to spot the occasional burnt-out shop and minibus amid the thousands of shops and minibuses still plying their trade on the endless streets.

Nor is Karachi a particularly violent city by world standards. Even if political and ethnic violence are included, the murder rate in Karachi at the last count put it twenty-fifth among the great cities of the world. Remove these elements, and the rate goes down to well below that of several large cities in the US. Despite the killings of April 2009, Karachi is still – God willing – much more peaceful than it was when I knew it in the late 1980s. As of 2010, killings are chiefly targeted, aimed at the activists and 'hard men' on either side; the killings are part of the polit-ical game, of the 'negotiated state'. Then, there were mass killings, with bomb attacks and pillion riders on motorbikes firing Kalashnikovs into crowds, leaving dozens dead at a time, and pointing towards outright ethnic civil war. This improvement in the country's greatest city has to be set against the growing violence of the Pathan areas of northern Pakistan. As usual, Pakistan is stumbling along, worse in some ways, better in others.

For that matter, even in its worst years Karachi was very far from the anarchy of West Africa, let alone Somalia or the Congo. Indeed, anyone who has done no more than visit Karachi airport can tell the difference. Since 2000, under two generally honest, efficient and dynamic city governments, the city's infrastructure has considerably improved. All the same, there have been moments in Karachi when I was tempted to kiss the Rangers (a temptation strongly to be resisted).

Finally, it is worth noting that none of the major outbreaks of conflict in Karachi over the past generation has involved the Taleban, or Islamist extremism in general. There have been isolated terrorist attacks by Sunni Islamist extremists in the city, including serious terrorism against local Shia, the murder of Daniel Pearl and the bomb attack on the US consulate; and Jamaat Islami students have been involved in armed clashes with other student groups in the university, but Karachi's tensions are overwhelmingly ethnic, not sectarian.

In fact, the Taleban stand about as much chance of taking over Karachi as I do, given the make-up and culture of most of its inhabitants. Rather, the dangers to Karachi from the Taleban are twofold. The first is that Taleban terrorist attacks attributed to members of the Pathan minority in the city may exacerbate ethnic tensions to the point where they are beyond the power of the army and Rangers to contain, and the economic life of the city – and of Pakistan – is severely damaged.

The second, more remote possibility is that developments elsewhere will split the army and weaken the state to the point where their control over Sindh and Karachi will collapse altogether, and this region will be delivered over to its own inner demons. On the basis of my own researches, I can state with melancholy confidence that the ability of Sindh's populations to regulate their differences peacefully in the absence of the Pakistani state would be low to non-existent.

Looming behind the short- to medium-term threat of ethnic violence is an even greater long-term danger – that of water: not enough of one kind, and too much of another. For the past 5,000 years and more, human civilization in this region has been a gift only of the River Indus, which flows through what would otherwise be desert and semi-desert.

After the British conquered Sindh in the 1830s, their first census recorded a population of barely 1.3 million people. One hundred and seventy years later, the population has soared to around 50 million people – and 50 million people cannot live in a desert.

This growth was thanks above all to massive British irrigation projects, which turned large areas of semi-desert into some of the most fertile land on earth. But almost all the water that flows down these canals still comes from the same old source: the Indus, that 'capricious and incalculable river'; and through a mixture of over-use and appalling wastefulness, in the decade leading up to 2010 the Indus no longer flowed into its delta for much of the year, and the sea crept in to replace it.

The great floods of 2010 have replenished the delta and promised Sindh's farmers a bumper crop in 2011, but this is likely to be a purely temporary effect – unless, on the one hand, Sindh can develop an infrastructure to conserve and use its water properly; or, on the other hand, such floods become a frequent occurrence, in which case much of Sindhi agriculture will be reduced to a subsistence level. By driving hundreds of thousands of Sindhi and Pathan peasants from their swamped lands and wrecked villages into Mohajir-dominated Karachi, the 2010 floods have also threatened Sindh's precarious ethnic peace – a tendency that can only get much worse if ecological disasters become a regular pattern.

As to the consequences of a really serious rise in sea levels as a result of climate change, you only have to stand on the low sea wall at Karachi and look at the city with its millions of inhabitants stretching back across miles of low-lying land (Karachi's average height above sea level is 26 feet) to imagine what would happen.

Caught between the hungry sea and the thirsty land, and with both pressures in danger of drastically intensifying as a result of climate change, Sindh needs nothing less than a revolution in its system of land use and water management over the next decades if human civilization in this region is not to be seriously threatened. Given the centrality of landownership to Sindhi political society, and the centrality of water to usable land, such a revolution would probably need to be not only technological and economic but also social and political; and whether one of the most stagnant societies in Asia is capable of such change seems highly doubtful.

THE HISTORY OF SINDH

The Indus (in Sanskrit, *Sindhu*) gives its name to Sindh, to India and also to the oldest civilization in Sindh, and one of the oldest on earth: the Indus Valley civilization, which existed in various forms between around 3300 and 1300 BCE. That civilization was destroyed, presumably by Aryan invaders from Central Asia, around 3,000 years ago, and no visible link exists between it and the Sindh of today.

However, it is rather depressing, when visiting the excavated ruins of the city of Mohenjo Daro in upper Sindh, to note that its clay bricks were better made and better laid than those of most Sindhi towns and villages of the present, though both are made from the same mud. Samina Altaf remarks that Mohenjo Daro's water supply also seems to have been better than those of many Pakistani cities today.[2]

Equally depressing is the fact that waterlogging because of rice cultivation in the surrounding fields and neglect by the Pakistani government means that by far the greater part of Mohenjo Daro, and all its earliest levels, are now lost for ever, melted back into the mud from which they came. In fact, Mohenjo Daro is apt to arouse bitter musings on cycles of historical decline in anyone with a reverence for the past and its exploration.

A traveller of 1842 described the homes of ordinary rural Sindhis:

> All the houses here are built of clay; they are scarcely twenty feet high, have flat roofs, from which a kind of ventilator sometimes rises, and air holes supply the place of windows. Long continued rain would destroy these huts and sweep away whole villages.[3]

Just as nothing much about the dwellings of ordinary people had changed in the thousands of years of human habitation in Sindh prior to this description, so nothing much seems to have changed in the 168 years since. This is one reason why the floods of 2010 were not as destructive as appeared at first sight. To put it bluntly: mud huts are easy to rebuild.

The ruins of Mohenjo Daro are topped by the much later stupa of a Buddhist monastery, representing the religion which for 1,000 years or so partially displaced the Hindu system created by the Aryans. Muslim rule began in the region with the conquests of Mohammed bin Qasim, an

Arab general, after 710 CE, though it was not until some 500 years later that the bulk of the Hindu population was converted to Islam. Though the original conquest was extremely violent, the subsequent conversion was largely peaceful, and was above all the work of the 'Sufi' saints described in Chapter 4, whose worship still predominates in interior Sindh. Around 20 per cent remained Hindu until the partition of India in 1947, and Sindh still contains by far the largest number of Hindus in Pakistan.

Sindh was the original gateway of Islam into the Indian subcontinent, spreading by sea from Arabia. In subsequent centuries, however, the importance of the sea links to Arabia faded, and the main Muslim route of invasion, migration and trade came to be from Iran and Central Asia through Afghanistan to Punjab and on to the plains of the Ganges. Cut off by the deserts of Balochistan to the west and the Thar to the east, and by the swamps of the Rann of Kutch to the south-east, Sindh developed in partial isolation from the main currents of Muslim life in the subcontinent. This isolation has strongly marked Sindhi culture down to the present.

From the early sixteenth century to the early eighteenth, Sindh was incorporated in the Mughal empire, though actual control by the central government was very loose. With the decline of the Mughals in the early eighteenth century, power was progressively seized by their local governors, the Kalhoras. In the later eighteenth century, the Kalhoras transferred their allegiance first to Nadir Shah of Iran, then to the Durrani dynasty of Afghanistan. Towards the end of the eighteenth century, the Kalhoras were themselves displaced by a new dynasty, that of the Talpurs, who ruled until the British conquest of 1843. The glory of the Talpurs is still recalled by the magnificent tiled and painted palaces of their secondary capital of Kot Diji, a place that cries out for conservation and tourism development but which, like Mohenjo Daro, has been quite shamefully neglected by the government.

The Kalhoras and Talpurs represented traditions which remain of central importance in much of Sindh today. The Kalhoras represented the hereditary descendants of the saints and of the Prophet (highly improbably in this as in most cases, since they are generally thought to have been descended from converted Hindus). The Talpurs represented the tribes of Baloch origin, which had always been present in Sindh but which increased their numbers greatly in the disorders which followed the end of Mughal rule.

These two groups provide many of the great landowner-politicians who continue to dominate the politics of 'interior Sindh'. Both the Kalhoras and the Talpurs also illustrate the vagueness of religious distinctions among the Sindhis, since the Kalhora saints were worshipped by both Sunnis and Shia, while the Talpurs include both Shia and Sunni branches. The shrines of the saints, large and small, extend across the Sindhi countryside. As Sarah Ansari writes: 'By the end of the eighteenth century, it had become virtually impossible to travel more than a few miles in Sindh without coming across the shrine of one saint or another.'[4]

Like the Seraiki belt of southern Punjab described in the last chapter, Sindh is the area of Muslim South Asia most dominated by the worship of *pirs*. As to the Baloch tribes, their migration from the deserts and semi-deserts to the west has contributed to the extreme conservatism of Sindhi rural society, its violent obsession with honour, and its tendency to cattle-lifting, banditry and tribal feuds.

In previous centuries, these Baloch tribes of Sindh, like the Mazaris, could field hundreds or even thousands of armed men each. The fort-like appearance of Sindhi villages, with their thorn fences and blank exterior walls with holes that do duty both for ventilation and as loopholes, attest to the traditional insecurity of Sindhi rural life, and the long lineage of Sindhi dacoity (banditry). In previous centuries, all the settled populations and traders were at risk from tribal raiders, but especially at risk were the Hindu merchants, bankers and moneylenders who dominated Sindh's commercial economy.

Under British rule, the Sindhi Hindu commercial classes profited greatly from increased law and order, an end to tribal raids, the development of a modern civil code governing commercial transactions, and the overcoming of Sindh's traditional isolation through the construction of railways and the great port of Karachi – which, when the British arrived, had been a small town of 14,000 people, dependent chiefly on fishing. Especially in Karachi, the Hindus were joined by Muslim immigrants from Gujarat and elsewhere in India, chiefly from ethnic and religious groups with strong commercial traditions such as the Memons, Khojas and Bohras, as well as Parsis.

By the later British period, these came to make up the bulk of the middle classes in Sindh. This movement was facilitated by the fact that until 1936 Sindh was not a separate province, but was part of the Bombay Presidency, ruled from the great commercial metropolis of that name. The father of Pakistani independence, Mohammed Ali Jinnah, came from a Khoja family of Gujarat, which settled in Karachi, and which contained Ismaili and orthodox ('Twelver') Shia branches.

As a result of this influx, Karachi emerged as a city which even before independence had a very different culture and ethnic character from that of the rest of Sindh, of which it (and not the Talpurs' Hyderabad) became the capital. In 1947, a majority of Karachi's inhabitants were Hindu. Karachi grew partly as a result of the enormously increased agricultural exports first of Punjab (from the 1890s) and then Sindh (from the 1930s) as a result of British irrigation projects.

Its greatest single boost under the Raj, however, came from the First World War, when it became one of the greatest points of transit for troops and supplies from British India to the British campaigns against the Ottoman empire in the Middle East. By independence Karachi had a population of some 350,000. By the census of 1961 this had risen to more than 2 million, by 1981 to 5 million, and today to some 18 million.

INDEPENDENCE AND MOHAJIR–SINDHI RELATIONS

The moment that conclusively wrenched Karachi into a separate path of development from 'interior Sindh' came with independence and partition. The very phrase 'interior Sindh' is suggestive, especially in the mouths of Urdu-speaking Karachiites, when it takes on some of the overtones of mid-Victorian references to the interior of Africa. Millions of Urdu-speaking Muslim 'Mohajirs' (a Muslim term meaning refugees for the sake of religious belief, after those who followed the Prophet from Mecca to Medina) left India for Pakistan, and by far the greater number settled in Karachi, and to a lesser extent in Sindh's second city of Hyderabad, both of which they came to dominate.

The resulting growth in Karachi's population was explosive even by the standards of the developing world – and it often seems a miracle that this growth did not overwhelm it completely, and that it manages to function better than most cities in Africa and many in Asia and South America. As of 2010, Karachi generates around a quarter of Pakistan's state revenues and GDP, and contains more than half of Pakistan's banking assets and almost a third of Pakistan's industry.

This economic dynamism was above all a result of the influx of non-Sindhis. As a result of this migration, in 1998, according to the census, Urdu-speakers made up 21 per cent of the population of Sindh, compared to 59 per cent Sindhi-speakers. In Karachi, they were 48 per cent, with around another 8 per cent made up of Gujarati, who also left India after 1947 and so come under the same heading of Mohajir.

The balance was made up mainly of other migrants to Karachi: almost 14 per cent Punjabis (including a number whose ancestors were settled in the countryside under British rule) and 11 per cent Pashto-speakers in Karachi in 1998 (certainly higher today). Only 7.22 per cent of the population of Karachi in 1998 was Sindhi-speaking. The balance was largely made up of Muslim emigrants from Gujarat in India, who speak their own languages but as Mohajirs tend to identify with the Urdu-speakers and the MQM. In Sindh as a whole, although so many Sindhis are of Baloch origin, most speak the Sindhi language, meaning that Balochi-speakers account for only 2 per cent of the population.

The Sindhis helped the process by which Urdu-speakers came to dominate the main cities by their attacks on the Hindu minority, which, though not nearly as savage as in Punjab, nevertheless led to the flight of most of them by 1950, and of all their wealthy and influential elements. Sindhi Hindu refugees went to swell the commercial prosperity of Gujarat and Bombay, but also to increase anti-Muslim chauvinism in India. The leader of the Hindu nationalist Bharatiya Janata Party (BJP), Lal Krishna Advani, was born in Karachi in 1927.

Like Punjab, Muslim Sindh came round to supporting the partition of India very late, and might indeed easily have wrecked the entire idea. The strongest support for the Muslim League in Sindh before independence came from ethnic non-Sindhis: the urban middle classes and dynamic Punjabi farmers who had settled in Sindh to exploit the new lands made fertile by British irrigation projects. Opposition to the League came from the Sindh United Party, which, like the Unionist Party in Punjab, tried to bridge the gap between Muslims and Hindus and preserve a united India with increased provincial autonomy. The United Party's Muslim membership was dominated by big 'feudal' landowners including Sir Shah Nawaz Bhutto, father of Zulfikar Ali Bhutto and grandfather of Benazir Bhutto.

The Muslim League encouraged and exploited a wave of anti-Hindu feeling in the 1940s to defeat the United Party, but then itself split into two factions. The former President of the League in Sindh, G. M. Syed, clashed bitterly with Jinnah over Syed's demands for Sindh to be fully autonomous within a loose Pakistani confederation. He left the party to found a Sindhi nationalist party, which still exists under the leadership of his son.

The nationalism of Syed and his followers was greatly increased by the influx of Mohajirs to Karachi and Hyderabad after 1947, taking over homes and property abandoned by the Hindus. The Sindhis dubbed the Mohajirs *makhar* – after the locusts which still sometimes devastate parts of the Sindhi countryside. The Mohajirs hit back with *paindu* ('villager', with a connotation of 'country bumpkin') or even *choupaya* (domestic animal, beast of burden).

The Mohajirs were and remain far better educated than the mainly rural Sindhis, and came mostly from middle-class urban backgrounds in India. According to the 1951 census, only 15 per cent of Mohajirs were unskilled labourers, with almost 40 per cent classified as clerical or sales workers, and 21 per cent as skilled workers. More than 5 per cent were from professional and managerial backgrounds. Karachi in consequence has the highest literacy rate of any city in Pakistan – which at 65 per cent is admittedly not saying very much. These origins continue to mark the Mohajirs out not merely from Sindhis but from the vast majority of Pakistanis, and the self-identification as a modern urban middle class is at the heart of Mohajir cultural and – later – political identity:

> The middle-class faction of Mohajirs has defined the core characteristics of Mohajir cultural identity: education, Urdu, resistance, urbanism. These characteristics are the privileges and qualities that were taken for granted for decades but were threatened in the 1960s and 1970s. These privileges and qualities are of central importance in the reading of history and have become part of Mohajir culture. Therefore, all Mohajirs are considered middle class – even the slum-dwellers in Usmania Mohajir Colony and the men who take their lunch in five-star hotels.[5]

The Mohajirs spoke Pakistan's new national language, Urdu, at home. This gave them a colossal advantage in competition for government jobs, which was increased still further by their residence in Karachi, which until 1958 was Pakistan's capital and a separate federally administered district. Mohajirs naturally also dominated the Urdu- and English-language educational establishments in Karachi, relegating Sindhis to a severely underfunded Sindhi university in Hyderabad. Sindh itself was dissolved as a province from 1955 to 1970, and incorporated in the 'one unit' of West Pakistan, intended to create a balance against the other unit of East Pakistan, with its somewhat larger population. Under 'one unit', Mohajirs and to a lesser extent Punjabis dominated the bureaucracy and police in Sindh at the expense of Sindhis.

RISE OF THE MQM (MOHAJIR QAUMI MAHAZ OR MOHAJIR PEOPLE'S MOVEMENT)

By the early 1970s, however, the advantage had swung back heavily in favour of the Sindhis. The shift of the national capital to Islamabad in the 1960s had reincorporated Karachi in the province of Sindh and reduced the Mohajirs' access to government positions; and the rise of the Sindhi Z. A. Bhutto's Pakistan People's Party (PPP) for the first time gave the Sindhis a grip both on a national political party and (from 1971 to 1977) on national government. Bhutto established quotas in education and government service for people from the rural areas of Sindh – in other words, ethnic Sindhis – that drastically reduced Mohajir opportunities in these fields.

Bhutto's anti-capitalist rhetoric was particularly directed at the non-Sindhi commercial elites of Karachi, and his establishment of Sindhi as the official provincial language hurt Mohajir prospects in Sindh. In the words of Feroz Ahmed, this confronted the Mohajirs with 'a sudden need to face the reality of Sindh'.

> For 23 years the Mohajirs of Karachi had never even thought of being in Sindh; a majority of them had never seen a Sindhi nor heard their language being spoken. Their youth had grown up thinking that Karachi was a Mohajir enclave or a world unto itself. In everyday speech, as in the press, the expression 'Karachi and Sindh' was in vogue [it still is – AL] ... For many Mohajirs, the return of Karachi to Sindh was nothing less than surrendering a homeland for the second time.[6]

This reinforced a sense among Mohajirs that they were losing the country – Pakistan – that 'they had founded', as the Punjabi elites had increasingly taken over from Mohajirs in the central bureaucracy – a shift symbolized and reinforced by the move of the capital to the new Punjabi city of

Islamabad. By the 1980s, the Mohajirs also found their ethnic dominance of Karachi under pressure from growing numbers of Punjabi and especially Pathan migrants.

This decline has continued since. In 1981, Mohajirs made up 24.1 per cent of the population of Sindh compared to 55.7 Sindhis, 10.6 per cent Punjabis and 3.6 per cent Pathans. By 1998, the Mohajir proportion had fallen to 21 per cent and the Sindhi proportion had risen to 59 per cent. The next census is going to be an explosive issue, because it will almost certainly show that the Mohajir proportion has dropped still further. In addition, there is a well-founded suspicion that a desire to evade registration for taxes means that a large part of the Pathan population of Karachi does not even appear in the census.

The Mohajirs lack the inward migration of the Pathans, and their higher level of education has also meant a lower birth-rate than that of both the Pathans and the Sindhis. Part of the explanation of the ruthlessness of the MQM can be explained by the perceived need to compensate for inexorable demographic decline by rigid political control, and by the fact that, in the words of one MQM activist, 'We cannot afford to give an inch, because we have our backs to the sea. The Sindhis have Sindh, and the Pathans can go back to their mountains; but we have nowhere but Karachi.' The new influx of Sindhis and Pathans displaced by the 2010 floods has increased this Mohajir fear still further.

The break-off of East Pakistan in 1971 seemed to destroy the premise of Muslim nationalism on which Pakistan had been founded, in which most Mohajirs had passionately believed, and for the sake of which they had sacrificed so much. Most had genuinely thought that the different ethnicities of Pakistan would merge themselves in one Urdu-speaking Muslim nation – though one in which those who had 'left their homes for Pakistan' would have an especially distinguished place.

The symbolic moment when Mohajirs began to think of themselves as a separate nationality within Pakistan, rather than simply as the best Pakistanis, came in August 1979, when a young student activist, Altaf Hussain, burned a Pakistani flag at Jinnah's tomb in Karachi, after making a speech on Mohajir rights – for which he was imprisoned and flogged by Zia-ul-Haq's military regime. He went on to found the Mohajir Qaumi Mahaz (Mohajir People's Movement), the political party that still dominates Karachi.

The result was a growth in ethnic violence between Sindhis and

Mohajirs in Karachi and Hyderabad, language riots that split Karachi University, and the beginning of Mohajir organization along ethnic lines. Previously, the dominant party among the middle- and lower-middle-class Mohajirs had been the Jamaat Islami, with its mixture of Islamist politics, anti-feudalism and Pakistani nationalism. The Jamaat remains to this day strongly marked by its Mohajir middle-class and urban origins.

Strong Mohajir support for the protest movement against Bhutto's government, and for the military regime of Zia-ul-Haq that followed, contributed further to Sindhi–Mohajir tension. Sindhi loyalty to the PPP, and dislike of the Punjabi-dominated army, made Sindh the centre of opposition to Zia's rule. Extensive protests in interior Sindh in the early 1980s led to a military crackdown in which some 1,500 people were killed. This is still described by Sindhi nationalist intellectuals (with gross exaggeration) as 'a genocide of the Sindhi people'. The movement was crushed, but left an enduring legacy of violent crime in interior Sindh, as fugitives from military law fled into the jungles to swell the bandit gangs of the region. Meanwhile, thousands of Sindhi PPP supporters were purged by Zia from the bureaucracy, and from the staffs of the state companies as these were reprivatized.

Meanwhile Mohajir radical groups came together in the MQM – allegedly with covert support from Zia's regime and the ISI, which wished to strengthen opposition to the Sindhi PPP in the province. The first major ethnic violence in Karachi under Zia, however, was not Mohajir against Sindhi, but Mohajir against Pathan, the start of a history of intermittent violence between these two communities which surfaced again during my stay in Karachi in April 2009.

As today, Mohajir resentment and fear of the Pathans was fuelled by cultural differences, by the Pathans' grip on passenger and freight transport in the city – an ethnic monopoly often enforced by violence – and, above all, by a growth in Pathan numbers and claims on public land. As today, this was due to a mixture of economic factors and war. The Soviet occupation of Afghanistan and the struggle against it sent some 3 million mainly Pathan refugees into Pakistan, a proportion of whom made their way to join the Pathan community of Karachi. With them came a great increase in the heroin trade, and in the number of automatic weapons in the city. In the 1970s, ethnic clashes in Karachi had been fought with knives, clubs and the occasional pistol. By the late 1980s the combatants were equipped with Kalashnikovs and, sometimes, rocket-propelled grenades and light machine-guns. The effect on the casualty figures can be imagined.

The first major outbreak of violence came in April 1985, when a Mohajir schoolgirl, Bushra Zaidi, was killed by a speeding Pathan-driven minibus. This sparked murderous attacks by Mohajirs and Punjabis on Pathans, leaving at least fifty-three dead in all. Much of the violence was orchestrated by young activists of the student wing of the Jamaat Islami, the Islami Jamaat-e-Taleba – though apparently without the approval of the party leadership.

In the succeeding years, many of these activists – including the MQM's founder, Altaf Hussain himself – left the Jamaati student groups to join the MQM. That party's origins lay among students of lower-middle-class origin. In this, it resembles the Jamaat but is radically different from all the other major Pakistani parties, which were formed by rural or urban magnates. Altaf Hussain founded the MQM in 1984, and in August 1986 the party held its first mass rally, in Nishtar Park, at which he declared the Mohajirs a separate nation within Pakistan. Already, the party's influence had spread so far that the rally was attended by hundreds of thousands of Mohajirs. Pictures of Altaf Hussain addressing this crowd are central parts of MQM iconography.

In the following years, hundreds more people were killed on all sides in ethnic violence. In 1987, the MQM defeated the Jamaat – in what you could call a kind of matricide, given the Jamaati origins of the MQM leadership – and swept to victory in local elections in both Karachi and Hyderabad, reigniting Sindhi fears of the Mohajirs. By 1988, this Sindhi–Mohajir violence was also occurring on a large scale, with Sindhi extremist groups allegedly receiving covert help from RAW, the Research and Analysis Wing of the Indian intelligence service. Hyderabad was even worse affected than Karachi, and its neighbourhoods became completely distinct ethnically as a result of what almost amounted to ethnic cleansing. Mohajirs fled from the rest of the towns of Sindh, deepening the ethnic divide in the province still further.

The MQM built up a powerful armed wing, which targeted not only Sindhi and Pathan militants but journalists and others who dared to criticize the MQM in public. Torture chambers were established for the interrogation of captured enemies. Every morning would see its harvest dumped by the roadside: murdered activists from the various sides, or unlucky passers-by.

By 1992, violence had grown so severe and was having such a bad effect on the economy of Pakistan's greatest city that (whatever its previous links to the MQM may have been) the army decided that basic order must be restored. First under Nawaz Sharif and then under the second administration of Benazir Bhutto, a tough crackdown was carried out. The operation proceeded in typical Pakistani fashion, through a mixture of ruthless force and diplomacy. On the one hand, the military, police, Rangers and intelligence agencies made widespread use of torture and 'encounter' killings against the militants.

On the other hand, great effort was devoted to splitting the MQM. Radical elements, which thought the leadership was making too many compromises with other parties and ethnicities, were covertly encouraged to split off into the 'Real MQM', which then launched ferocious attacks against its former comrades. The military (or rather the paramilitary Rangers, which are under the command of the army) were then able to crush the extremists, while eventually making peace with the chastened MQM leadership, which was released from prison in return for promises to keep their men under control.

Murders have continued, but at a greatly reduced rate – though the MQM–Pathan strife of 2009–2010 has led to fears that Karachi may return to the dark days of the early 1990s. The latest round of fighting began in May 2007, when the MQM, who had become close allies of President Musharraf, used their armed men to attack a rally to welcome Musharraf's arch nemesis Chief Justice Iftikhar Chaudhry, triggering violence in which dozens were killed.

Altaf Hussain had left Pakistan after an assassination attempt at the end of 1991, and ever since has lived in London. Like Benazir Bhutto and Nawaz Sharif during their periods of exile – but much more effectively – he maintains control over his party from a distance. Altaf Hussain is officially wanted by the Pakistani courts on charges including conspiracy to murder; but he is also regularly visited by Pakistani politicians and officials, including in April 2009 by President Asif Ali Zardari.

Despite its partial suppression by the state in the mid-1990s, the MQM has re-established an overwhelming grip on the government and politics of Karachi. However, its ability to use its dominance to develop the city is restricted by the very limited powers accorded to municipal government in Pakistan. Given that Karachi's demographic and economic structures are so different from those of the rest of Sindh, it would in fact make much more sense for Karachi to be a province of Pakistan, as in effect it was from 1947 to 1958, when it was Pakistan's capital and a separate federal district.

This would, however, lead to extremely violent protests by Sindhis, which would worsen still further Pakistan's security problems and probably make civilian rule impossible: These protests would be both by the nationalists, who would see this as theft of Sindhi land, and by the landowner-politicians and their followers, who would stand to lose a very large proportion of their powers of patronage – since Karachi accounts for less than half Sindh's population but around two-thirds of Sindh's GDP.

Sindh and Karachi are therefore trapped in an unhappy but relatively stable marriage, held in place by a mixture of patronage and fear. The MQM dominates Karachi electorally and therefore usually has to be included in any coalition government of the province of Sindh, while Sindhi landowners and tribal chieftains dominate the rest of the province and milk Karachi's economy for their own benefit. These landowners are mostly PPP, but include a very large number of opportunists who switch sides depending on who is in power in Islamabad – which is why the military administrations of both Zia and Musharraf were able to attract enough Sindhi support to form coalition governments in Sindh.

KARACHI'S ETHNIC FRONT LINES

The MQM's headquarters is known, with a kind of urban hipness, as Nine-Zero, after the last two digits of the telephone number of Altaf Hussain's house where the party had its beginnings, and which is now preserved as a kind of shrine. It is in Azizabad, a typical middle-class Mohajir neighbourhood, and by both nature and design it breathes the particular MQM spirit.

Like most of Karachi, the neighbourhood itself is *urban*, in a way that most other Pakistani cities are not. In most cities, outside the downtown areas, the houses of ordinary people are one-storey buildings of mud-brick or concrete, not essentially different from those of villages, and often built around gated compounds, while the houses of the rich are villas set in gardens. The general impression is of the country come to town – which given that most of the families moved from the countryside fairly recently, and keep close contacts with their relatives in the country, is literally true. Azizabad by contrast features taller, narrower but much more solid individual houses set next to each other, and small apartment blocks of four or five storeys. Elsewhere in the city, though there are few tower blocks and no skyscrapers, big blocks of flats line the main roads.

Four blocks around the HQ are sealed off by security barriers, but, thanks to some PR person, the barrier through which I entered is brightly painted with fruit and flowers and a sign proclaiming 'Street of Love and Peace'. This was thanks to a 'Concept by Husaini Electrics'. Beside it, a large poster proclaimed that 'On the occasion of the 25th anniversary of the founding of the MQM, the people of this area salute the Great Leader Altaf Hussain.' Beyond it was a second security barrier, with electronically operated bollards embedded in the roadway. Getting in required a telephone call and an escort – all very far from the disastrously sloppy Pakistani norm.

Opposite is a small, well-kept park, the Bagh-e-Afza, with a children's playground decorated with statues of giraffes and horses. The houses around were fairly shabby two- and three-storey buildings, but in reasonably good shape, and there was very little rubbish on the streets. 'The MQM tries to keep its neighbourhoods clean – that is very sacred for them,' my assistant told me. White, green and red MQM flags were everywhere, interspersed with the black flags of the Shia, because a large Shia prayer hall is just down the road.

The Youth Minister of Sindh, Faisal Sabzwari, took me to see Altaf Hussain's two-rooms-up, two-down house, with its tiny sitting-room, 'where Benazir Bhutto, Nawaz Sharif and any of the other leaders came to meet him and sat on this sofa'. Behind is a small courtyard, with no garden – a million miles from the mansions of PPP, PML(N) and ANP leaders, but also, it must be said, from those of some contemporary MQM leaders I visited.

The house now forms part of a headquarters complex including a media centre where young volunteers monitored a bank of thirty television screens and manned a telephone switchboard. Mr Sabzwari told me that they have a twenty-four-terabyte computer storage facility – 'which we are going to double soon' – an e-mail server with 50,000 addresses, and a desktop TV editing machine for making films. 'From here, we try to monitor whatever is published or broadcast in Karachi and the world about us.' Once again, the contrast with the amateurish and sometimes comical efforts of the other parties in this regard could hardly be more striking.

In a nearby building, I interviewed the mayor of Karachi, Sycd Mustafa Kamal – only thirty-eight years old in 2009 (but still older than the MQM's first mayor, Abdul Sattar, who was only twenty-four when he took office) and dressed for his age, in blue jeans and a checked shirt, with a closely cropped beard around his mouth and chin – in fact, he could have been a software manager in London. He sat with Mr Sabzwari in a small plain office with peeling blue walls and the inevitable pictures of Altaf Hussain: rather remarkably modest for the mayor of the seventh largest city on earth. In fact, the only unprofessional thing about the mayor is that he talks so fast it is difficult to take everything in. Together with his deep melodious voice, and pounding delivery, the impression is rather of being addressed by a bass drum.

He denounced the 'feudal' leadership and character of the other parties, and spoke of the MQM as a progressive middle-class alternative for all Pakistanis:

> For the past sixty years, forty families have ruled Pakistan. They have been re-elected seven times in one form or another, but in all that time they have never done anything for the people even on their own estates. They send their children to school in London, but they have never built a single school in their own villages . . . The MQM is the hope for the people of Pakistan, in which ordinary people will rule, and not these forty families.[7]

Concerning Karachi, his main refrains were his administration's commitment to building infrastructure, the hopelessness of the other parties in this regard, and the dysfunctionality of Pakistan's federal system, which left responsibility for the city's development and services in many different institutional hands, only some of them his:

> All our efforts are being undermined by the law and order situation, but I have no control over the police – not even the traffic police. So we build roads, and then we film the police holding up traffic and taking bribes along them.

Much of this is true, by the way, even if not the whole truth. He continued:

> Karachi generates 68 per cent of all the revenues of Pakistan, yet until we came to power, the city never had a master plan, even as its population

grew to 18 million. So you can imagine the job facing me. Forty-five per cent of neighbourhoods never even had a service plan. Four out of five industrial zones had no water or sewage provision . . .

Our aim has been not to develop Karachi so as to compete with the rest of Pakistan, but to make it internationally competitive – a far harder job. To achieve this, the first thing we need is world-class infrastructure. We have done more in four years than the other parties in fifty, but I know very well that it is only a beginning. We have to struggle and struggle just to keep pace with the growing population.

The MQM administration does indeed have a good reputation among independent observers and journalists in the city, and its achievements are visible: above all in the construction of new roads and flyovers to alleviate the previously dreadful traffic jams, in improvements to sewage and drainage which have reduced the flooding which used to follow the heavy rains, and in the creation of parks – the mayor's particular pride. Some of these projects were started under the Jamaat administration that ruled after the MQM boycotted the first elections under Musharraf – but then, the Jamaat in Karachi is also very much a Mohajir middle-class organization. Desperately needed metro-rail systems are planned, but their scale is beyond the constitutional competence of the municipal government and, as in Lahore, they are therefore held up in endless political infighting, battles over patronage, and bureaucratic lethargy at the levels of the Sindh and national governments.

After the meeting with the mayor, I drove along one of his new motorways, a 13-kilometre-long 'signal-free corridor' with underpasses for pedestrians and cross-traffic, and a belt of trees and greenery down the middle; once again, not a remarkable road by Western or East Asian standards, but a very remarkable road for Pakistan, and a vast improvement on what was there before.

This road also led me back from the mayor's optimistic vision to the other side of Karachi, and of the MQM: the ethnic violence which constantly threatens to tear the city apart. An MQM party worker, Nasir Jamal, took me to see some of the scenes of the violence between Mohajirs and Pathans which had cost several dozen lives in previous days – and which the MQM was accused of having orchestrated. The tragic element to this is that the MQM and the leading Pathan party, the ANP, were coalition partners at the time in both the national and the Sindh governments, and were also ideological allies against the Taleban.

In the 2008 elections, the ANP for the first time won two provincial assembly seats in Karachi. This is not many out of 130 seats in the assembly (and they won no National Assembly seats at all) but it seems to have severely rattled the MQM, which had got used to a monopoly of the Karachi seats. It was after this that MQM denunciations of the supposed Taleban infiltration of the Pathan community in Karachi really took off.

The MQM also genuinely disapproved of ANP-sponsored peace deals with the Taleban, and in the preceding months had warned with increasing vehemence of the alleged growth of Taleban influence among the Pathans of Karachi – something which ANP leaders denounced as a mere 'plot to seize Pathan property and businesses', as the ANP leader in Karachi, Syed Shahi, told me.

While Taleban terrorism could certainly make the ethnic situation in Karachi worse, the tension between Pathans and Mohajirs in the city has other roots, which Nasir Jamal sketched for me as we drove through the northern suburbs. On either side, great greyish-white apartment buildings rose like castles – and, like castles, they were topped with fluttering banners: red, green and white for the MQM, red for the ANP, green, red and black for the PPP, and the sinister red flag of the Jiye Sindh nationalist party, with in the centre a black hand holding a black axe: party flags which are also the badges of ethnic allegiance, and which marked most of the apartment blocks as now inhabited by a single ethnicity.

In between the apartment blocks were patches of wasteland with the occasional fine tree left over from the days when it was countryside, some of it covered in roughly built shanty towns, vehicle parks or impoverished-looking markets. This, Jamal said, was evidence of the way in which the Pathans were 'encroaching' on municipal and state land in the city. His words were a litany of standard MQM and Mohajir complaints about the Pathans:

> Those ANP flags on that *kachi abadi* [shanty town] are to show that Pathans have seized the land and will never let it go. The ANP seek to support every Pathan, even Taleban, demand in order to claim a share in the government of the city . . . You see those trucks and buses over there,

half blocking the road? When our government tried to get them to move to a proper vehicle park that we had built, they refused, because then they would be registered and would have to pay taxes . . . As it is, they use drugs gangs and other criminals to take over more and more property by force, then use the ANP to demand that the municipal government give them services for their new colonies, but pay no taxes. We are not against Pathans, but we have to be against these illegal occupations because they are a threat to everybody . . . You see those fine new housing complexes over there? They were built for Urdu-speakers but now they are empty because our people were threatened by the Pathans and had to leave . . . And there are more and more Pathans all the time. Pathans are barely educated, and none of their women can read or write at all. So their birth-rate is very high compared to our educated women.[8]

I suggested that since the MQM and ANP were coalition partners and allies against the Taleban, and since after all the Pathans were a large reality in Karachi which could not be removed, a compromise really should be possible: a deal whereby the MQM would agree to allocate the ANP certain municipal lands and apartment buildings for the Pathans, and a guaranteed share of political influence, through a certain number of seats in the provincial and national assemblies. Jamal replied in words that had become depressingly familiar to me from interviews with much more senior MQM figures over the previous weeks:

No, that is completely unacceptable. It would mean Mohajirs paying taxes to build houses for them, who pay no taxes at all. Not because they can't but because they won't. We are ready for compromise, but it has to be on the basis of accepted principles, not just giving them shares – they would only demand a share in every project in the city . . . As to parliamentary seats, we have free and fair elections here, and they can stand for them and win them if they can.

At this, I had to cover a smile, given what I had heard about election rigging by MQM activists – and heard from journalists and analysts who in other ways admired the MQM as a party. The real reason for the MQM's intransigence seems to be that they feel that time and demographics are against them, and that if they give even an inch to the steadily growing Pathan population they will end up losing control of Karachi altogether.

Jamal took me to Zarina Colony, a Mohajir settlement in the shadow of the low hills that fringe northern Karachi, which had seen several deaths in the latest fighting. Mohajir and Pathan fighters have repeatedly battled to control these insignificant hills, like a slow-motion, low-level urban gang version of the battle of Ypres; and as the sky darkened, the MQM guards became visibly uneasy.

As we entered the colony, we moved from Karachi to rural South Asia. Decrepit one-storey mud houses haphazardly lined the roads, and the street was dotted with heaps of rubbish. Looking up at the summit of the closest hill, I could see ANP flags against the sunset, the hill having been occupied by the Rangers, however, when they stepped in to end the fighting. The crowd that met us seemed to have been carefully put together to blame the ANP and present the MQM case over the latest fighting and, as far as I could judge, some of their stories were highly exaggerated. To Jamal's embarrassment, however, they departed from script by admitting that their colony was illegal. 'We will be registering it very soon,' he cut in. Many of them, like Jamal himself, were Urdu-speakers who had fled Bangladesh in the 1970s – twenty-five years after most of the Mohajirs, which helps explain why they were still unhoused.

They grew silent and looked uneasily at each other and at Jamal when I asked if they were satisfied with the city government. 'Well, the local *nazim* has done something,' Bilquis, a fat, formidable-looking local woman replied. 'At least we have a sewage line now [which according to my nose was not sufficient] and we have been promised a water pipe.' In one way, however, Zarina Colony was still Karachi, and not the rest of Sindh – in the way that the women like Bilquis pushed forward past their men to shout their complaints at me.

In previous days, I had visited Pathan areas to get their side of the story. Before the latest fighting, I saw Syed Shahi, the ANP president, at his home. Shahi is a self-made businessman who made a fortune in various enterprises after coming to Karachi in the 1970s, and had become a community leader. His luxurious home is decorated in eye-wateringly bad taste even by Pakistani standards, with a huge illuminated photograph of a Canadian lake dominating the glaringly lit, quasi-rococo drawing-room. Next to the drawing-room is a large *hujra*, or traditional Pathan male gathering place, set out in traditional style with cushions along the walls, a sign that, whether from culture or astuteness, Mr Shahi remained close to his community roots. Indeed, he looks that way, with a small moustache set in an enormous face, craggy and extremely tough-looking. His English is poor, and his son – who is studying in England to be a doctor and says he probably will stay there – had to translate for him.

Syed Shahi said that his aim is to 'defend Karachi as place where all different peoples can live'. He claimed that of these people, 4 million are Pathan – which most people say is a gross exaggeration, though none of them can agree on what the real figure is. He complained bitterly that 'the MQM says that other peoples can come here, but in fact they try to stop them from getting jobs, businesses, or an education.' He said the ANP is against the Taleban, but that the MQM's warnings of Taleban penetration of Karachi are just an excuse to seize Pathan land and business.

Asked about ANP mobilization of the community, Mr Shahi said that two weeks earlier his party had set up a Ladies' Wing. 'They will go to homes and register females to vote. We have never done this before because Pashtun women don't want to leave their homes or are not allowed to by their husbands.' Asked about social work and urban renewal, he didn't seem to understand what I was talking about:

> We can only do something like this once we are in power here. Only then can we set up NGOs. At the moment we are focused on getting access to education and government jobs for our people. In any case, most of our people are workers. They have no money, so can't do anything like this for themselves.[9]

The contrast with the MQM leadership could hardly have been more marked.

The longer-established middle-class Pathans of Karachi do however have a rather different face. After the fighting, I visited the ANP president for eastern Karachi, Yunus Buner, who owns a smallish construction business and whose family has been in Karachi for three generations. His home is an apartment in a small block, with a *hujra* furnished with armchairs rather than cushions, and decorated with artificial flowers. A small, clean-shaven man with glasses and an urbane manner, he introduced with great pride his two English-speaking teenage sons. About the MQM however he was not polite.

> We would have won several more seats from Karachi, but in mixed areas like this one the MQM seized the polling stations with heavily armed

gunmen. When I went to cast my own vote, the polling staff said that my vote had already been cast. That happened to thousands of our people, and there was nothing we could do about it – we would have been killed. We don't have enough weapons to fight with them. Whatever the MQM says, we are not armed the way Pashtuns are on the Frontier, and the MQM have the whole administration, police, army and intelligence agencies to back them up. The police refuse even to register FIRs [First Information Reports – see Chapter 3] against their men, while eleven of our men have been arrested . . .

I am on the peace committee with MQM, ANP and PPP members to try to keep the peace, but in fact there is no point talking to the MQM politicians here about this, because they just deny everything and anyway don't control the killers. The MQM's armed wing is controlled by Altaf Hussain in London . . .

As a businessman here, I want to keep the peace. I don't want a war that would destroy this city, but we won't accept this for ever. If our businesses go on being burned, we will have nothing to lose, and then there could be an Afghan situation here.[10]

He bitterly denounced the Taleban, saying that his own relatives in Buner District of the NWFP had been targeted by them, and he was helping refugees from there in Karachi; but that there were very few Taleban sympathizers in Karachi. 'Just because you are Pashtun and have a beard does not mean you are Taleban. The MQM are just using this to attack the ANP and Pashtuns in general.'

Mr Buner took me to the ANP office for east Karachi, a rather astonishing building. It stands entirely alone on the furthest eastern edge of Karachi, in a desolate suburb which is just beginning to be developed, and is painted inside and out in the ANP colour, bright red. The whole scene reminded me of something, and then I realized that it was scenes of Hollywood gangster films set in the 1920s or '30s, with dreary roadhouses and brothels standing alone in similarly half-empty suburbs. The recollection was so clear that I half expected Al Pacino and Robert de Niro to turn up.

Which in a way they had. Above the door was a neat line of bullet holes from two days earlier. I was told that this was the third time the building had been shot up by MQM gunmen, though nobody had been wounded. Elsewhere, however, thirteen ANP party workers had been killed in east Karachi in the first four months of 2009. 'They want to kill us all,' one of the ANP men said.

The bullet holes, however, seemed to me to tell a different story, of a warning not a murder attempt. If the MQM gunmen are as competent as the rest of their party, they are probably pretty good shots; and anyway, given the resources at their disposal, they could have destroyed the building and everyone in it – the more so as the ANP men did not appear to be armed. Neither Mr Shahi nor Mr Buner had heavily protected residences, and the MQM headquarters in east Karachi was not especially well defended.

If these leaders really expected to be attacked, such negligence would be suicidal. It seemed to me, therefore, that rather than a war to the death, what was happening in Karachi in the first half of 2009 was a war of maneouvre, part of the Pakistani 'negotiated state' in which violence is part of the negotiations: always in the background, and sometimes in the foreground, but in which usually it is only a few pawns who get killed. The greatest risk of Taleban terrorism in Karachi is that it will provoke the MQM into counter-attacks which will then trigger an all-out struggle, in which the Taleban will replace the ANP as leaders of the local Pathans, and the MQM will use this Talebanization as an excuse to reduce the Pathans to a completely subordinate status. However, as an official of the Pakistani Intelligence Bureau (IB) told me,

> The mood among the Pathans in Karachi is very different from the mid-1980s when all this started and there were huge riots with dozens or hundreds dead. Then, they believed all the old Pathan stuff about how they are the bravest and the toughest and Mohajir city-dwellers are cowards who won't fight. But the MQM taught them different, and gave them a very bloody nose. Today, Pathan gunmen may clash with MQM gunmen, and pick off local MQM activists, but our analysis is that they'll be very careful about joining the Taleban and starting a full-scale war with the Mohajirs, because they think they'd lose. And if they don't start a war, then the MQM will also basically tolerate them – just push them back from certain places, teach them a lesson now and then. The MQM also don't want all-out war that would wreck their city.

For a great strength of the MQM is that like the Jamaat, but unlike any other Pakistani party including the ANP, they do have a dream that goes beyond patronage for themselves and their supporters. Their weakness is that this dream is almost certainly unattainable.

The dream is of Karachi as a Muslim Singapore on the Arabian Sea: modern, clean, orderly and economically dynamic, ruled by a form of relatively mild and benevolent totalitarianism. And if Karachi were an independent island, the MQM and the people they represent would probably be both ruthless and able enough to achieve this dream. But of course Karachi is not an independent island. It is part of mainland Pakistan, and inextricably linked to the problems, and the peoples, of the rest of Pakistan. The danger is that the effort to maintain the MQM's vision and rule in Karachi in the face of the Pathans and Sindhis will feed the ruthless and chauvinist sides of the organization until its positive sides are drowned in the resulting bloodshed.

INTERIOR SINDH

The extent to which Karachi differs from its immediate hinterland in Sindh is absolutely staggering, even in a region of stark social and ethnic contrasts like South Asia – just as, beyond the city limits, the mayor's great motorway becomes the misnamed 'superhighway' between Karachi and Hyderabad, which is mostly a potholed two-lane country road. The bridge between these two worlds is the Sindhi *wadero* landowning class, tied to Karachi by its urban upper-class lifestyle and by the parliament and government of Sindh which *waderos* dominate, and which are situated in Karachi. I asked a Sindhi journalist to explain the difference between a *wadero* and a non-*wadero* landowner. The answer came down yet again to kinship and hereditary prestige:

> A *wadero* has to have a lot of land, but he has to have other things as well. He has to be the leader of a tribe, or from a *pir* family, and here in Sindh the family has to be an old one if he wants real respect. He has to have gunmen and dacoits working for him, and to play a role in politics. Otherwise, no matter how much land he has, he's just a big farmer.

I have met a considerable number of *waderos* during various travels in Sindh. The Unar Khans, tribal chiefs and politicians from northern Sindh, are not part of my acquaintance (though as the testimonies below indicate, I am sure they are perfectly splendid people). I did however meet a variety of their dependants during my travels in Sindh, and these meetings provided a frame for the world that the Unar Khans represent.

Of these encounters, the last was in some ways the most striking, because a statement of loyalty and respect that could have taken place 500 years ago was in fact delivered in the modern surroundings of Karachi airport, and by a man in a quintessentially modern service. The other places in the airport café being full, I asked if I could share the table of a middle-aged, balding man in the uniform of an official of Pakistan International Airlines. With typical hospitality, he offered me a share of his pudding, and asked about my travels in Pakistan. When I mentioned the Unars, his eyes lit up:

> The Unars are good people. They are a small tribe, but more powerful than all the other tribes put together because they are the bravest and help each other. If one of them is in trouble, all the others come together to help, with guns, people, money, whatever is necessary. Everyone knows that they are very generous, very loyal to their friends. They have done so much for my own family.

My PIA interlocutor grinned slightly, but made no comment, when I mentioned my previous indirect encounter with the Unars, a few days earlier. I had gone to a police station in Clifton, Karachi, to meet an officer known as an 'encounter specialist' – in other words a policeman tasked with the extra-judicial execution of prisoners. A youngish man was sitting on the floor with his hands together to one side, closer examination revealing that they were in fact chained to the barred window frame. His face was lean and gloomy, but also composed and even dignified despite his position, and what must have been some well-based fears as to what was going to happen to him.

The policemen told me that he was a member of a notorious dacoit gang from Larkana, picked up in Karachi on a tip-off, in return for a reward of Rs100,000. According to the police, he had been a bodyguard of the Unar Khans. The police, and journalists whom I asked about the Unars, also spoke of their 'courage' – though they often added other words as well. Visiting Sindh twenty years earlier, I had been told in admiring tones how Ghulam Ishaq Khan Unar, elected in 1988 for the PPP, had had three men from a rival family killed in revenge after his brother was shot down in a family feud in Larkana bazaar in 1986. A senior policeman in Sukkur told me on that occasion:

Half the people here are protecting dacoits. So what do you do? You try to round them up, and if they are killed, fine, and if you can keep them behind bars, also fine. And if a minister or politician turns up and tells you to release them, well, relax and enjoy, what else is there to do? This isn't England. You have to accept these things.

A week or so before my meeting with the dacoit in Karachi, I had been outside the front gate of one of the Unar Khans' residences, in the village of Bakrani on the road between Larkana and Mohenjo Daro. The area was festooned with flags of the PML(Q) Party, which the Unar Khan family was currently supporting, and a large concrete arch at the entrance to the estate commemorated the late patriarch of that family, a PML(Q) member of parliament who had died recently. His son, Altaf Hussain Khan Unar, had succeeded to his father's land and his political role.

The PML(Q) was the 'King's Party' set up by General Musharraf to bolster his administration, on the basis of defectors from Nawaz Sharif's Muslim League. It had no popular or traditional roots in Sindh at all – but, like other past 'parties' of the same kind, did not initially need them, because it could always attract to its ranks by a variety of promises landowner-politicians like the Unar Khans.

Of eighteen people I spoke to in the village, all but four said that they had voted and would vote for the PML(Q), for a reason about which they were entirely candid: 'This is the village of Unar Sahib. His house is just over there. We vote how our *wadero* says, because we are his people. He gives us everything, so we follow him,' as Nizar Shaikh, a carpenter, told me. As I sat in the café in the gleaming surroundings of Karachi airport I thought back to this scene, in a dusty village of mud houses which seemed little changed from those of Mohenjo Daro – two worlds apparently so utterly different, but linked by invisible but immensely strong links of kinship and patronage.

HUNTING BOAR AND LEADING TRIBES

The purpose of the first days of my journey to interior Sindh was not supposed to be politics – but then, in the world of Pakistani landowners, as in that of their English equivalents in the past, everything is in fact politics, including deaths, births and above all marriages; and hunting parties, which was what this particular trip was about. Sardar Mumtaz Ali Bhutto, uncle of Benazir Bhutto and hereditary chief of the Bhutto tribe, had invited me to a hunt for wild boar, organized in a patch of jungle on the banks of the Indus by a landowning family called Khoshk, *waderos* of a village of that name. Mumtaz Ali Bhutto was providing most of the dogs, for the breeding of which he is famous, and the huntsmen.

The Sardar's love of animals can take some curious forms. As our vehicle passed an emaciated, exhausted-looking horse pulling an over-loaded cart, he told me how unhappy such sights make him: 'Sometimes, if I see a man beating his horse and donkey, I will stop the car, get out and give him a beating instead.' Since kindness to animals is not much of a South Asian tradition, this must be one of the more interesting combinations of British attitudes to animals and Sindhi 'feudal' attitudes to people.

Like fox-hunting in Britain, wild-boar hunting in Pakistan is a matter of pure sport, since in a Muslim country the animals cannot be eaten by the hunters. The carcasses are thrown to the dogs or given to one of the remaining groups of low-caste, formerly tribal Hindus who live along the Indus. I was offered one myself, but declined; because driving around interior Sindh like a motorized Obelix, with an enormous putrefying pig tied to the roof of my car, while it would undoubtedly have attracted attention, would probably not have contributed to my prestige.

As was the case for millennia in Europe, hunting is an important means of maintaining connections and forging new bonds among the landowner-politicians in Sindh. Hunting in Sindh twice played a part in the rise of Zulfikar Ali Bhutto: once in 1955 when President Iskandar Mirza brought General Ayub Khan to Larkana to hunt and introduced Bhutto to him; once in January 1971 when a joint duck-shooting trip with President Yahya Khan helped bring them together in the moves which led to the horrible events surrounding Bangladeshi independence.

I had wanted to go on a boar hunt ever since I had had to turn down an invitation in southern Punjab in 1989, despite the incentive added by my host that two local landowning families were covertly at odds and might use the occasion to shoot each other rather than the boar. No such possibility was present on this latter occasion, if only because it turned out that the boar were to be hunted not with guns, but with spears.

At this news, my joy at being invited to this absolutely quintessential 'feudal' event was rapidly overtaken by the comical mental image of myself holding a spear, and the less comical one of my doing so while facing a large and understandably irritated boar. However, I needn't have worried. Only one huntsman carried a spear, to deliver the *coup de grâce* after the boar had been brought down by the hounds. The rest of us were spectators, with a very slight chance of becoming participants if the boar charged us directly.

As perhaps in hunting for sport everywhere, the quarry on this occasion seemed in part an excuse for getting up early in the morning to see the countryside at its best – and the countryside of Sindh in early summer is definitely at its best at dawn and not at midday. The sun popped up through the mist as a pale disk, looking much more like the moon, and for a while it was blissfully impossible to imagine the dreadful heat of a few hours later.

The dogs, so I was told, were a variety of lurcher: a cross between greyhounds and bull terriers, with ugly, formidable heads but graceful bodies. Each couple of hounds was held in leash by a huntsman, all three of the group looking with raised heads and fixed attention into the jungle, the huntsmen seeming to quiver with eagerness along with the dogs. The huntsmen, mostly young, looked intensely proud at being responsible for such splendid animals, and in the service of so splendid a lord as Sardar Mumtaz Ali Bhutto. They also looked markedly better fed than the ragged peasantry who provided the beaters. And indeed there was no pretence of egalitarianism about this hunt. As the guest of honour and provider of the dogs and huntsmen, Mumtaz Ali Bhutto sat directly facing the jungle. His younger son Ali and I sat some distance behind. Everyone else was firmly to one side.

However, in the subcontinent hierarchical organization is always only a step or so away from anarchy, whether cheerful or malignant, and it was certainly no proof against the mass excitement when the boar broke cover. This was especially so when one enterprising beast plunged into the Indus, pursued to the bank – and nearly over it – by a mob of yelling huntsmen and spectators, stirring the powdery dust into a maelstrom. Half-way over, a fishing boat tried to head it off, and a fisherman, whether overcome by excitement or in hope of a reward, actually dived into the river, grasped the boar round its neck, and guided it back to shore – a sight to remember. On reaching land, it shook him off indifferently along with the water and disappeared into the jungle. Four more boar succeeded in outrunning the dogs and knocking over or shaking off those that came close; so that in the end the entire bag for some five hours of hunting was one medium-sized female; which shows that the boar had a sporting chance.

The patches of jungle like the one in which we hunted are the remains of the great *shikargahs* (noble hunting reserves) of the past. They consist of low scrub and tall grasses, fertilized annually by the water and silt brought down by the melting of the Himalayan snows, and by the monsoon. This is the original natural cover of the Indus valley before human cultivation. In the past – and very likely in the future too – the ferocity of the floods and the frequently changing course of the river meant that the riverine areas themselves could not be cultivated, and so were never registered for ownership and taxation. Canals and dams have to a large extent reduced this threat, and landowners in recent decades have illegally encroached on the riverine areas, greatly increasing their wealth in the process – but still paying no tax.

However, some patches of jungle still remain, used as hunting reserves for boar and deer – and as the favourite hideouts of bandits; though whether with the knowledge and protection of the *waderos*, as is universally believed, I cannot say. One feature of the boar hunt, however (which I hardly noticed at the time, because it is so much a feature of the life of the rural nobility that you forget about it), was the bodyguards with their Kalashnikovs; not because most of the time there is any expectation that they will be needed, but as an insurance policy, and also of course as a source of prestige.

Not that Mumtaz Ali Bhutto apparently needed much to boost his prestige. The ancestral home in Mirpur Bhutto is one of the most magnificent that I have visited in rural Pakistan. More than 150 years old, it is also an example of how far local architecture has fallen since the days of the British, let alone the days of the Mughals. The old aristocratic architecture is not just beautiful, but efficient. The tall ceilings and ventilation windows make it habitable even during electricity cuts, when modern rooms become unendurable without fans or air-conditioning.

The drawing-room contains a throne-like silver chair on which the Sardar's grandfather was inaugurated, and a family tree which shows only male members – thereby omitting Benazir Bhutto! Beside the front gate is the exquisite eighteenth-century mausoleum of a family saint. In front of the house, facing a garden with the inevitable lawn for political meetings, an open hall between columns provides a space where the Sardar holds court, with his two sons sitting on either side of him and his steward standing respectfully to one side. Before him, a variety of petitioners appear to touch his feet and wait with hands clasped, as if in prayer, to receive an order or a judgment. Having received it, most sit to one side for a longer or shorter period to show respect, and by their presence and numbers help boost their lord's prestige.

The morning that I was a witness seemed fairly typical – and was almost identical to an audience by Mumtaz Ali Bhutto on the same spot when I had visited him twenty years before. Sharecroppers and local 'incharges' received orders for planting crops; participants in a land dispute were told to stop work on the land pending a decision; and two sheepish-looking peasants received a sharp response, tried to argue, and were sent packing by one of the gunmen. 'They are sharecroppers of a neighbouring landowner,' Amir Bhutto told me:

> He took away their land for various reasons and they have come to us for help getting it back. But this man is our political rival and they have always voted for him. So my father said, 'You never came to me in the past, you voted for my opponent. What can I do to help you? He is in another party and not in my influence.'[11]

When the circumstances are right, such discussions are often the prelude to a change of allegiance, or to new bargaining based on the threat of it. All over rural Sindh, and much of the rest of Pakistan as well, such scenes happen every day – the basic stuff of Pakistani politics, though rarely played out against such a magnificent background.

'FEUDAL' DOMINATION

One very proud member of a *wadero* family – but a highly educated one with an MA from Cambridge – was scathing about his fellow 'feudals':

> The Sardars in Sindh are changing, but not as fast as they should. Many are not interested in education. They don't think it helps them to run their estates or manage politics. So even the children of the bigger landowners are often surprisingly uneducated; and that of course also means that they

don't understand new agricultural techniques and have no idea or interest in any kind of wider development or improvement, beyond traditional charity. And because they dominate politics and government, that means that Sindh society in general is also changing very slowly.

Local journalists in the nearby town of Larkana recounted for me a litany of recent actions by 'feudals' in their region. One, a local chieftain, had been using his gunmen and dacoits to seize packets of land from small farmers, 'people without links to feudals and from weak tribes'. He was protected from police retaliation, I was told, because his brother was a provincial minister from the PPP. A much worse case involving local chieftains and PPP politicians will be recounted in the next chapter, on Balochistan. During the floods of 2010, landlord-politicians in western Sindh were credibly accused of opening local barrages so that the flood waters would spare their lands and inundate those of rivals.

I asked the Larkana journalists how Sindhi society and economy had changed over the past twenty years. There was a very long pause. 'Not much,' one said. Another said that there was now more education. In the industrial sector, they mentioned a considerable growth of small rice-processing units, with 200–300 of these in Larkana District alone; but then their remarks quickly turned to complaints about monopolization and price-rigging by the rice processors in league with the central bureaucracy in Islamabad.

Of the state industrial plants set up by Zulfikar Ali Bhutto to benefit his home district and since privatized, the textile mill has collapsed and been sold off for scrap – 'because of corruption and bad management'. The sugar mill, I was told, operates seasonally, but it looked quite derelict when I passed it. Local people blame non-PPP governments for lack of support – but private management has also failed. In other words, yet another tale of 'Third World' state-led industrial development which failed to take root.

People in Larkana told me that the PPP-led government which took power in 2008 had started a few road-building projects in Larkana, but that their main help to the town and district had been to create thousands of new jobs in the local bureaucracy, police, health and education systems and distribute them to their supporters. This pleased most of the people I talked to, because 'jobless people who were ignored by governments for the past twelve years have been given jobs. Some are from my village,' as Ghulam Abbas, a farmer, told me.

However, when asked if the newly appointed people were qualified for these jobs he did not even to pretend that this was the case. When a new government comes to power, these useless jobs will either be abolished, or – more likely – redistributed to their own followers, leaving the area with absolutely nothing in terms of real development. For there is nothing unique to the PPP about this. G. M. Morai, who runs a Sindhi television channel in Hyderabad, told me:

> Education is the only thing that can produce a bigger Sindhi middle class, but this is happening only very slowly. Sindhi education was put in the doldrums by Zia-ul-Haq, and since his time it has been the plaything of the *waderos*. Most of the teachers have been appointed by local *wadero* politicians from among their relatives and followers. Most have no training at all. Our whole education system is terribly backward. In 1999, I still did not know how to use a computer because there was nowhere in Hyderabad to learn. That has changed, but much more slowly than it should have. This also means that most of our politicians have no real education and no administrative or technocratic skills. All they can do is make speeches. The PPP has always been the biggest party in Sindh, but they reward loyalty and courage, not ability. Of course, it's admirable to have gone to gaol for five or ten years under Zia or Musharraf but it doesn't make you a good minister.[12]

Certainly Larkana, which given the PPP's periods in government should be one of the most developed towns in interior Sindh, is not visibly different from the others: a mass of higgledy-piggledy brick and mud houses with barely paved roads and heaps of uncollected rubbish. In the centre of one busy road was a frightful sight: what appeared to be a heap of rags was in fact a squatting beggar, inviting death and alms at the same time, with cars swerving to avoid him.

EXISTENTIAL THREATS?

On the whole, most Sindhis seem not unhappy with the existing social order, and that also seems true of the middle classes, such as they are. Like my Pakistan Airlines acquaintance, if they condemn *waderos* in general, they are very often attached to one *wadero* family in particular, or to a *pir* family which plays the same role. Outside some of the small radical nationalist groups, demands for land reform are extremely rare.

The potentially disastrous element in all this, however, is that in two respects Sindh is not in fact static: the population is growing ever bigger, largely because of the lack of education for women; and the water is ever diminishing, largely because the people are too uneducated, apathetic, conservative, divided along tribal lines and distrustful of one another and of the authorities to improve their agriculture or build their own local water infrastructure. If this goes on, and is not reversed by increased monsoon rains due to climate change, there is a real chance that Sindh one day will cease to exist as an area of large-scale human habitation.

One should, however, think twice about advocating a revolution against the *waderos*. In the first place, it is by no means certain that a ruling class made up of the wealthier peasants would be any more progressive economically or culturally. Certainly those more enterprising *waderos* whom I met complained constantly about the blind conservatism of their tenants and workers, very much in the fashion of Russian nineteenth-century landowners – though there is doubtless a self-serving element in their complaints.

Secondly, the *waderos* are by far the most important barrier against a Sindhi nationalism which, if given free rein, would not only destroy Pakistan, but plunge Sindh itself into ethnic conflict that would tear the province apart and wreck any hope of progress. The *waderos* are not attached to Pakistan by affection, with the exception of the Bhuttos. Even *wadero* members of the PML(N) whom I met – in other words, members of a Punjabi-led party – spent much of their time complaining about Punjabi domination and exploitation. Rather, the *waderos* are attached to the Pakistani state by ties of patronage, circulated and recirculated through the 'feudal' landowning elite by changes of government in Islamabad. In turn, as my experiences with the Unar Khans demonstrate, the *waderos* then circulate this patronage and protection downwards through society; small shares, but enough to help them go on dominating that society.

This charge of national treason for the sake of patronage is precisely the charge made against the *wadero* class by nationalist parties like Jiye Sindh; but even Jiye Sindh's former leader, G. M. Syed, was persuaded by General Zia's administration to modify his hostility to Pakistan by the offer to his son of a pilot's job with Pakistan Airlines. A movement against the *waderos* would have to be a middle-class one, and its ideology would inevitably be Sindhi nationalist.

My meetings with Sindhi intellectuals in Hyderabad were not encouraging as to the likely character of that nationalism. Like their East European equivalents in the past, their principal occupations appear to be folklore, nationalistically coloured religion (in this case, Sindhi Sufism), and what might be described as folkloric historiography – an approach now extended from the glorious past of the Indus Valley civilization and the Talpurs to the martyrs of the Bhutto dynasty. These have a huge gallery devoted to them in the Folklore Museum of Hyderabad University, where you pass from the exquisite traditional embroidery of Sindh to Zulfikar Ali Bhutto's worshipfully preserved socks.

With rare exceptions, repeated attempts on my part to discuss social, economic and ecological issues with Sindhi intellectuals led to a few platitudinous statements of concern, followed by a rapid reversion to the eternal topics of Mohajir and Punjabi exploitation of Sindh. The eventual collapse of Pakistan was taken as a given by most of them, but very few had thought seriously as to what would come next, beyond a wonderful independent Sindhi national existence in 'the most fertile part of Asia', as Sindh was repeatedly described to me.

If all this was depressingly familiar from conversations in Yugoslavia and the Soviet Union before their collapse, even more depressing was the light-hearted way in which a number of people on all sides talked of forthcoming ethnic war. The landowner brother of a PPP member of parliament described Sindh's prospects to me as follows:

> We are a peace-loving people, but if you look at our history, we are also the greatest fighting people in Pakistan, and we have the Pathans and Baloch on our side. I tell you that if there is war with the Mohajirs, Sindhis may receive the first blow, but then we will kill the Mohajirs like rats. They will be like the Jews in World War II, hiding in cellars and being hunted down. And in any case, Karachi could not live a week without Sindh's food and water.

Hearing this, I remembered similarly vainglorious words the previous week from a Mohajir doctor in Karachi: 'If Pakistan breaks up, the Mohajirs would conquer the whole of Sindh in a week and take their water. These *waderos* and their slaves will never fight.' All this recalls an old German proverb, 'He who speaks like this, also shoots.'

At the moment, however, all this remains just ugly talk. The leaderships of the various parties, the *wadero* class in the interior, and the businessmen of Karachi all know how much they have to lose from the disintegration of Pakistan. The tragedy of interior Sindh therefore does resemble that of some of the former Communist states – the revolution it so desperately needs would also spell its destruction.

Thus I remember Sindhi nationalists declaring back in 1989 how there would soon be a 'war to the death' against the Mohajirs. A debauched and repulsive younger member of the Soomro clan told me: 'We have only one choice. Either we lose Sindh or we kick those bloody bastard Mohajirs into the sea.' But twenty years on, no war to the death has occurred. And he was the least impressive nephew of a couple of pretty formidable brothers whom I met – both of them proud Sindhis but also completely pragmatic individuals who continue to draw patronage from the Pakistani state – which in Sindh, as elsewhere, has somehow managed to stumble on.

9

Balochistan

Might was right in days gone by, and the position of the party
aggrieved was the principal factor in determining the price to be
paid for blood; hence the compensation for a mullah, a said or a
person belonging to a leading family was ordinarily double that
for a tribesman. The ordinary rate of compensation (for a death) at
present among the Jamalis, Golas and Khosas is a girl and Rs200;
Umranis, a girl and Rs200 or Rs1,500 if no girl is given.
(*District Gazetteers of Balochistan*, 1906)[1]

Quetta is a garrison town in an oasis, on a high desert frontier. Wind-blown dust is everywhere, covering the world with a fine, gritty film, and turning the coarse grass and dry shrubs to a uniform grey, so that from the air it sometimes seems as if you are flying over the moon. Every now and again, whirlwinds stir the dust up into looming towers, which spread out and fall again in a stinging grey rain. At the end of the broad, straight streets of the cantonment, bare tawny mountains rise against the hard blue sky. In summer, the sun burns with a searingly dry heat. In winter, it is freezingly cold.

The kepis of the Foreign Legion would not feel out of place here, and as for the sola topees of the British Raj – well, they built the place. Their dead rest in the bleak, windswept Christian cemetery on the outskirts of the cantonment. Many of them are from the Welch Regiment, which served in Quetta in what seem to have been the especially unhealthy years of 1905 and 1906. By an odd chance, both the Welsh when they were conquered by the English and Indians when they converted to Christianity often took Christian names as their surnames. So

Private William Hughes rests beneath the carved ostrich feathers of his regiment next to Martin Williams, a Punjabi Christian clerk. Pairs of old British cannon and mountain guns stand outside the gates of the Pakistani generals who have succeeded them; and many of the challenges that those guns were dragged on to this high plateau to face continue to face those Pakistani generals, though in new forms.

But Quetta, like Ougadougou or Fort Lamy, is today a garrison town with elephantiasis. For reasons that will appear, people in Balochistan are even vaguer about figures than in the rest of Pakistan, but the general assumption is that Quetta has between 2 million and 2.5 million people – almost a quarter of Balochistan's sparse population. It contains not just the government and the military headquarters, but the vast majority of Balochistan's institutions of higher education and almost the whole of whatever little the province has of manufacturing industry.

Like so many colonial creations, Quetta sometimes seems like a ship moored to the land on which it sits, rather than growing from it. Its ethnic mixture, its economy and its official and commercial architecture all differ radically from those of Balochistan as a whole and have always done. According to the census of 1901, there were more speakers of European languages (mostly British soldiers and their families) in Quetta than there were speakers of the local languages, Baloch, Brahui and Pathan. The biggest number of inhabitants consisted of Punjabis, followed by Urdu-speakers.

The city used to be known to its educated inhabitants as 'Little Paris'. This is about as staggering a statement as one could well imagine, and not one that I would like to make in Paris itself – except perhaps to a Roman frontier official in Lutetia Parisorum 2,000 years ago, who might have seen some similarities. The notion of Quetta as Paris certainly brings home the distance between most of Quetta and the rest of Balochistan.

Outside Quetta begins the world which Quetta was built to quell and hold at bay: the world of the tribes. Drive out along the Saryab Road, and, between the edge of the city and the ridges that fringe the Quetta valley, you find yourself amid villages of yellow-grey mud, which from the outside could be the first human towns of the Middle East 12,000 years ago. Regular driving on the Saryab Road is not, however, a good idea these days. This is the poor Baloch area of Quetta, where the patrols of the Frontier Corps clash nightly with Baloch nationalist militants; quite apart from the threat of common-or-garden banditry and kidnapping. The tribal frontier is now within the boundaries of the garrison city, just as the tribal leaders sit in the government buildings of the cantonment.

On 11 August 2009, on which day the militants had vowed to hold their own Baloch Independence Day, I drove out on the Saryab Road with the Frontier Corps in a Flag March – an old British tradition which is exactly what it says it is. The soldiers hoisted large Pakistani flags on their jeeps and armoured cars and drove slowly up and down the road and around the outskirts of the city.

I asked an officer what all this was for. 'To show everyone that we are still here, and no one is going to push us out,' he replied. More specifically, the Frontier Corps was there to tear down any Baloch nationalist flags, which pro-independence parties had sworn to fly on that day. So beside the tribes, around them, and watching them from without and within sits another power in the land, the Pakistan army, flexible, pragmatic, restrained – most of the time; but implacably determined that in the end, and in all essential matters, its will should prevail.

However, since 2001, Balochistan has been menaced from another direction: the overspill of the war in Afghanistan, which has brought the Afghan Taleban to the Pathan areas of Balochistan – and Pathans make up as much as 40 per cent of Balochistan's population, and are a majority in Quetta itself. According to US intelligence, much of the Taleban leadership itself, grouped in the so-called 'Quetta Shura', was still based in Balochistan in late 2009. So far, this hasn't been bad for Balochistan. On the contrary, the Afghan Taleban seem to have struck a deal with the Pakistani security forces whereby they will not stir up militancy among the Pathans of Balochistan, in return for being left alone.

Given Pakistan's problems with Baloch militancy, Islamabad considers it especially important to keep the Pathans of Balochistan loyal. This is an additional reason for the shelter that Pakistan gives to parts of the Afghan Taleban leadership in Balochistan. Until early 2007, local journalists told me, the presence of these leaders was so open that it was very easy for Pakistanis (not Westerners) to gain interviews with them. Since then, however, US pressure has made Pakistan more careful, and the 'Quetta Shura' has been moved out of Quetta to more discreet locations in the Pathan areas in the north of the province.

The Afghan Taleban's presence risks provoking the US into launching the kind of cross-border attacks that have been going on for years in FATA to the north; and there is also the risk that US and British military actions in southern Afghanistan will lead to a major influx of Taleban fighters into Pakistani Balochistan. This could well be disastrous for the province.

If the Pathans of the province are stirred up against the Pakistani state, their latent tensions with the Baloch would also be awakened, above all concerning who should rule Quetta itself. Baloch nationalists who say that an independent Balochistan would be prepared to let the Pathan areas break away to join a new Balochistan fall very silent when you ask them what then would happen to Quetta. With Pathans against Pakistan and Baloch (and other Pathans), and Baloch against Pathans, Pakistan and Iran (and other Baloch), and Hazaras and others caught in the middle, that would have all the makings of a really unspeakable mess.

DISPUTED HISTORY, DISPUTED POPULATION

Balochistan is closely linked to the Sindh of the previous chapter – indeed, as previous chapters made clear, many 'Sindhis' and southern Punjabis are in fact from Baloch tribes, which retain their tribal loyalties and much of their tribal way of life. Like the Sindhis, the Baloch tribes worship saints and shrines, and most have so far been impervious to the appeals of modern radical Islamist thought. Neither the Islamist political parties nor the Taleban have made any serious inroads among the ethnic Baloch. There does however seem to be some Baloch support for the anti-Shia Sipah-e-Sahaba movement, which has carried out savage terrorist attacks on the Shia Hazara community in Quetta.

Balochistan is both much bigger and much smaller than Sindh – in fact it is both the biggest and smallest of Pakistan's provinces. With 134,000 square miles and some 43 per cent of Pakistan's land area, it is by far the biggest in terms of territory. With only some 9–11 million people and around 7 per cent of Pakistan's population, it is by far the smallest in terms of people.

Until 2010, the Pakistani central state allocated its support to provincial budgets according to population, resulting in a very small share for Balochistan. By the new National Finance Commission Award of that year, however, the allocation was rebalanced to take account of poverty and revenue generation. This meant that Balochistan's share went up from 7 per cent to 9.09 per cent, around 50 per cent above Balochistan's share of Pakistan's population. This was not nearly enough to satisfy more radical Baloch nationalists, but increased Pakistan's appeal to more moderate Baloch.

The contrast between territory and population largely shapes Balochistan's particular situation and problems. Balochistan's huge territory is home to the greater part of Pakistan's mineral and energy resources (with the colossal exception of the Thar coalfields of Sindh). Its tiny population means that it has little say in Pakistani national politics and little control over how its huge resources are developed.

Up to now, Baloch grievances have centred on the gas fields (of which the biggest are around Sui in Bugti tribal territory), which provide around a third of Pakistan's energy. Disputes over benefits from the field for the local tribal population sparked the latest Baloch insurgency. In future the giant copper mine under development at Reko Diq in western Balochistan may also be a fertile source of anger.

Plans have long been under consideration for two great overland energy corridors taking Iranian, Turkmen and Persian Gulf oil and gas across Pakistan. The first would go to India, to feed India's rapidly growing economy. Should a settlement between India and Pakistan ever permit this to be built, much of it would cross Balochistan. This would give Baloch militants great new opportunities for pressure on the Pakistani government; but, on the other hand, it would also give India a strong incentive to withdraw its support from those militants.

Another energy pipeline is already being built by China from Iran through Pakistan and across the Himalayas along the route of the famous Karakoram Highway. It is intended to help China to escape the threat of blockade of its seaborne energy routes by the US or Indian navies. The great new port of Gwadar which China built at General Musharraf's request in south-western Balochistan (as part of what has been called China's 'string of pearls' strategy in the Indian Ocean), near the entrance to the Persian Gulf, is intended as the starting point of that route. Gwadar could in future be of great benefit to the province in terms of Pakistani trade not only with China but with Iran, Afghanistan, Central Asia and India.

Together with the road from Karachi through Quetta to Afghanistan,

Gwadar makes Balochistan of great strategic importance as a supply route to the Western forces fighting in Afghanistan. So far, however, the development of Gwadar has only led to bitter Baloch nationalist complaints that non-Baloch are being settled in Quetta and that ethnic Baloch are not benefiting from the port. Pakistani officials retort that the local tribesmen in fact sold their land for a great profit, and are living off the proceeds. As so often in Pakistan, objective truth on this seems impossible to determine.

The ethnic Baloch are certainly the least developed and least privileged of all Pakistan's ethnic groups – or, at least, they are when they stay in Balochistan. Elsewhere, as noted, Baloch tribes which moved hundreds of years ago to Sindh and southern Punjab have provided a range of leading Pakistani politicians, including two presidents – Sardar Farooq Khan Leghari and the present incumbent (as of 2010), Asif Ali Zardari. This, however, has done almost nothing to benefit Balochistan itself.

Great dams ('*gabrbands*') from previous eras attest to the presence of civilizations long ago, but since the last round of climate change, Balochistan's desert soil has not generated its own civilization. Instead, poverty has mixed with tribal tradition to keep the Baloch poorly educated and unable to participate fully in the economy, administration and development of their own province. This has been left to other ethnicities – who are then blamed by the Baloch for 'exploiting' them.

Radical Baloch nationalists see their nation almost as the Red Indians of the American West in the middle decades of the nineteenth century – their territory dotted with mining camps and patches of alien settlement guarded by the forts of the US cavalry, and in imminent danger of ethnic swamping and extinction. This is exaggerated, and for most of their problems the Baloch have their own culture and social structures to blame. It is true, however, that they have been dealt a rather poor hand by modern history, and that they have not generally been treated with vision or generosity by Pakistani governments.

Baloch legends say that they originally moved into their present territories from the Middle East. Modern nationalism by contrast has sought to claim that they have lived where they are now for thousands of years. One very curious feature suggests that some of them at least may in fact have been around for that long: the fact that the Baloch are divided between two different languages, the main one being of Indo-European origin like those of all the surrounding peoples, but the smaller,

Brahui (or Brouhi), being largely Dravidian, which is the language-group of southern India, and – so it is presumed – of the Indus Valley civilization.

The Baloch, since records began, have been divided into several dozen tribes. At various times either outside empires or local princes exercised a loose hegemony over some of these tribes. In the late fifteenth century, the leader of one such short-lived tribal confederation, Mir Chakar, chieftain of the Rind tribe (1487–1511 CE), briefly conquered parts of Punjab and Sindh, laying the basis for large-scale Baloch migration into those lands.

However, the principality which Baloch nationalists regard as the historic Baloch national state was that of Kalat, founded in 1638 around another oasis like that of Quetta, fed by two natural springs (now dry because of tube-wells and the radical sinking of the water table). The British arrived in the region in the 1830s, and from 1839 to 1847 fought a fierce war with the Bugti tribe, which in many ways prefigured the present Pakistani war with the Bugti that began in 2005.

In 1876, the British frontier official Sir Robert Sandeman signed a treaty with the Khan bringing Kalat and its dependent territories under British suzerainty. According to the Pakistan state, this placed Kalat in the same position as the other princely states of British India, which after 1947 were voluntarily or involuntarily annexed to India or Pakistan. Baloch nationalists, however, claim that the relationship with the British empire was closer to that of the British protectorate of Nepal, which after 1947 became an independent state. There seems a good deal of truth in this – but, so far, the Pakistani army has been in a position to rule on this question.

The British put together the territories of what is now the Pakistani province of Balochistan for geographical, administrative and security reasons, but out of historically and ethnically disparate elements; in fact the province is almost as much of an artificial creation as Pakistan itself. Moreover, just as was the case with the Pathans and Afghanistan to the north, the British drew a frontier with a neighbouring state which cut the ethnic Baloch lands in two, dividing them between the British empire of India and the Persian empire to the west (with a small number in the deserts of Afghanistan to the north).

Baloch nationalists today claim a large chunk of Iran as part of the 'Greater Balochistan' that they hope to create – thereby guaranteeing the undying hostility of the Iranian as well as the Pakistani state. The

Jundallah movement for the independence of Iranian Balochistan is active in the western parts of Pakistani Balochistan on the Iranian border, in alliance with the Baloch tribal gangs who smuggle heroin from Afghanistan to Iran and the Gulf states through Pakistani territory. Pakistani and Iranian officials both firmly believe (though with little real evidence) that the US and British intelligence services are supporting Jundallah so as to put pressure on Tehran over its nuclear programme. In October 2009 Jundallah killed several senior Iranian officers in a suicide bombing in Iranian Balochistan. The Iranian government accused US, British *and* Pakistani agents of being behind the attack. Pakistan hit back by arresting what it said were several Iranian intelligence agents operating in Balochistan.

However, in a sign of the hellish complexity of this part of the world, Jundallah and the Baloch smugglers are also responsible for smuggling weapons and recruits to the Taleban and Al Qaeda. Thirteen suspected international Islamist volunteers, including three from Russia (apparently Tatars), were intercepted by the Pakistani army during my stay in Balochistan. One was a doctor, seemingly on the way to boost the Taleban's primitive medical services. I do not know what happened to them.

To the Kalat territories and those of the independent tribes, the British added Pathan territories to the north. These were taken from the nominal sovereignty of Afghanistan and, like the tribes of FATA, the tribes of northern Balochistan were split in two by the Durand Line drawn by the British to divide their sphere of influence from Afghanistan. They retain close tribal links to southern Afghanistan, and strong sympathies for the Afghan Taleban.

Some of the leading Pathan tribal families of northern Balochistan originated in what is now Afghanistan, and fled to British territory to escape from the ruthless state-building of Emir Abdur Rahman towards the end of the nineteenth century. After 1977, Pathan numbers in Balochistan were swelled greatly by a new wave of Pathan Afghan refugees, this time from the wars which erupted after the Communist takeover and the Soviet and Western occupations of Afghanistan.

Balochistan's third major ethnicity, the Hazara, also fled from Afghanistan to escape from Abdur Rahman. They are Shia of Mongolian origin from the central highlands of Afghanistan, and between 200,000 and 300,000 of them now live in Quetta and a few other towns. The only moment when I thought that Quetta might be, if not

Paris, then a transmogrified provincial town in southern France in a particularly hot summer, was when I visited the Hazara cemetery.

Like the Mohajirs of Sindh, their uprooting from their ancestral territory in Afghanistan has helped turn the Hazaras of Quetta into a remarkably well-educated and dynamic community (possibly also with the help of aid from Iran, though they deny this fervently). They have by far the best hospitals and schools outside the cantonment, and their cemetery breathes a sort of Victorian municipal pride in their community's heroes. They are especially proud of their prominence in the Pakistani military, and of the fact that a Hazara woman has become the first female fighter pilot in the Pakistani air force. Tragically, though, their cemetery also bears witness to the many Hazara killed in recent years in anti-Shia terrorist attacks by the Sunni sectarian extremists described in previous chapters.

Finally, there are the Punjabi and Mohajir 'settlers' (as they are known by the Baloch), who moved to the region under British and Pakistani rule. Put all these other ethnicities together, and the ethnic Baloch (i.e. the Baloch- and Brahui-speakers) are at best a small majority in Balochistan. In Quetta itself, Baloch may be as little as a quarter of the population, with Pathans the majority. But nobody really knows for sure. In 1901 British officials conducted a census which recorded down to the last child the population of all but the most remote tribes in Balochistan. More than a century later, in 2009, the Commissioner Quetta Division could not tell me within half a million people the population even of Quetta itself. This, however, was not mostly his fault. Apart from the general weakness of the Pakistani bureaucracy when it comes to gathering information, the main parties among the Pathans successfully urged their Pathan followers to boycott the last census in 1998, in the hope that this would help the Pathan Afghan refugees to merge with the local Pathan population, become Pakistani citizens, and boost Pathan political weight in Balochistan.

This boycott meant that the official figure of 6.5 million people for that year (4.9 per cent of Pakistan's population) was almost certainly a serious underestimate. According to the 1998 census, ethnic Baloch formed 54.7 per cent and Pathans 29.6 per cent, with the rest divided between Punjabis, Hazaras and others. But the Pathans claim to be 35–40 per cent of the population, and they may well be right. Almost as many ethnic Baloch live outside Balochistan as within it, though the figures are very hard to determine because many no longer speak Baloch but, while retaining Baloch tribal customs, consider themselves Sindhi or Punjabi.

Fear of ethnic swamping has been one factor in repeated Baloch revolts in both Iran and Pakistan, and the development of Gwadar has only increased these fears. In Pakistan, until the Islamist revolts after 2001, the Baloch were the most persistently troublesome of all the ethnic groups. There was armed resistance in 1948–9, after Kalat's accession (under considerable duress) to Pakistan; unrest again in the late 1950s, after Balochistan was merged into the 'one unit' of West Pakistan and the promises of full autonomy to Kalat state were broken; and a serious revolt between 1973 and 1977, after Zulfikar Ali Bhutto dismissed the moderate nationalist government of Balochistan as part of his moves to centralize power in his own hands, and arrested its leading members.

In all of these cases, however, most of the unrest was concentrated chiefly in one tribal group, and only parts of that group – in the late 1940s and 1950s, parts of the Mengel and other tribes of the old Kalat state and, in the 1970s, parts of the Marri tribe with certain allies. This allowed the Pakistani state to play on the deep traditional rivalries between the tribes and between sub-tribes of the same tribe, and eventually through a mixture of force and concessions to the Sardars of the rebel tribes, to bring these revolts to an end. In all of these cases, it was also never entirely clear if the rebellions concerned were themselves really aiming at full independence, at greater autonomy within Pakistan, or at benefits and redress of grievances for the particular tribes concerned.

THE BALOCH INSURGENCY AFTER 2000

Initially, this also seemed to be the case with the recent round of violent unrest which began after General Musharraf took power in 1999. Baloch fears were aroused by what may have been basically well-intentioned projects on the part of the Musharraf administration for the construction of the new deep-water port at Gwadar in south-western Balochistan near the Iranian border, and for the construction of new military cantonments in the province. These were intended to increase ethnic Baloch recruitment into the armed forces and spread employment in their neighbourhoods. Things were made worse by the high-handed way in which local land was bought for these projects and distributed to workers and officials from elsewhere in Pakistan.

Lack of consultation and intelligence meant that the administration was unaware of the risk that many Baloch would see these projects as increasing Punjabi immigration into Balochistan and threatening them with new 'swamping'. Islamabad seems to have been unsympathetic to Baloch demands that many of the jobs in these projects be reserved in advance for ethnic Baloch.

The result was a growth in armed protest – which was initially limited to some of the Marri tribe, and was led by a younger member of its Sardari family, Balach Marri. He later based himself in Afghanistan, where he was killed in obscure circumstances, probably by Pakistani intelligence, possibly by a misdirected US air strike, or – a remoter possibility – by an accurately directed US strike at Pakistan's request.

The insurgency took on a more serious aspect when it spread to parts of the Bugti tribe, led by their Sardar, Nawab Akbar Bugti. Nawab Bugti was not an inveterate enemy of Pakistan. On the contrary, he pursued throughout his life an opportunist course. After spending many years in gaol under Ayub Khan, in 1973 he sided with Zulfikar Ali Bhutto in dismissing the moderate nationalist government of Balochistan – thereby sparking the Baloch rebellion of that year – and was rewarded with the post of governor, which he held for a year before falling out with Bhutto. In 1989–90 he was chief minister. Bugti therefore demonstrates not implacable nationalist separatism, but rather the old tribal tradition of alternating between rebellion and participation in government, depending on circumstances. The old Italian principle that 'he who draws sword against his king should throw away the scabbard' has never applied in Balochistan, at least as the tribes see things.

Much of the Pakistani army, however, does not see rebellion simply as another form of legitimate political pressure, and this has led to what one might call fatal misunderstandings. They certainly proved fatal in the case of Nawab Bugti. The details of Bugti's rebellion after 2005 have been obscured by rival propaganda and myth-making, but the two main versions are as follows. According to Baloch nationalists, Bugti launched increasingly strong protests against the Musharraf administration's policies and in favour of a greatly increased share of revenues from Sui Gas for Balochistan. When these were rejected, he eventually took to the hills with his armed followers, where he was killed by the military in August 2006.

Alternatively, according to officials of Sui Gas, officers of the Pakistan army and rival Baloch politicians, Bugti was interested only in increased money and favours for his immediate family, and opposed a new military cantonment in Sui because it would threaten his control of the Bugti tribe. He ordered his men to start sabotaging the gas pipelines in order to blackmail the state; and when Musharraf failed to yield to this blackmail, Bugti took to the hills, where he was killed by accident in the course of military operations, or even – depending on which military version you listen to – killed himself and the Pakistani military delegation sent to negotiate with him. The supposed reason for this was that he knew that he was, in any case, dying of disease.

Senator Mushahid Husain Syed, who led a parliamentary delegation which negotiated with Bugti on behalf of the Musharraf administration, told me that the administration and high command were divided between those who wished to go on negotiating with Bugti, and hardliners who had become exasperated with what they regarded as his blackmail and who were determined to crush armed rebellion by force. In the senator's view, however, Bugti was not out for personal gain, but to defend his honour and his leadership of his tribe, which he regarded as threatened by the increasing military presence in his area; and to receive guaranteed jobs for Bugtis in the gas fields.

Two incidents pushed matters from skirmishing between the Bugtis and the military into full-scale revolt: in January 2005 a woman doctor in the military base in Bugti's area was raped. The military immediately alleged that a Bugti tribesman was responsible. Bugti took this as a personal insult and broke off talks with the government. As with Bugti's death, the actual facts of the case have been completely obscured by misinformation on all sides. The second critical incident came in December 2005, when Musharraf visited Kohlu in Balochistan (the first Pakistani leader to visit the region in many years), and rockets were fired at his helicopter. No one knows which Baloch group was responsible, but this attack in turn gave hardliners in the Pakistani military the chance to argue to Musharraf that no further concessions should be made to Bugti.

Fighting in the Bugti areas escalated, and on 26 August 2006 Bugti was killed, or died, along with three Pakistani officers when an explosion destroyed the cave where he had taken refuge. It is a mark of just how disastrous this was that every Pakistani officer with whom I have spoken has sought to absolve the army of responsibility. However, since they have come up with several different and incompatible accounts of what actually happened, it is difficult to attach too much credence to what they say.

What is certain is that senior Pakistani officials – including most probably Musharraf himself – had developed a deep personal contempt and loathing for Bugti. This is in part a matter of class and culture, and of a very different set of attitudes to the authority of the state. Representing both the Pakistani state and what they see as modernity, Pakistani generals were infuriated by Bugti's mixture of aristocratic contempt for them, democratic posing, economic blackmail and authoritarian and retrograde rule over his own tribe.

The result of Bugti's death was a surge of support for his even more radical grandson (and, in the view of the Pakistani military, evil genius) Baramdagh Bugti, who is now leading one wing of the Baloch insurgency from bases in Afghanistan. According to both Pakistani and Western intelligence sources, this is with the covert support of Indian intelligence. The resulting fighting in Balochistan has caused almost 1,000 deaths among militants, Pakistani soldiers and police, and local Punjabi and other 'settlers'. Between 600 and 2,500 suspected militants were arrested and held without charge by the Pakistani intelligence services (the figures differ wildly depending on whom you listen to), and, while most were eventually released again, some have disappeared for good. Many of the militants supposedly killed in battles with the Frontier Corps have also undoubtedly been subjected to extra-judicial execution.

When it comes to the Bugtis themselves, the Pakistani military has done a pretty effective job of divide and rule – just as previously in the case of the Marris, who are also split into several sub-tribes most of which are siding with Pakistan against the insurgency. The Kalpur sub-tribe of the Bugtis is still in arms against Sardar Akbar Bugti's family for control of the benefits of Sui Gas; and in that family, apart from Baramdagh in Afghanistan, there are two other claimants to the leadership of the Bugtis. The eldest son of Akbar Bugti's eldest son, Sardar Ali Bugti, holds the family base in Dera Bugti, though only under heavy military protection; and one of Bugti's sons, Talal Bugti, holds the family mansion in Quetta and the leadership of what is left of Bugti's Jamhoori Watan Party. Talal Bugti spent most of his life in Karachi, and only returned to Balochistan after his father's death.

When I attended a meeting of the party in Quetta, the not very resolute-looking Sardar Talal Bugti on the platform was rather cast into the shade by the fierce features and impressively bristling beard of his nephew Baramdagh, whose large picture was being held aloft by two fifteen-year-old children from – of all places – the elite St Mary's School. And this illustrates the most worrying aspect of the insurgency as far as the Pakistani state is concerned: that it seems to have spread from sections of the Marri and Bugti tribes to parts of the new Baloch educated youth who have emerged in recent years.

As in so much of the developing world, there are not nearly enough state jobs to provide for these people, and their often worthless education certificates do not equip them for modern technical or managerial jobs in gas, mining or at Gwadar – which they believe that they should be given as representatives of the indigenous ethnicity. The more moderate elements try to use their Sardars and the Pakistani political system to force the state to give them jobs; the more radical ones have turned to armed revolt.

So far, this revolt has not been impressive in military terms (which also means that Indian help to the insurgents must so far be at a pretty low level). Attacks on the army, the Frontier Corps and even the wretched police (many of whom in Balochistan are still armed with Second World War-era Lee Enfield bolt-action rifles) are still relatively infrequent. The great majority of the militants' targets are 'soft' ones – the Punjabi and other 'settlers' who have moved to Balochistan over the past 150 years to work in a variety of technical occupations for which the Baloch lack the education (like teachers) or which they consider beneath them (like barbers).[2]

What is happening is a sort of low-level ethnic cleansing, with more than 250 'settlers' killed across Balochistan in the year before my visit in August 2009. The district of Kalat was typical. In the first seven months of 2009, the militants had killed three Kashmiri bakers (together with a Baloch customer), three Punjabi tube-well drillers, one Punjabi teacher and one Baloch policeman.

The result naturally has been an exodus of non-Baloch teachers and technicians from villages and small towns in the ethnic Baloch areas, except where (as in the case of Sui Gas, the mining camps and the cantonments) settlements are under the direct protection of the army. The result has been to depress both Baloch educational levels and the Baloch economy still further, but, unlike the Taleban in FATA, this less than heroic insurgency does not as yet pose a serious threat to the control of the Pakistani military.

BALOCH TRIBALISM

Whether this remains the case will depend largely on how far Baloch tribal society is changing, and generating the kind of frustrated new class which will identify with Baloch nationalism rather than their own tribe. From the point of view of government, Baloch tribalism, like Pathan tribalism, was always an infernal nuisance, but it was also a containable nuisance susceptible to bribes. Among the Pathan tribes, social change and disruption helped to bring about the Taleban movement. It is not clear yet if social change among the Baloch is capable of creating a modern nationalist movement.

In many respects, Baloch tribal culture is close to that of the Pathans. Like the *pashtunwali*, the traditional Baloch code requires tribesmen:

> To avenge blood.
> To fight to the death for a person who has taken refuge with them.
> To be hospitable.
> To refrain from killing a woman, a Hindu, a servant or a boy not yet in trousers.
> To cease fighting on the intervention of a woman, Sayyid or mullah bearing the Koran on her or his head.
> Not to kill a man who takes refuge in a shrine.
> To punish an adulterer with death.[3]

This last provision – extended to illicit sexual relations in general or the mere suspicion of them – has been responsible for the ghastly and continual stream of 'honour killings' among the Baloch tribesmen, who have an obsession with the purity of their female kinsfolk which is extreme even by the pathological standards of their Pathan neighbours.

In one respect, however, Baloch tribalism is very different from that of the Pathans: its leadership is hereditary, hierarchical and even monarchical, whereas the Pathan tradition is meritocratic and even in a sense demo-cratic. In the Baloch tradition (and that of the Pathan tribes of northern Balochistan which are influenced by the Baloch), the position of Sardar – in principle at least – always passes from eldest son to eldest son. The ceremony of 'turbanning' the new Sardar resembles a coronation. Beneath the Sardar, a hierarchy of subordinate chieftains called *waderos* (the same word as for a 'feudal' landowner in Sindh, illustrating the close links between the provinces) and *mirs* rule over sub-sections of the tribe. Sardars can be savagely tyrannical in a way that Pathan chieftains are not; yet in one way both are alike. Over them stands a greater tyrant, which is tribal custom.

That said, the Baloch system in practice seems to have been more flexible than its formal appearance would suggest. Historical records suggest that, before the arrival of the British, tribes repeatedly either split into smaller tribes or grew by assimilating other tribes or bits of tribes. Leaders of sub-tribes revolted against their Sardars and founded separate tribes of their own. This was partly the result of migration from place to place, which British rule prevented. The British *Gazetteer* of 1906 describes the situation among some of the tribes near the Afghan border:

> The local tribe is nominally subject to Sardar Rustam Khan of Jebri, but he has no real influence over any Mamasani clan north of Kharan. The Mamasani tumandar or headman who appears to exercise most power over these wild tribes is Shah Khan Gul, Siahezai Mamasani, but even he has little influence except over his immediate followers.[4]

In fact, it has been suggested that the whole structure of single auto-cratic Sardars ruling over clearly marked tribes was in part at least a creation of the British, who found this convenient from the point of view of bribing and controlling the tribes. If this is so, then the process one can see today in Balochistan (and which is being encouraged by the army), of rival Sardars breaking up tribes into smaller feuding elements, is not really new, but a return to the pre-British norm.

One central feature of Baloch tribalism, however, was certainly not created by the British: the blood feud. As the *Gazetteer* has it:

> A Baloch tribe is not a homogeneous group, but has attained its growth by the gradual assimilation of a number of alien elements, the process

being admission to participation in common blood-feuds, then admission to participation in the tribal land, and lastly admission to kinship with the tribe . . . In other words, common blood-feud is the underlying principle uniting a tribe, but the conception merges into that of common blood, i.e. connection by kinship.[5]

The tradition of the feud is alive and well in Balochistan today. The process of becoming Pakistani politicians and ministers does not seem to have reduced one bit the enthusiasm for this tradition among the Baloch Sardars, whose penchant for murdering fellow politicians makes Baloch politics in some respects closer to those of the Sicilian mafia than the 'social democratic' politics officially espoused by the political parties over which they rule.

What is more, to tribal traditions of violence the Baloch Sardars seem to add a more aristocratic sense of touchy personal honour which makes them even more trigger-happy – quite apart from their feudal (as opposed to tribal) sense of personal entitlement, including the right to kill anyone who offends them. Indeed, if I were to make a distinction within the terms of Baloch culture between a good Sardar and a bad one, it would be that a good Sardar doesn't kill anyone without what he thinks is a good reason.

Thus the late Nawab Akbar Bugti once declared:

> You must remember that I killed my first man when I was twelve . . . The man annoyed me. I've forgotten what it was about now, but I shot him dead. I've rather a hasty temper you know, but under tribal law of course it wasn't a capital offence, and in any case as the eldest son of the Chieftain I was perfectly entitled to do as I pleased in our own territory. We enjoy absolute sovereignty over our people and they accept this as part of their tradition.[6]

The Nawab in fact seems to have been exaggerating somewhat for the sake of the effect on his British interviewer. A Sardar who repeatedly shot his own followers without serious provocation would soon enough find himself without followers, or would be shot in the back himself. Nonetheless, as Paul Titus writes, 'The Bugtis remain entrenched in a world in which honour, expressed through the forceful and uncompromising response to challenges to oneself, remains a pre-eminent value. Specific acts of assertion and vengeance follow from and constitute Bugti cultural logic and history.'[7]

In recent decades, the Bugtis have been involved in several feuds, which have helped to define the politics of Balochistan as a whole. There is a longstanding feud between the Sardars and the Kalpur sub-tribe, whose lands cover much of the gas field. The Kalpurs want to keep more of the benefits for themselves and out of the hands of the Bugtis. In the 1980s, Hamza Khan Kalpur was killed during an election campaign, allegedly by the Bugtis. In the early 1990s, the Kalpurs in revenge allegedly killed Akbar Bugti's youngest son Salar, which in 2003 led Akbar Bugti to kill the Kalpur candidate in the elections of that year. One of the reasons for the Chief Minister (as of 2010), Nawab Mohammed Aslam Khan Raisani, to have stayed loyal to Pakistan and joined the government is that he also has a feud with the Bugtis, and accuses Akbar Bugti of having arranged the murder of his father by members of his party from the Rind tribe.

The Bugtis are also involved in a bloody feud with the family of the hereditary Sardar of the Marri tribe, Khair Baksh Marri – a feud which has helped split the Baloch radical nationalists into different tribal camps, since Khair Baksh Marri is another radical nationalist who led the revolt against Pakistan in the 1970s. His family also has a feud with one of the Marri sub-tribes, the Bijranis, which has helped lead that tribe to join the present government and reject the insurgency. And so on, and on, and on.

Chief Minister Nawab Mohammed Aslam Khan Raisani has a notoriously hot temper, and is accused of responsibility for at least half a dozen murders. The only living member of the Provincial Assembly not to hold a position in government cannot do so because he cannot set foot in Quetta – for Raisani has publicly sworn to kill him if he does. The aggressively bristling beards and upturned moustaches of the men of Sardari families would have a comically theatrical effect were it not for the fact that they say something very real about the men who sport them.

If you want to live in Balochistan – and indeed Pakistan as a whole – without going crazy, it is probably a good idea to try to cultivate an anthropologist's approach to the issue of Sardari feuding, as Sylvia Matheson did when researching her remarkable book *The Tigers of Balochistan*. After all, murder by mutual cultural consent is in a certain sense a kind of blood sport. Those Sardars who don't want to participate can always leave their traditional power and their traditional territories and go to live in London or wherever (Karachi isn't far enough, as the Minister for Excise, Sardar Rustam Jamali, discovered when he was gunned down there in August 2009).

When it comes to Baloch tribal tradition, cultural broadmindedness has however two limits, as far as I am concerned. The first is Baloch independence. It seems all too probable that Baloch tribalism would soon reduce this to a Somali-style nightmare, in which a range of tribal parties – all calling themselves 'democratic' and 'national' – under rival warlords would fight for power and wealth. The task of the Pakistani Frontier Corps on the 'national day' proclaimed by existing pro-independence parties was made easier by the fact that the nationalist parties could not even agree what flag to fly, let alone who should lead them.

In these circumstances, independent Balochistan would revert to its pre-British condition of unrestrained tribal warfare, but this time the wars would be fought not with swords and single-shot muskets, but with AK-47s, machine-guns, rocket-propelled grenades, and whatever heavier weaponry could be acquired with the proceeds of the heroin trade. Claims on the territory of all Balochistan's neighbours would lead to economic blockade and make dependence on heroin and smuggling even more complete. Ethnic chauvinism would kill or chase out the ethnic minorities which provide whatever there is of a modern economy. Quetta would be wrecked in fighting with the Pathans and Hazara. As in Somalia, Al Qaeda and its allies would fish happily amid the ruins: a version of Somalia on the Persian Gulf.

At the end of Sylvia Matheson's book, after recounting the killing of yet another lesser Bugti chief by his enemies, she asks:

> And how and where can it end? Can these traditionally lawless tribes, so cussedly and illogically proud that they consider it more praiseworthy to steal cattle and grain than to demean themselves by working and earning money – can such men as these ever fit into the pattern of modern, democratic civilization as we know it, or must this dream be left for the coming generation?[8]

Her book was researched in the 1950s and published in 1967. Almost two generations have passed since then, but there is still very little sign of this 'dream' coming true among the Baloch tribes.

THE TREATMENT OF WOMEN

The second area where anthropological tolerance should have its limits is in the treatment of women. This is not universally bad, and it may have been better in the past. According to Sylvia Matheson:

> In the early days of tribal society, women enjoyed a tremendous amount of liberty ... The women folk of the leading Khans of Kalat were noted for their activities in politics and warfare; segregation of the sexes is in fact fairly recent, probably introduced since the gradual opening up of the country to strangers.[9]

I did indeed meet one formidable aristocratic lady politician from the Kalat royal family, Mrs Rubina Irfan, a deputy from the formerly pro-Musharraf PML(Q) Party (in a sign of the irrelevance of national party labels in Balochistan, her husband, Agha Irfan Karim, is a deputy from the PPP). Unusually, her development fund has been responsible for some successful projects in Kalat. Even more unusually, she is the leading force in promoting women's football in Pakistan. This has to be played by single-sex teams, indoors, and only in the presence of women and family members – still, a step forward.

Mrs Irfan also stressed that in really traditional Baloch tribal society women had more freedom than in partially modernized society, where male anxiety has been stirred up to pathological levels. Another very impressive lady (though a Mohajir, not an ethnic Baloch), Surriya Allahdin from the great Habibullah industrial family, described to me her charity's success in setting up two girls' schools in rural Balochistan, and how in one area this had led to the average age of girls at marriage going up from twelve to fifteen in the course of thirteen years. 'So give us another generation, and hopefully we will have helped bring the marriage age up to a civilized level, and as a result of this and education we will also help to bring down the birth-rate, which is vital.'

All the same, much of the treatment of women in the Baloch tribal society of today is nothing short of appalling, even by Pakistani standards; and, what is more, some of the most atrocious actions against women in Sindh and southern Punjab are carried out by local tribes of Baloch origin. Quite apart from 'honour killings', as described in the first chapter of this book, the giving of minor girls in marriage as part of the settlement of feuds is still commonplace.

I must confess that several times during my visit to Balochistan I found myself muttering the famous words of General Sir Charles Napier, then Commander-in-Chief in India, when informed that suttee (the burning of widows) was an ancient Rajput custom:

> You say that it is your custom to burn widows. Very well. We also have a custom: when men burn a woman alive, we tie a rope around their necks and we hang them. Build your funeral pyre; beside it, my carpenters will build a gallows. You may follow your custom. And then we will follow ours.

Fortunately, or unfortunately, I do not have General Napier's power, or at least three Baloch politicians would find themselves dangling from lamp-posts – if Quetta had lamp-posts, which of course it doesn't outside the cantonment. No, make that four or five.

These particular thoughts were inspired by a particularly ghastly case of 'honour killing', which occurred on 13 July 2008 in Babokot village, Nasirabad District, near the borders of Sindh. Three teenage student girls of the Umrani tribe were shot by order of a tribal jirga for trying to marry men of their own choice rather than their family's, and then buried while still alive. Two female relatives who tried to save them were killed as well. It is alleged that a chieftain of the tribe, Mir Abdul Sattar Umrani, chaired the jirga which ordered the killings.[10]

According to a police official with whom I spoke, his brother, Balochistan Minister of Communications Sadiq Umrani, put strong pressure on the police not to investigate. Amusingly – if your sense of humour runs that way – on 13 August 2009 a court in Sindh finally issued an arrest warrant for Sadiq Umrani and his brothers; not, however, for the case of the buried women, but for the alleged murder of five people of the Palal tribe of northern Sindh, including a woman and two children, in a dispute over land in 2008.

Sardar Israrullah Zehri, a PPP senator of Pakistan's upper house of parliament, defended the burial of the Umrani women, saying that 'these are centuries-old traditions and I will continue to defend them. Only those who commit immoral acts should be afraid.' The Zardari administration later made him Minister of Posts. The acting chairman of the Senate – another Baloch chieftain, Sardar Jan Mohammad Jamali – described the killings as having been blown out of proportion by the media.[11] All of these politicians belong to the PPP, a party dedicated, according to its programme, to women's rights, social progress and the rule of law. None has been expelled from the government or the party.

Another Baloch minister (for Sports and Culture) from a Sardari family, Mir Shahnawaz Khan Marri, told me:

> The burying of those girls alive was a conspiracy against Balochistan. There is no report on who killed them and why. The Supreme Court has not produced a report. It has not been proved yet that they were killed. These kinds of things are designed so as to create a scenario against Balochistan. The Afghans are here, they get millions of dollars to create subversion here, all different international agencies are working here . . .[12]

After this, the minister plunged into a rant lasting more than five minutes, during which a paranoid account of the conspiracies of the outside world against Balochistan somehow ended with the statement that 'I don't believe in nationalism. The world has become a global village and we should all love each other.'

All of these politicians have claimed either that the girls were not killed at all, killed but not buried alive, or that they had engaged in 'immoral acts' and therefore deserved their punishment, or all of these together. None of this is true. I interviewed the police surgeon who dug up and examined the bodies of the three girls, Dr Shamim Gul. They had all been buried alive, and they were all virgins.

Dr Gul – the only police surgeon for the whole of Balochistan – is the most remarkable person I met during my travels in Pakistan. Among other things she is very much more of a man than the vast majority of the men I encountered – if I may be forgiven a Baloch-sounding comment. This fifty-eight-year-old Pathan grandmother, deaf as a post in one ear (our conversation was conducted in bellows on my side), spends her professional life travelling around Balochistan at night (because there are a great many people of course who do not exactly favour her investigations), digging up rotting corpses and examining them in makeshift morgues in temperatures which can reach 50 degrees Celsius. 'Sometimes the bodies fall to pieces and I have to put them back together again,' she told me.[13]

Dr Gul does her work without a police escort – for reasons that will come as no surprise to anyone who knows the police of Pakistan. And she goes on doing her duty despite the fact that of the ten or fifteen bodies of women murdered in 'honour killings' which she examines each year, not one case has ever been successfully prosecuted, though a few people may have been embarrassed a bit; and those she examines are in her estimate only around 5 per cent of the total killed, because the vast majority are never reported.

Dr Gul retired in 2008 but then took up the job again in 2009 because no one else wanted it. For myself, if I had Napier's powers I would begin by making her the Inspector-General (i.e. provincial chief) of police in Balochistan, and then promote her upwards from there. She certainly deserves a senior job more than any other local politician or official whom I met.

VISIT TO A BUGTI

Nawabzada Jamil Bugti, son of Nawab Akbar Bugti by his second wife, took a rather more restrained – and coherent – line on the murder of the girls when I visited him on his estate outside Quetta. He also said that there was no proof that they had been buried alive, but then immediately changed his line to say that, if indeed it had happened, it was contrary to Baloch tradition:

> If there is a case of adultery then in our tradition you have to kill the man as well as the woman involved; and if you do so without sufficient evidence then you have a blood feud on your hands. Salik Umrani is not even the real head of his tribe. He is neither partridge nor quail, that is why he didn't follow tribal tradition in this case ... I remember a case that my father once deputed me to judge. A man had killed his wife and her lover and volunteered to walk through a fire to prove that they had been having an affair. The lover's family had denied it and demanded compensation, or they would have launched a blood feud. And the husband took his seven steps through the fire as if on rose petals! So the lover's family withdrew their demand and I closed the case.[14]

This was strange stuff to hear in an elegant modern living-room lined with vaguely Impressionist still-life paintings, and from a man with some at least of the manners and appearance of an English gentleman; but then, there was a good deal that was strange – and revealing – about our meeting.

Nawabzada Bugti's house is set in an artificial, tube-well-fed oasis near the village of Miangundi, a few miles outside Quetta. The area has been developed by various Baloch nobles as a commercial venture of orchards, with their mansions set in the middle of them. The contrast between his garden, with its green lawns and rose-beds, and the arid, savage mountains behind added to the slightly surreal air of our conversation.

The Nawabzada complained that the conservatism of Baloch farmers meant that they would not accept drip technology even though almost the whole cost of installing it is covered by the Asian Development Bank – though I could not help noticing that his own garden was being watered by the old, horribly wasteful technique of flooding the whole lawn several inches deep. In one corner of the vast garden, a new swimming pool was under construction.

Like his father and most of his family, Jamil Bugti at fifty-nine is a tall, handsome, aristocratic-looking man with aquiline features and a modified version of the bristling Baloch beard. He towered over his lawyer, a squat, rubber-faced and obsequious Punjabi who had driven out with us from Quetta as a partial safeguard against nationalist banditry. The sense of racial difference was even starker when it came to the Nawabzada's small, thin, dark-skinned servants. These are 'Mrattas', descendants of Marathas from central India, captured in war by the Mughal emperors and given to their Bugti troops as slaves in lieu of wages.

Traditionally, their women have served as concubines to the Bugti ('their women were regarded as fair game for all Bugtis' in Matheson's words) but there was no sign of Bugti blood in the faces of the Nawabzada's servants. The Mrattas were officially made equal citizens of Pakistan after 1947, and the Nawabzada insisted that 'they have merged completely with the Bugti and no one can tell the difference any more' – given all the circumstances a real whopper. On the other hand, the British official and ethnographer R. Hughes Buller stated in 1901 that,

> Many Baloch tribes consist chiefly of elements which have been affiliated to the Baloch and have afterwards set up for themselves. As time passes, their origin is forgotten and with it any social inferiority which may have originally existed. An instance of a group which has only lately asserted

Baloch origin, is the Golas of Nasirabad. Though enumerated with the Baledis they are looked upon by other Baloch as occupying a low place in the social scale. Common report assigns them a slave origin, and as the word gola means slave in Sindhi, it is quite possible that this belief has some foundation in fact.[15]

So just possibly something of the sort may indeed very gradually be happening in the case of the Mrattas, even if it obviously hasn't happened yet.

Like most of the members of Sardari families whom I met, the Nawabzada talked a fiercely pro-independence and anti-Pakistani talk, accentuated by his deep booming voice and frequent use of English obscenities. His resentment of the Pakistani state seemed genuine enough when he spoke of his father's death at the hands of the Pakistan army, of how, at the age of nine, he had seen his father arrested for the first time ('When he was released in 1969 I had already graduated'), and of his fury at seeing pictures of Pakistani officers posing in his ancestral home at Dera Bugti. He accused the Pakistani army of committing 'genocide' in Balochistan, and declared that 'I don't see how any honourable Baloch can celebrate Pakistani independence. For us it has been sixty years of slavery, barbarism and torture.'

He expressed utter contempt for Pakistan-led development in Balochistan, declaring of Musharraf's new port at Gwadar,

> We don't want to develop Gwadar or other ports – we don't want another Dubai in Balochistan. What is Dubai? A bloody whorehouse like the Hira Mandi ['Diamond Market', or red-light district] in Lahore. Why should we allow millions of outsiders to come here and take our land?

At first hearing, then, this is an example of the Pakistani state's utter failure to retain or cultivate the loyalty of many of the Baloch tribal aristocracy. At the second hearing, however, certain questions began to arise. If he was so committed to independence, why had he not taken sides in the conflict over the leadership of the Bugti tribe between his two nephews, Nawabzada Ali Bugti, the officially turbaned head of the tribe sitting in Dera Bugti under army protection, and Nawabzada Baramdagh Bugti, leading the pro-independence forces from exile in Afghanistan (whom he described as 'following my father's line and doing a pretty good job')?

And, above all, of course, why had he not been arrested by the

Pakistani security forces, and why in fact was he still sitting in a paid position on the board of Pakistani Petroleum, to which he had been restored after a period of suspension? To these questions the Nawab-zada's responses became rather less fluent. Concerning his non-arrest, he declared that 'I suppose given all my medical problems, they do not want another dead Bugti on their hands', though I must say he looked in fine fettle to me.

By the end of the interview, therefore, the Nawabzada seemed to me to represent not an unqualified failure on the part of the Pakistani state, but rather a sort of qualified success – a success, that is for the old twin imperial policies of divide and rule and co-optation of elites, something that every successful empire-builder from Rome to Victorian Britain has understood perfectly. In the case of the British empire on the Baloch frontier, this involved financial subsidies to the Sardars to keep their tribes quiet, subsidies which could then be withdrawn from those who stepped out of line. Military action was very much a last resort.

PAKISTAN AND BALOCHISTAN

The Pakistani approach has generally been the same in essence but different in form. It is summed up in the remarkable fact that, as of 2009, out of sixty-five members of the Baloch Provincial Assembly, sixty-two were in the provincial government as ministers, ministers without portfolio or advisers with ministerial rank. Nor did the remaining three deputies constitute much of an opposition. Two had not occupied ministerial chairs by virtue of being dead, which is an obstacle to government service even in Balochistan. The third cannot visit Quetta because of the blood feud with the chief minister, mentioned above.

This is the kind of thing which has led me to place the word 'democracy' in this book in inverted commas; and perhaps I should do the same for 'development'; because the point of this whole set-up is that on top of their ministerial salary and staff, every member of the government gets a Rs50 million (£385,000) personal share of Balochistan's development budget, to spend on projects in his own district.

Irrational? Not at all. From the point of view of serious development, yes of course completely crazy. As a new way of co-opting the tribal leadership (in an age when you can't just have political agents handing out bags of gold coins), eminently sensible – and effective. It is above all thanks to the Pakistani state's ability to hand out this kind of personal largesse – as well as some hard blows when necessary – that as of 2009 all but three of the eighty-odd tribal Sardars or claimants in Balochistan were ranged with the government, and had not joined the anti-Pakistan insurgency. For that matter, even members of Nawab Bugti's own Jamhoori Watan Party continued to sit in the provincial assembly!

The priorities of Baloch ministers took on an almost comically obvious shape in the already mentioned interview I had with the Minister of Sports and Culture. Outside his office, his four staff sat around drinking tea, chatting, reading the papers and otherwise doing absolutely nothing – not that they could have done very much, since neither they nor the minister had a computer or even a typewriter. The minister complained bitterly that Balochistan has a quota of state jobs according to its small population, when instead – in his view – it should get the same proportion of jobs as it has of Pakistani territory – i.e. almost half of all jobs in the central bureaucracy, a thought which made me choke into my tea. For the population in general, he demanded that Islamabad create 60,000 junior administrative jobs in Balochistan, and distribute them to graduates. As of early 2010, this is being negotiated between the governments in Islamabad and Quetta, with 30,000 jobs a frequently mentioned compromise figure.

Completely unprompted by me, the minister also complained three times in the course of the interview that ethnic Baloch should be given more Pakistani ambassadorships, which seemed to me a pretty clear indication of what was on his own mind as far as jobs were concerned. The idea that merit or qualifications should play any part in appointments to any these jobs appeared nowhere in his remarks – nor does it, apparently, in the negotiations between Quetta and Islamabad.

Rather than the old British strategy, this then is closer to the Roman approach of making smaller local tribal chieftains into local officials, and bigger ones into Roman senators. By making them responsible for tax collection, these local leaders were also given a share in state revenues. The Romans, though, had the advantage of representing not just overwhelming military force and an efficient state bureaucracy, but also a great state-building idea, summed up in the values of *Romanitas*.

It would be quite a stretch to suggest that there exists a civilizing concept called *Pakistanitas* – if only because Pakistanis differ so radically over what it is or should be. However, sitting in Quetta and looking at the alternatives does bring home the fact that there is at least a certain kind of *modernità alla Pakistanese*. In Balochistan, this is to be found above all in three places: among the Hazara; in the gas fields and mines; and in the army. The last element in a way embraces the other two. The Hazara are both deeply attached to the armed forces and proud of their prominent role in them, and look to those armed forces for protection; and the gas fields and mines also depend wholly on the army for protection. Inevitably, therefore, and despite a determined effort on their part to pretend otherwise, the responsibilities of the Pakistani army in Balochistan go far beyond the purely military.

This appeared strongly from my interview with the Pakistani general commanding in Balochistan, Lt-General Khalid Wynne. I am not qualified to judge his qualities as a general; but when it comes to relative modernity, I must confess that I was greatly prejudiced in his favour by his daughter – whom I have never met, but who is studying for a PhD in molecular biology in the US. The general admitted disarmingly that 'my wife and I wanted to arrange her marriage but she insisted on doing research instead, so we gave in, and sold some property to pay for her education. Then she won a top scholarship, which makes us very proud.'

My interview with General Wynne illustrated the way in which the Pakistani army is repeatedly drawn into managing wider areas of the state. This is not always because the generals want this, but because of an iron logic proceeding both from the fact that the armed forces constitute by far the most efficient and coherent institution of that state, and that in the NWFP and Balochistan economic development has a critical security dimension. It has to be protected from insurgency, and it can contribute to defeating insurgency.

Thus our conversation began with the usual ritualistic declaration on the part of the general that the army has no interest in once again becoming involved in politics and government, and wishes to concentrate on its core tasks of defending the country against external aggression and defeating domestic insurgency. He said that while the army is ultimately responsible for internal security within Balochistan, it is not involved in operations against the present insurgency, which are the business of the Frontier Corps.

The interview ended with the general describing how the army is closely involved in the management of the big coal mine being developed at Chamalang near Balochistan's border with Punjab and Sindh, which in 2007–9 produced around 1 million tons of coal. This is in a mixed Pathan–Baloch area, where Marri tribesmen have traditional grazing rights, and a violent dispute broke out between them over access to benefits from the mine, which for many years held up its development. In 2006 the army was invited to settle this dispute, and to guarantee the resulting agreement.

This involved recruiting and paying Marri tribesmen as local police (levies), and a development fund from the profits of the mine to be spent on schools, roads and health care to benefit both the Pathans and the Marris. 'This is something that I am really proud of, that we are involved in nation-building,' the general told me. All this also has a security dimension. In the general's view, the deal over Chamalang has contributed greatly to persuading Marris not to join the present insurgency.[16] It will be very interesting to see if – as has been proposed – the army now starts taking a key part in running other mining projects in Balochistan and elsewhere, and distributing the benefits to the local population. The army will in any case have to be present at these sites in order to protect them from the insurgents.

The question of just how much wealth lies underneath Balochistan is the subject of crazed nationalist myth-making, with stories abounding of Balochistan 'having more oil than Kuwait', and so on. Having talked to geologists, the truth appears to me to be that Balochistan probably has very little oil, and few major new gas fields left to discover. What it does have, however, is very large amounts of copper, together with lesser amounts of gold.

The Chinese corporation running the Saindak mine as of 2010 processes around 15,000 tonnes of ore a day. Informed (as opposed to mythical) estimates for the Reko Diq field near the borders with Afghanistan and Iran range up to 16 million tonnes of pure copper and 21 million ounces of gold, which if developed would make Pakistan one of the world's largest producers of copper (though still far behind Chile), and a serious gold producer. A joint Canadian–Chilean consortium (Tethyan Copper) plans to invest up to $3 billion in Reko Diq's development (leading to the inevitable paranoid headline on the pakalert website, 'Reko Diq Mystery: Why Neocons and Zionists are after Balochistan?').[17]

Reko Diq could be of great benefit to Pakistan and Balochistan – or it could lead to explosive disputes between them, and among the Baloch themselves, as has been the case with both Sui Gas and Gwadar Port. The most obvious solution to distributing the benefits of mines like Reko Diq would be something like the Alaska Permanent Fund, which invests a proportion (in effect 11 per cent) of the proceeds of Alaskan oil for the long-term benefit of the population of Alaska, above all in terms of investment in infrastructure, services and water conservation.

Especially water conservation. Although Balochistan's population is so small, it is still far too large for the province's water resources, unless the use of water is radically improved. At present, the Quetta valley in particular is beginning to look like my grim prediction for Sindh and even Pakistan a few decades down the line: millions of people trying to survive in a desert. Over the past fifty years, water experts in Quetta told me, draining by tube-wells has made the local water table sink from 40 feet to more than 800 feet below the ground. In 'Settler Town', in the mid-1990s, the water table was at 200 feet. Now it is at 1,200 feet, and there is in any case less and less to bring up. Many of the local tube-wells and manual wells are now dry, and much of the population has to buy its water from tankers. Settler Town contains approximately 200,000 people. It goes without saying that the state's water-pipe system is now permanently dry. In the grim judgement of Andrew Arthur of the UNHCR, 'In another ten years or so, the water table in parts of the Quetta valley will be below 2,000 feet and people will start to migrate out, as has already happened in Sibi, Chaghi and Dalbandia, where the situation is even worse.'[18]

The two natural springs which created an oasis in the Quetta valley and were responsible for the creation of Quetta itself have both long since dried up. A new water pipeline is being built from the hills to supply drinking water to the city, but what will become of local agriculture if this goes on no one likes to think. Moreover, corruption and changes of government mean that this pipeline is already three years behind schedule. An urgent need is for more small earthen dams to trap rainwater, since what little there is in Balochistan at present mostly goes to waste, and for the replacement of private tube-wells with metred government windmill-pumps that bring up a little at a time and cannot be used for the dreadfully wasteful 'flood irrigation'.

So there would be an immense amount of valuable work to be done by a long-term infrastructure fund drawing on the profits of Balochistan's

gas and mineral wealth. The problem is that, left to Baloch Sardari politicians to administer such a fund, there is no way that most would save
anything for the future, or for the benefit of Balochistan as a whole.
Everything would be spent on short-term gains for themselves and their
followers. This would actually increase discontent both among educated
Baloch and in the tribes in the immediate vicinity of the mines.

If the army or some other Pakistani national institution were made
responsible for distributing the benefits of extractive industries to the
population, their task would therefore involve a huge and perhaps impossible degree of diplomacy. This is something at which the Pakistani army
and state in Balochistan have a decidedly mixed record. In general they
have not done too badly, aided by the fragmentary and feuding nature of
Baloch tribal society. Sometimes, however, they have slipped up very
badly indeed, as in the death of Sardar Akbar Bugti.

Like other senior officers, General Wynne now admits that the army
seriously mishandled its treatment of Bugti and Bugti's death. Like
them, he claims that the Pakistani army did not in fact kill Bugti (which
is highly doubtful) and (which has been confirmed to me by several different sources) that they were in fact negotiating with him to the very
end. The general was open in his personal contempt for Bugti, whom he
described as interested only in his own family and followers and doing
nothing to spread the benefits of Sui Gas among his tribesmen, let alone
Balochistan as a whole. He said that when, as a young officer, he had
asked Bugti about his representatives stealing the workers' wages, Bugti
had just laughed at him dismissively.

On the other hand, the general said, there is no good seeing things in
Balochistan in terms of black and white:

> Everything here is shades of grey. Here you have to be street smart. Or to
> put it another way, you need to be a little bit of a rascal to understand this
> part of the world. You always have to be prepared to negotiate with your
> enemies – who knows, they may change sides and become your allies
> tomorrow. That is something the Americans still haven't understood in
> Afghanistan ... That is why you can meet in Quetta many nationalist
> politicians who have declared themselves to be rebels against Pakistan, but
> who we deliberately haven't touched.

When it comes to dealing with Akbar Bugti, the overwhelming majority of Pakistani political, media and elite opinion – including liberal

opinion – agrees with General Wynne that the state and army should have gone on negotiating with him even after he took up arms and started killing Pakistani soldiers. Indeed, there have even been demands not just from Baloch nationalists but from liberal human rights lobbyists that Musharraf be tried for his murder. Certainly everyone sensible agrees that it is necessary to negotiate with radical-sounding Baloch nationalists in an effort to wean them away from the real hardliners. Given that these Baloch rebels are not exactly progressive people, this makes an interesting contrast with the attitude of Pakistani liberals to the attempts of the state and army to negotiate with Islamist militants in the Pathan areas and elsewhere. These attempts have been denounced not just as foolish and hopeless but as evidence of sinister hidden sympathy and co-operation between the military and the Pakistani Taleban.

The reality seems to me rather different, and will be explored in the following chapters. Certain sympathies and strategic calculations concerning the Taleban have existed; but the main underlying theme has been a different one, characteristic of the Pakistani state in many areas including Balochistan. This theme involves a chaotic but often in the end fairly effective mixture of continual negotiation and bargaining, with intermittent brutal force. As is obvious, this mixture failed in the end when dealing with the Pakistani Taleban; but as will be seen in the following chapters, the *way* in which it failed has also been crucial to Pakistan's success against the Taleban.

10

The Pathans

The very name Pakhtun spells honour and glory,
Lacking that honour what is the Afghan story?
In the sword alone lies our deliverance,
The sword wherein is our predominance,
Whereby in days long past we ruled in Hind;
But concord we know not, and we have sinned.

(Khushal Khan Khattak)[1]

One way of looking at the Pathans of Pakistan is as eighteenth-century Scots without the alcohol.[2] Here we have a people with a proud history of independence, often bitterly resentful of their incorporation in a new state – and yet many of whom at the same time draw tremendous advantages from membership of that state, most of which is much richer than their own stony pastures. The already poor province has been impoverished still further in recent years, first by the war with the Pakistani Taleban, then by the floods of 2010 which hit this region worst of all. A Pakistani Dr Johnson could well say of his Pathan compatriots that 'the noblest prospect a Pathan ever sees is the high road that leads him to Punjab.'

Not that many Pathans would admit that, even the ones actually living in Punjab. Pathan ethnic pride is notorious. Just as completely integrated Scots in the British establishment have often at heart remained proud and even resentful Scots, so I heard a senior Pakistani civil servant in Peshawar railing against the Punjabis whose industrialists, he said, were sucking the North West Frontier Province dry and who had blocked his own advancement within the central civil service. And yet this man would as soon have wished for an independent Pakhtunkhwa linked to Afghanistan as he would have wished for a union with Pluto. Nor indeed was his own family united on this: his daughter, employed in Islamabad, growled in response, 'And what have Pashtuns ever done for themselves? They just sit there asking Islamabad for subsidies.'

It should be noted that every single senior civil servant, serving or retired, whom I met in the province was himself an ethnic Pathan, and an attempt has been made to ensure that the most senior military commanders in the province and FATA are also usually ethnic Pathans. This marks a major difference from Balochistan; and from this point of view at least the notion of the NWFP as a Punjabi colony is quite wrong.

On the other hand, at a dinner party in Peshawar, I listened to two members of the Pathan elites, a retired army colonel and a senior local journalist for a Pakistani TV channel, discussing the possibility of Pakistan breaking up into its ethnic regions. Neither of them wanted this outcome, and both would suffer from it very badly indeed; but they were prepared to discuss it with a cool detachment which you would never find among Punjabis of their rank and position.

The complexity of Pathan links to Pakistan is illustrated by an anecdote told me by a leading politician for the nationalist Awami National Party (ANP), Bashir Bilour. The Bilours are strong Pathan nationalists, but have also sided at different times with all Pakistan's national parties, as part of factional fighting within the ANP. All the same, I was quite surprised to learn that his family has intermarried with that of the late Ghulam Ishaq Khan (1915–2006), veteran Pakistani bureaucrat, President from 1988 to 1993 and an ardent Pakistani patriot. Nonetheless, when in 1993 Ghulam Ishaq appealed to Bilour to support him against Nawaz Sharif, he did so with the words, 'After all, we Pashtuns should stick together, not go with the Punjabis!'

Along similar lines, a retired Pathan officer, Brigadier Saad, described to me how his uncle, an ANP veteran, over dinner one day had cursed the Afghans as savages. 'How can you say this, Uncle?', he asked. 'Haven't you been saying for years that they are our Pashtun brothers and we should unite with them?'

'Oh, that wasn't serious! It's just a way of frightening those damned Punjabis so that they don't beat us up.'

In the Pathan highlands, an insurrection is raging against the national government, fed in part by Pathan national sentiment. Yet as with the

Scottish rebellions of 1715 and 1745, the motivation of this rebellion is not nationalism as such, but a mixture of ancient clan unrest against any government with religious differences; and the stated goal is not Pathan independence, but a change of regime in Pakistan as a whole.

Of course, the parallel is very far from exact. It does not include the crucial importance of developments in neighbouring Afghanistan for the affairs of Pakistan's Pathans. Equally importantly, the society of the Pathan areas, and the tribal areas in particular, is rougher by far than that of eighteenth-century Scotland, and this in turn produces a much rougher kind of religious radicalism. Alas, there is no great modern Enlightenment culture to produce a contemporary Pathan Adam Smith or David Hume.

A young, highly educated Pathan woman of my acquaintance, from an elite background, described to me in 2008 how a girlfriend of hers from a similar background had recently called off her arranged marriage at the last moment in order to marry instead a former suitor: 'There was a terrible scandal of course, but in the end the parents saw that there was nothing to be done, and agreed.' I said that I found this an encouraging sign of progress, if only at the elite level. 'Yes,' she replied, looking aside with an extremely bitter face, 'but if that had happened in my family there would have been half a dozen deaths by now between us and the other families involved, starting with the girl.'

The provincial office of the Pakistan People's Party – at the time of writing Pakistan's ruling party – stands on University Road, Peshawar's high street, lined with fairly modern-looking shops and offices. Just opposite, a side road leads to the Tehkal quarter – and within a few feet turns into a rutted dusty track, unpaved and lined with filthy-looking shops, barrows with flyblown fruit and vegetables, and concrete shacks roofed with corrugated iron. Every woman on this street when I visited it was wearing a black or blue burqa.

'You can tell the Afghan girls because they wear a more modern type of burqa than our local women – more fashionable and stylish,' a Peshawari woman told me; something which one could find tragic, comic or even heroic, according to taste. 'Was this road ever paved?' I asked. 'Once upon a time', was the answer.

In other words, in trying to create a strict Shariah-based system in the Pathan areas the Taleban are not trying to impose something completely new. They are trying to develop something partly new out of elements that are very old indeed. And the cruelty for which the Taleban are rightly reproached has to be seen in the context of what at the best of times can be a very hard society indeed, especially as far as women are concerned.

Peshawar itself is a hard enough city, and looks it: a sprawl of dusty grey brick and concrete slums interspersed with the extravagant villas of the well-off, shrouded in dust and pollution; searingly hot in summer and grindingly cold in winter. When I think of the city, I often remember the sign for an angiography centre (heart clinic) at the entrance to the road where my usual guest-house is situated in University Town. In the West, such a sign would probably have featured a handsome elderly man, with some saccharine message about taking care of your heart for the sake of your grandchildren. The sign in Peshawar featured a huge colour photograph of a human heart, streaked with blood and rimmed with glistening fat. One of the great charms of the Pathans, acknowledged by all observers, is that they are nothing if not candid. After this, when I saw a sign for 'Brains School, Peshawar', I half expected it to be accompanied by a picture of a raw brain.

Peshawar's only grace-notes are the neat and elegant official military cantonment, the beautiful gardens of its schools and colleges, built by the British on Mughal patterns, and the occasional exquisitely shaped minaret, pointing towards a better world than that of Peshawar. Yet by the standards of the rest of the province, Peshawar is wealthy indeed, with banks, luxury stores, an international hotel, even a halal McDonald's. Now and then, if you look down a straight street, or over some low roofs, you see the outlines of an even poorer, harder world, which both hates and envies Peshawar – the tawny sentinels of the Frontier mountains, graveyard of armies.

THE MOUNTAINS AND THE PLAINS

I thought of those mountains when I attended a service at St John's Cathedral, the old British garrison church of Peshawar. My fellow congregants were not Pathans, but descendants of low-caste Hindus, converted under the British Raj. The memoirs of the Reverend T. L. Pennel attest to the extreme resistance of the Pathans to any effort to convert them to Christianity. In fact it says a great deal for the spirit of missionaries like Pennel that they made the attempt at all.[3]

So the noses of the congregation were much flatter than those of the rest of the city's population, the skins darker, and the bodies shorter. In fact, the whole service made a contrast to the dour face of Pathan public life. After three weeks in the NWFP the sight of the unveiled women in their brightly coloured *shelwar kameezes* and the occasional sari – though for the most part decorously seated apart from the men – was profoundly refreshing.

Although traditionally an impoverished and despised community, and today an increasingly endangered one, the Christians in Pakistan have done comparatively well in recent years, thanks to strong community co-operation, help from international Christian groups and, perhaps most importantly, commitment to education. Many of the men had pens clipped to their front pockets as a sign that they were employed in some literate profession.

The cheerful beat of the Anglican hymns, transformed almost out of recognition by India and accompanied by drums and cymbals, had a fine martial air, appropriate to a profoundly embattled and endangered community in an increasingly embattled city. A tiny girl with an enormous grin sat on the altar steps, clapping her hands in time to the music. Fans waved to and fro in a vain effort to reduce the sweltering heat, for it was August and we were in the middle of one of Peshawar's eternal power cuts, so the giant overhead fans were still. Outside, a dozen armed police stood guard against the terrorists who have attacked so many Christian churches (and Shia mosques) in recent years. Reassuring, but, as we have seen again and again, alas, in the face of a really large-scale assault not enough to do much more than die bravely – which the poor devils have done often enough, usually unremarked by the Western media.

It was strange to sit in such heat in a red-brick neo-Gothic church below a fine Victorian hammer-beam roof, listening to a fire and brimstone sermon in Urdu; but much stranger to think of the faces that would have filled the church sixty years before – the white (or rather also brick-red) faces of the British garrison, administrators and the tiny non-official British community. Outside the main entrance, one of the greatest of the British in India is commemorated by a tall cross and an inscription which still has the power to move, because it was erected not by a state or government but by a friend, and for no reason save friendship: To Field Marshal Auchinleck, 'In affection and admiration to the memory of this great gentleman, great soldier and great man. From his devoted friend General Sher Ali Pataudi, 1984'.

Auchinleck's comrades and predecessors, whose names adorn the walls of the cathedral, might well have been surprised by the congregation and the music, but I doubt that much else that is happening on the Frontier today would have surprised them. The reason is summed up in their memorials: Major Henry MacDonald, Commandant of Fort Michni, 'cruelly murdered by Afridis, 21st March 1873'; Lt Colonel James Loughan O'Bryen, commanding 31st Punjab Infantry, 'killed in action at the head of his regiment at Agran, Bajaur, 30th September 1897'; Leslie Duncan Best OBE MC IPS, Political Agent Dir, Swat and Chitral, 'killed in action near Loe Agra, 11th April 1935'.

Tablet after tablet of this kind stretch along the cathedral walls, commemorating a hundred years of British warfare with the Pathan tribes of the North West Frontier and Afghanistan. These ghosts testify that Pathans do not take kindly to an infidel military presence in their territories. Soviet monuments could have told the same story, if a Soviet Union had survived to commemorate its dead in Afghanistan. The surprising thing, therefore, about the present Taleban insurgency in the Pathan areas of Afghanistan and Pakistan is not that it is happening, but that it was not more widely predicted.

Looking at the attractive, unveiled women in the church, my mind travelled back twenty years to another city under threat from tribal warriors fighting for Islam: Kabul in the summer of 1989, with the Mujahidin (then anti-Communist 'freedom fighters' according to the Western media, but in their own presentation warriors for Islam) beginning to tighten their grip after the Soviet military withdrawal. I visited the university there and, talking to the women students and professors, I remembered what a grizzled, middle-aged *mujahid* from a ruined village in the hills had told me around a camp fire in Nangrahar a few months earlier, when I asked him what he meant to do when the Communists were defeated and the cities fell. 'I mean to capture an educated wife,' he had said.

I remembered the narrowed eyes and lean, hard faces of the Mujahidin as they stared into Ghazni from the hills around the town. I remembered them again three years later, when I was a journalist stationed in the Soviet Union during its fall, and read what had in fact happened to Afghanistan's cities and especially their women when the Mujahidin captured them; and when I returned to Afghanistan after 9/11 and learned at first hand what the Mujahidin victory had meant for the people of Kabul. To be fair to the Taleban, it was precisely because they offered a version of peace and order after the horrors of Mujahidin anarchy that their rule was welcomed by so many Afghan Pathans in the mid-1990s. Yet for the educated classes in the cities, and for many non-Pathans, the cure was even worse than the disease.

THE PATHAN TRADITION AND PATHAN NATIONALISM

The Taleban in both Afghanistan and Pakistan are as of 2010 first and foremost a Pathan phenomenon, with deep roots in Pathan history and culture. Whenever the tribes rose in the past, whether against the British or Afghan authorities, this was for their tribal freedoms but always in the name of Islam and usually under the inspiration of local religious figures. For most of Afghan history, the Afghan kings also called their people to war in the name of Islam – in between launching their own ferocious campaigns against dissident mullahs preaching rebellion against those same kings. The religious theme has therefore long flowed together with tribal yearning for freedom from authority – any authority, but above all of course alien and infidel domination. Or, as a Pathan saying has it: 'The Afghans of the Frontier are never at peace except when they are at war.'

The Taleban therefore have a rich seam of instinctive public sympathy to mine in the Pathan areas. So far in both Afghanistan and Pakistan they have, however, drawn on Pathan ethnic sentiment without co-opting it completely and becoming a Pathan nationalist force. Indeed, they have not attempted to take this path. The reasons for this relate to Taleban ideology and ambitions, and also to the complicated geopolitical situation in which the Pathan ethnicity has found itself over the past 150 years.

For according to most standard models of modern nationalism the Pathans, like the Somalis, are a paradox or anomaly. They are an ethno-linguistic group with a very strong consciousness of common ethnic culture and identity, and with an ancient ethnic code of behaviour (the *pashtunwali*) to which most Pathans still subscribe, at least rhetorically. As in Somalia, all the elements would seem to be in place to create a modern ethno-linguistic nation-state; and yet the Pathans like the Somalis have never generated a modern state-building nationalism; and have indeed played a leading part in tearing to pieces whatever states have been created on their territory.

There are thought to be somewhere between 35 and 40 million Pathans in the world today, of whom considerably more than half live in Pakistan. This gives the Pakistani state a vital interest in what happens to the Pathans of Afghanistan. As Pakistani officials and officers have argued to me, it also means that the Pakistani state simply cannot afford to take a line on Afghanistan (for example, actively helping the US presence there) with which a majority of Pathans strongly disagree.

The vagueness of the figures on Pathan numbers illustrates the fact that no reliable Afghan national census has *ever* taken place, precisely because the issue of ethnic percentages is so explosive. Thus most educated Afghan (and Pakistani) Pathans with whom I have spoken have put the Pathan proportion of the Afghan population at 60–70 per cent. Non-Pathan Afghans have put it at 30–40 per cent. A Pakistani Pathan army officer described this to me as 'statistical genocide' on the part of the other Afghan nationalities – who say the same thing about Pathan figures.

Pathans have always regarded Afghanistan as an essentially Pathan state, and they have some reason. The dynasty which created the Afghan state was indisputably Pathan, and 'Afghan' is simply the Persian word for 'Pathan'. As Tajuddin Khan, General Secretary of the ANP, put it, 'Every Pakhtun is an Afghan, though not every Afghan is a Pakhtun.' Throughout modern Afghan history, until the overthrow of the Communists in 1992, the central state and army were almost always dominated by Pathans – and the shock of the four years from 1992–6 when non-Pathans dominated Kabul was indeed one factor in generating mass support for the Taleban among Pathans.

And yet the Pathan claim to Afghanistan was always shot through with ambiguities, which have helped cripple Pathan nationalism as a state-building force. The Pathan ruling dynasty in fact spoke a dialect of Persian (Dari), as did the army and bureaucracy. Dari, not Pashto (or Pakhto), was the lingua franca of Afghanistan both formally and informally. As far as the great majority of rural Pathans (i.e. the great majority of Pathans in general) were concerned, loyalty to family, clan and tribe always took precedence over loyalty to the Afghan state.

The tribes could be rallied for a time behind jihads against alien invaders of Afghanistan (or earlier, behind campaigns to conquer and plunder parts of India or Iran); but equally, Pathan tribes repeatedly rose in revolt against Pathan rulers of Afghanistan in the name of Islam and tribal freedom, and those rulers in response carried out some of their most savage repressions in Pathan areas.

Above all, from the early nineteenth century on, the Afghan monarchy never came anywhere near making good its claim to rule over all or even most Pathans. This was due first and foremost to the way in which first the Sikh rulers of Punjab in the first half of the nineteenth century, and then their British successors, had conquered extensive Pathan territories (and especially the most fertile and heavily populated of them all, the Peshawar valley).

It is also because Afghanistan has always been much poorer either than British India or than Pakistan, and since the late 1970s has also been racked with incessant warfare. Or, as an ANP activist admitted to me after a few drinks, 'Our old programme of union with Afghanistan is dead and everyone knows it, because no one in their senses wants to become part of Afghanistan, today or for all the future that we can see. Pakistan is bad, but Afghanistan is a nightmare, and has been for a generation.'

Until the nineteenth century, the Pathans had also never been united under one effective state, but had rather owed a vague and qualified allegiance to a variety of different dynasties, ruling from India, Kabul and sometimes Iran. Equally, however, they had never been divided between different effective states with real frontiers, let alone ruled by non-Muslim infidels. That began to change with the rise of Sikh power in Punjab in succession to the collapsing Mughal empire, and the fall of Peshawar to the Sikhs in 1823.

In the late 1830s the British appeared on the scene. In an effort to create an Afghan client state to resist Russian expansion in Central Asia, the government of British India sent a military expedition to overthrow the then Afghan ruler and replace him with a British puppet. This led to the memorable Afghan victory of 1842, when a British army attempting to retreat from Kabul to Jalalabad in midwinter was completely destroyed. The memory of Sir Alexander Burnes, a British official whose arrogance was held by both Afghans and British to have contributed to the disaster (and who paid for it with his life), is still commemorated in a Pathan phrase used to someone who is getting above himself: 'Who do you think you are, Lati [Lord] Barness?'

After a second costly war in Afghanistan in 1878–80, the British gave up any ambition to establish a permanent military presence in Afghanistan. Instead, they chose to build up a former Afghan enemy from the Durrani clan, Abdurrahman Khan, as Emir of Afghanistan and bulwark against Russia. A mixture of Abdurrahman's ruthless ability and British guns and money then consolidated a rudimentary modern Afghan state within the borders Afghanistan occupies today – borders imposed by and agreed between the British and Russian empires.

Meanwhile, the British defeated the Sikhs and incorporated their territories into the Indian empire, and then gradually pushed forward their military power into the Pathan territories lying between Afghanistan and British India. After a variety of experiments (some of them bloody failures), the British opted for a dual approach. The Peshawar valley and certain other 'settled' areas were incorporated into districts of British India. In 1901 the Pathan districts of Punjab were grouped in a chief commissioner's division; and in 1932 this was separated from the province of Punjab and turned into the new North West Frontier Province (NWFP). This province was placed under regular British Indian administration and law. Until 2010, when it was renamed Khyber-Pakhtunkhwa, the province retained its British geographical name, much to the irritation of Pathan nationalists.

Today, the NWFP covers 29,000 square miles and has a population of some 21 million, some 13 per cent of Pakistan's total population. Apart from the 3 million or so Hazara (who speak Hindko, a language more closely related to Punjabi, Hindi and Urdu), the great majority are Pathan and Sunni. Peshawar city has ancient minorities of Shia and Hindko speakers, though these have been greatly reduced in terms of proportion over the past generation by the influx of Sunni refugees from Afghanistan. Ethnic divisions are in any case somewhat blurred compared to religious and tribal ones. Many Hindko-speakers in Abbotabad are descendants of Pathans who adopted the language after they migrated to the area, while in other parts tribes originally believed to be Hindko-speaking adopted Pashto.

Other Pathans live in the territories which after Pakistani independence became the province of Balochistan, the northern parts of which are overwhelmingly Pathan and which overall may be as much as 40 per cent Pathan in population. It is here that much of the leadership of the Afghan Taleban is thought to have based itself since 2001. Balochistan is Pakistan's poorest province, and the NWFP the second poorest, with much lower rates of literacy and health care than in Punjab. As recorded in Chapter 8 on Sindh, a Pathan community thought to number between 1 and 3 million lives in Karachi, making that city the third largest Pathan city in the world.

Smaller Pathan communities are scattered across Pakistan, with members often employed in some branch of the transport industry or as security guards. In addition, a number of important tribes of north-western Punjab are Pathans, though they now mostly speak Punjabi. The family of the famous cricketer-turned-politician Imran Khan comes from one of these tribes, the Niazis, settled around the Punjabi town of Mianwali. He is an MP from Mianwali, but his Pathan origins and condemnation of the US presence in Afghanistan gives him some popularity in the NWFP as well. As of 2010, however, this has not led to his party, the Tehriq-e-Insaf (Movement for Justice) being able to make any serious progress against the long-established parties of the province – because, as many ordinary people who admire him but will not vote for him have told me candidly, they do not think that he will ever have any favours to distribute.

After partition in 1947 some Pathans moved to Pakistan from territories in India, such as Rohilkand, which their ancestors had conquered centuries before. These, however, though very proud of their Pathan origins, speak Urdu at home and are mostly to be found in Punjab or Karachi. They include the famous Pakistani Foreign Minister under Zia and Benazir Bhutto, Sahabzada Yaqub Khan.

In addition, there were the three Pathan princely states of Chitral, Dir and Swat, whose princes owed allegiance to the British but otherwise ruled their territories independently, in accordance with a mixture of local custom and personal whim. These three states were incorporated into the NWFP in the late 1960s as 'provincially administered tribal areas'. The judicial system in these territories has never been definitively settled, and the Pakistani system has never been fully accepted as legitimate by the population. This has helped provide fertile soil in recent decades for Islamist groups demanding the full implementation of the Shariah.

In the case of Swat, the personality of the last ruler Miangul Jahan-zeb was so impressive that the memory of his rule continues to undermine Pakistani rule to this day, and to boost support for the Taleban. The past remoteness of these areas is also worth remarking. The beautiful Swat valley in the 1960s and 1970s was a famous hippy destination, and since then developed as a holiday spot for the Pakistani elites; and yet the first European had set foot in Swat fewer than eighty years before. In 1858 and again in the 1890s, Swat and the adjoining areas were the sites of major tribal jihads against the approach of the British Raj to their borders.

THE FEDERALLY ADMINISTERED TRIBAL AREAS (FATA)

Swat and Chitral apart, the focus of armed Islamist revolt in British days, as since 9/11, has always been in the tribal areas of the mountains along the border with Afghanistan. The tribes living between British India and Afghanistan were formally cut off from Afghanistan in the 1890s by the frontier drawn by Sir Mortimer Durand, and named after him. In the British conception, however, this was meant to be a good deal less than a regular international frontier with Afghanistan, and that is still how the tribes themselves see it. In the words of a British report on Waziristan of 1901, 'The Durand Line partitions the *sphere of influence* [my italics] of the two governments concerned, and is not intended to interfere in any way with the proprietary and grazing rights of the tribes on either side.'[4]

The tribes of the frontier were considered by the British to be too heavily armed, too independent-minded, and too inaccessible in their steep and entangled mountains to be placed under regular administration. Instead, the British introduced a system of indirect rule, which was inherited by Pakistan and remains officially in force today in the seven Federally Administered Tribal Areas (FATA) – though in practice it has largely collapsed in the face of the Taleban insurgency. Limited administrative and judicial authority is still exercised by the local Political Agent and his subordinates. The PA is appointed by the government, and rules largely through local councils (jirgas) of tribal notables (*maliks*).

This system was intended not to govern, but to manage the tribes, and contain both their internal feuds and any potential rebellion against the central government. The British usually responded to tribal rebellions and raids not with attempts at permanent conquest, but by a strategy cynically described by British officers as 'butcher and bolt', or 'burn and scuttle'; punitive expeditions would enter a given territory, burn down villages and the forts of *maliks* and religious figures held to be responsible for the attacks, kill any tribesmen who resisted, distribute subsidies to allies, and then return again to their bases. Some British officials denounced this in favour of an intensified 'forward policy' of extending direct British rule up to the Afghan border; but in general 'the issue on which almost all administrators and soldiers agreed was that a permanent military presence inside tribal territory was not a feasible option.'[5]

In 1947–8, the new state of Pakistan, believing that the Muslim tribes would not revolt against a Muslim state, withdrew regular troops from the tribal areas. Security there was left to the locally recruited Frontier Corps, a system that remained generally in place until the launch of the campaign against the Afghan Taleban in Waziristan in 2004. The new Pakistani state felt that the tribes had demonstrated their loyalty by the enthusiasm with which many, and especially the Mahsuds of Waziristan, had joined in the 'jihad' in Kashmir in the autumn of 1947.

The population of FATA is overwhelmingly Pathan with a few Hindko-speakers. Apart from the Turi tribe in the Kurram Agency, who are Shia, the whole population of FATA are Sunni Muslims. FATA covers 10,500 square miles, and has a population of some 3.5 million. Its development indices are far lower even than those of the NWFP, with only 30 per cent male literacy and 3 per cent female. These miserable figures have been widely blamed on FATA's peculiar system of government (or non-government) – which is doubtless true; but they can also be attributed to the inaccessible nature of the territory and the intense conservatism and xenophobia of its people.

An ANP dissident, Juma Khan Sufi, summed up the problem for FATA and Pathans more widely in words which are harsh but which are also a necessary antidote to the endless self-pity, self-praise and paranoid conspiracy theories that I heard during my time on the Frontier:

> Pukhtoons are happy with their archaic tribal culture. A large part of our society is content living in its tribal particularism, which people cherish as freedom ... The attitude of the ordinary Pukhtoon does not at all tally

with the modern world. Illiteracy and poverty are common. Most of us don't send our children to school. Female education is still disliked by a majority of Pukhtoons . . . The empowerment of women is anathema. They have no rights in their society. During elections, village elders belonging to opposing parties try to reach a consensus on not allowing womenfolk to exercise their right to vote . . .

We take pride in these things, which in reality should be a cause of shame. Hence the claim of most Pukhtoons: whatever good is found, is there because of us and whatever bad is found in society is the creation of aliens.[6]

Or as Noman Wazir, CEO of Frontier Foundries, put it with deep bitterness: 'There is all this talk of helping bring Pashtuns into the twenty-first century, but this is nonsense. It's too much of a leap. What we need to do is bring them from the Bronze Age to the Iron Age.' Admittedly, he is a steel manufacturer.

The Political Agent rules in FATA – or used to – through the *maliks*, a term usually translated as tribal chiefs but better understood as tribal notables. These are not chiefs in a traditional sense, but are chosen by the government, and are very numerous: some 35,000 in all throughout FATA. They include many local religious figures. The theory behind the system is that government would pick men of real moral and political authority in their tribe, but there are many stories of Political Agents appointing men who had bribed them, or even appointing their own servants. Political parties are banned from standing for election in FATA, and full adult suffrage in national elections was introduced only in the 1990s.

Legally, the Political Agent governs on the basis of the Frontier Crimes Regulations (FCR), which are themselves drawn chiefly from the *pashtunwali*. These differ greatly from the British-derived state code of Pakistan, especially in providing for collective punishment of clans and tribes for crimes committed by one of their members. This provision sounds and indeed is harsh, but is also a traditional and logical response to a situation in which ties of tribal solidarity mean that criminals can always be assured of refuge among fellow tribesmen.

The demolition of the houses of enemies as a reprisal is an old Pathan custom; it degrades the prestige of an enemy but because it does not involve killing it does not automatically lead to blood feuds. In the past, it was widely employed both by the British and by many of the leaders of Islamist revolts against the British. The FCR are often pointed to as a key obstacle to progress and development in the tribal areas, and doubtless this is true; but deciding what to replace them with is another matter. On one thing the great majority of inhabitants of FATA with whom I have spoken are united: they do not want to come under Pakistani state law in its existing form.

PATHAN POLITICAL CULTURE

The political culture of the Pathan areas of Pakistan is related to that of other parts of the country, but with particular local features which are in part bound up with the *pashtunwali*. The first, especially marked in FATA, is a much stronger tradition of revolt and war, not just against outside invasion, but against government in general. This is related to the greater role both of religion and of tribes and makes Pathans – even to some degree in the 'settled areas' – very different from the much more docile populations of Punjab and Sindh.

It was a Sindhi superintendent of police who told me that the police in the NWFP committed the fewest abuses against the population, and especially against women, of any of the Pakistani forces,

> because up there, if you rape a woman she has relatives who will avenge her with a bullet through your head – not just brothers, but even distant cousins. Whereas in Sindh and even more Punjab, people are far more beaten down, and much more accepting of whatever the police do, and kinship bonds are weaker.

The key cultural importance of clan solidarity and collective revenge (*badal*) in the *pashtunwali* is obviously of key importance here.

The second, closely related feature is the greater egalitarianism and individualism of the Pathans – once again, chiefly in the tribal areas, but to some extent throughout the province. As a friend in the FATA Secretariat told me:

> In Balochistan, people owe unconditional obedience to one hereditary Sardar. That has never been true among the Pashtuns. Here, there have always been lots of lesser chiefs within one tribe. Even in the settled areas

and Swat, where the power of the khans was traditionally much greater, people could and did often switch allegiance from one khan to another. As for the tribal areas and especially Waziristan, there have been no long-standing political dynasties, and even the greatest *malik* was always only a first among equals.

The lesser importance of hereditary loyalty compared to Punjab and Sindh increases the importance of personal prestige (in Pashto, *nom*, or literally 'name', as in 'reputation', or as we would say in English, 'having a name' for something), which may initially be inherited, but which then has to be constantly renewed by the individual leader. This is where the Taleban's targeting of *maliks* in FATA and political leaders in the NWFP has been so frighteningly effective. As my FATA acquaintance put it:

> So many *maliks* have been killed by the Taleban that they are scared, and with good reason. In public, they denounce military actions against the Taleban, while in private they beg us to continue them. The problem is that everyone knows they are scared, and if you are scared, you cannot be a *malik* in anything but name. You know how this society values physical courage more than anything else.

The same is true of the politicians in the NWFP, who have to keep running in national or local elections, and therefore to keep appearing at public rallies. If they have opposed the Taleban, then such appearances are standing invitations to suicide bombers – who have indeed claimed several political victims. The problem is that even if the politicians can afford bullet-proof glass screens like the leading politicians in Pakistan and India, that makes them look scared. I was told that the *nom* of Asfandyar Wali Khan, leader of the ANP, suffered a terrible blow when, after an assassination attempt against him in Charsadda in October 2008 which killed one of his guards, he left town immediately in a helicopter and did not attend the guard's funeral.

Finally, and related to the individualism of the Pathans, is the even greater fissiparousness of Pathan politics, even within the same family. So universal is rivalry between cousins that it even has a formal name: *taburwali*. In Swat, Fredrik Barth studied how the rigid institutionalization of faction permeated local politics. In the past, and to some degree up to the present, this rivalry often spilled over into violence, which the *pashtunwali* acted to mediate and restrain, but never could and never was intended to prevent. The *pashtunwali*, in other words, is not a code of law, but rather a set of guidelines for regulating what is known in anthropology as 'ordered anarchy'.

Feuds between families (or, rather, often rival bits of the same family) are not often as violent as in the past, but the possibility is always there. Above all, however, this tradition means that parties in the NWFP are even more likely to split and split again than is the case elsewhere in Pakistan. Several local leaders of the ANP and PPP whom I visited spent much of the interviews abusing not their party's opponents, but their own party colleagues.

In Afghanistan in the 1990s, the Taleban succeeded in crushing local feuds with their own harsh and rigid version of the Shariah – though only after these feuds had assumed a really monstrous character in the wake of the collapse of the Communist state and the triumph of the Mujahidin. If the Taleban in Pakistan can succeed in binding their tribal followers together through the discipline of their version of the Shariah, they will have gained a frightening advantage over their mainstream political opponents in the Pathan territories.

The social and cultural difference between most of the tribal areas on the one hand, and the Peshawar valley and Swat on the other, can be summed up in the nature of their *hujras*. This absolutely central Pakistani social, cultural and political institution is hard to translate, having elements of the feudal audience chamber, the men's club, the village hall, the debating society, the barracks for political workers, and the guesthouse.

In a sexually segregated society where it is out of the question for any men but the closest relatives to attend mixed gatherings within houses, the *hujras* are where the men of a given area meet to discuss everything under the sun. Occasionally they are collectively maintained, but usually they are owned by some local big man, and attendance at his *hujra* is to a greater or lesser extent a sign of allegiance or at least deference to him.

In the tribal areas of Pakistan and Afghanistan that I have visited, *hujras* are generally part of the house itself, though firmly separate from it. As far as I can see from the very few family quarters I have been allowed to visit, the *hujras* generally do not differ in style from the family quarters: guests and host all sit on carpets on the ground, leaning on cushions arranged in a rectangle round the walls. Of course the quality of the carpets, the stove and the roof will differ according to the wealth and power of the host, and everyone there will know that wealth and power very precisely; but cultural norms dictate an appearance both of equality and of common culture.

It is quite otherwise with the *hujras* of the big political landlords and bosses in the Peshawar valley and Swat. These tend to be clearly distanced from the main house, and clearly poorer, and they have broken chairs and sofas, not carpets and cushions. This marks the social, economic and to some extent cultural differentiation of the Pathan elites in the 'settled areas' and Swat, which the Taleban have used to increase their support among the poor. Anecdotal evidence suggests that big landlord politicians spend less and less time in their *hujras*, preferring to stay in the luxury of their family quarters.

This somewhat resembles the process in England between the sixteenth and eighteenth centuries by which first the nobility, then the lesser gentry and finally the bigger farmers ceased to eat in halls or kitchens, together with their servants and followers, and ate instead in their own dining-rooms. However, in those days the English gentry did not need to appeal to their followers for votes, and were not faced with a popular revolt against their rule.

THE AWAMI NATIONAL PARTY (ANP)

Hereditary members of the landowning elites dominate the Awami National Party (ANP), the moderate Pathan nationalist party of the region; and class hostility to their dominance has fuelled support for the Taleban in Swat and elsewhere and may in the long run help to destroy the ANP. The party has alternated in government and opposition since independence, and in 2008 for the first time formed the NWFP government on its own (though with PPP support) after winning the provincial elections of that year. The ANP's political ancestors came together on the basis of resistance to British rule. It has been led from its beginnings by yet another South Asian political dynasty, the Wali Khans, a landowning family from the Peshawar valley.

Neither the ANP nor the Islamist JUI can be said to dominate NWFP politics, because no party has been able to do this. The main national parties – the PPP and Muslim League – also have a strong presence in the province, and with help and patronage from Islamabad have often been able to lead coalition governments. To judge by my interviews with ordinary people in the NWFP in 2008–9, it is possible that the Muslim League, with its greater Islamic identity and dislike of the US, may improve its vote in the Pathan areas, despite its close identification with the province of Punjab. In part this is because it retains a distance from the Pakistani army, on which the ANP now depends for protection.

All the parties have, however, been plagued by one of the perennial curses of Pakistani politics – an endless tendency to split when particular leaders do not receive enough patronage to reward their kinsmen and supporters, or when they clash with other leaders over issues of status and prestige. Thus the politician who was the mainstay of the Musharraf administration in the province, national Interior Minister Aftab Khan Sherpao, was leader of what had been a famous local PPP political landowning dynasty in the province, and had been chief minister of a PPP-led government in the early 1990s. Sherpao split from the PPP and founded his own PPP (Sherpao) either because he was not rewarded sufficiently by the party during its periods of government in the 1990s, or because he had lost faith in Benazir Bhutto's leadership, or both. The ANP has also repeatedly split along lines of family allegiance and advantage.

Compared to the PPP and Muslim League, however, the ANP's Pathan nationalism, ostensibly left-wing, populist ideology and deep roots in local society should make the ANP a principal obstacle to the spread of the Taleban among Pakistani Pathans. Indeed, its victory over the Islamist parties in the February 2008 elections was portrayed by most Western observers in precisely this light.

Perhaps, after Western forces leave Afghanistan, the ANP will indeed be able to play this role. So far they have been crippled in this regard by a range of factors. Firstly, the ANP has always been dominated by landowning khans from the Peshawar valley. Of course, this allows them to rely on support from the traditional followers of those khans, but it also puts them at a disadvantage when faced with the egalitarian and even socially revolutionary message of the Taleban. Moreover, while the Taleban can at least appeal to Pathan nationalist feeling in the struggle against the hated American presence in Afghanistan, the ANP's Pathan nationalism has become an increasingly threadbare rhetorical fiction.

Above all, the ANP were long hindered in confronting the Taleban by the views of the vast majority of their own supporters and activists, who, to judge by my interviews with many of them, regard the US presence in Afghanistan as illegitimate and who see ANP support for a military crackdown on the Taleban as essentially launching a Pathan civil war on the orders of the United States. As Fakhruddin Khan, the son of the ANP General Secretary, said to me, 'one main reason for sympathy for the Taleban is that every Pashtun has been taught from the cradle that to resist foreign domination is part of what it is to do *Pashto*' – in other words, to follow the Pathan Way.

Part of the ANP's problem in fighting the Taleban is that to be seen to help even indirectly the US military presence in Afghanistan goes against its own deepest instincts, both Pathan nationalist and anti-colonialist. The party's founder, Abdul Ghaffar Khan (1890–1988), whose grandson leads the party today, was ostensibly a Gandhian pacifist, but his poetry is more reminiscent of the warlike Khattak:

> If I die, and lie not bathed in martyr's blood,
> None should this [Pashtun] tongue pollute,
> Offering prayers for me.
> Oh mother, why should you mourn for me,
> If I am not torn to pieces by British guns?[7]

The history of the origins of the ANP under British rule illustrates both the power of Pathan nationalism and its weakness in the face of appeals which mix nationalism with religion. Thus, remarkably, Abdul Ghaffar Khan was able to found a Pathan mass nationalist movement, the Khudai Khidmatgars, or Servants of God (popularly known as the Red Shirts, from their uniforms), dedicated to alliance with the overwhelmingly Hindu Indian National Congress and, in principle at least, committed to Gandhian principles of non-violence.

No more unlikely product of Pathan culture can easily be imagined. The explanation is, however, obvious. So deeply did most Pathans loathe British rule that they were prepared to ally with the main Indian force struggling against that rule, the Congress. They opposed Mohammed Ali Jinnah's Muslim League, which, though made up of fellow Muslims, was regarded quite rightly as much more interested in doing deals with the British in order to safeguard Muslim interests than in seeking to expel the hated alien rulers. This sentiment allowed the Red Shirts and their political allies to dominate NWFP politics in the last fifteen years of British rule, and Ghaffar Khan's brother, Dr Khan Sahib, became chief minister of the province.

When in 1946–7 it became apparent that the British really were preparing to quit, the position of the Khan brothers and their followers quickly collapsed in the face of the religious-based propaganda of the Muslim League in favour of an independent Muslim state of Pakistan. The idea of living in a Hindu-dominated India proved absolutely unacceptable to most Pathans, and the Congress leader, Jawaharlal Nehru, was almost lynched by a Pathan mob on a visit to the province. Undermined by both the Muslim League and the departing British, a last-ditch attempt at an independent 'Pakhtunkhwa' linked to Afghanistan also failed.

Thereafter, the relations of Abdul Ghaffar Khan and his movement with the Pakistani state were naturally deeply troubled, since that state and army had good reason to doubt their loyalty. He and his leading followers spent many years in Pakistani jails, with their party banned, under both military and civilian governments, including that of the PPP in the 1970s. In part because of the rigging of elections against them, they never succeeded before 2008 in forming the provincial government of the NWFP, though they several times took a share in government.

The links of the ANP and its predecessor parties to Afghanistan, though dictated by their Pathan nationalism, have also over the years proved a disastrous liability. Afghanistan proved enough of a threat to Pakistan to terrify the Pakistani security establishment and deepen their opposition to enhanced Pathan autonomy within Pakistan; but not remotely enough of an attractive force to win over large numbers of Pakistani Pathans to union with Afghanistan; and from the late 1970s the ANP also became in part hostage to the dreadfully radical and violent swings of the Afghan domestic spectrum.

First, in the 1950s, Ghaffar Khan and his followers became associated with the campaign of the Afghan Prime Minister (and later President) Sardar Daud Khan to mobilize Pathan nationalism so as to bring about the union of the NWFP and FATA with Afghanistan – a campaign which included providing funds and armed support for tribal rebels against Pakistan. Then, after 1979, Abdul Ghaffar Khan became closely tied to the Soviet occupation of Afghanistan and its Afghan Communist allies. He lived in Afghanistan under Soviet occupation and is buried in the Afghan city of Jalalabad. Because of the ANP's anti-British legacy, and because the Pakistani state and military had generally been allied with the United States, ANP ideology took on an anti-American cast.

Today, this mutual hostility between the ANP and Washington has of necessity greatly diminished, and the US of course greatly welcomes ANP ties to the Afghan administration of Hamid Karzai. The problem is that – to judge by my own interviews with Pakistani Pathans – Karzai is despised by most of the ANP's own activists and voters as a US colonial stooge, and the association with him does nothing for ANP prestige among Pakistani Pathans, and weakens the party vis-à-vis the Taleban.

The ANP shares certain features with its main political rival within the province, the Islamist Jamiat-e-Ulema-e-Islam (JUI). Both are ostensibly radical anti-establishment parties which nonetheless have involvements in electoral politics stretching back decades, and have often formed part of coalition governments. Both are deeply integrated into Pakistan's system of political patronage and corruption. Yet both only formed their own governments in the NWFP very recently: the JUI as part of the Muttahida Majlis-e-Amal (United Action Council) Islamist coalition which won the elections of 2002 in the Frontier; the ANP as a result of the crushing defeat of the MMA in the elections of 2008.

In both cases, the victories were hailed as crucial political turning points, for good or evil. In neither case does this appear to have been true. To judge by my own interviews with ordinary voters in the NWFP, the truth was closer to what Sikander Khan Sherpao (a member of the Provincial Assembly and son of the aforementioned Aftab Sherpao), told me in August 2008:

> The people who say that the religious parties have been smashed for good and the moderate parties have triumphed are wrong. If you look at the issues on which the MMA got their votes in 2002 and the ANP this year, the most important ones are the same. This year, people voted for the ANP because they were against Musharraf, and too much of the MMA was seen as pro-Musharraf. And they voted for the ANP because, like the MMA before, they are hostile to the American presence in Afghanistan and promised peace with the militants and a bigger role for the Shariah.[8]

Apart from the issue of Afghanistan and the Taleban, the changes in government in 2002 and 2008 were also part of the rather melancholy cycle of Pakistani political life, in which incumbent governments are voted out because of their failure to fulfil their promises, to be replaced by their opponents – who then also fail. Both the ANP and JUI are deeply divided internally, partly along purely factional and family lines, but also over ideology and strategy. This constant, time- and energy-consuming infighting helps swallow up any potential for reform and good governance that may originally have existed.

Businessmen with whom I talked in the NWFP said that there had been absolutely no difference between the last three governments (PML(Q), MMA and ANP) in terms of corruption. The level of bribe-taking had remained the same – in other words extremely high. Indeed, a Western businessman in the security construction field said that even in the Middle East he had never seen anything quite like the level of corruption that he had experienced in Peshawar, under both the MMA and ANP: '*Everyone* wants a bribe. And the worst of it is, the government is so chaotic and faction-ridden that even when you pay half a dozen people you can't be sure of getting a result, or that some new guy won't pop up asking for his share.'

The voters have little real expectation of radical improvement, but hope that things will get a bit better, and above all that their neighbourhoods or families may draw some specific benefit. As far as the JUI is concerned, taking over the government proved as much of a curse as a blessing. As a result, many ordinary Pathans have come to see the party and its allies as just as corrupt and incompetent as the Pakistani national parties, and no sort of radical alternative to them.

A common answer on the streets of every NWFP town I visited, when I asked people how they had voted in the last elections, was either that they had not voted at all, because 'the parties are all the same – none of them keep their promises,' as Sayyid Munawar Shah, a shopkeeper in Peshawar, told me; or, if they had voted for a given party, it was because 'my father and grandfather voted for them', or 'we are followers of such and such Khan, and so we vote for him'. Any kind of convinced support for any of the parties was extremely hard to find.

This was true even outside the front door of the ANP's headquarters on Pashaggi Road in Peshawar, where the shopkeepers told me that they had not voted in the last elections. 'Why should we? They are thieves, all of them. They promise and promise, and then do nothing,' as one told me. The doing nothing was rather obvious. The street was deeply pot-holed, without street lamps, and littered with stinking rubbish. The idea that enlightened self-interest and party propaganda alone might have dictated an attempt to improve the neighbourhood did not seem to have occurred to any of the party activists lounging listlessly inside their cavernous headquarters – and the same was true of the other party headquarters I visited. With the exception of the Jamaat Islami and the MQM, this is not how Pakistani parties think.

Looking at the condition of Peshawar, I asked several ANP leaders if they had ever thought of trying to initiate some kind of urban renewal scheme like the Orangi Pilot Project in Karachi. No one even seemed to understand what I was talking about. However, in this they are only reflecting their own society – for, after all, the shopkeepers on Pashaggi Road might have organized themselves to clean up the rubbish from their front doors, and it hadn't occurred to them either.

As of 2009, the same fate that befell the MMA seems to threaten the ANP. The party stood for election in February 2008 on a platform of negotiating peace deals with the Islamist militants, gaining increased autonomy for the NWFP, changing the name of the province to Pakhtunkhwa (in line with the other four provinces, which all have a name related to that of the chief local ethnicity) and restoring the judges sacked by Musharraf. All of these demands, including talks with the Taleban, were extremely popular with the ANP supporters and activists with whom I have spoken.

However, the ANP set out no detailed or coherent economic policy or plan for social reform – though to be fair that is difficult for any provincial government when the powers of the provinces are so limited. As of 2010, its hopes of extracting more powers from the centre had – as so often in the past – been frustrated by stonewalling in Islamabad. As a result, the party's programme has in practice been limited to attempts at peace with the Taleban and to the demand that the NWFP be officially renamed Pakhtunkhwa. The PPP-led government in Islamabad agreed to this (in the form of 'Khyber-Pakhtunkhwa') in April 2010 – a decision which immediately sparked riotous protests by the Hindko-speaking Hazara minority in the NWFP which left seven people dead in the town of Abbotabad. The protesters were demanding a new Hindko-speaking province of their own – another example of the way in which separatism in Pakistan is held in check by local ethnic opposition.

In one respect, however, the position of the ANP altered radically in the course of 2008–9: for the first time in its history, the party was forced by the Taleban revolt not just to make a covert deal with the Pakistani army, but to ally with them publicly and explicitly; and, since the ANP leadership is now completely dependent on the army for protection against assassination by the Taleban, this relationship is likely to remain. It represents a complete reversal of the party's previous Pathan nationalist and anti-military positions, and a key political question among Pakistani Pathans for the next generation will be whether ANP activists and voters stick with the party regardless, or whether they move away to found other parties – or even are drawn by Pathan nationalism to join the Taleban, as the last Pathan nationalist force left standing.

JAMIAT-E-ULEMA-E-ISLAM (JUI, COUNCIL OF ISLAMIC CLERICS)

The contrast between public rhetoric and actual addiction to deal-making is if anything even more true of the other mainstream Pakistani party based in the Pathan areas, the Islamist JUI. In its origins this party was not Pathan, but rather a continuation of the tradition of Islamist groups from elsewhere finding fertile soil for growth on the Frontier. The party grew out of the pro-Pakistan wing of the Jamiat-e-Ulema-e-Hind, the leading Islamist group in India under British rule. The JUH stemmed from the revivalist religious tradition established by the Deoband madrasah in what is now the Indian state of Uttar Pradesh, and known as 'Deobandi'.

For several decades the different branches of the JUI have become more and more overwhelmingly Pathan – unlike the other leading Islamist political party in Pakistan, the Jamaat Islami, which has a much more all-Pakistani character. The JUI also differs from the Jamaat in being far less intellectual and in having a far looser organization and leadership structure. In fact, rather than a modern Islamist party it resembles the ANP in being an alliance of local notables, though in the case of the JUI the notables are religious figures rather than local khans, and there is no hereditary dynasty to hold it together. Instead, there has been a succession of charismatic leaders, which has led to the party splitting into two wings, the JUI(F) led by Maulana Fazl-ur-Rehman, and another branch led by Maulana Sami-ul-Haq.

As Joshua White writes:

> Key decisions by the JUI-F are routinely made by Fazlur Rehman and a traveling coterie of personal advisors, and the party has only recently invested in a well-equipped headquarters. The combination of charismatic leadership and decentralized party structure has led to nearly constant dissension within the JUI-F, most of which is dealt with informally in Pashtun-style shuras and quiet deals.[9]

The JUI's Islamism, like the ANP's nationalism, has – or had – a socialistic tinge, and the party remains strongly committed in principle to spreading development among the poor. In 1972, the JUI formed a brief government of the NWFP in coalition with the ANP (or NAP as it was then known), with a programme of economic populism and of strengthening the rules of the Shariah. Alcohol and gambling were banned in the province, and the JUI attempted unsuccessfully to pass laws forcing women to wear veils in public. At the same time, the JUI often co-operated with the ostentatiously secular Zulfikar Ali Bhutto, leading to a subsequent history of intermittent alliances with the PPP, and charges of hypocrisy, opportunism and treachery from other Islamist parties, and now from the Taleban.

The full 'Pashtunization' of the JUI was above all the product of the 1980s and the jihad against the Soviet forces in Afghanistan and their Afghan Communist allies. Support for the Islamist groups among the Afghan Mujahidin, both from the Pakistani state and from Saudi Arabia and private donors in the Gulf, led to a huge influx of money to madrasahs in the Frontier where many of the Afghan Mujahidin were educated and shaped ideologically, and to an enormous growth in the number of those madrasahs. Both the JUI and the Jamaat became heavily involved in various forms of support for the Afghan jihad, and profited greatly as a result.

In one way the ANP and JUI resemble each other. They both began as 'revolutionary' parties in a Pakistani context: the ANP for the abolition of Pakistan itself, or at least its transformation into a very loose democratic federation; the JUI for a revolutionary transformation of the Pakistani state and society along Islamist lines. Both, however, have in practice long since become 'mainstream' political players, forming coalitions for political and above all patronage advantage. Both in consequence are at risk of being outflanked ideologically and politically by the Taleban.

Thus, despite its deep ideological opposition – in theory – to the US presence in Afghanistan and to Pakistani help to the US, the JUI functioned as a de facto supporter of Musharraf's administration, and at the time of writing is a partner in government of President Zardari's PPP – a government whose programme it says it detests for a whole set of reasons, including most of all its alliance with the US!

In July 2009 I asked the JUI spokesman Jalil Jan why in view of his party's bitter opposition to Zardari's policies they did not leave the government. He replied:

> Our ministers stand in parliament and criticize the government of which they are part. Don't you think that is brave of us? . . . It is not *kufr* [disbelief, or disobedience to God] that people voted for us in order to get jobs for them. So it isn't bad that we are in power at the centre and in Balochistan, and are able to give jobs to our people.[10]

Of course, like everyone else I always knew this about the JUI – but it is nice to have it confirmed from the horse's mouth. 'Money doesn't smell,' a Peshawari journalist quoted cynically when I asked about this. The JUI's problem is that American money does increasingly smell in Pathan nostrils – in fact it stinks to high heaven. The victory of the Muttahida Majlis-e-Amal (MMA) Islamist coalition in the 2002 elections in the NWFP and the Pathan areas of Balochistan was due in part to favouritism by the Musharraf administration in order to defeat the PPP and PML(N); and in part to the fact that the PPP and ANP simply could not agree to co-operate either against Musharraf or against the Islamists.

To judge by my own observations and public opinion polls, however, by far the most important factor in their victory was mass Pathan anger at the US invasion of Afghanistan and overthrow of the Taleban there. In the succeeding years, the MMA's de facto support for Musharraf – even as he forged a closer and closer alliance with the US and abandoned the jihad in Kashmir – did not go unnoticed among Pathan voters. Repeatedly on the streets of Peshawar people told me that they had voted MMA in 2002 but not 2008, because 'the JUI support Musharraf and Musharraf helps the Americans'.

In addition, leading the government from 2002 to 2008 meant that the JUI, like the ANP after 2008, was exposed to the standard accusations against all Pakistani governments: of not having fulfilled their campaign promises of better government and more development; of engaging in corruption; and of not giving my brother/cousin/uncle/ nephew a job, contract, or whatever.

The JUI – a bit like Communists in the past – also suffered from their own inflated promises. They had promised to introduce true Shariah rule in the Frontier, and thereby to transform society. Since by definition the Shariah – being the Word of God – cannot suffer from inherent flaws as far as conservative Pathans are concerned, the explanation of the MMA's failure in this regard could only be attributed by voters to the failings of the MMA and its leaders.

The MMA had its very origins in Pakistani Islamist outrage at the US invasion of Afghanistan, and took shape in 2001–2 as the 'Pakistan–Afghan Defence Council'. Its six parties included the two wings of the JUI, the JI, three smaller Sunni parties and one Shia party. The inclusion of the Shia and a party belonging to the Barelvi theological tradition (old rivals of the Deobandis) marked the 'broad church' nature of the alliance, and also drew a line between the JI and JUI on the one side and extreme anti-Shia Sunni radical groups like the Sipah-e-Sahaba on the other.

The record of the MMA in government between 2002 and 2008 reflected a number of features which say a good deal about the 'mainstream' Islamists in Pakistan, about the balance of power between the centre and the provinces, and about Pakistani politics in general. The first was confusion. The government took a long time to put a legislative programme together and, even when it did, no one was quite sure what was and was not a law. Secondly, the only really radical Islamist laws that the MMA government passed (for example, extending the writ of the Shariah in the state legal system) were in any case blocked by the Supreme Court and the government in Islamabad – something that has happened to every provincial government that has attempted serious change.

Lastly, there is the actual content of the MMA's legislation and governance, which in some respects was very different from the standard view of Islamist politics in the West, and showed an interesting mixture of what in the West would be called 'progressive' and 'reactionary' elements. The more progressive sides of the MMA government mark the alliance off very clearly from the Taleban, in both its Afghan and Pakistani manifestations. Thus, while on the one hand the MMA tried to bring in a range of measures enforcing public standards of dress for women, and its activists launched vigilante attacks on video stores and other sources of 'immorality', on the other hand its government did more than most previous administrations to increase education for girls. This was due not to the JUI, but to the presence in the MMA coalition of the Jamaat Islami and a Shia political party.

When I visited the MMA's Minister for Local Development, Asif Iqbal Daudzai, in May 2007, he was at pains to emphasize his government's progressive agenda. This included community participation in developing local infrastructure projects, Rs50 million for improvements in sanitation in Peshawar, and a great increase in primary education, including for girls. While this was doubtless mostly for Western consumption, it did not seem wholly so. He and other government officials laid special stress on their moves to end the negative features of the *pashtunwali* as far as women are concerned, and in particular what he described as the 'hateful' practice of giving girls in compensation as part of the resolution of disputes.

The problem was and is that, as with both previous and later governments, resources are so limited. This was rubbed home by the minister's own office, which I approached up a flight of broken stairs with hardly a lamp working, barking my shins in the process, to sit on a broken chair in a bleak office with cracked windows and peeling walls. This was in its way impressive, since it indicated that if there was corruption in this ministry the officials had not spent it on their own offices; but it also illustrated the deep poverty of the province and its government.

However, the reputation of the MMA alliance both in the West and with officials in Pakistan was deeply tarnished by its murky relations with the radicals who later went on to found the Pakistani Taleban, and by its ambiguous attitude to jihad within Pakistan. In 2007 the alliance split over this issue, with the JUI condemning the radicals who took over the Red Mosque complex in Islamabad, while the Jamaat Islami supported them (see next chapter). However, the JUI retained close private links to some of the Taleban, who supposedly helped Fazl-ur-Rehman in the February 2008 election campaign, even as other Taleban rejected the electoral process altogether. On the other hand, the JUI was tainted in the eyes of more-radical Muslims, and indeed of much of the population in general, by its continued association with Musharraf – thereby ending up with the worst of all worlds.

In August 2008, after they had been defeated in the elections, the information secretary of the JUI, Abdul Jalil Jan, came to drink tea with me in my guest-house in University Town, Peshawar. Echoing the words of many people in the NWFP (including voters for the ANP and PPP), he asked me:

> Why have Beitullah Mahsud and Fazlullah declared war on the Pakistani government and army? Wouldn't you do so if someone invaded your territory and killed your women and children? It doesn't matter if it is the US or Pakistan who have done the killing. They have been attacked . . . So we support talks aimed at peace. The previous peace negotiations were a success, but then they were violated, and by whom? By the government and army on the orders of America. If there is to be peace, then the government must stick to the terms of peace and not launch new attacks . . . As to Afghanistan, that is the Afghans' own business, but naturally people here have strong feelings about what is happening and what the US is doing there. After all, like many people here, I am an Afghan Pashtun myself by origin: my ancestors came here long ago from Kunar.[11]

Within the NWFP, both the JUI and JI thus opposed any strong action against the radicals who gained an increasing grip on Swat during the MMA period in government. Indeed, many of the Swat radicals had previously been Jamaat cadres and retained close links to the party. The MMA parties did not favour the more brutal and retrograde actions of these forces (including attacks on police, vigilante executions and floggings, and the burning down of girls' schools) but seem to have found it impossible publicly to take action against groups claiming to act in the name of the Shariah and the Afghan jihad. This inaction on the part of the MMA, and the failure of the JUI and MMA government to consolidate their support, helped open the way for the rise of the Taleban among the Pathans of the Frontier.

Meanwhile, JUI links to hated governments in Islamabad were also losing it local support. In 2008 I heard this about the party in the context of its support for Musharraf. Even a few days before Musharraf's resignation, both the Fazl-ur-Rehman and Sami-ul-Haq wings of the party were still very hesitant about supporting his impeachment, as Sami-ul-Haq himself told me in August 2008 – using as his excuse that 'if Musharraf should be impeached, then so should many of the other politicians. All have committed crimes.'

By 2009, ordinary people in Peshawar were cursing the party's membership of the government of the hated Zardari. It is highly questionable, therefore, whether the patronage extracted by the party really compensates any more for this growth in unpopularity. The JUI's alliance with Pakistani national parties and aspirations to share power in Islamabad, either for patronage or to change the Pakistani system, also mean that there are clear limits on how far it can exploit Pathan nationalism. As Abdul Jalil told me:

> We support greater autonomy for the NWFP and other provinces, but on one condition: that this demand must not be based on hatred and must not encourage conflicts with Punjabis, Baloch or other ethnic groups in Pakistan. If this plan is based on good relations and agreements with our ethnic neighbours, then we will support it. But ANP ideas create a real danger of ethnic conflict. That is especially true of all this talk of a Greater Pashtunistan taking in huge bits of Balochistan and Punjab. Of course other nationalities will oppose this.

For many years, the thoroughly pragmatic Islamism of the JUI and the equally pragmatic nationalism of the ANP have helped ensure that the great majority of Pathans have lived peacefully and not too unhappily within Pakistan. However, with both these parties now seriously discredited by their association with President Zardari and his alliance with the USA, the future of electoral politics in Khyber-Pakhtunkhwa is now an open question.

PART FOUR

The Taleban

11

The Pakistani Taleban

There arose one of those strange and formidable insurrections among the Pathans which from time to time sweep across the Frontier mountains like a forest fire, carrying all before them. As on previous occasions there followed a reaction, but the fire is not wholly put out. It continues to smoulder dully until a fresh wind blows.

(Olaf Caroe)[1]

As described in earlier chapters, the world of Sunni Islamist extremism in Pakistan embraces a range of different groups, with significantly different agendas. The sectarian extremists described have long been carrying out terrorist attacks against Pakistani Shia and Christians. These and others in 2008–10 also turned to increasingly savage terrorist attacks in alliance with the Pakistani Taleban against state targets, 'Sufi' shrines and the general public, in response to growing military offensives in Bajaur, Swat and Waziristan. The terrorist threat from Islamist extremists is therefore now present across Pakistan. It will almost certainly grow further, and may end by radically changing the Pakistani state.

As of 2010, however, Islamist *rebellion* is not widespread. So far, mass insurrection has been restricted to parts of the Pathan areas of Pakistan, and has been due more to specific local factors and traditions than to wider Islamist and Pakistani ones. Among the Pathans, the Taleban can draw upon traditions of Islamist resistance to the Soviets, and long before that to the British; and indeed on a hostility, which dates back to time immemorial, to the rule of any state. Just as the backbone of the Taleban and their allies in both Afghanistan and Pakistan is to be found among the Pathans, so any settlement of the conflict with the Taleban in both countries will have to be one which brings a majority of the Pathan population on board.

As explained in previous chapters, the deeper religious, ethnic and tribal roots of the Pakistani Taleban date back hundreds of years, and were revived by the Soviet invasion of Afghanistan and the struggle against it. The upsurge of militancy among the Pakistani Pathans after 2001 was due overwhelmingly to the US invasion of Afghanistan, and the influence of the Afghan Taleban.

Contrary to a widespread belief, Pakistan was not responsible for the creation of the Taleban in Afghanistan. As recounted by Mullah Abdul Salam Zaeef, a member of the core Taleban leadership, they had their origin in groups of madrasah students from Kandahar and surrounding provinces, who came together in the early 1980s to fight against the Soviet occupation and the Communist government. They were trained by the Pakistani military – but with arms supplied by the US. Men from these formations then gathered spontaneously in Kandahar province in 1994, in response to the dreadful anarchy which had gripped the region after the Mujahidin's overthrow of the Afghan Communist regime in 1992.[2]

As of 1994, the Afghan group which was being supported by Pakistan was the radical Islamist and ethnic Pathan Hezb-e-Islami of Gulbuddin Hekmatyar, which the Taleban later defeated in their drive north to Kabul. By then, however, Hekmatyar had been at war for two years with other Mujahidin parties mainly representing the non-Pathan nationalities but, despite terrible bloodshed, had failed either to capture Kabul or to bring order to the Pathan areas. When the Taleban consolidated their authority in Kandahar, and protected Pakistani trade in the area, a section of the Pakistani security establishment led by the Interior Minister in the Bhutto government, General Nazeerullah Babar, identified them as a force worth supporting.

There were a bizarre few months in 1994 and 1995 during which the Pakistani Intelligence Bureau (responsible to the Interior Minister) and the ISI (Inter-Services Intelligence, responsible to the military) were supporting the Taleban and Hekmatyar against each other; but by 1996 Pakistan was fully committed to the Taleban, and Pakistani arms supplies, military advisers, training and Islamist volunteers played an important part in their subsequent victorious campaigns.

The Pakistani security services also encouraged some of their old Pathan allies in the war against the Soviets to join the Taleban – notably the formidable Jalaluddin Haqqani and his clan along the Afghan border with Pakistani Waziristan, who continue as of 2010 to play a key part in fighting against Western forces and the Kabul government and to enjoy close ties to the Pakistani military. According to Western intelligence sources, the ISI encouraged and helped the Haqqani group to carry out a destructive attack on the Indian embassy in Kabul in July 2008. Nonetheless, as Mullah Zaeef's memoir also makes clear, the Taleban leadership never fully trusted Pakistani governments and the Pakistani military, and since 2001 there has been in some Taleban circles active hatred of the Pakistani military because of the way in which they sided with the US after 9/11.

The reasons for the Pakistani security establishment's support for the Taleban are not complicated, and as far as the high command are concerned stem from strategic calculations and not Islamist ideology (which is not to say of course that the strategy has been a wise one). Lower-level operatives, however, engaged since the 1980s in helping the Afghan Islamist groups on the ground undoubtedly developed their own strong local allegiances.

The strategic root of support for the Taleban is witnessed by the fact that the initiator of the strategy, General Babar, was a minister in Benazir Bhutto's PPP government, and that Pakistan's approach continued unchanged under governments with very different attitudes to Islamism. Certainly General Musharraf, a convinced Westernizing modernizer, can by no stretch of the imagination be accused of ideological sympathy for the Taleban.

Musharraf, however, did for most of his career share in the basic reason for Pakistan's Afghan strategy, which is fear of encirclement by India, and of India using Afghanistan as a base to support ethnic revolt within Pakistan. This fear is exaggerated, but is held with absolute conviction by almost all the Pakistani soldiers with whom I have spoken, and indeed by most of the population in northern Pakistan. In the words of Major-General Athar Abbas, head of military public relations in 2009 (and one of the most intelligent senior officers in the army):

> We are concerned by an Indian over-involvement in Afghanistan. We see it as an encirclement move. What happens tomorrow if the American

trainers are replaced by Indian trainers? The leadership in Afghanistan is completely dominated by an India-friendly Northern Alliance. The Northern Alliance's affiliation with India makes us very uncomfortable because we see in it a future two-front war scenario.[3]

In consequence, Pakistani governments and military leaderships have believed that Pakistan must have a friendly government ruling in Kabul or, failing that, at least friendly forces controlling the Pathan areas of Afghanistan adjacent to the Pakistani border. This was necessary also because of the perceived threat that Kabul, backed by India, would return to the Afghan strategy of the 1950s, of supporting Pathan separatist revolt within Pakistan.

This fear has been kept alive by the support of the Kabul government and India – albeit very limited – for Baloch rebels in Pakistan; and by the Karzai administration's refusal to recognize the 'Durand Line' between Afghanistan and Pakistan. Hence the absurd but passionately held belief among many Pakistanis that India is the principal force behind the Pakistani Taleban. In the 1990s there was also a belief among Pakistani strategists that Afghanistan could become a corridor for the expansion of Pakistani trade and influence in former Soviet Central Asia. Today, however, this hope is held only by Pakistani Islamists.

Despite the Taleban's striking military successes, it was obvious to more intelligent Pakistani officials as early as 1998 that its Afghan strategy was going badly wrong. This was above all because of the entry on to the scene of Osama bin Laden and Al Qaeda. Forced to leave their former refuge in Sudan, they had returned to Afghanistan, where they had fought against the Soviets and Communists and forged close links with local Pathan Islamists.

Al Qaeda ingratiated themselves with the Taleban partly though ideological affinity (and the prestige which Arab origins have long possessed in this part of the world); partly through money; and partly because they came to serve as shock troops for the Taleban in their campaigns in northern Afghanistan, where many of their Pathan troops were unwilling to fight.

On 7 August 1998 Al Qaeda carried out bomb attacks against the US embassies in Nairobi and Dar-es-Salaam, killing more than 200 people. In response, the Clinton administration ordered cruise missile attacks on Al Qaeda bases in Afghanistan, passing across Pakistani territory. In the following years, both the Nawaz Sharif and Musharraf governments asked the Taleban to expel Al Qaeda and seek better relations with the US. Pakistani officials whom I have interviewed have also claimed credit for the Taleban's drastic reduction of heroin production in Afghanistan in 2000–2001, aimed at persuading the West to recognize the Taleban's rule.

These Pakistani moves, however, were not backed by real pressure (for example by withdrawing Pakistani military assistance or restricting Afghanistan's vital trade through Pakistan). The bankruptcy of Pakistan's policy, and the greater influence of Al Qaeda, were drastically revealed when in March 2001 the Taleban destroyed the great Buddhist statues at Bamian, despite a strong personal appeal by Musharraf.

Nonetheless, the Musharraf administration could still see no alternative to Taleban rule in Afghanistan that would be favourable to Pakistan, and Pakistan was therefore still linked to the Taleban when, on 11 September 2001, as a Pakistani general said to me, 'the roof fell in on us'. Musharraf's statement that US Deputy Secretary of State Richard Armitage threatened to 'bomb Pakistan back to the Stone Age' if Pakistan failed to co-operate in the US attack on Afghanistan seems to have been greatly exaggerated; but if the language was more diplomatic than that reported by Musharraf, the threat from the US to Pakistan in the immediate wake of 9/11 was undeniable.[4] Given the mood in America and in the Bush administration at that time, hesitation by Pakistan would indeed have been very dangerous for the country.

With the agreement of the rest of the Pakistani High Command, Musharraf therefore agreed to help the US by establishing two US air bases in Pakistan to support the campaign against the Taleban in Afghanistan; supplying US forces in Afghanistan through Pakistan; arresting Al Qaeda members in Pakistan; and blocking Taleban forces from retreating from Afghanistan into Pakistan. The first two promises were substantially kept, but the third only to a very limited extent.

Musharraf was apparently able to extract from Washington one major concession in Afghanistan: the evacuation by Pakistani aircraft of an unknown number of Pakistani military advisers and volunteers with the Taleban, trapped in the northern city of Kunduz by the advance of the Northern Alliance and in danger of being massacred. This made good sense, as such a development would have been hideously embarrassing to both Washington and Islamabad. Many of those Taleban fighters who surrendered to the Northern Alliance forces near Mazar-e-Sharif were indeed massacred, or herded into containers in the desert and baked to death.[5] An unknown number of Taleban fighters were also evacuated by the Pakistanis from Kunduz.

Along the border with Afghanistan, the Pakistani army fought with and arrested some Arab and other foreign fighters trying to escape Afghanistan, but seem often to have turned a blind eye to Afghan and Pakistani fighters. It is not known how exactly Osama bin Laden, Aiman al Zawahiri and other Al Qaeda leaders were able to escape into Pakistan. If Pakistani troops were lax or complicit, so too were the Afghan troops which the West employed to capture Al Qaeda's stronghold of Tora Bora on the Pakistan border in December 2001. In the end, there were simply not enough troops on either side of the Durand Line to control one of the most rugged frontiers in the world.

Musharraf was able for a while to sell his policy of helping the US in Afghanistan to the Pakistani establishment and people by his convincing argument that America would otherwise join with India to destroy Pakistan. In other words, it was a continuation of the general Pakistani view that India is Pakistan's greatest challenge. However, the alliance with the US over Afghanistan was never a popular strategy in Pakistan, and between 2002 and 2004 it was loaded with new elements which increasingly crippled Musharraf's popularity and prestige.

Firstly, the US insisted that Pakistan extend its withdrawal of support for the Afghan Taleban to the Pakistan-backed groups fighting India – which have a much deeper place in the hearts of many Pakistanis and especially Punjabis. Secondly, the US invasion of Iraq raised the already high level of hostility to America in the Pakistani population until it was among the highest in the Muslim world. Finally, the withdrawal of the Afghan Taleban from Afghanistan into the Pathan tribal areas of Pakistan, and the mobilization of Pakistani Pathans in support of them, led the US to demand that Pakistan launch what became in effect a civil war on its own soil.

While Pakistan was beginning to create one enemy for itself in the Pathan areas on Washington's orders, it was also more and more being required to suppress the anti-Indian militants which it had backed since 1988. Washington's insistence that Pakistan extend its opposition to Islamist militancy to Pakistan-backed groups in Kashmir and India was inevitable, given the general terms in which the Bush administration framed the 'Global War on Terror'.

American pressure was greatly accelerated by the actions of the terrorists themselves. On 13 December 2001, terrorists linked to the Pakistan-based groups Lashkar-e-Taiba and Jaish-e-Mohammed launched a suicide attack on the Indian parliament. In response, India massed troops along the border with Pakistan. Under intense pressure from Washington, in January 2002 Musharraf banned these two groups, and in a major new departure declared that Pakistan was opposed not just to the Taleban and Al Qaeda but to Islamist militancy in general.

He promised India and the US that his administration would prevent further terrorism against India from Pakistani soil, but also demanded that India and the international community move to solve the Kashmir issue, which 'runs in our blood'.[6] The Musharraf administration did move effectively to stop militants crossing into the province from Pakistan, and the following year declared a ceasefire along the Line of Control. Musharraf wound up a number of militant training camps, and declared an official ban on Lashkar-e-Taiba, Jaish-e-Mohammed and other groups. In practice, however, these groups remained in existence under other names. Lashkar-e-Taiba's parent organization, Jamaat-ud-Dawa, retained and expanded its large network of schools and charitable organizations, and in 2005, with military encouragement, played a leading part in helping the victims of the terrible Kashmir earthquake. After 2002 the Pakistan government's moves against the militants did lead to a drastic reduction in violence within Indian Kashmir, and a limited warming in Indo-Pakistan relations.

Musharraf himself stated his administration's approach as follows:

Al Qaeda has to be defeated militarily, period. They are foreigners who have no right to be in Pakistan. With the militant Taleban, it is more complicated. They are local people who are not so easily recognized, and they have local roots. So we have to deal with them militarily when necessary, but we also need to wean the population away from them by political means and through social and economic development, and negotiate so as to draw away more moderate elements. This is not an easy job. We may be double-crossed. We may fail. But we have no choice but to pursue this course because we cannot use military means against the whole population ... After all, previously I was the only one saying about Afghanistan too that the West needed a political strategy there to wean away some parts of the Taleban from the terrorists. Now Western leaders also accept this.[7]

In the wake of 9/11, Musharraf's administration did therefore take strong action against Al Qaeda operatives in the heartland of Pakistan, arresting hundreds, including some of the group's leaders, together with Pakistani sympathizers. This was later to help destroy Musharraf's administration, when the Supreme Court demanded an account of what had happened to some of these 'disappeared' people (the general assumption in Pakistan being that many had been illegally handed over to the US and were being held at US bases in Afghanistan).

For almost three years the Musharraf government avoided taking strong action against Al Qaeda and the Taleban in Pakistan's tribal areas along the Afghan border. One reason was the strategic calculation of the Pakistani security establishment concerning future Pakistani influence in Afghanistan. The view of important parts of the army and the political establishment is that a Taleban-ruled Afghanistan, though problematic in many ways, would still be vastly preferable to one dominated by Afghanistan's non-Pathan nationalities, in alliance with India.

On the other hand, such an outcome is in the view of the Pakistani establishment clearly not worth risking the existence of Pakistan by provoking a US attack on Pakistan; so while the leadership of the Afghan Taleban has enjoyed a measure of *shelter* in Pakistan (especially in northern Balochistan and the city of Quetta, where several of them are credibly reported to be based), Pakistan has not actually *supported* the Afghan Taleban, in the way that Pakistan, the US, Britain, Saudi Arabia and other countries supported the Afghan Mujahidin against the Soviets. This is obvious from the Taleban's lack of sophisticated weaponry and training. Indeed, even in June 2010, according to a briefing by the British military which I attended, they were still far behind the Iraqi insurgents even in the construction of Improvised Explosive Devices (IEDs).

This evidence strongly contradicts a report of Matt Waldman of June 2010 alleging close Pakistani military assistance at the highest level to the Afghan Taleban (a report based on exclusively Afghan sources and containing some highly improbable anecdotes, including a personal meeting between President Zardari and Taleban leaders in which he pledged Pakistani support). It should also be a reminder of how much more the Pakistani military *could* do to help the Afghan Taleban (and other anti-Western groups) if the relationship between Pakistan and the US were to collapse completely.[8]

The Musharraf administration adopted a strategy of trying to placate the Americans by encouraging local tribesmen to drive out foreign Islamist fighters aligned with Al Qaeda (Arabs, Uzbeks, Chechens and others), while leaving fellow-Afghan Pathans alone. In mid-2004 the administration changed this strategy somewhat, partly in response to assassination attempts against Musharraf which were traced to militants in Waziristan; but much more importantly because the Afghan Taleban, using Pakistani territory as a base, had begun their successful counter-offensive against the US and its allies in Afghanistan. The Taleban were enormously helped in this by the diversion of US military effort to the war in Iraq, and by the failure to create a working administration in Afghanistan. Pakistan therefore came under intense growing US pressure to launch an offensive in its tribal areas, and especially in Waziristan, the heart of Taleban support. Musharraf was accused by the US media and members of Congress of 'double-dealing', and the long-standing links between the Pakistan army and the Taleban were repeatedly brought up for discussion.

This much is obvious. A much more difficult question is how far, and how many, ISI operatives on the ground actively sympathize with and help the Taleban and other militant groups. Indeed, this question would be impossible to answer without access to the top-secret files of Pakistani Military Intelligence (MI – not to be confused with the ISI), which monitors internal discipline in the armed forces. Some of them must have such sympathies, given the public attitudes of retired senior officers such as former ISI chief Hamid Gul, and a number of retired lower-ranking officers with whom I have spoken.

This personal closeness of parts of the military to some of the Islamists stemmed from three campaigns: the Zia-ul-Haq administration's sponsorship of the Pathan Islamist Mujahidin groups who fought against the Soviets in Afghanistan after 1979; the Pakistani military's mobilization of Islamist radical groups to fight against the Indians in Kashmir after 1988; and the belated decision of the government of Benazir Bhutto in 1994 to back the Afghan Taleban in their campaign to conquer Afghanistan and create Islamic order there.

On the other hand, Musharraf made a determined effort to weed out radical Islamists from the senior ranks of the army and ISI, and there is no evidence whatsoever that his successor as Chief of Staff, General Ashfaq Kayani, has any Islamist sympathies. On the contrary, the heavy fighting with the Pakistani Taleban which broke out in 2007 and intensified in 2009 has, I am told, led to still further vigilance against possible Taleban sympathizers in the officer corps. 'After all, we are not suicidal idiots,' an officer told me.

The really important difficulty with Pakistani military attitudes to the Taleban from 2001–10, it seems to me, goes deeper. It stems from the fact that, while the Pakistani military is deliberately shaped so as to make its members – of all ranks – feel a caste apart, they are still in the end recruited from Pakistani society. They have parents, grandparents, siblings, in-laws. They go back to live with them on leave. Most of Pakistani society – especially in those areas of northern Punjab and the NWFP from which the rank and file of the army are recruited – is not Islamist. That is obvious from the election results. What it is, is bitterly anti-American, for reasons set out in earlier chapters. This anti-American feeling did not lead most of the population, even in the Pathan areas, to support the Pakistani Taleban, and terrorism and Islamist revolution within Pakistan. It did, however, contribute to overwhelming – indeed, in many Pathan areas, universal – sympathy for the Afghan Taleban in their struggle against the US presence in Afghanistan.

THE RISE OF THE PAKISTANI TALEBAN

An additional factor in delaying Pakistani military intervention in FATA was that, with very brief exceptions, neither the Pakistani military nor the full authority of the Pakistani government had ever been extended to the tribal areas. Pakistan had continued the indirect British form of rule there, but, remembering the repeated bloody campaigns that the British had had to launch in the region, in 1947 withdrew most regular Pakistani troops from FATA. The Pakistani military move into Waziristan in 2004 was therefore not exactly the *restoration* of Pakistani authority in the region, but in some ways represented something radically new.

There was a widespread fear in the military that to invade FATA (which is what it amounted to) might be a military and political debacle;

and one can believe this version, because a debacle was what it turned out to be. Remembering the repeated tribal revolts against the British military presence in the region, Pakistan had always kept a light military presence there, relying on the Pathan-recruited Frontier Corps rather than regular soldiers. Waziristan in particular has long been famous for armed defiance. A British report of 1901 declared of the Waziris that: 'From the early days of our rule in the Punjab, few tribes on the frontier have given greater or more continuous trouble, and none have been more daring or more persistent in disturbing the peace of British territory.'[9]

When in March 2004 the Pakistani army moved into south Waziristan to attack the Afghan Taleban and Pakistani militants, the result was a revolt of local tribesmen under the leadership of radical local mullahs. In fierce battles, several villages were destroyed and hundreds of local people killed, including women and children. The army too suffered hundreds of casualties; and, most worryingly of all, there were instances of units refusing to fight. Several officers were reportedly dismissed from the military as a result. Meanwhile the army's assumption of political responsibility for an area of which it knew little helped destroy what was left of the delicate mechanism of 'indirect rule' inherited from the British.

Faced with a sharply deteriorating situation, the government made the first of several peace deals with the militants led by a local mullah, Nek Mohammed Wazir, guaranteeing the withdrawal of troops and an amnesty in return for a promise to exclude foreign militants and cease attacks into Afghanistan. These deals were always inherently fragile, however. The militants were ready enough not to attack Pakistan, but insisted on their right to go on helping the Taleban's jihad in Afghanistan. When the US struck back against them with missile strikes – or persuaded Pakistan to attack them – they alleged treachery on the part of the Pakistani government, and abrogated the agreement. This happened for the first time when, two months after the April 2004 peace deal, Nek Mohammed was killed by a US hellfire missile.

Heavy fighting in south Waziristan then continued intermittently until, in February 2005, the government signed a second deal along the same lines with Nek Mohammed's successor, Beitullah Mahsud. In September 2006, this truce was extended to north Waziristan. These agreements prevented major battles, but intermittent skirmishes continued; and the militants used the withdrawal of the army to extend their local power, execute or expel local enemies, and impose their version of Shariah law. They also of course continued to help the Afghan Taleban conduct their war against the US and the Karzai administration in Afghanistan. In response, the US continued to strike targets in the tribal areas with missiles.

The tribal areas in these years presented a bewildering picture to Western eyes, of local truces with the militants in some places even as heavy fighting took place elsewhere. This was widely assumed in the West to be the result of the duplicity of the Pakistani government and military. It certainly reflected a deep unwillingness to launch a general assault in the whole region, partly for fear of the internal consequences for Pakistan, and partly because, with most of the army deployed against India, there were simply not enough troops available for this task.

The mixed picture on the Frontier also reflected local realities, which the British learned to understand and manage during their hundred years in the region. It always made sense to try to play divide and rule, because the tribal society of the Pathans meant that the enemy was naturally divided; and if the Pakistani state was attacking some militant groups while seeking agreements with others, this was also true the other way round – that is to say, the Pakistani Taleban were attacking in some areas while seeking accommodation in others.[10]

Raising local *lashkars* (independent militias) to fight is an ancient Pathan tradition – indeed, the Taleban in Afghanistan operate largely through temporarily raised local *lashkars* – and was also much used by the British. Like the Pakistani army today, they would raise a *lashkar* from one tribe or clan who were local rivals of another clan which had revolted. As of 2008–9 this was being touted by the Pakistani military as a key part of their new strategy, but it carries obvious risks both of multiplying local civil wars and of creating Frankenstein's monsters.

Until mid-2007, militant attacks outside the tribal areas were restricted to individual acts of terrorism, such as the murder of Daniel Pearl, and attacks on French technicians and the US Consulate in Karachi. In July 2007, however, an incident took place at the Red Mosque (Lal Masjid) complex in Islamabad, which led to the end of the truce, to an explosive growth of militant action in the tribal areas and beyond, and to the formation of the Pakistani Taleban, or Tehriq-e-Taleban Pakistan (TTP), under the leadership of Beitullah Mahsud.

Since January 2007 the Red Mosque complex had become a base for militants who were launching vigilante raids on video stores and Chinese-run 'massage parlours' in adjacent areas of the city. In the NWFP and FATA this kind of thing was happening constantly without the government taking action, but the Red Mosque is situated less than 2 miles from the presidential palace and the parliament. The damage to the government's prestige was becoming intolerable.

On the other hand, the mosque is the oldest in Islamabad, and the clerical family which ran it was exceptionally well connected within the Pakistani establishment. Moreover, the complex included a religious college for women, and many of the militants engaged in vigilante actions in Islamabad were women from this college. The government was extremely afraid – and, as it turned out, with good reason – of the effects on public opinion of a battle in the mosque leaving women dead. However, when Chinese massage girls were arrested by the militants, the Chinese government sent a strong message to President Musharraf that he had to act. Given China's importance to Pakistan both as a strategic ally and as a source of development aid, that message was listened to (in response, militants killed three Chinese engineers in the NWFP).

On 10 July 2007, after repeated negotiations for surrender had failed, Pakistani troops stormed the complex. According to official figures, a total of 154 people, including 19 soldiers and some of the women militants, were killed in the ensuing battle, during which militants retreated to the cellars of the building and fought to the death.

The Red Mosque affair illustrates some of the appalling dilemmas faced by Pakistani governments in confronting Islamist militancy. In the months leading up to the military action, the Musharraf administration was constantly reproached by the Pakistani media for its failure to take action. He was accused not merely of negligence, but of deliberately helping the militants in order to prove to Washington that he was facing an Islamist revolt and therefore needed unconditional US support – something for which there is no actual evidence whatsoever.

When Musharraf finally ordered an assault there was a storm of condemnation from the media and civil society. Leading members of the Human Rights Commission and of the Lawyers' Movement have told me that, even after resigning from office, Musharraf should be imprisoned or even hanged for 'murdering thousands of people at the Lal Masjid', and that 'this issue could have been resolved through negotiations but

General Musharraf intentionally spilled the blood of innocent people to please his foreign masters'.

The then Prime Minister, Shaukat Aziz, saw this coming. He told me in early May 2007:

> It's true that we shouldn't have allowed things to go so far at the Lal Masjid, but you see we really don't want to see body-bags of the people there appearing on television, least of all of women from the age of ten up. Then the same editors who are criticizing us for inaction would criticize us for brutality, ordinary people would be disgusted, and terrorism and extremism in the country would certainly increase enormously. So far, these people at the mosque are not carrying out terrorist attacks. They are an irritant, not a menace, and so we will try to negotiate a peaceful end to all this if we possibly can.[11]

Much criticized at the time by Pakistani and Western liberals, these turned out in retrospect to have been very sensible words.

As Shaukat Aziz predicted, the storming of the mosque led to a wave of insurgency in the Pathan areas, a huge increase in terrorism, and a revulsion in Pakistani public opinion which helped lead to the downfall of the Musharraf administration. In reaction, militants in Waziristan called off a truce with the army, in force for the previous ten months, and launched a new wave of attacks on military and official targets. All over Pakistan, sympathizers with the Taleban with whom I talked used this incident to justify Taleban terrorism against the state.

In December 2007, different militant groups operating in the Pathan areas came together to form the Pakistani Taleban (TTP), a loose alliance with Beitullah Mahsud as *amir* or overall leader. The TTP declared itself to be an ally both of the Afghan Taleban and of Al Qaeda in a defensive jihad against the US occupation of Afghanistan. Their statements on Pakistan have varied considerably. On occasions they have declared that they have no quarrel with Pakistan and are only fighting the Pakistani army because it attacked them on US orders. On other occasions, however, they have declared their hostility to the existing Pakistani state as such, and their determination to achieve an Islamic revolution in Pakistan.

As a senior Pakistani general said to me, 'We on our side should avoid calling these Pakistani militants "Taleban". It's exactly what they want. It means that they are associated with religion, study of religion and above all what our people see as the legitimate jihad against the foreign occupation of Afghanistan.' And indeed, the view of the mass of the Pakistani population on Afghanistan was summed up pretty well by Maulana Sami-ul-Haq, leader of one faction of the JUI:

> If a dog fell into your well, would you remove the dog or would you empty the well? Once a red dog fell into the Afghan well, and the international community helped to get the dog out. Now a white dog has fallen in, and what are they doing? Trying to empty the well, one bucket at a time. Haven't they learned anything from Afghan history? But our people, the Pakistanis, support those who are trying to remove the dog.

In order to understand the growth of militancy in the tribal areas of Pakistan, it is essential to understand the weak nature of the border dividing the Pathan tribes of Afghanistan and Pakistan: weak in terms of physical control by the two states, but even more importantly in the minds of the tribesmen themselves. As noted, the anti-Soviet war of the 1980s weakened this border still further, with Pakistani Pathans encouraged by both Pakistan and the West to see Afghan refugees and the Afghan Mujahidin as their brothers and to fight alongside them.

Furthermore, while the Afghan Taleban have not explicitly drawn on Pathan nationalism since 2001, and their propaganda avoids insults against other ethnicities (in the hope of winning over the non-Pathan ethnicies of Afghanistan), their identity and propaganda are nonetheless suffused with Pathan culture, imagery and identity. The importance of motifs of resistance and Islam in that culture gives the Taleban a very strong appeal. A speech by Mullah Omar the day before the start of the US bombing campaign in 2001, refusing to surrender Al Qaeda to the US and vowing to resist US attack, has, for many Pathans, a Shakespearean or Churchillian force. He stressed that victory would come only in the long run, and in the short term the Taleban could expect defeat and death:

> I know that my power; my position; my wealth; and my family are in danger ... However, I am ready to sacrifice myself and I do not want to become the friend of non-Muslims, for non-Muslims are against all my beliefs and my religion ... I insist on sacrificing myself, and you should do likewise ... [I am] ready to leave everything and to believe only in Islam and in my Afghan bravery.[12]

The militants who later formed the Pakistani Taleban revolted in 2004 against the Pakistani army in order to defend what they saw as the legitimate jihad in Afghanistan, their sacred code of hospitality for Muslims and Pathans fleeing from infidel attack, and their own ancient tribal freedoms. We may well argue that what they did went horribly against the real interests of their own people. We cannot argue that they betrayed their own code.

So while the Afghan and Pakistani Talebans have separate leaderships and face in different directions, they draw their inspiration from the same sources. However, it does seem that as the struggle with the Pakistani state and army intensified after the storming of the Red Mosque in 2007, the Pakistani Taleban leadership may have become obsessed with this struggle to the detriment of the Afghan jihad.

Mullah Omar declared several times that the Pakistani state was not the enemy, and that Muslims should concentrate on fighting the real enemy, which he says is US forces and their allies in Afghanistan. This presumably reflected pressure on Mullah Omar from the Pakistani army, but by the same token it probably reflected genuine fear that the Pakistani Taleban might wreck his relationship with that army, and with it his chances of long-term victory in Afghanistan.

THE NATURE OF THE PAKISTANI TALEBAN

The Pakistani Taleban is not nearly as tight a movement as the decentralized Afghan Taleban, but is, rather, a loose alliance of autonomous Islamist radical groups and commanders, under the nominal leadership of an *amir*. The first *amir* was Beitullah Mahsud; when he was killed by a US drone in August 2009, Hakimullah Mahsud took over. Both are from the notoriously unruly and fanatical Mahsud tribe of south Waziristan, which was a thorn in the British empire's flesh for 100 years.

Pakistani journalists who have travelled in the tribal areas have described needing passes and permissions from as many as half a dozen different local Taleban commanders in order to move from one Agency to another. Some of the local Pakistani Taleban groups are close to Al Qaeda and are heavily influenced by international jihadi agendas. Others, especially in Swat, have agendas more focused on local power and the transformation of local society. All, however, are committed to supporting the jihad in Afghanistan, and most seem capable of co-operating effectively against the Pakistani army when it penetrates their territory. While all now say that they are committed to Islamist revolution in Pakistan, all also claim – and probably believe – that their movement began as a defensive action against the Pakistani army's 'invasion' of Waziristan in 2004, and against US drone attacks on FATA.

The Pakistani Taleban draw much of their funding from taxing the heroin trade and other illegal activities, and some are directly involved in kidnapping and other crimes. In the Taleban case the distinction between 'taxation' of local transport and business and 'extortion' is impossible to draw. In most areas of FATA it seems that their demands are not too heavy, or at least not heavy enough to drive the population into revolt against them.

After their association with what is seen as a legitimate jihad in Afghanistan, the other reason which every Taleban sympathizer I met gave for his support was the Taleban's implementation of Shariah law. This is not the same as support for revolution and, what is more, the 'law' that the Taleban enforce is often not really the Shariah at all, but a sprinkling of the Shariah mixed with the *pashtunwali* and a rough form of communal justice. However, for reasons set out in Chapter 3, a great many people see this as preferable to the appallingly slow, opaque, alien and corrupt Pakistani judicial system.

The Taleban also gain credit for crude but tough and effective enforcement of their version of the law. One of the reasons why the Taleban is popular, including with many small businessmen from FATA and Peshawar with whom I talked, is that they have cracked down very hard on freelance kidnapping, and on local drug-dealing which helps fuel crime. They also sort out small-scale business disputes. In Peshawar, I talked to a ceramics trader from Landi Khotal in the Khyber Agency. He deeply disliked the Taleban, and despite his limited means had sent his son to study in Britain for fear that he might fall under their influence or just be conscripted to help them. However, he also described how for almost fifteen years he had been trying to recover a Rs800,000 debt from another businessman through the Pakistani courts: 'bribe after bribe, and nothing happened; because of course the other side was bribing too, and so the case was delayed and delayed'.

Eventually, he went to the Taleban, 'and they sorted it out in a week'.

His erstwhile partner had to pay him Rs500,000. The Taleban asked for 10 per cent of that as a fee for their help, 'but I thought it wise to give them 15 per cent,' he said with a rather melancholy twinkle. This kind of thing can sometimes be accompanied by a rough humour which appeals to Pathan sensibilities. Faced with two cousins who had been quarrelling for many years over some land, an independent Islamist warlord named Mangal Bagh locked them in the same room and told them that they would stay there till they came to an agreement – which they did.

My friend in ceramics said that while the Taleban tax the drugs trade passing through their territories ('because they don't care if Westerners take drugs'), they crack down very hard on local drug-dealing, thereby earning much credit in the local population and especially from parents. So if the Taleban are bandits, they are often what Max Weber called 'rational bandits' – and rational banditry in his view was the original basis of taxation and the state.

It is critically important to remember that in the propaganda of the Pakistani Taleban, and in the view of the majority of Pathans and Punjabis with whom I have spoken, the Pakistani Taleban war is not intended as a war against Pakistan and was not initiated by Beitullah Mahsud and his allies but by the Pakistani government and army. These Pakistanis portray this struggle as a defensive action to protect the legitimate Afghan jihad from a treacherous stab in the back by the Pakistani servants of America, who also 'massacred innocent Muslims' at the Red Mosque.

This is not to say that a majority of the people with whom I spoke in Peshawar, Abbotabad and the towns of the Peshawar valley actively support the Pakistani Taleban – if that were so, then the situation in the region would be much worse than it is. The overwhelming level of sympathy for the Afghan Taleban does not result in similar levels of support for the Pakistani Taleban. Outside the tribal areas, a large majority of the people I met denounced both the harshness of the Taleban's implementation of the Shariah, and their terrorism and attacks on the Pakistani army and police – even if, as stated, they often qualified this by saying that such attacks are really the work of Indians or Americans, since 'Muslims would not do this.'

Rather, the notion of a defensive jihad helps create a sense of moral equivalence between the Pakistani Taleban and the Pakistani army, in which people criticize both sides, and mass support for tough military action against the Pakistani Taleban is undermined to the point where fewer than 20 per cent of the people I surveyed in the NWFP in the summer of 2008 were prepared to support it, with the rest demanding peace talks.

From one point of view the idea that the Pakistani Taleban is acting from purely defensive motives is nonsense, since plots to assassinate Musharraf by militants based in Waziristan predated the army offensive in the region and were partly responsible for that offensive. Moreover, the propaganda of the Pakistani Taleban also speaks of their goal of creating an Islamist revolution in Pakistan. However, a very large number of ordinary Pakistanis believe that the struggle of the Pakistani Taleban is 'defensive', and this has a powerful effect in wrecking their support for military action against them. Again and again, on the streets of Peshawar, Rawalpindi, Lahore, Faisalabad and Multan, people told me that, in the words of one Lahori shopkeeper, 'The Taleban are doing some bad things, but you have to remember that they are only doing them in self-defence, because the army took American money to attack them.'

The revolt of the Pakistani Taleban therefore stems in the first instance from the Western presence in Afghanistan and the struggle of the Afghan Taleban against that presence and the Afghan forces it supports. The movement, however, has much deeper and older roots. These lie in ancient Pathan traditions of religiously justified resistance to outside rule; in the Soviet occupation of the 1980s and the Afghan resistance against that occupation; in the nature of the support given by Pakistan and parts of the Arab world to that resistance; and in social change on the Frontier, which has undermined the old British–Pakistani system for managing the tribes.

THE LINEAGE OF THE PAKISTANI TALEBAN

The marriage of tribal revolt and religious revival is not specific to the Pathans, but is one of the oldest traditions of the Muslim world, including the Maghrib, West Africa and the Arabian peninsula itself. As Ernest Gellner remarks, echoing the great fifteenth-century Arab sociologist Ibn Khaldun:

> What would happen if bellicose tribesmen outside the walls had designs on the city? Most often nothing at all, for these tribal wolves are generally

at each other's throats, and their endless mutual feuds, often fostered by the
ruler, neutralize them. They lust after the city anyway, but their internal divisions prevent them from satisfying their desire ... But what would happen if
some authoritative cleric, having with some show of plausibility denounced
the impiety and immorality of the ruler, thereby also provided a banner, a
focus, a measure of unitary leadership for the wolves? What if he went into
the wilderness to ponder the corruption of the time, and there encountered,
not only God, but also some armed tribesmen, who responded to his message?[13]

Ibn Khaldun wrote of this coming together of religious purification and
plunder in the history of the Bedouin tribes of North Africa:

It is their nature to plunder whatever other people possess. Their susten-
ance lies wherever the shadow of their lances falls ... When they acquire
superiority and royal authority, they have complete power to plunder as
they please. There no longer exists any political power to protect property,
and civilization is ruined.[14]

Yet at the same time, in Khaldun's analysis, when united under the banner
of religious puritanism and regeneration, these plundering but courageous
tribes are also the force that overthrows corrupt and decadent kingdoms
and refounds them – for a while – on a stronger basis. The Wahabis in
eighteenth-century Arabia, in alliance with the tribe of Saud, were a late
but impressive manifestation of this tradition. In Gellner's words:

The manner in which demanding, puritan unitarianism enters tribal life,
and the manner in which tribes are induced on special occasions to accept
overall leadership, are the *same*. The exceptional crisis in the tribal world
provides the opening, the opportunity, for that 'purer' form of faith which
normally remains latent, respected but not observed.[15]

Tribal dissidence and religious radicalism have therefore been partners
in the Muslim world for many centuries. On the one hand there is the
anarchy of the tribes, ordered only by their own traditions: in the Arabic
of the Maghrib the *bled-es-siba*, in the Pathan lands and Iran *yaghestan*:
the land of unrest (or 'the land of defiance', as Afghanistan has sometimes been called in both the Persian and Indian traditions): opposed to
the *bled-es-makhzen* or *hukumat*, the land of government. A rather
gloomy Pathan proverb sums up the disadvantages of both ways of life:
'Feuding ate up the mountains, and taxes ate up the plains.'

The great majority of the Pathan tribal revolts against the British were orchestrated by religious figures in the name of jihad: all of them, naturally, described by the British as 'mad'. These included the Akhund of Swat in the 1860s, the Hadda Mullah, the Manki Mullah, the Fakir of Buner and the Powindah Mullah in the 1890s, and in the 1930s the Fakir of Ipi, against whose rebellion the British deployed two divisions (including my maternal uncle's Gurkha battalion).

The Fakir of Ipi's rebellion took place in Waziristan, later the heartland of Taleban support after 9/11 and the US overthrow of the Taleban. Incidentally, all these revolts were influenced to a greater or lesser extent by news from other parts of the Muslim world (albeit often extremely twisted) about clashes between Muslims and the Christian imperial powers; so the notion that Pakistanis being influenced by developments in Palestine or Iraq marks a new departure is completely wrong.

Waziristan was also the site of major uprisings in the 1890s, and in 1919 when the Wazirs and Mahsuds rose in support of the Afghan invasion of India. It may be noted incidentally that just as at the time of writing the US and Pakistani forces have not yet killed or captured much of the top leadership of Al Qaeda or the Taleban, so, despite deploying some 40,000 troops in Waziristan, the British never caught the Fakir of Ipi, who died in his bed in 1960 – by that stage, interestingly enough, preaching Pathan nationalism and an independent Pashtunistan.

Almost forty years before the emergence of the Afghan Taleban, the great anthropologist of the Pathans, Fredrik Barth, wrote the following about the orchestration of revolt in the name of Islam:

> A more temporary organization [than the regular relationship between a local saint and his followers] may be built around persons of less established sanctity, based on the Islamic dogma of the holy war and the blessings awaiting the soldier (*ghazi*) who figures in one. This line of appeal requires considerable demagogic powers and is mainly adopted by mullahs. Essentially, it depends for its success on the presence of a fundamental conflict in the area, and the ability to play on ideals of manliness and fearlessness so as to whip up confidence among the warriors of the community.[16]

The Taleban, however, are a new variation of this old pattern. They are an alliance of newly risen younger mullahs, rather than single 'authoritative clerics' possessing individual *baraka*. Their chief leaders, like Beitullah Mahsud and Fazlullah, emerged to prominence when they were in their late twenties or early thirties. This is not quite such a shift as the Pakistani elites make out. The Pathan tradition in general is far more egalitarian in spirit than those of the other parts of Pakistan, and, within that tradition, those of some of the tribes of the Frontier have always been famous for the unwillingness of the tribesmen to bow to hereditary chieftains. 'Traditionally, the dominant characteristic of the Mahsud was his independence – in a sense, every man was his own malik.'[17] Leadership has generally been through merit, and especially courage and skill in fighting. Though of course the leaders of the Pakistani Taleban are very pious Muslims, unlike previous leaders of revolt against the British such as the Mullah of Hadda they are not regarded as saints by their followers, but only as especially able and tough military commanders.

The Taleban are much more effective than previous religiously led revolts, above all because they have far more organization, discipline and therefore stamina. The revolts against the British arose suddenly and spread rapidly, but were also mostly rather brief. A few bloody defeats and the tribesmen melted back to their villages. The Taleban by contrast have gone on absorbing very heavy casualties for many years. As I was told when travelling with the Afghan Mujahidin in the 1980s, 'Pashtuns are brave, but not deliberately suicidal.' That has obviously changed, as far as some of the Taleban fighters are concerned.

Relative Taleban discipline and endurance probably owe a great deal to the unprecedented network of local cadres provided by young local mullahs. This in turn has been part of a social upheaval in FATA whereby, through the Taleban, members of this previously powerless and even despised class have seized local power from the landowning *maliks*.

I am reminded of something said by Imam Shamil, the great nineteenth-century Islamist resistance leader in the north Caucasus, after he finally had to surrender to Russia – that the Russians should really be grateful to him for making their rule possible; because by rigorous implementation of the Shariah he had accustomed the Chechen tribes to government, where previously none had existed. Shamil's Islamic state in Chechnya and Daghestan lasted for almost twenty-five years, in a much smaller territory than the Pathan tribal areas, and against far larger numbers of Russian troops than the British ever had to deploy against their rebels – who (like Shamil's Chechens) were fighting largely to prevent any kind of state being imposed on them.

Unlike many previous leaders, the Taleban leaders also do not derive their prestige from deep Islamic learning, but only from rigorous practice. Rather than simply leading a movement of tribal chieftains, they have replaced those chieftains with their own rule. Inspired in part by the Wahabis, their rule has been far more consistently dogmatic in their insistence on their version of the Shariah than any previous movement among the Pathans.

Previously, while religious figures led tribal revolts in the name of Islam, the struggle was also very much in defence of the tribal customs summed up in the *pashtunwali* – many of them pre-Islamic. They were certainly not encouraged to try to change those customs in accordance with strict Koranic Islam. The few who tried generally came to a bad end, as with Syed Ahmed Barelvi, abandoned by his followers after he interfered with their marriage customs – though in his case, the fact of being a non-Pathan from India doubtless also played a part. In fact, there is a Pathan saying that 'Pathans are always ready to die for Islam, but find it very difficult to live by Islam.'

All the same, the Taleban are close enough to Khaldun's and Gellner's picture to make clear that what we are facing among the Pathans is not simply a product of the last thirty or for that matter the past 150 years of Pathan history, but has roots which go back to the very origins of Islam, and have never failed yet to put out new shoots in each new era. In the Frontier territories, this has run together throughout modern history with a determination to maintain tribal independence from outside control. As Sana Haroon writes:

> This hinterland of successive, contradictory jihads in support of Pakhtun ethnicism, anti-colonial nationalism, Pakistani territorialism, religious revivalism and anti-American imperialism generated, in turn, fluid and fluctuating political allegiances within the Tribal Areas. Only the claim to autonomy persisted unchanged and uncompromised, and within that claim the functional role of religious leaders as social moderators and ideological guides was preserved. From outside, patrons recognized and supported that claim, reliant in their own ways on the possibilities that the autonomous Tribal Areas and its mullas afforded.[18]

These possibilities were quickly recognized by the US, Pakistani and Arab backers of the Afghan jihad against the Soviets after 1979. The tribal areas of Pakistan, and to some extent the Pathan areas in general, became the safe havens of the Afghan Mujahidin, just as they are the safe havens of the Taleban today. The distinction between the Pathans on different sides of the Afghan–Pakistan border – never very strong – was blurred as more than 3 million (mainly Pathan) refugees from Afghanistan fled into Pakistan. In these areas the Mujahidin were housed, armed and trained by the Pakistanis, Saudis and Americans.

The training was both military and ideological, as thousands of young Afghans studied alongside Pakistanis and Arabs in Deobandi madrasahs in the Pathan areas of Pakistan, funded by Arab money and, in consequence, increasingly influenced by Wahabi thought and culture. The first leader of revolt in Waziristan, Nek Mohammed, was the product of such a madrasah, and had fought with the Mujahidin in the 1980s and the Taleban in the 1990s.

The importance of the Afghan jihad of the 1980s for subsequent history cannot be exaggerated. The Frontier was flooded with international arms, many of which, lovingly preserved, are still in use by the Taleban in Afghanistan and Pakistan. After decades in which the Pakistani state had tried to build up a Pakistani Pathan identity separate from Afghanistan, young Pakistani Pathans were now told that Afghanistan's war was their war, and that it was their religious and ethnic duty to fight alongside their Afghan brothers.

Today, many Pakistani Taleban fighters did not originally intend to fight in Pakistan, but volunteered to fight with the Taleban in Afghanistan – with the full support of their communities, and the tacit acquiescence of the Pakistani authorities. But, of course, they came home radicalized, and deeply bitter at the Pakistani government for, as they see it, stabbing the Taleban and their jihad in the back.

Because of the prestige they earned as 'Mujahidin', they are now used by the Pakistani Taleban as the first-line cadres when it comes to spreading propaganda and influence in their home areas of the Frontier. From the propaganda point of view, the dead are just as important as the living. In the years after 2001, the funerals of 'martyrs' (*shahids*) killed in Afghanistan became important and well-attended events in FATA and the NWFP, and in some cases their tombs have become places of pilgrimage. This is a tradition which goes back through the war with India in Kashmir in 1947–8 and to revolts against the British, but which also received a tremendous boost from the Pakistanis who fought and died in the war against the Soviets, when of course their public funerals received full state support and approval.

Finally, the local mullahs of the region not only were radicalized by their exposure to Wahabi influences and Arab Wahabi volunteers such as Osama bin Laden and his comrades, but saw their social prestige – hitherto usually very low – greatly increased by their association with the jihad in Afghanistan. Many younger ones actually fought with the radical Mujahidin in Afghanistan, alongside the Arabs. This change coincided with wider social changes in FATA as traditional tribal structures of authority were undermined by the influx of new money both from the Afghan jihad and the drugs trade.

One aspect of the Pathan tradition on which the Taleban have built with great success is the role of religious figures in resolving or limiting disputes and, on occasions, uniting the tribes in jihad. The absence of any other authority over the tribes meant that 'it was almost impossible for opposing factions to approach each other through any other means than mulla-led arbitration'.[19]

The British administrator W. R. H. Merk wrote:

> Mians and Mullahs fulfil much the same secular purposes as the monks of Europe did in the middle ages; they act as trustees and custodians of property, as the protectors of women and children committed to their charge, and are the mediators of messengers in family or tribal strife. Their intimate cohesion and the ramifications of their class through the tribes makes them an admirable instrument for organizing a popular movement.[20]

The line you often hear from the Pathan upper classes, that traditionally mullahs had little prestige in Pathan society, being little better than common village servants, paid in kind to perform prayers at marriages and funerals, is therefore only partially correct.

Or rather, it is correct enough as far as the lowly village mullah is concerned. As with your average Catholic parish priest in the Mediterranean in the past – semi-literate, venal and living in sin with his 'housekeeper' – the population needs their sacred services, but not their advice. They are in fact regarded rather like a service caste, one step above the potters and plumbers (or how plumbers would be regarded if there were any plumbing). This is especially true because, as in the villages of traditional Catholic Europe, the population knows very well not only all the mullah's personal failings, but also how much he is under the thumb of the local landlords. 'You wife of a mullah' is a common Pathan insult. Or as another saying has it, 'The mullah should have his milk, be it from a bitch or a donkey.'

As with medieval Catholic Europe, however, this ironical attitude to the local priest in no way implies mockery of the sacred as such, or blocks admiration for figures who seem to have a direct relationship with the sacred. In the Pathan lands, as elsewhere, this is associated originally with a successful claim to be a Sayyid, or descendant of the Prophet. Such figures never become village mullahs, or 'imams' of local mosques – this is far beneath them. Sayyids have always played an immensely important and prestigious role in local society. According to Barth:

> The status of saints makes them particularly suited to the role of mediator or arbitrator . . . In making political use of their role as peacemakers, saints must take numerous variables into account and in fact be rather clever. In the words of one prominent saint, 'I look like a simple man; I live simply – but oh! The things I do!' The settlements which a saint proposes must be justified by reference to some rule or ideal. They must also take cognizance of de facto situations, and the saint must be skilled in inventing compromises and face-saving devices . . . But without some force to back them, such manipulations sooner or later fall to the ground. The necessary force derives from several sources, but if the saint himself disposes of some military power, however little, this greatly enlarges his field of manoeuvre.[21]

One last element must be mentioned in the historical genealogy of jihad on the Frontier. This is the role of non-Pathan Islamists from elsewhere, who move to the region partly to find safe havens, and partly to mobilize the warlike Pathans to join in wider international struggles and agendas. From the early nineteenth century, radical Islamists in India intermittently moved to the tribal areas, as the only unconquered areas of the Indian subcontinent, and home to famously warlike people who might be inspired to join in jihad, first against the Sikhs, then against the British. A century later, in the wake of the First World War, another Islamist, Maulana Hussain Ahmad Madni, wrote of his group's anti-British strategy:

> Without violence, evicting the *angrez* from Hindustan was impossible. For this, a centre, weapons and mujahidin were necessary. Hence it was thought

that arrangements for weapons and recruitment of soldiers should be conducted in the area of the 'free tribes'.[22]

The veteran Frontier political agent and last British governor of the NWFP, Sir Olaf Caroe, wrote that such forces from outside, as well as the Pathans' own religious leaders, were unable to sustain jihad for long:

> A leader appears, and unites tribal sentiment in a surge of enthusiasm that carries all before it. For a while internal jealousies are laid aside, and an enthusiastic loyalty is forthcoming. Individuals are found ready to face death for a cause, and no one counts the cost. The idea of sacrifice is in the air. The crest of the wave bursts over the barrier, and the victory seems won. Then the leader gives way to vainglory, the stimulus which gave unity fails, envy and malice show their heads. The effort, steady and sustained, which is needed to maintain the position won proves to be beyond the tribal reach. The ground won is lost, and the leader forfeits confidence and is discarded.[23]

In this respect, however, the Taleban do seem to represent something new. Western writing likes to dwell on their internal divisions, but by the standards of any previous Pathan jihad – our own Mujahidin of the 1980s included – they have so far displayed formidable unity and stamina. One explanation for this would seem to be that while certain Pathan cultural and ideological traditions have continued little changed, Pathan society has in some respects changed quite radically.

In particular, the power of the greatest traditional source of Pathan fragmentation – the tribes and their chieftains – has been greatly diminished as a result of thirty years of war in Afghanistan and its overspill in Pakistan. With the power of the *maliks* greatly reduced, the local mullah is really the only available semi-educated leader of local society – unless you count the drugs lords, of course. So, politically incorrect though it may be to say it, the Western and Pakistani official policy of trying to re-energize the tribes and tribal chieftains, and of creating tribal *lashkars* under traditional command, actually represents a step backwards in historical terms, compared to Taleban organization.

These changes in Pathan society have also produced a new feature of the Taleban, which marks them out from the old jihads. They are an alliance not of a handful of prominent religious figures from Sayyid backgrounds and allied chieftains, but of many ordinary local mullahs and religious students from poor and simple backgrounds. Speaking of another ostensibly Islamist warlord on the borders of Peshawar, Mangal Bagh Afridi, again and again educated people in Peshawar would ask me rhetorically, 'Who on earth can respect a former bus conductor as a leader?' Those readers who have not already guessed the answer can turn to the next paragraph for the solution – one which had never occurred to my educated Peshawari interlocutors.

The answer of course is *another bus conductor*. In other words, it is precisely the lowly origins of the Taleban and related figures which endear them to the Pathan masses. A strong though mainly unstated element of class feeling has therefore also entered into the struggle. By contrast, all the non-Islamist parties in the Frontier – the ANP, the different branches of the PPP and Muslim League, and Imran Khan's followers – are overwhelmingly dominated by khans and *maliks*, and the JUI is linked to this class in many ways. Because so many of the Pakistani elites – even in the Frontier – are so obviously Westernized, as well as being deeply corrupt, a certain feeling exists in the population, as in Iran in the 1970s, that 'it is the *poor* who are Muslims'.

THE MOHMAND AGENCY

At least in Peshawar a large majority of the ordinary people with whom I spoke on the street and in the bazaars denounced terrorism, and said that although they supported the rule of the Shariah in principle, they opposed Taleban attempts to impose it by force. It was very different in the part of FATA that I visited. On what seemed to me to be reasonable grounds of self-preservation, I did not go to those tribal agencies like Waziristan, where the Pakistani Taleban have been in effective control for several years.

A visit to a relatively peaceful part of the Mohmand Agency in September 2008 was quite alarming enough, in terms not of any visibly direct threat to me (though, on this one occasion, I did have a sense that such a threat would have appeared if I had stayed for a few days), but of the opinions of the people. Following the Red Mosque battle in July 2007, the Taleban in the agency had come into the open and established a headquarters at Kandhura and a number of training camps in parts of the agency closer to Bajaur in the north and the Afghan border in the west. These areas had seen repeated clashes with the army and the Frontier Corps, in which sometimes one side and sometimes the other had got the upper hand, but the areas closer to the Peshawar valley were still supposedly under fairly firm government control.

That many Mohmands sympathize with the Taleban would, once again, not have come as a surprise to those British officials who were once responsible for keeping them in hand. The Durand Line cut the tribe in half, but failed as elsewhere to cut tribal ties of sympathy with the Mohmands of Afghanistan. Nor, as elsewhere, did it create anything like a regular international frontier. Throughout the years following 2001, the mountainous parts of the Mohmand Agency have been an important route for Taleban infiltration into north-eastern Afghanistan.

The great tribal rising of 1897 was led in these parts by the Mullah of Hada, whose religious authority extended to both sides of the line, and who was imprisoned by the Amir of Afghanistan just as he was pursued by the British. For a long time, trade on the roads was taxed not by the two states but by the clans themselves – just as, today, it is taxed by the local militias making up the Pakistani Taleban, and the occasional independent warlord like Mangal Bagh Afridi (who, however, also acts in the name of Islam).

Between the British arrival in the region in the 1840s and the creation of the Durand Line, in the words of the British official W. R. H. Merk, 'by the tacit consent of the governments concerned, those of [British] India and of Kabul, a *modus vivendi* was established by which either government dealt with the clans as if the other [government] did not exist.'[24] A quaint formulation but, to judge by the experience of recent years, perhaps the only way the Afghan and Pakistani states of today will ever find to co-exist in this region.

I went to the Mohmand Agency to visit a local *malik* family of my acquaintance, whose father is a senior official in Islamabad but who maintain a house in their ancestral village near the town of Shapqadar. This town itself is a monument to the British Raj, having grown up around the fort which the British built to bar the entrance from the Mohmand territories into the Peshawar valley.

The villages around Shapqadar were founded by rebellious Mohmands from the hills, resettled by the British under the guns of the fort, and placed under the regular British Indian legal code, not the Frontier

Crimes Regulations. So the area is one of the numerous anomalies of the Frontier – a 'settled' part of a tribal agency, but one whose inhabitants retain the legends of their old unsettled past. In 1897 the fort was attacked by the followers of the Mullah of Hada, who left 300 of their number dead before its walls – part of the campaign described by Winston Churchill in 'The Malakand Field Force', which he accompanied as an officer-cum-war correspondent.[25]

The prestige and wealth of the 'Akhundzada' family whom I visited near Shapqadar came originally from their descent from another local 'Sufi' religious figure, Akhund Zafar, who led yet another revolt under the banner of jihad against the infidel. 'His shrine is only thirty minutes' drive from here, but now it is Taleban territory and too dangerous for us to visit,' I was told. Like many saints, he is also famous for having cast out demons, and people with psychologically disturbed relatives will take them to his shrine to be exorcised, a fact mentioned deprecatingly by the family.

As with the Gailanis of Afghanistan, there is an old and familiar irony here: the semi-Westernized noble family whose local influence originally came from an anti-Western struggle, a new version of which is aimed at them and their class, and from 'superstitious' beliefs which they now disown, trying to maintain their power in the face of a new wave of 'fanaticism', with which their ancestor would probably have been wholly in sympathy.

Shapqadar is still a barrier to getting out of or into the Mohmand Agency, but now the reasons are the roads and the traffic. Bypass roads are unknown in small towns in Pakistan and we had made the mistake of travelling on a market day. Traffic jam doesn't begin to describe the results – more like a double reef knot. The crossroads in the centre of town was a maelstrom of dust and exhaust fumes, apparently sucking into it cars, buses, trucks, scooter rickshaws, horse-carts, donkey-carts, men pushing carts, men on horseback and one understandably depressed-looking camel, all mixed up with a simply incredible number of people on foot for such a small town, as if the heavens had opened on a Sunday morning and rained humanity on Shapqadar. Out of the dust-shrouded mêlée the brightly painted lorries with their great carved wooden hoods loomed like war elephants in an ancient battle.

In the middle, two policemen in a state of frenzy were lashing the cars with their sticks as if they were recalcitrant animals, while a third leant exhausted against a column. 'Sometimes you even have to feel sorry for the police in this country,' the daughter of my host – an elegant, attractive lady from Islamabad – said with a sigh, adjusting her head-scarf against any inquiring glances from the men practically jammed against our windows.

> Everyone is afraid of them but no one actually listens to them. They are not really monsters, they just lash out from frustration at their miserable lives . . . As to Shapqadar, you could come back here twenty years from now and nothing will have changed except that the traffic will have got even worse. After all, nothing has changed in the past twenty.

It took us almost an hour and a half to get through this insignificant place; a long study of the grim, drab concrete ugliness of most Pakistani urban life. So universally grey and dust-coated were the buildings that I could not immediately tell a local landmark from the houses on either side – four blackened music and video shops torched by the Taleban a few months before as part of their campaign against vice.

This is a common step in the Taleban campaign to take over a given area, once they feel they have enough local support. Because the video shops often do show pornographic films in their back rooms, even those men who frequent them may be ashamed of the fact and feel obliged to denounce them in public; and, for the same reason, they are also very unpopular with local wives and mothers – who of course never set foot in them but deeply fear the effects on their menfolk.

Half an hour further on, the village to which we were travelling lay snoozing in the baking heat of early September, looking very much on the outside as if it hadn't changed in twenty years, or even twenty centuries. The khaki colour of its walls was set off nicely by the rather beautifully coloured viscous green scum on the stinking stream running through its middle. We swept through a gate – really more a gap in a mud wall – and were in the family's compound. A lengthy wait ensued, while the key of the main house was sought – for the rest of the family had not arrived yet – and I had leisure to look around, through the sweat which began to pour down my face as soon as I left the car's air-conditioning.

The wide outer court had a small mosque on one side, and on the other sides the *hujra* (male guest-house or gathering place), and a sort of open pavilion where the family's workers sprawled on charpoys in the stupefying heat, some attended by their small sons. The buildings were all whitewashed, or at least had been at some point in their history. In one corner of the court, the shafts of an old broken-down horse-drawn carriage drooped with a melancholy air.

The *maliks* had not long ago dominated the village economically, but their holdings had been radically reduced by land reform and repeated divisions between brothers, and now the compound of the elder was only one of several belonging to brothers and cousins on the old family property. The eldest son – whom I was visiting – now held only 180 *kanals* of land (43 acres), and his influence had presumably also suffered from his being absent most of the time at his job in Islamabad, though on the other hand this also enabled him to use his influence to get some local people jobs.

The main house, in the inner court, bore clear signs of the family being absent much of the time. Much of the furniture was under dust covers, and damp stains stretched down some of the walls. Rich by the standards of the local peasantry, it was poor and simple by the standards of the urban elites – a reminder once again not to use the word 'feudal' as if it implied wallowing in luxury. Power cuts meant that the atmosphere inside was stifling, and that there was nothing cold to drink.

In fact, I was just about to sink hopelessly into slumber when I was jerked awake by the sight of a very familiar acquaintance from another life, or even as it seemed to my superheated brain another planet: a small tapestry of that absolute staple of the Soviet middle-class household, that emblem of respectable Russian domesticity, Ivan Shishkin's *Morning in a Pine Forest* (with mist and bear cubs) – at 100 degrees or so in the shade. This was one of those not infrequent moments in Pakistan when I wondered whether sanity is not a much-overrated attribute which it would be easier simply to abandon.

In the car on the way from Peshawar a certain Russian, or at least Chekhovian-Gogolesque, atmosphere had already begun to grow, as my hostess complained of the rise of the lower classes in the village:

> I loathe these new people. I know it's wrong but I can't help it. They should be shown their place. My father got their sons jobs in the junior civil service, and now that they have made money from bribes they build themselves big brick houses and try to set themselves up as *maliks*, deciding on local disputes. My father has threatened to have some of them thrown out of those houses – after all, he owns the land they're built on.

As will become apparent, he would probably be very unwise to do any such thing.

The Chekhovian impression deepened with the appearance of the family's steward or general factotum, Shehzad, a scrawny middle-aged individual with a long horse face, greying hair, crooked teeth, a pen clipped to the outside of the breast pocket of his shirt as a mark of status, and a manner which mixed the ingratiating and the overbearing – not, as is usually the case, when dealing with people of different status, but in talking to a person of higher status; a small, offbeat sign of Pathan egalitarianism.

No sooner were we out of the car than he began to harass my hostess unmercifully about a new mobile phone that he said that she had promised him. 'You gave me your word more than a year ago and still I am stuck with this rubbish. This is not Muslim behaviour!' This promised cell-phone hung around for the whole of my stay, emerging every time the conversation threatened to flag. 'What can I do?' my hostess asked with an only half-comical sigh, 'He harasses me unmercifully, but he has been with my father for ever. We can't possibly get rid of him.'

Then Shehzad took me out to the *hujra* to meet the agricultural labourers and tenant farmers, at which point things ceased to be comical, and I was in no danger of falling asleep. Just as the impending Russian revolution formed the looming background to Chekhov's gentry, so it turned out that my hosts – without fully realizing it themselves – were sitting on the crust of a river of lava.

Shehzad himself, as he told me with complete candour, like the vast majority of the tenants and the village in general, is a strong sympathizer of both the Afghan and the Pakistani Taleban – something of which his master and mistress were wholly unaware, but which he revealed to me with no hesitation whatsoever. In fact, he went further than most sympathizers with the Taleban:

> It is not terrorism when you attack Pakistani government employees like at the Wah factory because they were making weapons so the army can kill their own people. The government is taking American money to do this, and they should be fought. Ninety-nine per cent of people in this village support the Taleban, because the Taleban just want to fight the American occupiers of Afghanistan and bring Islamic Law, and everyone agrees with that.

As we sat there on broken chairs on the verandah of the *hujra*, more figures drifted up to support these views. The keeper of the *hujra* – not a very dutiful one, to judge by its appearance – came and sat with us. Under his thick black beard he had a naive smile and a surprisingly boyish face, almost as if the beard had been stuck on that morning at a village fête. He told me that his brother was fighting with the Taleban, 'maybe in Bajaur against the Pakistani army, maybe in Afghanistan against the Americans. Wherever they send him on jihad, he will go.'

I asked why his brother had joined the Taleban.

He joined the Taleban because he believes in Islam, and because the Americans attacked Afghanistan without cause. Afghanistan is an occupied country like Kashmir. He and the other Taleban do not want to fight the Pakistani army, but they have no choice because the army is attacking them on the orders of America. The Taleban would like to make an agreement with the government here so that they can go and fight in Afghanistan. But America doesn't allow the government to do that. It wants war in Pakistan so that Muslim will kill Muslim.

I asked about Taleban pay.

Yes, it is true that the Taleban pay him Rs12,000 a month, and the police only get Rs6,000. That is a reason. For two years he could not find any steady work. Then the Taleban came and offered to take him. Our family are very happy that he went, because he is on jihad against America and everyone here supports that . . . It is true that some of our relatives have jobs with the Pakistani state. For example, I have a cousin in the police. But I am not worried about him being killed by the Taleban. He is fighting for America, and it is better that he should be killed. No one here wants to join the police or army any more.

A tenant farmer, Tazmir Khan, a solid-looking middle-aged man with a sort of universal farmer's look and huge hands planted on his thighs, joined the conversation. He farms 30 *kanals* (3.75 acres), 4 *kanals* of which he rents from the *malik*, to his unhappiness. 'I work, work and then I have to pay here.' Tazmir has been quoted in Chapter 3, on justice, explaining why the Taleban are better than the state courts and police. He added:

The Taleban have driven out criminals and bad characters. They are doing much good work stopping drug-dealing and kidnapping. There has been no more of that since they came here. We can travel in the middle of the night without problems. Before, everyone was home by 10.00 p.m. for fear of dacoits. And mothers want their sons to join the Taleban. Yes, it is dangerous, but it is honourable and for Islam, and it is better than joining some gang and getting into God knows what dirty business . . .

In Bajaur, Musharraf and the government have killed too many people. The Taleban are just killing Pakistani soldiers in response. The Taleban are good. If the government targets them, only then they will fight back. Otherwise they will just fight the Americans and not trouble the Pakistani army. Everyone here is against the Americans.

I asked Shehzad about how the Taleban spread their influence and enforced their authority.

They started with a few men, often ones they had recruited from round here coming back here, and going round the *hujras* and mosques, talking quietly about the Taleban and what they want, and persuading people to support them. Then, when they thought they had enough support and could start acting, they put up banners and posters all over this area saying what they will not allow, telling people to be good Muslims. If you sell alcohol or drugs or do other bad behaviour, the Taleban will warn you twice and then if you don't change or leave, they will take you to a Shariah court and execute you, or maybe let you off with a fine and a beating. In Mansuqa, a nearby village, a local mullah publicly mocked the Taleban and was killed by them a few weeks ago.

Although appointed by the *maliks*, the mullah of the family mosque, Zewar, endorsed these views.

That afternoon, I went out to talk to people on the streets and in the shops of the village and, with rare exceptions, it was the same picture. I talked to forty-eight people in all in that village, and every single one of them sympathized with the Afghan Taleban. All but seven also sympathized with the Pakistani Taleban. Those seven – local shopkeepers plus one visiting minor civil servant – condemned them categorically for their attacks on the Pakistani army and police. But it was difficult to say just how deep this condemnation went, since they too – as far as I could make out from the shouting match which developed on several occasions – often blamed such actions on Indian agents.

As afternoon drew towards evening, I sat with my hosts on their verandah as the family of the mullah came to pay their respects, with a mixture of deference and affectionate familiarity. Some of the herd of clerical offspring came to be admired and patted on the head. Afterwards, my host, a compact middle-aged man in the neatly pressed *shelwar* of the civil servant, with a military-style clipped moustache, began to speak in confident tones of the struggle against the Taleban – and indeed it seemed that he had little idea of the state of feeling in the village, or even among his own servants.

He said that he had not heard of any preaching or other activity by the Taleban in the neighbourhood, and he was sure they did not have majority support. 'If the government really wants to get rid of the Taleban it can; it just needs to be ruthless. In the end, they are just a few troublemakers.' But as the shadows lengthened, so his mood darkened:

> It is true that the local police have largely given up, so nobody is doing much to stop the Taleban. People think that the present government and all the political parties are corrupt, and do nothing for the people, and the worst thing is that it is true. So people may not support the Taleban, but they have become indifferent, and that is also bad . . .

This, remember, as of September 2008 was supposed to be not a Taleban area, but a peaceful area under government control. By the end of my stay I had come to the conclusion that all this really meant was that, unlike in Swat or other areas, the Pakistani Taleban had not publicly announced their takeover or attacked government positions. Yet already, in a nearby village, the Taleban had seized the *hujra* of a local *malik* politician from the ANP and turned it into a Shariah court, and the *malik* and his family had had to flee to Peshawar. 'And they will never come back,' I was told, 'because once you have shown that you are scared, people don't respect you any more, so you can no longer lead even if the Taleban are defeated one day.' I was reminded of a saying I had once heard about life in an American prison, that this was a world in which, 'if you once take a step back, you will never take another step forward'.

As far as public opposition, state authority or the power of the *maliks* and their mullahs were concerned, there seemed little enough to stop the Taleban if they did decide to take over in that village. Remembering my Russian landowning ancestors in similar circumstances, I was left with the hope that perhaps old ties of kinship and respect would mean that the local Taleban would not directly target their *maliks*, or at the least would eventually allow them to depart in peace.

However, as will be described in the next chapter, this pessimism proved exaggerated. The Pakistani state and army still do have the resources to fight back effectively against the Taleban; and perhaps, equally importantly, the Taleban, like many revolutionary movements, are chronically given to overestimating their strength and overplaying their hand. In the spring and summer of 2009, this hubris led to nemesis for the Taleban of the Swat valley.

12

Defeating the Taleban?

No patchwork scheme, and all our recent schemes, blockades, allowances etc. are mere patchwork, will settle the Waziristan problem. Not until the military steam roller has passed over the country from end to end will there be peace. But I do not want to be the person to start the machine.

(Lord Curzon, Viceroy of India 1898–1905)[1]

By the summer of 2008 things were therefore looking fairly bad in the Pathan areas. It was not of course as bad as the Western media portrayed it – I had been warned before travelling to Peshawar that the city was 'under siege' and close to falling, but in fact I spent a month based in the city and never felt under direct personal threat.

Nonetheless, the sense of crisis was real. It was to be felt above all in the business community, many of whose members were making plans to leave if it became necessary. For example, smaller businessmen who would never have dreamed of this in the past were beginning to sell property to finance their sons' education in Britain or America, so as to lay the basis for the whole family to move later. Even a tough ex-brigadier of my acquaintance admitted to me later that he had sold some of his land and bought property in Karachi instead, 'just in case'.

Big businessmen were also seriously worried. When I visited Noman Wazir, CEO of Frontier Foundries, the biggest steel-mill in the NWFP, he broke off in the middle of our interview to give orders to his chief of staff, a retired military officer, about buying Kalashnikovs. 'We have to get arms. Talk to the SSP [Senior Superintendent of Police]. Use any kind of political pressure to get the licences. You know what to do.'

Mr Wazir's factory is situated on the Jamrud Industrial Estate in

Hayatabad, the western suburb of Peshawar on the very edge of the Khyber Tribal Agency. Naturally, therefore, of all the areas of Peshawar Hayatabad is the most lawless and the most penetrated by the Taleban. Beside the main road I saw a sign – a common one in Peshawar these days: 'My husband Shahir Ishaq has been kidnapped for three months and the government has done nothing.'

I asked Mr Wazir if he had given up completely on the police. 'No, not completely,' he replied.

> But they desperately need help. Look, there are about 22,000 police in the NWFP, with about 8,000 modern weapons for all of them, very few vehicles, very poor communications and terrible pay. So it's hardly surprising they are not doing well. Even if the government had much more money, it would take years to improve them. So the private sector has to look after itself.

When I returned to Peshawar almost a year later, in July 2009, the mood had improved considerably. This was odd in a way, because terrorism in the city had actually got much worse. The Pearl Continental Hotel had been wrecked by a car bomb despite its heavy security, suicide bombings were growing in scale and becoming more indiscriminate, and the number of kidnappings and murders had risen to the point where I was told even by more resilient friends that to stay in my usual guest-house would be extremely dangerous (so I stayed most gratefully at the Frontier Constabulary Mess instead). Since then, bombs on an unprecedented scale have caused hundreds of casualties. The terrorists have also become far more indiscriminate, planting bombs in bazaars and outside hospitals, rather than, as before, concentrating on state and military targets.

The difference was not the level of violence, but the end of the sense of helpless drift that had gripped the city during my visit in 2008: the feeling that the army and the government (state and provincial) were more and more losing the initiative to the Taleban, and had no plan at all for getting it back. In fact, a determined counter-offensive had already begun in the Bajaur Agency to the north of Peshawar, but it was not clear if it would continue or would end in negotiations like so many military offensives before it. Above all, the growing Taleban hold on the district of Swat seemed to herald a move of the rebels out from FATA (which after all had never been under real state authority) and into the 'settled areas' of the NWFP.

In July and August 2009, by contrast, despite the insecurity and violence, there was a general feeling that the military and the authorities had finally got a grip on the situation and demonstrated that they were determined to fight, and that, whatever happened, the Taleban would not be allowed to seize control of Peshawar and its valley. Business confidence had returned, and there was less talk of people leaving. For this, a range of new state policies and actions was responsible – but above all, it was due to the military counter-offensive in Swat in the late spring and summer of 2009.

The counter-offensive against the Taleban indeed provides something of a classic example of the Pakistani response to really serious threats: the eventual selection, from the hordes of more or less useless Pakistani public servants, of a small number of brave and able men; the concentration, from Pakistan's heaps of squandered public finances, of enough money to support a major operation; the belated unity of the political, economic, administrative and military elites in the face of a common existential danger; the brutal but in the end brutally effective manner in which the struggle has been conducted; the way in which most of the operation has been conducted outside the constitution, the law and the regular administrative and political structures; and the central role of the army not just in the military operation but every other area.

Unity among the elites was essential, because the near-paralysis of the summer of 2008 in the Pathan areas affected every area of the state, and was largely due to the bitter divisions between the political parties, the military and the civil service. For this various factors were responsible: the slow death of the Musharraf presidency (he resigned on 18 August 2008) and the struggle over the succession, which dominated the attention of the political party leaderships and governments; the tradition of bitter distrust between the military and the ruling parties in both Islamabad and Peshawar; and the awareness of everyone concerned that tough military operations against the Taleban were opposed by the majority of the population, especially in the Pathan areas.

PUBLIC OPINION AND THE TALEBAN

The following fact has been widely ignored in the West, probably because it raises a very uncomfortable issue: namely, that Western governments and the Western media believe that they want to promote democracy in Pakistan, but that they have pressed upon Pakistani governments a co-operation with the West in the 'war on terror' which most Pakistani voters detest. Pakistani politicians, however – who need those voters' votes – obviously could not be indifferent to this dilemma, or, at least, not until the threat from the Taleban to themselves became so grave and so obvious that they felt that they had no choice but to fight back. For a long time, therefore, all the main actors on the Pakistani political stage, including Musharraf, the military, the intelligence agencies and the political parties, tried to avoid tough action against the Pakistani Taleban, while at the same time not breaking with the United States. Each at the same time tried to put the blame on the others for the failure to confront the Taleban.

For reasons that have already been explained, these feelings were especially strong among the Pathans, and are closely related to their opinions of the Afghan Taleban struggle. I thought that I might find some more hopeful signs at Peshawar University, which is both a centre of ANP and PPP support, and the site of whatever progressive feeling exists among Pathan youth in the province. In any case, it is always nice to visit Peshawar University. Its green and beautiful grounds are like a drop of perfume squeezed out as if by God's hand from the hard and gritty fabric of Peshawar. They remind one why, for all the great monotheistic religions that emerged from the arid Middle East, paradise is a garden.

Next door is the Islamia College, from which the university originally grew, a magnificent complex of British buildings in neo-Mughal style, set in even more beautiful gardens under the shade of giant chenars (oriental plane trees). The whole represents a successful attempt by the British to blend Oxford or Cambridge with the lost glories of Peshawar before the Sikh conquest, glories still lamented by Peshawaris. A successful attempt architecturally, that is – not, alas, intellectually. I visited the university and Islamia College twice, in May 2007 and August 2008, and if things did not seem to have got much worse between those two dates as far as student and faculty opinion was concerned, that was only because they were so bad already.

In May of 2007, thanks to the kind invitation of Professor Taqi Bangash, I spoke with thirty-one history students at the university. Just over half were girls. Eight of them wore the *niqab*, which half veils the face up to the nose, a bit like a bandit's mask, three were in full *burqas*, and four wore headscarves but with faces uncovered. Only one went wholly unveiled, in sharp contrast to old photographs from the 1960s and 1970s I saw in the department, where many of the girls were unveiled.

Despite repeated invitations from me, the women on this occasion played very little part in the conversation. One exquisitely beautiful girl with perfectly chiselled features in a bright pink *shelwar kameez* and headscarf sat throughout in perfect stillness and silence, so like a rose in every way that I was sorely tempted to giggle. The only voluble and intelligent exception was a visiting student from Iran – another small sign that as far as women's rights and participation are concerned, the West has not understood the nature of the balance between Iran and the 'pro-Western' states of the region.

There were considerable differences among the students concerning the level of their sympathy for the Afghan Taleban and their Pakistani allies; but on two things there was unanimity. I asked them the following: 'If there are free and fair elections and a democratic government is elected; and if this government agrees with Washington to launch a military operation against the Taleban in FATA, would you support or oppose this?' The response was, by a show of hands: oppose, twenty-nine; support, nil. By the same token, all of them supported peace deals between the Pakistani government and the militants; and all said that if the US sent troops into FATA, the Pakistani army should fight them. This group of students included Jamaat and JUI supporters, but also PPP and ANP activists.

There was unanimity too in the loud burst of applause which greeted the words of one of the Islamist students, Gul Ahmed Gul, a handsome young man with a neatly clipped beard, more like an old school left-wing student activist:

> When you go back to Washington, please tell the Americans to leave Afghanistan and let us sort out our own problems, because, as long as they are there, people will fight against them. The Americans must pay more attention to what local people want. We do not want more Americans to die, but we also do not agree to Americans coming to this part of the world to kill our fellow Muslims, whatever American reasons for this may be.

With the obvious exception of the Iranian girl, all of the students agreed that 'We and the Afghans are one people.'

Perhaps because the students spent most of the time asking me questions rather than giving their own views, the conversation on that occasion proceeded along more or less rational lines. In August 2008 I revisited the university and the Islamia College to meet with both students and staff, and I'm afraid that my notebook contains a suggestion of mine for their joint motto: 'Unity in Idiocy'. This was despite the fact that the Islamia College, as its name suggests, is a hotbed of Jamaat and JUI support, while the Area Studies Centre of the university, where I spoke in the morning, is a leading intellectual centre of the ANP.

The previous day, an acquaintance of mine, the chief political officer at the US Consulate in Peshawar, had been ambushed by Taleban gunmen on the same street as my guest-house in University Town, and saved by her armoured limousine. I can't say that my patience during the discussions at the Centre was improved by hearing in the opening remarks by the Centre's head, Professor Azmat Hayat Khan, that, 'Of course, the Americans carried out that attack themselves so as to give themselves an excuse to invade Pakistan.' To approving murmurs from his colleagues, he added:

> Four thousand American mercenaries are operating in FATA. They are the ones carrying out the ruthless killings there, not the Taleban. We have proof of this. Four days ago, eighteen bodies of Americans were brought to the morgue in Peshawar. We know that they are not Taleban or Muslim because they are not circumcised. Russians, Chinese, Iranians are all supporting the Taleban against us, for their own reasons. As for Britain and the US, Professor Lawrence Freedman predicted that it is their policy to cause anarchy in Pakistan so as to achieve their goals.[2]

It was easy to check on this, since Sir Lawrence happens to be the vice-principal of my college in London. There was of course no truth in it – but then, there was no truth in the morgue story either. As to the American mercenaries, if Peshawari opinion is to be believed, FATA must be getting pretty crowded, since people there think that thousands of Indian Sikhs and Israeli agents are also there pretending to be Taleban, alongside the Russians, Chinese and Iranians. I also heard stories to the effect that the entire battle between the Pakistani military and the Taleban was faked and that *all* terrorist attacks were in fact being carried out by the ISI – and the people who told me this included not just uneducated people on the street but a lawyer and member of Pakistan's Human Rights Commission!

In fact, to my considerable chagrin as a British subject, the only major country not accused in my presence of sending its troops to pretend to be Taleban was Britain. I'd hoped that this was the result of Pathan hospitality and unwillingness to offend a guest, but I'm sorry to say that when I asked a Pathan friend about this he replied that 'I'm afraid that it's really that people here now see America and Britain as the same thing.'

That afternoon, I got another dose of conspiracy theory from someone at the other end of the political spectrum, Syed Zahir Shah, Professor of Botany at the Islamia College, a charming old man with a silken white beard, who his students told me is a member of the Jamaat party. To the same murmur of approval from colleagues as at the Area Studies Centre, he told me:

> The Pakistani Taleban were created by the big powers, the US, Russia, Israel and India, so as to destroy Pakistan. It is not Pakistanis who are carrying out these terrorist attacks. It was the same with Benazir Bhutto. No Pakistani or Muslim killed her. She was killed because she was a strong political leader, and India, Israel and other foreign forces don't want Pakistan to be stable.

Like many other people in Peshawar he produced for me 'proof' of a secret plan by the Bush administration to partition Pakistan. This turned out to be a map published by Ralph Peters, a retired US lt-colonel who writes a column for the *New York Post*, a tabloid, who has held no official position in any US administration. When I pointed out to the professor that the Pakistani Taleban had in fact taken public responsibility for the terrorist attack on the Pakistani munitions factory at Wah the previous week, which had killed almost 100 ordinary Pakistani workers, he changed tack and declared: 'Yes, but they have their reasons. Their women and children have been killed by Pakistani bombs dropped on the orders of America.'

If these were the views and the intellectual standards of professors from both the secular and the Islamist parties, then it is hardly surprising that much of the general public also had much sympathy for the Taleban and none at all for the US, and that the entire public discourse in the NWFP is so sodden with ludicrous conspiracy theories as often to be barely minimally rational.

In part these conspiracy theories are the work of the army itself, which (so I have been told by senior officers in private) has been spreading the line about India's role in an effort to discredit the Pakistani Taleban. This, however, seems to have backfired badly, in that so many people can now blame Taleban terrorism on 'foreign hands', and thereby continue to believe in the 'good' Taleban which does not do such things. Echoing similar views from a great many ordinary people, the correspondent for the *Nation* newspaper in Faisalabad, Ahmed Jamal Nizami, told me in January 2009:

> All the suicide bombings in Pakistan are the result of operations in which Pakistani or US forces kill women and children; and some of them like the Marriott were carried out by RAW [the Indian government's Research and Analysis Wing – i.e. the Indian intelligence service]. Pakistani agencies have proof that the truck came from the Indian embassy.[3]

This sort of attitude was very widespread among Pakistani journalists with whom I talked in 2008–9, and was obviously reflected or at least hinted at in their reports and analyses – with disastrous results for the willingness of their audiences to support military action against the Taleban. This explains why the army's action after April 2009 in getting a grip on the Pakistani media was so important to the struggle against the Pakistani Taleban.

THE ANP AND THE TALEBAN

Responding to the views of its own followers, and of the Pathan and indeed Pakistani electorate in general, the ANP therefore stood in the elections of February 2008 on a platform of negotiating peace with the Taleban. This corresponded to the ANP's Pathan nationalism, and horror at the thought of conducting what would amount to a Pathan civil war within Pakistan. The ANP was also influenced by its traditional hostility to both the United States and the Pakistani army, and its unwillingness to launch such a war in alliance with these forces.

These attitudes were so deeply rooted that they persisted for more than a year after ANP politicians in Swat and elsewhere began to be killed by the Taleban in large numbers. From their election to the NWFP government in February 2008 to the counter-offensive in Swat in May 2009 the ANP's policy towards the Taleban therefore presented a picture of utter confusion, of calling for tougher military action while bitterly condemning every action that caused civilian casualties, and of attacking the military for covert links to the Taleban while continuing to pursue talks with the Taleban themselves. In the end, for political and cultural reasons that I will describe, this approach turned out much better than might have been expected; but in the summer of 2008 it contributed greatly to the mood of paralysis and pessimism gripping Peshawar.

This was very apparent from a debate on the conflict in Swat on 19 August 2008 in the Provincial Assembly in Peshawar that I attended. The building itself is splendid but also somewhat confusing, as so often in the former colonial territories of the Muslim world: gleaming white neo-classical columns support an ornate neo-Mughal roof covered with Urdu calligraphy. Somewhat to my alarm, my British passport and white face led to my car being waved through the security checkpoint with no search for explosives or weapons.

Speaker after speaker, from government and opposition alike, rose to lament the situation in Swat. The only things that almost all agreed on were that the Americans should withdraw from Afghanistan; that within Pakistan, the central government and above all the army were to blame, either for causing collateral damage, or for secretly helping the Taleban, or both; and that the Pakistani justice system needed radical reform, including through the extension of the Shariah.

Abdul Akbar Khan, the leader of the PPP in the assembly, took the strongest anti-military line of all – though he was the man who in theory should have been representing the central government, which had declared its desire for the closest co-operation with the military. In fact, though, as I sensed from Abdul Akbar, and as I found openly in talking to other PPP deputies, as well as PPP activists on the street, their loathing of Zardari was such that they no longer really saw themselves as linked to the central government, and they certainly tried to play this link down in private.

Abdul Akbar even hinted that it was the army itself, and not the Taleban, who were destroying girls' schools in Swat (despite the fact that the Taleban had publicly taken responsibility, and in a number of cases had expelled the pupils and seized the schools as headquarters instead of destroying them). This was a charge which an ANP leader had made explicitly to me in private the previous week. 'Why are the schools being destroyed not during the day, but in the night when there is a curfew and only the military can move freely?' he had asked. 'Isn't the answer obvious?'

Perhaps the most striking example of the extremely complex ANP attitude to the Taleban and the army came in an interview I had in January 2009 with Bushra Gohar, an ANP member of the national parliament in Islamabad and a distinguished Pakistani feminist. Here, if anywhere, I expected to find a really tough approach to dealing with the Taleban, given their own savage hatred of everything that she represented.

Ms Gohar is indeed a striking individual, with an intelligent, humorous face, short iron-grey hair and a general style that reminded me somewhat of my younger sister, a barrister in London. Burbles and hoots from a small relative in the background were a cheerful descant to our rather grim discussion. For the first half hour we spoke about women's issues, and she displayed a most impressive mixture of intelligence, commitment and pragmatism.

Then we got on to the Taleban, and for me at least the rationality of her views disintegrated. She declared that 'we can't talk to the Taleban unless they lay down their arms', but on the question of how to make them do that, it seemed that the Pakistani army should do everything and nothing. She blamed the military for not attacking the Taleban, but also for using too much violence and killing civilians. She declared that the Pakistani army should act to shut the Afghan Taleban training camps in Waziristan, but also that she was firmly opposed to military operations in Waziristan. When I asked her how then the camps could be shut, she replied that 'Everyone knows that they are run by the ISI. The ISI has only to give the order, and the camps will be shut.'[4]

THE POLICE AND THE ARMY

Given attitudes like these in the NWFP government, it was not surprising that morale in the NWFP police in the summer of 2008 had reached dangerously low levels. As one of the force's commanders admitted:

> We have largely lost the institutional memory that we used to have, and we have very little good intelligence coming in ... Real policing, going out and finding out what is happening, has become virtually non-existent. We are policing by the seat of our pants, not going about it in an organized and professional manner, but just reacting to what happens.

I interviewed some of the same junior police officers in both August 2008 and July 2009, and the change in their mood was a useful indicator of how things in general had changed in the city over the intervening year. In August 2008 I spoke to two assistant sub-inspectors of police (ASIs) from Hayatabad, the western suburb of Peshawar, about the situation in what the London police would call their 'manor'. Both men were in their early twenties: Asif with a round, bearded face like a cheerful pirate, Mushtaq clean-shaven, darker and more formidable-looking. 'Security here is getting worse day by day,' Mushtaq said. 'The Taleban drive by our police station in pick-up trucks, showing off their Kalashnikovs and rocket-propelled grenades, and we are not allowed to do anything about it. Our orders are not to arrest them, to shoot only if they shoot at us first. It's terrible for our prestige!'

To which Asif replied urgently, 'Yes, but, Mushtaq, they are so much better armed than we are! If we attacked them, you know what would happen. Even if we won that fight, they would come back at night and destroy our station. Much better to ignore them.' Humiliating, no doubt, but also without doubt entirely correct. As a righteous Westerner I should have supported Mushtaq; actually my human sympathies were all with Asif.

But when I met Asif again in July 2009, his mood had improved considerably.

> A year ago, things were getting worse day by day, but now they are a bit better. For example, we have orders to open fire on the Taleban on sight. This order came after the military operation started in Swat. There was a wave of shootings and bombings in response, but still it is better that we began to fight ... The public mood has also changed. In the past, when we asked people for information about the Taleban they would shut their doors. Now, when the Taleban come to an area we are quickly informed about them ... Our pay has also increased, though not nearly enough. With bonuses, an ASI now gets Rs14,000 a month and a constable Rs9,000 [compared to a mere Rs6,000 in 2008]. It is not nearly enough for the risks we run, but better than it was. Though it is still not as much as the Taleban pay their fighters – they get Rs12,000–15,000.

What Asif told me reflected what a top police officer in Peshawar had told me eleven months earlier about what the police needed to do:

> We have to reoccupy the land, start policing places on the ground and delivering security to the people. The US has given us two computers, but that doesn't help much and nor do Western police advisers – what the hell

do they know about the realities of this society? Whenever you give us something we just come up with highfalutin' phrases which satisfy you, and you have no idea whether anything has really changed. This isn't what is necessary. What's necessary is that the IG [Inspector-General – head of the provincial police] and other senior officers should pick up guns and go out themselves on operations. A constable on Rs7,000 a month won't risk his life if his officers are not there with him.

I mentioned the plaques to fallen British police officers in the cathedral. 'Exactly,' he replied. As so often when meeting with senior policemen in Pakistan and India, a slightly uneasy, even uncanny feeling came over me at the contrast between this highly intelligent, courteous and candid figure and the reputation of the force to which he belongs.

In this case, the uncanny feeling was increased by the fact that the officer with whom I was speaking bore a quite remarkable resemblance to the late David Niven in middle age: aquiline, humorous features, balding head, clipped moustache and equally clipped accent. In fact, being rather light-headed from running around in the heat of a Peshawar August, there were moments during the interview when I imagined that I actually was watching David Niven playing a police officer of the British Raj; and, for that matter, if such an officer had been suddenly reincarnated and joined in our conversation, I do not suppose that he and his Pakistani successor would have found much to disagree about.

This officer was a leading proponent of the creation of special police brigades to hold territory against the Taleban after the army has cleared it. These would be paid at higher rates than the rest of the police (whose pay should also be raised radically) and equipped to the same level as the Rangers and other paramilitary units under the army. He said that the creation of such brigades would improve morale and reduce what he admitted was a really serious problem – the leaking of information to the Taleban by police sympathizers. 'Only a few really support the Taleban ideology, but a great many share the view of the population that this is not Pakistan's war.'

I was reminded of what a senior policeman in Karachi had told me a few years before: that when he received orders to carry out an operation to catch Islamist terrorists, he made the plans with only two trusted colleagues. 'All the rest get the orders when they are already in the jeeps and close to the destination – otherwise, every operation we planned would be blown in advance.'

By July 2009, the Inspector-General of Police in the NWFP, Malik Naveed Khan, said that 2,500 elite police had been trained, and had contributed to a great improvement in the situation. The police were also training and equipping special community police to defend their areas against the Taleban – 'not like *lashkars*, because these are chosen, armed and controlled by us, so there is no risk of them changing sides or becoming dacoits'. He said that, thanks to all this, the increase in pay and the sense of new determination from the top, police morale had improved enormously over the previous few months. Above all, though, he said, the change in mood was due to the Swat operation, and the transformation of civil–military relations which it reflected.

As of the summer of 2008 these had been as bad as could well be imagined. The politicians' views of the army have already been described. A retired colonel of my acquaintance exploded in response:

> Those bastards! If we are supporting the militants in secret, how come more than 1,500 of us have been killed fighting them? It is the politicians who are running scared and doing deals with the militants. They just don't know who they are more scared of, Washington or the Taleban. So they run to Washington and whine and grovel, and then they come back and order us to fight harder. Then when we do and people are killed, they get scared of their voters and put all the blame on us. They declare a truce and start peace negotiations again with the Taleban, and all the gains we have made at God knows what cost in lives go up in smoke. For months now, Kayani [General Ashfaq Kayani, chief of the army staff in succession to Musharraf] has been asking for clear political support for military operations and from all the ANP and most of the PPP has got nothing but shuffling excuses. Are you surprised we have military coups in this country?

A senior serving officer speaking in Peshawar in August 2008 was more measured:

> We have never received clear political backing for military operations against the Taleban because no one is willing to take responsibility for civilian deaths and displacement. After all, it is not easy for any government to take responsibility for creating hundreds of thousands of refugees among its own people. But I must say that this was also true of Musharraf, not just of the civilian politicians who have taken over. That is also why we need special anti-terrorism forces which don't cause so much collateral damage

as the army, because we are trained for full-scale war and don't really know how to do things any other way, though of course we try to keep civilian casualties as low as possible.

Another problem to which the general drew attention was the unreliability of the Frontier Corps, the locally recruited paramilitary police, or *khassadars*, and the Frontier Constabulary, who are supposed to patrol the line between FATA and the NWFP.

> The Frontier Corps men are linked to local tribal society. That is why they are essential, because they know what is happening, so provide vital intelligence. Also, using non-Pashtun troops is very unpopular, as we found in 2004. But the problem is that they hate killing their own people, above all when many people say that this is for the sake of America. If enough of them are killed by the militants, they will often fight back; but they have been fighting for five years now and are very tired and becoming demoralized. As for the *khassadars* and the Constabulary, they are now useless. They just sit in their posts and do nothing.

This tension between local knowledge and local loyalty is an old one. The British, who created the units out of which the Frontier Corps was formed, fully recognized the desirability of using local troops whenever possible, and most of the troops stationed in the region were in fact locally recruited. This also meant that the British faced repeated mutinies and desertions whenever really serious trouble flared with the local tribes, and often had to disband their Pathan units.[5] Similarly, since 2004, the Frontier Corps has seen repeated incidents of units refusing to fight or even deserting en masse to the Taleban. This reflected not just Pathan affinities but also a history of the Frontier Corps being underfunded and poorly equipped compared to the regular army (and not included in the benefits of the Fauji Foundation). By 2010 this was beginning to change, but, like the NWFP police, the FC had still received astonishingly limited help from the US – even in the area of effective modern body armour.

THE TURNING POINT

Faithful to its electoral promise of making peace with the Taleban, and responding to the will of its electorate, in February 2009 the ANP government of the NWFP negotiated a settlement with the Taleban of Swat based on the adoption by the national government of the Nizam-e-Adl ('System of Justice') regulation for Swat and the adjoining districts of the Malakand administrative division. This stipulated the exclusive rule of Islamic justice in Swat District, as well as an amnesty for all Taleban fighters there – in effect conceding Taleban control of much of the district. In return, the Taleban were to cease attacks on the army, police and local population.

According to the agreement, they were also supposed to lay down their arms, though no one seriously expected this to happen. On the contrary, there was a widespread expectation that the Taleban would use Swat as a training ground for the jihad in Afghanistan. On 13 April, the agreement was passed into law by the National Assembly in Islamabad, and signed by President Zardari. To judge by media reports and my own interviews, it enjoyed the support of the overwhelming majority of Pakistanis, the Mohajirs of Karachi being the only large-scale exception.

As will be seen, on paper at least the Nizam-e-Adl agreement was much less unprecedented, radical and extensive than appeared at first sight. The local Taleban certainly saw it that way, pointing out that it only covered justice, whereas a true Islamic system covers all aspects of life, including government, politics and economics. Responding to the will of the electorate, all the parties in the National Assembly except for the MQM voted for the agreement. However, it elicited immense criticism in the Western media and among Pakistani liberals, who saw it as a catastrophic defeat for the Pakistani state, as the de facto surrender of control over Swat to the Taleban, and even as part of an inexorable march of the Taleban that could take them to power in Islamabad, just as the Taleban in Afghanistan had swept from province to province in the 1990s.

In fact, however, the Nizam-e-Adl agreement proved to be the start of what appears to be an important turning point in the Pakistani state's struggle with the Taleban – not the beginning of the end, but at least the end of the beginning, as Churchill said. Oddly enough, this was because the Taleban shared the liberals' and the Western media's assessment of the extent of the government defeat; and because both the Taleban and the West ignored the critical role of Pakistani and Pathan public opinion in the shaping of events and of policy.

On that score, two Pathans who played critical roles in the fight against the Taleban said very similar things to me in August 2008. One was Afrassiab Khattak, the most famous ANP intellectual and chief adviser to the ANP chief minister. The other was Lt-General Masoud Aslam, officer commanding XI Corps in Peshawar in 2008–9 and therefore in effect commander of the army's fight against the Taleban in FATA and Swat.

At that point, Dr Khattak was ferociously critical of the military's performance, and General Aslam for his part, though more discreetly, criticized the politicians for their failure to 'take ownership' of the fight against the Taleban. Both however emphasized the vital importance in Pathan culture of being seen to try sincerely to negotiate a peace settlement before resorting to arms – if you wanted to have public opinion on your side in the battle. General Aslam had served in Waziristan in 2004–5 and had this to say about dealing with the Taleban:

> The problem is this damned *pashtunwali*, which the people follow, and everyone who wants to operate effectively here has to respect. Most of the ANP are deeply influenced by it, progressives though they say they are. The *pashtunwali* includes this tradition that if people come asking for peace, you have to talk to them whatever has happened before. So then a jirga is held. And they talk. You know how they talk. They talk not just all day and all night, but all week and all month. And even if the army has started in a position of strength, with time your position gets weaker and your prestige goes down. Your men are sniped at, your vehicles are burned. And the morale of your men goes down, because they are just sitting there being shot at and not allowed to do anything in response. Meanwhile the militants say, 'Oh, it wasn't us, we will try to catch the miscreants, who knows who they are, maybe the ISI is responsible.' In Waziristan in 2005 the talks went on for three months, and by the end of it we were in a much weaker position than when we started ...

It's true that you do have to be seen to talk genuinely and honestly before you strike really hard. Many of our own men are Pashtuns and they expect this. It is essential to put the militants in the wrong, to convince ordinary people that it is the other side which is breaking the peace. So the ANP government is right to negotiate. But to negotiate from a position of weakness is a disastrous mistake. The tribesmen respect *nang* [honour] but *nang* is based on *nom* [name, prestige]. And that means showing that you can use force: use it early, use it hard, but use it discriminately. That is why burning the houses of miscreants is a good old Pashtun tradition. This is how the religious leaders enforced their authority. It is not something that you wicked Brits thought up. The tribesmen see this, and say to themselves, 'Ah, they know who did what. I had better be careful.'[6]

From the point of view of Pathan culture and public opinion, the Nizam-e-Adl agreement, so much criticized at the time, contributed enormously to the reversal in the Taleban's fortunes – but only because the Taleban also misinterpreted it to mean that they were winning and the army was on the run. Four Taleban actions in particular were responsible for transforming public opinion concerning the need to fight against the Taleban.

First, the Taleban and other Islamist groups allied to them began to extend their campaign of terrorism from the Pathan areas to Punjab. The bombing of the Marriott Hotel in Islamabad on 20 September 2008 was a forerunner of this, and a shattering blow to the complacency that had hitherto reigned among many of the Pakistani elites. In the winter and spring of 2009, attacks began in Lahore, including most notably an attack on the visiting Sri Lankan cricket team on 3 March that left six policemen dead, and an attack on the police training academy on 30 March that killed twelve.

These attacks cruelly exposed the unpreparedness and vulnerability of the Punjab police, and brought home to the ruling classes in Lahore that the Taleban were not just a bunch of traditionally unruly Pathan tribesmen on the far-off Frontier, but were a real threat to themselves. When I visited Lahore in September 2008 immediately after my stay in the NWFP, I was shocked by the complacency and indifference of Lahoris of every class of society. When I returned in January 2009 this had begun to change a bit, but the real transformation came between then and my next visit in July 2009.

The second Taleban mistake – though one that was so bound up with their ideology and revolutionary purpose as to be inevitable – was the public caning of a seventeen-year-old girl for 'immorality' in Swat by the Taleban. Captured on a mobile phone camera, this film was very widely shown on Pakistani television in early April (with strong urging by the government and military), and caused general revulsion. However, the responses of the elites and of ordinary people with whom I spoke were rather different. Educated Pakistanis were outraged that it had happened at all; ordinary Pakistanis, that such punishment had been carried out in public before a male audience, when such punishments should be carried out in private and by the girl's own family.

On 19 April, Sufi Muhammad Hassan, an Islamist leader whom the government had released from jail in return for a promise to negotiate a settlement with his son-in-law, Swati Taleban leader Maulana Fazlullah, made a speech in Swat in which he declared that 'We hate democracy . . . We want Islam in the entire world. Islam does not permit democracy or election.' He also stated that there could be no appeal from Shariah courts in Swat to Pakistan's higher courts (he had been saying the same things for many years, but the Pakistani media had never really taken notice before). Also widely reported in the media, this showed Pakistanis that the Taleban were by no means just good Muslims interested in promoting Islamic behaviour and Islamic justice (which many non-Islamists throughout the NWFP and Punjab had persisted in believing), but aimed at overthrowing the existing state and imposing their own rule.

It must be said, though, that, to judge by my interviews, the effect of all this among the Pakistani masses was somewhat less than government and military propaganda have suggested. So these developments alone would not have provoked a mass backlash or a strong counteroffensive against the Taleban. The tipping-point came in the second week of April 2009 when the Taleban sent hundreds of their fighters from Swat across the mountains into the neighbouring district of Buner, to the south-east. A completely insignificant place in itself (historically part of the Swat princely state) Buner therefore came to play an important role in Pakistani history.

Although Buner is only 70 miles from Islamabad, there are an awful lot of mountains in between, and no one in Pakistan seriously thought that its fall indicated that the Taleban were simply going to sweep on and take the capital. However, the capture of Buner brought the Taleban much closer to the motorway linking Islamabad and Peshawar, and to the Tarbela dam, which provides northern Pakistan with much of its electricity. The immediate and complete collapse of the local police in the face of the Taleban, and the easy routing of a local *lashkar*, were profoundly worrying. 'They really seemed all set to go on to take Mansehra and Abbotabad,' Major Tahir, a staff officer in Swat, told me later.

Most of all, I was told by officers, the fall of Buner produced a feeling in the army high command that the military's prestige was now on the line; that if they failed to fight back now, people would begin to think that they would never fight. Not just ordinary Pakistanis but even Pakistani soldiers (especially in the Frontier Corps) would begin to look on the Taleban as the winning side, whom it would be wise to conciliate or even to join. At the same time, the army was encouraged by what officers described to me as a '180-degree change' in the attitude of the ANP government and local politicians to military action.

Finally, the fall of Buner made it even more difficult to resist the growing pressure from Washington to take tougher action against the Pakistani Taleban. Pakistanis were stung by a speech by Secretary of State Hillary Clinton on 6 March describing the internal security situation in Pakistan as 'threatening' and hinting that it might collapse as a state. The fact that Pakistan desperately needed US aid, and goodwill in producing international aid, of course contributed greatly to the belief in the Pakistani establishment that something had to be done to please Washington. China, too, previously fairly relaxed about the growth of militancy in Pakistan, reportedly became alarmed by the Taleban's takeover in Buner, and communicated this alarm to the Pakistani government.[7] However, this outside pressure would not in itself have brought about a change in Pakistani behaviour, if the actions of the Taleban themselves had not produced a new sense of will in the political and military establishments, backed by a significant shift in public opinion.

It is difficult to say whether it was the army, the federal government under the PPP and President Zardari, or the NWFP government of the ANP who took the initiative in pressing for a counter-offensive, because, when it turned out to be a success, all tried to claim the chief responsibility. In fact, what seems to have happened is that all of these groups contained leading figures who for the past year had been pressing for a counter-attack; and the Taleban seizure of Buner empowered them to push this through against the resistance of hesitant colleagues.

The result was not just a counter-offensive in Buner and Swat, and then in south Waziristan, the Mohmand Agency and elsewhere, but a general tightening of policy and behaviour across the board. The army rigorously excluded journalists from the fighting zones, ensuring that they could not report Taleban views. Moreover (so I have been told by journalists) they used commentators and television anchors with military links to persuade or pressure them into supporting the military operations, making the same approach to media owners – who by this stage were themselves becoming alarmed by the Taleban's rise, and the possible effects on their own fortunes.

A senior journalist in Peshawar described to me how on 27 April General Kayani invited him and eleven other Pathan journalists to see him and asked them for their backing in the coming military operation in Swat. Above all, he asked them in their reporting to play down the issue of collateral damage and civilian casualties, which had made previous operations so unpopular, and this they promised to do.

The change in media coverage was crucial to the change in Pakistani public opinion. Prior to this, the media had given extensive coverage to Taleban statements, and indeed had often given them equal time with official statements by the government and military. Contrary to allegations by Pakistani liberal publications like the *Friday Times*, this was not in general because of outright ideological support for the Taleban, but rather a reflection of Pakistani public opinion in general, which was prepared to see certain good sides in the Taleban and which tended to blame the Taleban and the government equally for violence.

The media of course also love a good scoop, which interviews with the Taleban often gave them. Finally, the media are just as addicted to conspiracy theories as the rest of Pakistani society and, like that society, for years had tended to accompany reports of Taleban terrorism with heavy hints about 'foreign hands' and conspiracies by the Pakistani intelligence services – which is only to say that before April 2009 the Pakistani media in their coverage of the Taleban were neither better nor worse than the society from which they came. All of this changed considerably when the army and state finally put their feet down.

The ANP also belatedly began to exercise real leadership as far as its own supporters and activists were concerned, ordering them to support the military operation and to stop criticizing the military for civilian casualties or alleged ties to the Taleban. Instead, ANP propaganda began stressing the number of ANP politicians who had been killed by the Taleban, and the Taleban's threat to democracy in the NWFP. The change in the language of my ANP acquaintances concerning the army between August 2008 and July 2009 was truly astonishing. An additional reason, in the view of Major-General Ishfaq Ahmed, commanding the army in the Malakand division, was that 'the new Chief of Army Staff [i.e. General Kayani] played a big part in this, because he made clear that he is not interested in a political role, so the politicians are no longer scared of us'.[8]

THE BACKGROUND TO REVOLT IN SWAT

The Islamist militants' takeover in Swat in 2007–9 was widely seen as a sign that they could extend their control from the tribal areas into the 'settled areas' of the NWFP, and further towards Islamabad. Much was made of the fact that Swat had previously been a tourist destination (I was told in August 2009 that I was the first Western tourist to visit the bazaar in Mingora for more than two years), and even, in the 1960s and 1970s, a stop on the 'hippy trail'. All of this was rather misleading. Swat has a very specific history, different alike from the tribal areas and from the rest of the NWFP. The Islamists' takeover was not a question of the 'Taleban' moving into Swat from outside, but of an overwhelmingly local movement which, while it placed itself under the name and banner of the Pakistani Taleban, remained completely autonomous.

Key to understanding the militants' temporary success in Swat are three factors: a tradition of Islamist militancy in the region stretching back to the mid-nineteenth century; the nature of the princely state of Swat, which retained a semi-independence until 1969; and the way in which Swat was incorporated into Pakistan.

Despite social change in recent decades, Swat remains to a considerable extent a tribal society in which the Yusufzai Pathans dominate. As elsewhere in the Pathan lands, religious figures have wielded great authority. The Akhund of Swat (1794–1877) in the mid-nineteenth century was followed by the remarkable religious dynasty of the Mianguls, who for the first time created stable monarchical rule over the Swat valley. The British accepted and backed the Mianguls as rulers, partly because they were effective in crushing or expelling Islamist extremists (the 'Hindustan fanatics' or 'Mujahidin') who wished to use Swat as a base to carry out jihad against the British. Pakistan inherited the British protectorate, but in 1969 (twenty years after India had abolished its princely states), princely rule was ended and Swat was incorporated into Pakistan.

The law the princes exercised was based on a mixture of local tribal custom and the Shariah called *rivaj*, but – especially under the last prince (or Wali), Jehanzeb – they also created an autocratic but enlightened government which did a great deal to bring education and economic development to Swat. The small size of the population meant that the Walis could hand out judicial and administrative decisions directly to much of the population.

Justice was *be Dalila, be Wakila au be Apela* (without argument, without advocate, and without appeal) but was quick, cheap, transparent, generally fair, and above all in accordance with the local people's own conceptions of justice. In a telling comment, Behrouz Khan, a native of Swat and correspondent for Geo TV in Peshawar, described the last Wali as 'basically a kind of aristocratic Mangal Bagh' (in a reference to the Islamist warlord mentioned in the last chapter) – dealing out autocratic, ruthless but popular justice leavened with humour.[9]

It is a very depressing comment on the quality of the Pakistani governmental, political and legal systems that every single person with whom I spoke in Swat – every single one, including Pakistani officials and officers – said that Swat had been better run under the last Wali, and that, in particular, the administration of justice had been far superior. As an army major (not a Swati) told me:

> The merger of 1969 had a very bad effect on Swat. The Wali ruled with justice and fair play. He guaranteed all the amenities of life for the people. But from 1969 to the present, every Pakistani government has failed to administer justice and meet the needs and the aspirations of the people. So older people in Swat used to tell their sons and daughters how much better things had been before.

This deep public respect for the Wali's memory led the Taleban to spare the homes of the old royal family in Saidu Sharif, despite their hatred for the landowning class in general. A certain Pathan nationalist element was also present in the nostalgia for independent Swat. It had been a Pathan state under Pathan princes, using the Pashto language for administration and justice; whereas in the NWFP as in the rest of Pakistan, the local language had been eclipsed in government, higher education and social status by either English or Urdu.

A historian of Swat, Sultan-i-Rome, writes that while under the old system the Wali and officials took direct responsibility for government, under the Pakistani system no one did. Merger led to ruthless exploitation of forests and plunder of natural resources and a huge increase in corruption. This amounted to 'a sort of colonization of Swat by which it lost its separate identity, which had stood for centuries, if not millennia'.[10]

This history is of immense importance in explaining what happened in Swat, and why the militants' temporary seizure of power in Swat is not necessarily a forerunner of similar developments elsewhere. Maulana Fazlullah, who in 2007 placed his movement under the aegis of the Pakistani Taleban, seems to have dreamed of re-creating the princely state as an independent Islamic emirate like Afghanistan under the Taleban, with himself as Emir.

The memory of Swat state left the population with a deep sense not only of the corruption and injustice but of the basic illegitimacy of the Pakistani judicial system. In consequence, within a couple of years of the merger with Pakistan, local figures were already calling for the adoption of the Shariah instead of Pakistani state law. These included men such as Dani Gul, who had led the democratic opposition to the Wali's autocracy, but soon became bitterly disillusioned with Pakistan.

These feelings were increased by the twists and turns in Swat's constitutional position within Pakistan, and especially its judicial system. From 1969 until 1974, Swat had no constitutionally recognized judicial code at all. In 1974, Swat and the other former Pathan princely states were named Provincially Administered Tribal Areas, or PATA. They came under the NWFP, but had a different legal system, including a stronger role for jirgas. Then in 1994, the Pakistani Supreme Court declared this arrangement unconstitutional and decreed the full incorporation of these territories into the Pakistani judicial order.

In response, in 1995, a local Islamist group, the Tehriq-e-Nifaz-e-Shariat-e-Mohammedi (TNSM) or Movement for the Enforcement of Islamic Law, launched mass protests in Swat and other areas of the Malakand Division in support of their demand for Shariah law. The protests blocked roads and government offices were seized. Several dozen people were killed, mostly in the resulting state crackdown. However, the national government of Benazir Bhutto backed down and agreed to a limited role for the Shariah in the administration of justice in the Malakand. The Nizam-e-Adl agreement of 2009 was therefore not nearly as new or as radical as most people assumed.

The TNSM's founder, Maulana Sufi Muhammad, was a former local

Jamaat Islami leader who had split from the party in 1992 in disgust at its opposition to armed revolution. Sufi Muhammad was arrested in 1994 but later released when he ordered his followers to call off their protests, and (doubtless with official encouragement) in the course of the 1990s became a prominent local mobilizer of support for the Afghan Taleban.

The TNSM also had close links with the Pakistani militant groups in Kashmir, where one of Sufi Muhammad's chief lieutenants, Ibn-e-Amin, fought with Jaish-e-Mohammed in the 1990s. He and other TNSM commanders had previously fought with the Mujahidin in Afghanistan in the 1980s – and one reason, I was told, why agitation for Shariah law had not happened much earlier was that so many local militants were away in Afghanistan.

The role of TNSM leaders in these conflicts involved close links to the ISI; and while I do not believe that the ISI promoted the TNSM in Swat for nefarious reasons of its own, there is a great deal of anecdotal evidence to suggest that they intervened on occasions in 2007–8 to save particular TNSM leaders (presumably old allies) from being arrested by the army or police. Less clear is whether these links played any part in discouraging the army from taking tougher action.

In 2001, when the US invaded Afghanistan, Sufi Muhammad inspired thousands of his followers and new volunteers to fight there, and a very large number perished. In November 2001, at US insistence, the Musharraf administration imprisoned him again, and in February 2002 the TNSM was banned, together with other Islamist organizations.

However, the ban was not strictly enforced, and Maulana Fazlullah, Sufi Muhammad's son-in-law, took over as the TNSM's leader. He forged links with the emerging revolt in FATA, and gradually strengthened and armed the movement in Swat. Fazlullah and the TNSM made effective use of the Kashmir earthquake in 2005, partly by effective relief work, but also by portraying it as God's punishment for Pathan sins. He spread the TNSM's message partly though effective broadcasts on his local secret radio station, which gained him the nickname 'Mullah FM'.

The expansion of TNSM power was made possible in part by the presence of the MMA Islamist government in Peshawar, which strongly discouraged tough action against them, and in particular by the MMA-appointed Commissioner of the Malakand division, Syed Muhammad

Javed, who is widely accused of having been a Taleban sympathizer. He was arrested in May 2009 for abetting the rebellion (though some officials have told me that he had been made an innocent scapegoat and that he was simply implementing government policy), and was released again in October 2009.

In July 2007, infuriated by the government's attack on the Red Mosque in Islamabad, Fazlullah led the TNSM in open revolt, gained control of much of Swat and instituted Shariah courts under TNSM control. He had first declared war on the government in Swat in January 2006, when his brother, who was fighting with the Taleban on the Frontier, was killed in the US drone attack on a suspected Al Qaeda headquarters at Damadola in Bajaur. Fazlullah blamed the Pakistan government for helping the US, and vowed to take revenge.

Initially, as elsewhere, the TNSM/Taleban won much local popularity by eliminating local drug-dealers, kidnappers and other criminals whom the Pakistani police had been unwilling or unable to deal with. However, the Taleban then began attacks on local officials, policemen, military personnel and politicians. Their campaign of attacks on girls' schools – which they declared un-Islamic – was so ferocious that even a spokesman for the Tehriq-e-Taleban Pakistan (TTP) begged them to desist. After the formation of the TTP, Fazlullah announced the adherence of the TNSM to the Taleban, while retaining full local autonomy.

In November 2007, the Pakistani army launched a major counter-offensive, which captured and destroyed Fazlullah's headquarters and drove him and his men into the hills, from where they continued terrorist attacks. However, following the election of the ANP in February 2008, the new ANP government of the NWFP insisted on ending the operation and beginning negotiations with the Taleban. Sufi Muhammad was released from jail after renouncing violence and promising to mediate in negotiations. He did indeed manage to negotiate a ceasefire in May 2008, but the result was that Fazlullah and his followers returned to the Swat valley in force and took a savage revenge on local people who had supported the military actions against them. The local population not surprisingly became convinced that neither the politicians nor the army was serious about fighting the Taleban, and would not protect local people who opposed them. In the words of Major Tahir of the army staff, 'people decided that the Taleban were here to stay and they had better get along with them'.

The result was increasing TNSM/Taleban control of Swat. Clashes with the military resumed in the summer and continued for the next six months, with hundreds killed and hundreds of thousands fleeing to the plains. Among the dead were a number of local leaders of the ANP and PPP, and many other local politicians and their families were driven out of Swat. In all, 238 schools were destroyed (mainly those for girls but including some for boys) out of 1,540 in Swat, and others were occupied and turned into militant bases.

The TNSM/Taleban forces which created this mayhem do not seem to have been especially well armed, at least to judge by the captured weapons which the army showed me in Mingora. As one would expect, their most dangerous asset by far was the Improvised Explosive Device (IED), several of which were on display, in some cases with remote-control mechanism. There were several dozen AK-47s and a few rocket-propelled grenades. However, there were also a large number of old bolt-action rifles, shotguns and pistols, some of them dating back to the Victorian era. In Swat at least it does not seem to have been TNSM/Taleban weaponry that brought them their successes, but their ability to melt into the population, strike at unguarded or lightly guarded targets, terrify the police into inactivity, and run rings round the army.

This violent stand-off with the army in Swat continued until the negotiation of the Nizam-e-Adl agreement in February 2009, by which Shariah law became the only legal code in the Malakand Division. This agreement was welcomed by the great majority of ordinary Pakistanis with whom I have spoken, and the overwhelming majority of Swatis. In the case of the Swatis, this was not only because they wanted peace between the Taleban and the army, but also because they actively prefer the Shariah to the Pakistani legal system. Indeed, as of early 2010 the Nizam-e-Adl is still in force in Swat, and most people wish for it to remain so.

Interestingly, however, Fazlullah and the local TNSM/Taleban seem to have interpreted this agreement in exactly the same way as the West and the Pakistani liberal media – namely, as a sign that the Pakistani state and army were on the run and could be driven from one district after another. The resulting hubris led to their move into neighbouring Buner, which triggered their nemesis – the massive counter-offensive of the army against them.

By mid-summer of 2009, the military had driven the TNSM/Taleban from the Swat valley, captured hundreds of their activists, and – according to military figures – killed some 1,200 of them. However, the cost to the civilian population had been high. Though the military seems to have done its best to keep civilian deaths to a minimum, and damage in the city of Mingora itself was slight, villages where the TNSM/Taleban made a stand were heavily bombarded. Estimates of civilian casualties range from several dozen to several hundred, and more than 1.5 million people – a majority of the district's population – fled from the fighting. By the end of the year almost all had returned – only to be displaced again the following August by the floods which swept down the Swat valley from the deforested mountains, destroying much of the region's remaining infrastructure.

VISIT TO SWAT

I visited Swat again (more than twenty years after I had gone there for a peaceful holiday) in August 2009, over two months after the army counter-offensive had begun. The army had cleared the Taleban from the Swat valley itself, and according to military figures by mid-August had killed or captured some 2,000 militants, while losing almost 200 of their own men; but another 3,000–4,000, led by their chief commanders, had taken refuge in the surrounding hills, and began to launch suicide bombings and occasional assassinations. However, in the four days that I spent in Swat and Buner I did not hear a single shot or explosion – a sign of the extent to which the army had regained control of the valley. Over the following months, the army managed to kill or capture many of the remaining Swati commanders.

The road leading up to Swat from Mardan and the plains is itself a reminder of the region's turbulent past. To reach the Swat valley, you have to cross the dramatic Ambela pass, where in 1863 local tribesmen under the banners of Islam fought a long battle against a British invading army. The British eventually dislodged them from the heights, but accepted a compromise settlement and did not occupy the valley itself (three centuries earlier, a Mughal army dispatched by the Emperor Akbar had met disaster in an attempt to subdue the Yusufzais of Swat).

The reason for the British expedition had been to force the expulsion from the region of a group of Islamist militants (the surviving followers of Syed Ahmed Barelvi, mentioned in Chapter 1), whom the British called 'Wahabis' and 'Hindustan fanatics'. These had been raiding Brit-ish-controlled territory and attempting to stir up rebellions among other Pathans. How the hopelessly outgunned Swatis managed this is easy enough to see: the bare mountains rise almost sheer from the valley below, and a road hacked out from the mountainside crawls along their face. Viewed from the opposite hillside, the trucks carrying refugees back to their homes in Swat looked small as beetles. Then you cross the pass, and look down into the beautiful Swat valley, a sort of giant oasis with the Swat river meandering through it, fringed by willows and clumps of waving feather grass. In August 2010, this river became a raging torrent of destruction.

One of the reasons the floods of 2010 were so destructive is that the population has grown so much and settled in places always known to be vulnerable to flooding. The capital, Mingora – still quite a small town when I visited it in the 1980s – has suffered like everywhere else from the runaway growth of Pakistan's population, and now is just another overcrowded semi-slum with between 300,000 and 450,000 people (as usual, no one knows for sure). When I first arrived, it smelled terrible, because of uncollected rubbish; but, by the time I left, municipal workers in laminated jackets were beginning to clear things up. Damage in Mingora itself was very limited; the Taleban had not tried to make a stand in the town, and the army had taken care not to bombard it.

Talking to people on the streets in Mingora was not very enlighten-ing. Fear of the army was very obvious, and I had a strong sense of everyone looking over their shoulders to see who might be listening. Everyone said that they supported the military and hated the Taleban. Interviews with people from Swat in the Jalozai camp for displaced people near Peshawar a fortnight earlier had given a rather different impression (the ones conducted out of the hearing of the camp admin-istration, that is).

They all described how popular the TNSM had been when the move-ment first started, because of their advocacy of the Shariah, their administration of harsh but fair justice, and their actions against cor-rupt and oppressive local politicians and landlords; but also because of the great prestige that many local people attached to their participation in the jihads in Afghanistan and Kashmir. All said that they supported Shariah law for Swat and wanted the Nizam-e-Adl agreement to remain in force.

A large majority said that their sympathy for the Taleban had declined sharply over the previous year. For this they gave various reasons. Among the most common were that after the Nizam-e-Adl agreement the Taleban had shown that they were not really interested in the Shariah but in power for themselves. Many people mentioned the petty and not-so-petty harassment of local people and the offences against local traditions of dancing and singing at weddings, and so on. Particular offence had been caused by young Taleban boys stopping older men in the street in front of their families and ordering them to stop trimming their beards. 'In our Pashtun culture, we show respect to our elders,' one man growled.

The TNSM/Taleban also established a growing reputation for savagery, which frightened people into silence but also deeply shocked them. The IDPs (Internally Dispaced Persons) mentioned two cases in particular (not, interestingly enough, the public caning of the girl which caused so much offence among educated people elsewhere in Pakistan). One was when the Taleban publicly hanged four local policemen in the main bazaar in Mingora to frighten the rest of the police into surrender – 'and they were just local men, we didn't know anything bad that they had done,' as one IDP said.

The other incident that caused great disgust was the TNSM/Taleban's treatment of Pir Samiullah. He was a leading hereditary religious figure from the Barelvi tradition and guardian of his family shrine at Mangal Dagh, and had led local opposition to the Taleban. It was not the fact that the TNSM/Taleban killed him that caused the disgust, but the fact that they later dug up his body, hung it in public for three days, and then blew it up with explosives, scattering bits for hundreds of yards – in order to shatter the mystique attached to the body of a *pir*. 'To kill your enemy is one thing,' I was told by local people, 'but to desecrate his body, that is not Muslim and not Pashtun.'

On the other hand, quite contrary to government propaganda, sympathy for the Taleban had by no means evaporated altogether. A majority of those I spoke with in the Jalozai IDP camp near Peshawar, albeit a small one, still blamed the army and the Taleban equally for the violence and destruction that had taken place, and said that the government should still try to make peace with the Taleban. 'In the end, this is all America's doing,' an old man said. 'They have brought this war to Pakistan.'

This impression was confirmed by a local schoolteacher to whom we gave a lift on the way to Swat from Ambela. He said that when the TNSM first appeared, the vast majority of the local population supported them, but that most had changed their minds as a result of their fanaticism and when it became apparent that they wanted power for themselves. Still, he said that 15–20 per cent of people continued to support them, and this estimate was backed in private by officers and local journalists with whom I talked.

MINGORA TO DOROSHKHEL

Some of the reasons why a good many local people blame the army and the TNSM/Taleban equally became apparent on a drive up the Swat valley from Mingora to the village of Doroshkhel near Matta about a third of the way up the valley, where I went to see a local ANP leader, Afzal Khan Lalla. Along the way, we passed numerous destroyed buildings, some on their own, others clustered together where battles had been taking place.

As we went, my guide gave me a running commentary:

> That building there was a hotel owned by an ANP politician. The Taleban burned it last year ... That was a Taleban madrasah which the army destroyed ... Those houses over there were destroyed by shelling when the army attacked in June ... That used to be a girls' school which the Taleban destroyed ... Those shops over there were owned by a Taleban sympathizer. The army blew them up last month ...

I began to see the differences between houses destroyed from above by bombs or shellfire and those blown up from below by explosives. Major Tahir told me candidly:

> We have demolished more than 400 houses belonging to Taleban members. Destroying houses in this way is an old punishment among Pashtuns. And seeing their homes demolished, local people are encouraged. They see that this time we are really serious about fighting the Taleban.[11]

No doubt this is true, but it is also easy to see how an ordinary inhabitant of the Swat valley might feel that his or her neighbourhood was suffering equally from the two sides and call a plague on both their houses. In addition, according to a solidly researched report of Human Rights Watch published in July 2010, the army in Swat has been carrying out a very considerable number of extra-judicial executions of captured Taleban and suspected Taleban supporters. Human Rights Watch said it had firm evidence of 50 such killings, and had been told of 238 in all.[12]

The widespread use of extra-judicial executions was confirmed for me in an off-hand way by Afzal Khan. Immediately after my interview with him, he went to sit in a jirga with elders from the nearby Sakha side-valley. They were trying through Afzal Khan to negotiate the surrender of the local Taleban commander in their valley, named Gul Yar (whom most of them had reportedly supported), so as to avoid attack by the army. I asked what terms they were trying to negotiate: 'Well, firstly of course that the army should not shoot him out of hand, because that is what they do with most Taleban commanders they capture,' I was told.

I met Afzal Khan in his ancestral village of Doroshkhel. Afzal Khan is not in fact the staunch ANP loyalist that ANP propaganda since 2008 has tried to make out. Like so many Pathan landowning politicians, he has repeatedly moved between parties, and sometimes stood as an independent, depending on circumstances and personal and family advantage. In 2009, a nephew was a minister in the ANP government in Peshawar and other relatives were scattered through the national and provincial assemblies.

Long before I visited Swat, ANP leaders whom I met in Peshawar were presenting Afzal Khan as an iconic ANP figure, for one reason and one reason only: he had stood his ground in the face of the Taleban, when most of the ANP and other politicians in the area had been driven out by them. This flight was very understandable in view of the number of politicians killed by the Taleban, but in a culture which has traditionally prized physical courage above any other virtue, it has nonetheless done them and the ANP terrible damage.

Afzal Khan's reputation for courage was not undeserved. It is true that his village and the compound of his extended family were defended not only by his own followers but by the Pakistani army; but it is also true that this determined eighty-two-year-old great-grandfather stayed on leading his men after he had been wounded in an ambush in which two of his guards and his nephew were killed. It probably helps his public image that he certainly looks the part of a chieftain. The garden of his home in Doroshkhel could have been an English garden, on an English summer afternoon – if you can imagine an English garden with a machine-gun nest in one corner, and sitting in the other an owner who bears a strong resemblance to a giant bald-headed eagle.

Pathan features are often on a large scale (and the noses of ANP politicians sometimes seem to be growing in sympathetic if hopeless emulation of the epic hereditary protuberances of their ruling dynasty, the Wali Khans), but whether in reality, or because of his rather overwhelming character, Afzal Khan's nose, ears and eyebrows seemed truly enormous. I must also say, however, that if set of eyes and shape of mouth are anything to go by, like many a chieftain Afzal Khan owes his leadership not only to his courage and determination but to a very considerable capacity for ruthlessness.

This was indeed his reputation in Swat long before the TNSM began their rebellion, and it brings me to one key element in the Taleban's appeal, which seems especially marked in Swat: that of class resentment and even of class war. This was of course fervently denied by Afzal Khan and other politicians with whom I spoke, but I heard it from a great many other sources, including Pakistani army officers. Since the end of Swat state, as agriculture has become more commercialized, so certain landowning khans have used their power to encroach on the lands of weaker neighbours. This also helped to increase loathing of the Pakistani judicial system.

As I was told:

> A khan politician would use his gunmen to seize some poor farmer's land and his political connections to stop the administration doing anything about it. Then he would say to the farmer, 'Sure, take me to court. You will pay everything you have in bribes, you will wait thirty years for a verdict, and the verdict will still be for me. So what are you going to do about it?' Well, when the TNSM came up, that farmer could do something about it. He joined them.

Such behaviour was by no means true of all or even most khans, but it was widespread enough to cause great resentment.

The TNSM/Taleban never adopted land reform as a formal part of their programme, but they used their power to redress local grievances like the one just described, recover seized land for the poor and drive out unpopular landlords. This social radicalism was related in complex ways to their appeal to non-Pathan communities in Swat, the Gujjars and Kammis, who make up a large though undefined proportion of Swat's population.

The Gujjars were originally a nomadic tribe in the plains of northern India. In Swat, they had traditionally been tenants of the Yusufzai Pathan tribe which had dominated the valley since the sixteenth century (indeed, in Swat and elsewhere, 'Pathan' and 'landowning farmer' were traditionally synonyms). The Kammis were a service caste of bakers, barbers, butchers, artisans, and so on, probably of Hindu origin. They had traditionally not farmed land or even owned their houses. However, with the breakdown of the old order, Gujjars and even Kammis had acquired land of their own, while remaining especially vulnerable to oppression by the Pathan khans.

The TNSM/Taleban never made an explicit public appeal to Gujjars and Kammis against the Yusufzai Pathans – they could not possibly have done, being overwhelmingly Yusufzais themselves. Given Yusufzai dominance, such an appeal would also have been fatal to the militants' chances. Rather they did two things: by stressing their ideological commitment to an egalitarian community of all Muslims, they appealed to Gujjar and Kammi sentiments in a looser and vaguer way; and they redressed – often savagely – particular acts of oppression by khans against these communities.

Thus I was told that more than a decade before the TNSM rebellion began, the son of a khan had abducted and raped a Kammi girl, and had of course never been prosecuted for this. He had already fled, but the Taleban burned down his family home and drove them out, saying that this was overdue punishment for the rape, 'and, of course, that got all the Kammis of the neighbourhood on their side'.

As a result of the army crushing the Taleban in Swat in 2009, the old khan families, good and bad, are coming back – and it remains to be seen if the bad ones have learned a lesson from what happened to them, or whether they will simply use the army to restore their power, take revenge on their enemies and resume their old oppressions. This is a danger which has some Pakistani soldiers of my acquaintance seriously worried. Structures of local wealth and authority in Swat have been further damaged by the floods of 2010. All of this suggests that while the army's reconquest of Swat in the summer of 2009 has proved that it will fight to preserve Pakistan and that Pakistan will therefore be preserved, it will not be the end of Islamic militancy in this region.

This is also demonstrated by the progress of fighting in FATA. The Pakistan army's reconquest of Swat was followed by offensives in south Waziristan and other areas of FATA which regained much territory and killed some 570 Pakistani Taleban fighters (76 soldiers also died). The Pakistani Taleban response was greatly to intensify their terrorist attacks inside Pakistan and make them even more indiscriminate.

By February 2010, according to official figures, 7,598 civilians had died in Pakistan, as a result of terrorist attacks, Taleban executions, military action, or US drone attacks. It is worth noting that this figure is two and a half times the number of Americans killed on 9/11. By that time, 2,351 soldiers had been killed – two and a half times US military deaths in Afghanistan.[13] According to Pakistani official estimates (which may of course be exaggerated) by mid-2010 the conflict with the Pakistani Taleban and their allies had cost Pakistan some $35 billion dollars in state spending and economic losses – almost twice the $18 billion in US aid that Pakistan had received by that date.

During the same period, according to the Pakistani military, the Pakistani Taleban and their allies had lost 17,742 men killed or captured – though how many of these were real fighters rather than sympathizers is impossible to say. What can be said is that, despite all this, as of late 2010 the militants remained in control of much of FATA; and, also, that the Pakistan military seemed highly unwilling to attack them in some areas like north Waziristan – apparently because this would risk bringing the Pakistani forces into conflict with the Afghan Taleban and their allies (especially the followers of the Haqqani clan) based in these areas. So despite the much tougher approach to Pakistan's own Taleban threat in 2009–2010, action against the Afghan Taleban continued to be limited by all the factors set out in this book, and this in turn limited to some extent action against Pakistani militants, at least in FATA.

The continued strength of militancy in these areas is, however, not due chiefly to constraints on the Pakistani military. As in many other Pathan territories in Pakistan and Afghanistan, the roots of Taleban support are far too old and deep to be eradicated by military action alone – yet the Pakistani political parties, civilian bureaucracy and private businessmen all seem very far from being able to back up military action with real local development, let alone a more equitable political and judicial system. By 2010, the threat that militants would push the Pakistani state into collapse had been defeated – in so far as it had ever existed; but terrorism and local unrest will be with Pakistan for the foreseeable future.

Conclusions

It should be clear from this book that Pakistan, though a deeply troubled state, is also a tough one; and that, barring catastrophic decisions in Washington, New Delhi – and of course Islamabad – it is likely to survive as a country. In the long run, the greatest threat to Pakistan's existence is not insurgency, but ecological change. However, Pakistani farmers are also tough and adaptable, and while some areas like the Quetta valley are likely to suffer disastrous water shortages in the near future, in the country as a whole, drought will take several decades to become truly catastrophic; and floods, though devastating in the short term, can also be controlled and harnessed given determination, organization and money. This allows time for human action to ameliorate the impending crisis, if the West, China and of course Pakistan itself have the will to take this action.

The rest of the world should work hard to help Pakistan, because, as I have emphasized, long after Western forces have left Afghanistan, Pakistan's survival will remain a vital Western and Chinese interest. This should encourage co-operation between Beijing and Washington to ensure Pakistan's survival. By contrast, a Sino-US struggle for control over Pakistan should be avoided at all costs, as this would add enormously to Pakistan's destabilization.

In the short term, of course, Western policy towards Pakistan will be shaped by developments in Afghanistan, but this policy should not be dictated by those developments. For Pakistan is in the end a great deal more important and potentially dangerous than Afghanistan. Whatever strategy the US ends up adopting in Afghanistan, Pakistan will be critical to its success. Quite apart from Islamabad's strategic calculations, this is made inevitable by the fact that more than half of the Pathan ethnicity lives in Pakistan, while maintaining a strong interest in what happens to the Pathans on the other side of the Durand Line.

Whatever happens, Pakistan will therefore insist both that Pathans are strongly represented in any Afghan regime, and that Islamabad has a share of influence in Afghanistan, at least to the point where other countries – meaning above all India – cannot use Afghanistan as a base from which to threaten Pakistan.

No conceivable short-term gains in the Western campaign in Afghanistan or the 'war on terror' could compensate for the vastly increased threats to the region and the world that would stem from Pakistan's collapse, and for the disasters that would result for Pakistan's own peoples. Though many Indians may not see it this way, the collapse of Pakistan would also be disastrous for India, generating chaos that would destabilize the entire region. Western and Indian strategy towards Afghanistan and Pakistan should therefore be devised with this fact firmly in mind.

This should include recognition, at least in private, that it has above all been the US-led campaign in Afghanistan which has been responsible for increasing Islamist insurgency and terrorism in Pakistan since 2001. By this I do not mean to advocate a humiliating US and British scuttle from Afghanistan, nor to suggest that a Western withdrawal from Afghanistan would end the extremist threat to Pakistan, a threat which has long since developed a life of its own. Nonetheless, concern for the effects of the US military presence in Afghanistan on the situation in Pakistan is one of the strongest arguments for bringing that presence to an end as soon as this can honourably be achieved, and against conducting more wars against Muslim states under any circumstances whatsoever.

This also implies that the US should observe restraint in its pressure on Pakistan. Drone attacks on Pakistan's tribal areas have killed many Taleban and Al Qaeda leaders, but they have not noticeably impaired the Afghan Taleban's ability to go on fighting effectively, while causing outrage among Pakistanis – especially because of the very large numbers of women and children who have also been killed by the attacks. The US ambassador to Pakistan, Anne Patterson, discussed the risks of the drone strategy in a cable sent to the State Department in 2009 and revealed by WikiLeaks. She acknowledged that drones had killed ten out of twenty known top Al Qaeda leaders in the region, but stated that they could not entirely eliminate the Al Qaeda leadership and, in the meantime:

> Increased unilateral operations in these areas risk destabilizing the Pakistani
> state, alienating both the civilian government and military leadership, and

provoking a broader governance crisis within Pakistan without finally achieving the goal [of climinating the Al Qaeda and Taleban leadership].[1]

The well-substantiated belief that – despite official denials – the Pakistani high command and government have provided information to the US in return for strikes against Pakistani Taleban leaders has also been confirmed by WikiLeaks. As Prime Minister Yusuf Raza Gilani told US officials in August 2008, 'I don't care if they do it as long as they get the right people. We'll protest in the National Assembly, then ignore it.'[2]

Pakistani acquiescence in the drone strikes, however, damaged the prestige of the military in society and the morale of ordinary soldiers, and encouraged the perception of the military as a 'force for hire'. There should therefore be no question of extending the attacks to new areas of Balochistan or Khyber-Pakhtunkhwa, which would further enrage local society, spread the Pakistani Taleban insurgency to new areas, and reduce existing Pakistani co-operation with the US.

Even more dangerous is the presence of US special forces on the ground in Pakistan. Reports of this in Pakistan are greatly exaggerated. According to the US embassy cables released by WikiLeaks, as of October 2009 only sixteen such US soldiers were deployed in Pakistan, to two Pakistani military bases in north and south Waziristan. While they are doing some useful work against the Taleban, they are also potential hostages to fortune, and likely to provoke mass anger at their presence in the population and the military.[3]

Above all, as this book has argued, there must be no open intervention of US ground forces in FATA, as this risks outright mutiny in the Pakistani army. This restraint should be observed even if the US comes under new terrorist attack. Britain should use whatever influence it possesses in Washington to oppose any such interventions, which could have the most disastrous effects on both terrorism and ethnic relations within Britain itself.

Pakistan's links to the Afghan Taleban, hitherto seen in the West overwhelmingly as a problem, should also be seen as potentially a critical asset in the search for an exit from Afghanistan. We might as well try to use Pakistan in this way, since, as the US embassy in Islamabad reported gloomily but accurately in September 2010:

> There is no chance that Pakistan will view enhanced [US] assistance levels in any field as sufficient compensation for abandoning support to these

groups [i.e. the Afghan Taleban and their allies] which it sees as an important part of its national security apparatus against India. The only way to
achieve a cessation of such support is to change the Pakistani government's
perception of its security requirements.[4]

The US and other Western countries fighting in Afghanistan should
use Pakistan as an intermediary to initiate talks with the Taleban in the
hope of eventually reaching a settlement, if, as seems highly probable,
the attempt to defeat the Taleban by force does not succeed. Because of
its links with the Taleban, Pakistan will have to play a key role in bringing about such negotiations. In 2010 the Obama administration began
to move towards the idea of talks, but still seemed very far away from
a recognition of what such talks would really entail. In the words of a
senior Pakistani diplomat:

> The US needs to be negotiating with the Taliban, those Taliban with no
> links to al-Qaida. We need a power-sharing agreement in Afghanistan and
> it will have to be negotiated with all the parties . . . The Afghan government
> is already talking to all the stakeholders, the Taliban, the Haqqani network,
> Gulbuddin Hekmatyar, and Mullah Omar. The Americans have been setting
> ridiculous preconditions for talks. You can't lay down such preconditions
> when you are losing.[5]

Such a Western strategy should also stem from a recognition that Pakistan's goals in Afghanistan are in part legitimate – even if the means by
which they have been sought have not been – and this legitimacy needs
to be recognized by the West. The US and EU should work hard to try
to reconcile legitimate Pakistani goals in Afghanistan with those of
India, and to draw other regional states into a consensus on how to
limit the Afghan conflict. China, close to Pakistan and fearful of Islamist
extremism, could be a key player in this regard.

The US needs to continue to limit Indian involvement in Afghanistan
if it is to have any hope of a long-term co-operative relationship with
Pakistan. The West also needs to seek a peaceful solution to the Kashmir
dispute, despite all the immense obstacles in both Pakistan and India. As
Ambassador Patterson told her government:

> Most importantly, it is the perception of India as the primary threat to the
> Pakistani state that colours its perceptions of the conflict in Afghanistan
> and Pakistan's security needs. The Pakistani establishment fears that a

pro-Indian government in Afghanistan would allow India to operate a proxy war against Pakistan from its territory . . . Increased Indian investment in, trade with, and development support to the Afghan government, which the USG [US government] has encouraged, causes Pakistan to embrace Taliban groups as anti-India allies. We need to reassess Indian involvement in Afghanistan and our own policies towards India . . . Resolving the Kashmir dispute would dramatically improve the situation.[6]

The overall question of the future of US–Indian relations is far too broad to be discussed here. What can be said is that a balance needs to be struck between the economic and security benefits to the West of closer ties to India and the security threats to the West stemming from a growth of Islamist militancy in Pakistan. In the end, not even the greatest imaginable benefits of US–Indian friendship could compensate for the actual collapse of Pakistan, with all the frightful dangers this would create not just for the West but for India too.

We should also not dream – as US neo-conservatives are apt to do – that India can somehow be used by the US to control Pakistani behaviour. The truth, as outlined by Ambassador Patterson, is exactly the opposite. Only Pakistanis can control Pakistan, and the behaviour of the Pakistani security establishment will always be determined by what they see as the vital needs of Pakistan and the Pakistani army.

A new approach to Pakistan over the future of Afghanistan should therefore be part of a much deeper long-term engagement with Pakistan by the West in general, and one tied not to the temporary war in Afghanistan but to the permanent importance of Pakistan as a state. This is crucial for Britain in particular, whose large minority of Pakistani origin retains extremely close ties with Pakistan and forms an enduring organic link between the two countries, and, through Britain, to Europe and North America.

Whatever happens, this human link is not going to go away. To help make it a force for good rather than a danger, the west needs to develop a much deeper knowledge of Pakistan, a much deeper stake in Pakistan, and a much more generous attitude to helping Pakistan. I hope that by showing Pakistan in all its complex patchwork of light and shadow, this book will help to bring about such a new approach.

Notes

I INTRODUCTION: UNDERSTANDING PAKISTAN

1. Tariq Ali, *Can Pakistan Survive? The Death of a State* (Penguin, London, 1983).
2. Pierre Lafrance, in Christophe Jaffrelot (ed.), *Pakistan: Nation, Nationalism and the State* (Vanguard Books, Lahore, 2002), p. 339.
3. Interview with the author, Lahore, 8/1/2009.
4. My attention was drawn to this fascinating statistic by Dr Shandana Mohmand of the Lahore University of Management Sciences (LUMS).
5. Alison Shaw, *Kinship and Continuity: Pakistani Families in Britain* (Harwood Academic Publishers, Amsterdam, 2000), p. 99.
6. Ibid., p. 154.
7. Stephen M. Lyon, *An Anthropological Analysis of Local Politics and Patronage in a Pakistani Village* (Edwin Mellen, Lewiston, NY, 2004).
8. Quoted in Muhammad Azam Chaudhary, *Justice in Practice: The Legal Ethnography of a Pakistani Punjabi Village* (Oxford University Press, 1999).
9. Sudeep Chakravarti, *Red Sun: Travels in Naxalite Country* (Penguin, New Delhi, 2009).
10. Chaudhary, *Justice in Practice*; Lyon, *Anthropological Analysis*.
11. On the initiative of the ANP provincial government, the province was officially renamed Khyber-Pakhtunkhwa in April 2010, to reflect its majority Pathan population, known in their own language as Pakhtuns or Pashtuns. However, since it was known as the North West Frontier Province during the period of research for this book, and during the historical and recent events I describe, I have kept the old name.
12. See Joshua T. White, *Pakistan's Islamist Frontier: Islamic Politics and US Policy in Pakistan's North-West Frontier* (Centre on Faith and International Affairs, Washington, DC, 2007).
13. Graham Greene, *Our Man in Havana* (Penguin, London, 1978), p. 151.
14. Pervez Musharraf, *In the Line of Fire: A Memoir* (Free Press, New York, 2006), p. 126.
15. *Broken System: Dysfunction, Abuse and Impunity in the Indian Police*, published 4 August 2009, on http://www.hrw.org. See also a book on police and

criminals in Mumbai: Suketu Mehta, *Maximum City* (Alfred A. Knopf, New York, 2005). And see also the reports of the International Committee of the Red Cross on the Indian treatment of Kashmiri detainees, as stated to US diplomats and revealed by WikiLeaks in the *Guardian* (London), 17 December 2010.

16. Figures from the Population Association of Pakistan website: http://www.pap.org.pk/statistics/

17. John Briscoe and Usman Qamar, *Pakistan's Water Economy: Running Dry* (Oxford University Press, Oxford and the World Bank, Washington, DC, 2006), p. xiv.

18. Michael Kugelman and Robert M. Hathaway (eds), *Running on Empty: Pakistan's Water Crisis* (Woodrow Wilson Center, Washington, DC, 2009), Introduction, p. 24.

19. This point is made well in an engaging memoir about an American student's life in Pakistan: Ethan Casey, *Alive and Well in Pakistan: A Human Journey in a Difficult Time* (Grand Central Publishing, New York, 2005).

20. The answer, I eventually discovered, is the charmingly named demoiselle crane. In an interesting example of human (male) minds working in the same way across very different cultures, while some Western naturalist named them after young French girls, in Baloch poetry they are used to symbolize girls bathing (French or otherwise).

21. John Wyndham, *The Kraken Wakes* (Penguin, London, 1956), pp. 203–6.

22. Sir Denzil Ibbetson, *Panjab Castes* (Civil and Military Gazette Press, Lahore, 1883, reprinted Sang-e-Meel, Lahore, 2001), p. 1.

2 THE STRUGGLE FOR MUSLIM SOUTH ASIA

1. Faiz Ahmed Faiz, 'You tell us what to do', in *The True Subject: Selected Poems of Faiz Ahmed Faiz*, translated by Naomi Lezard (Vanguard Books, Lahore, 1988), p. 63.

2. Iqbal Akhund, *Trial and Error: The Advent and Eclipse of Benazir Bhutto* (Oxford University Press, Karachi, 2000), p. 116.

3. This was true both of architecture and of human cultural resources. At partition, India got to keep the greater part of the Muslim cultural intelligentsia and – most miserably of all for most Pakistanis – of the nascent film world. India's Bollywood film industry would not exist in its present form without the contribution of great Muslim actors, actresses, directors and composers: Nargis, Waheeda Rehman, Shabana Azmi, Naseeruddin Shah, the greatest male hearthrob of the present age Shah Rukh Khan, and many others. On the other hand, in Saadat Hasan Manto, who left for Pakistan, Bollywood lost what could have been its greatest writer.

4. Indeed, Muslim forces were as responsible for the fall of the Mughal empire as Hindus, Sikhs or the British. The single most shattering moment in the Mughal collapse was the capture and sack of Delhi itself in 1739 by the

Persian and Afghan forces of Nadir Shah, an event so ghastly that it is still commemorated by an Urdu word for atrocity, *nadirshahi*. In 1761, the city was sacked again by the founder of Afghanistan, Ahmed Shah Durrani.

5. This belief also permeates the Pakistani diaspora in Britain; and not just ordinary people, but members of the educated elites as well. Thus at a meeting of the Pakistan Society of University College London which I addressed on 3 February 2010, the great majority of students who spoke thought that the US or Israel had carried out the 9/11 attacks. If this is true of students in Britain, then the chances of the West persuading students in Pakistan to support Western policy would seem negligible.

6. Cited in Penderel Moon, *Divide and Quit* (Chatto & Windus, London, 1964), p. 11.

7. Cited by S. M. Burke, *Landmarks of the Pakistan Movement* (Punjab University Press, Lahore, 2001), p. 182.

8. Ayesha Jalal, *The Sole Spokesman: Jinnah, the Muslim League and the Demand for Pakistan* (Cambridge University Press, Cambridge, 1985).

9. A curious last echo of Muslim League hopes for a united confederal India is to be found in the fact that the inscriptions on the tombs of Jinnah and his deputy Liaquat Ali in Karachi are in both Urdu and Hindi.

10. Peter Hardy, *The Muslims of British India* (Cambridge University Press, Cambridge, 1972), p. 239.

11. Ian Talbot, *Pakistan: A Modern History* (Hurst & Co., London, 2005), p. 120.

12. Cited in Shafqat Tanveer Mirza, *Resistance Themes in Punjabi Literature* (Sang-e-Meel, Lahore, 1992), p. 162. I have changed the English translation slightly to eliminate bad grammar.

13. Liaquat's assassination in 1951 was the first in a long series of unexplained killings of Pakistani politicians, which have contributed greatly to the conspiracy-mindedness which is one of the biggest curses of intellectual life and public debate in Pakistan.

14. Figures at http://www.tradingeconomics.com/Economics/GDP-Growth.aspx?Symbol=PKR.

15. For a description and analysis of the concept of modern 'Sultanism', see H. E. Chehabi and Juan J. Linz, *Sultanistic Regimes* (Johns Hopkins University Press, Baltimore, MD, 1998).

16. Interview with the author, Lahore, 15/10/1988.

3 JUSTICE

1. Cited in G. C. J. J. van den Bergh, 'The Concept of Folk Law in Historical Context: A Brief Outline', in Alison Dundes Renteln and Alan Dundes (eds), *Folk Law: Essays in the Theory and Practice of Lex Non Scripta*, vol. I (University of Wisconsin Press, Madison, WI, 1995), p. 7.

2. Interview with the author, Mohmand Agency, 2/9/2008.

3. Ibid.
4. Akbar Hussain Allahabadi (1846–1921), in *The Best of Urdu Poetry*, translated with an introduction by Khushwant Singh (Penguin Viking, New Delhi, 2007), p. 81. And he, by the way, was a British judge in India!
5. Interview with the author, Karachi, 17/4/2009.
6. Sir Cecil Walsh, KC, *Crime in India* (Ernest Benn, London, 1930), p. 31.
7. Ibid., p. 45.
8. Muhammad Azam Chaudhary, *Justice in Practice* (Oxford University Press, Oxford, 1999), pp. 25–6.
9. Interview with the author, Karachi, 17/4/2009.
10. Cited in C. van Vollenhoven, 'Aspects of the Controversy on Customary Law', in Renteln and Dundes (eds), *Folk Law*, vol. I, p. 254.
11. Interview with the author, Peshawar, 25/7/2009. See also Aurangzaib Khan, 'Judge Thy Neighbour', *The Herald* (Karachi), 40 (4), April 2009.
12. M. P. Jain, 'Custom as a Source of Law in India', in Renteln and Dundes (eds), *Folk Law*, vol. I, p. 75.
13. W. H. Sleeman, *Rambles and Recollections of an Indian Official*, ed. Vincent A. Smith (1844; reprinted Oxford University Press, Karachi, 1980), p. 388.
14. Interview with the author, Karachi 2/5/2009.
15. Interview with the author, Multan, 18/1/2009.
16. James Traub, 'Lawyers' Crusade', *New York Times* magazine, 1 June 2008.
17. *District Gazetteers of Balochistan*, 1906, edited and compiled by Mansoor Bokhari (reprinted Gosha-e-Adab, Quetta, 1997), vol. I, p. 94.
18. Jain, 'Custom as a Source of Law', p. 70.
19. Stephen M. Lyon, *An Anthropological Analysis of Local Politics and Patronage in a Pakistani Village* (Edwin Mellen, Lewiston, NY, 2004), p. 24.

4 RELIGION

1. Muhammad Iqbal, *Mazhab*, cited in Ayesha Jalal, *Self and Sovereignty: Individual and Community in South Asian Islam since 1850* (Routledge, London, 2000), p. 578.
2. Koran, Sura 2 (The Cow), verse 172.
3. Major Aubrey O'Brien, 'The Mohammedan Saints of the Western Punjab', *Journal of the Royal Anthropological Institute*, 41 (1911), p. 511.
4. Francis Robinson, *Islam and Muslim History in South Asia* (Oxford University Press, New Delhi, 2006), p. 52.
5. Ian Talbot and Shinder Thandi, *People on the Move: Punjabi Colonial and Post-Colonial Migration* (Oxford University Press, Oxford, 2004), p. 183.
6. Saifur Rehman Sherani, 'Ulema and Pir in Pakistani Politics', in Hastings Donnan and Pnina Werbner (eds), *Economy and Culture in Pakistan: Migrants and Cities in a Muslim Society* (Macmillan, London, 1991), p. 221.

7. Interview with the author, Karachi, 7/11/1988.
8. Pnina Werbner, 'Stamping the Earth with the Name of Allah: Zikr and the Sacralising of Space among British Muslims', *Cultural Anthropology*, 11 (1996), pp. 309–38.
9. Interview with the author, Lahore, 1/8/2009.
10. Carl W. Ernst, *The Shambhala Guide to Sufism* (Shambhala, London, 1997), p. 213.
11. Interview with the author, Lahore University of Management Sciences (LUMS), 4/1/2009.
12. O'Brien, 'The Mohammedan Saints', p. 509.
13. Katherine Pratt Ewing, '*Malangs* of the Punjab: Intoxication or *Adab* as the Path to God?' in Barbara Daly Metcalf (ed.), *Moral Conduct and Authority: The Place of Adab in South Asian Islam* (California University Press, Berkeley, 1984), p. 363.
14. Hasan al-Banna, cited in Hamid Enayat, *Modern Islamic Political Thought*, with an introduction by Roy P. Mottahedeh (I. B. Tauris, London, 2005), p. 85.
15. http://www.jamaat.org.
16. Interview with the author, Abbotabad, NWFP, 12/8/2008.
17. Interview with the author, Faisalabad, 12/1/2009.
18. http://www.jamaat.org/new/english.
19. Interview with the author, Mansura, Lahore, 4/1/2009
20. Ibid.
21. Interview with the author, Islamabad, 30/4/2007.
22. Interview with the author, Peshawar, 2/5/2007.

5 THE MILITARY

1. Interview with the author, Karachi, 1/5/2009.
2. Interview with the author, Quetta, 1/8/2009.
3. Hasan-Askari Rizvi, *Military, State and Society in Pakistan* (Sang-e-Meel, Lahore, 2003), p. 8.
4. Shuja Nawaz, *Crossed Swords: Pakistan, Its Army and the Wars Within* (Oxford University Press, Oxford, 2008), pp. 446–58.
5. As recorded by US diplomats and revealed by WikiLeaks. See the *Guardian* (London), 1 December 2010.
6. Figures from *The Military Balance 2009*, published by the International Institute for Strategic Studies, London, and Owen Bennett-Jones, *Pakistan, Eye of the Storm* (Yale University Press, London, 2009), pp. 270–72.
7. See Ayesha Siddiqa, *Military Inc. Inside Pakistan's Military Economy* (Oxford University Press, Karachi, 2007).
8. Ibid., p. 212.
9. Interview with the author, Karachi, 1/5/2009.

10. Adnan Adil, 'Pakistan's Post 9/11 Economic Boom', 21 September 2006, cited in Brian Cloughley, *War, Coups and Terror: Pakistan's Army in Years of Turmoil* (Pen and Sword Books, Barnsley, 2008), p. 157.

11. Interview with the author, Rawalpindi, 27/7/2009.

12. Interview with the author, Peshawar, 28/7/2009.

13. Tan Tai Yong, *The Garrison State: Military, Government and Society in Colonial Punjab, 1849–1947* (Sage Publications, Lahore, 2005), p. 26.

14. Quoted in Rizvi, *Military, State and Society in Pakistan*, p. 62.

15. Zahid Hussain, 'Kayani Spells out Terms for Regional Stability', Dawn.com, 2 February 2010.

16. Interview with the author, Lahore, 2/8/2009.

17. Nawaz, *Crossed Swords*, pp. 570–71.

18. As Abida Husain once remarked to me, 'All our military capos have been personally pleasant, unassuming people, easy to get on with – very different from many of our politicians with their arrogance and edginess. Probably this is something to do with the democracy of the officers' mess, and not seeming to be too clever. Zia was the cleverest of them all, but got where he did precisely by pretending to be stupid.'

19. Stephen M. Lyon, *An Anthropological Analysis of Local Politics and Patronage in a Pakistani Village* (Edwin Mellen, Lewiston, NY, 2004), p. 2. Things were just the same in Europe in the past. Nonetheless, the Pakistani (and Indian) style of deference to superiors can become a little tiresome to modern Western ears, and certainly does not encourage the free exchange of ideas. A typical telephone conversation between an inferior and superior in the bureaucracy or any political party goes 'Ji Sir, ji Sir, ji . . . Bilkul [absolutely] Sir, bilkul, bilkul . . . Sain [right] Sir, sain . . . Yes, Sir, yes . . .' Sometimes the inferiors run out of breath altogether and are reduced to little orgasmic gasps of deference and submission, until you want to slap both parties over the head with alternate volumes of *Das Kapital*.

20. Interview with the author, Karachi, 1/5/2009.

21. Interview with the author, Rawalpindi, 9/10/2001.

22. This is derived from Aristotle via Hegel, though somewhat misrepresents both.

23. Z. A. Bhutto, *Foreign Policy of Pakistan* (Pakistan Institute of International Affairs, Karachi, 1964), p. 13.

24. Ibid.

25. For a small example of the inflexible mindset of many Pakistani soldiers concerning Kashmir, see an article in the Pakistan military's monthly magazine, *Hilal*, of August 2009: Colonel Dr Muhammad Javed, 'Kashmir: An Unfinished Agenda of Partition'.

26. Interview with the author, Islamabad, 4/8/2008.

27. Stephen Tankel, *Storming the World Stage: The Story of Lashkar-e-Taiba* (Columbia University Press, New York, 2010).

28. Hafiz Abdul Salam bin Muhammad, 'Jihad in the Present Time', http://web.archive.org/web/20030524100347/www.markazdawa.org.

29. Tankel, *Storming the World Stage*.

30. Nawaz, *Crossed Swords*, p. 551.

31. Mark Fitzpatrick (ed.), *Nuclear Black Markets: Pakistan, A. Q. Khan and the Rise of Proliferation Networks* (IISS, London, 2007), p. 116.

6 POLITICS

1. Lewis Namier, *The Structure of Politics at the Accession of George III* (Macmillan, London, 1970), p. 2.

2. Sir William Sleeman, *Rambles and Recollections of an Indian Official* (1844; reprinted Oxford University Press, Karachi, 1980), p. 238.

3. Interview with the author, Jhang, 5/10/2002.

4. On Akram Khan Alizai; Mountstuart Elphinstone, *An Account of the Kingdom of Caubul* (1819; reprinted Sang-e-Meel, Lahore, 1998), vol. II, p. 285.

5. Interview with the author, Islamabad, 3/11/1990.

6. Interview with the author, Karachi, 23/10/1990.

7. Iqbal Akhund, *Trial and Error: The Advent and Eclipse of Benazir Bhutto* (Oxford University Press, Karachi, 2000), p. 135.

8. Interview with the author, Gujrat, 9/11/1988.

9. Interview with the author, Islamabad, 10/12/1988.

10. Readers may have noticed one inevitable omission, which did not even begin to approach the subconscious depths of our conversation and which I certainly wasn't going to drag to the surface – namely, the idea that she might use a vacuum-cleaner herself.

11. Interview with the author, Jhang, 5/10/2002.

12. Interview with the author, Rawalpindi, 17/7/2009.

13. This may be apocryphal. I have heard it repeated many times, but have never been able to track down the original.

14. Interview with the author, Mirpur Bhutto, 24/4/2009. On the other hand, he had used almost exactly the same words to me twenty years earlier, and not a great deal appears to have changed in the meantime as far as *wadero* power in Sindh is concerned.

15. *Gazetteer of the Attock District* (Government Printing, Lahore, 1930; reprinted Sang-e-Meel, Lahore, 2003), p. 95.

16. Akhund, *Trial and Error*, p. 53.

17. Interview with the author, Shikarpur, 15/11/1990.

18. As I wrote in my notebook while accompanying Abida Husain, an elderly 'feudal' from a Shia *pir* family in Jhang, in baking heat, during the 2002 elections: 'These feudal politicians are not spoiled aristocrats. Some can show iron discipline when politics requires. I'm lounging in my seat half asleep, with flies settling on my nose, kept awake only by the state of my bladder. This is the

eighth meeting we've been to and there she is, bolt upright on the platform for the past hour, looking cool as a cucumber, completely attentive to what the audience is saying.'

19. Mosharraf Zaidi, 'When the News Becomes News', *The News*, Karachi, 5 January 2010.
20. Interview with the author, Karachi 17/4/2009.
21. Interview with the author, Karachi, 3/10/1990.
22. Interview with the author, Islamabad 4/12/1988.
23. Maqsood Jafri, *The Ideals of Bhutto* (privately published, 2002), pp. 55, 59.
24. Special supplement 'honouring anniversary of birth of Shaheed Z. A. Bhutto', *Pakistan Times*, 5 January 1990.
25. Interview with the author, Karachi, 2/10/1990.
26. For accounts of these cases, see Human Rights Watch, *World Report 2009*, Pakistan section, pp. 290–91; Asian Human Rights Commission statement of 4 March 2009: 'Order an honour killing – become a minister'; Rubina Saigol, 'Women and Democracy', *Dawn News*, 3 December 2008; 'Sindh High Court Adjourns Saira Jatoi's Case', *Daily Times*, 30 October 2008; Hasan Mansoor, 'Pakistani couple married for love, hiding in fear of tribal justice', *Hindustan Times*, 11 June 2009.
27. Interview with the author, Karachi, 3/5/2009.
28. Interview with the author, Lahore, 30/12/2008.
29. Interview with the author, Lahore, 2/8/2009.
30. 'Pak government should hold talks with Taliban', Dawn.com, 3 July 2010.
31. 'C. M. Shahbaz Wants Taliban to Spare Punjab', Dawn.com, 15 March 2010.
32. Interview with the author, Karachi, 17/4/2009.
33. Interview with the author, Karachi, 3/5/2009.
34. Iftikhar H. Malik, 'Ethno-Nationalism in Pakistan: A Commentary on the Muhajir Qaumi Mahaz (MQM) in Sindh', *South Asia Bulletin*, 18 (2) (1995), p. 44.
35. Interview with the author, Karachi, 3/5/2009.
36. Oskar Verkaaik, *Migrants and Militants: 'Fun' and Urban Violence in Pakistan* (Princeton University Press, Princeton, 2004), p. 62.

7 PUNJAB

1. Bapsi Sidhwa, *The Bride* (Futura, London, 1984), p. 19.
2. According to this award the allocation of revenue was divided up according to the following criteria: population, 82.00%; poverty, 10.30%; revenue, 5.00%; IPD (Inverse Population Density) 2.70%. See www.einfopedia.com/nfc-award-national-finance-commission-award-of-pakistan.php.
3. Quoted in Ayesha Jalal, *Partisans of Allah: Jihad in South Asia* (Sang-e-Meel Publications, Lahore, 2008), p. 41.

4. See, for example, Eugen Weber, *Peasants into Frenchmen: The Moderniza-tion of Rural France, 1870–1914* (Stanford University Press, Stanford, 1976).
5. The names are imaginary.
6. Moni Mohsin, *Diary of a Social Butterfly* (Random House, Karachi, 2009).
7. Figures in Ian Talbot, 'The Punjabization of Pakistan: Myth or Reality?', in Christophe Jaffrelot (ed.), *Pakistan: Nation, Nationalism and the State* (Van-guard, Lahore, 2005), p. 56.
8. Figures in J. Briscoe and U. Qamar, *Pakistan's Water Economy: Running Dry* (Oxford University Press, Oxford, and the World Bank, Washington, DC, 2006); and 'World Bank Report on Pakistan's Water Resources', *Daily Times*, Lahore, 18 January 2006.
9. Chaudhury Shujaat Hussain, interview with the author, Gujrat, 9/11/1988.
10. 'Meat is very seldom eaten except by the better class, and except on occa-sions of rejoicing or by way of hospitality', *Gazetteer of the Multan District 1923–24* (Government Printing, Lahore, 1926; reprinted Sang-e-Meel, Lahore 2001), p. 129.
11. Interview with the author, Faisalabad, 14/1/2009.
12. *Gazetteer of the Multan District*, p. 121.

8 SINDH

1. Kamila Shamsie, *Kartography* (Bloomsbury Publishing, London, 2003), p. 259.
2. Samina Altaf, 'Public Health, Clean Water and Pakistan: Why We Are Not There Yet', in Michael Kugelman and Robert M. Hathaway (eds), *Running on Empty: Pakistan's Water Crisis* (Woodrow Wilson Center, Washington, DC, 2009).
3. Captain Leopold von Orlich, *Travels in India*; quoted in H. T. Sorley, *Shah Abdul Latif of Bhit: A Study of Literary, Social and Economic Conditions in 18th Century Sind* (Ashish Publishing House, New Delhi, 1984), p. 95.
4. Sarah Ansari, *Sufi Saints and State Power: The Pirs of Sind, 1843–1947* (Vanguard Books, Lahore, 1992), p. 22.
5. Oskar Verkaaik, *A People of Migrants: Ethnicity, State and Religion in Karachi*, Comparative Asian Studies, 15 (VU University Press, Amsterdam, 1994), p. 47.
6. Feroz Ahmed, 'Ethnicity and Politics: The Rise of Muhajir Separatism', *South Asia Bulletin*, 8 (1988), pp. 37–8.
7. Interview with the author, Karachi, 28/4/2009.
8. Interview with the author, Karachi, 28/4/2009.
9. Interview with the author, Karachi, 29/4/2009.
10. Interview with the author, Karachi, 30/4/2009.
11. Interview with the author, Mirpur Bhutto, 17/4/2009.
12. Interview with the author, Hyderabad, 20/4/2009.

9 BALOCHISTAN

1. *District Gazetteers of Balochistan,* 1906 (ed. and compiled by Mansoor Bokhari), 2 vols (reprinted Gosha-e-Adab, Quetta, 1997), vol. II, p. 1028.

2. 'Balochistan Militants Killing Teachers', report by Human Rights Watch, issued 13/12/2010 at http://www.hrw.org/en/news/2010/12/13/pakistan-balochistan-militants-killing-teachers.

3. *District Gazetteers of Balochistan,* vol. I, p. 128.

4. Ibid., p. 102.

5. Ibid., vol. II, p. 994.

6. Sylvia Matheson, *The Tigers of Balochistan* (Oxford University Press, Karachi, 1967), pp. 1–3.

7. Paul Titus, 'Whither the Tigers?', Introduction to the 1995 edition of *The Tigers of Balochistan* by Sylvia Matheson, p. 25.

8. Matheson, *Tigers,* p. 204.

9. Ibid., p. 48.

10. See 'A Statement by the Asian Human Rights Commission', 4 March 2009 (at www.humanrightsblog.org/pakistan).

11. Quoted in Human Rights Watch World Report, 2009, pp. 290–1.

12. Interview with the author, Quetta, 12/8/2009.

13. Interview with the author, Quetta, 16/8/2009.

14. Interview with the author, Miangundi, Balochistan, 14/8/2009.

15. *District Gazetteers,* vol. II, p. 1001.

16. See also Brigadier (retd) Tughral Yamin, 'Chamalang: Winning Hearts and Minds', *Hilal* (Pakistan armed forces magazine), May 2009.

17. http://pakalert.wordpress.com/2009/06/06/reko-diq-mystery.

18. Interview with the author, Quetta, 15/8/2009.

10 THE PATHANS

1. Khushal Khan Khattak, translated by Sir Olaf Caroe, in Caroe, *The Pathans* (1958; reprinted Oxford University Press, Oxford, 2006), p. 238.

2. For an explanation of why I have chosen to use the Hindustani name (taken over by the British) 'Pathan' to describe this people, rather than 'Pakhtun' or 'Pashtun' (depending on which Pathan dialect you are using), see the Introduction, p. 22.

3. T. L. Pennel and Earl Roberts, *Among the Wild Tribes of the Afghan Frontier: A Record of Sixteen Years' Close Intercourse with the Natives of the Indian Marches* (1908; reprinted Kessinger Publishing, Whitefish, MT, 2005).

4. *Report on Waziristan and its Tribes* (Punjab Government Press, 1901, republished by Sang-e-Meel Publications, Lahore, 2005), p. 9.

5. See Brian Robson, *Crisis on the Frontier: The Third Afghan War and the*

Campaign in Waziristan, 1919–20 (Spellmount, Staplehurst, 2004), p. xiii. 'Butcher and Bolt' was also taken by the BBC correspondent David Loyn as the title of his book on outside interventions in Afghanistan and its borderlands, published in 2008.

6. Juma Khan Sufi, *Bacha Khan, Congress and Nationalist Politics in NWFP* (Vanguard Books, Lahore, 2005), pp. 1–2.

7. Quoted in Ahmad Hasan Dani, *Peshawar: Historic City of the Frontier* (Sang-e-Meel Publications, Lahore, 2002), p. 172.

8. Interview with the author, Peshawar, 24/8/2008.

9. Joshua T. White, *Pakistan's Islamist Frontier: Islamic Politics and US Policy in Pakistan's North-West Frontier* (Centre on Faith and International Affairs, Washington, DC, 2007), p. 39.

10. Interview with the author, Peshawar, 21/7/2009.

11. Interview with the author, Peshawar, 26/8/2008.

11 THE PAKISTANI TALEBAN

1. Sir Olaf Caroe, *The Pathans* (1958; reprinted Oxford University Press, Oxford, 2006), p. 300.

2. Abdul Salam Zaeef, *My Life with the Taleban*, ed. Alex Strick van Linschoten and Felix Kuehn (Hurst & Co., London, 2010), pp. 21–80.

3. Interview with the *Indian Observer* online, 16/11/2009, at www.observerindia.com.

4. Pervez Musharraf, *In the Line of Fire: A Memoir* (Free Press, New York, 2006), p. 201.

5. Seymour Hersh, 'The Getaway', *New Yorker*, 28 January 2002; Ahmed Rashid, *Descent into Chaos: How the War against Islamic Extremism is Being Lost in Pakistan, Afghanistan and Central Asia* (Allen Lane, London, 2008), pp. 91–3.

6. Text of speech at transcripts.cnn.com/TRANSCRIPTS/0201/12/smn.21.html.

7. Meeting with the media and experts in London, 28/1/2008 (my notes).

8. Matt Waldman, 'The Sun in the Sky: The Relationship between Pakistan's ISI and Afghan Insurgents', Discussion Paper no. 18, Crisis States Discussion Papers, London School of Economics, June 2010.

9. *Report on Waziristan and its Tribes* (Punjab Government Press, 1901; reprinted Sang-e-Meel Publications, Lahore, 2005), p. 22.

10. Some vivid anecdotes of this approach (albeit carried out by a Pathan official in the British service) are to be found in John Bowen, *Plain Tales of the Afghan Border* (Springwood Books, London, 1982).

11. Interview with the author, Islamabad, 2/5/2007.

12. Quoted in Claudio Franco, 'The Tehrik-e-Taleban Pakistan', in Antonio Giustozzi (ed.), *Decoding the New Taleban: Insights from the Afghan Field* (Hurst, London, 2009), p. 272.

13. Ernest Gellner, 'Flux and Reflux in the Faith of Men', in Gellner, *Muslim Society* (Cambridge University Press, Cambridge, 1981), p. 45.

14. Ibn Khaldun, *The Muqadmimah: An Introduction to History*, trans. Franz Rosenthal, ed. N. J. Dawood (Routledge & Kegan Paul, London, 1967), p. 118.

15. Gellner, *Muslim Society*, p. 53.

16. Fredrik Barth, *Political Leadership among Swat Pathans* (London School of Economics Monographs on Social Anthropology, London, 1959), pp. 61–2.

17. Brian Robson, *Crisis on the Frontier: The Third Afghan War and the Campaign in Waziristan, 1919–20* (Spellmount, Staplehurst, 2004), p. 212.

18. Sana Haroon, *Frontier of Faith: Islam in the Indo-Afghan Borderland* (Hurst, London, 2007), p. 3.

19. Ibid., p. 79.

20. W. R. H. Merk, *The Mohmands* (1898; reprinted Vanguard Books, Lahore, 1984), p. 12.

21. Barth, *Political Leadership*, pp. 98–9.

22. Hussain Ahmad Madni, 1953, quoted in Haroon, *Frontier of Faith*, p. 93.

23. Caroe, *Pathans*, pp. 305–6.

24. Merk, *The Mohmands*, p. 33.

24. In Winston S. Churchill, *Frontiers and Wars* (reprinted Eyre & Spottiswoode, London, 1962).

12 DEFEATING THE TALEBAN?

1. Quoted in J. G. Elliott, *The Frontier 1839–1947* (London, Cassell, 1968), p. 229.

2. My notebook, 28/8/2008.

3. Interview with the author, Faisalabad, 12/1/2009.

4. Interview with the author, Islamabad, 19/1/2009.

5. See, for example, Brian Robson, *Crisis on the Frontier* (Spellmount, Staplehurst, 2004), pp. 84, 98; and Sir Olaf Caroe's reminiscences of an incident of mutiny in the South Waziristan Militia in 1905 with which he was personally involved, in his *The Pathans* (1958; reprinted Oxford University Press, Oxford, 2006), Appendix D, pp. 468–78.

6. Interview with the author, Peshawar, 19/8/2008.

7. Andrew Small, 'China's Caution on Afghanistan-Pakistan', *Washington Quarterly* (July 2010), pp. 81–97.

8. Interview with the author, Mingora, Swat, 7/8/2009.

9. Interview with the author, Peshawar, 10/8/2008.

10. Sultan-i-Rome, *Swat State from Genesis to Merger, 1915–1969* (Oxford University Press, Karachi, 2008), pp. 323–4.

11. Interview with the author, Mingora, Swat, 8/8/2009.

12. Human Rights Watch, 'Pakistan: Extrajudicial Executions by Army in Swat', 16 July 2010, at www.hrw.org.

13. http://www.ummid.com/news/2010/February/18.02.2010/cost_of_war_against_terror.htm.

CONCLUSIONS

1. Cable from US Embassy in Islamabad to State Department, 25/9/2010, WikiLeaks extract 224303, published in the *Guardian* (London), 1 December 2010, p. 6.
2. Reported via WikiLeaks in the *Guardian* (London), 1 December 2010, p. 7.
3. Ibid.
4. US Embassy cable of 23/9/2010.
5. Ewen MacAskill and Simon Tisdall, 'Barack Obama Shifts Towards Talks with Taliban', *Guardian* online, 19 July 2010, at www.guardian.co.uk/world/2010/jul/19/obama-afghanistan-strategy-taliban-negotiate.
6. US Embassy cable of 23/9/2010.

Books Consulted

CHAPTER 2 THE STRUGGLE FOR MUSLIM SOUTH ASIA

Iqbal Akhund, *Trial and Error: The Advent and Eclipse of Benazir Bhutto* (Oxford University Press, Karachi, 2000)

M. Athar Ali, *Mughal India: Studies in Polity, Ideas, Society and Culture* (Oxford University Press, New Delhi, 2006)

Alyssa Ayres, *Speaking Like a State: Language and Nationalism in Pakistan* (Cambridge University Press, Cambridge, 2009)

Sartaj Aziz, *Between Dreams and Realities: Some Milestones in Pakistan's History* (Oxford University Press, Karachi, 2009)

Owen Bennett-Jones, *Pakistan: Eye of the Storm* (Yale University Press, London, 2009)

Benazir Bhutto: Daughter of the East: An Autobiography (Pocket Books, London, 2008)

Zulfikar Ali Bhutto, *If I Am Assassinated* (Vikas, New Delhi, 1979)

Shahid Javed Burki, *Pakistan: Fifty Years of Nationhood* (Vanguard, Lahore, 2004)

M. Ikram Chagatai, *Shah Waliullah: His Religious and Political Thought* (Sang-e-Meel Publications, Lahore, 2005)

H. E. Chehabi and Juan J. Linz (eds), *Sultanistic Regimes* (Johns Hopkins University Press, Baltimore, MD, 1998)

Stephen P. Cohen, *The Idea of Pakistan* (Brookings Institution Press, Washington, DC, 2004)

William Dalrymple, *The Last Mughal: Fall of a Dynasty, Delhi 1857* (Bloomsbury Publishing, London, 2007)

Emma Duncan, *Breaking the Curfew: A Political Journey Through Pakistan* (Michael Joseph, London, 1989)

Altaf Gauhar, *Ayub Khan: Pakistan's First Military Ruler* (Sang-e-Meel Publications, Lahore, 1993)

Irfan Habib, *The Agrarian System of Mughal India 1556–1707* (Oxford University Press, Oxford, 1963)

Peter Hardy, *The Muslims of British India* (Cambridge University Press, Cambridge, 1972)

Christophe Jaffrelot (ed.), *A History of Pakistan and Its Origins* (Anthem Press, London, 2004)

Ayesha Jalal, *Partisans of Allah: Jihad in South Asia* (Harvard University Press, Cambridge, MA, 2008)

——, *The Sole Spokesman: Jinnah, the Muslim League and the Demand for Pakistan* (Cambridge University Press, Cambridge, 1985)

John Keay, *India: A History* (Grove Press, Canongate, 2001)

Sir Syed Ahmed Khan, *The Causes of the Indian Revolt* (Oxford University Press, Karachi, 2000)

Roedad Khan, *Pakistan: A Dream Gone Sour* (Oxford University Press, Karachi, 1997)

Dennis Kux, *The United States and Pakistan 1947–2000: Disenchanted Allies* (Woodrow Wilson Center Press, Washington, DC, 2001)

Christina Lamb, *Waiting for Allah: Benazir Bhutto and Pakistan* (Hamish Hamilton, London, 1991)

David Lelyveld, *Aligarh's First Generation: Muslim Solidarity in British India* (Oxford University Press, New Delhi, 2003)

Anthony Mascarenhas, *The Rape of Bangladesh* (Vikas, New Delhi, 1972)

T. R. Metcalf, *The Aftermath of Revolt: India, 1857–1870* (Princeton University Press, Princeton, NJ, 1964)

William B. Milam, *Bangladesh and Pakistan: Flirting with Failure in South Asia* (Hurst, London, 2009)

Penderel Moon, *The British Conquest and Dominion of India, Parts I and II* (India Research Press, New Delhi 1999)

——, *Divide and Quit* (Chatto & Windus, London, 1964)

Sharif al Mujahid, *The Ideology of Pakistan* (Islamic Research Institute, Islamabad, 2001)

Shuja Nawaz, *Crossed Swords: Pakistan, Its Army and the Wars Within* (Oxford University Press, Oxford, 2008)

Omar Noman, *The Political Economy of Pakistan, 1947–85* (Kegan Paul International, London, 1985)

Francis Robinson, *The Mughal Emperors and the Islamic Dynasties of India, Iran and Central Asia, 1206–1925* (Thames & Hudson, London, 2007)

——, *Separatism Among Indian Muslims: The Politics of the United Province's Muslims, 1860–1923* (Cambridge University Press, Cambridge, 2008)

Farzana Shaikh, *Making Sense of Pakistan* (Hurst, London, 2009)

Ian Talbot, *Pakistan: A Modern History* (Hurst, London, 2005)

——, *Provincial Politics and the Pakistan Movement: The Growth of the Muslim League in Northwest and Northeast India, 1937–1947* (Oxford University Press, Oxford, 1988)

Romila Thapar, *A History of India*, Vol. I (Penguin, London, 1990)

Sir Archibald Wavell, *The Viceroy's Journal* (Oxford University Press, Oxford, 1973)

Stanley Wolpert, *Jinnah of Pakistan* (Oxford University Press, Oxford, 1998)

———, *A New History of India* (Oxford University Press, New York, 2008)

———, *Shameful Flight: The Last Years of the British Empire in India* (Oxford University Press, New York, 2006)

———, *Zulfi Bhutto of Pakistan: His Life and Times* (Oxford University Press, Oxford, 1993)

Lawrence Ziring, *Pakistan in the Twentieth Century: A Political History* (Oxford University Press, Oxford, 1997)

CHAPTER 3 JUSTICE

Paul Bohannon (ed.), *Law and Warfare: Studies in the Anthropology of Conflict* (Natural History Press, New York, 1967)

Muhammad Azam Chaudhary, *Justice in Practice: The Legal Ethnography of a Punjabi Village* (Oxford University Press, Oxford, 1999)

Bernard S. Cohn, 'Law and the Colonial State in India', in Cohn, *Colonialism and Its Forms of Knowledge* (Princeton University Press, Princeton, 1996)

A. S. Diamond, *Primitive Law: Past and Present* (Routledge, reprinted London, 1984)

Alison Dundes Renteln and Alan Dundes (eds), *Folk Law: Essays in the Theory and Practice of Lex Non Scripta*, 2 vols (University of Wisconsin Press, Madison, WI, 1995)

E. E. Evans-Pritchard, *The Nuer: A Description of the Modes of Livelihood and Political Institutions of a Nilotic People* (Oxford University Press, New York, 1987)

E. Adamson Hoebel, *The Law of Primitive Man: A Study in Comparative Legal Dynamics* (Harvard University Press, Cambridge, MA, 1967)

Suketu Mehta, *Maximum City: Bombay Lost and Found* (Vintage Books, New York, 2005)

Sir Penderel Moon, *Strangers in India* (Faber & Faber, London, 1945)

V. S. Naipaul, *Among the Believers: An Islamic Journey* (Picador, London, 2003)

Major-General Sir W. H. Sleeman, KCB, *Rambles and Recollections of an Indian Official*, ed. by Vincent A. Smith (1844; reprinted Oxford University Press, Karachi, 1980)

Harry Holbert Turney-High, *Primitive War: Its Practice and Concepts* (University of South Carolina Press, Chapel Hill, 1991)

Sir Cecil Walsh, KC, *Crime in India* (Ernest Benn, London, 1930)

CHAPTER 4 RELIGION

Imtiaz Ahmad (ed.), *Ritual and Religion among Muslims in India* (Manohar, New Delhi, 1981)

Khurshid Ahmad (ed.), *Islamic Perspectives: Studies in Honour of Mawlana Sayyid Abul Ala Mawdudi* (Islamic Foundation, Leicester, 1979)

Aziz Ahmed, *Islamic Modernism in India and Pakistan* (Oxford University Press, London, 1967)

——, *Studies in Islamic Culture in the Indian Environment* (Oxford University Press, New Delhi, 1998)

Sarah Ansari, *Sufi Saints and State Power: The Pirs of Sind, 1843–1947* (Cambridge University Press, Cambridge, 1992)

Abdul Sattar Edhi, *A Mirror to the Blind: An Autobiography*, as narrated to Tehmina Durrani (Edhi Foundation, Karachi, 1996)

Hamid Enayat, *Modern Islamic Political Thought*, with an introduction by Roy P. Mottahedeh (I. B. Tauris, London, 2005)

Carl W. Ernst, *The Shambhala Guide to Sufism* (Shambhala, London, 1997)

Clifford Geertz, *Islam Observed: Religious Development in Morocco and Indonesia* (Yale University Press, New Haven, CT, 1968)

Ernest Gellner, *Muslim Society* (Cambridge University Press, Cambridge, 1981)

——, *Saints of the Atlas* (Weidenfeld & Nicolson, London, 1969)

David Gilmartin, 'Religious Leadership and the Pakistan Movement in the Punjab', *Modern Asian Studies*, 13 (1979), pp. 485–517

Ayesha Jalal, *Partisans of Allah: Jihad in South Asia* (Sang-e-Meel, Lahore, 2008)

——, *Self and Sovereignty: Individual and Community in South Asian Islam since 1850* (Routledge, London, 2000)

Gilles Kepel, *Jihad: The Trail of Political Islam* (Harvard University Press, Cambridge, MA, 2002)

——, *The War for Muslim Minds: Islam and the West* (Harvard University Press, London, 2004)

Peter Mayne, *Saints of Sind* (J. Murray, London, 1956)

Barbara Daly Metcalf (ed.), *Moral Conduct and Authority: The Place of Adab in South Asian Islam* (California University Press, Berkeley, CA, 1984)

Sharif Al Mujahid, *Ideology of Pakistan* (Islamic Research Institute, Islamabad, 2001)

Katherine Pratt Ewing, 'The Politics of Sufism: Redefining the Saints of Pakistan', *Journal of Asian Studies*, 42 (1983), pp. 251–68

Muhammad Amir Rana, *A to Z of Jehadi Organizations in Pakistan*, translated by Saba Ansari (Mashal, Lahore, 2009)

Francis Robinson, *Islam and Muslim History in South Asia* (Oxford University Press, New Delhi, 2006)

Olivier Roy, *The Failure of Political Islam* (I.B. Tauris, London, 1994)

Annemarie Schimmel, *Mystical Dimensions of Islam* (University of North Carolina Press, Chapel Hill, NC, 1975)

Farzana Shaikh, *Making Sense of Pakistan* (Hurst, London, 2009)

Ian Talbot (ed.), *The Deadly Embrace: Religion, Politics and Violence in India and Pakistan, 1947–2001* (Oxford University Press, Karachi, 2007)

Anita Weiss (ed.), *Islamic Reassertion in Pakistan: The Application of Islamic Laws in a Modern State* (Vanguard, Lahore, 1987)

CHAPTER 5 THE MILITARY

Sumantra Bose, *Kashmir: Roots of Conflict, Paths to Peace* (Harvard University Press, Cambridge, MA, 2003)

Shahid Javed Burki and Craig Baxter, *Pakistan Under the Military* (Westview Press, Boulder, CO, 1991)

Pervaiz Iqbal Cheema, *The Armed Forces of Pakistan* (Oxford University Press, Karachi, 2002)

Brian Cloughley, *War, Coups and Terror: Pakistan's Army in Years of Turmoil* (Pen and Sword Books, Barnsley, 2008)

Stephen P. Cohen, *The Pakistan Army* (Oxford University Press, Karachi 1999)

Gordon Correra, *Shopping for Bombs: Nuclear Proliferation, Global Insecurity, and the Rise and Fall of the A. Q. Khan Network* (Oxford University Press, Oxford, 2006)

Mahmud Ali Durrani, *India and Pakistan: The Cost of Conflict and the Benefits of Peace* (Oxford University Press, Karachi, 2001)

Ayesha Jalal, *The State of Martial Rule* (Cambridge University Press, Cambridge, 1990)

Mohammad Ayub Khan, *Diaries, 1966–72*, ed. Craig Baxter (Oxford University Press, Karachi, 2007)

Alastair Lamb, *Crisis in Kashmir, 1947–1966* (Pan Books, London, 2000)

Adrian Levy and Catherine Scott-Clark, *Deception: Pakistan, the United States and the Global Nuclear Weapons Conspiracy* (Atlantic Books, London, 2007)

Pervez Musharraf, *In the Line of Fire: A Memoir* (Free Press, New York, 2006)

Shuja Nawaz, *Crossed Swords: Pakistan, Its Army and the Wars Within* (Oxford University Press, Oxford, 2008)

Sher Ali Pataudi, *The Story of Soldiering and Politics in India and Pakistan* (Bakhtyar Press, Lahore, 1983)

George Perkovich, *India's Nuclear Bomb: The Impact on Global Proliferation* (Oxford University Press, Oxford, 2000)

Hasan-Askari Rizvi, *Military, State and Society in Pakistan* (Sang-e-Meel, Lahore, 2003)

Victoria Schofield, *Kashmir in Conflict: India, Pakistan and the Unending War* (I. B.Tauris, London, 2002)

Ayesha Siddiqa, *Military Inc. Inside Pakistan's Military Economy* (Oxford University Press, Karachi, 2007)

Sten Widmalm, *Kashmir in Comparative Perspective* (Oxford University Press, Oxford, 2002)

Tan Tai Yong, *The Garrison State: Military, Government and Society in Colonial Punjab, 1849–1947* (Vanguard Books, Lahore, 2005)

CHAPTER 6 POLITICS

Saghir Ahmad, *Class and Power in a Punjabi Village* (New York and London, 1977)

Iqbal Akhund, *Trial and Error: The Advent and Eclipse of Benazir Bhutto* (Oxford University Press, Karachi, 2000)

Hamza Alavi, 'Kinship in West Punjabi Villages', *Contributions to Indian Sociology* (1972)

———— and F. Halliday (eds), *State and Ideology in the Middle East and Pakistan* (Macmillan, London, 1977)

Sartaj Aziz, *Between Dreams and Realities: Some Milestones in Pakistan's History* (Oxford University Press, Karachi, 2009)

Owen Bennett-Jones, *Pakistan: Eye of the Storm* (Yale University Press, London, 2009)

Benazir Bhutto: Daughter of the East: An Autobiography (Pocket Books, London, 2008)

Zulfikar Ali Bhutto, *If I Am Assassinated* (Vikas, New Delhi, 1979)

Zekiye Eglar, *A Punjabi Village in Pakistan* (Columbia University Press, New York, 1960)

Michael D. Fischer, 'Marriage and Power: Tradition and Transition in an Urban Punjabi Community', in H. Donnan and P. Werbner (eds), *Economy and Culture in Pakistan: Migrants and Cities in a Muslim Society* (London: Macmillan, 1991)

Richard G. Fox, *From Zamindar to Ballot Box* (Cornell University Press, Ithaca, NY, 1969)

Michael Gilsenan, *Lords of the Lebanese Marches* (I. B. Tauris, London, 1996)

Husain Haqqani, *Pakistan between Mosque and Military* (Carnegie Endowment, Washington, DC, 2005)

Michael Hicks, *Bastard Feudalism* (Longman, London, 1995)

David C. Kang, *Crony Capitalism: Corruption and Development in South Korea and the Philippines* (Cambridge University Press, Cambridge, 2002)

Roedad Khan, *Pakistan: A Dream Gone Sour* (Oxford University Press, Karachi, 1997)

Charles Lindholm, *Generosity and Jealousy: The Swat Pukhtun of Northern Pakistan* (Columbia University Press, New York, 1982)

Harban Mukhia, 'Was There Feudalism in Indian History?', *Journal of Peasant Studies*, 8 (3) (1981)

Omar Noman, *The Political Economy of Pakistan, 1947–85* (Kegan Paul International, London, 1985)

J. G. Peristiany (ed.), *Honour and Shame: The Values of Mediterranean Society* (Weidenfeld & Nicolson, London, 1965)

Joyce Pettigrew, *Robber Noblemen: A Study of the Political System of Sikh Jats* (Routledge & Kegan Paul, London, 1975)

Declan Quigley, *The Interpretation of Caste* (Oxford University Press, Oxford, 1993)

L. Roniger and A. Günes-Ayata (eds), *Democracy, Clientelism, and Civil Society* (L. Rienner, London, 1994)

CHAPTER 7 PUNJAB

Muhammad Akbar, *The Punjab under the Mughals* (Ripon Press, Lahore, 1948)

Muhammad Azam Chaudhary, *Justice in Practice: The Legal Ethnography of a Pakistani Punjabi Village* (Oxford University Press, Oxford, 1999)

W. L. Conran and H. D. Craik, *The Punjab Chiefs* (Civil and Military Gazette Press, Lahore, 1909; reprinted Sang-e-Meel, Lahore, 1993)

Zekiye Eglar, *A Punjabi Village in Pakistan* (Columbia University Press, New York, 1960)

H. L. O. Garrett, *The Punjab a Hundred Years Ago* (Government Printing, 1934; reprinted by Book House, Lahore, 2002)

Gazetteer of the Attock District (Government Printing, Lahore, 1930; reprinted Sang-e-Meel, Lahore, 2003)

Gazetteer of the Chenab Colony (Government Printing 1911; reprinted Sang-e-Meel, Lahore, 1996)

Gazetteer of the Multan District, 1923–24 (Government Printing, Lahore, 1926; reprinted Sang-e-Meel, Lahore, 2001)

Sir Denzil Ibbetson, *Panjab Castes* (Civil and Military Gazette Press, Lahore, 1883; reprinted Sang-e-Meel, Lahore, 2001)

Stephen M. Lyon, *An Anthropological Analysis of Local Politics and Patronage in a Pakistani Village* (Edwin Mellen, Lewiston, NY, 2004)

Joyce Pettigrew, *Robber Noblemen: A Study of the Political System of the Sikh Jats* (Routledge & Kegan Paul, London, 1975)

Bapsi Sidhwa (ed.), *Beloved City: Writings on Lahore* (Oxford University Press, Karachi, 2005)

Gurharpal Singh and Ian Talbot, *Punjabi Identity: Continuity and Change* (Manohar Publishers, New Delhi, 1996)

Ian Talbot and Shinder Thandi, *People on the Move: Punjabi Colonial and Post-Colonial Migration* (Oxford University Press, Oxford, 2004)

Tan Tai Yong, *The Garrison State: The Military, Government and Society in Colonial Punjab, 1849–1947* (Vanguard Books, Lahore, 2005)

CHAPTER 8 SINDH

Feroz Ahmed, 'Ethnicity and Politics: The Rise of Muhajir Separatism', *South Asia Bulletin*, 8 (1988)

Hamza Alavi, 'Nationhood and the Nationalities in Pakistan', in Hastings Donnan and Pnina Werbner (eds), *Economy and Culture in Pakistan: Migrants and Cities in a Muslim Society* (Macmillan, London, 1991)

Sarah Ansari, 'Partition, Migration and Refugees: Responses to the Arrival of Muhajirs in Sind during 1947–48', *South Asia Bulletin*, 18 (2) (1995)

———, *Sufi Saints and State Power: The Pirs of Sind, 1843–1947* (Vanguard Books, Lahore, 1992)

Charles H. Kennedy, 'The Politics of Ethnicity in Sindh', *Asian Survey*, 31 (10) (1991)

Iftikhar H. Malik, 'Ethno-Nationalism in Pakistan: A Commentary on the Muhajir Qaumi Mahaz (MQM) in Sindh', *South Asia Bulletin*, 18 (2) (1995)

H. T. Sorley, *Shah Abdul Latif of Bhit: A Study of Literary, Social and Economic Conditions in 18th Century Sind* (Ashish Publishing House, New Delhi, 1984)

Oskar Verkaaik, *Migrants and Militants: 'Fun' and Urban Violence in Pakistan* (Princeton University Press, Princeton, 2004)

———, *A People of Migrants: Ethnicity, State and Religion in Karachi*, Comparative Asian Studies, 15 (VU University Press, Amsterdam, 1994)

Akbar Zaidi, *Regional Imbalances and the National Question in Pakistan* (Vanguard Books, Lahore, 1992)

CHAPTER 9 BALOCHISTAN

Martin Axmann, *Back to the Future: The Khanate of Kalat and the Genesis of Baloch Nationalism, 1915–1955* (Oxford University Press, New York, 2008)

Balochistan: Conflicts and Players (Pakistan Institute for Peace Studies, Islamabad, 2008)

Taj Mohammed Breseeg, *Baloch Nationalism: Its Origin and Development* (Royal Book Company, Karachi, 2004)

District Gazetteers of Balochistan, 1906 (ed. and compiled by Mansoor Bokhari), 2 vols (reprinted Gosha-e-Adab, Quetta, 1997)

Selig Harrison, *In Afghanistan's Shadow: Baloch Nationalism and Soviet Temptations* (Carnegie Endowment for International Peace, 1980)

Sylvia Matheson, *The Tigers of Balochistan*, Introduction by Paul Titus (Oxford University Press, Karachi, 1967)

Robert N. Pehrson, *The Social Organisation of the Marri Baloch* (Wenner-Gren Foundation, Chicago, 1966)

Paul Titus (ed.), *Marginality and Modernity: Ethnicity and Change in Post-Colonial Balochistan* (Oxford University Press, Karachi, 1996)

CHAPTERS 10, 11 AND 12 THE PATHANS, THE PAKISTANI TALEBAN, DEFEATING THE TALEBAN?

Akbar S. Ahmed, *Millennium and Charisma among Pathans: A Critical Essay in Social Anthropology* (Routledge & Kegan Paul, London, 1967)

Amineh Ahmed, *Sorrow and Joy among Muslim Women: The Pukhtuns of*

Northern Pakistan (Cambridge University Press, Cambridge, 2006)

Fredric Barth, *Political Leadership among Swat Pathans* (London School of Economics monographs on Social Anthropology, London, 1959)

John Bowen, *Plain Tales of the Afghan Border* (Springwood Books, London, 1982)

Sir Olaf Caroe, *The Pathans* (1958; reprinted Oxford University, Press, Oxford, 2006)

Winston S. Churchill, 'The Malakand Field Force', in *Frontiers and Wars* (Eyre & Spottiswoode, London, 1962)

Steve Coll, *Ghost Wars: The Secret History of the CIA, Afghanistan and Bin Laden* (Penguin, London, 2005)

Robert D. Crews and Amin Tarzi (eds), *The Taliban and the Crisis of Afghanistan* (Harvard University Press, Cambridge, MA, 2008)

Ahmad Hasan Dani, *Peshawar: Historic City of the Frontier* (Sang-e-Meel Publications, Lahore, 2002)

Gilles Dorronsoro, *Revolution Unending* (Hurst, London, 2005)

David B. Edwards, *Before Taliban: Genealogies of the Afghan Jihad* (California University Press, Berkeley, 2002)

———, *Heroes of the Age: Moral Fault Lines on the Afghan Frontier* (University of California Press, Berkeley, CA, 2005)

Antonio Giustozzi (ed.), *Decoding the New Taleban: Insights from the Afghan Field* (Hurst, London, 2009)

———, *Koran, Kalashnikov and Laptop: The Neo-Taleban Insurgency in Afghanistan* (Hurst, London, 2007)

——— and Noor Ullah, *Tribes and Warlords in Southern Afghanistan 1980–2005* (Crisis States Research Centre, London, Working Paper series 2, no. 7)

Benedicte Grima, *Secrets from the Field: An Ethnographer's Notes from Northwest Pakistan* (Oxford University Press, Oxford, 2004)

Sana Haroon, *Frontier of Faith: Islam in the Indo-Afghan Borderland* (Hurst, London, 2007)

Miangul Jehanzeb, *The Last Wali of Swat: An Autobiography as Told to Fredrik Barth* (White Orchid Press, Bangkok, 1995)

Jehanzeb Khalil, *The Mujahideen Movement in Malakand and Mohmand Agencies, 1900–1940* (Area Studies Centre, Peshawar University, 2000)

Are Knudsen, *Violence and Belonging: Land, Love and Lethal Conflict in the North West Frontier Province of Pakistan* (NIAS Press, Copenhagen, 2007)

Anatol Lieven, *Chechnya: Tombstone of Russian Power?* (Yale University Press, New Haven, CT, 1998)

Magnus Marsden, *Living Islam: Muslim Religious Experience in Pakistan's North West Frontier* (Cambridge University Press, Cambridge, 2005)

John Masters, *Bugles and a Tiger* (Cassell, London, 2002)

W. R. H. Merk, *The Mohmands* (1898; reprinted Vanguard Books, Lahore, 1984)

T. L. Pennel and Earl Roberts, *Among the Wild Tribes of the Afghan Frontier: A Record of Sixteen Years' Close Intercourse with the Natives of the Indian*

Marches (1908; reprinted Kessinger Publishing, Whitefish, MT, 2005)

Muhammad Amir Rana, *A to Z of Jehadi Organisations in Pakistan* (Mashal Books, Lahore, 2009)

Brian Robson, *Crisis on the Frontier: The Third Afghan War and the Campaign in Waziristan, 1919–20* (Spellmount, Staplehurst, 2004)

James W. Spain, *The Pathans of the Latter Day* (Oxford University Press, Oxford, 1995)

——, *The Way of the Pathans* (Oxford University Press, Oxford, 1962)

Sultan-i-Rome, *Swat State from Genesis to Merger, 1915–1969* (Oxford University Press, Karachi, 2008)

Joshua T. White, *Pakistan's Islamist Frontier: Islamic Politics and US Policy in Pakistan's North-West Frontier* (Centre on Faith and International Affairs, Washington, DC, 2007)

Glossary

alim (plural *ulema*)	Religious scholar learned in the Shariah.
badal, badla	Revenge.
baraka, barkat	Spiritual power.
Barelvi	Islamic religious tradition tracing its descent from the madrasah of Bareilly in the United Provinces (now Uttar Pradesh) of India, and including reverence for shrines and saints.
biradiri	Local kinship group.
Caliphate	The ideal universal government of the world's Muslim community; assumed to be the epitome of just and righteous rule. The title held by the Ottoman sultans until 1923.
Chaudhury	A term of respect among the Jats.
dacoit	Bandit, brigand.
Deobandi	Islamic religious tradition tracing its descent from the madrasah of Deoband in the United Provinces (now Uttar Pradesh) of India, focused on strict adherence to the Koran and generally hostile to the worship of saints.
diya	Compensation paid by the guilty party for murder or injury.
dupattas	Scarves.
encounter killing	Extra-judicial execution by the police or intelligence services.
Frontier Force	Paramilitary force staffed by military officers but under the control of the Federal Ministry of the Interior, responsible for external and border security in the Federally Administered Tribal Areas and Balochistan. Recruited from local Pathans.
ghairat	Honour, pride; (in women): modesty, purity, respectability.

hadith	An established and recorded saying or story of the Prophet.
Hajj	The pilgrimage to Mecca, incumbent on all Muslims of sufficient means.
hujra	Traditional Pathan male gathering place.
ijtihad	The process of making a decision on a case of Shariah law by individual interpretation of the scriptural sources. More broadly, reinterpretation of the Muslim tradition in the light of reason.
izzat	Honour, prestige, reputation.
jawan	Lad, youth; informal term for the military rank and file.
jihad	Struggle for the sake of Islam; divided between the 'Greater Jihad', for personal and social purity, faith and justice, and the 'Lesser Jihad' of armed struggle.
jirga	(Pathan, Baloch and Sindhi), a council of elders and notables.
kafir	Infidel, pagan.
khan	Lord (Turkic); the formal or informal title of a respected man among the Pathans and other Pakistani ethnicities and tribes.
madrasah	Religious school.
malangs	Dervishes, devotees of a Sufi saint.
malik	A Pathan notable. In the tribal areas, one officially recognized by the state as one of the representatives of a given clan.
maulana	Graduate of a religious school, a learned cleric.
Mohajir	A person who migrates for the sake of Islam; in Pakistan, applied to those who migrated from India after partition.
Moharram	The first month of the Islamic calendar, especially sacred to Shia because of the anniversary of the death of Imam Hussain on the 10th Moharram (Ashura).
mujahid	A warrior of Islam.
mullah	Muslim cleric; usually, the cleric of a village mosque.
murid	Follower of a saint.
nom (Pashto)	Name, reputation, prestige.
panchayat	(Punjabi), a village council.
pashtunwali	The traditional moral and behavioural code of the Pathan tribes.
pir	A hereditary saint (in the Maghrib, *marabout*).
qaum	Community, ethnicity, nation.
qazi	Islamic judge.

Quaid-e-Azam	Great Leader: The honorary title of Muhammad Ali Jinnah, founder of Pakistan.
Raj	Rule, kingdom.
Rangers	Paramilitary force under the Ministry of the Interior, responsible for internal and border security in Sindh and Punjab.
sajjada nashin	Literally, he who sits on the prayer carpet; the hereditary guardian of a shrine.
Sardar	A hereditary tribal chieftain.
Sayyid (or Syed)	A descendant of the Prophet.
Seraiki	Language widely spoken in southern Punjab and part of northern Sindh.
Shariah	Islamic law.
Talib	A religious student.
taqiyya	Shia tradition permitting the concealing of your true faith in times of persecution.
tehsil	Administrative sub-division of a district.
thana	Local police station.
Ummah	The universal world community of Muslims.
urs	Death anniversaries of saints
wadero	A hereditary landowner in Sindh.
Wahabi	Islamic tradition based in Saudi Arabia, adhering to an ultra-strict version of the Koran and Shariah and bitterly hostile both to Shia and to the worship of shrines.
zamindar	A landowner (in Punjab and northern India).

Appendix One: Chronology of Muslim South Asia

c. 3300 BCE – 1300 BCE   Indus Valley civilization in what is now Pakistan.

After 1500 BCE   Aryan migrations into South Asia (presumed).

Sixth–fifth centuries BCE   Life of Siddhartha Gautama (Buddha).

Fifth–fourth centuries BCE   Afghanistan and Punjab come under the dominion of the Persian empire (satrapies of Gandhara and Kamboja).

327/326 BCE   Alexander the Great invades Afghanistan and Punjab, and defeats the Indian king Porus. Alexander founds Greek settlements in Afghanistan (Bactria) which survive for several hundred years.

321–185 BCE   Mauryan empire conquers most of northern India and Afghanistan. Under this and subsequent dynasties, the Gandharan Buddhist civilization flourishes in what is now Afghanistan and northern Pakistan.

First century BCE–sixth century CE   Kushan and Gupta empires.

632 CE   Death of the Prophet Mohammed.

Late seventh century CE   Muslim invasions of Sindh.

711 CE   Mohammed bin Qasim, a general of the Muslim Ummayad dynasty, invades Sindh by sea and initiates Muslim rule in South Asia. He extends Muslim rule as far north as Multan in southern Punjab.

971–1030   Life of Mahmud of Ghazni (in Afghanistan), the first Muslim invader of northern India.

c. 990–1077   Life of Abul Hassan Ali Hajvery (Data Ganj Baksh), a Sufi Muslim saint who initiates conversion of people of northern Punjab to Islam and is buried in Lahore.

1162–1206   Muhammad of Ghor (in Afghanistan) leads Muslim campaigns in northern India. In 1186 he captures Lahore.

1193   Muhammad of Ghor's general Qutb-ud-Din Aybakh captures Delhi. He founds the Delhi sultanate, and is buried in Lahore.

1206–1526   A succession of Muslim dynasties rule northern India from Delhi.

1398   Tamerlaine sacks Delhi.

1469–1538   Life of Guru Nanak, founder of Sikhism.

1526   Zahiruddin Babur invades India through Afghanistan, defeats the last Lodhi sultan of Delhi, and founds the Mughal empire.

1556–1605 Rule of the Mughal emperor Jalaluddin Akbar 'the Great'.

1703–62 Life of the great South Asian Muslim religious thinker and reformer Shah Waliullah.

1707 Death of the last great Mughal emperor, Aurangzeb.

1739 Delhi sacked by the Persian ruler Nadir Shah.

1761 Delhi sacked by Ahmed Shah Abdali, founder of the Durrani kingdom in Afghanistan.

Eighteenth century Rise of Sikh power in Punjab.

1801–39 Rule of the Sikh Maharaja Ranjit Singh in Punjab.

1803 The Mughal ruler Shah Alam II accepts the protection of the British East India Company, which by now rules most of India.

1817–98 Life of the Muslim reformist educator and politician Sir Syed Ahmed Khan.

1840–42 First British–Afghan war.

1843 British conquest of Sindh.

1845–9 British defeat the Sikhs and conquer Punjab.

1856 British annex Awadh, the last major autonomous Muslim state in northern India.

1857 Muslim and Hindu revolt against British rule, called by the British the 'Indian Mutiny'. Delhi and Lucknow are largely destroyed. The last Mughal emperor is deposed. Savage reprisals against the Muslims of north India.

1866 Shah Waliullah's spiritual descendants found a madrasah at Deoband in northern India and lay basis for Deoband movement in South Asian Sunni Islam.

1875 Sir Syed founds the Mohammedan Anglo-Oriental College (later Aligarh Muslim University) at Aligarh, south-east of Delhi.

1876–1948 Life of Mohammed Ali Jinnah, founder of Pakistan.

1878–80 Second British–Afghan war.

1885 Foundation of the Indian National Congress.

1893 British draw the 'Durand Line' marking the frontier between British India and Afghanistan. It is never accepted by the Afghans.

1896 Jinnah joins the Congress.

1896–9 Major revolts in the name of Islam among the Pathan tribes against British domination.

1906 Foundation of Muslim League in Dhaka, east Bengal (now Bangladesh).

1914–18 First World War.

1916 Jinnah becomes president of the Muslim League and initiates 'Lucknow Pact' with the Congress.

1919–24 Khilafat movement of South Asian Muslims against British rule and in defence of the Ottoman Caliphate (formal leadership of the Muslim world community, or Ummah).

1920 Jinnah resigns from the Congress.

1930 Sir Muhammad Iqbal, president of the Muslim League, speaks for the first time of the possibility of a separate Muslim state in north-western India.

1936–9   The British conduct major campaigns in Waziristan against Islamist rebels led by the Faqir of Ipi.

1938   Elections under British rule. Split between Congress and the Muslim League after the Congress refuses to include the League in provincial governments.

1939–45   Second World War.

1940   Muslim League passes 'Lahore Resolution' calling for an 'autonomous and sovereign' state of Pakistan.

1946   British Cabinet Mission fails to negotiate an agreement with Congress and the Muslim League on a united independent India with a loose federal constitution and guaranteed power-sharing between Hindus and Muslims.

August 1947   Independence of India and Pakistan: communal massacres in Punjab and Bengal claim between 200,000 and 1 million lives. Around 12 million people become refugees in India or Pakistan.

October 1947   Beginning of conflict between India and Pakistan over Kashmir.

September 1948   Death of Jinnah.

1951   Assassination of his successor, Liaquat Ali Khan.

1952   Language riots in East Pakistan initiate movement for the separation of the region from West Pakistan.

1953   Riots in Punjab against the Ahmadi religious minority show the strength of the Islamist parties on the streets. Martial law declared. Pakistani army enters into internal politics.

1958   Military coup by the commander-in-chief, General Mohammed Ayub Khan.

1958–69   Administration of Ayub Khan. The economy grows successfully. Limited land reform carried out in West Pakistan. In foreign policy, Ayub aligns Pakistan closely with the United States, but also cultivates ties with China. The capital is moved from Karachi to the new city of Islamabad, near Rawalpindi in northern Punjab.

1965   War with India over Kashmir ends in stalemate, seen in Pakistan as a defeat. Opposition to Ayub Khan grows, increasingly led by his former Foreign Minister, Zulfikar Ali Bhutto.

1969   Ayub Khan resigns in the face of growing public protests against his rule, and is succeeded by the army chief of staff, General Muhammad Yahya Khan.

1969–71   Growth of agitation for de facto independence of East Pakistan.

1970   National elections lead to the victory of Sheikh Mujib-ur-Rehman's pro-independence Awami League in East Pakistan (with a majority in Pakistan overall) and of Bhutto's Pakistan People's Party in West Pakistan.

March 1971   Pakistan army begins a savage campaign against the separatist movement in East Pakistan. Civil war begins. Millions of refugees flee to India.

December 1971   'Bangladesh War'. India invades East Pakistan, and defeats and captures the Pakistani forces there. East Pakistan becomes independent as Bangladesh. Resignation of Yahya Khan.

1971–7 Government of Zulfikar Ali Bhutto and the Pakistan People's Party. The government carries out limited land reform and a more radical nationalization of banks and industries. The dismissal of the provincial government of Balochistan leads to a Baloch revolt which is suppressed by the army. Bhutto distances Pakistan from the United States and moves closer to China.

1977 Allegations of the rigging of elections by the government lead to a mass movement against Bhutto's rule.

July 1977 The army chief of staff, General Zia-ul-Haq, carries out military coup.

1977–88 Administration of Zia-ul-Haq. His government greatly extends Bhutto's moves to make Pakistan an Islamic state. The role of the Shariah in the legal system is strengthened. Partial reversal of Bhutto's populist economic measures.

April 1979 Bhutto hanged after being convicted of responsibility for the murder of a political opponent (charges which are fiercely contested by Bhutto's supporters). His daughter Benazir succeeds to leadership of PPP.

December 1979 Soviet invasion of Afghanistan. The United States extends massive aid to Pakistan as a bulwark against supposed Soviet expansionism. Together with Saudi Arabia and other states, the US and Pakistan build up the Afghan Mujahidin forces to fight against the Soviet troops and Afghan Communist government. First beginnings of the Taleban in southern Afghanistan. Some 3 million Afghan refugees flee to Pakistan.

1981 Violent protests in Sindh against Zia's rule are suppressed by the military, leaving around 1,500 dead.

1984 Foundation of the Muhajir Qaumi Movement to represent Urdu-speaking migrants from India in Karachi and other cities of Sindh.

1985 Ethnic riots in Karachi begin years of ethnic violence in that city.

1988 Protests against rigged elections in Indian Kashmir are bloodily suppressed by Indian troops, leading to a long-running insurgency in which tens of thousands are killed. Pakistan supports the insurgents with arms and volunteers from Islamist militant groups.

August 1988 General Zia and leading staff killed in an air crash, generally presumed to be sabotage. The military and civil service manage a 'transition to democracy'.

November 1988 The Pakistan People's Party (PPP) under Benazir Bhutto wins national elections and forms a coalition government. The IJI (Islami Jamhoori Ittehad) coalition, led by the Muslim League headed by Mian Nawaz Sharif, wins the provincial elections in Punjab and forms the government there.

January 1989 Soviet forces withdraw from Afghanistan. In March, a Mujahidin attempt to defeat the Communist forces there suffers a bloody setback at Jalalabad.

April 1989 Riots against the publication of Salman Rushdie's *Satanic Verses* leave five dead in Islamabad.

1990   The US imposes economic sanctions against Pakistan after it fails to show that it is not conducting a nuclear weapons programme. President Ghulam Ishaq Khan dismisses the PPP government on charges of corruption and incompetence. Caretaker administration. The Muslim League wins the subsequent national elections and forms a coalition government.

1991–3   First government of Nawaz Sharif begins liberalization of the economy. A military campaign launched in Karachi to bring ethnic conflict there to an end.

March 1992   Fall of the Communist government of Afghanistan. Mujahidin parties seize power and soon begin bloody civil war among themselves. Pakistan backs the Pathan forces of Gulbuddin Hekmatyar's Hezb-e-Islami.

December 1992   A Hindu mob encouraged by the Bharatiya Janata Party (BJP) destroys the Babri Mosque in the north Indian city of Ayodhya, on the grounds that it was originally the site of a Hindu temple. This increases Hindu–Muslim tension and violence in India.

1993   Ishaq Khan and Nawaz Sharif fall out. After prolonged political confusion, both are forced to resign by the military. The PPP wins the subsequent national elections.

1993–96   Second government of Benazir Bhutto. The government regains control of Karachi. Pakistan switches its support in the Afghan civil war to the newly reformed Taleban of Kandahar.

1994   Taleban capture Kabul.

1996   President Farooq Leghari dismisses PPP government on charges of corruption. Elections lead to a sweeping victory for the Muslim League of Nawaz Sharif.

1997–9   Second government of Nawaz Sharif. The government carries out important economic reforms, but becomes increasingly autocratic. The Chief Justice is forced from office and opposition journalists are targeted.

May 1998   India explodes nuclear devices. Pakistan follows suit, leading to intensified US sanctions.

April 1999   Benazir Bhutto and her husband, Asif Ali Zardari, are convicted of corruption. Ms Bhutto stays abroad. Mr Zardari spends several years in jail.

May 1999   After Pakistani forces occupy positions across the Line of Control at Kargil in Kashmir, India counter-attacks. Pakistan eventually withdraws under heavy US pressure.

October 1999   After Nawaz Sharif attempts to dismiss the Army Chief of Staff, General Pervez Musharraf, he is overthrown in a military coup. Musharraf takes power.

1999–2008   Musharraf administration. Musharraf institutes stern measures against corruption, and rolls back some of the Islamist laws passed by Zia and Sharif. He liberalizes media laws, allowing a vast growth in private television channels, and institutes policies intended to improve the position of women.

However, like previous military rulers, Musharraf becomes increasingly dependent on the existing political elites.

September 2001   Al Qaeda launches terrorist attacks on New York and Washington. Musharraf given ultimatum by the Bush administration to support US invasion of Afghanistan. Musharraf agrees to allow two US air bases in Pakistan and to allow supplies for the US forces in Afghanistan to cross Pakistan.

November–December 2001   Backed by massive US airpower and some special forces, the anti-Taleban warlords in Afghanistan overthrow Taleban rule. The leadership of the Taleban and Al Qaeda escape to Pakistan and go into hiding.

December 2001   Pakistan-based Islamist militants launch a terrorist attack on the Indian parliament in New Delhi. India masses troops on its border with Pakistan.

January 2002   Under heavy US and Indian pressure, Musharraf bans the SSP and LeJ, together with Lashkar-e-Taiba and Jaish-e-Mohammed, Islamist militant groups formerly sponsored by the Pakistani military. Over the next years, violence in Kashmir diminishes greatly.

February–March 2002   Muslim activists in India attack a train containing Hindu nationalist pilgrims to Ayodhya, killing fifty-nine. In response, some 2,000 Muslims are massacred in the Indian state of Gujarat by Hindu militants linked to the ruling Bharatiya Janata Party (BJP), and encouraged by the local BJP government.

May–June 2002   Terrorist attacks in Karachi against French technicians and the US Consulate.

October 2002   National elections. The pro-Musharraf Muslim League (Qaid-e-Azam) wins most seats and forms a coalition government. The MMA Islamist coalition wins the elections in the North West Frontier Province and Balochistan and forms the governments there.

November 2003   India and Pakistan announce a ceasefire in Kashmir. Pakistan and India resume air links and other ties.

March 2004   Under US pressure, the Pakistani military launches a major campaign in Waziristan, on the border of Afghanistan, against local allies of the Afghan Taleban. In this and subsequent offensives, hundreds are killed, including many civilians. Increase of support for militancy in the tribal areas. In April 2004, after the military campaign reaches stalemate, the Pakistani government makes a peace deal with the local Islamist leader Nek Mohammed. This is abrogated by the militants in June when Nek Mohammed is killed in a US airstrike. The government goes on to make a similar deal with his successor, Beitullah Mahsud.

January 2005   Start of a new insurgency in Balochistan, initially by members of the Bugti tribe.

October 2005   Massive earthquake in Pakistani Kashmir leaves tens of thousands dead. Islamist groups lead the relief effort.

January 2006 A US missile strike on suspected Al Qaeda members at Damadola in the Bajaur Tribal Agency of Pakistan kills seventeen people, including civilians. This marks the beginning of intensified US strikes from unmanned aircraft against suspected Al Qaeda and Taleban leaders in the Pakistan tribal areas which kill many senior figures but also infuriate the local population.

August 2006 Baloch rebel leader Nawab Akbar Bugti is killed in mysterious circumstances, together with Pakistani troops. Baloch insurgency intensifies, partly led by his grandson, Baramdagh Bugti.

January–July 2007 Islamist radicals turn the Red Mosque (Lal Masjid) complex in Islamabad into an armed base and begin enforcing Shariah law in parts of the capital. In July, security forces storm the Red Mosque, in a battle in which (according to official figures) 154 people are killed. In protest, militants in the tribal areas abrogate their peace agreement with the government.

March 2007 Start of clash between Musharraf and the Chief Justice, Iftikhar Chaudhry, who demands that the government account for Pakistanis who have 'disappeared' at the hands of the security forces in Balochistan and elsewhere. Many Pakistanis believe that suspected Islamist militants have been secretly and illegally transferred to US custody. The Chief Justice also challenges other measures by the Musharraf administration. Musharraf dismisses the Chief Justice, who then leads a protest movement of lawyers, with increasing mass support.

May 2007 Several dozen people killed in Karachi when activists of the Mohajir Qaumi Movement (allied to Musharraf) block a visit by the Chief Justice to the city.

September 2007 Formation of the Pakistani Taleban (Tehriq-e-Taleban Pakistan, or TTP), a loose alliance of mainly Pathan militant groups. Militants in the Swat District of the NWFP increasingly threaten local government.

October 2007 Musharraf wins a presidential election generally thought to be rigged.

November 2007 Under increasing pressure from the Lawyers' Movement and other public protests, Musharraf declares martial law, but is soon forced to withdraw this under US pressure. Musharraf is forced to resign as Army Chief of Staff. Nawaz Sharif and Benazir Bhutto are allowed to return from exile. The US promotes an alliance between Musharraf and Ms Bhutto.

27 December 2007 Ms Bhutto is assassinated at a public rally in Rawalpindi, apparently by the Pakistani Taleban. According to the alleged terms of her will (which is, however, not made public), her widower, Asif Ali Zardari, succeeds her as co-leader of the Pakistani People's Party, in tandem with their underage son Bilawal, a student at Oxford.

February 2008 Parliamentary elections. The PPP wins most seats and forms a coalition government at the centre. Yusuf Raza Gilani becomes Pakistani prime minister. The Muslim League of Nawaz Sharif wins a majority in Punjab and forms the government there. The moderate Pathan nationalist Awami National Party (ANP) forms the government of the NWFP.

July 2008 The Pakistani army launches an offensive against the Pakistani Taleban in the Bajaur Tribal Agency.

August 2008 Musharraf resigns as president.

September 2008 Zardari is elected president by members of the national and provincial assemblies. He breaks his promise to re-appoint Iftikhar Chaudhry Chief Justice.

20 September 2008 The Marriott Hotel in Islamabad is badly damaged by a car bomb, in the first major terrorist attack in the capital. Over the next eighteen months, terrorist attacks by the Pakistani Taleban and their allies intensify across Pakistan, becoming increasingly indiscriminate and claiming thousands of victims among civilians as well as among Pakistani troops and police.

November 2008 Relations between India and Pakistan worsen drastically again after terrorists from the Pakistan-based (though officially banned) Lashkar-e-Taiba carry out terrorist attacks in the Indian city of Mumbai, leaving 185 dead. Pakistan is forced to take intensified measures against LeT, but refuses Indian demands to extradite suspects to India.

February 2009 The national government and the government of the NWFP reach the 'Nizam-e-Adl' agreement with the Pakistani Taleban in Swat, providing for the extension of Shariah law in the province in return for the Taleban abandoning their campaign of violence.

March 2009 The Zardari administration ousts the Sharif government in the Punjab, after the Supreme Court (appointed by Musharraf and Zardari) declares the election of Nawaz and Shahbaz Sharif illegal. The Muslim League leads a mass march on Islamabad. Zardari is forced to back down, allow Iftikhar Chaudhry back as Chief Justice, and allow the Muslim League to resume the government in Punjab.

April 2009 The Taleban in Swat take over the neighbouring district of Buner, closer to Islamabad.

May 2009 The Pakistani army launches a massive offensive to retake Swat and Buner. Hundreds of Taleban are killed or captured, but hundreds of thousands of civilians are also forced to flee their homes.

August 2009 Pakistani Taleban leader Beitullah Mahsud is killed in a US airstrike. He is succeeded by Hakimullah Mahsud. Hamid Karzai is re-elected president of Afghanistan in elections which are widely seen as deeply flawed by rigging and corruption.

September 2009 The US Senate passes the Kerry–Lugar Bill, providing for greatly increased US assistance to Pakistan. However, it causes great offence to many Pakistanis by the strict conditions it sets concerning Pakistani action against the Taleban, and Pakistan's nuclear programme.

October 2009 The Pakistani military begins a major offensive against the Pakistani Taleban in south Waziristan.

10 October 2009 Taleban militants attack the headquarters of the Pakistani army in Rawalpindi, killing ten.

December 2009 US President Barack Obama announces a 'surge' in US troops in Afghanistan, and intensified operations against the Taleban there. The Supreme Court declares illegal an amnesty passed by President Musharraf giving Zardari and other leading PPP figures immunity for prosecution for corruption.

31 December 2009 National Finance Commission Award, agreed between the national government and the provinces, rebalances the allocation of revenue in favour of Sindh, the NWFP and especially Balochistan.

1 January 2010 More than ninety people killed by Taleban suicide bomb at a volleyball game in Laki Marwat district of the NWFP.

14 January 2010 Jamaat-ud-Dawa condemns the killing of Muslims by suicide bombing as unislamic and says that such attacks 'played into the hands of the US, Israel and India'.

19 April 2010 President Zardari signs into law sweeping constitutional reforms transferring powers from the President to the Prime Minister, thereby reversing changes introduced by Presidents Zia-ul-Haq and Musharraf. In accordance with a longstanding demand of the Awami National Party (ANP), the North West Frontier Province is renamed Khyber-Pakhtunkhwa. This move sets off violent protests in the Hindko-speaking area of the province in which several people are killed.

1 May 2010 Faisal Shehzad, a Pakistani-American, attempts to detonate a car bomb in Times Square, New York. US Secretary of State Hillary Clinton subsequently warns Pakistan that there would have been 'very severe consequences' had the bomb exploded.

1 July 2010 Suicide bombers kill more than forty worshippers at the shrine of Data Ganj Baksh in Lahore.

29 July 2010 The heaviest monsoon rains on record cause catastrophic floods in Pakistan (starting with Swat and the northern mountains), which eventually leave 1,900 dead and more than 20 million displaced. The Zardari administration comes under strong criticism for failures in the relief effort.

September–October 2010 Pakistan temporarily blocks NATO supplies to Afghanistan via the Khyber Pass in protest against a US helicopter attack that killed Pakistani soldiers on the Afghan border.

November–December 2010 WikiLeaks reveals details of Pakistani co-operation with the US including the presence of limited numbers of US special forces in Pakistan. Leaked cables also record unflattering US opinions of President Zardari, and the diversion and misuse of US military aid to Pakistan.

4 January 2011 Salman Taseer, liberal Governor of Punjab (appointed by President Zardari) is assassinated by one of his own bodyguards, a Barelvi conservative Muslim outraged by Mr Taseer's criticism of Pakistan's harsh blasphemy law and its use to persecute religious minorities.

Appendix Two: Pakistani Statistics

Population growth

1951 census: 33,816,000 (17.80 per cent urban)

1961 census: 42,978,000 (22.46 per cent urban)

1972 census: 65,321,000 (25.40 per cent urban)

1981 census: 84,254,000 (28.28 per cent urban)

1998 census: 130,580,000 (32.51 per cent urban)

2010: 180,000 to 200,000 (estimate)

Annual rate of population growth (2010 estimate)

2.2 per cent (down from 3.1 per cent in the 1980s)

Infant mortality (2009 estimate)

62 per 1,000 births

Age distribution (2008)

0–14 years: 42 per cent

15–64 years: 55 per cent

65 and over: 4 per cent

Life expectancy (2007 estimate)

Men: 66.5 years

Women: 67.2 years

Literacy (2010)

Total population: 55.9 per cent

Men: 68.2 per cent

Women: 43.6 per cent

Population by province (1998 census)

Punjab: 56 per cent (approximate)

Sindh: 22 per cent (approximate)

North West Frontier Province (NWFP):   13 per cent (approximate)
Balochistan: 7 per cent (approximate)
Federally Administered Tribal
   Areas (FATA):   2.5 per cent (approximate)

Territory of Pakistan

803,940 square kilometres (340,000 square miles) plus 85,000 square kilometres (32,818 square miles) for Azad Kashmir and the Northern Areas, both disputed with India

Territory by province

Balochistan: 347,000 square kilometres
Punjab: 205,000 square kilometres
Sindh: 140,000 square kilometres
NWFP: 74,000 square kilometres
Federally Administered Tribal
   Areas (FATA):   27,000 square kilometres
(Azad Kashmir):   13,000 square kilometres)
(Northern Areas):   72,000 square kilometres)

Human Development Index (2006)

Pakistan: 0.539 (comparable to Ghana)
Urban: 0.656 (comparable to South Africa)
Rural: 0.496 (comparable to Togo)

Urban Punjab: 0.657 (comparable to Tajikistan)
Urban Sindh: 0.659
Urban NWFP: 0.627 (comparable to India)
Urban Balochistan: 0.571
Rural Punjab: 0.517 (comparable to Sudan)
Rural NWFP: 0.489
Rural Balochistan: 0.486
Rural Sindh: 0.456 (comparable to Eritrea)

Index

ANATOL LIEVEN is professor of international relations and terrorism studies in the War Studies department of King's College, London, and a senior fellow of the New America Foundation in Washington, D.C. As a journalist, he reported from South Asia, the former Soviet Union, and Eastern Europe for the *Times* and other publications. His books include *Chechnya: Tombstone of Russian Power* (1998); *America Right or Wrong: An Anatomy of American Nationalism* (2004); and *Ethical Realism: A Vision for America's Role in the World* (with John Hulsman) (2006).